REFLECTIONS ON MAN

Readings in Philosophical Psychology from
Classical Philosophy to Existentialism

The Harbrace Series in Philosophy

UNDER THE GENERAL EDITORSHIP OF
Jesse A. Mann and Gerald F. Kreyche

REFLECTIONS ON MAN
Readings in Philosophical Psychology from
Classical Philosophy to Existentialism

PERSPECTIVES ON REALITY
Readings in Metaphysics from
Classical Philosophy to Existentialism

APPROACHES TO MORALITY
Readings in Ethics from
Classical Philosophy to Existentialism

REFLECTIONS ON MAN

Readings in Philosophical Psychology from Classical Philosophy to Existentialism

UNDER THE GENERAL EDITORSHIP OF

Jesse A. Mann, *Georgetown University*
Gerald F. Kreyche, *DePaul University*

CONTRIBUTING EDITORS:

Elizabeth G. Salmon, *Fordham University*
Richard T. De George, *The University of Kansas*
Robert J. Kreyche, *Rockhurst College*
Margaret Gorman, R.S.C.J., *Newton College of the Sacred Heart*
Robert Sokolowski, *The Catholic University of America*

Harcourt, Brace & World, Inc.
New York / Chicago / Burlingame

Library of Congress Catalog Card Number: 66-16062

Printed in the United States of America

The experience of past ages, the progress of the sciences, and the treasures hidden in the various forms of human culture, by all of which the nature of man himself is more clearly revealed and new roads to truth are opened, these profit the Church, too. For, from the beginning of her history she has learned to express the message of Christ with the help of the ideas and terminology of various philosophers, and has tried to clarify it with their wisdom, too.

From the text of the Second Vatican Council's Pastoral Constitution on the Church in the Modern World, promulgated December 7, 1965.

The philosophical disciplines are to be taught in such a way that the students are first of all led to acquire a solid and coherent knowledge of man, the world, and of God, relying on a philosophical patrimony which is perennially valid and taking into account the philosophical investigations of later ages. This is especially true of those investigations which exercise a greater influence in their own nations. Account should also be taken of the more recent progress of the sciences. The net result should be that the students, correctly understanding the characteristics of the contemporary mind, will be duly prepared for dialogue with men of their time.

From the text of the Second Vatican Council's Declaration on Priestly Training, promulgated October 28, 1965.

Foreword

Most Christians sooner or later decide that philosophy solves no ultimately important problems by itself.

I hasten to add that only the dullest anti-intellectual, dull to the point of perverse, would be tempted on that account to hold philosophy in anything less than solid esteem. I also add that the Catholic Christian acknowledges that, in principle at least, philosophy could come up with rational solutions to many (theoretically, perhaps, most) of the natural problems which embarrass or intrigue human reason.

The First Vatican Council confirmed what the Apostle Paul had suggested concerning the power of reason (the philosopher's proper and characteristic tool) to solve with considerable certainty even the "problem of God," at least as far as God's existence and some of His essential attributes are concerned. But in the concrete human condition the Christian may well conclude that pure philosophy (to the extent that philosophy can be isolated from the total experience of man made in God's image, fallen from original justice, supernaturally redeemed) raises more questions than it can possibly solve and that, unaided, it solves practically none.

The unbeliever arrives at a like conclusion more often than not, and, if the conclusion be bleak, the unbeliever sometimes expresses it with wistful beauty. Edward Fitzgerald echoes Omar Khayyám:

> *Myself when young did eagerly frequent*
> *Doctor and Saint, and heard great Argument*
> *About it and about: but evermore*
> *Came out by the same Door as in I went.*

But the Christian's conclusion need not be so bleak. His love for philosophy may—indeed, should—be as passionate as that of the unbeliever, but his dependence on it is never more than partial. Not only for salvation hereafter but for sanity here, he has the light of faith to illumine the testimonies of reason and the resources of theology to supply for the inadequacies of philosophy.

For example, he may see no possibility of a satisfactory philosophy of history, as I, for one, see none. However, the Incarnation (which utterly

exorable – persuaded or moved by pleas

eludes the domain of reason) gives history such meaning as a Christian can bring to his meditations upon it; but the Incarnation is the object of faith and reflection upon it provides the stuff of a theology of history. Philosophy brings cold comfort to the problem of evil; only the Cross (which is, for the philosophers, still the foolishness that Paul confessed it to be) lifts from this mystery the dreadful burden it places on the human heart.

The very "problem of God," mentioned above, illustrates how pathet- ically inadequate, however certain, are the answers of philosophy to the demands of the devout heart, let alone of the unbelieving mind. The "God of the philosophers," the neat and convenient God who emerges patly as the logical conclusion from lines of cold reasoning much as a mathematical formula emerges, inevitably and inexorably, from a mass of data— this sterile God of the debating halls is by no means to be denied by reason or rejected out of hand by the believer. But He, like reason itself, is only a part of total reality and a meager answer to our total need; He is a poor thing, however logically necessary, beside the God of Abraham, the God of Job, and above all the God of Jesus Christ and His saints.

pitiful

unavoidably; certainly

unrelenting; inflexible

The Christian perceives a mutual need between philosophy and theology, between reason and revelation, that is satisfied only in the integral wisdom that comes from the interplay of faith asking reason and reason asking faith for their respective witnesses. Hence his special regret when confronted by the excessive mutual exclusions between reason and faith set up by those in whom the method of Descartes speedily resulted in a mood which has permeated our culture to the hurt, the Christian considers, of both philosophy and theology. Hence, too, the special temptation of the devout sometimes to fuse with excessive simplicity the concerns and functions of philosophy and theology. The unity of philosophical experience is an attainable goal for the sophisticated traveler equipped with reliable maps; otherwise, it can be a mirage, a pot of fool's gold at the end of a rainbow that has many broad bands but, in fact, no end. *Myself when young. . . .*

spread through; diffuse

But whatever the abstract power of philosophy in the face of the questions which excite or torment the human spirit, it is not, I submit, the business of philosophy to solve problems. Even in their best efforts to answer the riddles of life, the philosophers make their chief contribution when they succeed, as they have done, in pounding out more clear and pointed statements of the questions. It is probably not the vocation of the philosopher to give *answers,* least of all *final answers;* it is, one suspects, his essential task and his most valuable contribution to uncover, to phrase, and to press the *questions.*

In the present crisis of our culture, this may be of all vocations the most difficult, and one of the most urgent. When Gertrude Stein was dying, she wearily asked the friends clustered about her bed: *What is the answer?* No one replied; no theologian was present. *In that case,* she

characterized by a lack of simplicity or naturalness; refined to the point of artificiality; worldly-wi not naive

insisted, *what is the question?* The silence remained unbroken: philosophy, too, was without a representative. It has become the (imperative) role of philosophers to help us at least to state the question in an age of the dusty answers that "gets the soul when hot for certainties in this, our life."

Herein lies both the justification and great merit for Christian students of the present comprehensive collection of readings from widely differing philosophers. These volumes bring together historic attempts to answer perennial problems which engage human speculation. But the chief value of the publication lies (as it should) not in the enduring worth of any answers suggested, but in the contribution that each tentative answer inevitably makes to the posing of the so elusive questions, to the clarification of the elements of problems—a full answer to which may never be (afforded) by philosophy but the analysis of which is a built-in demand of the human intellect and an incomparable delight of the human spirit.

No small achievement this, the clarification of the terms of the problems. One suspects that most of the ultimate answers will turn out to be somehow *simple,* with the simplicity that traditional Christian philosophical speculations about God attribute to the Divine Nature. It is the statement of the questions that is tough—that plus, perhaps, the acceptance of the consequences, moral and intellectual, of some of the answers.

And so, if the Church is grateful to the philosophers for stating so many of the questions before which men, in bewilderment, turn to her, it is no less true that the sensitive philosopher is grateful to the Church for the manner in which she, even when lacking specific answers, somehow herself serves as the answer to the master-knots of human fate. She does so by her teaching concerning the Incarnation and the consequent premises for salvation history. She does so by her preaching of Christ, the Alpha and Omega of human experience, and especially of Christ Crucified. She does so supremely in the recollection of the mystery of the Resurrection.

But in all this there is that reciprocity between faith and reason required by the mutual dependencies to which we refer above. The Church, therefore, looks to the philosophers, in varying degrees and with varying profit but to them all without exception, not only for help in stating the questions but for guidance in the phrasing of the (articulated) responses of the Spirit. This is the clear sense of the Second Vatican Council's Constitution on the Church in the Modern World when it says:

> Just as it is in the world's interest to acknowledge the Church as an historical reality, and to recognize her good influence, so the Church herself knows how richly she has profited by the history and development of humanity.
>
> The experience of past ages, the progress of the sciences, and the treasures hidden in the various forms of human culture, by all of which the nature of man himself is more clearly revealed and new roads to truth are opened, these profit the Church, too. For from the beginning of her history she has learned to express the

message of Christ with the help of ideas and terminology of various philosophers, and has tried to clarify it with their wisdom, too. . . . [And] thus the ability to express Christ's message in its own way is developed in each nation, and at the same time there is fostered a living exchange between the Church and the diverse cultures of people. To promote such exchange, especially in our days, the Church requires the special help of those who live in the world, are versed in different institutions and specialties, and grasp their innermost significance in the eyes of both believers and unbelievers. With the help of the Holy Spirit, it is the task of the entire People of God, especially pastors and theologians, to hear, distinguish and interpret the many voices of our age, and to judge them in the light of the divine word, so that revealed truth can always be more deeply penetrated, better understood and set forth to greater advantage.

The editors of these volumes have acted in response to the implicit plea of the Council's pastoral declaration. That is not the least of the reasons why their work is so welcome.

✠ JOHN WRIGHT
BISHOP OF PITTSBURGH

Epiphany, 1966

Preface

anything inherited, as a trait or a character [margin note]

The three text-anthologies in the Harbrace Series in Philosophy—*Reflections on Man, Perspectives on Reality,* and *Approaches to Morality*—offer a genuinely pluralistic approach to the basic issues in Philosophy of Man, Metaphysics, and Ethics. Their publication comes at a time when this approach is being encouraged within the entire Christian world. As His Excellency, Bishop John Wright, has pointed out in the Foreword, the Church "looks to the philosophers, in varying degrees and with varying profit but to them all without exception, not only for help in stating the questions but for guidance in the phrasing of the articulated responses of the Spirit." *publish or make known officially; make wide spread* [annotation]

An openness to truth wherever it may be found is revealed in various documents (promulgated) at the Second Vatican Council. In the Declaration on Priestly Training, for example, no one system is singled out for (exclusive) treatment; rather, seminarians are urged to study the "philosophical (patrimony) which is perennially valid" and to become acquainted with those investigations that have influenced their own country. *not shared or divided; sole, single; snobbish; undemocratic* [margin note]

The pluralistic attitude affirmed by the Council has, in recent years, been the dominant approach in many Catholic colleges and universities in the United States. The significance of the *aggiornamento* in philosophy is that the philosophical pluralism initiated by some is now (enjoined) upon all. Such a positive attitude is in keeping with the demands of the society in which we live. Students of philosophy must know the dynamic currents of thought which are expressed in a free society. It is obvious that valuable insights are to be gained from considering more than one philosophical approach, especially when the pluralism exists within the framework of Christian philosophy itself. The fact that by design Aquinas is systematic and Marcel is unsystematic does not deprive the student from gaining wisdom from both. It is just as true that one can benefit philosophically from a study of philosophies beyond the Christian tradition or even hostile to it. Aquinas did not feel he had to baptize Aristotle before he could study him with profit. *command; order, urge or impose upon; all parts, all end; prohibit; forbid* [margin note]

Clearly there is no substitute for reading the philosophers themselves. The great thinkers have a right to be heard on their own; they present their own cases most effectively and are their own best interpreters. The objection is sometimes raised that primary sources are too difficult for the beginning student. This is not the case, however, when the readings have been carefully chosen by specialists in their respective fields and are accompanied by detailed commentary. Such a judicious selection of texts enables the introductory student to read the works of the great philosophers and to study their conception and development in a historical context.

The text-anthologies in this series give the beginning student a substantial introduction to different philosophical perspectives that are relevant to the contemporary American scene. Accordingly, each volume in the series presents materials from Classical and Scholastic Thought, Dialectical Thought, American Naturalist and Pragmatic Thought, Analytic and Positivist Thought, and Existentialist and Phenomenological Thought. A number of other traditions (Cartesian Rationalism and Utilitarianism, for example) have great historical value, but are not directly and dynamically relevant to the contemporary American scene. Although such traditions are not represented in the readings, they are covered in the General Introduction and are discussed in the section introductions where pertinent.

The series has been planned so that one volume does not presuppose the others. There is no fixed order in which the books have to be studied, although in most colleges the courses in Philosophy of Man and Metaphysics are taught to freshmen and sophmores while Ethics is usually a junior- or senior-level course. The five sections of each book have been edited by expert philosophers and teachers, each of whom has worked and written in the subject matter of his field. The Contributing Editors have chosen readings for their respective sections that are both representative of key issues and are within the competence of the beginner. Each selection is an ample, self-contained unit that provides a full argument and an adequate sampling of the philosopher's style. Some of the readings (Brunner's and Husserl's selections in *Reflections on Man* and the sections of the *Vienna Manifesto* in *Perspectives on Reality*) appear in English for the first time, thus making available important works that would be otherwise inaccessible to the vast majority of undergraduate students.

The editors introduce their sections with long essays that discuss the basic issues and place the readings in their historical and philosophical framework. As a further aid to the student's understanding of the subject, the editors provide a glossary of important philosophical terms for each section. No attempt has been made to include all terms or to give exhaustive definitions. The definitions are brief and descriptive, and are intended to serve as a convenient reference for the student as he reads the primary sources. Other editorial aids include headnotes that provide biographical data on each philosopher; footnotes (identified by the initials of the philosopher, editor, translator, or section editor) that clarify references, foreign phrases, or difficult terms; and annotated bibliographies of primary sources and commentaries, selected with the beginning student in mind.

Within each section are questions that test the student's comprehension of the selections he has read. In addition, there are two sets of questions at the end of each section: the first set is for the section as a whole; the second relates the section to other parts of the book. These questions may be used as topics for term papers or as guidelines for those classes conducted in the dialogue or Socratic method; they also are an excellent means of review.

The volumes can be used in the classroom in a variety of ways. Some instructors may want to cover the entire book in the course semester, while others may choose to concentrate on certain sections and assign remaining ones for home study. Because of the extensive editorial aids included, such assignments are feasible. Moreover, the sections do not have to be taken up in the order in which they appear in the books. Most instructors will want to begin with the General Introduction, which explains the nature and historical development of philosophy and analyzes the basic problems, topics, and issues of the particular subject of the volume. Once the student has had this orientation, the teacher may take up any philosophical tradition he chooses. In fact, the pluralistic approach of the volumes makes it possible for teachers with different areas of specialization to collaborate in teaching the course. They can also take advantage of the many excellent films now available that are related to the teaching of philosophy.[1]

practicable,
possible?
likely,
reasonable?
probable,
suitable!

The General Editors assume overall responsibility for the three books in the Harbrace Series in Philosophy; their specific responsibility was in writing the General Introduction and Preface for each volume and in coordinating the program of study aids. The Contributing Editors wrote the introductory essays and selected the readings for their respective sections. The series represents a genuinely collaborative effort on the part of seventeen editors to present philosophy as a meaningful enterprise for students. The attitude of pluralistic openness makes it possible for students to enter into the act of philosophizing with initiative, spontaneity, and enthusiasm; it also prevents philosophy from being a subject easily contained in a parcel of memorized formulas. Great philosophers have not been interested in the tidy definition but in a disciplined reflection on the world of truth and value. Students who resist memorized formulas will respond to philosophical materials that have obvious relevance to the world in which they find their problems and project their own solutions. It is precisely such materials that the editors have sought to include in these volumes.

J.A.M.
G.F.K.

January, 1966

---

[1] A very helpful list of films, and their distributors, has been compiled by Caroline E. Schuetzinger of Mercy College, Detroit. This list appeared in *The New Scholasticism*, XXXIX, 2 (April, 1965), 224–29.

Contents

PART I
CLASSICAL AND SCHOLASTIC THOUGHT:
Plato, Aristotle, Aquinas

EDITED BY Elizabeth G. Salmon, *Fordham University*

PART II
DIALECTICAL THOUGHT:
Hegel, Marx, Engels, Schaff

EDITED BY Richard T. De George, *The University of Kansas*

PART III
AMERICAN PRAGMATIC-NATURALIST
  THOUGHT:
Peirce, James, Dewey, Santayana

EDITED BY Robert J. Kreyche, *Rockhurst College*

PART IV
ANALYTIC-POSITIVIST THOUGHT:
Hume, Carnap, Russell, Ayer, Ryle, Wittgenstein, Moore, Strawson, Hampshire

EDITED BY Margaret Gorman, R.S.C.J., *Newton College of the Sacred Heart*

PART V
EXISTENTIALIST AND PHENOMENOLOGICAL THOUGHT:
Husserl, Merleau-Ponty, Sartre, Brunner, Marcel, Heidegger

EDITED BY Robert Sokolowski, *The Catholic University of America*

General Introduction

BY *Jesse A. Mann* AND *Gerald F. Kreyche*

natural
↑
~~in~~herent - innate, basic, inborn

belonging to the real nature of the thing; essential, inherent;

The principal concern of this book is to present the key ideas and issues
faced by a number of thinkers attempting to formulate a philosophy of
man. These thinkers can be highly individualistic, yet this does not prevent
our being able to place them in broad traditions or schools of thought. Although this is done more for the sake of convenience than for the intrinsic
demands of the subject matter, such classification serves a useful purpose.

Although relatively few men in history have given us a coherent and
thoroughgoing philosophy of man, it is safe to assert that no thinking adult
has ever failed to formulate for himself some philosophy of man, however
unrefined. More often than not, the person making such an implicit formulation would not even be aware of his doing so. Yet if he were asked to
respond to some key questions, it would be immediately apparent that he
had broached the subject.

Let us ask him, for example, whether he thinks man is free, and if so, to
what extent. Or we might inquire of him the meaning that he ascribes to
freedom as it is applied to man. If such questions are posed Socratically,[1]
the answers are bound to be forthcoming, since everyone has given at least
peripheral consideration to these and to similar questions.

An intelligent person will not attempt to pursue these questions in a
vacuum or to base them on personal experience only, although the latter
should not be ignored. The thinking man will want to see what others have
said on the topic in order to see how they square with his own views. If he
is prudent, he will consider the answers of others in an open fashion and be
ready to learn from any and all sources. He will be particularly interested
in those who have had an influence on the thought of contemporary times.
He will be operating under the generally safe assumption that views which

---

[1] Socrates (470–399 B.C.), the teacher of Plato, asked questions of his fellow citizens
and philosophers in such a way that a hint to the possible answer was partly contained in the question itself. This encouraged the perceptive listener to offer a reply
to the problem. Yet the one who replied generally did not realize at first that Socrates' technique was a method designed toward getting the listener deeper and deeper
into the problem itself. The first answer given would probably see eventual rejection
as the problem gradually unfolded.

1

have persisted over time are likely to have some contact with the truth of
the matter. *a collection of poems, stories, etc.*

This volume is an (anthology) of such views, for it brings together some
of the major influences relevant to contemporary philosophic thought. The
readings include the views of men who lived well over two thousand
years ago; they also include the views of those who are still actively engaged in philosophical writing, one of whom is a recent winner of a Nobel
prize.[2] A variety of views in this volume are presented so that the reader
can draw freely from pluralistic sources, using a number of their insights
(while rejecting others) to assist him in formulating his own philosophy of
man. The resulting philosophy of man will then be an (explicit,) organized,
and technical exposition, instead of an (implicit,) chaotic, and "armchair"
viewpoint.

But before even the outlines of a philosophy of man can be arrived at,
it will be wise to discuss the larger picture of philosophy itself. The philosophy of man, after all, is but part of the whole fabric of philosophy.
explicit - clearly stated, distinctly expressed; leaving nothing implied; definite, outspoken

An Initiation into Philosophy

Man has searched for many precious things in the history of civilization.
Among these are gold, silver, new lands, and (artifacts) of bygone civilizations. But the most precious search conducted by man has been the
search for wisdom—philosophy. Philosophy has proved to be an unending
quest, and we have inherited the legacy of the great minds of history as
guides to help us pursue it. The search for the good life has been termed
ethics; the search for meaning of reality and God, *metaphysics;* and the
search for who man is, *philosophy of man.*

Perhaps the philosopher can best be described as one who loves truth
in its deepest meaning. This is in keeping with the literal meaning of the
word "philosophy," a love of wisdom. The study of philosophy is a continual encounter, a dialogue carried on in search of truth wherever it may be
found.

Philosophy has been called the "speciality of the general." It has been
characterized as "beginning in wonder and ending in mystery," and also
has been viewed as more appropriate to the gods than to man, for it seeks
out the divine. But philosophy is not a study of the (occult,) although it does
reach the plane of natural mysteries. It is not religion, nor a substitute for
it, although some thinkers in history have tried to make it such. Unlike
supernatural theology, it cannot appeal to revelation and faith as intrinsic
aids in its quest.

All of the above descriptions of philosophy are true, though necessarily

implicit - implied, inherent; unquestioning, absolute.

[2] Jean-Paul Sartre (b. 1905). However, he rejected this honor and became the first
Nobel prize winner in history to refuse the award of his own (volition.)

incomplete. The questions philosophy poses are simple to formulate, but exceedingly difficult to answer to the full satisfaction of the inquirer.

Philosophy may sound strange and remotely archaic to the twentieth-century mind, so caught up in the marvelous technology and science of the age. To some, it has been mistakenly viewed as an intellectual game, invented by old and bearded men to pass the time of day. Yet of all studies, it is the most relevant to man, for it concerns *man as man*—not man as scientist or as artist or as laborer. What could be more proper to the study of mankind than man himself?

The tools of the philosopher are not geiger counters, scalpels, or paint brushes. His tools are ideas, and they have moved more than mountains, whether for good or for ill. In the final analysis, the world is moved, not by a lever and fulcrum, but by ideas. It is the battle for men's minds and the conflict of ideologies that have characterized the progress and decline of cultures and civilizations. The work of the philosopher can be noted in all.

Philosophy does not have all the answers, but it does grasp and raise the important questions and problems of life, and it proposes solutions to many of them. The reader should not expect philosophy to make him content and then send him out to pasture. To the contrary, philosophy forces one to become restless, in the healthy way that liberal education seeks to make one restless. It does this by encouraging in the inquirer an ever increasing desire to know and to love the truth. Socrates summed up the feeling of the philosopher when he declared, "The unexamined life is not worth living."

There are several ways in which we can determine what philosophy is. One is to see historically what contributions philosophers have made in the past and to sample their views on what constitutes the nature of philosophy. Another is to examine the contemporary scene and observe present-day philosophers at their work, for by so doing we can also see what philosophy is. Strange though this may appear, both methods of inquiry reveal much the same data. To a large extent, the questions philosophers are asking today are quite similar (although the language is different) to those posed by philosophers in the past.

A careful study reveals that at some points in history the answers given to these questions are divergent; at others they are in agreement. This is not to imply that philosophical progress has been neglected; rather it is to state that its forward motion has been "seesaw" in character. If we look for progress, it is important that we search for it in the right places. Unlike that found in many other disciplines, philosophical progress is marked principally by progress in depth. Its advance can be described more aptly as vertical rather than horizontal.

The riches of the ages, the legacy of many centuries, have given contemporary man greater insights into the same problem than those had by the men who first posed the questions. There is, then, a continuity in the philosophical enterprise despite sharp and wide divergencies between individual schools of thought. The continuity philosophy manifests in history permits at least a summary definition. Philosophy can be termed an inquiry which seeks to encompass the whole of reality by understanding its most basic causes and principles insofar as these are acceptable to reason and experience.

The Beginnings of Philosophy: The Pre-Socratics

Philosophy as a science, that is, as a systematic attempt to uncover the causes of things, traces its beginnings to the Greeks nearly twenty-six centuries ago. This is not to say that other cultures lacked their own philosophical ideas. Yet it was the Greeks who were the first to separate philosophy from religion and mythology in order to pursue it as a study in its own right.

Philosophy had its beginnings in the sixth century B.C., not in Athens as one might suspect, but in the Greek colonies. More particularly, it began in Ionia, which was located in Asia Minor on the Mediterranean coast of what is now Turkey. It was here that East was to meet West; a veritable cradle of the intermingling of Egyptian, Babylonian, and Greek cultures was to be found.

But why, we might ask, should philosophy begin when it did—comparatively late in the civilization of man? Why, too, should it begin in Ionia instead of in Athens? The explanation lies in the fact that philosophy as a kind of necessary intellectual luxury could only be afforded by those who had time to wonder. Any culture that begins philosophizing would have to be quite developed before it could afford such a luxury. Prior to this time, man had been too busy working out the day-to-day problems of subsisting to bother with philosophy. It began in Ionia rather than in Athens because the citizens of Athens were too embroiled in practical political difficulties to have time for it. Philosophy, as reflective thinking, needed a suitable environment and Athens simply could not provide it at the time.

So it was that the first philosophers were historically grouped together and labeled as the Ionian school, even though many years separated their respective lives. What did they philosophize about? What causes did they seek to discover? As one might guess, they were interested in uncovering the basic principles of the world in which we live. Their philosophy was largely an attempt to account for the similarities and differences of things. They observed that the world manifests a unity amid variety, that despite its myriad aspects, it was a uni-verse. In short, they raised the problem of "the one and the many," as it applied to the material world they knew. Their effort and their raising of the problems should be credited, rather than their solutions. Today their answers appear naive.

For example, Thales (*c.* 624–546 B.C.), the "father of philosophy," looked for the basic principle of unity to which all material reality could be reduced. He was convinced that change demands a fundamental common ground, a basic constituent from which change proceeds and to which it returns. He observed that everything in the world is some form of a liquid, solid, or gas. Further observing that water could be evaporated, frozen, or liquefied, he thought he uncovered the root principle of reality. Water is the element common to all things; everything is some variation of it.

Others thought that air or some indeterminate principle could be the basis of things. Air was given because it too could take on different aspects of reality through rarefaction and condensation.

Meanwhile, in Southern Italy a semisecret society claimed that basically things are nothing more than numbers and geometrical forms. These philosophers were known as the Pythagoreans, after their leader Pythagoras (580–500 B.C.).[3] The reasoning in part that led to their position was this: Everything we observe appears to be some combination of points, lines, and surfaces, hence mathematical. Further, musical harmony and pitch can be accounted for by lengthening or shortening the strings of the lyre, a musical instrument of the day. Hence, reality is explainable by mathematics, for reality is fundamentally numbers. Number two represents the female; number three, the male; number five, marriage. In this way they accounted for the harmony and for the unity and diversity of reality. Following their inspiration, Plato later claimed that fire is so painful because it is composed of tiny solid triangles (tetrahedrons). Consequently, wherever one touches it, one is pricked by an angle point. Earth is bulky because it is a cube, and so on.

Early in the fifth century B.C., another philosopher, Heraclitus (*c.* 540–475 B.C.), focused his attention on the empirical fact of change. Since everything seems to be changing, he felt that reality is fundamentally change itself. Fire, for example, ceases to exist unless it is changing. The same is true of observable living things; hence, for Heraclitus, to be is to be changing. He is reported to have said that no man can put his foot into the same stream twice, for since the stream is changing, it will never be the same. His disciples went even further by concluding one could not put his foot into the same stream even once!

As might be expected, another philosopher, Parmenides (530–444 B.C.), disagreed with Heraclitus and held a contrary position. For Parmenides, man is the constant victim of sense illusions, such as "seeing" the mirage of water on a desert plain. Change is only one more such illusion. In truth, he claimed, nothing changes—everything simply is. All apparent differences between things are illusory. If things are not different,

---

[3] The reader may recall the Pythagorean theorem from geometry. Its formulation can be traced to this group of philosophers.

then they must all be the same. Hence, Parmenides' thought led in the direction of pantheism, namely, that everything is simply an aspect of God, who alone is real.

Next came a man who provided a synthesis to some of these earlier views. His name was Empedocles (*c.* 490–430 B.C.) and he held that the four elements—earth, air, fire, and water—plus certain natural forces, account for all. Just as paint colors can be mixed to get new colors (e.g., blue and yellow produce green), so the elements can mix to give us the new aspects of reality that we all observe. In brief, quantitative changes explain qualitative changes.

At this point, we see that philosophy was beginning to develop and paving the way to advance beyond views of the cosmos to views on man. From a cosmologically oriented philosophy, we can detect a shift to an anthropologically oriented one. Up to now, none of the philosophers seemed able to explain the differences between living and nonliving things, or the fact that order is present in the world. Entering the scene at this juncture was a man named Anaxagoras (*c.* 500–428 B.C.), who spoke of a principle of mind or intelligence as having something to do with reality. Unfortunately, he only hinted at the role it plays, but a breakthrough had been made and would be carried on by others.

Also about this time another school of thought termed Atomism burst upon the Greek scene. Its leaders were Leucippus (*fl.* 460 B.C.) and Democritus (*c.* 460–370 B.C.) and they provided a framework for a more extensive and complete philosophical vision. They held that ultimately matter is indestructible and is composed of tiny particles of matter designated as atoms. They were not, however, thinking of what the modern-day physicist refers to as atoms.

According to the Atomists, these fundamental particles of matter differ only in their shapes. All are in motion, often proceeding in different directions. When they collide by chance, they either stick together, thus accounting for generation and birth, or they break other combinations apart, thereby accounting for corruption and death. Here for the first time was a thoroughgoing materialism, and the Atomists applied their doctrine to all known areas of philosophy. In the philosophy of man and in ethics, they held that man is simply an aggregate union of material particles for whom death is an absolute dissolution.

Athens now awakened to philosophy, and a famous threesome introduced a golden age for philosophy. They were Socrates (470–399 B.C.), Plato (*c.* 427–347 B.C.), and Aristotle (384–322 B.C.), in each case, the earlier serving as the teacher of the man following. Despite this continuity, however, their views, especially with respect to a philosophy of man, were quite dissimilar. With this trio philosophy came of age and its basic divisions were outlined. Although the reductionist error, that is, reducing all subsequent philosophical problems to the categories proposed by these men, must

coming after; following in time, place, or order.

be avoided, it is safe to assert that most of the key problems in classical philosophy were set down and discussed by them.[4]

Apart from the triumvirate of Socrates, Plato, and Aristotle, a period of intellectual chaos and moral decline can be noted in the fifth and fourth centuries of pre-Christian Greece. It is aptly described in Thucydides' *History of the Peloponnesian War.*

> Words had to change their ordinary meaning and to take that which was now given them. Reckless audacity came to be considered the courage of a loyal ally; prudent hesitation, specious cowardice; moderation was held to be a cloak for unmanliness; ability to see all sides of a question, inaptness to act on any. Frantic violence became the attribute of manliness; cautious plotting, a justifiable means of self-defence. The advocate of extreme measures was always trustworthy; his opponent a man to be suspected. To succeed in a plot was to have a shrewd head, to divine a plot a still shrewder; but to try to provide against having to do either was to break up your party and to be afraid of your adversaries. Oaths of reconciliation, being only proffered on either side to meet an immediate difficulty, only held good so long as no other weapon was at hand; but when opportunity offered, he who first ventured to seize it and to take his enemy off his guard, thought this perfidious vengeance sweeter than an open one, since, considerations of safety apart, success by treachery won him the palm of superior intelligence.[5]

The comedies of Aristophanes portray the same scene.

At this time a group of teachers known as the Sophists emerged in Greece. Originally, a "sophist" meant a wise person, but the appellation was applied to these men in a derogatory way. They taught students in the professions how to succeed at any cost. Basically, they were sceptics and relativists. Protagoras (480–410 B.C.), one of their principal spokesmen, held that "man is the measure of all things, of what is, that it is, of what is not, that it is not." In effect, this meant that things are the way they appear to the subjective mode of the knower. All absolutes are automatically ruled out as well as the entire realm of the objective. Science, truth, and moral norms retain at best a purely subjective status and, accordingly, they differ with each man. The useful becomes the criterion of truth and action.

The Sophist position was aptly and succinctly summed up by Aristotle in his remark that "they have the appearance of knowledge without the reality."

---

[4] It will be the task of this essay to state the basic problems as pertaining to a philosophy of man and to draw implications from the answers given. But before this is attempted, we will continue to survey the history of philosophy. Philosophy, after all, is often reactionary. Never does it arise in a vacuum; it is born and bred in an historical and empirical setting, even though it normally attempts to go beyond both.

[5] Thucydides, *History of the Peloponnesian War,* trans. by R. Crawley (London: J. M. Dent, 1910), Book III, 82, 83, pp. 224–25.

Such is the brief picture, then, in which a philosophy of man began taking shape in the Western world during classical times. In a number of respects, it parallels our own times.

The Maturation of Greek Philosophy: The Athenian Period

Opposition to the Sophist mentality, which makes philosophy all but impossible, came from Socrates. Socrates never wrote a line, but his ideas were immortalized for us by Plato, especially in the latter's early dialogues. While previous philosophy had been chiefly concerned with cosmological and, to some extent, psychological inquiry, Socrates advanced philosophy to the level of ethical inquiry. His principal concern was with the nature of virtue and whether or not it could be identified with knowledge. Although no absolute resolution was made, he was inclined to believe that no man could do moral wrong knowingly, for if he did he would be acting contrary to his nature as a rational being.

Plato, who studied under Socrates, continued the moral inquiry and found himself in basic agreement with this Socratic position. In later years, however, Plato became more and more interested in political philosophy, as witness his dialogues, the *Republic* (a treatment of the ideal state) and the *Laws*. Plato also extended philosophy more deeply into the area of metaphysics. This branch of philosophy is interested in ascertaining the nature of reality, truth, goodness, and unity.

Yet, it was the genius of Aristotle that systematized the inquiry of metaphysics to the status of a science, whose object is called "being" or "the real." By probing into the nature of the real as real, Aristotle attempted to clarify and to answer the problems of change, stability, plurality, oneness, multiplicity, and unity.

In addition, Aristotle gave new rigor to scientific and philosophical inquiry by insisting that all such efforts be directed at discovering the manifold causes of the object under investigation, seeking to answer why things are and why they act the way they do. Accordingly, he fathered the science of logic which formulated the method of demonstration and valid reasoning. In addition to logic and metaphysics, he developed a science of physics and philosophy of nature, a philosophical psychology and a system of ethics. He also made rich contributions to nearly all of the then known fields of knowledge, sharpening their insights and extending their frontiers. His definition of tragedy in the *Poetics* still stands as a classic position in literature.

After the death of Aristotle, minor schools continued in the philosophical tradition of Aristotle, Plato, and the pre-Socratics, mainly by way of attempting syntheses of their viewpoints. By and large, however, Greek philosophy came to a standstill after the third century B.C. Engaged in futile wars, the Greeks themselves were eventually conquered by the Romans, who took the leading Greek philosophers to Rome. These philosophers, called Stoics, taught young Roman students, especially in the domain of politics and law. Their influence can best be seen in the field of natural law.

Around the second or third century A.D., an important school of philosophy arose called Neoplatonism. Its most important spokesman was Plotinus (205–70). His position is in the tradition of Plato, but it adds to the latter a strongly mystical and religious flavor.

St. Augustine (354–430) was greatly influenced by the movement of Neoplatonism and, although more of a theologian than a philosopher, he helped to "christianize" Platonic philosophy, making it acceptable to the Church.

Medieval Philosophy:
Continuation of the Greek Tradition

In the period between Augustine's death and the Middle Ages, philosophy made scant progress beyond preserving its own tradition. However, with the religious and secular challenges faced by the Church in the Middle Ages, with the rise of the universities, and with the accessibility of Greek primary sources being opened up by the Crusades, philosophy once again made sharp advances.

In the early Middle Ages, a loose philosophical-theological system based on an Augustinian-Platonic tradition was in the forefront. However, in the thirteenth century, the general philosophical tradition prevailing in the West (albeit with some important variations) was that of Aristotle. The man who did the most to develop and continue this Aristotelian intellectual tradition in the Latin West was St. Thomas Aquinas (1225–74). If Augustine "christianized" Plato, then certainly Aquinas "baptized" Aristotle. One cannot overemphasize the difficulties Aquinas had in doing so, especially in light of the fact that for the previous eight centuries the Augustinian-Platonic synthesis prevailed. Yet, history bears witness to the success of Aquinas' efforts. Aquinas brought the rigorous Aristotelian methodology as well as Aristotle's key ideas to bear upon philosophy and Christian theology. Aquinas' adaptation of Aristotle came to be known as Thomism.

Many other great minds besides St. Thomas were active at the time: St. Anselm (1033–1109), St. Albert the Great (1206–80), St. Bonaventure (1221–74), Duns Scotus (1265–1308), and, later, William of Ockham (c. 1280–1349). To be fully appreciated these men need to be studied in depth, something which cannot be done here. Together they bear witness to a vigorous philosophical pluralism that marked medieval thought.

After the high-water mark of medieval thought, a period of philosophical decline set in, partly because the great religious orders did not encourage original thinking in philosophy. Many of the orders sought simply to consolidate their own philosophical position (as given by an important figure in the order) and would not tolerate philosophical "novelty." The Dominicans, for example, stressed the thought of St. Thomas; the Franciscans, that of Duns Scotus. It is unfortunate that the spirit of independent thought so carefully nurtured and so vigorously defended in the thirteenth century was to be so quickly abandoned.

Modern Philosophy: The New Era

Unlike medieval philosophy, modern philosophy was largely the work of laymen. Its point of departure was not the God of the medievals, or the world of the Greeks, but man. Its method, initially, was introspective and reflective.

René Descartes (1596–1650), who desired philosophy to be as certain as mathematics (in which he was a master, having invented analytic geometry), laid down a method for future philosophical enquiry. The method sought to determine as true only those ideas that are clear and distinct to the reflective mind. Descartes felt that man, prior to experience, was endowed with innate (inborn) ideas. Hence, Descartes began philosophizing with the innate idea he had of himself as a "thinking thing." This, in turn, led to the innate idea of God. Both inborn ideas were then employed to verify the reality of the world in which we live. While Aquinas proceeded from the world to self, and from the two to God, Descartes commenced with the self, then with God, both ideas leading to the world.

Descartes' method of looking for the clear and distinct idea as a guarantee of certitude evolved into philosophical rationalism. This tradition emphasizes mind over matter and feels confident that nearly all problems can be resolved by subjecting mind to their consideration. It tends to deemphasize sense experience and the singular by focusing its attention on laws of thought and on the universal. The tradition was carried on by Benedict Spinoza (1632–77), who attempted to formulate ethics according to geometrical demonstration, Gottfried Wilhelm Leibniz (1646–1716), the coinventor of calculus, and Immanuel Kant (1724–1804), a formulator of the nebular hypothesis as an explanation of the world's origin.

On the other hand, a sharp reaction to rationalism was led successively and progressively by such men as Thomas Hobbes (1588–1679), George Berkeley (1685–1753), John Locke (1632–1704), and David Hume (1711–76). With the exception of Berkeley, all rejected innate ideas. All insisted on testing the validity of an idea by tracing that idea to the initial experience from whence it was derived. All denied the ability of the understanding of man to abstract essences from objects, in effect making intellectual knowledge differ from sense knowledge in degree rather than in kind. Philosophy was clearly delimited by this viewpoint which has been termed the empiricist tradition; yet, like Descartes, the philosophers of this tradition were very interested in developing a philosophy of man.

Immanuel Kant eventually drew from both the rationalists and the empiricists and, in a limited way, closed the period of modern philosophy. From the rationalists he accepted intellectual knowledge as universal and necessary; from the empiricists he insisted that all genuine knowledge be drawn from experience. Contrary to the rationalists, however, he argued that man is incapable of knowing the essences or natures of things; contrary to the extreme empiricists, he held that scientific knowledge is possible and that one need not lapse into scepticism and relativism.

G. W. F. Hegel (1770–1831) crowned the rationalistic aspect of Kantian thought. For Hegel, all reality is to be viewed as the development of a rational principle—Mind—which is the totality of reality. Everything must be seen as one or another phase of Mind as it runs the course of history. Reality, or Mind, accordingly is always becoming and things are forever capable of further development and perfection. Hegel brought out this idea in a momentous synthesis termed the *Phenomenology of Mind*. It is generally regarded as the high point of philosophical idealism.

Contemporary Philosophy: Reaction to Hegel

The existentialist movement and those allied with its basic ideas reacted strongly to Hegelian philosophy. Søren Kierkegaard (1813–55), Arthur Schopenhauer (1788–1860), Friedrich Nietzsche (1844–1900), Gabriel Marcel (b. 1889), and others insisted that an element of the irrational be present in the world and especially in the actions of man. *Will*, rather than *intellect* or mind, came to be emphasized, along with its corresponding call for freedom, commitment, and engagement. Jean-Paul Sartre, although an existentialist, is one of the few to remain partially under the positive influence of Hegel. Sartre insists on dialectical development in the world and even uses Hegelian terminology at times. Yet Sartre's emphasis on the irrational and absurd and his rejection of an Absolute sharply separate him from further Hegelian ideology.

The phenomenological method of the existentialists, although drawn initially from Edmund Husserl (1859–1938), who had strong tendencies to idealism, is also employed in an anti-Hegelian manner. Basically, the method constitutes an attempt to describe rather than define the objects of knowledge and the states of consciousness of the knower. Maurice Merleau-Ponty (1907–61) uesd it to great advantage in discussing the body, perception, etc.

Karl Marx (1818–83) also used Hegel, but only in methodology. Marx insisted that matter, not mind, is what is developing in history; but it is developing according to laws formulated by Hegel. Those laws are basically opposing forces (thesis and antithesis) clashing to produce new realities (syntheses), which retain the richness of the old but add the perfection of the new. For Hegel, the clash of non-being and being gives rise to change or becoming; for Marx, the clash of the proletariat (thesis) and the bourgeoisie (antithesis) will eventually give rise to the classless society (synthesis).

Naturalism and pragmatism, particularly as manifested in the British and American philosophies, also react against the rationalistic tradition. Philosophical naturalism refuses to see meaning in any order but the natural order. It brooks no interference by the supernatural order or by mind seen as a spiritual phenomenon. Pragmatism often provides the method for naturalism with the criterion of truth being offered as that which is useful and which produces fruitful results. Naturalism and pragmatism insist once again on experience as the only source of meaning. The importance of the physical sciences, especially since the evolutionary breakthrough by Darwin, became paramount, and naturalistic-pragmatic thought replaced the armchair speculative attitude so prevalent previously. Charles Sanders Peirce (1839–1914), William James (1842–1910), and John Dewey (1859–1952) long occupied the forefront of this general movement. Yet Sidney Hook (b. 1902), George Santayana (1863–1952), Abraham Edel (b. 1908), and others worked within its framework and helped to refine and develop its ideas.

Somewhat akin to the naturalists and pragmatists in their reaction to speculative and rationalistic thought are the analytic and positivistic philosophers of the present day. The early Vienna Circle of Rudolf Carnap (b. 1891), Herbert Feigl (b. 1902), Moritz Schlick (1882–1936), and Ludwig Wittgenstein (1889–1951) sought to put a stop to philosophical theorizing of the rationalistic type. They, together with A. J. Ayer (b. 1910), Gilbert Ryle (b. 1900), and other counterparts of the Oxford-Cambridge school, held that language clarification would dissolve the philosophical problems on which philosophers had been impaled for centuries. The body-soul problem, the subject-object problem, and other problems arose because of syntactical errors. The proper use of language would change all this and leave philosophy a skeleton of its former self. Science would henceforth take over what had previously been accorded the domain of philosophy.

This, then, summarizes the major periods of the history of philosophy. It will be noted that emphasis shifts among men and within different epochs, as to both the point of departure for philosophy and the problems regarded as central to it. Having surveyed the history of philosophy, however briefly, we are not prepared to delve more directly into the topic of our major concern—a philosophy of man.

Toward a Philosophy of Man: The Key Problems

What is a philosophy of man? Basically it may be described as an overview on the nature, activities, and destiny of man. It attempts to assess his place in and his relationship to the world. Through such an overview, an understanding of what man is and who he is will emerge. In short, a philosophy of man hopes to see man as a totality within a totality. In some respects, a philosophy of man constitutes a metaphysics of man, for it is a probe of the deepest causes and meaning of man.

Such a philosophy cannot begin with the "what" of man, any more than the physicist can begin with the essence of matter. It must commence operationally; that is, a philosophy of man must look first to the activities that characterize man in an historical setting. It must begin with the manifestations of the things that a man does, how he acts privately and socially, as an isolated individual and in a group.

To look for such clues as will lead us to a philosophy of man, we must adopt certain guidelines so that our search will be an orderly one and not a meandering effort. These guidelines can be proposed as a series of questions to certain key problems. The answers will help fit together the pieces making up the mosaic for a philosophy of man. To look for such answers, we will consult a variety of sources. No philosophy of man could lay claim to being complete in its essentials, to say nothing of being honest with itself, if it did not take into consideration other philosophies of man to test its conclusions.

Although hosts of problems can be cited, all are reducible to four key problems or to implications derived therefrom. Sometimes only the smaller part of the problem manifests itself in a particular epoch, but as problems, they persist through the history of philosophy. The first is the problem of *knowledge;* the second, *freedom;* the third, man's *unity;* and the last, *immortality*.

The Problem of Knowledge

All men agree that man is a knowing being. No one can deny this, especially in the light of today's "knowledge explosion." In certain areas man has learned more in the past fifty years than in the previous five thousand years. We can also find agreement that the brute animal is likewise capable of knowing. Here, however, general agreement stops. When it comes to asking how man knows, what he does know, and what he can know, philosophers offer different answers.

To bring the problem more sharply into focus, let us consider one aspect of the problem as applied to contemporary science. Today in science we know through the use of instruments, rather than through direct observation. With instruments as intermediaries, the question may be raised as to what extent the scientist grasps the real in knowing. Does he necessarily alter the object in knowing it, so that what he knows is only what he has changed?

Werner Heisenberg (b. 1901) suggests that such is the case.[6] For example, one cannot measure the speed and position of an electron simultaneously, for in measuring one the scientist affects the other. (This principle is termed the Heisenberg principle of indeterminacy or uncertainty.)

The German philosopher, Immanuel Kant, held a similar, although much more generalized, view. According to Kant, in order to know an object we must change it (owing to the demands that the conditions of knowledge must meet—demands that are imposed by the nature of the knower). For example, said Kant, we do not know things in space and time as though space and time really exist "outside" the knower. Rather, space and time are categories (a priori forms of sensibility) of the knower. Their function is to help organize at a sensory level the raw datum of knowledge that the knower obtains from the world. Therefore, says Kant, we cannot know the real order of things as it is in itself, that is, as outside the knower. To draw an analogy, one might inquire how we know that the light in the refrigerator is off when the door is closed. The only way to find out would be to open the door, but in so doing we have triggered the switch and so have caused the light to be seen as on. Now, if the switch were hidden, and if it operated simultaneously with the slightest opening of the door, would we ever really know if we caused the light to turn on, or whether perhaps the light had been on all along? Would we know, at least in this case, the way reality was, before we affected and changed it?

In science today, we often proceed mathematically and with logical constructs, that is, we set up some kind of archetype or blueprint in our mind and then attempt to explain reality on its basis. Hence we can use different mathematical systems to explain the same physical phenomenon. Such would be the case when we apply Euclidian or non-Euclidian geometry to a specific problem. We can also view light under a particle or a wave theory, depending on which suits the convenience of our explanation and enables us to predict more accurately. Studying matter at the macroscopic level, Newtonian laws can be applied, but these same laws are often denied at the subatomic level of inquiry.

In such cases, have we made reality conform to our mind, instead of having our mind conform to reality? From the viewpoint of mathematics, for instance, an object is more or less circular, depending on the degree of conformity it has to the perfect circle present in our mind. If the method of the scientist is primarily a mathematical one, then we can see that a larger question is before us, namely, to what extent does the scientist grasp the real on its own terms? Has he, perhaps, fashioned reality in his image, instead of the converse?

---

[6] Heisenberg is a Nobel prize winner in physics. He has written extensively on philosophical scientific problems. See especially his *Physics and Philosophy* (New York: Harper & Bros., 1958), pp. 129, 143–45, and *passim*.

Now the pragmatist will not quarrel with the above procedure as long as it produces fruitful results. Yet many will carry the theory over to all knowledge, and applications of the principle will be made to the entire life situation. Utility will then become the sign, if not the criterion of truth, and truth will be reduced to a purely relative status. Such a view paves the way for man to become a constructor of truth rather than a discoverer of truth.

The problem of knowing the real is also a problem for certain of the existentialists. Jean-Paul Sartre, for example, designates man as in the category of *pour soi* (for itself), as opposed to the category of *en soi* (in itself). That is, man is basically a *subject* residing in a hostile world of *objects*. Sartre will admit to man's ability to know himself as a subject, for man can see within himself. Indeed, a subject is what man is principally and primarily. But can man know other men as subjects, or can he only know them as objects? And what of other men knowing him? Can they know him except as object? To know another man as an object is to falsify him, for he is principally a subject. This, among other reasons, is why Sartre rules out God, for God's knowledge would so objectify man as to destroy man.

Sartre sets up two categories of knowing, subjective and objective, and sees them as fundamentally irreconcilable when applied to knowledge of ourselves and of other men. In knowing other men, we are doomed to regard them as objects and to employ our knowledge as a kind of dragnet device, destroying their basic dignity as subjects.

Perhaps a clearer and more broadened view of the problem of knowledge can be had by glancing briefly at Plato's position here. Plato sharply distinguished between two types of knowing activity enjoyed by man— sensory and intellectual. Each possesses its own special characteristics.

Sensory knowledge deals with the *material, individual, changing,* and *accidental* characteristics of things. That which the eye sees or the ear hears is something material and singular, subject to the fluctuations found in the world about us.

Intellectual knowledge, on the other hand, deals with *immaterial, universal, unchanging,* and *essential* features. For example, the common notions of beauty or of humanity apply to many individual things, hence they are universal ideas. Once these concepts are grasped, they are grasped for all time and so are unchanging. They also contain the essential and necessary characteristics of the objects represented and so are quite different from the kind of information that the senses reveal. The senses, for example, tell us that a man is two hundred pounds, handsome, and dark-haired, but the senses never reveal what a man as man essentially and necessarily is. It is clear that the man will still be a man even though his appearances as grasped by the senses change. He can lose weight, become ugly, lose his hair, and still remain essentially what he is—a man. The senses do not reveal what a thing necessarily is; they only portray the changing appearances.

Accordingly, Plato asked if intellectual knowledge could be derived from sensory knowledge. But to ask this is to ask how the universal could come from the individual, the immaterial from the material, the unchanging from the changing, and the essential from the accidental. Since the two orders of knowledge seemed so far removed from each other, Plato could not allow that intellectual knowledge was derived from the sensory order. (He would not even claim that the senses give us "knowledge"; in his view, they produce only opinion and conjecture.) Hence, he reasoned, if a world of objects exists that corresponds to my sense knowledge (and from which this knowledge is somehow derived)—the world I live in and see about me—then, *a fortiori,* a world of intelligible objects must exist that corresponds to my intellectual ideas and from which the latter are derived. So it is that Plato argued to his famous "world of ideas" that have a reality apart from the mind of man and apart from the world of sense.

Aristotle offered a solution to the problem posed by Plato without "going out of this world" to do so. Aristotle accepted Plato's distinguishing characteristics of the two orders of knowledge, yet saw the intellectual order as derived from the sensory order. Although for Plato there are two different sources of knowledge, for Aristotle there is but one. Yet Aristotle still claimed for man both intellectual and sensory knowledge. He accounted for the former, however, by assuming an intellectual faculty in man that can "abstract" from the sensory order the data of intellectual knowledge. This ability to abstract and to understand serves as one of the principal distinctions between man and the brute. Hence, man's ability to think abstractly and to sense concretely both bear on the same world, the one in which we live.

St. Augustine harkened back to the spirit of Platonism by attempting to see the truth from within. An interior glance reveals innate ideas or contact with eternal truths. Augustine faced the same problem Plato did. How could the sensory order affect the intellectual and spiritual side of man, when the latter seems to be so far above the former? There is in both thinkers a clear distaste for the sensory world and things within it. Their knowledge theory bears this out, for even sensory knowledge has a touch of spirituality about it.

The scholastic tradition of the Middle Ages, while containing elements of Augustinian-Platonic knowledge theory, is heavily oriented to Aristotelian views, particularly as modified and developed by St. Thomas Aquinas.

In modern philosophy, René Descartes accepted an innate theory of knowledge ultimately verified by God. That is, we are born with some basic ideas whose clarity and distinctness reveal their truth to us. They are further guaranteed by God, whose existence we arrive at by considering the innate idea implanted in us.

Subsequent thinkers went down either the path of idealism and rationalism (e.g., Spinoza, Leibniz, and, to some extent, Kant and Hegel), or empiricism (e.g., Hobbes, Locke, Hume, and, to some extent, Berkeley). If empiricism accepts intellectual knowledge at all, it is because this position reduces it to an extension of sense knowledge. This means that there is no essential distinction between the knowledge enjoyed by the brute and that possessed by man. Association of ideas supplanted the Aristotelian doctrine of abstraction. Present-day positivists acknowledge themselves as largely derived from this empiricist tradition. The Vienna Circle, for example, an early twentieth-century group that played an important role in resurrecting empiricism, traces its heritage to Hume.

Two questions present themselves at this point; they are larger questions that provide the framework in which the positions cited above are located. The first is: Do we know the real or only our own impressions, regardless of whether these impressions be sensory or intellectual? The second question follows closely upon the first: If it is the real which we know, how deeply can we know it?

Let us examine the first of these. Do we know the real or only our own impressions of it? To take the example of seeing, an inverted retinal image appears in the eye, together with a corresponding stimulation in the optic center of the brain. Do we sense the image (or the electrical brain stimulation), or do we sense the thing (object) that the image represents?

Should the former be the case, how could we determine whether our image corresponds adequately to the object and truthfully represents it? In short, if it is the image that we know, rather than the object, how could we ever be sure it portrays the object as it really is? How could we ever know we are correct in talking about the object in terms of our impressions of it? Wouldn't it always be *our* impression and no one else's? If so, could anyone else ever *know* our impression (image)? Wouldn't they only know their own impressions? How could there be truth or falsity in such a situation?

If the above is the case, then for practical purposes things would *have to be* the way they *seem to be* according to the knower. All knowledge would be relative to the knower, who would forever lack any ability to check out the correspondence of his impressions with things. Such a position can be catalogued as phenomenalism, which asserts that we can only know the appearances of things. One might even claim, as did George Berkeley, that there is no reality "behind" the appearances; the impressions in us alone are what are real. Logically Berkeley had to deny the material world; however, he still maintained that the ideas or impressions have to come from some source, and this source is God. Reality for Berkeley, then, is entirely spiritual.

Opposed to phenomenalism and idealism is the realism held by Aristotle and Aquinas. They claimed that what we know first of all is not the image, but the *object* re-*presented* by the image. An analogy might be employed to show their point. When we look into a mirror, what do we see—

the mirror or ourselves? The normal response would be "ourselves," for we aren't even aware we're looking into a mirror until we see something by means of it. If we see the mirror, there is but one thing to do—take a rag and clean it, for the mirror ordinarily is not seen. The role and purpose of the mirror is such that it is primarily meant to convey and to point to something other than itself. This is why a large mirror in a small room makes the room seem much larger. It points away from itself to that which it re-*presents*. The sense impression and the idea are signs that make us aware of things before they make us aware of themselves. Thus, things do not depend on the knower (Berkeley), but the knower depends on things.

To the above dispute, the pragmatist might reply that there is no difference between the two positions, because neither one *makes* a difference in the practical order of things. For the pragmatist, to *be* a difference, a thing must *make* a difference. The analytic philosopher would likewise respond that only a pseudoproblem has been raised, for there is no way in which either position can be verified. Hence, previous philosophers have dreamt up this non-sense, meaningless pseudoproblem.

Yet an answer to the problem does have implications for a philosophy of man. To say that we know only our impressions is to enclose each of us in his own little world, always unable to escape its confines. The severe limitations that this imposes upon man are obvious in every inquiry he undertakes. The answers to all inquiries would be fundamentally the same—that is the way it *seems* to me. The absolute, the universal, the ethical norms —all would have to fall by the wayside. Could order of any kind prevail in such a world of subjectivism? Would not arbitrariness be the rule of the day?

Let us now investigate the second question, that is, if we do know the real order of things, how deeply can we know it? Can we know it only as grasped by the sense experience, or do we possess intellectual insights into it as well? Certainly the brute has sense knowledge. The dog recognizes its food, its master, its natural enemies. But does the brute recognize meaning? Arguing that it can be trained to respond to a command does not indicate an awareness of meaning, but only an association of sounds and conditioned response.

Man grasps meaning. He can understand what a thing is for, what an *end* is, and why particular *means* must be subordinated to it (as, for example, shutting the door to keep out a draft of air). The use of tools also indicates an understanding of which the brute seems incapable. Man sees their meaning in the abstract; the brute grasps significance only in the concrete. It is on the basis of man's intellectual insight into meaning, which differs from mere sensory knowledge, that human progress can be accounted for. The only progress observable in the animal kingdom is fundamentally biological in character.

The implications for an understanding of man are very great. They depend on which basic position one assumes with respect to man's knowledge, whether it is sensory or intellectual, and whether it is of a different quality as well. Like the scientist, the philosopher can only base his conclusions on evidence; if man reveals no traits essentially different from the brute, then there is no ground for concluding that man is essentially different from the brute. If man is not essentially different from the brute, his treatment of fellowmen should be no different from his treatment of other brutes. Although unfortunately this is sometimes the case, it is not usually. The evidence points in the direction that man does grasp meaning in the abstract and the concrete. Hence, man must be something essentially different from the brute. Since some of the actions of man differ essentially from those in the animal kingdom, man must contain within himself some principle accounting for this difference. This principle is usually called by those who accept the distinction a rational soul.

The Problem of Freedom

Having briefly considered some aspects of the problem of knowledge, we can now move into the area of action that is specifically human, namely, free activity. Freedom has been a goal of man since he first existed. It has taken many forms and has acquired diverse meanings, but throughout history a constant factor has remained in its understanding. The desired freedom of the caveman to be protected from the forces of natural disaster, of the slave and the serf to escape their state of subservience, of the colonized peoples to rule themselves, of the minority groups to obtain full civil rights—they all point to this.

Political freedom, economic freedom, social freedom, and academic freedom strike a common note and presuppose something more basic, namely, moral freedom. Without the latter, all derived freedoms would prove to be meaningless. Moral freedom implies an ability to make a commitment, regardless of whether or not that commitment may be implemented and carried out. The problem of moral freedom, or the problem of free will, is a major problem in any philosophy of man. Again, one must either deny it or affirm it on the basis of the available evidence.

The various philosophical positions with respect to the problem of free will can be reduced to three: (1) freedom is an illusion; (2) freedom is man's highest activity; (3) freedom is rooted in reason.

FREEDOM IS AN ILLUSION. The first position that freedom is an illusion has been held by different philosophers and at various times. Logically, all materialists must acknowledge themselves as holding to this viewpoint. If matter is governed exclusively by purely deterministic laws and if man is nothing more than matter (regardless of how complex his make-up may be), then man must be governed exclusively by purely deterministic laws.

The early Atomists, for example, could not logically opt for human freedom. Neither could the strict empiricist, although the latter might be open to the possibility of freedom. The materialist and the strict empiricist generally see man as simply one more part of nature, following mechanical laws in a world of sheer determinism.

It should be pointed out that the denial of human freedom can be found in philosophers who are neither materialists nor empiricists, as the Stoics, a group of philosophers living in ancient Greece and Rome around the beginning of the Christian era. They maintained that freedom basically consists in conforming our wills to accept the inevitable. In effect, they held that regardless of what we do, what will happen will happen. We do not control our destiny; choice consists primarily in accepting our fate. Whether or not we accept it, fate will be the same. Following the Stoic understanding of natural law, we can only live according to nature and accept our destiny. That is why a person is called "stoical" or is said to assume a "stoic" attitude if he remains impassive and unconcerned about the adversities and joys of life. The Stoic rationale can be more easily grasped if we consider their ideas on freedom within the pantheistic framework of their philosophy.

Benedict Spinoza, who like the Stoics was pantheistically inclined, also denied the freedom of man. Each man is required to act according to the deterministic laws that rule him.

The sixteenth-century English philosopher, Thomas Hobbes, held a similar view. He considered freedom as a name used to disguise our ignorance of the laws of nature which force us to act the way we do. He viewed chance as a name to cloud our ignorance of the laws of nature that bring about an unusual event. Many positivists and analytical philosophers imply much the same thing.

Those who deny freedom are generally termed behaviorists, determinists, or fatalists. Yet seldom do they deny freedom to man in any outright fashion. Often they will claim that man is free in much the same way that a ball is free to roll downhill if one removes all obstacles in its path. Or they will point out that man is free as a brute is free. A dog can be trained to obey and to conform to a command; so too man can be trained through social pressures.

For a person to do something as a result of persuasion, even pressure, is quite different from physically forcing him to do it. In short, there is an important distinction which must be observed between disposing and determining someone. To dispose a person favorably toward some line of action is only to incline him toward it, to give him a definite leaning toward a particular mode of behavior. To determine is to necessitate, to force, or to coerce a person to a particular behavior. Dispositions and habits do not necessarily cancel out freedom; in fact, they may be the result of freedom and its very adornment, when such habits are good or virtuous.

Now man is not born in a vacuum. He has many hereditary factors that include more than genes and chromosomes, for they take in the entire human history that man has bequeathed to man. Consequently, it may well be the case that collectively, and historically, certain groups have been propelled to certain ends. As the Marxists point out, the history of man reveals an important impetus given to his development or retardation by economic and other historical factors and pressures. Man's freedom has certainly seen severe limitations in particular epochs and for a variety of reasons. Certainly in many respects man is not free, but determined. He must obey any number of physical laws, for part of him, at least, is physical and material. But may one not concede all this without denying the essential trait of freedom to man?

FREEDOM IS MAN'S HIGHEST ACTIVITY.   Let us now examine the second position with respect to freedom, that is, it is real and operates independently of reason. In sharp contrast to the first position which negates freedom, this view upholds freedom as an absolute, if not *the* absolute. While recognizing the order of reason, this position places freedom above that order. It is characteristically described as voluntarism and regards the will as man's highest power or function. Among the scholastics, Duns Scotus accepted this position. In the last analysis so does Descartes, who reduced all error to a fault of the will.[7]

Those upholding the supremacy of freedom, or will, in man generally do so because of its importance to the practical order. We find, for example, in Hobbes, Niccolò Machiavelli (1469–1527), Schopenhauer, and Nietzsche, a fundamental stress on will to power. Whether this be toward personal or political power is of no concern here. What is to be noted is their stress on the will as the highest of powers.

William James stressed the will to believe and the favorable consequences that follow upon this concentration. As James never tired of pointing out, it makes a great difference in our lives if we will believe, for it makes possible that which may in all other circumstances prove to be impossible.

Much of the emphasis on will in contemporary philosophy can be traced back to Immanuel Kant. With respect to knowledge, Kant was convinced of man's inability to reach the real order. Cognition is restricted to the order of phenomena, or appearances. If man is to be considered phenomenally, Kant argued, we are obliged to see his actions as unfree and determined, following the same physical laws of all other things. However, it is difficult for the philosopher to live as though the real order is unreachable. Since Kant accepted such a real order (that of noumena or things in themselves as opposed to phenomena or things as they appear), we find he then tried to break into it—not by understanding, but by will. Hence,

---

[7] "Whence, then, spring my errors? They arise from this cause alone, that I do not restrain the will." (René Descartes, *Meditations on First Philosophy,* in *Philosophers Speak for Themselves,* ed. by T. V. Smith and Marjorie Grene [Chicago: University of Chicago Press, 1957], I, 88.)

almost by a tour de force of the will, we find Kant postulated freedom, God, the world, and immortality.[8]

Since Kant's time, philosophers have stressed this brute impetus of the will. We see it in Kierkegaard, the Danish religious existentialist, and especially in Jean-Paul Sartre, the contemporary French existentialist. Stated quite simply, Sartre considers freedom the very nature of man, for through freedom and choice we determine ourselves to be and to become what we are. The necessity for commitment and engagement, the immorality of neutrality—both follow from this.

For Sartre, however, the free choice by which we are self-determined is one based upon a fundamental absurdity, for there is no God, and without God the world is meaningless. Somehow we must justify ourselves; since we can find no rational basis for our choice, it is then absurd, but it is nonetheless a choice. In such a situation, any choice is better than none, for life does not admit of neutrality. *What* we choose is not as important as *that* we choose and thereby exercise our human prerogative. So it is for Sartre that "man is condemned to be free"; in the vacuum created by the absence of God in the world, we must choose to become a god.

Freedom is then the distinguishing characteristic of man, but it can only be exercised in a situation. Such a situation may be an absolute or a relative "limit-situation," to use Karl Jaspers' (b. 1883) term. That each man must die is an example of an absolute limit-situation, for no man operates outside such a framework. On the other hand, a temporary sickness may place man in a relative limit-situation, which is only momentarily confining.

The implications of the Sartrean position on a philosophy of man are many. It makes every man jealous of the other who is always attempting to usurp his freedom. This freedom has an insatiable appetite ever seeking new areas of conquest. If freedom is an absolute, then so is each man; hence each is condemned to be aggressive, defensive, and suspicious toward others. The implications for man's social character are overwhelming; one is led to wonder if the Sartrean position does not lead us back to Hobbes, who declared the natural state of men to be one in which all are at war with one another.

FREEDOM IS ROOTED IN REASON. The third position with respect to freedom, that is, a reality rooted in reason and, in the proper order of things, subordinated to reason, will now be considered. This view predominates in Thomistic-Aristotelian philosophy. It holds that free will is an appetitive power, which, to avoid being arbitrary and meaningless, must be under the direction of its cognitive counterpart, reason or intellect. Freedom follows upon intelligence; man is free because he is intellectual, not

---

[8] In Christianity, there has long been a Kantian emphasis on duty, striven for by the practical reason (will) that has given rise to the "will-power" Christian. Unfortunately, such a position has often obscured the aim of the Christian to be a lover primarily.

the converse. This position acknowledges many factors that affect freedom and will but cites the need for virtues (good habits) to direct lower inclinations to the good of the whole man. Accordingly, it seeks to obtain freedom from the rule of passion.

Knowledge provides the basis for choice and opens up its field. It sees the root of freedom in reason. Freedom, therefore, is enlarged in a manner that is proportionate to the enlargement of knowledge. Hence, the greater man's wisdom, the greater his freedom. Generally, we find both parents and teachers exercising this rule of thumb: The greater knowledge and responsibility that their protégés reveal, the greater latitude of freedom is given them.

This is not to commit oneself to psychological determinism—the view that whatever reason presents as the greater good will automatically receive a rubber stamp approval by the will. Contrary to Plato, knowledge of what is right never insures the doing of what is right. The Thomistic-Aristotelian position recognizes the semiautonomous character of freedom, but stresses the necessity for its subordination to reason for the well being of the whole man. Intellect, rather than will, is seen as the root power in man here, although in the practical order, a complementary relationship should always exist between the two.

In such a view, freedom acts in accord with law, not against it, for law is an ordinance of reason. Law assists freedom to maintain its true character, and not to degenerate into license. The existentialist Marcel will generally agree with this position, but he stresses the results of freedom, such as love and friendship. These help reveal who man is more than any consideration of the abstract notion of freedom.

Although freedom is a personal experience and cannot be dissected in a laboratory or put under a microscope, there is no reason for denying its reality. Those who look for freedom in this way will not find it, any more than they will discover what life is by dissecting an animal. Failure to recognize the facticity of man's freedom, then, can easily lead to an absolutism in the social order that can provide the basis for slavery, paternalism, or both.

The Problem of Man's Unity

All philosophers are agreed that in some way man is a whole, a unity. The facts of consciousness testify to this. However, different interpretations of what kind of unity is possessed by man run through the history of philosophy. In exploring this topic, we will first explain the two basic kinds of unity that may be found in the world about us—aggregate unity and essential unity; then we will see how these are applicable to the basic positions that can be held with respect to man's unity.

AGGREGATE UNITY. An aggregate unity is a whole in which the parts all retain their respective identity as parts. The whole is nothing more than the sum of its parts. The aggregate unity can be very crude or very refined.

For example, there are immense differences between an old Model T Ford and its new expensive counterpart, the T-Bird, but, despite the differences in unity, both are aggregate wholes. Or to take another example, a painting done by the master Rembrandt differs sharply from one done by a child, yet both are aggregate wholes.

ESSENTIAL UNITY. On the other hand, an essential unity or whole is one in which the parts have lost their identity precisely as parts and are subsumed by the whole. Somehow that whole is more than the mere sum of its parts. The whole assumes new characteristics that were not present in the parts from which it came to be. Take as an example a chemical compound such as water: water is a new and different reality from hydrogen and oxygen; although it comes from those two elements, it possesses characteristics or properties of its own. It exists normally in a liquid state, freezes at 32° F., and boils at 212° F. Hydrogen does not have these characteristics; neither does oxygen. Both elements have their own distinctive properties. A chemical compound is a true essential unity, as opposed to a colloid, which is but an aggregate whole.

Any organism then is an essential unity, a whole that is more than an aggregate of its physicochemical parts. It possesses, in distinction to nonorganic things, peculiar characteristics, the most important of which is its self-initiating activity—its immanent activity. Take as an example the phenomenon of growth. An icicle "grows" only by adding water from without; like a snowman, it only gets bigger by having something packed onto it. But growth—true growth—of an organism proceeds from an internal principle. Although food is needed for growth, the activity of growth is principally from within the organism, not from without.

Bearing these distinctions in mind, we will now survey the possible positions that may be taken regarding the unity and make-up of man.

It is clear that man is either an aggregate or an essential unity, but before deciding which, we must reach some conclusions about his constitutive make-up. Three positions seem possible: (1) man is basically material; (2) man is basically spiritual; (3) man is some combination of both spirit and matter. Let us now examine each position in detail.

MAN IS BASICALLY MATERIAL. This position has found many adherents, from the early Atomists to the current Marxists. Summarily this position holds that while man may well be the highest example of organized matter in the world, he still is nothing more than matter. Although we cannot as yet explain all of man's complex activities, we will eventually be able to do so as we progress scientifically. Studies in comparative psychology show us the amazing similarities between man and the brute. Recent investigations of amino acids, DNA, and others, lead us to believe that life will be produced synthetically, if not soon, at least in the remote future. Hence, man's unity and make-up can be explained without having recourse to principles other than matter. It is only of late that we have become more and more cognizant of the dynamic and evolving character of matter. This rejection of the previous view that matter is static opens the door to a full explanation of man in purely material terms. Evolution virtually clinches the argument, say those who hold man to be exclusively material. The unity of man, then, in such a position, may be an aggregate unity, or an essential unity. Yet it is a thoroughly monistic unity, for only one principle makes up man, matter.

MAN IS BASICALLY SPIRITUAL. Apart from George Berkeley, almost no philosopher has interpreted this to mean that there is no connection of man with matter. Nonetheless, a number of philosophers have seen man as a fundamentally spiritual being encumbered by presence in or with a body. Body and spirit (soul) are seen as two different things, even though they are somehow tied together.

Plato represented this position well when he gave his view of man as a soul entombed in a body, as an "oyster in its shell." Basically, man *is* a soul *having* a body. The reality that is man is really the soul; it is the soul that thinks and senses, looking out as it were through the organs of the body. The body is unnatural to man, even relatively evil for him, and constitutes a moral and intellectual hindrance to his perfection.

It is easy to detect the influence of Plato's ideas on St. Augustine, who coupled them with the background of Manicheism (a philosophical-religious sect that held that matter is evil), to which he had been subjected for over a decade.

Accordingly, those who subscribe to the Augustinian-Platonic bent of mind look for truth within man, not in the world. By transplanting Plato's "world of ideas" into the mind of God, and by having contact with these eternal truths through possession of a spiritual nature, Augustine could consult the "Inner Master" to determine truth. Hence, there is in this position a natural tendency to accept inborn ideas, that is, innatism. A general ignoring of, if not a positive disdain for, things material normally follows upon the general position that man is basically spiritual. The body of man is simply some sort of appendage attached to man in his present state.

In modern times, Descartes pursued a somewhat similar theme, for he held man to be primarily "a thinking thing." Since thought is the essence of man or spirit, man is principally spirit.[9] Yet, like Plato and Augustine, Descartes had to account for the factual presence of the body to man. The essence of matter (the body) is extension, and despite its antithesis to the realm of spirit in his philosophy Descartes nonetheless joined it unnaturally to the soul. In brief, Descartes wanted an essential unity to obtain in the mind-matter (soul-body) relationship, but his principles permitted only an aggregate union.

Today, there are few adherents to the Platonic-Augustinian-Cartesian brand of spiritualization of man, yet it has had its appeal to Eastern mystics as well as to many within Westernized Christianity. It goes hand in

---

[9] Jacques Maritain has characterized the thought of Descartes as an "angelism," for Descartes saw man as an embodied angel.

hand with what John Courtney Murray (b. 1904) terms an "eschatological humanism," which sees man as "in the world, but not of the world." Contemporary existentialists and phenomenologists such as Merleau-Ponty, Martin Heidegger (b. 1889), and Marcel issue vigorous protests against the historical "slighting" of man's body. What is needed today, Marcel says, is a metaphysics of incarnation.

The unity of man as comprising body and soul in the Platonic tradition is at best an aggregate union. The soul and body are seen as two separate but somehow joined entities. The one can often operate independently of the other, in an almost schizophrenic fashion. If the materialist and the empiricist tend to see man simply as a "thing among things," the rationalist tends to see man as being "above the world." Could it be that man is in some way both?

MAN IS SOME COMBINATION OF BOTH SPIRIT AND MATTER. This is the common tradition of the Thomistic-Aristotelian school, although it is not restricted to that school. According to this view, since man is an organized being, there must be a principle within man to account for this phenomenon of organization. That the organization proceeds from a principle internal to man is clear, in that growth, sensing, thinking, etc., all can be characterized as immanent activities. The principle accounting for such organization is a form, or soul. In fact, the argument is applicable to all organic beings, which, then, must have forms or souls. But besides the principle of organization, there is obviously that which is organized, and this principle is matter. Organic beings therefore possess two principles, matter and form, which complement each other and are seen as thoroughly integrated.

To make this clearer, one might employ the following: Cloth (matter), given a principle of organization (form), becomes a suit; wood (matter), given a principle of organization (form), becomes a chair. Together, the matter and the form constitute one whole.

The analogy is weak, however, for it does not point up the position that the unity of matter and form in organic beings is a substantial unity, an essential unity. Current existentialist terminology of man as "incarnate soul" stresses this latter point more fully. Man is not two things, antitheses accidentally and synthetically joined in an aggregate whole; he is one thing, or essential unity derived from two principles, but principles that by themselves are incomplete.

More especially in reference to man (although Aristotle's thought is ambiguous on this), certain operations are exhibited, which, although operating through matter, are not intrinsically dependent upon matter. An example would be that of thinking or willing. These human operations transcend matter and argue to the form (soul) in man as having nonmaterial, immaterial, spiritual qualities. Yet because man also exhibits psychosomatic activities (sensing, growing, and the like), it is clear that man is not essentially soul but a substantial union of matter and soul (form). Unlike the Augustinian-Platonic school, this position holds that matter is essential to man and natural to him, but the same is true of the spiritual soul. Accordingly, he is less than an angel, but more than a brute, straddling, as it were, the thresholds of both worlds.

Consciousness testifies to this essential unity and self-identity, for every action of man, whether psychic or psychosomatic, is seen as *my* activity, and not simply as the activity of a particular power operating in isolation from the whole man.

In regard to the two previous positions, which say that man is basically material or basically spiritual, Thomistic-Aristotelianism is in general agreement with what they hold, but in disagreement with what they deny. It is in what the two previous positions *don't* say that the principal quarrel is found.

For example, materialists accept the fact of man's organization, but instead of explaining it, they prefer to ignore it. Yet organization is clearly an effect, and hence demands some cause to account for it—not merely an initiating, extrinsic cause, but an interior one as well.

The Augustinian-Platonic tradition recognizes some degree of interaction of matter on mind (body on soul), but its principles are unable to account for this phenomenon. An example is our inability to think clearly when we are physically fatigued. Another example in a reversed vein is the physically fatiguing character that thinking has on man's material side.

Further, the Thomistic-Aristotelian argues (against the Augustinian-Platonic tradition): If the union of body and soul is unnatural and a hindrance, why should we not look forward to death (the separation of the two)? However, the fact is that normally death is not viewed as desirous in itself.

Man is not only an individual, but because he enjoys an essential unity, having as the principle of that unity an intellectual form, man is a person. But it is only through man's operation and activities, such as knowing and acting freely, that we come to be aware of this. Although man is free because he is intellectual, he is intellectual because he has the kind of soul (form) that he possesses. To possess a lower form, such as that organizing the plant or the brute, would be to lack intellectuality and hence freedom. Consequently, it is in this that he enjoys rights (and duties) and can live the moral and human life. Hence, man, as Marcel puts it, is a being who can make promises—one in whom we can believe.

The problem of man's unity has been a thorny one for philosophers, especially with respect to those who opt for some spiritual principle in man as at least partially constitutive of man's make-up. The theory of evolution, if not fully accepted at the moment, is accumulating sufficient support to force even the most conservative thinker to cope with the possibility of its becoming a fully established fact.

The Thomistic-Aristotelians are generally favorably inclined toward evolutionary theory, but normally qualify it so that the soul of man, being spiritual, could not evolve, but had to come to man from without—infused into matter at a moment in history when man first emerged. Yet, certain difficulties on this point prevail within the Thomistic-Aristotelian philosophy of man. Unless they are inwardly Platonists, they cannot say simply that the body of man evolved although the soul did not. For in their theory, the "body" is made to be a human body by the information of the human soul. In short, the human "body" did not exist prior to the existence of a human soul.

Thus, too, the Thomistic-Aristotelians seem to posit a "break" in nature's progression and continuity by holding against evolutionary theory regarding the soul of man.

Interestingly enough, Pierre Teilhard de Chardin (1881–1955), who in some respects might be classified as existentialist and naturalist in his thinking, was unalterably opposed to such a "break" and to the discontinuity in natural process that a nonevolving spiritual soul seems to require. Yet Teilhard de Chardin offered no theoretical solution to the problem; he simply left it hanging.

The existentialists generally see man's unity as that of a subject. This is unique, surrounded as man is by a world of objects.

The Marxist can be placed in the camp of materialism and has provided no developed philosophy of the person. Marxist faith is rooted in the species "humanity," not in the persons who make up humanity.

The solution to the problem of man's unity and nature must be based on answers given to the earlier questions about man's knowledge and freedom. In addition, we find that quite often the philosopher's views on man's immortality have some bearing on his answers to the problem of unity. The influence is psychological, however, for the latter question cannot be answered philosophically until the former is accounted for.

The Problem of Immortality

This problem is of greater personal interest to the average reader than the previous ones, for so much hinges on its answer. However, an attempt to solve it cannot be made in a vacuum. One must first pose solutions to the other problems cited and then draw out their implications with respect to immortality.

If man is simply an aggregate (or even an essential) unity of refined matter and nothing more, then death is the end for man. Immortality of any kind, other than continuance of the same atoms of matter that were present before, is logically meaningless. At best, what might be salvaged is some kind of impersonal immortality, which is nothing more than the continuance of the species to which man contributes. Hence, one might piously conclude that man lives on through the perpetuation of the human species, or through his work. But with the evolutionary theory, the idea of fixed species continuing forever is doomed. Immortality as rooted in the species is then a tenuous thing.

Bertrand Russell (b. 1872) views the idea of personal immortality as a fundamentally limited historical notion, which arose in an aristocratic society. In the golden age of Greek philosophy, when slaves were regarded as less than fully human, such a society prevailed. The notion of immortality resulted from society's extolling the individual free man. In a democratic society, charges Russell, such a notion has become obsolete; we should instead devote our attention to a democratic salvation of the masses, not the individual.

Somewhat similar is the Marxist idea of working not toward the immortality of the individual, but toward the classless society. A trace of one type of humanism can be seen as running throughout this position, and it is discussed and defended by many naturalists, including John Dewey and Corliss Lamont (b. 1902). It is social salvation—society—that counts, not the individual, who may or may not be sacrificed for its good.

Immortality, as used philosophically, generally implies some kind of afterlife for man. It may refer to man, whole and entire, or only to a part of man. It may involve a continuity of the person retaining his own identity or may simply refer to his impersonal absorption into a higher principle.

In early times, primitive man in the Biblical tradition had only vague notions regarding immortality, as is borne out in the Old Testament. The New Testament, however, makes a definite advance by promising a "resurrection of the dead."

Yet, the immortality of man, whole and entire, was often seen as gratuitous. No thought was given to a "natural" immortality or to the possibility that only a part of man, his soul, was immortal. Immortality referred to the whole person, as "resurrection of the dead" implies. This follows, too, for man was never seen as a unity composed of dualistic principles, something foreign to concrete, existential Jewish thinking.

Although his position is never seen as clear and definitive, Plato did make an attempt to grapple with the problem of immortality of the soul, remembering, of course, that the soul *is* the Platonic man. This immortality is tied up with ethical considerations, particularly in the early *Dialogues,* in which the thought of Socrates exercises a major influence.

A number of arguments are offered in defense of a limited kind of immortality for some men, if not for all. One of the arguments proceeds from the Platonic assumption that men have innate ideas. Since man is born with these ideas, he must have derived them from a previous existence in which the soul was unencumbered by the body (given to it later as some vague punishment). Tying this to the broad theory of metempsychosis, Plato suggested that the soul should continue to exist after death, perhaps in a manner similar to its existence before birth, although he did not appear to have reached firm conclusions on this point. (Plato's view on man as essentially a soul leaves him no problem on personal immortality, provided he accepts immortality of the soul, which would then be immortality of the man.)

The position of Aristotle is still more obscure. It seems that Aristotle would reject a prior existence of the soul (before its union with matter), for its very meaning is to be the form of matter. Without matter, the soul would have no *raison d'être*. Whether Aristotle held for immortality of the individual soul is a moot point. At best, he seems to have accepted the possibility of only a part of the soul, the intellect, being immortal.

St. Thomas presented a number of arguments purporting to prove that the human soul is immortal. Basically, it is immortal because it is spiritual. We know it is spiritual because it has operations or activities that surpass matter (intellection and willing, for example). Since it has activities ultimately proper to itself, it must have some entitative status, even apart from matter. Therefore, though death corrupts man, it does not corrupt the soul, which continues in existence.

Yet it is clear that not all Thomists accept the demonstrability of the immortality of the human soul. Gaetano Cardinal Cajetan (1469–1534), for example, rejected the arguments as proof. The arguments further do not establish personal immortality, in the sense that the person is immortal. Only an element of the person remains immortal, namely, the soul. For Aquinas the human soul can never be considered a person, for it is incomplete unless united with matter.

Part of the difficulty in Thomism lies in opting for the essential union of matter and form (soul), or man, while at the same time making the soul a substance (or a particular thing) as well. To some observers, Aquinas attempted to reconcile Plato and Aristotle on this problem, when their positions appear to be philosophically irreconcilable.

Interestingly enough, Aquinas began his argument for the immortality of the soul where Plato did, namely, with intellectual knowledge. While Plato argued on the basis of man's cognitive operations (the knowing of universals) that man, namely, the soul, previously existed, Aquinas argued to the continued existence of the soul. But for Aquinas even the separated soul still maintains a transcendental orientation to matter. As theologian, he saw this aptitude for matter giving credibility to the doctrine of resurrection of the body.

Immanuel Kant stated that the question of the soul's immortality can be answered positively, but that this answer is speculatively unverifiable. However, it must be posited by the practical reason to preserve the order of morality. The moral order becomes meaningless unless we accept the assumption that the soul is immortal.

Some of the pragmatists, especially William James, hold that the doctrine of immortality cannot be established, but belief in immortality can be consoling and may produce fruitful results. John Dewey, however, saw it as having harmful results, for it orients man to a life and world other than the one in which he lives.

The analytic philosophers, by and large, declare the problem to be somewhat non-sensical, for there is no way of submitting it to verification procedures. It is neither true nor false to say that man or some aspect of him is immortal, for the sentence expresses a wish that is disguised as a factual statement. In short, the sentence has emotive value, but it lacks cognitive value. It is in the same category as the declaration parents might make to their children, "God will be angry if you don't obey me."

Among the existentialists, Sartre accuses those who take refuge in a doctrine of personal immortality as being guilty of "bad faith," ignoring what is of consequence here and now. Marcel, however, has a Christian commitment to some type of immortality for man, claiming that man has a natural tendency to immortality and that such tendencies cannot be frustrated. But immortality is revealed more through experiences of hope and fidelity than through philosophical demonstration. In short, Marcel attempts to get back to personal experience and connatural knowledge and away from scientific proof.

Representative Philosophies of Man

In order to assist the reader to develop his own philosophy of man, the essays and readings in this volume will explore five basic philosophies with respect to their views on man. The traditions represented in the readings have been chosen because they are all relevant to the contemporary scene and have influenced current-day thought.

The Classical and Christian Philosophy of Man

The first part of the book is given over to what is termed the "classical and Christian" philosophy of man. The thread of unity that runs through it is the Thomistic-Aristotelian tradition. However, the views of Plato, St. Augustine, and a number of others are also surveyed, for they have made important contributions to this tradition and, in some respects, they have even sharply opposed it.

Readings in this section include the knowledge problem as posed and answered by Plato, Aristotle, and Aquinas. Of especial concern is the dichotomy and unity of sensory and intellectual cognition.

While there is relatively little that can be found in Plato regarding the will of man, the readings reflect his viewpoint on the freedom of man to live the good life and to follow the dictates of reason. The selections from Aquinas on will and freedom echo the further development of Aristotelian thought on this topic.

The problems of unity and immortality are taken up successively in Plato, Aristotle, and Aquinas. Plato seems inclined to accept a limited kind of immortality, at least for the good man, while Aristotle prefers to leave the problem unanswered, although he does supply certain hints for its possible resolution. Aquinas' views are definitive here, and he presents them as the logical conclusions of an Aristotelian philosophy of man and as consonant with the entire Christian tradition.

The Collectivist View of Man

The second division concerns itself with the Hegelian-Marxist philosophy of man, which could be termed a "collectivist" view of man. Great divergencies of thought mark this section, yet the historical orientation of both systems and other common bonds enable us to collate these views at least in part. Although Hegel's thought terminates in idealism, and Marx's thought ends in materialism, both are monists to the core. That is, both accept only a single principle as the ultimate source of explanation for man. For Marxists, that principle is matter; for Hegelians, the principle is mind. It should be pointed out that the philosophy of Marxism is considerably wider than the philosophy of Marx. The same may be said of Hegel and Hegelianism. The introductory essay and readings have noted this and have been oriented to the "school" rather than simply to the leader of the school of thought.

Selections in the readings reveal the kind of knowledge that Hegel envisioned as most appropriate to man, namely, self-consciousness. Yet this self-consciousness is shown to be one that sees the individual mind as part of the whole realm of Absolute Mind. The progressive understanding by man of himself in his historical picture is represented in the readings taken from Marx. Man's unity and nature as constituted by matter which is evolving, as well as his human character which is viewed as primarily social, are also stressed. Hence, man outside the collective is not truly human.

The excerpt from Engels reveals the Marxist position on freedom. Basically it is an insight into necessity and calls for man to recognize the laws that determine his destiny. This recognition will enable man to work with rather than against nature, helping him to achieve his end more quickly than would otherwise be possible.

The theme of immortality is of little consequence to Marxists, for they see death as simply the dissolution of the material unity that was man. Hegel, however, appears to argue for an impersonal absorption of man into the Absolute Mind. Yet, this can hardly be regarded as opting for personal immortality.

The Pragmatic-Naturalist Philosophy of Man

The third division, which deals with the pragmatic-naturalist philosophy of man, is generally American in outlook. It might be simply described as a "naturalistic" philosophy of man, for the pragmatists often find themselves using naturalistic principles. Charles Sanders Peirce, William James, John Dewey, and George Santayana serve as its principal spokesmen, but others have extended their views and this tradition.

Readings in this division cover Peirce's exposition on the necessity for and the method of making our ideas clear. In this selection one can see why the analytic movement has recently seen in Peirce the germinal views of their own position.

The readings also reveal what the naturalists and pragmatists understand by truth as "happening" to an idea. The selections from James are particularly relevant on this point. The general position of knowledge as an interaction of mind with experience is highlighted. How we test for meaning and fruitful results is discussed by Peirce, James, and Dewey.

The passages taken from James point up his great interest in freedom and will. His "voluntarism" here is very much in evidence, and he ties up this theory of freedom and belief quite neatly in the selections. His call for openness to new ideas and his condemnation of absolutism is a minor classic.

This tradition is not particularly concerned with the problem of man's unity, except to view it occasionally as a pseudoproblem. However, the interest of James in the problem of immortality is reflected in the selections given. A different viewpoint is revealed in a careful reading of Dewey, perhaps one more consonant with the scientific method which the readings in Dewey explain. Here one sees that man's destiny is to be part of a changing and evolving cosmos. Nonetheless, man is one who can influence and who is influenced by such a world. Belief in immortality, for Dewey, is characterized as harmful to the humanistic vision that he depicts.

The Analytic-Positivist Philosophy of Man

The fourth division surveys the analytic-positivist philosophy of man. At times, their philosophy is an antiphilosophy, yet this movement exerts a powerful influence on philosophical thought, especially in England and in America. Some of the men represented in this tradition are A. J. Ayer, Gilbert Ryle, and Ludwig Wittgenstein. They often see their contributions as therapeutic in character, cutting out of philosophy those problems that they describe as cognitively and factually meaningless.

In the readings by Ayer there are excellent examples of this therapy, particularly as applied to the problem of knowledge of oneself and of other minds. We also see Russell bring this view to bear on the mind and matter problem, a key issue of classical and contemporary philosophy. The problem of freedom and necessity is elaborated in the selections taken from Ayer. He sees it as a pseudoproblem, for neither position is verifiable in terms of analytic philosophy criteria. Statements on the issue are reducible to non-sense.

The excerpts taken from Hume treat the problem of man's unity, especially as put in terms of the problem of self-identity. The question that Hume raises is whether I can be certain I endure as anything more than a stream of consciousness, a bundle of perceptions and images. Stuart Hampshire (b. 1914) does not find total agreement with the Humean view, and selections taken from the latter's works indicate his view of man as more than a machine.

The problem of immortality as a philosophical issue is obviously not tolerated by the analytic and positivist movement. The readings reveal the fundamental reasons for this being regarded as one more pseudoproblem capable of dissolution by the analytic method.

The Existentialist-Phenomenological Philosophy of Man

The fifth and last division is that of the existentialist-phenomenological philosophy of man. Its impact had been felt long before its technical character became known. European in origin, it has strong advocates in America. The readings for this area also cover men widely divergent in their conclusions, though generally united in methodology. Represented are Husserl, Heidegger, and Sartre, and a number of others.

The selections from Husserl reveal both the phenomenological method and its application to the problem of knowledge, consciousness, and intentionality, but selections taken from others indicate sharp divergencies of opinion on this topic. Husserl's thought led him in the direction of idealism, a position thoroughly excoriated by Marcel.

Language and speech as revelatory of knowledge is treated by the Merleau-Ponty selections. The same readings point out through a phenomenology of man's body the meaning that things have in relation to it. Marcel likewise stresses an incarnational approach to a philosophy of man.

The freedom of man is a theme that runs through the selections taken from Sartre, August Brunner (b. 1894), and Marcel. Yet Sartre alone views freedom as the very nature of man, for it constitutes his "nothingness" whereby he is able to become other than what he is. Without this freedom, man would be another thing among things, an "in itself" instead of a "for itself."

Man's unity and character as a person are stressed by Brunner and Marcel. Man as person opens up the possibility of an "I-Thou" relationship which can obtain between men, instead of the "I-It" structure governing man and other things.

The reading from Heidegger emphasized man as the locus of being and how all reality must be viewed in this light. As an example, Heidegger discusses time and its meaning revealed as a mode of man's being in the world.

Conclusion

We have now reviewed the five major movements which have a bearing on a contemporary philosophy of man, and we have also indicated how these movements stand with respect to the four major problems of knowledge, freedom, unity, and immortality. The details of each can be garnered from the essays and readings to follow.

Once the reader has gone over the essays and the selections he will be in a position to develop his own philosophy of man. At the very least, he will have a base on which to build such a philosophy, for the answers one gives to the key problems discussed will determine the future direction of one's thought. The implications of the conclusions to the basic problems, however, will need to be worked out in further detail and in a more sophisticated form. This is an unending task and emphasizes the need for continued growth in a philosophy of man. No matter which "school of thought" one chooses for a guide, insights and assimilation of truth must be taken from all quarters. Nevertheless, a coherent picture rather than a mere eclecticism should be the goal of one attempting to formulate a philosophy of man.

Instead of taking over any predigested philosophy of man, each thinking person has the right and duty to work out his own philosophy. That this will be generally in the broad framework of a previous school of thought is of no consequence, for the thinking person will have assimilated such views to the extent that although shared by many, the insights will now be made his own and belong to him in a personal way.

To do this will be to engage in the enterprise of philosophy, the search for wisdom. This search will reveal that philosophy is an on-going process, a continuing dialectic of the past with the present, oriented to the future. The search will reveal in the words of Etienne Gilson a "unity of philosophical experience."

PART ONE

Introduction
___

Historical Background

Plato: Man as Soul

Aristotle: Man as Composite of Body and Soul

Aquinas: Man as Embodied Spirit

Conclusion: A Return to Dualism

Readings
___

PLATO: *On the Nature of Man* (from *Phaedo*)

ARISTOTLE: *On the Nature of Man* (from *De Anima*)

AQUINAS: *On the Nature of Man* (from *On Spiritual Creatures, The Soul, Summa Theologica,* Part I, *and Truth*)

CLASSICAL
AND SCHOLASTIC
THOUGHT:

Plato
Aristotle
Aquinas

EDITED BY

Elizabeth G. Salmon

FORDHAM UNIVERSITY

CLASSICAL AND SCHOLASTIC THOUGHT:
Plato
Aristotle
Aquinas

Introduction.

Historical Background

The classical and Christian philosophy of man embraces in its tradition various thinkers whose diverse views span many centuries. While the great Greek pagan thinkers—Socrates, Plato, and Aristotle—enunciated the basic problems of this tradition and elaborated in various ways highly philosophical reflections on man, the ultimate complexity of man was much more fully realized and philosophically elaborated in medieval Christianity, especially in the works of St. Thomas Aquinas. The unity of the tradition is not one of synchronization of various views but one of recurring problems that the Greeks saw were raised by that unique reality, man.

Before we examine the specific positions of the principal men making up this tradition, it will be helpful to view the tradition as a whole. Then we can understand the continuity of the problems, which runs throughout and allows the whole to be characterized as the classical and Christian tradition.

The early pre-Socratic thinkers gave birth to philosophy slowly and laboriously. The interpretation of their work by recent historians has been quite varied. For example, John Burnet emphasizes their interest in physical sciences, or how things are made from the primal matrix. Francis M. Cornford sees their efforts as an attempt to rationalize traditional myths, and Werner W. Jaeger sees them as an intellectual attempt to seek and elucidate the divine or ultimate first principle. Aristotle, writing in the fourth century B.C., saw that these thinkers primarily observed the phenomena of nature and sought the ultimate material cause (matter or stuff).

The matter or stuff being itself vital but distinguished by opposing qualities offered an explanation of the process of cosmic development.

Pythagoras (580–500 B.C.) and his followers explained the living cosmos in mathematical terms, which gave rise to Plato's notion of cause as reason or formal implication, as distinct from cause as agent. It is also said that the Pythagoreans considered ethical notions such as moral virtue as a harmony or proportion. Their doctrine of the transmigration of souls brought about the idea of a certain independence of the vital principles. An echo of these doctrines of Pythagoras is evident in Plato's *Phaedo*.

Of the early Greek thinkers, however, Heraclitus (*c.* 540–475 B.C.) and Parmenides (530–444 B.C.) had the greatest influence on Plato and Aristotle. Heraclitus influenced them by his doctrine of "flux," though the extreme exponents of this position were Protagoras and Cratylus in the fifth century B.C. Heraclitus is also credited by some as having introduced the basic ethical problem, that is, the possibility of an absolute standard in a constantly changing existence. This certainly was Plato's problem, and in the *Phaedo* he developed a philosophy of man as a foundation for the ethical concepts of Socrates (*c.* 470–399 B.C.).

The sought-for idea of necessity and immutability was suggested to Plato by Parmenides. He saw the world of his experience as what is, and what is cannot not be, for man cannot know what is not and what is can only be thought of as being. This insight into the necessity of being formed the basis of metaphysics for later thinkers. Plato (427–347 B.C.) juxtaposed the positions of Heraclitus and Parmenides and synthesized the problems of both in his theory of knowledge. Aristotle reconciled the two aspects of reality in material being itself by the composition of matter and form. Actually, however, there is no proof that Heraclitus and Parmenides themselves elaborated their philosophies in opposition to one another.

From Parmenides' arguments Zeno (*fl.* 464 B.C.) and Melissus (*fl.* 450 B.C.) developed further arguments and logical conclusions that at least marked the difference between the conditions of reasoning and the conditions of reality. Their work led to further elaboration in the study of logic, especially by Aristotle.

In the face of the Parmenidean argument that being is permanent, pre-Socratic cosmological tradition was carried on by Empedocles (*c.* 490–430 B.C.), who spoke of four elements: fire, water, earth, and air. These are all considered as having within them from the beginning a vital principle and their combination begets a related cosmos. There is permanence through these elements and difference through their combinations. The concept of matter, even in the unrelated atoms of Democritus (*c.* 460–370 B.C.), is not mechanistic; life, soul, and mind are in this matter. Thus Empedocles spoke of thought as a vital corporeal function; since we are of the living earth, particles given off by earth can vitally affect us. So it is said one knows like by like, a formula elaborated by Empedocles.

Only in Anaxagoras (*c.* 500–428 B.C.) was mind spoken of as self-ruling and mixed with nothing; he also spoke of mind as an extended thing, and he explained knowledge by the meeting of opposites.

Aristotle (384–322 B.C.), educated by Plato and influenced by his own biological studies, re-elaborated in the *De Anima* a philosophy of man explanatory of man's typical organic unity.

The last great expression of Greek thought and also a synthesis of it is found in the work of Plotinus (205–270). This work is basically Platonic, although it attempts to resolve Aristotelian problems in order to present a unified philosophical view of reality. It stresses the problem of the one and the many, that is, of God and the world. This view has its own unique character and has come to be known as Neoplatonism.

St. Augustine (354–430), seeking truth and happiness, gave credit to Plotinus for showing him the way from mere material existence to an appreciation of spirit. Through St. Paul he learned he could not in practice make the ascent to the Ultimate without grace. Augustine's writing is an expression of Christian wisdom; its primary purpose is to explain to fallen man the way to reach God and beatitude. The speculative elements of this wisdom which were considerably developed have their roots in Neoplatonism. Of Aristotle, Augustine knew only the *Categories,* one of Aristotle's treatises in logic, which had only an indirect bearing on his philosophy of man.

In light of Aristotle's idea of science St. Thomas (1225–74) developed within his theological work a much more autonomous philosophy, one dominated by a metaphysics that, through the influence of Plotinus and Arab thinkers and of the doctrine of creation, stresses the ultimate perfection of being as existence. The conception that man is not just a biological organism but a created person destined to see God led St. Thomas to rethink the philosophy of man in order to express this unity of a person. But at the outset the Aristotelian realism and naturalism offered basic principles more acceptable than those of Platonic dualism.

Plato: Man as Soul

Plato's philosophy of man is embodied in his portrait of Socrates; its main facets can be found in his dramatic dialogue, the *Phaedo,* which recounts Socrates' discourse before his execution. Socrates is portrayed as a religious man who feels himself to be in the hands of the gods, as a man who believes in a hereafter where the just or unjust will be accorded due reward or punishment, and as a courageous man who finds his courage in the pursuit of wisdom.

Wisdom—Contemplation of Platonic Forms

During his youth, Socrates recalls, he sought wisdom in the physical sciences. These sciences, absorbing as they were, considered only the conditions and elements that went into the forming of things, such as the generation of man. What was more important were the principles that helped Socrates understand what man should be and the end for which he should act in order to be more fully man. These principles are the *best* reasons for man's existence; they are the absolute values in which man shares, and should seek further to share in order to be more fully. In the *Phaedo,* the dialogue from which the reading selections are taken, Plato explained that these reasons or principles are the basis of ethical action.

The *Phaedo* opens with Socrates serenely maintaining that death fulfills the wishes of a philosopher. But life (not suicide) is a condition for death, since a man's life is not his but the gods'. Life is a training for death; it is a constant effort to purify the soul that entails a gradual nonreliance on the body. In the order of knowledge, life implies a turning to pure thought, which is not concerned with our ever changing sense experience but with the absolute immutable insights of intellectual knowledge. The soul is pictured as striving for independence and for separation from the body to achieve the contemplation of the absolute. In this endeavor the soul turns not in upon itself but toward the absolute form.

In other words, real wisdom seeks the best reasons or principles, the contemplation of which is what constitutes the true life of man. Plato was convinced that the changing world which men encounter in sensation is not as real or as perfect as another world of absolute values which some men can know by the disciplined use of the highest powers of their minds. Such absolute values as truth, justice, goodness, and beauty are the patterns and ideal types of all the things that can be called just or good, true or beautiful in the world of sense-knowledge. They are called *forms* because they are the very pattern and ideal according to which everything in the universe of sense experience is structured.

Although it is not emphasized in the *Phaedo,* in the later works of Plato we see that knowledge of the forms, inasmuch as such forms are participated in by the concrete things, demands that the soul use sensible experience to make it turn to its intellectual vision. The body in this sense has a certain necessary association with the soul.

In the *Phaedo* the nature of the soul is described as the very opposite of that of body—immutable, invisible, noncomposed, seeking pure thought. There is a sharp dichotomy: life is of the soul, death is of the body. In fact, life seems to be identified with the soul, and soul with the intellect. Thinking is emphasized as the work of the soul, while sensing and feeling, as passions and desires, seem to be affections of the body.

The soul, as rational, seeks death, which is separation from the body. The body and its pleasures can only blind the soul. Concomitantly, fear of death is consequent upon the attachment to the body and its pleasures. Some men may seem to have courage, but such courage arises more from fear of greater evils than from the detached wisdom of the soul. Wisdom is true virtue.

In fact the true tendency, and so the character, of the soul becomes evident if we consider its search for wisdom. Bodily senses are no aid, or only incidentally an aid, since the soul reaches truth only insofar as it is released from contact with the body. In many of the dialogues Socrates' contemporaries equate knowledge with perception. In perception man is the measure because things are as he experiences them. For Plato, true knowledge is never equivalent to mere perception; rather, as Socrates recalls to his companions, man can know absolute justice and goodness without the perception of bodily eyes.

Immortality of the Soul

The purification of the soul can be carried on only insofar as the thinker is convinced that the soul has an existence of its own. Hence Socrates develops reasons for the immortality of the soul.

FIRST ARGUMENT: GENERATION FROM OPPOSITES. The first argument is on the level of the observation of physical change. It stresses the necessary cycle from sleeping to waking and from waking to sleeping, from the dead to the living and the living to the dead. This is merely an instance of a general principle of the generation of all things from their opposites. Our experience shows that all things come from something else—therefore there must be a something from which things come. In turn, this something must be replenished if it itself is finite.

SECOND ARGUMENT: RECOLLECTION, KNOWLEDGE OF FORM, PREEXISTENCE. The first argument is reinforced by Socrates' doctrine of recollection. Learning, he had taught, is a matter of recalling what the soul once knew. In the *Phaedo*, Plato stressed that it is knowledge of absolute equality that permits us to judge the equality of two concrete, perceived things. This is true of our judgments of what is great and good, for they are made only in terms of absolute greatness and goodness. If the soul has such absolute knowledge, it must have had a previous existence. Thus, recollection, knowledge of the forms, and preexistence are linked.

Actually, the soul's seeing the absolute ideas of equality or goodness proves that the soul is unchanging and is akin to the pure, the eternal, the immortal—resembling the divine—while the body is mortal and perishable. Only the soul, which in this life flees the body in order to reach wisdom, will in the end belong to the race of the gods; but the soul, penetrated by the body, will be drawn back to the haunts of the visible world.

Philosophy is what leads the soul to the pure state, encouraging it to turn from its incidental use of the body and to trust in itself and in the contemplation of the absolutely true, divine, and real.

Socrates' companions are not content to know only that the soul preexists. They feel that he should also show that the soul will not in the future be dissolved like the body. In reply, Socrates points out that only a composite thing can be broken up and dispersed. Socrates had learned from the physical sciences that material things of this world, including the body, are constituted of particles of matter with opposite qualities or elements of different kinds. The cosmic process combines such elements but it can also, as experience shows, destroy such combinations. However, mind as an act of contemplation of an absolute form is an act as simple and immutable as the form itself. Mind, as such an act of contemplation, entails no composition and so also no possibility of decomposition.

This kinship of soul with the immutable and nonvisible forms shows that the soul has an entirely different nature than the body. The soul, being pure thought, is of the divine and so rules the body. In other words, since the soul is not material, it cannot perish as does the body.

Objections to the Immortality of the Soul

SOUL IS A HARMONY. Yet Plato admitted that no matter what his belief may be, and despite the strength of Socrates' arguments, there are powerful objections to the immortality of the soul. The most important objection is that the soul is but a harmony resulting from the bodily elements, just as music is a harmony of the strings of the lyre.

Answer: Contradicts recollection. Still, to say that the soul is a harmony contradicts knowledge as recollection, an already firmly established position. Recollection presupposes preexistence and so an independence of the soul from the body. Harmony admits of degrees, as is evident from the attunement of the lyre. However, a soul, as soul, cannot have degrees. If you say the soul is a harmony, you cannot have within it two harmonies, one of virtue and the other of vice, for they are contradictory. Neither can you say that all souls have only the harmony of virtue. Besides, we see the soul ruling the body, sometimes opposing the tendencies of the body. If soul were but a bodily harmony, it could not so oppose the body.

SOUL IS EXPENDABLE ENERGY. Another objection says that the soul, even though it is a principle of life, is an expendable energy, that is, it will be dissipated at some time after death.

Answer: Develops new methods. Instead of trying to understand what things are by observing the elements and conditions of their corruption, Plato proposed a supposition or a hypothesis as a reason, cause, or principle that will explain why they are what they are. He supposes that if the form, for example, absolute beauty, exists, things can be said to be beautiful by participating in beauty. The concrete sensible thing can be said to be caused to be beautiful by participation or sharing in beauty. The point Plato is making is that for us to understand that a thing is beautiful or an act is just, we must first possess an ideal or standard of beauty or justice. The individual thing or act is then rendered intelligible through the reason or cause by being seen as an existence that shares or participates in the ideal.

In this argument Plato is saying that the soul, by participating in life, cannot at the same time participate in death. Here we come upon the difficulties of this very central doctrine of participation with regard to the soul. Is the soul itself life or is it merely a participation in the form of life? It seems it should have the simplicity of the form of life to be immortal. In another way it could be asked: Is the soul contemplating identical with the object contemplated?

Conclusion: Warning Against Scepticism

No matter how difficult it may be to prove the immortality of the soul, Socrates warns us not to be sceptical of all argument, for the appreciation of the character and life of the soul is of the utmost importance in the conduct of our moral life. Our afterlife depends upon this life. Some things are difficult to prove to the complete satisfaction of mind. Hence, we must often be content with probable opinion in such matters; this is clearly the way Socrates feels as he faces death at the end of the *Phaedo,* though Plato in myth envisions the afterlife.

Aristotle: Man as Composite of Body and Soul

Aristotle, Plato's student for nearly twenty years, held several views on the unity of man. In his early period he proposed a dualism of body and soul quite similar to that of Plato. In his mature period, influenced by his biological investigations, he expressed an organic conception of man in which he saw the soul as the entelechy of the body—that is, a substantial form that completes and perfects the body to make it a living thing. His classic study, *De Anima (Treatise on the Soul)*, is the work of this period. The problems it discusses can be compared with those of Plato's early work, the *Phaedo.*

In Aristotle's treatment of man, the ethical problem, which was so important to Plato, is no longer primary; rather, because of Aristotle's interests in biological studies, his viewpoint is predominantly scientific. The treatise does not focus on an individual as the *Phaedo* centers around Socrates. Aristotle, stressing the soul as the principle of any life, includes man within the order of living beings, although the function of intellect marks him as a special kind of living being. Plants, animals, and men all have soul, but in an analogous sense.

The most striking non-Platonic position is Aristotle's insistence not only on the fact that man is observed to act as a unit consisting of body and soul, but also on his understanding that to define his nature he must define it as the unity of body and soul. Through the influence of his biological studies, Aristotle conceived soul (the informing principle) and body (matter) as constituting one substance. From this conception arises the problem of *nous,* or intellect, as different and distinct from soul.

Nature of the Soul

In Book I of *De Anima* Aristotle stressed the problems and difficulties confronted in studying the soul. Nevertheless, the study is of utmost importance in our understanding of nature because, as he said, soul is the "principle of animal life." For a scientific study of animal life there must be an investigation of the soul, both to determine something of the soul's essential nature and to detail its properties.

Some of these properties pertain to the soul itself and others to the unit of body and soul. The soul with its properties seems to exist independent of the body and not just as a principle that determines and informs the body. However, the majority of properties arise from the composite unit, for in most cases the soul cannot act or be acted upon without the involvement of body. Thinking is the one exception. As Aristotle noted, "If there is any way of acting or being acted upon proper to soul, soul will be capable of separate existence; if there is none, its separate existence is impossible."

These two kinds of properties (of soul alone or of body and soul) also raise the question whether the whole study of the soul is embraced by the philosophy of nature, or whether, if there is some "part" independent of the body, metaphysics treats of that part.

Before attempting to state his own position, particularly concerning the nature of the soul, Aristotle turned back to study what his predecessors had said in order to garner their positive findings and to avoid their mistakes. The pre-Socratics considered something be-souled if it originates movement and has sense perception. The chief conclusions Aristotle drew from this study are that all previous positions involve the absurdity that "they all join the soul to a body, or place it in a body, without any specification of the reason of this union, or the bodily condition required for it."

Aristotle also noted that it is incorrect to say that the soul is angry or learns. On the basis of his biological studies of animals and men, he considered it more correct to say that it is a man, the composite of body and soul, who is angry or learns. Some pre-Socratics, Empedocles, for example, held that man has to be composed of elements in order to know the elements, because only "like can know like." Anaxagoras alone maintained that mind has nothing in common with anything else. But then, Aristotle asked, how can it know? Others held that the soul is but the harmony or unifying principle of the elements, and that this harmony disappears with the death of the body.

This raises the question: Are the attributes or functions of the soul identical with the soul? If they are not, do they arise from the soul as a whole, or does each arise from a different part of the soul?

Matter and Form: Act and Potency

In Book II of *De Anima* Aristotle, seeking a solution to this question, first expounded his general philosophical principles. He noted that *substance,* in the sense of *being,* can be predicated in the following ways:

1. Of *matter,* in this case *body,* as "that which in itself is not a 'this' " —meaning not a concrete individual such as a dog, but that which

potentially is able through form to become an individual "this."
2. Of *form,* in this case *soul,* as "that in virtue of which a thing is called a 'this.' "
3. Of the *composite,* body and soul—a "this." It is in this last sense that substance is most properly used, for to Aristotle substance meant a concrete individual. In its primary meaning substance refers either to a material existent such as an animal composed of matter and form, or to a pure self-subsistent form.

In addition to the primary meaning of substance, Aristotle discussed being as *accidents,* that is, those appearances of beings, such as qualities, quantities, and relations, that exist only in a subject in which they are found. Thus John the individual subject, is a substance whose qualities of courage and brilliance and whose quantity of two hundred pounds are modifications, or accidents. The word "accident" here is an unfortunate one for the modern reader. Aristotle did not mean by it anything tragic and unexpected. He simply meant the *ways* in which an existing individual subject happens to manifest itself. Thus John appears to us as brilliant or courageous and as large in build.

In the composite of body and soul, the body (matter) is the potential element, while the soul (form) is the actual. In other words, the living body as just *body* is matter or the subject of life; by the soul, its form, it is living. So the "soul must be a substance (or being) in the sense of the form of a natural body having life potentially in it."

Soul as actuality can have two meanings: either soul possessed of actuality, or soul exercising actuality. Soul possessed of actuality, the principle of life, is considered by Aristotle as the "first grade of actuality of a natural organized body." If then the soul is spoken of as the act of body, it is absurd to ask if body and soul are one. Body and soul should only be spoken of in the manner in which they exist, that is, as the principles of the unit—man.

Body and soul are to each other as wax is to the shape given it by the stamp. The soul then is "inseparable from its body, or at any rate certain parts of it are, if it has parts." Though Aristotle was not definitive here in his investigation of the proper nature of the soul, he suggested that we study what is more known to us, that is, the properties, functions, or powers of the soul. This study might give us an insight into the rational basis from which the definition of soul springs. The chief functions of the soul are nutrition, sensation, reasoning, and movement. Not all living things have all these functions, but plants, animals, and men have soul in some sense.

Viewing the soul as actuality, but stressing actuality as the source of its functioning, Aristotle considered the ways in which the soul is the "cause" of an organic body: first, it is cause in the sense that it is the essence of the whole living body; second, it is cause in the sense that it is the end, the ultimate purpose, for the sake of which the body exists; third, it is cause in the sense that it moves and alters the body. In the first meaning Aristotle implied that the essence of a living thing is form, although he said that the substance of man is the composite body and soul. Form and matter would then be correlative.

PRIMARY MATTER. Primary matter was one of the basic notions that Aristotle employed throughout his philosophy. While form is active and determining, matter is purely passive and without determinations of its own. Being of itself pure potentiality, it possesses no actual determinations and so never exists of itself. Prime matter can be explained by the analogy of the conditions seen as necessary in the making of a statue. The bronze is the matter out of which the statue is molded; considered as metal, it is formless. When it is molded into the statue it is given a form that determines it, or makes it to be a statue of a god. If this statue is in turn melted down, the bronze is still present but it no longer has the form of a god. Aristotle observed a somewhat similar process in nature, especially in the radical change from life to death. For example, a dog having been killed, the "dead body" presented a certain continuity of "matter" but a change from the active, living form to a non-living form. That principle in the thing that marked the continuity he termed "matter"; that principle that marked the differing, determinate character he termed "form."

Any material body that has a soul tends to preserve itself. By nutrition and reproduction plants realize this end of self-preservation. Since animals have sense perception including imagination (which, because it involves the sense of touch, begets pleasure or pain, and so desire), they can of themselves be the source of movement. In addition to nutrition and sensation, man has reasoning, which may arise either from the soul itself or from something other than the form of body, or it may be a function of a "part" transcending the role of form; we shall dwell more on this later.

SENSE PERCEPTION. Sensation in all animals is a movement or effect from without, begetting a change in quality in the animal sensing. Sensation is not produced without an external agent which impresses the potentiality of the sense as a signet ring impresses wax. Wax as impressed is one with the impression without the matter of the gold remaining. Hence the sense in potency is actuated by the object proper to that sense, but is limited to that object.

Sensation could also be called a ratio; it is as hearing is to what is heard. Thus the activity of the sensible object and the act of the percipient sense are for Aristotle one and the same activity; yet the distinction between their being remains. This combination cannot be considered as a mere physical one.

Just as we spoke of life possessed and exercised, we also speak of an animal as having sensation in two ways: as power, such as the living eye, or as activity, the actual seeing. In this manner Aristotle spoke of life possessed as potency and life exercised as act. In like fashion he spoke of sensation, both as the power to sense (*potency*) and as the exercise of sensation or sensing (*act*).

Sense perception can have a double aspect: it entails an alteration caused by an object, and it can be seen as the effect brought by this alteration. Aristotle distinguished three different objects of perception: first, the objects proper to one of the five senses, namely, touch, taste, sight, hearing, smell (touch being fundamental to all); second, the common sensibles that do not correspond to a special organ but affect the sensibility of two or more organs, such as size or shape. These also suppose a consciousness of the temporal unity of the sense activities in man, which is memory. The third object of perception is not strictly a sense object; it is an accidental sensible. For example, we perceive something green which happens to be a plant; we perceive the color, but only accidentally can it be said that we perceive the plant. Within his treatment of sense he studied in detail each proper sense, as well as the object and media of the sense; to a lesser degree he studies the sense organ itself.

IMAGINATION. Besides sense perception, Aristotle treated imagination, which he distinguished from perception and from rational thought. Imagination is an activity that includes sense perception in the widest sense, that is, both proper and common sensibles; these, together with memory, form an organic whole. Yet imagination is not simply the passive effect of sensation in general; it tends in both animal and man to "fabricate." This act of fabrication is particularly marked in man, for in him imagination not only reproduces the images he senses, but it forms its own. All imaginative constructs, Aristotle held, are strongly influenced by the emotions, which are reactions concomitantly elicited by immediate sense perception.

Imaginative constructs should be distinguished from opinion. What one imagines and what one thinks (in the sense of having an opinion) may seem to express a similar kind of knowledge; actually, though, opinion is a more complicated stage of knowledge than imagination. Opinion entails belief, and belief entails conviction resulting from a degree of discursive thinking which may indeed include the work of imagination but is not identical with it.

The subject of imagination was barely touched on before Aristotle. Plato mentioned it only as an activity that evaluated sensation. Yet in Aristotle's treatment of imagination, it is surprising that he did not clearly integrate it as a factor in the organic structure of the soul's cognitive activity which he emphasized up to this point. Instead, he spoke of it as resulting from the influence of emotion over perception.

Mind *or* Nous

In Book III of *De Anima* there are the classic Chapters 4 and 5 in which Aristotle considered the *nous,* that "part" of the soul with which the soul knows and thinks. He was concerned with whether the *nous* is or is not "part" of soul, in what sense it is spoken of as different and separable, and how thinking, the activity of *nous,* takes place.

In trying to answer these questions, Aristotle began with an analysis of thinking. He said that if it is like perceiving, it must in some way be *potential* and thus capable of receiving the form or essence of an object. That is, mind must "be related to the thinkable as sense is to the sensible." However, the potentiality of mind cannot be exactly like that of sense: first, because it is not attached to any physical organ; and, second, because it is not limited to the particular kind of object corresponding to an organ, such as sound to the ear or color to the eye. If all that exists is thinkable, then the mind must be universally potential to all that is. And so Aristotle described the mind as having in it nothing contradictory to the thinkable, which is to say that its character must be such that it can become all that is. Because sense perception is tied to a particular organ, it cannot grasp anything other than the proper object of that organ.

As was shown earlier with respect to life and sensation, Aristotle held that the mind could be considered as act in two ways: (1) mind having "become all things" has knowledge, but this state is as potency to (2) mind as exercising the power of understanding on its own initiative. Power (1) is to its operation (2) as potency is to act. But in this relationship mind differs from sensation in that in its "potential" state mind is able to know itself, for "in the case of objects that involve no matter, what thinks and what is thought are identical."

An objection to this description of mind as potential to all things is that such a potency would destroy the condition that renders the effect of one thing on another possible and so renders understanding impossible. For example, a physical thing can have a physical effect only on that which itself is physical. In other words, that which is affected (patient) and that which effects (agent) must have something in common.

Aristotle answered this objection by explaining that the potentiality of mind does not mean that it is indeterminate or without character, but rather that its character is such that it has something in common with everything. Mind itself as being can be actuated by all being. In so describing mind's potentiality Aristotle touched upon the essential character of mind and also upon the transcendental character of being.

OBJECT OF MIND. Through its senses the soul perceives concretely the qualities or the combined factors that constitute a material thing. Mind, Aristotle held, apprehends the form or essence, or what might be considered the essential unity or structure of the combined factors—its very being. In apprehending this unity, mind grasps an intelligibility that is separated from matter and is the "form" of the matter. Therefore, intellect itself, becoming an object that is nonmaterial, cannot be a power involving matter. The classic difficulty is that what is thinkable for us exists in the concrete, material thing. How then does mind really apprehend it in a nonmaterial fashion?

In Chapter 5 of Book III—a section that has greatly puzzled the commentators—Aristotle presented us with his answer to this difficulty. He first pointed out that in the soul, as in the whole of nature, there is "that which is what it is by becoming all things" (first form of intellect), and there is that which is "what it is by virtue of making all things" (second form of intellect).

TWO FORMS OF INTELLECT. The problem is not only how the mind apprehends the intelligible essence or form, but also what is the relation between the above two forms of intellect.

The creative, or making, intellect seems to be just what is demanded to make thought possible in the human condition in which intellect is in potency, and the intelligible is only potentially present in the concrete material thing.

But whether the role of the creative intellect is to make intelligible what is potential in the material thing is a matter of speculation among Aristotelian scholars. One of the foremost scholars, W. D. Ross, interprets Aristotle as having maintained that all thought is active but has two roles: the "passive reason recognizes the presence of universals in particular things"; while "the active reason divines the existence of abstractions that are never present in experience." [1] The passive reason is considered passive only because it has a certain dependence on sense experience, whereas active or creative reason forms intelligible notions from other universal notions and so is not dependent on sense. Intellect is activity itself. Freed from the body, it would appear just as it is: it alone would be immaterial, immortal, and eternal. In this interpretation, active intellect seems like Plato's soul. It is still not clear how this function or "part" of soul is related to soul, the form of body. With St. Thomas we shall see another interpretation, influenced in part by Greek commentators and Arabian thinkers.

Power of Movement and Appetite

After developing the main features of the soul as knowing, Aristotle asked: What is it in the soul that originates movement? Is it a power that is one or many? As was noted previously, nutrition and reproduction are those powers that have for their end the self-preservation of the living. Aristotle now stressed that all powers of the soul and the soul itself—whether of animals or men—have for their end the preservation of their own nature. This is to say that all powers of nature have a teleological character. Beyond this, however, he asked what power of the soul accounts for locomotion or self-movement in an animal or man? There is, Aristotle said, only one power which moves to action, and that is desire, or appetite in a very broad sense. In explaining it he noted that desire is always desire for an end. Although he held that desire has different manifestations—*will* in

[1] Aristotle, *De Anima,* ed. by W. D. Ross (Oxford: Clarendon Press, 1961), pp. 46–47.

the rational part and *appetite* in the sensible part of the soul—he did not treat them separately.

From one point of view the object of desire is primary: for example, imagination moves the power of locomotion by presenting an object of desire, that is, an appetible good. In turn, the power of locomotion moves imagination and the whole man to obtain that appetible good. The complicated relations of sense perception and sense appetite, of reason and rational appetite, were never fully worked out by Aristotle in his extant writings.

In the *Nicomachean Ethics,* Aristotle spoke of desire as a movement of pursuit or avoidance. He emphasized that here, in respect to man's moral action, there is the influence of reason. Thus it is possible to speak of choice, which by Aristotle's definition, is an act of practical intellect whose object is "truth in agreement with right desire." Only in man is there found "desiderative reason" or "rationative desire," which extends only to those things that man is able to accomplish. Thus desire is limited to human ends.

Conclusion: The Unity of Man

Plato, in the *Symposium,* described man's drive for self-completion. In this drive, desire for what will fulfill his nature is the primary directive of man's activity. However, besides this desire for possession, the desire for procreation suggests both desire for giving and love of another. Insofar as Plato freed desire from being a tendency to this or that self-good and spoke of it as a tendency of the form of the good, he spoke of the movement of desire toward an object that transcends limited human objects.

In neither Plato nor Aristotle do we find *will* clearly described as a pure intellectual power. In Plato there is the movement of desire toward a transcendent object. In Aristotle there is the indication that man as knowing controls his desire through choice. However, in neither one is there a notion of will as pure intellectual love combining a transcendent object with choice. Such an intellectual love would not be just a desire of fulfillment, but would also be a love of the object for itself. This view is not possible until the whole concept of man more clearly incorporates within it an intellectual immortal principle that has as its object the transcendental notion of being and the good.

Plato may have left us with a more personal concept of man and his immorality through the appealing figure of Socrates, along with his suggestive description of knowledge and the afterlife. Basically he stressed the life of the soul as the source of intellectual immutable knowledge, as against changing perception, with desire not too distinct from appetite.

Aristotle, because of his scientific interests, left us with a less personal picture of man, yet with one that presented him as having the unity of a living organism, marked by the oddity of a soul or a function of his soul that transcends the mere role of vivifying a body. This intellectual principle or power is nonmaterial, immortal, and unchangeable, but it is difficult to see it as assuring personal immortality. In Aristotle the individual man is not a soul but the composite, body and soul. And one cannot speak of the composite as immortal.

St. Thomas Aquinas: Man as Embodied Spirit

St. Thomas came to the study of man first as a Christian, and then as a Christian theologian. Christian theology had absorbed much of the Platonic concept of the soul, and spoke of it as a being independent and separable from the body. With the introduction of the works of Aristotle to the West, the soul was presented, with the exception of the *nous,* as the vitalizing and informing principle of the body. St. Thomas synthesized these seemingly contradictory views of man: man as a spiritual soul and man as a material being of nature. His position is understandable only in the light of his deepest metaphysical insights.

While Plato approached the philosophy of man from a moral point of view and Aristotle from a scientific, St. Thomas came to it primarily from a metaphysical point of view. However, his metaphysical principles had their source in the experience of man, and his philosophy of man began from that experience. Once developed, his metaphysics deepened this philosophy. The end result is a position expressive of the reciprocal influence of a philosophy of man and metaphysics. In another sense, man philosophically is the center of St. Thomas' thought insofar as it is man who, through the activity of his highest powers, intellect and will, becomes the source of the philosophical knowledge of the world, himself, and God.

Historically, the setting in which St. Thomas developed the philosophy of man in the *Summa Theologica* is that of theology. Following the theological order, his treatment of man is preceded by the proofs of God's existence, an explanation of God's attributes, and a discussion of the Trinity. After the treatise concerning God, he considered the works of God and the procession of creatures from his creative act—first the angels or pure spiritual creatures and then the world. Only then did he treat of man as composed of spirit and body. An emphasis on the existence of spirit thus preceded his study of man.

In this study St. Thomas first treated man's nature or essence, and second his origin. A theologian, he explained, tends to embrace one feature of man's nature only, namely, his soul, because he is primarily interested in the immortal principle. Moreover, he sees the soul as being immediately connected with God's creative action. All Christian writers before St. Thomas had accepted that the soul is a spiritual substance; what spiritual substance meant for St. Thomas will be seen in terms of his philosophical explanation. Man's body is considered only in its relation to the soul and insofar as it is necessary to it.

Unity of Man

In the light of this theological emphasis on the nature of the soul, it is surprising that from the outset St. Thomas stressed in an Aristotelian fashion the organic unity of man. Despite what is meant by the term "substantiality of the soul," the soul cannot be considered in any way that would lead to the destruction of this organic concept. A Platonic dualism, even in its least radical form, is alien to his realism.

St. Thomas maintained that the form of man must be a subsistent spiritual principle, that is, a formal principle that exists in its own right, not in and through the existence of the composite man. In a sense he saw this principle as a nonmaterial "this" in the Aristotelian sense of an individual, but only insofar as its existence is of itself spiritual. On the other hand, this form is a principle of the individual man; it is that by which a man is and understands. St. Thomas' position was necessitated by two aspects of man: first, man is a unit, and, second, man is a particular unit who understands. Understanding is an activity that transcends the conditions of matter. Time and again he insisted that it is "this man" Socrates or "this man" Plato who exists. Man, the actively rational being with self-determining love, is the fundamental data. Man the person has a unity deeper than the biological unity of Aristotle.

In Article II of *On Spiritual Creatures* St. Thomas raised the problem whether a spiritual substance can be united to a body. In the first question of the *Disputed Questions: On the Soul* he asked whether man's soul can be the form of man as well as a spiritual substance. This is the same problem approached from a different angle. One approach considers whether a spiritual substance can be the form of a body, and the other whether the form of a body can be a spiritual substance. The difficulty lies in the fact that a spiritual substance is considered a self-subsistent thing whereas, as we have seen in Aristotle, the primary idea of form as the act and perfection of matter conveys the idea of a correlative principle.

The soul must be seen as more than form in the sense of correlative principle because thinking is man's thinking; it is his activity. Activity, St. Thomas held, arises from the existence of that which acts; it is what it is because of the character of the existent from which the action flows. Through the analysis of man's action and with particular stress on his intellectual action, as the typical human activity, St. Thomas was led to insist, in the face of the many Aristotelian interpretations, that the form and act of body as human must at the same time be a principle not totally immersed in matter and the conditions of matter.

If intellectual activity is the activity of this man, it must arise from the perfection that makes him man, or from his form. Still, if it is an activity that can reflectively consider the material conditions of itself as a material thing and reflectively direct its action, it must be an activity that transcends those corporeal conditions. St. Thomas saw man's highest personal activity, thinking, stemming from man's total nature and in a degree conditioned by it, but not itself an operation performed by a bodily organ.

As we have seen, both Plato and Aristotle noted that the activity of thinking is different from bodily activities, such as sensing, and their emotional reactions. Thinking has a character that is noncorporeal, though Aristotle was not clear as to the connection of the *nous* with the soul, nor its connection in general with man.

Nature of the Soul

Like Aristotle, St. Thomas first spoke of soul in the wider sense of a general principle of life. In Part I of the *Summa Theologica* he stated that "body can be spoken of as a principle of life if we consider a particular kind of body, that is, a living body; but it is such a body through the act and perfection of life." So the "first principle of life is not body but the act of body."

When he spoke of the vegetative and sensitive soul as well as the rational soul, his words might lead us to think that he was referring to a self-subsistent principle in all three cases. This is not so. Soul in general refers to the form or act of matter. When St. Thomas treated the sensitive soul he clearly maintained that of itself it has no operation; its operation belongs as such to the composite. Since it is the composite that lives and senses, this activity bespeaks the activity of a material thing that has a limited degree of formal perfection, that is, life but not a self-subsistent soul. "Forms themselves do not have being, but composites have being through forms," and such "corporeal forms . . . are caused . . . by the reduction of matter from potentiality to act by some composite agent." Of course, the first production entails no transmutation but rather creation. It is creation, not of material forms but of a material composite, in which "the seeds of forms are implanted that they may be able to be brought by movement into act."

Thus vegetative and sensitive souls are not spiritual principles but are forms, that is, acts that give a determinate character to this material thing. If form is a determining principle of matter, how did St. Thomas speak of matter?

Matter and Form: Act and Potency

Matter for St. Thomas, meaning prime matter, is never a subject in the sense that matter preceded form, for "to say that matter preceded, but without form, is to say that being actually existed, but without act, which is a contradiction in terms."

Although not a subject, matter is yet a potency, that is, an openness to the effect of modifying physical agents in those things that we designate as material subjects or substances; but "one never finds in nature a potency that is not perfected by some act and on this account there is always some form in prime matter." What actually exists are material things: beings that, because of the changes they undergo, are beings essentially potential to such change. They are each a definite kind of thing and yet open to the effect of that agent that corresponds to their potentiality. In each kind of thing "the potency of each individual being is such as its perfection is found to be." Thus prime matter is a potency within the essence of an existing material thing. The corresponding material form in this same material composite is act and perfection of this matter.

With respect to matter and form, the position of St. Thomas is beyond that of Aristotle. St. Thomas thought of reality as created existences and not as formally different instances of eternal matter. He spoke of the principles of matter and form, not to explain the multiplicity of individual beings as such, but only to explain the different kinds of material existents. Material existents are those whose essence or nature is to a degree indefinite or potential and so open to the determination or the informing of other physical agents.

Matter and form are thus principles primarily explanatory of change and not of the continuity of existence. They are no longer seen as the ultimate principles of being. Whereas for Aristotle matter is the eternal indefinite substrata of forms maintaining the permanence of existence, for St. Thomas existence makes the material essence to be, and only in terms of existent being can one speak of matter as a subject of forms.

With respect to the living, St. Thomas spoke of the vegetative and sensitive "soul" rather than of form, not only because of Aristotle's use of "soul" but because he considered that the formal perfection of life is something more than the form of the material elements. For where one observes an example of life there is the more perfect organic unity, evidenced through the living being's teleological self-movement. As the living being is a higher form of unity, its act or form is more clearly determinate in character. St. Thomas said that "to live is nothing else than for a substance, with such a nature, to be," though he did not see life as arising solely from the active and passive qualities or disposition of corporeal matter. As these corporeal elements with their qualities came to be structured or synthesized into more developed modes, he seemed to demand some other influence (such as that of the heavenly bodies), but not necessarily a creative action. However, of man he said, "The life of man, as being the most perfect grade, is not said to be produced, like the life of the other animals, by the earth or water, but immediately by God."

ONE FORM IN MAN. If it can be said that Socrates is a living animal, he is so through his soul or form; but if we say he understands through another soul or form, this man Socrates will not be one but two beings. "For a thing that is one in an unqualified sense does not come into being from two acts, but from potency and act inasmuch as that which is in potency comes into being actually. . . . Therefore . . . if there were a manifold of many substantial forms in one individual instance of substance, the individual instance of substance would not be one in an unqualified sense, but in a qualified sense. . . ." Thus the unity of man demands that there be in man but one formal principle—soul.

Man's Knowledge

First it must be said that man, Socrates for example, understands: understanding is *his* action. As a human action understanding is one of apprehending material things that are immediately present to man, but as an intellectual action it is not one by which man becomes in a material way like the material things he understands. Understanding is a reflection in which these spatio-temporal objects are seized in a nontemporal and nonspatial way.

From St. Thomas' study on *Truth* we can elicit the various degrees of reflection that develop as we move toward the knowledge of truth as truth. He says that "truth follows the operation of the intellect inasmuch as it belongs to the intellect to judge about a thing as it is." This conformity is known through the intellect's reflection on its act. In its act of judging the intellect not only knows, but knows that it knows, and therefore sees the entire process of knowledge as one unified experience.

It is the nature of the intellect to express the thing, or what is; mind's nature is to express all the thinkable. In this same act mind grasps that *being* is what is understandable and as such is the good of the intellect. Ultimately, mind understands that the being of the thing itself is mind's perfection and that the thing itself, in its degree of being, is good, independent of its relation to the mind.

In this realization of one's act as true, each man knows that he knows and this necessarily is an act that transcends the conditions of matter.

ABSTRACTION AND KNOWLEDGE AS IMMANENT ACTION. But how can it be said that the intellect knows being when, knowing in this nonspatio-temporal fashion, it cannot conceive the concrete singular but only the general, intelligible, and potentially universal aspect? In the *Summa Theologica* and in the *Commentary on the De Trinitate,* St. Thomas explained abstraction and its content. Abstraction may occur in two ways: first, by an absolute and simple consideration in which we may consider one thing without considering another, second, by "understanding that one thing does not exist in some other, or that it is separate from it."

In explanation of the first way, intellect grasps something of the nature of the species apart from its individuating principles as represented in the phantasm; that is, it grasps the thing as a something, a universal drawn from the particular. "Something" merely expresses the general unity of its formal or determinate character. For example, it grasps something of the nature of animal, leaving aside the individuating characteristics that mark it as this particular dog.

In the second way, intellect, already having grasped something of the nature of the species, can judge that the formal principle of that nature is not the potential or material principle of the nature. In this act, intellect says to itself: one principle is not the other. This is abstraction through judging. For example, we can understand that the soul of man as form is a different principle from his body as matter.

We have difficulty understanding abstraction because we tend to think of the abstract as a general picture. This is partly due to the influence of the English empirical philosophy, which described abstraction as the making of a composite picture or of an image of the most common features.

Such abstraction is not what St. Thomas meant. For him, intellectual knowledge is an immanent act of the mind, that is, an act terminating in and perfecting the mind. It is mind saying to itself what the thing is. This nonimaginative character of intellectual activity is stressed in his work *Truth,* where Aquinas said that "to understand is as if to read within (*intus legere*)." Sense and imagination know only exterior accidents; it is only the intellect that reaches something of the essence of a thing. He did not mean that the intellect in this abstractive insight, by which it apprehends the essence or quiddity, thoroughly comprehends this "what," or the nature of the thing that the intellect grasps. He meant only that we understand those things that are immediately known to our intellect upon a quidditative grasp, giving rise to formation of terms expressive of this grasp. Such is the first principle of philosophy which states that a thing is, or is something.

A second meaning of intellectual activity stresses the development of intellectual knowledge leading through reasoning and inquiry to a developed comprehension. The difference between the two is further emphasized by the fact that the simplicity of the first act eliminates the possibility of error, while the complexity of reasoning and inquiry allows for its possibility.

Does, however, this "reading within" mean that the intellect "goes out to the thing known"? Not exactly, for since understanding is an immanent act it does not terminate in the thing known. For any action follows the condition of the form of the one acting, as the form is the principle of the action.

The problem then is how the immanent action of knowing arises within the intellect, unless intellect somehow actually becomes the thing it knows.

By the effect of the thing on us—through the proper and common senses with their emotional reaction and through organization of this sense perception in the continuity of consciousness that entails memory—we have in a way become the thing. However, the thing experienced at this level is still subject to the conditions of space and time. St. Thomas interpreted Aristotle's active intellect as a power of our intellect, which transforms this causal activity of the thing affecting us into that which can spiritually inform our intellect in its potential state. Our intellect thus informed is capable of an immanent expression of the mode of being of the affecting material thing. As St. Thomas said in Part I of the *Summa Theologica,* "It cannot be said that sensible knowledge is the total and perfect cause of intellectual knowledge, but rather [it] is in a way the matter of the cause." The intellect itself in contact with matter must be the informing cause of its own potency so that its immanent operation can be of its own nature.

KNOWLEDGE OF SINGULARS. However, the causality of the intellect which is necessarily abstractive does not seem to allow for an intellectual knowledge of the existent singular. The intellectual would seize something of the nature of man but not Socrates, this man.

Although St. Thomas did not say we are conscious of the agency of the intellect, he did say we know the unity of the knowing process. We judge, through this unified process, our conception of the nature of Socrates to be an expresssion of the mode of being of the individual man, Socrates.

That the intellect cannot intellectually express the singular material existent is because a thing of nature can act on us only inasmuch as it is actual. Its action flows from it inasmuch as it exists; but it is the kind of action it is because of its essence or nature. If that nature is to a great degree potential, we shall be able to understand it only in a general fashion expressive of its formal principles. Thus it is not possible for our intellect to express intellectually the material singular. This does not mean that man, whose consciousness is one, is not intellectually aware in a reflective fashion that his intellectual expression of the formal aspect is one that results from an existential whole, existentially experienced. Therefore, that aspect of the thing that is rendered actually intelligible is, in total context of consciousness, in continuity with the sense-experienced individual. Man knows the singular; but intellectually he seizes in the first kind of abstraction only that aspect that can be rendered intelligible. Through abstraction as judgment he renders understandable the total situation. St. Thomas can say that it is Socrates, the man, who understands, and understands the concrete material thing, not just intelligible forms.

Incorruptible Principle—The Immortality of Man

Thus, because man is an organic whole, human understanding of the spatiotemporal through a non-spatiotemporal reflection is possible. St. Thomas spoke of understanding as an operation rooted in a power, or as we might say, in a function of man; but as a metaphysician he could not speak of a function that is not a function of something that is. He thus held that such a function bespeaks an existing source that must be the very act or form of man. Since the function is non-spatiotemporal, so is the source. Man then is man by the actuality of a spiritually existing form that informs an organic body and makes it a human body.

St. Thomas emphasized that a being is by the act of "to be." He saw man to be by an act that is not strictly the act of a material composite, but the act of his spiritual principle. Since the dissolution of the body cannot strictly affect a nonmaterial principle, he held man in this principle to be immortal. On the other hand, he was speaking of the immortality of a principle that is forever a form correlative to matter and in the genesis of its operation conditioned by matter, for the body is for the good of the soul, not vice versa. Hence the immortal soul is never an angelic form. His philosophy of man may establish it as incorruptible form; a metaphysics of created being eliminates the possibility of the annihilation of being, spirit, or matter.

Having made man's own soul the cause of his intellectual knowledge and having made evident that man knows that he knows and knows the truth of his knowing, St. Thomas brought out, as his predecessors did not, that our intellectual nature has an immediate inclination to the good of our nature, which is being itself. Thus in every intellectual nature there is will, or intellectual appetite, that must love the good. Awakened by knowledge, will tends to being as it exists, not as it is known. This intellectual love of a creature has two aspects: the love of being as its good—its fulfillment, and the love of being as it is in itself. However, nothing singular that we experience in life embodies the total perfection of what is; so nothing is seen as absolutely good. Each thing is seen as good within the total desire of the good and each becomes an end or a point of rest for our love only as we choose to accept it as absolute or as a means to our ultimate fulfillment. In the context of love man becomes, as it were, personally conscious that he transcends the conditions of space and time. His free choice becomes the pivotal point of his development as spirit, and entailed in that development is the whole of nature. The philosophy of man for St. Thomas can terminate only in moral philosophy, or how man ought to act.

Conclusion: A Return to Dualism

With the definite beginning of modern philosophy in the seventeenth century, St. Thomas' unitary conception of man was no longer prevalent. The change came about for various reasons, but there was one definite line of development from St. Thomas to René Descartes (1596–1650).

St. Thomas' view of man, Aristotelian as it may seem in many aspects, was one formulated in opposition to the Arab interpreters of Aristotle's work, whose views were studied particularly in the Faculty of Arts of the University of Paris. It was this trend, and not St. Thomas, that was indirectly to influence Descartes' idea of soul as *cogito,* the I think.

With respect to the position of the Arabs, St. Thomas rejected both the position of Avicenna (980–1037), who made the active intellect of Aristotle one for all men and the source of the illumination of the possible intellect, and the position of Averroës (1126–98), who made the spiritual *nous* (both possible and active intellect) one and separate from man.

St. Thomas' chief objection to both these positions was that they denied that the particular man, Socrates, for example, is the cause of his own knowledge and that he himself understands.

The Averroistic current passed from Paris to the universities of northern Italy, and with other Aristotelian and Platonic currents influenced Renaissance thought.

Pompanazzi of Padua (1462–1526), in his *De Immortalitate Animae,* raised for the sixteenth and seventeenth centuries the question of the soul and its immortality in terms of all the Aristotelian difficulties. He saw the Greek commentor, Alexander of Aphrodisias, upholding Aristotle's idea of the soul as form; in so doing he said it was correlative to matter, and the soul would be corrupted when the material composite was corrupted. Pompanazzi objected to Aristotle's Arab interpreters because in different fashions they separated man and intellectual activity. He realized that St. Thomas had said the soul was both form and spiritual substance, but for him this was unintelligible. It was contradictory because he thought of being only as form. If form makes a thing to be what it is, the thing could not formally or essentially be, at one and the same time, spiritual substance and material co-principle. However, if one thinks of being as the act of existence, as St. Thomas did, then an existent of a spiritual mode of being could play the role of vitalizing, as a form, an organic body and the body would exist through this spiritual principle.

The debate on immortality continued throughout the sixteenth century until the time of Descartes. Descartes was not primarily motivated by this problem, but he saw that what gave him a key to the nature of science also offered a solution to the current debate on the incorruptibility of the soul.

Descartes' fundamental notion is the unity of science. He equated mind actually thinking with the thinking of a simple notion, such as a mathematical ratio or an identity that expressed unity for him. Such ideas were perfectly clear to him; they were also an act of an existent mind because relation is established through an act of mind. So the *cogito,* the I think, in the act of thinking is clear and certain. The "I" is the act of thought and this act of thought exists. I, existing, has nothing to do with body because this thought, like a simple mathematical idea, is perfectly intelligible, even if body does not exist. Hence man is defined in terms of the *cogito,* and the *cogito* is distinct, including in its intelligibility nothing of body and its corruption.

Descartes' position marked a return to a radical dualism and a rejection of the biological unity of man, not to justify ethical values but to found a mechanistic physics. Even though Descartes did not intend it, he bequeathed to his immediate followers the problem of the unity of man—body and soul.

Glossary

ABSTRACTION:

In St. Thomas the intelligible species (or nature as intelligible) is abstracted from the phantasms by the power of the agent intellect, and thus results a certain likeness in the possible intellect. Primarily, the likeness is related to the possible intellect as that by which it understands things; secondarily, it is that which is understood. Example: the nature of animal is primarily understood as existing in particular animals, but this same nature, understood as existing in the mind, is the universal. Elements of this position are Aristotelian, but not the position as a whole. See also *Phantasm*.

ACT AND POTENCY:

Change in a sensible thing is the basis for these correlative ideas, but their meaning, in an analogous fashion, goes beyond change. An essentially changeable thing is one potential to the action of a suitable agent, but at the same time it exists as some kind (act) of thing. Here, potency and act are principles of the essence itself. If an existent is, and yet is only a degree of perfection of being, it cannot of itself account for being that degree, and so its existence is not of its essence. Thus this essence, even though it be a pure form, is as potency to the act of existence. If a substance is not identical with its operation, its operation is as act to the potency of that substance.

The varied uses must be seen in each text. Potency is also equivalent to passive power, and operation to active power.

CAUSE:

The meaning of cause is involved in the meaning of being. Plato stressed cause as the reason or intelligible principle (the idea) that renders other things intelligible. In the practical order this is the "best reason" or end—the "why" a thing is done. Aristotle, having stressed the understanding of sensible things and seeking to explain change, spoke of four causes as real physical principles. The *material* cause is that out of which something is made or becomes, as the bronze of a statue. The *formal* cause is the character or determination given to the material (bronze) to make the statue. The *efficient* cause is that which produces the statue. The *final* cause is the end or purpose of the production. Ultimately, Aristotle seems to have reduced these causes to the idea of formal cause as the final cause of change. St. Thomas, going beyond Aristotle, spoke primarily of a cause as cause of existence; insofar as a thing is, it is able to cause or produce being or make something be.

ENTELECHY:

In Aristotle's philosophy of man, soul is spoken of as act, form, or entelechy. The Greek word stresses the idea of form as dynamic and as the principle of the full realization of the thing's actuality. The soul as entelechy (form) is that which completes and perfects the body to make it a living body and is seen as inseparable from the body. Entelechy is derived from the Greek word *entelechia* (actuality).

ESSENCE (*Essentia*) and EXISTENCE (*Esse*):

Correlative principles of a being (*ens*) answering to the questions: *What* is it (essence)? *Is* it (existence)?

FACULTIES:

In St. Thomas faculties are powers that either have the soul as their subject or the composite as informed by the soul. Powers are defined through the being's acts or operations and these acts are distinguished by their objects. The objects are related to passive powers as their moving or actuating cause and to active powers as their end or term. Citing Aristotle, St. Thomas said that powers can be classed under five heads: vegetative, sensitive, appetitive, locomotive, and intellectual.

INTELLECT:

For Aristotle, any form without matter is a mind, *nous,* or intellect. In man, what in the soul is called mind or intellect is that whereby the soul thinks and judges. This part of the soul (and it is not clear whether Aristotle considered intellect to be a part of the soul) may or may not be separable from the body. For St. Thomas, the intellect is the power of the soul through whose operation of apprehension, judgment, and reasoning one can reflectively understand it as a power correlative to, and expressive of, what is (or being). He considered the intellect in its act of understanding and of reflecting as transcending the conditions of matter and so inferred that the principle of such an operation, the soul, is immaterial. For the meaning of agent intellect and possible intellect, see *Abstraction.*

NATURE:

Aristotle described natural beings as having an innate principle of motion. In contrast to manufactured or artificial beings, natural beings act according to what they are, and so nature can express the actual essence of a thing as the source of its activity. Thus it is the nature of a plant to grow and of man to think.

PHANTASM:

It is the unified perceptual image formed by the "common sense" (*sensus communis*), which is an internal sense, the unifying center of the five senses. Through this "common sense," sensible qualities are perceived both as distinct objects and yet as aspects of a single object.

PRIME MATTER:

In Aristotle, but especially in St. Thomas, prime matter is not a thing; it is, in a material thing, a principle correlative to substantial form. It is understood as the potentiality within the very essence of a being that can, through the agency of another being, be essentially changed. Since in itself it is not a being, the properties and manifestations of being, such as quantity and quality, cannot be ascribed to it. St. Thomas related the human body to the soul as prime matter to substantial form, which composite is potential to change through other physical agents.

SOUL:

In the *Phaedo,* Plato spoke of the soul as a spiritual being imprisoned in a body; it is identified with the person. In later works he spoke of the soul as having parts. In Aristotle soul is the substantial form, the vital principle of activity in any living being from plants to man, having in each case different powers or faculties. St. Thomas also spoke of soul as the principle of life; in beings below man, however, he saw soul as a grade of corporeal form. In man, soul is a spiritual principle existing in its own right but vivifying the body through its act of existence.

SUBSTANCE:

A being to which it is given to exist in itself and not in another as in a subject. Socrates is a subject and exists in himself, whereas his complexion, stature, and virtues are not subjects but require Socrates as the subject in which they inhere. Substance is thus contrasted with accidents, or appearances of being such as quantity, quality, place, and posture, which are not themselves existing subjects. St. Thomas stressed that substances are subjects through the act of existence, but they are constituted as the kinds of substance they are (animal or man) through their substantial form.

SUBSTANTIAL FORM:

The act or determination of a material composite that constitutes the composite to be the kind of substance it is. Substantial form is not a shape or an externally perceived form; it is act with respect to the potency of matter in the essence of a being. For St. Thomas, beings have existence *through* their form, but not by virtue of it. Only in man is the substantial form, the rational soul, seen as spiritual.

WILL:

For a finite thing, to be is always to tend to be. Since the object of the intellect is the understanding of what is, this understanding actuates its intellectual desire or will, which then immediately tends to being as the good. Thus, will is the rational appetite whereby human beings necessarily seek the good. This love of the good, in conjunction with the intellectual understanding of particular good things in the context of the idea of the total good, is the source of mind's free choice or free rejection of any particular thing as *its* good. Only man is considered to be endowed with will; all other beings are directed to their proper good by either innate tendencies or instincts.

Plato

On the Nature of Man

From *Phaedo*

[Phaedo, a disciple of Socrates who was present at the death of Socrates, is recalling for others the conversation Socrates carried on with his friends the day of his death. Socrates asks that his friends convey a message to Evenus, another philosopher disciple of Socrates.]

V   Tell Evenus this, Cebes, and bid him farewell from me; and tell him to follow me as quickly as he can, if he is wise. I, it seems, shall depart today, for that is the will of the Athenians.

61   And Simmias said, What strange advice to give Evenus, Socrates! I have often met him; and from what I have seen of him I think that he is certainly not at all the man to take it, if he can help it.

What, he said, is not Evenus a philosopher?

Yes, I suppose so, replied Simmias.

Then Evenus will wish to die, he said, and so will every man who is worthy of having any part in this study. But he will not lay violent hands on himself; for that, they say, is wrong. And as he spoke he put his legs off the bed on to the ground, and remained sitting thus for the rest of the conversation.

Then Cebes asked him, What do you mean, Socrates, by saying that it is wrong for a man to lay violent hands on himself, but that the philosopher will wish to follow the dying man?

What, Cebes? Have you and Simmias been with Philolaus, and not heard about these things?

Nothing very definite, Socrates.

Well, I myself only speak of them from hearsay, yet there is no reason why I should not tell you what I have heard. Indeed, as I am setting out on a journey to the other world, what could be more fitting for me than to talk about my journey and to consider what we imagine to be its nature? How could we better employ the interval between this and sunset?

Then what is their reason for saying that it is wrong for a man to kill VI
himself, Socrates? It is quite true that I have heard Philolaus say, when he was living at Thebes, that it is not right; and I have heard the same thing from others, too, but I never heard anything definite on the subject from any of them.

You must be of good cheer, said he, possibly you will hear something 62
some day. But perhaps you will be surprised if I say that this law, unlike every other law to which mankind is subject, is absolute and without exception; and that it is not true that death is better than life only for some persons and at some times. And perhaps you will be surprised if I tell you that these men, for whom it would be better to die, may not do themselves a service, but that they must await a benefactor from without.

Oh indeed, said Cebes, laughing quietly, and speaking in his native dialect.

Indeed, said Socrates, so stated it may seem strange, and yet perhaps a reason may be given for it. The reason which the secret teaching gives, that man is in a kind of prison, and that he may not set himself free, nor escape from it, seems to me rather profound and not easy to fathom. But I do think, Cebes, that it is true that the gods are our guardians, and that we men are a part of their property. Do you not think so?

I do, said Cebes.

Well then, said he, if one of your possessions were to kill itself, though you had not signified that you wished it to die, should you not be angry with it? Should you not punish it, if punishment were possible?

Certainly, he replied.

Then in this way perhaps it is not unreasonable to hold that no man has a right to take his own life, but that he must wait until God sends some necessity upon him, as has now been sent upon me.

Yes, said Cebes, that does seem natural. But you were saying just now VII
that the philosopher will desire to die. Is not that a paradox, Socrates, if what we have just been saying, that God is our guardian and that we are his property, be true? It is not reasonable to say that the wise man will be content to depart from this service, in which the gods, who are the best of all rulers, rule him. He will hardly think that when he becomes free he will

take better care of himself than the gods take of him. A fool perhaps might think so, and say that he would do well to run away from his master; he might not consider that he ought not to run away from a good master, but that he ought to remain with him as long as possible, and so in his thoughtlessness he might run away. But the wise man will surely desire to remain always with one who is better than himself. But if this be true, Socrates, the reverse of what you said just now seems to follow. The wise man should grieve to die, and the fool should rejoice.

63   I thought Socrates was pleased with Cebes' insistence. He looked at us, and said, Cebes is always examining arguments. He will not be convinced at once by anything that one says.

Yes, Socrates, said Simmias, but I do think that now there is something in what Cebes says. Why should really wise men want to run away from masters who are better than themselves, and lightly quit their service? And I think Cebes is aiming his argument at you, because you are so ready to leave us, and the gods, who are good rulers, as you yourself admit.

You are right, he said. I suppose you mean that I must defend myself against your charge, as if I were in a court of justice.

That is just our meaning, said Simmias.

VIII   Well then, he replied, let me try to make a more successful defense to you than I did to the judges at my trial. I should be wrong, Cebes and Simmias, he went on, not to grieve at death, if I did not think that I was going to live both with other gods who are good and wise, and with men who have died and who are better than the men of this world. But you must know that I hope that I am going to live among good men, though I am not quite sure of that. But I am as sure as I can be in such matters that I am going to live with gods who are very good masters. And therefore I am not so much grieved at death; I am confident that the dead have some kind of existence, and, as has been said of old, an existence that is far better for the good than for the wicked.

Well, Socrates, said Simmias, do you mean to go away and keep this belief to yourself, or will you let us share it with you? It seems to me that we too have an interest in this good. And it will also serve as your defense, if you can convince us of what you say.

I will try, he replied. But I think Crito has been wanting to speak to me. Let us first hear what he has to say.

Only, Socrates, said Crito, that the man who is going to give you the poison has been telling me to warn you not to talk much. He says that talking heats people, and that the action of the poison must not be counteracted by heat. Those who excite themselves sometimes have to drink it two or three times.

Let him be, said Socrates; let him mind his own business, and be prepared to give me the poison twice, or, if need be, thrice.

I knew that would be your answer, said Crito, but the man has been importunate.

Never mind him, he replied. But I wish now to explain to you, my judges, why it seems to me that a man who has really spent his life in philosophy has reason to be of good cheer when he is about to die, and may well hope after death to gain in the other world the greatest good. I will try to show you, Simmias and Cebes, how this may be.   64

The world, perhaps, does not see that those who rightly engage in philosophy study only dying and death. And, if this be true, it would be surely strange for a man all through his life to desire only death, and then, when death comes to him, to be vexed at it, when it has been his study and his desire for so long.   IX

Simmias laughed, and said: Indeed, Socrates, you make me laugh, though I am scarcely in a laughing humor now. If the multitude heard that, I fancy they would think that what you say of philosophers is quite true; and my countrymen would entirely agree with you that philosophers are indeed eager to die, and they would say that they know full well that philosophers deserve to be put to death.

And they would be right, Simmias, except in saying that they know it. They do not know in what sense the true philosopher is eager to die, or what kind of death he deserves, or in what sense he deserves it. Let us dismiss them from our thoughts, and converse by ourselves. Do we believe death to be anything?

We do, replied Simmias.

And do we not believe it to be the separation of the soul from the body? Does not death mean that the body comes to exist by itself, separated from the soul, and that the soul exists by herself, separated from the body? What is death but that?

It is that, he said.

Now consider, my good friend, if you and I are agreed on another point which I think will help us to understand the question better. Do you think that a philosopher will care very much about what are called pleasures, such as the pleasures of eating and drinking?

Certainly not, Socrates, said Simmias.

Or about the pleasures of sexual passion?

Indeed, no.

And, do you think that he holds the remaining cares of the body in high esteem? Will he think much of getting fine clothes, and sandals, and other bodily adornments, or will he despise them, except so far as he is absolutely forced to meddle with them?

The real philosopher, I think, will despise them, he replied.

In short, said he, you think that his studies are not concerned with the body? He stands aloof from it, as far as he can, and turns toward the soul?

I do.

Well then, in these matters, first, it is clear that the philosopher releases   65 his soul from communion with the body, so far as he can, beyond all other men?

It is.

And does not the world think, Simmias, that if a man has no pleasure in such things, and does not take his share in them, his life is not worth living? Do not they hold that he who thinks nothing of bodily pleasures is almost as good as dead?

Indeed you are right.

LIFE OF THE SOUL: WISDOM

X But what about the actual acquisition of wisdom? If the body is taken as a companion in the search for wisdom, is it a hindrance or not? For example, do sight and hearing convey any real truth to men? Are not the very poets forever telling us that we neither hear nor see anything accurately? But if these senses of the body are not accurate or clear, the others will hardly be so, for they are all less perfect than these, are they not?

Yes, I think so, certainly, he said.

Then when does the soul attain truth? he asked. We see that, as often as she seeks to investigate anything in company with the body, the body leads her astray.

True.

Is it not by reasoning, if at all, that any real truth becomes manifest to her?

Yes.

And she reasons best, I suppose, when none of the senses, whether hearing, or sight, or pain, or pleasure, harasses her; when she has dismissed the body, and released herself as far as she can from all intercourse or contact with it, and so, coming to be as much alone with herself as is possible, strives after real truth.

That is so.

And here too the soul of the philosopher very greatly despises the body, and flies from it, and seeks to be alone by herself, does she not?

Clearly.

And what do you say to the next point, Simmias? Do we say that there is such a thing as absolute justice, or not?

Indeed we do.

And absolute beauty, and absolute good?

Of course.

Have you ever seen any of them with your eyes?

Indeed I have not, he replied.

Did you ever grasp them with any bodily sense? I am speaking of all absolutes, whether size, or health, or strength; in a word, of the essence or real being of everything. Is the very truth of things contemplated by the body? Is it not rather the case that the man who prepares himself most carefully to apprehend by his intellect the essence of each thing which he examines will come nearest to the knowledge of it?

Certainly.

And will not a man attain to this pure thought most completely if he goes to each thing, as far as he can, with his mind alone, taking neither sight nor any other sense along with his reason in the process of thought, to be an encumbrance? In every case he will pursue pure and absolute being, with his pure intellect alone. He will be set free as far as possible from the eye and the ear and, in short, from the whole body, because intercourse with the body troubles the soul, and hinders her from gaining truth and wisdom. Is it not he who will attain the knowledge of real being, if any man will? XI

Your words are admirably true, Socrates, said Simmias.

And, he said, must not all this cause real philosophers to reflect, and make them say to each other, It seems that there is a narrow path which will bring us safely to our journey's end, with reason as our guide. As long as we have this body, and an evil of that sort is mingled with our souls, we shall never fully gain what we desire; and that is truth. For the body is forever taking up our time with the care which it needs; and, besides, whenever diseases attack it, they hinder us in our pursuit of real being. It fills us with passions, and desires, and fears, and all manner of phantoms, and much foolishness; and so, as the saying goes, in very truth we can never think at all for it. It alone and its desires cause wars and factions and battles; for the origin of all wars is the pursuit of wealth,[1] and we are forced to pursue wealth because we live in slavery to the cares of the body. And therefore, for all these reasons, we have no leisure for philosophy. And last of all, if we ever are free from the body for a time, and then turn to examine some matter, it falls in our way at every step of the inquiry, and causes confusion and trouble and panic, so that we cannot see the truth for it. Verily we have learned that if we are to have any pure knowledge at all, we must be freed from the body; the soul by herself must behold things as they are. Then, it seems, after we are dead, we shall gain the wisdom which we desire, and for which we say we have a passion, but not while we are alive, as the argument shows. For if it be not possible to have pure knowledge while the body is with us, one of two things must be true: either we cannot gain knowledge at all, or we can gain it only after death. For then, and not till then, will the soul exist by herself, separate from the body. And while we live, we shall come nearest to knowledge, if we have no communion or intercourse with the body beyond what is absolutely necessary, and if we are not defiled with its nature. We must live pure from it until God himself releases us. And when we are thus pure and released from its follies, we shall dwell, I suppose, with others who are pure like ourselves, and we shall of ourselves know all that is pure; and that may be the truth. For I think that the impure is not allowed to attain to the pure. Such, Simmias, I fancy must needs be the language and the reflections of the true lovers of knowledge. Do you not agree with me? 66

67

Most assuredly I do, Socrates.

---
[1] Cf. *Republic* 373d. [F.J.C.]

XII   And, my friend, said Socrates, if this be true, I have good hope that, when I reach the place whither I am going, I shall there, if anywhere, gain fully that which we have sought so earnestly in the past. And so I shall set forth cheerfully on the journey that is appointed me today, and so may every man who thinks that his mind is prepared and purified.

That is quite true, said Simmias.

And does not the purification consist, as we have said, in separating the soul from the body, as far as is possible, and in accustoming her to collect and rally herself together from the body on every side, and to dwell alone by herself as much as she can, both now and hereafter, released from the bondage of the body?

Yes, certainly, he said.

Is not what we call death a release and separation of the soul from the body?

Undoubtedly, he replied.

And the true philosopher, we hold, is alone in his constant desire to set his soul free? His study is simply the release and separation of the soul from the body, is it not?

Clearly.

Would it not be absurd then, as I began by saying, for a man to complain at death coming to him, when in his life he has been preparing himself to live as nearly in a state of death as he could? Would not that be absurd?

Yes, indeed.

In truth, then, Simmias, he said, the true philosopher studies to die, and to him of all men is death least terrible. Now look at the matter in this way. In everything he is at enmity with his body, and he longs to possess his soul alone. Would it not then be most unreasonable if he were to fear and com-

68   plain when he has his desire, instead of rejoicing to go to the place where he hopes to gain the wisdom that he has passionately longed for all his life, and to be released from the company of his enemy? Many a man has willingly gone to the other world, when a human love or wife or son has died, in the hope of seeing there those whom he longed for, and of being with them: and will a man who has a real passion for wisdom, and a firm hope of really finding wisdom in the other world and nowhere else, grieve at death, and not depart rejoicing? Nay, my friend, you ought not to think that, if he be truly a philosopher. He will be firmly convinced that there and nowhere else will he meet with wisdom in its purity. And if this be so, would it not, I repeat, be very unreasonable for such a man to fear death?

Yes, indeed, he replied, it would.

XIII   Does not this show clearly, he said, that any man whom you see grieving at the approach of death is after all no lover of wisdom, but a lover of his body? He is also, most likely, a lover either of wealth, or of honor, or, it may be, of both.

Yes, he said, it is as you say.

Well then, Simmias, he went on, does not what is called courage belong especially to the philosopher?

Certainly I think so, he replied.

And does not temperance, the quality which even the world calls temperance, and which means to despise and control and govern the passions —does not temperance belong only to such men as most despise the body, and pass their lives in philosophy?

Of necessity, he replied.

For if you will consider the courage and the temperance of other men, said he, you will find that they are strange things.

How so, Socrates?

You know, he replied, that all other men regard death as one of the great evils to which mankind is subject?

Indeed they do, he said.

And when the brave men of them submit to death, do not they do so from a fear of still greater evils?

Yes.

Then all men but the philosopher are brave from fear and because they are afraid. Yet it is rather a strange thing for a man to be brave out of fear and cowardice.

Indeed it is.

And are not the orderly men of them in exactly the same case? Are not they temperate from a kind of intemperance? We should say that this cannot be; but in them this state of foolish temperance comes to that. They desire certain pleasures, and fear to lose them; and so they abstain from other pleasures because they are mastered by these. Intemperance is defined to mean being under the dominion of pleasure, yet they only master certain pleasures because they are mastered by others. But that is exactly what I said just now—that, in a way, they are made temperate from intemperance. 69

It seems to be so.

My dear Simmias, I fear that virtue is not really to be bought in this way, by bartering pleasure for pleasure, and pain for pain, and fear for fear, and the greater for the less, like coins. There is only one sterling coin for which all these things ought to be exchanged, and that is wisdom. All that is bought and sold for this and with this, whether courage, or temperance, or justice, is real; in one word, true virtue cannot be without wisdom, and it matters nothing whether pleasure, and fear, and all other such things are present or absent. But I think that the virtue which is composed of pleasures and fears bartered with one another, and severed from wisdom, is only a shadow of true virtue, and that it has no freedom, nor health, nor truth. True virtue in reality is a kind of purifying from all these things; and temperance, and justice, and courage, and wisdom itself are the purification. And I fancy that the men who established our mysteries had a very real meaning: in truth they have been telling us in parables all the time that whosoever comes to Hades uninitiated and profane will lie in the mire, while he that has been purified and initiated shall dwell with the gods. For "the thyrsus-bearers are many," as they say in the mysteries, "but the inspired few." And by these last, I believe, are meant only the true philosophers. And I in my life have striven as hard as I was able, and have left nothing undone, that I might become one of them. Whether I have striven in the right way, and whether I have succeeded or not, I suppose that I shall learn in a little while, when I reach the other world, if it be the will of God.

That is my defense, Simmias and Cebes, to show that I have reason for not being angry or grieved at leaving you and my masters here. I believe that in the next world, no less than in this, I shall meet with good masters and friends, though the multitude are incredulous of it. And if I have been more successful with you in my defense than I was with my Athenian judges, it is well.

THE SOUL IS IMPERISHABLE: PREEXISTENCE

XIV When Socrates had finished, Cebes replied to him, and said I think that for the most part you are right, Socrates. But men are very incredulous of
70 what you have said of the soul. They fear that she will no longer exist anywhere when she has left the body, but that she will be destroyed and perish on the very day of death. They think that the moment that she is released and leaves the body, she will be dissolved and vanish away like breath or smoke, and thenceforward cease to exist at all. If she were to exist somewhere as a whole, released from the evils which you enumerated just now, we should have good reason to hope, Socrates, that what you say is true. But it will need no little persuasion and assurance to show that the soul exists after death, and continues to possess any power or wisdom.

True, Cebes, said Socrates; but what are we to do? Do you wish to converse about these matters and see if what I say is probable?

I for one, said Cebes, should gladly hear your opinion about them.

I think, said Socrates, that no one who heard me now, even if he were a comic poet, would say that I am an idle talker about things which do not concern me. So, if you wish it, let us examine this question.

GENERATION FROM OPPOSITES

XV Let us consider whether or not the souls of men exist in the next world after death, thus. There is an ancient belief, which we remember, that on leaving this world they exist there, and that they return hither and are born again from the dead. But if it be true that the living are born from the dead, our souls must exist in the other world; otherwise they could not be born again. It will be a sufficient proof that this is so if we can really prove that the living are born only from the dead. But if this is not so, we shall have to find some other argument.

Exactly, said Cebes.

Well, said he, the easiest way of answering the question will be to consider it not in relation to men only, but also in relation to all animals and
plants, and in short to all things that are generated. Is it the case that everything which has an opposite is generated only from its opposite? By opposites I mean the honorable and the base, the just and the unjust, and so on
in a thousand other instances. Let us consider then whether it is necessary
for everything that has an opposite to be generated only from its own
opposite. For instance, when anything becomes greater, I suppose it must
first have been less and then become greater?

Yes.

And if a thing becomes less, it must have been greater, and afterward   71
become less?

That is so, said he.

And further, the weaker is generated from the stronger, and the swifter
from the slower?

Certainly.

And the worse is generated from the better, and the more just from the
more unjust?

Of course.

Then it is sufficiently clear to us that all things are generated in this
way, opposites from opposites?

Quite so.

And in every pair of opposites, are there not two generations between
the two members of the pair, from the one to the other, and then back
again from the other to the first? Between the greater and the less are
growth and diminution, and we say that the one grows and the other dimin-
ishes, do we not?

Yes, he said.

And there is division and composition, and cold and hot, and so on. In
fact, is it not a universal law, even though we do not always express it in so
many words, that opposites are generated always from one another, and
that there is a process of generation from one to the other?

It is, he replied.

Well, said he, is there an opposite to life, in the same way that sleep is   XVI
the opposite of being awake?

Certainly, he answered.

What is it?

Death, he replied.

Then if life and death are opposites, they are generated the one from
the other: they are two, and between them there are two generations. Is it
not so?

Of course.

Now, said Socrates, I will explain to you one of the two pairs of opposites of which I spoke just now, and its generations, and you shall explain
to me the other. Sleep is the opposite of waking. From sleep is produced

the state of waking, and from the state of waking is produced sleep. Their generations are, first, to fall asleep; secondly, to awake. Is that clear? he asked.

Yes, quite.

Now then, said he, do you tell me about life and death. Death is the opposite of life, is it not?

It is.

And they are generated the one from the other?

Yes.

Then what is that which is generated from the living?

The dead, he replied.

And what is generated from the dead?

I must admit that it is the living.

Then living things and living men are generated from the dead, Cebes? Clearly, said he.

Then our souls exist in the other world? he said.

Apparently.

Now of these two generations the one is certain? Death I suppose is certain enough, is it not?

Yes, quite, he replied.

What then shall we do? said he. Shall we not assign an opposite generation to correspond? Or is nature imperfect here? Must we not assign some opposite generation to dying?

I think so, certainly, he said.

And what must it be?

To come to life again.

72   And if there be such a thing as a return to life, he said, it will be a generation from the dead to the living, will it not?

It will, certainly.

Then we are agreed on this point: namely, that the living are generated from the dead no less than the dead from the living. But we agreed that, if this be so, it is a sufficient proof that the souls of the dead must exist somewhere, whence they come into being again.

I think, Socrates, that that is the necessary result of our premises.

XVII   And I think, Cebes, said he, that our conclusion has not been an unfair one. For if opposites did not always correspond with opposites as they are generated, moving as it were round in a circle, and there were generation in a straight line forward from one opposite only, with no turning or return to the other, then, you know, all things would come at length to have the same form and be in the same state, and would cease to be generated at all.

What do you mean? he asked.

It is not at all hard to understand my meaning, he replied. If, for example, the one opposite, to go to sleep, existed without the corresponding opposite, to wake up, which is generated from the first, then all nature would at last make the tale of Endymion meaningless, and he would no longer be conspicuous; for everything else would be in the same state of sleep that he was in. And if all things were compounded together and never separated, the Chaos of Anaxagoras would soon be realized. Just in the same way, my dear Cebes, if all things in which there is any life were to die, and when they were dead were to remain in that form and not come to life again, would not the necessary result be that everything at last would be dead, and nothing alive? For if living things were generated from other sources than death, and were to die, the result is inevitable that all things would be consumed by death. Is it not so?

It is indeed, I think, Socrates, said Cebes; I think that what you say is perfectly true.

Yes, Cebes, he said, I think it is certainly so. We are not misled into this conclusion. The dead do come to life again, and the living are generated from them, and the souls of the dead exist; and with the souls of the good it is well, and with the souls of the evil it is evil.

RECOLLECTION OF THE ABSOLUTES

And besides, Socrates, rejoined Cebes, if the doctrine which you are fond of stating, that our learning is only a process of recollection, be true, then I suppose we must have learned at some former time what we recollect now. And that would be impossible unless our souls had existed somewhere before they came into this human form. So that is another reason for believing the soul immortal.

XVIII

73

But, Cebes, interrupted Simmias, what are the proofs of that? Recall them to me; I am not very clear about them at present.

One argument, answered Cebes, and the strongest of all, is that if you question men about anything in the right way, they will answer you correctly of themselves. But they would not have been able to do that unless they had had within themselves knowledge and right reason. Again, show them such things as geometrical diagrams, and the proof of the doctrine is complete.[2]

And if that does not convince you, Simmias, said Socrates, look at the matter in another way and see if you agree then. You have doubts, I know, how what is called knowledge can be recollection.

Nay, replied Simmias, I do not doubt. But I want to recollect the argument about recollection. What Cebes undertook to explain has nearly brought your theory back to me and convinced me. But I am nonetheless ready to hear you undertake to explain it.

In this way, he returned. We are agreed, I suppose, that if a man remembers anything, he must have known it at some previous time.

---

[2] For an example of this see *Meno* 82a ff., where, as here, Socrates proves the doctrine of Reminiscence, and therefore the Immortality of the Soul by putting judicious questions about geometry to a slave who was quite ignorant of geometry, and, with the help of diagrams, obtaining from him correct answers. [F.J.C.]

Certainly, he said.

And are we agreed that when knowledge comes in the following way, it is recollection? When a man has seen or heard anything, or has perceived it by some other sense, and then knows not that thing only, but has also in his mind an impression of some other thing, of which the knowledge is quite different, are we not right in saying that he remembers the thing of which he has an impression in his mind?

What do you mean?

I mean this. The knowledge of a man is different from the knowledge of a lyre, is it not?

Certainly.

And you know that when lovers see a lyre, or a garment, or anything that their favorites are wont to use, they have this feeling. They know the lyre, and in their mind they receive the image of the youth whose the lyre was. That is recollection. For instance, someone seeing Simmias often is reminded of Cebes; and there are endless examples of the same thing.

Indeed there are, said Simmias.

Is not that a kind of recollection, he said; and more especially when a man has this feeling with reference to things which the lapse of time and inattention have made him forget?

Yes, certainly, he replied.

Well, he went on, is it possible to recollect a man on seeing the picture of a horse, or the picture of a lyre? Or to recall Simmias on seeing a picture of Cebes?

Certainly.

And it is possible to recollect Simmias himself on seeing a picture of Simmias?

No doubt, he said.

74

XIX   Then in all these cases there is recollection caused by similar objects, and also by dissimilar objects?

There is.

But when a man has a recollection caused by similar objects, will he not have a further feeling and consider whether the likeness to that which he recollects is defective in any way or not?

He will, he said.

Now see if this is true, he went on. Do we not believe in the existence of equality—not the equality of pieces of wood or of stones, but something beyond that—equality in the abstract? Shall we say that there is such a thing, or not?

Yes indeed, said Simmias, most emphatically we will.

And do we know what this abstract equality is?

Certainly, he replied.

Where did we get the knowledge of it? Was it not from seeing the equal pieces of wood, and stones, and the like, which we were speaking of just now? Did we not form from them the idea of abstract equality, which is different from them? Or do you think that it is not different? Consider the question in this way. Do not equal pieces of wood and stones appear to us sometimes equal and sometimes unequal, though in fact they remain the same all the time?

Certainly they do.

But did absolute equals ever seem to you to be unequal, or abstract equality to be inequality?

No, never, Socrates.

Then equal things, he said, are not the same as abstract equality?

No, certainly not, Socrates.

Yet it was from these equal things, he said, which are different from abstract equality, that you have conceived and got your knowledge of abstract equality?

That is quite true, he replied.

And that whether it is like them or unlike them?

Certainly.

But that makes no difference, he said. As long as the sight of one thing brings another thing to your mind, there must be recollection, whether or no the two things are like.

That is so.

Well then, said he, do the equal pieces of wood, and other similar equal things, of which we have been speaking, affect us at all this way? Do they seem to us to be equal, in the way that abstract equality is equal? Do they come short of being like abstract equality, or not?

Indeed, they come very short of it, he replied.

Are we agreed about this? A man sees something and thinks to himself, "This thing that I see aims at being like some other thing, but it comes short and cannot be like that other thing; it is inferior"; must not the man who thinks that have known at some previous time that other thing, which he says that it resembles, and to which it is inferior?

He must.

Well, have we ourselves had the same sort of feeling with reference to equal things, and to abstract equality?

Yes, certainly.

Then we must have had knowledge of equality before we first saw equal things, and perceived that they all strive to be like equality, and all come short of it.

That is so.

And we are agreed also that we have not, nor could we have, obtained the idea of equality except from sight or touch or some other sense; the same is true of all the senses.

Yes, Socrates, for the purposes of the argument that is so.

At any rate it is by the senses that we must perceive that all sensible objects strive to resemble absolute equality, and are inferior to it. Is not that so?

75

Yes.

Then before we began to see, and to hear, and to use the other senses, we must have received the knowledge of the nature of abstract and real equality; otherwise we could not have compared equal sensible objects with abstract equality, and seen that the former in all cases strive to be like the latter, though they are always inferior to it?

That is the necessary consequence of what we have been saying, Socrates.

Did we not see, and hear, and possess the other senses as soon as we were born?

Yes, certainly.

And we must have received the knowledge of abstract equality before we had these senses?

Yes.

Then, it seems, we must have received that knowledge before we were born?

It does.

XX   Now if we received this knowledge before our birth, and were born with it, we knew, both before and at the moment of our birth, not only the equal, and the greater, and the less, but also everything of the same kind, did we not? Our present reasoning does not refer only to equality. It refers just as much to absolute good, and absolute beauty, and absolute justice, and absolute holiness; in short, I repeat, to everything which we mark with the name of the real, in the questions and answers of our dialectic. So we must have received our knowledge of all realities before we were born.

That is so.

And we must always be born with this knowledge, and must always retain it throughout life, if we have not each time forgotten it, after having received it. For to know means to receive and retain knowledge, and not to have lost it. Do not we mean by forgetting, the loss of knowledge, Simmias?

Yes, certainly, Socrates, he said.

But, I suppose, if it be the case that we lost at birth the knowledge which we received before we were born, and then afterward, by using our senses on the objects of sense, recovered the knowledge which we had previously possessed, then what we call learning is the recovering of knowledge which is already ours. And are we not right in calling that recollection?

Certainly.

76   For we have found it possible to perceive a thing by sight, or hearing, or any other sense, and thence to form a notion of some other thing, like or unlike, which had been forgotten, but with which this thing was associated. And therefore, I say, one of two things must be true. Either we are all born with this knowledge and retain it all our life; or, after birth, those whom

we say are learning are only recollecting, and our knowledge is recollection.

Yes indeed, that is undoubtedly true, Socrates.

Then which do you choose, Simmias? Are we born with knowledge or do we recollect the things of which we have received knowledge before our birth? XXI

I cannot say at present, Socrates.

Well, have you an opinion about this question? Can a man who knows give an account of what he knows, or not? What do you think about that?

Yes, of course he can, Socrates.

And do you think that everyone can give an account of the ideas of which we have been speaking?

I wish I did, indeed, said Simmias, but I am very much afraid that by this time tomorrow there will no longer be any man living able to do so as it should be done.

Then, Simmias, he said, you do not think that all men know these things?

Certainly not.

Then they recollect what they once learned?

Necessarily.

And when did our souls gain this knowledge? It cannot have been after we were born men.

No, certainly not.

Then it was before?

Yes.

Then, Simmias, our souls existed formerly, apart from our bodies, and possessed intelligence before they came into man's shape.

Unless we receive this knowledge at the moment of birth, Socrates. That time still remains.

Well, my friend, and at what other time do we lose it? We agreed just now that we are not born with it; do we lose it at the same moment that we gain it, or can you suggest any other time?

I cannot, Socrates. I did not see that I was talking nonsense.

Then, Simmias, he said, is not this the truth? If, as we are forever repeating, beauty, and good, and the other ideas really exist, and if we refer all the objects of sensible perception to these ideas which were formerly ours, and which we find to be ours still, and compare sensible objects with them, then, just as they exist, our souls must have existed before ever we were born. But if they do not exist, then our reasoning will have been thrown away. Is it so? If these ideas exist, does it not at once follow that our souls must have existed before we were born, and if they do not exist, then neither did our souls? XXII

Admirably put, Socrates, said Simmias. I think that the necessity is the same for the one as for the other. The reasoning has reached a place of safety in the common proof of the existence of our souls before we were born and of the existence of the ideas of which you spoke. Nothing is so evident to me as that beauty, and good, and the other ideas which you spoke of just now have a very real existence indeed. Your proof is quite sufficient for me.

But what of Cebes? said Socrates. I must convince Cebes too.

THE SOUL'S SURVIVAL

I think that he is satisfied, said Simmias, though he is the most skeptical of men in argument. But I think that he is perfectly convinced that our souls existed before we were born.

XXIII   But I do not think myself, Socrates, he continued, that you have proved that the soul will continue to exist when we are dead. The common fear which Cebes spoke of, that she may be scattered to the winds at death, and that death may be the end of her existence, still stands in the way. Assuming that the soul is generated and comes together from some other elements, and exists before she ever enters the human body, why should she not come to an end and be destroyed, after she has entered into the body, when she is released from it?

You are right, Simmias, said Cebes. I think that only half the required proof has been given. It has been shown that our souls existed before we were born; but it must also be shown that our souls will continue to exist after we are dead, no less than that they existed before we were born, if the proof is to be complete.

That has been shown already, Simmias and Cebes, said Socrates, if you will combine this reasoning with our previous conclusion, that all life is generated from death. For if the soul exists in a previous state and if, when she comes into life and is born, she can only be born from death, and from a state of death, must she not exist after death too, since she has to be born again? So the point which you speak of has been already proved.

XXIV   Still I think that you and Simmias would be glad to discuss this question further. Like children, you are afraid that the wind will really blow the soul away and disperse her when she leaves the body, especially if a man happens to die in a storm and not in a calm.

Cebes laughed and said, Try and convince us as if we were afraid, Socrates; or rather, do not think that we are afraid ourselves. Perhaps there is a child within us who has these fears. Let us try and persuade him not to be afraid of death, as if it were a bugbear.

You must charm him every day, until you have charmed him away, said Socrates.

78   And where shall we find a good charmer, Socrates, he asked, now that you are leaving us?

Hellas is a large country, Cebes, he replied, and good men may doubtless be found in it; and the nations of the Barbarians are many. You must search them all through for such a charmer, sparing neither money nor labor; for there is nothing on which you could spend money more profitably. And you must search for him among yourselves too, for you will hardly find a better charmer than yourselves.

That shall be done, said Cebes. But let us return to the point where we left off, if you will.

Yes, I will: why not?

Very good, he replied.

Well, said Socrates, must we not ask ourselves this question? What kind of thing is liable to suffer dispersion, and for what kind of thing have we to fear dispersion? And then we must see whether the soul belongs to that kind or not, and be confident or afraid about our own souls accordingly.   XXV

That is true, he answered.

Now is it not the compound and composite which is naturally liable to be dissolved in the same way in which it was compounded? And is not what is uncompounded alone not liable to dissolution, if anything is not?

I think that that is so, said Cebes.

And what always remains in the same state and unchanging is most likely to be uncompounded, and what is always changing and never the same is most likely to be compounded, I suppose?

Yes, I think so.

ABSOLUTES UNCHANGEABLE

Now let us return to what we were speaking of before in the discussion, he said. Does the being, which in our dialectic we define as meaning absolute existence, remain always in exactly the same state, or does it change? Do absolute equality, absolute beauty, and every other absolute existence, admit of any change at all? Or does absolute existence in each case, being essentially uniform, remain the same and unchanging, and never in any case admit of any sort or kind of change whatsoever?

It must remain the same and unchanging, Socrates, said Cebes.

And what of the many beautiful things, such as men, and horses, and garments, and the like, and of all which bears the names of the ideas, whether equal, or beautiful, or anything else? Do they remain the same or is it exactly the opposite with them? In short, do they never remain the same at all, either in themselves or in their relations?

These things, said Cebes, never remain the same.

You can touch them, and see them, and perceive them with the other   79
senses, while you can grasp the unchanging only by the reasoning of the intellect. These latter are invisible and not seen. Is it not so?

That is perfectly true, he said.

Let us assume then, he said, if you will, that there are two kinds of   XXVI
existence, the one visible, the other invisible.

Yes, he said.

And the invisible unchanging, while the visible is always changing.

Yes, he said again.

Are not we men made up of body and soul?

There is nothing else, he replied.

And which of these kinds of existence should we say that the body is most like, and most akin to?

The visible, he replied; that is quite obvious.

And the soul? Is that visible or invisible?

It is invisible to man, Socrates, he said.

But we mean by visible and invisible, visible and invisible to man; do we not?

Yes; that is what we mean.

Then what do we say of the soul? Is it visible or not visible?

It is not visible.

Then is it invisible?

Yes.

SOUL PARTICIPATES IN THE ABSOLUTES

Then the soul is more like the invisible than the body; and the body is like the visible.

That is necessarily so, Socrates.

XXVII Have we not also said that, when the soul employs the body in any inquiry, and makes use of sight, or hearing, or any other sense—for inquiry with the body means inquiry with the senses—she is dragged away by it to the things which never remain the same, and wanders about blindly, and becomes confused and dizzy, like a drunken man, from dealing with things that are ever changing?

Certainly.

But when she investigates any question by herself, she goes away to the pure, and eternal, and immortal, and unchangeable, to which she is akin, and so she comes to be ever with it, as soon as she is by herself, and can be so; and then she rests from her wanderings and dwells with it unchangingly, for she is dealing with what is unchanging. And is not this state of the soul called wisdom?

Indeed, Socrates, you speak well and truly, he replied.

Which kind of existence do you think from our former and our present arguments that the soul is more like and more akin to?

I think, Socrates, he replied, that after this inquiry the very dullest man would agree that the soul is infinitely more like the unchangeable than the changeable.

And the body?

That is like the changeable.

XXVIII Consider the matter in yet another way. When the soul and the body
80 are united, nature ordains the one to be a slave and to be ruled, and the other to be master and to rule. Tell me once again, which do you think is

like the divine, and which is like the mortal? Do you not think that the divine naturally rules and has authority, and that the mortal naturally is ruled and is a slave?

I do.

Then which is the soul like?

That is quite plain, Socrates. The soul is like the divine, and the body is like the mortal.

Now tell me, Cebes, is the result of all that we have said that the soul is most like the divine, and the immortal, and the intelligible, and the uniform, and the indissoluble, and the unchangeable; while the body is most like the human, and the mortal, and the unintelligible, and the multiform, and the dissoluble, and the changeable? Have we any other argument to show that this is not so, my dear Cebes?

We have not.

Then if this is so, is it not the nature of the body to be dissolved   XXIX
quickly, and of the soul to be wholly or very nearly indissoluble?

Certainly.

You observe, he said, that after a man is dead, the visible part of him, his body, which lies in the visible world and which we call the corpse, which is subject to dissolution and decomposition, is not dissolved and decomposed at once? It remains as it was for a considerable time, and even for a long time, if a man dies with his body in good condition and in the vigor of life. And when the body falls in and is embalmed, like the mummies of Egypt, it remains nearly entire for an immense time. And should it decay, yet some parts of it, such as the bones and muscles, may almost be said to be immortal. Is it not so?

Yes.

And shall we believe that the soul, which is invisible, and which goes hence to a place that is like herself, glorious, and pure, and invisible, to Hades, which is rightly called the unseen world, to dwell with the good and wise God, whither, if it be the will of God, my soul too must shortly go—shall we believe that the soul, whose nature is so glorious, and pure, and invisible, is blown away by the winds and perishes as soon as she leaves the body, as the world says? Nay, dear Cebes and Simmias, it is not so. I will tell you what happens to a soul which is pure at her departure, and which in her life has had no intercourse that she could avoid with the body, and so draws after her, when she dies, no taint of the body, but has shunned it, and gathered herself into herself, for such has been her constant study—and that only means that she has loved wisdom rightly, and has truly prac-   81
ticed how to die. Is not this the practice of death?

Yes, certainly.

Does not the soul, then, which is in that state, go away to the invisible that is like herself, and to the divine, and the immortal, and the wise, where she is released from error, and folly, and fear, and fierce passions, and all the other evils that fall to the lot of men, and is happy, and for the rest of time lives in very truth with the gods, as they say that the initiated do? Shall we affirm this, Cebes?

Yes, certainly, said Cebes.

XXX   But if she be defiled and impure when she leaves the body, from being ever with it, and serving it and loving it, and from being besotted by it and by its desires and pleasures, so that she thinks nothing true but what is bodily and can be touched, and seen, and eaten, and drunk, and used for men's lusts; if she has learned to hate, and tremble at, and fly from what is dark and invisible to the eye, and intelligible and apprehended by philosophy—do you think that a soul which is in that state will be pure and without alloy at her departure?

No, indeed, he replied.

She is penetrated, I suppose, by the corporeal, which the unceasing intercourse and company and care of the body has made a part of her nature.

Yes.

And, my dear friend, the corporeal must be burdensome, and heavy, and earthy, and visible; and it is by this that such a soul is weighed down and dragged back to the visible world, because she is afraid of the invisible world of Hades, and haunts, it is said, the graves and tombs, where shadowy forms of souls have been seen, which are the phantoms of souls which were impure at their release and still cling to the visible; which is the reason why they are seen.

That is likely enough, Socrates.

That is likely, certainly, Cebes; and these are not the souls of the good, but of the evil, which are compelled to wander in such places as a punishment for the wicked lives that they have lived; and their wanderings continue until, from the desire for the corporeal that clings to them, they are again imprisoned in a body.

XXXI   And, he continued, they are imprisoned, probably, in the bodies of animals with habits similar to the habits which were theirs in their lifetime.

What do you mean by that, Socrates?

I mean that men who have practiced unbridled gluttony, and wantonness, and drunkenness probably enter the bodies of asses and suchlike animals. Do you not think so?

82   Certainly that is very likely.

And those who have chosen injustice, and tyranny, and robbery enter the bodies of wolves, and hawks, and kites. Where else should we say that such souls go?

No doubt, said Cebes, they go into such animals.

In short, it is quite plain, he said, whither each soul goes; each enters an animal with habits like its own.

Certainly, he replied, that is so.

And of these, he said, the happiest, who go to the best place, are those who have practiced the popular and social virtues which are called temperance and justice, and which come from habit and practice, without philosophy or reason.

And why are they the happiest?

Because it is probable that they return into a mild and social nature like their own, such as that of bees, or wasps, or ants; or, it may be, into the bodies of men, and that from them are made worthy citizens.

Very likely.

But none but the philosopher or the lover of knowledge, who is wholly   XXXII
pure when he goes hence, is permitted to go to the race of the gods; and therefore, my friends, Simmias and Cebes, the true philosopher is temperate and refrains from all the pleasures of the body, and does not give himself up to them. It is not squandering his substance and poverty that he fears, as the multitude and the lovers of wealth do; nor again does he dread the dishonor and disgrace of wickedness, like the lovers of power and honor. It is not for these reasons that he is temperate.

No, it would be unseemly in him if he were, Socrates, said Cebes.

Indeed it would, he replied, and therefore all those who have any care for their souls, and who do not spend their lives in forming and molding their bodies, bid farewell to such persons, and do not walk in their ways, thinking that they know not whither they are going. They themselves turn and follow whithersoever philosophy leads them, for they believe that they ought not to resist philosophy, or its deliverance and purification.

How, Socrates?

I will tell you, he replied. The lovers of knowledge know that when phi-   XXXIII
losophy receives the soul, she is fast bound in the body, and fastened to it; she is unable to contemplate what is, by herself, or except through the bars of her prison house, the body; and she is wallowing in utter ignorance. And philosophy sees that the dreadful thing about the imprisonment is that it is caused by lust, and that the captive herself is an accomplice in her own   83
captivity. The lovers of knowledge, I repeat, know that philosophy takes the soul when she is in this condition, and gently encourages her, and strives to release her from her captivity, showing her that the perceptions of the eye, and the ear, and the other senses are full of deceit, and persuading her to stand aloof from the senses and to use them only when she must, and exhorting her to rally and gather herself together, and to trust only to herself and to the real existence which she of her own self apprehends, and to believe that nothing which is subject to change, and which she perceives by other faculties, has any truth, for such things are visible and sensible, while what she herself sees is apprehended by reason and invisible. The soul of the true philosopher thinks that it would be wrong to resist this deliverance from captivity, and therefore she holds aloof, so far as she can, from pleasure, and desire, and pain, and fear; for she reckons that when a man has vehement pleasure, or fear, or pain, or desire, he suffers from

them not merely the evils which might be expected, such as sickness or some loss arising from the indulgence of his desires; he suffers what is the greatest and last of evils, and does not take it into account.

What do you mean, Socrates? asked Cebes.

I mean that when the soul of any man feels vehement pleasure or pain, she is forced at the same time to think that the object, whatever it be, of these sensations is the most distinct and truest, when it is not. Such objects are chiefly visible ones, are they not?

They are.

And is it not in this state that the soul is most completely in bondage to the body?

How so?

Because every pleasure and pain has a kind of nail, and nails and pins her to the body, and gives her a bodily nature, making her think that whatever the body says is true. And so, from having the same fancies and the same pleasures as the body, she is obliged, I suppose, to come to have the same ways, and way of life: she must always be defiled with the body when she leaves it, and cannot be pure when she reaches the other world; and so she soon falls back into another body and takes root in it, like seed that is sown. Therefore she loses all part in intercourse with the divine, and pure, and uniform.

That is very true, Socrates, said Cebes.

XXXIV

84

It is for these reasons then, Cebes, that the real lovers of knowledge are temperate and brave; and not for the world's reasons. Or do you think so?

No, certainly I do not.

Assuredly not. The soul of a philosopher will consider that it is the office of philosophy to set her free. She will know that she must not give herself up once more to the bondage of pleasure and pain, from which philosophy is releasing her, and, like Penelope, do a work, only to undo it continually, weaving instead of unweaving her web. She gains for herself peace from these things, and follows reason and ever abides in it, contemplating what is true and divine and real, and fostered up by them. So she thinks that she should live in this life, and when she dies she believes that she will go to what is akin to and like herself, and be released from human ills. A soul, Simmias and Cebes, that has been so nurtured and so trained will never fear lest she should be torn in pieces at her departure from the body, and blown away by the winds, and vanish, and utterly cease to exist.

XXXV

At these words there was a long silence. Socrates himself seemed to be absorbed in his argument, and so were most of us. Cebes and Simmias conversed for a little by themselves. When Socrates observed them, he said: What? Do you think that our reasoning is incomplete? It still offers many points of doubt and attack, if it is to be examined thoroughly. If you are discussing another question, I have nothing to say. But if you have any difficulty about this one, do not hesitate to tell me what it is, and, if you are of the opinion that the argument should be stated in a better way, explain your views yourselves, and take me along with you if you think that you will be more successful in my company.

Simmias replied: Well, Socrates, I will tell you the truth. Each of us has a difficulty, and each has been pushing on the other and urging him to ask you about it. We were anxious to hear what you have to say; but we were reluctant to trouble you, for we were afraid that it might be unpleasant to you to be asked questions now.

Socrates smiled at this answer and said, Dear me! Simmias; I shall find it hard to convince other people that I do not consider my fate a misfortune when I cannot convince even you of it, and you are afraid that I am more peevish now than I used to be. You seem to think me inferior in prophetic power to the swans, which, when they find that they have to die, sing more loudly than they ever sang before, for joy that they are about to depart into the presence of God, whose servants they are. The fear which men have of death themselves makes them speak falsely of the swans, and they say that the swan is wailing at its death, and that it sings loud for grief. They forget that no bird sings when it is hungry, or cold, or in any pain; not even the nightingale, nor the swallow, nor the hoopoe, which, they assert, wail and sing for grief. But I think that neither these birds nor the swan sing for grief. I believe that they have a prophetic power and foreknowledge of the good things in the next world, for they are Apollo's birds; and so they sing and rejoice on the day of their death, more than in all their life. And I believe that I myself am a fellow slave with the swans, and consecrated to the service of the same God, and that I have prophetic power from my master no less than they, and that I am not more despondent than they are at leaving this life. So, as far as vexing me goes, you may talk to me and ask questions as you please, as long as the Eleven of the Athenians [3] will let you.

Good, said Simmias; I will tell you my difficulty, and Cebes will tell you why he is dissatisfied with your statement. I think, Socrates, and I daresay you think so too, that it is very difficult, and perhaps impossible, to obtain clear knowledge about these matters in this life. Yet I should hold him to be a very poor creature who did not test what is said about them in every way, and persevere until he had examined the question from every side, and could do no more. It is our duty to do one of two things. We must learn, or we must discover for ourselves, the truth of these matters; or, if that be impossible, we must take the best and most irrefragable of human doctrines and, embarking on that, as on a raft, risk the voyage of life, unless a stronger vessel, some divine word, could be found, on which we might take our journey more safely and more securely. And now, after what you have said, I shall not be ashamed to put a question to you; and then I shall not have to blame myself hereafter for not having said now what I think. Cebes and I have been considering your argument, and we think that it is hardly sufficient.

85

---

[3] Officials whose duty it was to superintend executions. [F.J.C.]

OBJECTIONS TO IMMORTALITY

(1) *Soul Is a Harmony*

XXXVI   I daresay you are right, my friend, said Socrates. But tell me, where is it insufficient?

To me it is insufficient, he replied, because the very same argument might be used of a harmony, and a lyre, and its strings. It might be said that the harmony in a tuned lyre is something unseen, and incorporeal, and perfectly beautiful, and divine, while the lyre and its strings are corporeal, and with the nature of bodies, and compounded, and earthly, and akin to the mortal. Now suppose that, when the lyre is broken and the strings are cut or snapped, a man were to press the same argument that you have used, and were to say that the harmony cannot have perished and that it must still exist, for it cannot possibly be that the lyre and the strings, with their mortal nature, continue to exist, though those strings have been broken, while the harmony, which is of the same nature as the divine and the immortal, and akin to them, has perished, and perished before the mortal lyre. He would say that the harmony itself must still exist somewhere, and that the wood and the strings will rot away before anything happens to it. And I think, Socrates, that you too must be aware that many of us believe the soul to be most probably a mixture and harmony of the elements by which our body is, as it were, strung and held together, such as heat and cold, and dry and wet, and the like, when they are mixed together well and in due proportion. Now if the soul is a harmony, it is clear that, when the body is relaxed out of proportion, or overstrung by disease or other evils, the soul, though most divine, must perish at once, like other harmonies of sound and of all works of art, while what remains of each body must remain for a long time, until it be burned or rotted away. What then shall we say to a man who asserts that the soul, being a mixture of the elements of the body, perishes first at what is called death?

XXXVII   Socrates looked keenly at us, as he often used to do, and smiled. Simmias' objection is a fair one, he said. If any of you is readier than I am, why does he not answer? For Simmias looks like a formidable assailant. But before we answer him, I think that we had better hear what fault Cebes has to find with my reasoning, and so gain time to consider our reply. And then, when we have heard them both, we must either give in to them, if they seem to harmonize, or, if they do not, we must proceed to argue in defense of our reasoning. Come, Cebes, what is it that troubles you and makes you doubt?

I will tell you, replied Cebes. I think that the argument is just where it was, and still open to our former objection. You have shown very cleverly and, if it is not arrogant to say so, quite conclusively that our souls existed before they entered the human form. I don't retract my admission on that point. But I am not convinced that they will continue to exist after we are dead. I do not agree with Simmias' objection, that the soul is not stronger and more lasting than the body: I think that it is very much superior in those respects. "Well, then," the argument might reply, "do you still doubt, when you see that the weaker part of a man continues to exist after his death? Do you not think that the more lasting part of him must necessarily be preserved for as long?"

(2) *Soul Is an Expendable Energy*

See, therefore, if there is anything in what I say; for I think that I, like Simmias, shall best express my meaning in a figure. It seems to me that a man might use an argument similar to yours to prove that a weaver, who had died in old age, had not in fact perished, but was still alive somewhere, on the ground that the garment which the weaver had woven for himself and used to wear had not perished or been destroyed. And if anyone were incredulous, he might ask whether a human being, or a garment constantly in use and wear, lasts the longest; and on being told that a human being lasts much the longest, he might think that he had shown beyond all doubt that the man was safe, because what lasts a shorter time than the man had not perished. But that, I suppose, is not so, Simmias; for you too must examine what I say. Everyone would understand that such an argument was simple nonsense. This weaver wove himself many such garments and wore them out; he outlived them all but the last, but he perished before that one. Yet a man is in no wise inferior to his cloak, or weaker than it, on that account. And I think that the soul's relation to the body may be expressed in a similar figure. Why should not a man very reasonably say in just the same way that the soul lasts a long time, while the body is weaker and lasts a shorter time? But, he might go on, each soul wears out many bodies, especially if she lives for many years. For if the body is in a state of flux and decay in the man's lifetime, and the soul is ever repairing the worn-out part, it will surely follow that the soul, on perishing, will be clothed in her last robe, and perish before that alone. But when the soul has perished, then the body will show its weakness and quickly rot away. So as yet we have no right to be confident, on the strength of this argument, that our souls continue to exist after we are dead. And a man might concede even more than this to an opponent who used your argument; he might admit not only that our souls existed in the period before we were born, but also that there is no reason why some of them should not continue to exist in the future, and often come into being, and die again, after we are dead; for the soul is strong enough by nature to endure coming into being many times. He might grant that, without conceding that she suffers no harm in all these births, or that she is not at last wholly destroyed at one of the deaths; and he might say that no man knows when this death and dissolution of the body, which brings destruction to the soul, will be, for it is impossible for any man to find out that. But if this is true, a man's confidence about death must be an irrational confidence, unless he can prove that the soul is wholly indestructible and immortal. Otherwise everyone who is dying must fear that his soul will perish utterly this time in her separation from the body.

XXXVIII It made us all very uncomfortable to listen to them, as we afterward said to each other. We had been fully convinced by the previous argument; and now they seemed to overturn our conviction, and to make us distrust all the arguments that were to come, as well as the preceding ones, and to doubt if our judgment was worth anything, or even if certainty could be attained at all.

Echecrates. By the gods, Phaedo, I can understand your feelings very well. I myself felt inclined while you were speaking to ask myself, "Then what reasoning are we to believe in future? That of Socrates was quite convincing, and now it has fallen into discredit." For the doctrine that our soul is a harmony has always taken a wonderful hold of me, and your mentioning it reminded me that I myself had held it. And now I must begin again and find some other reasoning which shall convince me that a man's soul does not die with him at his death. So tell me, I pray you, how did Socrates pursue the argument? Did he show any signs of uneasiness, as you say that you did, or did he come to the defense of his argument calmly? And did he defend it satisfactorily or not? Tell me the whole story as exactly as you can.

89 *Phaedo.* I have often, Echecrates, wondered at Socrates; but I never admired him more than I admired him then. There was nothing very strange in his having an answer. What I chiefly wondered at was, first, the kindness and good nature and respect with which he listened to the young men's objections; and, secondly, the quickness with which he perceived their effect upon us; and, lastly, how well he healed our wounds, and rallied us as if we were beaten and flying troops, and encouraged us to follow him, and to examine the reasoning with him.

Ech. How?

Phaedo. I will tell you. I was sitting by the bed on a stool at his right hand, and his seat was a good deal higher than mine. He stroked my head and gathered up the hair on my neck in his hand—you know he used often to play with my hair—and said, Tomorrow, Phaedo, I daresay you will cut off these beautiful locks.

I suppose so, Socrates, I replied.

You will not, if you take my advice.

Why not? I asked.

You and I will cut off our hair today, he said, if our argument be dead indeed, and we cannot bring it to life again. And I, if I were you, and the argument were to escape me, would swear an oath, as the Argives did, not to wear my hair long again until I had renewed the fight and conquered the argument of Simmias and Cebes.

But Heracles himself, they say, is not a match for two, I replied.

Then summon me to aid you, as your Iolaus, while there is still light.

Then I summon you, not as Heracles summoned Iolaus, but as Iolaus might summon Heracles.

It will be the same, he replied. But first let us take care not to make a   XXXIX
mistake.

What mistake? I asked.

The mistake of becoming misologists, or haters of reasoning, as men
become misanthropists, he replied; for to hate reasoning is the greatest evil
that can happen to us. Misology and misanthropy both come from similar
causes. The latter arises out of the implicit and irrational confidence which
is placed in a man who is believed by his friend to be thoroughly true and
sincere and trustworthy, and who is soon afterward discovered to be a bad
man and untrustworthy. This happens again and again; and when a man
has had this experience many times, particularly at the hands of those
whom he has believed to be his nearest and dearest friends, and he has
quarrelled with many of them, he ends by hating all men and thinking that
there is no good at all in anyone. Have you not seen this happen?

Yes, certainly, said I.

Is it not discreditable? he said. Is it not clear that such a man tries to
deal with men without understanding human nature? Had he understood it
he would have known that, in fact, good men and bad men are very few   90
indeed, and that the majority of men are neither one nor the other.

What do you mean? I asked.

Just what is true of extremely large and extremely small things, he replied. What is rarer than to find a man, or a dog, or anything else which is
either extremely large or extremely small? Or again, what is rarer than to
find a man who is extremely swift or slow, or extremely base or honorable,
or extremely black or white? Have you not noticed that in all these cases
the extremes are rare and few, and that the average specimens are abundant and many?

Yes, certainly, I replied.

And in the same way, if there were a competition in wickedness, he
said, don't you think that the leading sinners would be found to be very
few?

That is likely enough, said I.

Yes, it is, he replied. But this is not the point in which arguments are
like men; it was you who led me on to discuss this point. The analogy is
this. When a man believes some reasoning to be true, though he does not
understand the art of reasoning, and then soon afterward, rightly or
wrongly, comes to think that it is false, and this happens to him time after
time, he ends by disbelieving in reasoning altogether. You know that persons who spend their time in disputation, come at last to think themselves
the wisest of men, and to imagine that they alone have discovered that there
is no soundness or certainty anywhere, either in reasoning or in things, and
that all existence is in a state of perpetual flux, like the currents of the
Euripus, and never remains still for a moment.

Yes, I replied, that is certainly true.

And, Phaedo, he said, if there be a system of reasoning which is true, and certain, and which our minds can grasp, it would be very lamentable that a man who has met with some of these arguments which at one time seem true and at another false should at last, in the bitterness of his heart, gladly put all the blame on the reasoning, instead of on himself and his own unskillfulness, and spend the rest of his life in hating and reviling reasoning, and lose the truth and knowledge of reality.

Indeed, I replied, that would be very lamentable.

XL First then, he said, let us be careful not to admit into our souls the notion that all reasoning is very likely unsound; let us rather think that we ourselves are not yet sound. And we must strive earnestly like men to become sound, you, my friends, for the sake of all your future life, and I, 91 because of my death. For I am afraid that at present I can hardly look at death like a philosopher; I am in a contentious mood, like the uneducated persons who never give a thought to the truth of the question about which they are disputing, but are only anxious to persuade their audience that they themselves are right. And I think that today I shall differ from them only in one thing. I shall not be anxious to persuade my audience that I am right, except by the way; but I shall be very anxious indeed to persuade myself. For see, my dear friend, how selfish my reasoning is. If what I say is true, it is well to believe it. But if there is nothing after death, at any rate I shall pain my friends less by my lamentations in the interval before I die. And this ignorance will not last forever—that would have been an evil—it will soon come to an end. So prepared, Simmias and Cebes, he said, I come to the argument. And you, if you take my advice, will think not of Socrates, but of the truth; and you will agree with me if you think that what I say is true; otherwise you will oppose me with every argument that you have; and be careful that, in my anxiety to convince you, I do not deceive both you and myself, and go away, leaving my sting behind me, like a bee.

XLI Now let us proceed, he said. And first, if you find I have forgotten your arguments, repeat them. Simmias, I think, has fears and misgivings that the soul, being of the nature of a harmony, may perish before the body, though she is more divine and nobler than the body. Cebes, if I am not mistaken, conceded that the soul is more enduring than the body; but he said that no one could tell whether the soul, after wearing out many bodies many times, did not herself perish on leaving her last body, and whether death be not precisely this—the destruction of the soul; for the destruction of the body is unceasing. Is there anything else, Simmias and Cebes, which we have to examine?

They both agreed that these were the questions.

Do you reject all our previous conclusions, he asked, or only some of them?

Only some of them, they replied.

ANSWER TO FIRST OBJECTION

Well, said he, what do you say of our doctrine that knowledge is recollection, and that therefore our souls must necessarily have existed somewhere else, before they were imprisoned in our bodies? 92

I, replied Cebes, was convinced by it at the time in a wonderful way; and now there is no doctrine to which I adhere more firmly.

And I am of that mind too, said Simmias; and I shall be very much surprised if I ever change it.

But, my Theban friend, you will have to change it, said Socrates, if this opinion of yours, that a harmony is a composite thing, and that the soul is a harmony composed of the elements of the body at the right tension, is to stand. You will hardly allow yourself to assert that the harmony was in existence before the things from which it was to be composed? Will you do that?

Certainly not, Socrates.

But you see that that is what your assertion comes to when you say that the soul existed before she came into the form and body of man, and yet that she is composed of elements which did not yet exist? Your harmony is not like what you compare it to: the lyre and the strings and the sounds, as yet untuned, come into existence first; and the harmony is composed last of all, and perishes first. How will this belief of yours accord with the other?

It will not, replied Simmias.

And yet, said he, an argument about harmony is hardly the place for a discord.

No, indeed, said Simmias.

Well, there is a discord in your argument, he said. You must choose which doctrine you will retain—that knowledge is recollection or that the soul is a harmony.

The former, Socrates, certainly, he replied. The latter has never been demonstrated to me; it rests only on probable and plausible grounds, which make it a popular opinion. I know that doctrines which ground their proofs on probabilities are impostors and that they are very apt to mislead, both in geometry and everything else, if one is not on one's guard against them. But the doctrine about recollection and knowledge rests upon a foundation which claims belief. We agreed that the soul exists before she ever enters the body, as surely as the essence itself which has the name of real being exists. And I am persuaded that I believe in this essence rightly and on sufficient evidence. It follows therefore, I suppose, that I cannot allow myself or anyone else to say that the soul is a harmony.

And, consider the question in another way, Simmias, said Socrates. Do you think that a harmony or any other composition can exist in a state 93 other than the state of the elements of which it is composed?

Certainly not.

Nor, I suppose, can it do or suffer anything beyond what they do and suffer?

He assented.

A harmony therefore cannot lead the elements of which it is composed; it must follow them?

He agreed.

And much less can it be moved, or make a sound, or do anything else in opposition to its parts.

Much less, indeed, he replied.

Well, is not every harmony by nature a harmony according as it is adjusted?

I don't understand you, he replied.

If it is tuned more, and to a greater extent, he said, supposing that to be possible, will it not be more a harmony, and to a greater extent, while if it is tuned less, and to a smaller extent, will it not be less a harmony, and to a smaller extent?

Certainly.

Well, is this true of the soul? Can one soul be more a soul, and to a greater extent, or less a soul, and to a smaller extent, than another, even in the smallest degree?

Certainly not, he replied.

Well then, he replied, please tell me this; is not one soul said to have intelligence and virtue and to be good, while another is said to have folly and vice and to be bad? And is it not true?

Yes, certainly.

What then will those who assert that the soul is a harmony say that the virtue and the vice which are in our souls are? Another harmony and another discord? Will they say that the good soul is in tune, and that, herself a harmony, she has within herself another harmony, and that the bad soul is out of tune herself, and has no other harmony within her?

I, said Simmias, cannot tell. But it is clear that they would have to say something of the kind.

But it has been conceded, he said, that one soul is never more or less a soul than another. In other words, we have agreed that one harmony is never more, or to a greater extent, or less, or to a smaller extent a harmony than another. Is it not so?

Yes, certainly.

And the harmony which is neither more nor less a harmony, is not more or less tuned. Is that so?

Yes.

And has that which is neither more nor less tuned a greater, or a less, or an equal share of harmony?

An equal share.

Then, since one soul is never more nor less a soul than another, it has not been more or less tuned either?

True.

Therefore it can have no greater share of harmony or of discord?

Certainly not.

And, therefore, can one soul contain more vice or virtue than another, if vice be discord and virtue harmony?

By no means.

XLII

Or rather, Simmias, to speak quite accurately, I suppose that there will be no vice in any soul if the soul is a harmony. I take it there can never be any discord in a harmony which is a perfect harmony.

Certainly not.

Neither can a soul, if it be a perfect soul, have any vice in it?

No; that follows necessarily from what has been said.

Then the result of this reasoning is that all the souls of all living creatures will be equally good if the nature of all souls is to be equally souls.

Yes, I think so, Socrates, he said.

And do you think that this is true, he asked, and that this would have been the fate of our argument, if the hypothesis that the soul is a harmony had been correct?

No, certainly not, he replied.

XLIII

Well, said he, of all the parts of a man, should you not say that it was the soul, and particularly the wise soul, which rules?

I should.

Does she yield to the passions of the body or does she oppose them? I mean this. When the body is hot and thirsty, does not the soul drag it away and prevent it from drinking, and when it is hungry does she not prevent it from eating? And do we not see her opposing the passions of the body in a thousand other ways?

Yes, certainly.

But we have also agreed that, if she is a harmony, she can never give a sound contrary to the tensions, and relaxations, and vibrations, and other changes of the elements of which she is composed; that she must follow them, and can never lead them?

Yes, he replied, we certainly have.

Well, now, do we not find the soul acting in just the opposite way, and leading all the elements of which she is said to consist, and opposing them in almost everything all through life; and lording it over them in every way, and chastising them, sometimes severely, and with a painful discipline, such as gymnastic and medicine, and sometimes lightly; sometimes threatening and sometimes admonishing the desires and passions and fears, as though she were speaking to something other than herself, as Homer makes Odysseus do in the *Odyssey,* where he says that

> He smote upon his breast, and chid his heart:
> "Endure, my heart, e'en worse hast thou endured."

Do you think that when Homer wrote that, he supposed the soul to be a harmony and capable of being led by the passions of the body, and not of a nature to lead them and be their lord, being herself far too divine a thing to be like a harmony?

Certainly, Socrates, I think not.

Then, my excellent friend, it is quite wrong to say that the soul is a harmony. For then, you see, we should not be in agreement either with the divine poet Homer or with ourselves.

That is true, he replied.

XLIV Very good, said Socrates; I think that we have contrived to appease our Theban Harmonia with tolerable success. But how about Cadmus, Cebes? he said. How shall we appease him, and with what reasoning?

I daresay that you will find out how to do it, said Cebes. At all events you have argued that the soul is not a harmony in a way which surprised me very much. When Simmias was stating his objection, I wondered how anyone could possibly dispose of his argument; and so I was very much surprised to see it fall before the very first onset of yours. I should not wonder if the same fate awaited the argument of Cadmus.

My good friend, said Socrates, do not be overconfident, or some evil eye will overturn the argument that is to come. However, that we will leave to God; let us, like Homer's heroes, "advancing boldly," see if there is anything in what you say. The sum of what you seek is this. You require me to prove to you that the soul is indestructible and immortal; for if it be not so, you think that the confidence of a philosopher, who is confident in death, and who believes that when he is dead he will fare infinitely better in the other world than if he had lived a different sort of life in this world, is a foolish and idle confidence. You say that to show that the soul is strong and godlike, and that she existed before we were born men, is not enough; for that does not necessarily prove her immortality, but only that she lasts a long time, and has existed an enormous while, and has known and done many things in a previous state. Yet she is not any the more immortal for that; her very entrance into man's body was, like a disease, the beginning of her destruction. And, you say, she passes this life in misery, and at last perishes in what we call death. You think that it makes no difference at all to the fears of each one of us, whether she enters the body once or many times; for everyone but a fool must fear death, if he does not know and cannot prove that she is immortal. That, I think, Cebes, is the substance of your objection. I state it again and again on purpose, that nothing may escape us, and that you may add to it or take away from it anything that you wish.

Cebes replied: No, that is my meaning. I don't want to add or to take away anything at present.

XLV Socrates paused for some time and thought. Then he said, It is not an easy question that you are raising, Cebes. We must examine fully the whole subject of the causes of generation and decay. If you like, I will give you

my own experiences, and if you think that you can make use of anything   96
that I say, you may employ it to satisfy your misgivings.

Indeed, said Cebes, I should like to hear your experiences.

ANSWER TO SECOND OBJECTION

Listen, then, and I will tell you, Cebes, he replied. When I was a young
man, I had a passionate desire for the wisdom which is called Physical Science. I thought it a splendid thing to know the causes of everything; why a
thing comes into being, and why it perishes, and why it exists. I was always
worrying myself with such questions as, Do living creatures take a definite
form, as some persons say, from the fermentation of heat and cold? Is it
the blood, or the air, or fire by which we think? Or is it none of these, but
the brain which gives the senses of hearing and sight and smell, and do
memory and opinion come from these, and knowledge from memory and
opinion when in a state of quiescence? Again, I used to examine the destruction of these things, and the changes of the heaven and the earth, until
at last I concluded that I was wholly and absolutely unfitted for these studies. I will prove that to you conclusively. I was so completely blinded by
these studies that I forgot what I had formerly seemed to myself and to
others to know quite well; I unlearned all that I had been used to think that
I understood; even the cause of man's growth. Formerly I had thought it
evident on the face of it that the cause of growth was eating and drinking,
and that, when from food flesh is added to flesh, and bone to bone, and in
the same way to the other parts of the body their proper elements, then by
degrees the small bulk grows to be large, and so the boy becomes a man.
Don't you think that my belief was reasonable?

I do, said Cebes.

Then here is another experience for you. I used to feel no doubt, when
I saw a tall man standing by a short one, that the tall man was, it might be,
a head the taller, or, in the same way, that one horse was bigger than another. I was even clearer that ten was more than eight by the addition of
two, and that a thing two cubits long was longer by half its length than a
thing one cubit long.

And what do you think now? asked Cebes.

I think that I am very far from believing that I know the cause of any
of these things. Why, when you add one to one, I am not sure either that
the one to which one is added has become two, or that the one added and   97
the one to which it is added become, by the addition, two. I cannot understand how, when they are brought together, this union, or placing of one by
the other, should be the cause of their becoming two, whereas, when they
were separated, each of them was one, and they were not two. Nor, again,
if you divide one into two, can I convince myself that this division is the
cause of one becoming two; for then a thing becomes two from exactly the
opposite cause. In the former case it was because two units were brought
together, and the one was added to the other; while now it is because they

are separated, and the one divided from the other. Nor, again, can I per-suade myself that I know how one is generated; in short, this method does not show me the cause of the generation or destruction or existence of any-thing. I have in my own mind a confused idea of another method, but I cannot admit this one for a moment.

XLVI   But one day I listened to a man who said that he was reading from a book of Anaxagoras, which affirmed that it is Mind which orders and is the cause of all things. I was delighted with this theory; it seemed to me to be right that Mind should be the cause of all things, and I thought to myself, If this is so, then Mind will order and arrange each thing in the best possi-ble way. So if we wish to discover the cause of the generation or destruc-tion or existence of a thing, we must discover how it is best for that thing to exist, or to act, or to be acted on. Man therefore has only to consider what is best and fittest for himself, or for other things, and then it follows neces-sarily that he will know what is bad; for both are included in the same sci-ence. These reflections made me very happy: I thought that I had found in Anaxagoras a teacher of the cause of existence after my own heart, and I expected that he would tell me first whether the earth is flat or round, and that he would then go on to explain to me the cause and the necessity, and tell me what is best, and that it is best for the earth to be of that shape. If he said that the earth was in the center of the universe, I thought that he would explain that it was best for it to be there; and I was prepared not to require any other kind of cause, if he made this clear to me. In the same way I was prepared to ask questions about the sun, and the moon, and the stars, about their relative speeds, and revolutions, and changes; and to hear why it is best for each of them to act and be acted on as they are acted on. I never thought that, when he said that things are ordered by Mind, he would intro-duce any reason for their being as they are, except that they are best so. I thought that he would assign a cause to each thing, and a cause to the universe, and then would go on to explain to me what was best for each thing, and what was the common good of all. I would not have sold my hopes for a great deal: I seized the books very eagerly, and read them as fast as I could, in order that I might know what is best and what is worse.

XLVII   All my splendid hopes were dashed to the ground, my friend, for as I went on reading I found that the writer made no use of Mind at all, and that he assigned no causes for the order of things. His causes were air, and ether, and water, and many other strange things. I thought that he was ex-actly like a man who should begin by saying that Socrates does all that he does by Mind, and who, when he tried to give a reason for each of my ac-tions, should say, first, that I am sitting here now, because my body is com-posed of bones and muscles, and that the bones are hard and separated by joints, while the muscles can be tightened and loosened, and, together with the flesh and the skin which holds them together, cover the bones; and that therefore, when the bones are raised in their sockets, the relaxation and contraction of the muscles make it possible for me now to bend my limbs, and that that is the cause of my sitting here with my legs bent. And in the same way he would go on to explain why I am talking to you: he would assign voice, and air, and hearing, and a thousand other things as causes; but he would quite forget to mention the real cause, which is that since the Athenians thought it right to condemn me, I have thought it right and just to sit here and to submit to whatever sentence they may think fit to impose. For, by the dog of Egypt, I think that these muscles and bones would long ago have been in Megara or Boeotia, prompted by their opinion of what is best, if I had not thought it better and more honorable to submit to whatever penalty the state inflicts, rather than escape by flight. But to call these things causes is too absurd! If it were said that without bones and muscles and the other parts of my body I could not have carried my resolutions into effect, that would be true. But to say that they are the *cause* of what I do, and that in this way I am acting by Mind, and not from choice of what is best, would be a very loose and careless way of talking. It simply means that a man cannot distinguish the real cause from that without which the cause cannot be the cause, and this it is, I think, which the multitude, groping about in the dark, speaks of as the cause, giving it a name which does not belong to it. And so one man surrounds the earth with a vortex, and makes the heavens sustain it. Another represents the earth as a flat kneading trough, and supports it on a basis of air. But they never think of looking for a power which is involved in these things being disposed as it is best for them to be, nor do they think that such a power has any divine strength. They expect to find an Atlas who is stronger and more immortal and abler to hold the world together, and they never for a moment imagine that it is the binding force of good which really binds and holds things together. I would most gladly learn the nature of that kind of cause from any man, but I wholly failed either to discover it myself or to learn it from anyone else. However, I had a second string to my bow, and perhaps, Cebes, you would like me to describe to you how I proceeded in my search for the cause.

I should like to hear very much indeed, he replied.

When I had given up inquiring into real existence, he proceeded, I thought that I must take care that I did not suffer as people do who look at the sun during an eclipse. For they are apt to lose their eyesight, unless they look at the sun's reflection in water or some such medium. That danger occurred to me. I was afraid that my soul might be completely blinded if I looked at things with my eyes, and tried to grasp them with my senses. So I thought that I must have recourse to conceptions, and examine the truth of existence by means of them. Perhaps my illustration is not quite accurate. I am scarcely prepared to admit that he who examines existence through conceptions is dealing with mere reflections, any more than he who examines it as manifested in sensible objects. However, I began in this way. I assumed in each case whatever principle I judged to be strongest; and then I held as true whatever seemed to agree with it, whether in the case of the cause or of anything else, and as untrue whatever seemed not to agree with it. I should like to explain my meaning more clearly; I don't think you understand me yet.

Indeed I do not very well, said Cebes.

XLIX   I mean nothing new, he said; only what I have repeated over and over again, both in our conversation today and at other times. I am going to try to explain to you the kind of cause at which I have worked, and I will go back to what we have so often spoken of, and begin with the assumption that there exists an absolute beauty, and an absolute good, and an absolute greatness, and so on. If you grant me this, and agree that they exist, I hope to be able to show you what my cause is, and to discover that the soul is immortal.

You may assume that I grant it you, said Cebes; go on with your proof.

Then do you agree with me in what follows? he asked. It appears to me that if anything besides absolute beauty is beautiful, it is so simply because it partakes of absolute beauty, and I say the same of all phenomena. Do you allow that kind of cause?

I do, he answered.

Well then, he said, I do no longer recognize nor can I understand these other wise causes: if I am told that anything is beautiful because it has a rich color, or a goodly form, or the like, I pay no attention, for such language only confuses me; and in a simple and plain, and perhaps a foolish way, I hold to the doctrine that the thing is only made beautiful by the presence or communication, or whatever you please to call it, of absolute beauty—I do not wish to insist on the nature of the communication, but what I am sure of is, that it is absolute beauty which makes all beautiful things beautiful. This seems to me to be the safest answer that I can give myself or others; I believe that I shall never fall if I hold to this; it is a safe answer to make to myself or anyone else, that it is absolute beauty which makes beautiful things beautiful. Don't you think so?

I do.

And it is size that makes large things large, and larger things larger, and smallness that makes smaller things smaller?

Yes.

And if you were told that one man was taller than another by a head, and that the shorter man was shorter by a head, you would not accept the
101   statement. You would protest that you say only that the greater is greater by size, and that size is the cause of its being greater; and that the less is only less by smallness, and that smallness is the cause of its being less. You would be afraid to assert that a man is greater or smaller by a head, lest you should be met by the retort, first, that the greater is greater, and the smaller smaller, by the same thing, and secondly, that the greater is greater by a head, which is a small thing, and that it is truly marvelous that a small thing should make a man great. Should you not be afraid of that?

Yes, indeed, said Cebes, laughing.

And you would be afraid to say that ten is more than eight by two, and that two is the cause of the excess; you would say that ten was more than eight by number, and that number is the cause of the excess? And in just the same way you would be afriad to say that a thing two cubits long was longer than a thing one cubit long by half its length, instead of by size, would you not?

Yes, certainly.

Again, you would be careful not to affirm that, if one is added to one, the addition is the cause of two, or, if one is divided, that the division is the cause of two? You would protest loudly that you know of no way in which a thing can be generated, except by participation in its own proper essence; and that you can give no cause for the generation of two except participation in duality; and that all things which are to be two must participate in duality, while whatever is to be one must participate in unity. You would leave the explanation of these divisions and additions and all such subtleties to wiser men than yourself. You would be frightened, as the saying is, at your own shadow and ignorance, and would hold fast to the safety of our principle, and so give your answer. But if anyone should attack the principle itself, you would not mind him or answer him until you had considered whether the consequences of it are consistent or inconsistent, and when you had to give an account of the principle itself, you would give it in the same way, by assuming some other principle which you think the strongest of the higher ones, and so go on until you had reached a satisfactory resting place. You would not mix up the first principle and its consequences in your argument, as mere disputants do, if you really wish to discover anything of existence. Such persons will very likely not spend a single word or thought upon that, for they are clever enough to be able to please themselves entirely, though their argument is a chaos. But you, I think, if you are a philosopher, will do as I say.

102

Very true, said Simmias and Cebes together.

Ech. And they were right, Phaedo. I think the clearness of his reasoning, even to the dullest, is quite wonderful.

Phaedo. Indeed, Echecrates, all who were there thought so too.

Ech. So do we who were not there, but who are listening to your story. But how did the argument proceed after that?

Phaedo. They had admitted that each of the Ideas exists and that Phe-   L
nomena take the names of the Ideas as they participate in them. Socrates, I think, then went on to ask:

If you say this, do you not, in saying that Simmias is taller than Socrates and shorter than Phaedo, say that Simmias possesses both the attribute of tallness and the attribute of shortness?

I do.

But you admit, he said, that the proposition that Simmias is taller than Socrates is not exactly true, as it is stated; Simmias is not really taller because he is Simmias, but because of his height. Nor again is he taller than

Socrates because Socrates is Socrates, but because of Socrates' shortness compared with Simmias' tallness.

True.

Nor is Simmias shorter than Phaedo because Phaedo is Phaedo, but because of Phaedo's tallness compared with Simmias' shortness.

That is so.

Then in this way Simmias is called both short and tall, when he is between the two; he exceeds the shortness of one by the excess of his height, and gives the other a tallness exceeding his own shortness. I daresay you think, he said, smiling, that my language is like a legal document for precision and formality. But I think that it is as I say.

He agreed.

I say it because I want you to think as I do. It seems to me not only that absolute greatness will never be great and small at once, but also that greatness in us never admits smallness, and will not be exceeded. One of two things must happen: either the greater will give way and fly at the approach of its opposite, the less, or it will perish. It will not stand its ground, and receive smallness, and be other than it was, just as I stand my ground, and receive smallness, and remain the very same small man that I was. But greatness cannot endure to be small, being great. Just in the same way again smallness in us will never become nor be great; nor will any opposite, while it remains what it was, become or be at the same time the opposite of what it was. Either it goes away or it perishes in the change.

103
LI

That is exactly what I think, said Cebes.

Thereupon someone—I am not sure who—said,

But surely is not this just the reverse of what we agreed to be true earlier in the argument, that the greater is generated from the less, and the less from the greater, and, in short, that opposites are generated from opposites? But now it seems to be denied that this can ever happen.

Socrates inclined his head to the speaker and listened. Well and bravely remarked, he said, but you have not noticed the difference between the two propositions. What we said then was that a concrete thing is generated from its opposite; what we say now is that the absolute opposite can never become opposite to itself, either when it is in us, or when it is in nature. We were speaking then of things in which the opposites are, and we named them after those opposites; but now we are speaking of the opposites themselves, whose inherence gives the things their names; and they, we say, will never be generated from each other. At the same time he turned to Cebes and asked, Did his objection trouble you at all, Cebes?

No, replied Cebes; I don't feel that difficulty. But I will not deny that many other things trouble me.

Then we are quite agreed on this point, he said. An opposite will never be opposite to itself.

No never, he replied.

Now tell me again, he said; do you agree with me in this? Are there not   **LII**
things which you call heat and cold?

Yes.

Are they the same as snow and fire?

No, certainly not.

Heat is different from fire, and cold from snow?

Yes.

But I suppose, as we have said, that you do not think that snow can ever receive heat, and yet remain what it was, snow and hot: it will either retire or perish at the approach of heat.

Certainly.

And fire, again, will either retire or perish at the approach of cold. It will never endure to receive the cold and still remain what it was, fire and cold.

True, he said.

Then, it is true of some of these things that not only the idea itself has a right to its name for all time, but that something else too, which is not the idea, but which has the form of the idea wherever it exists, shares the name. Perhaps my meaning will be clearer by an example. The odd ought always to have the name of odd, ought it not?

Yes, certainly.

Well, my question is this. Is the odd the only thing with this name, or is there something else which is not the same as the odd, but which must al-   104
ways have this name, together with its own, because its nature is such that it is never separated from the odd? There are many examples of what I mean: let us take one of them, the number three, and consider it. Do you not think that we must always call it by the name of odd, as well as by its own name, although the odd is not the same as the number three? Yet the nature of the number three, and of the number five, and of half the whole series of numbers, is such that each of them is odd, though none of them is the same as the odd. In the same way the number two, and the number four, and the whole of the other series of numbers, are each of them always even, though they are not the same as the even. Do you agree or not?

Yes, of course, he replied.

Then see what I want to show you. It is not only opposite ideas which appear not to admit their opposites; things also which are not opposites, but which always contain opposites, seem as if they would not admit the idea which is opposite to the idea that they contain: they either perish or retire at its approach. Shall we not say that the number three would perish or endure anything sooner than become even while it remains three?

Yes, indeed, said Cebes.

And yet, said he, the number two is not the opposite of the number three.

No, certainly not.

Then it is not only the ideas which will not endure the approach of their opposites; there are some other things besides which will not endure such an approach.

LIII   That is quite true, he said.

Shall we determine, if we can, what is their nature? he asked.

Certainly.

Will they not be those things, Cebes, which force whatever they are in to have always not its own idea only, but the idea of some opposite as well?

What do you mean?

Only what we were saying just now. You know, I think, that whatever the idea of three is in, is bound to be not three only, but odd as well.

Certainly.

Well, we say that the opposite idea to the form which produces this result will never come to that thing.

Indeed, no.

But the idea of the odd produces it?

Yes.

And the idea of the even is the opposite of the idea of the odd?

Yes.

Then the idea of the even will never come to three?

Certainly not.

So three has no part in the even?

None.

Then the number three is uneven?

Yes.

So much for the definition which I undertook to give of things which are not opposites, and yet do not admit opposites; thus we have seen that the number three does not admit the even, though it is not the opposite of the even, for it always brings with it the opposite of the even; and the num-

105 ber two does not admit the odd, nor fire cold, and so on. Do you agree with me in saying that not only does the opposite not admit the opposite, but also that whatever brings with it an opposite of anything to which it goes never admits the opposite of that which it brings? Let me recall this to you again; there is no harm in repetition. Five will not admit the idea of the even, nor will the double of five—ten—admit the idea of the odd. It is not itself an opposite, yet it will not admit the idea of the odd. Again, one and a half, a half, and the other numbers of that kind will not admit the idea of the whole, nor again will such numbers as a third. Do you follow and agree?

I follow you and entirely agree with you, he said.

LIV   Now begin again, and answer me, he said. And imitate me; do not answer me in the terms of my question: I mean, do not give the old safe answer which I have already spoken of, for I see another way of safety, which is the result of what we have been saying. If you ask me, what is that which must be in the body to make it hot, I shall not give our old safe and stupid answer, and say that it is heat; I shall make a more refined answer, drawn from what we have been saying, and reply, fire. If you ask me, what is that which must be in the body to make it sick, I shall not say sickness, but fever; and again to the question what is that which must be in number to make it odd, I shall not reply oddness, but unity, and so on. Do you understand my meaning clearly yet?

Yes, quite, he said.

Then, he went on, tell me, what is that which must be in a body to make it alive?

A soul, he replied.

And is this always so?

Of course, he said.

Then the soul always brings life to whatever contains her?

No doubt, he answered.

And is there an opposite to life, or not?

Yes.

What is it?

Death.

And we have already agreed that the soul cannot ever receive the opposite of what she brings?

Yes, certainly we have, said Cebes.

LV

Well; what name did we give to that which does not admit the idea of the even?

The uneven, he replied.

And what do we call that which does not admit justice or music?

The unjust, and the unmusical.

Good; and what do we call that which does not admit death?

The immortal, he said.

And the soul does not admit death?

No.

Then the soul is immortal?

It is.

Good, he said. Shall we say that this is proved? What do you think?

Yes, Socrates, and very sufficiently.

Well, Cebes, he said, if the odd had been necessarily imperishable, must not three have been imperishable?

106

Of course.

And if cold had been necessarily imperishable, snow would have retired safe and unmelted, whenever warmth was applied to it. It would not have perished, and it would not have stayed and admitted the heat.

True, he said.

In the same way, I suppose, if warmth were imperishable, whenever cold attacked fire, the fire would never have been extinguished or have perished. It would have gone away in safety.

Necessarily, he replied.

And must we not say the same of the immortal? he asked. If the immortal is imperishable, the soul cannot perish when death comes upon her. It follows from what we have said that she will not ever admit death, or be in a state of death, any more than three, or the odd itself, will ever be even, or fire, or the heat itself which is in fire, cold. But, it may be said Granted that the odd does not become even at the approach of the even; why, when the odd has perished, may not the even come into its place? We could not contend in reply that it does not perish, for the uneven is not imperishable; if we had agreed that the uneven was imperishable, we could have easily contended that the odd and three go away at the approach of the even; and we could have urged the same contention about fire and heat and the rest, could we not?

Yes, certainly.

And now, if we are agreed that the immortal is imperishable, then the soul will be not immortal only, but also imperishable; otherwise we shall require another argument.

Nay, he said, there is no need of that, as far as this point goes; for if the immortal, which is eternal, will admit of destruction, what will not?

LVI   And all men would admit, said Socrates, that God, and the essential form of life, and all else that is immortal, never perishes.

All men, indeed, he said; and, what is more, I think, all gods would admit that.

Then if the immortal is indestructible, must not the soul, if it be immortal, be imperishable?

Certainly, it must.

Then, it seems, when death attacks a man, his mortal part dies, but his immortal part retreats before death, and goes away safe and indestructible.

It seems so.

107   Then, Cebes, said he, beyond all question the soul is immortal and imperishable, and our souls will indeed exist in the other world.

I, Socrates, he replied, have no more objections to urge; your reasoning has quite satisfied me. If Simmias, or anyone else, has anything to say, it would be well for him to say it now; for I know not to what other season he can defer the discussion if he wants to say or to hear anything touching this matter.

No, indeed, said Simmias; neither have I any further ground for doubt after what you have said. Yet I cannot help feeling some doubts still in my mind; for the subject of our conversation is a vast one, and I distrust the feebleness of man.

You are right, Simmias, said Socrates, and more than that, you must re-examine our original assumptions, however certain they seem to you; and when you have analyzed them sufficiently, you will, I think, follow the argument, as far as man can follow it; and when that becomes clear to you, you will seek for nothing more.

That is true, he said.

But then, my friends, said he, we must think of this. If it be true that the soul is immortal, we have to take care of her, not merely on account of the time which we call life, but also on account of all time. Now we can see how terrible is the danger of neglect. For if death had been a release from all things, it would have been a godsend to the wicked; for when they died they would have been released with their souls from the body and from their own wickedness. But now we have found that the soul is immortal, and so her only refuge and salvation from evil is to become as perfect and wise as possible. For she takes nothing with her to the other world but her education and culture; and these, it is said, are of the greatest service or of the greatest injury to the dead man at the very beginning of his journey thither. For it is said that the genius, who has had charge of each man in his life, proceeds to lead him, when he is dead, to a certain place where the departed have to assemble and receive judgment and then go to the world below with the guide who is appointed to conduct them thither. And when they have received their deserts there, and remained the appointed time, another guide brings them back again after many long revolutions of ages. So this journey is not as Aeschylus describes it in the Telephus, where he says that "a simple way leads to Hades." But I think that the way is neither simple nor single; there would have been no need of guides had it been so; for no one could miss the way if there were but one path. But this road must have many branches and many windings, as I judge from the rites of burial on earth.[4] The orderly and wise soul follows her leader and is not ignorant of the things of that world; but the soul which lusts after the body flutters about the body and the visible world for a long time, as I have said, and struggles hard and painfully, and at last is forcibly and reluctantly dragged away by her appointed genius. And when she comes to the place where the other souls are, if she is impure and stained with evil, and has been concerned in foul murders, or if she has committed any other crimes that are akin to these and the deeds of kindred souls, then everyone shuns her and turns aside from meeting her, and will neither be her companion nor her guide, and she wanders about by herself in extreme distress until a certain time is completed, and then she is borne away by force to the habitation which befits her. But the soul that has spent her life in purity and temperance has the gods for her companions and guides, and dwells in the place which befits her. There are many wonderful places in the earth; and neither its nature nor its size is what those who are wont to describe it imagine, as a friend has convinced me.

. . .

A man of sense will not insist that these things are exactly as I have described them. But I think that he will believe that something of the kind is true of the soul and her habitations, seeing that she is shown to be im-

LVII

108

LXIII

---

[4] Sacrifices were offered to the gods of the lower world in places where three roads met. [F.J.C.]

mortal, and that it is worth his while to stake everything on this belief. The venture is a fair one, and he must charm his doubts with spells like these. . . . For these reasons a man should be of good cheer about his soul if in his life he has renounced the pleasures and adornments of the body, because they were nothing to him, and because he thought that they would do him not good but harm; and if he has instead earnestly pursued the pleasures of learning, and adorned his soul with the adornment of temperance, and justice, and courage, and freedom, and truth, which belongs to her and is her own, and so awaits his journey to the other world, in readiness to set forth whenever fate calls him. You, Simmias and Cebes, and the rest will set forth at some future day, each at his own time. But me now, as a tragic poet would say, fate calls at once; and it is time for me to betake myself to the bath. I think that I had better bathe before I drink the poison, and not give the women the trouble of washing my dead body.

LXIV   When he had finished speaking Crito said, Be it so, Socrates. But have you any commands for your friends or for me about your children, or about other things? How shall we serve you best?

Simply by doing what I always tell you, Crito. Take care of your own selves, and you will serve me and mine and yourselves in all that you do, even though you make no promises now. But if you are careless of your own selves, and will not follow the path of life which we have pointed out in our discussions both today and at other times, all your promises now, however profuse and earnest they are, will be of no avail.

We will do our best, said Crito. But how shall we bury you?

As you please, he answered; only you must catch me first and not let me escape you. And then he looked at us with a smile and said, My friends, I cannot convince Crito that I am the Socrates who has been conversing with you and arranging his arguments in order. He thinks that I am the body which he will presently see a corpse, and he asks how he is to bury me. All the arguments which I have used to prove that I shall not remain with you after I have drunk the poison, but that I shall go away to the happiness of the blessed, with which I tried to comfort you and myself, have been thrown away on him. Do you therefore be my sureties to him, as he was my surety at the trial, but in a different way. He was surety for me then that I would remain; but you must be my sureties to him that I shall go away when I am dead, and not remain with you; then he will feel my death less; and when he sees my body being burned or buried, he will not be grieved because he thinks that I am suffering dreadful things; and at my funeral he will not say that it is Socrates whom he is laying out, or bearing to the grave, or burying. For, dear Crito, he continued, you must know that to use words wrongly is not only a fault in itself, it also creates evil in the soul. You must be of good cheer, and say that you are burying my body; and you may bury it as you please and as you think right.

.   .   .

QUESTIONS FOR STUDY AND DISCUSSION

1. What does Socrates mean by declaring that "the philosopher is always dying"?
2. What specific remarks or ideas enunciated by Socrates indicate that man is "essentially a soul" which in this life is "appended to a body"?
3. How does Socrates view the effect of sense activity upon the soul in the latter's ability to reason?
4. Present in summary form the principal Platonic arguments tending to prove the immortality of the soul. Give your own critique of these, assessing their strengths and weaknesses.
5. What is meant by the adjective "absolute" in such phrases as "absolute beauty," "absolute good," and "absolute justice"?
6. Present Socrates' critique of the view that "the soul is a harmony."
7. If we grant the immortality of the soul, what implications can be made as to its proper care in this life?
8. Why does Socrates show disappointment with the question of Crito: "But how shall we bury you?"

Aristotle

ARISTOTLE was born in 384 B.C. in Stagira, and studied at the Macedonian court where his father was physician to the king. For a short time, he tutored the young Alexander the Great. Aristotle attended Plato's Academy for twenty years, but after Plato's death founded his own school, the Lyceum. He left Athens in 323 B.C. for Chalcis, where he died a year later. An astute observer, he contributed much to the natural sciences of his time, especially biology; this empirical bent gave the foundations of his philosophy a strongly realistic flavor. The inventor of logic and the father of numerous works, his thought is subtle and complex. The bulk of his technical writings remain the great heritage of the occidental world, and their influence on Christian, Jewish, and Arabian thought cannot be overestimated. Numerous commentaries on Aristotle's works have been written in nearly every generation.

On the Nature of Man

From *De Anima* (*On the Soul*)

BOOK I

402ª

1 Holding as we do that, while knowledge of any kind is a thing to be honoured and prized, one kind of it may, either by reason of its greater exactness or of a higher dignity and greater wonderfulness in its objects, be more honourable and precious than another, on both accounts we should naturally be led to place in the front rank the study of the soul. The knowledge of the soul admittedly contributes greatly to the advance of truth in general, and, above all, to our understanding of Nature, for the soul is in some sense the principle of animal life. Our aim is to grasp and understand, first its essential nature, and secondly its properties; of these some are thought to be affections proper to the soul itself, while others are considered to attach to the animal [1] owing to the presence within it of soul.

---

[1] The complex of soul and body. [R. MC K.]

From Aristotle, *De Anima*, in *The Oxford Translation of Aristotle*, vol. III, edited by J. A. Smith and W. D. Ross. Copyright 1931 by Clarendon Press, Oxford. Reprinted by permission of Clarendon Press, Oxford. This selection was edited by Richard McKeon in *Basic Works of Aristotle* (New York: Random House, 1941).

To attain any assured knowledge about the soul is one of the most difficult things in the world. As the form of question which here presents itself,
viz. the question "What is it?" recurs in other fields, it might be supposed
that there was some single method of inquiry applicable to all objects
whose essential nature we are endeavouring to ascertain (as there *is* for derived properties the single method of demonstration); in that case what we
should have to seek for would be this unique method. But if there is no
such single and general method for solving the question of essence, our
task becomes still more difficult; in the case of each different subject we
shall have to determine the appropriate process of investigation. If to this
there be a clear answer, e.g. that the process is demonstration or division,
or some other known method, difficulties and hesitations still beset us—
with what facts shall we begin the inquiry? For the facts which form the
starting-points in different subjects must be different, as e.g. in the case of
numbers and surfaces.

First, no doubt, it is necessary to determine in which of the *summa
genera* [2] soul lies, what it *is;* is it "a this-somewhat," a substance, or is it a
quale or a quantum, or some other of the remaining kinds of predicates
which we have distinguished? Further, does soul belong to the class of potential existents, or is it not rather an actuality? Our answer to this question
is of the greatest importance.

KINDS, PARTS, AND PROPERTIES OF SOUL

We must consider also whether soul is divisible or is without parts, and
whether it is everywhere homogeneous or not; and if not homogeneous,
whether its various forms are different specifically or generically: up to the
present time those who have discussed and investigated soul seem to have
confined themselves to the human soul. We must be careful not to ignore
the question whether soul can be defined in a single unambiguous formula,
as is the case with animal, or whether we must not give a separate formula
for each sort of it, as we do for horse, dog, man, god (in the latter case the
"universal" animal—and so too every other "common predicate"—being
treated either as nothing at all or as a later product [3]). Further, if what
exists is not a plurality of souls, but a plurality of parts of one soul, which
ought we to investigate first, the whole soul or its parts? (It is also a difficult problem to decide which of these parts are in nature distinct from one
another.) Again, which ought we to investigate first, these parts or their
functions, mind or thinking, the faculty or the act of sensation, and so on?
If the investigation of the functions precedes that of the parts, the further
question suggests itself: ought we not before either to consider the correlative objects, e.g. of sense or thought? It seems not only useful for the discovery of the causes of the derived properties of substances to be ac-

402ᵇ

---

[2] *Summa genera:* highest class. Genus and species: either a biological or logical classification. Genus is the class of which species is the subordinate class. [E.G.S.]
[3] As presupposing the various sorts instead of being presupposed by them. [R. MC K.]

quainted with the essential nature of those substances (as in mathematics it is useful for the understanding of the property of the equality of the interior angles of a triangle to two right angles to know the essential nature of the straight and the curved or of the line and the plane) but also conversely, for the knowledge of the essential nature of a substance is largely promoted by an acquaintance with its properties: for, when we are able to give an account conformable to experience of all or most of the properties of a substance, we shall be in the most favourable position to say something worth saying about the essential nature of that subject; in all demonstration a definition of the essence is required as a starting-point, so that definitions 403ᵃ which do not enable us to discover the derived properties, or which fail to facilitate even a conjecture about them, must obviously, one and all, be dialectical and futile.

COMPLEX OF BODY AND SOUL

A further problem presented by the affections of soul is this: are they all affections of the complex of body and soul, or is there any one among them peculiar to the soul by itself? To determine this is indispensable but difficult. If we consider the majority of them, there seems to be no case in which the soul can act or be acted upon without involving the body; e.g. anger, courage, appetite, and sensation generally. Thinking seems the most probable exception; but if this too proves to be a form of imagination or to be impossible without imagination, it too requires a body as a condition of its existence. If there is any way of acting or being acted upon proper to soul, soul will be capable of separate existence; if there is none, its separate existence is impossible. In the latter case, it will be like what is straight, which has many properties arising from the straightness in it, e.g. that of touching a bronze sphere at a point, though straightness divorced from the other constituents of the straight thing cannot touch it in this way; it cannot be so divorced at all, since it is always found in a body. It therefore seems that all the affections of soul involve a body—passion, gentleness, fear, pity, courage, joy, loving, and hating; in all these there is a concurrent affection of the body. In support of this we may point to the fact that, while sometimes on the occasion of violent and striking occurrences there is no excitement or fear felt, on others faint and feeble stimulations produce these emotions, viz. when the body is already in a state of tension resembling its condition when we are angry. Here is a still clearer case: in the absence of any external cause of terror we find ourselves experiencing the feelings of a man in terror. From all this it is obvious that the affections of soul are enmattered formulable essences.

Consequently their definitions ought to correspond, e.g. anger should be defined as a certain mode of movement of such and such a body (or part or faculty of a body) by this or that cause and for this or that end. That is precisely why the study of the soul must fall within the science of Nature, at least so far as in its affections it manifests this double character.

Hence a physicist would define an affection of soul differently from a dialectician; the latter would define e.g. anger as the appetite for returning pain for pain, or something like that, while the former would define it as a boiling of the blood or warm substance surrounding the heart. The latter 403ᵇ assigns the material conditions, the former the form or formulable essence; for what he states is the formulable essence of the fact, though for its actual existence there must be embodiment of it in a material such as is described by the other. Thus the essence of a house is assigned in such a formula as "a shelter against destruction by wind, rain, and heat"; the physicist would describe it as "stones, bricks, and timbers"; but there is a third possible description which would say that it was that form in that material with that purpose or end. Which, then, among these is entitled to be regarded as the genuine physicist? The one who confines himself to the material, or the one who restricts himself to the formulable essense alone? Is it not rather the one who combines both in a single formula? If this is so, how are we to characterize the other two? Must we not say that there is no type of thinker who concerns himself with those qualities or attributes of the material which are in fact inseparable from the material, and without attempting even in thought to separate them? The physicist is he who concerns himself with all the properties active and passive of bodies or materials thus or thus defined; attributes not considered as being of this character he leaves to others, in certain cases it may be to a specialist, e.g. a carpenter or a physician, in others (*a*) where they are inseparable in fact, but are separable from any particular kind of body by an effort of abstraction, to the mathematician, (*b*) where they are separate both in fact and in thought from body altogether, to the First Philosopher or metaphysician. But we must return from this digression, and repeat that the affections of soul are inseparable from the material substratum of animal life, to which we have seen that such affections, e.g. passion and fear, attach, and have not the same mode of being as a line or a plane.

2   For our study of soul it is necessary, while formulating the problems of which in our further advance we are to find the solutions, to call into council the views of those of our predecessors who have declared any opinion on this subject, in order that we may profit by whatever is sound in their suggestions and avoid their errors.

The starting-point of our inquiry is an exposition of those characteristics which have chiefly been held to belong to soul in its very nature. Two characteristic marks have above all others been recognized as distinguishing that which has soul in it from that which has not—movement and sensation. It may be said that these two are what our predecessors have fixed upon as characteristic of soul.

.   .   .

407ᵇ

Most [previous] theories about the soul involve the following absurdity: they all join in the soul to a body, or place it in a body, without adding any specification of the reason of their union, or of the bodily conditions required for it. Yet such explanation can scarcely be omitted; for some community of nature is presupposed by the fact that the one acts and the other is acted upon, the one moves and the other is moved; interaction always implies a *special* nature in the two interagents. All, however, that these thinkers do is to describe the specific characteristics of the soul; they do not try to determine anything about the body which is to contain it, as if it were possible, as in the Pythagorean myths, that any soul could be clothed upon with any body—an absurd view, for each body seems to have a form and shape of its own. It is as absurd as to say that the art of carpentry could embody itself in flutes; each art must use its tools, each soul its body.

SOUL IS HARMONY

4   There is yet another theory about soul, which has commended itself to many as no less probable than any of those we have hitherto mentioned, and has rendered public account of itself in the court of popular discussion. Its supporters say that the soul is a kind of harmony, for (*a*) harmony is a blend or composition of contraries, and (*b*) the body is compounded out of contraries. Harmony, however, is a certain proportion or composition of the constituents blended, and soul can be neither the one nor the other of these. Further, the power of originating movement cannot belong to a harmony, while almost all concur in regarding this as a principal attribute of soul. It is more appropriate to call health (or generally one of the good states of the body) a harmony than to predicate it of the soul. The absurdity becomes most apparent when we try to attribute the active and passive affections of the soul to a harmony; the necessary readjustment of their conceptions is difficult. Further, in using the word "harmony" we have one or other of two cases in our mind; the most proper sense is in relation to spatial magnitudes which have motion and position, where harmony means the disposition and cohesion of their parts in such a manner as to prevent the introduction into the whole of anything homogeneous with it, and the secondary sense, derived from the former, is that in which it means the ratio between the constituents so blended; in neither of these senses is it plausible to predicate it of soul. That soul is a harmony in the sense of the mode of composition of the parts of the body is a view easily refutable; for there are many composite parts and those variously compounded; of what bodily part is mind or the sensitive or the appetitive faculty the mode of composition? And what *is* the mode of composition which constitutes each of them? It is equally absurd to identify the soul with the ratio of the mixture; for the mixture which makes flesh has a different ratio between the elements from that which makes bone. The consequence of this view will therefore be that distributed throughout the whole body there will be many souls, since every one of the bodily parts is a different mixture of the elements, and the ratio of mixture is in each case a harmony, i.e. a soul.

From Empedocles at any rate we might demand an answer to the fol-

408ª

lowing question—for he says that each of the parts of the body is what it is in virtue of a ratio between the elements: is the soul indentical with this ratio, or is it not rather something over and above this which is formed in the parts? Is love the cause of any and every mixture, or only of those that are in the right ratio? Is love this ratio itself, or is love something over and above this? Such are the problems raised by this account. But, on the other hand, if the soul is different from the mixture, why does it disappear at one and the same moment with that relation between the elements which constitutes flesh or the other parts of the animal body? Further, if the soul is not identical with the ratio of mixture, and it is consequently not the case that each of the parts has a soul, what is that which perishes when the soul quits the body?

That the soul cannot either be a harmony, or be moved in a circle, is clear from what we have said. Yet that it can be moved incidentally is, as we said above, possible, and even that in a sense it can move itself, i.e. in the sense that *the vehicle* in which it is can be moved, and moved by it; in no other sense can the soul be moved in space. More legitimate doubts might remain as to its movement in view of the following facts. We speak   408ᵇ of the soul as being pained or pleased, being bold or fearful, being angry, perceiving, thinking. All these are regarded as modes of movement, and hence it might be inferred that the soul is moved. This, however, does not necessarily follow. We may admit to the full that being pained or pleased, or thinking, are movements (each of them a "being moved"), and that the movement is originated by the soul. For example we may regard anger or fear as such and such movements of the heart, and thinking as such and such another movement of that organ, or of some other; these modifications may arise either from changes of place in certain parts or from qualitative alterations (the special nature of the parts and the special modes of their changes being for our present purpose irrelevant). Yet to say that it is *the soul* which is angry is as inexact as it would be to say that it is the soul that weaves webs or builds houses. It is doubtless better to avoid saying that the soul pities or learns or thinks, and rather to say that it is the man who does this with his soul.What we mean is not that the movement is in the soul, but that sometimes it terminates in the soul and sometimes starts from it, sensation e.g. coming from without inwards, and reminiscence starting from the soul and terminating with the movements, actual or residual, in the sense organs.

MIND SEEMS IMPASSIBLE

The case of mind is different; it seems to be an independent substance implanted within the soul and to be incapable of being destroyed. If it could be destroyed at all, it would be under the blunting influence of old age. What really happens in respect of mind in old age is, however, exactly parallel to what happens in the case of the sense organs; if the old man could recover the proper kind of eye, he would see just as well as the young man. The incapacity of old age is due to an affection not of the soul but of its vehicle, as occurs in drunkenness or disease. Thus it is that in old age the activity of mind or intellectual apprehension declines only through the decay of some other inward part; mind itself is impassible. Thinking, loving, and hating are affections not of mind, but of that which has mind, so far as it has it. That is why, when this vehicle decays, memory and love cease; they were activities not of mind, but of the composite which has perished; mind is, no doubt, something more divine and impassible. That the soul cannot be moved is therefore clear from what we have said, and if it cannot be moved at all, manifestly it cannot be moved by itself.

411ᵃ

5   From what has been said it is now clear that knowing as an attribute of soul cannot be explained by soul's being composed of the elements, and that it is neither sound nor true to speak of soul as moved. But since (a) knowing, perceiving, opining, and further (b) desiring, wishing, and generally all other modes of appetition, belong to soul, and (c) the local movements of animals and (d) growth, maturity, and decay are produced by the soul, we must ask whether each of these is an attribute of the

411ᵇ

soul as a whole, i.e. whether it is with the whole soul we think, perceive, move ourselves, act or are acted upon, or whether each of them requires a different part of the soul? So too with regard to life. Does it depend on one of the parts of soul? Or is it dependent on more than one? Or on all? Or has it some quite other cause?

DIVISIBILITY OF SOUL

Some hold that the soul is divisible, and that one part thinks, another desires. If, then, its nature admits of its being divided, what can it be that holds the parts together? Surely not the body; on the contrary it seems rather to be the soul that holds the body together; at any rate when the soul departs the body disintegrates and decays. If, then, there is something else which makes the soul one, this unifying agency would have the best right to the name of soul, and we shall have to repeat for it the question: Is *it* one or multipartite? If it is one, why not at once admit that "the soul" is one? If it has parts, once more the question must be put: What holds *its* parts together, and so *ad infinitum?*

The question might also be raised about the parts of the soul: What is the separate rôle of each in relation to the body? For, if the whole soul holds together the whole body, we should expect each part of the soul to hold together a part of the body. But this seems an impossibility; it is difficult even to imagine what sort of bodily part mind will hold together, or how it will do this.

It is a fact of observation that plants and certain insects go on living when divided into segments; this means that each of the segments has a soul in it identical in species, though not numerically identical in the different segments, for both of the segments for a time possess the power of sensation and local movement. That this does not last is not surprising, for they no longer possess the organs necessary for self-maintenance. But, all the same, in each of the bodily parts there are present all the parts of soul, and the souls so present are homogeneous with one another and with the whole; this means that the several parts of the soul are indisseverable from one another, although the whole soul is [4] divisible. It seems also that the principle found in plants is also a kind of soul; for this is the only principle which is common to both animals and plants; and this exists in isolation from the principle of sensation, though there is nothing which has the latter without the former.

BOOK II

1 Let the foregoing suffice as our account of the views concerning the soul which have been handed on by our predecessors; let us now dismiss them and make as it were a completely fresh start, endeavouring to give a precise answer to the question, What is soul? i.e. to formulate the most general possible definition of it.

SUBSTANCE

412ᵃ

We are in the habit of recognizing, as one determinate kind of what is, substance, and that in several senses, (*a*) in the sense of matter or that which in itself is not "a this," and (*b*) in the sense of form or essence, which is that precisely in virtue of which a thing is called "a this," and thirdly (*c*) in the sense of that which is compounded of both (*a*) and (*b*). Now matter is potentiality, form actuality; of the latter there are two grades related to one another as e.g. knowledge to the exercise of knowledge.

Among substances are by general consent reckoned bodies and especially natural bodies; for they are the principles of all other bodies. Of natural bodies some have life in them, others not; by life we mean self-nutrition and growth (with its correlative decay). It follows that every natural body which has life in it is a substance in the sense of a composite.

But since it is also a *body* of such and such a kind, viz. having life, the *body* cannot be soul; the body is the subject or matter, not what is attributed to it. Hence the soul must be a substance in the sense of the form of a natural body having life potentially within it. But substance [5] is actuality, and thus soul is the actuality of a body as above characterized. Now the word actuality has two senses corresponding respectively to the possession of knowledge and the actual exercise of knowledge. It is obvious that the soul is actuality in the first sense, viz. that of knowledge as possessed,

---

[4] *Sc.* "in a sense, i.e. so as to preserve its homogeneity in even its smallest part." [R. MC K.]
[5] *Sc.* in the sense of form. [R. MC K.]

for both sleeping and waking presuppose the existence of soul, and of these waking corresponds to actual knowing, sleeping to knowledge possessed but not employed, and, in the history of the individual, knowledge comes before its employment or exercise.

DEFINITION OF SOUL

That is why the soul is the first grade of actuality of a natural body having life potentially in it. The body so described is a body which is organized. The parts of plants in spite of their extreme simplicity are "organs"; e.g. the leaf serves to shelter the pericarp, the pericarp to shelter the fruit, while the roots of plants are analogous to the mouth of animals, both serving for the absorption of food. If, then, we have to give a general formula applicable to all kinds of soul, we must describe it as the first grade of actuality of a natural organized body. That is why we can wholly dismiss as unnecessary the question whether the soul and the body are one: it is as meaningless as to ask whether the wax and the shape given to it by the stamp are one, or generally the matter of a thing and that of which it is the matter. Unity has many senses (as many as "is" has), but the most proper and fundamental sense of both is the relation of an actuality to that of which it is the actuality.

We have now given an answer to the question, What is soul?—an answer which applies to it in its full extent. It is substance in the sense which corresponds to the definitive formula of a thing's essence. That means that it is "the essential whatness" of a body of the character just assigned.[6] Suppose that what is literally an "organ," [7] like an axe, were a *natural* body, its "essential whatness," would have been its essence, and so its soul; if this disappeared from it, it would have ceased to be an axe, except in name. As it is,[8] it is just an axe; it wants the character which is required to make its whatness or formulable essence a soul; for that, it would have had to be a *natural* body of a particular kind, viz. one having *in itself* the power of setting itself in movement and arresting itself. Next, apply this doctrine in the case of the "parts" of the living body. Suppose that the eye were an animal —sight would have been its soul, for sight is the substance or essence of the eye which corresponds to the formula,[9] the eye being merely the matter of seeing; when seeing is removed the eye is no longer an eye, except in name—it is no more a real eye than the eye of a statue or of a painted figure. We must now extend our consideration from the "parts" to the whole living body; for what the departmental sense is to the bodily part which is its organ, that the whole faculty of sense is to the whole sensitive body as such.

412[b]

---

[6] Viz. organized, or possessed potentially of life. [R. MC K.]

[7] Instrument. [R. MC K.]

[8] Being an artificial, not a natural, body. [R. MC K.]

[9] Which states what it is to be an eye. [R. MC K.]

We must not understand by that which is "potentially capable of living" what has lost the soul it had, but only what still retains it; but seeds and fruits are bodies which possess the qualification.[10] Consequently, while waking is actuality in a sense corresponding to the cutting and the seeing,[11]   413ᵃ the soul is actuality in the sense corresponding to the power of sight and the power in the tool; [12] the body corresponds to what exists in potentiality; as the pupil *plus* the power of sight constitutes the eye, so the soul *plus* the body constitutes the animal.

From this it indubitably follows that the soul is inseparable from its body, or at any rate that certain parts of it are (if it has parts)—for the actuality of some of them is nothing but the actualities of their bodily parts. Yet some may be separable because they are not the actualities of any body at all. Further, we have no light on the problem whether the soul may not be the actuality of its body in the sense in which the sailor is the actuality [13] of the ship.

This must suffice as our sketch or outline determination of the nature of soul.

2   Since what is clear or logically more evident emerges from what in itself is confused but more observable by us, we must reconsider our results from this point of view. For it is not enough for a definitive formula to express as most now do the mere fact; it must include and exhibit the ground also. At present definitions are given in a form analogous to the conclusion of a syllogism; e.g. What is squaring? The construction of an equilateral rectangle equal to a given oblong rectangle. Such a definition is in form equivalent to a conclusion.[14] One that tells us that squaring is the discovery of a line which is a mean proportional between the two unequal sides of the given rectangle discloses the ground of what is defined.

We resume our inquiry from a fresh starting-point by calling attention to the fact that what has soul in it differs from what has not in that the former displays life. Now this word has more than one sense, and provided any one alone of these is found in a thing we say that thing is living. Living, that is, may mean thinking or perception or local movement and rest, or movement in the sense of nutrition, decay and growth. Hence we think of plants also as living, for they are observed to possess in themselves an originative power through which they increase or decrease in all spatial di-

---

[10] Though only potentially, that is, they are at a further remove from actuality than the fully formed and organized body. [R. MC K.]

[11] To the second grade of actuality. [R. MC K.]

[12] To the first grade of actuality. [R. MC K.]

[13] Actuator. [R. MC K.]

[14] It has nothing in it corresponding to a middle term. [R. MC K.]

A middle term is the term in a syllogism that appears in the major and minor premises but not in the conclusion, but it is the link that assures the connection of the terms in the conclusion. [E.G.S.]

rections; they grow up *and* down, and everything that grows increases its bulk alike in both directions or indeed in all, and continues to live so long as it can absorb nutriment.

This power of self-nutrition can be isolated from the other powers mentioned, but not they from it—in mortal beings at least. The fact is obvious in plants; for it is the only psychic power they possess.

413ᵇ   This is the originative power the possession of which leads us to speak of things as *living* at all, but it is the possession of sensation that leads us for the first time to speak of living things as animals; for even those beings which possess no power of local movement but do possess the power of sensation we call animals and not merely living things.

The primary form of sense is touch, which belongs to all animals. Just as the power of self-nutrition can be isolated from touch and sensation generally, so touch can be isolated from all other forms of sense. (By the power of self-nutrition we mean that departmental power of the soul which is common to plants and animals: all animals whatsoever are observed to have the sense of touch.) What the explanation of these two facts is, we must discuss later. At present we must confine ourselves to saying that soul is the source of these phenomena and is characterized by them, viz. by the powers of self-nutrition, sensation, thinking, and motivity.

Is each of these a soul or a part of a soul? And if a part, a part in what sense? A part merely distinguishable by definition or a part distinct in local situation as well? In the case of certain of these powers, the answers to these questions are easy, in the case of others we are puzzled what to say. Just as in the case of plants which when divided are observed to continue to live though removed to a distance from one another (thus showing that in *their* case the soul of each individual plant before division was actually one, potentially many), so we notice a similar result in other varieties of soul, i.e. in insects which have been cut in two; each of the segments possesses both sensation and local movement; and if sensation, necessarily also imagination and appetition; for, where there is sensation, there is also pleasure and pain, and, where these, necessarily also desire.

We have no evidence as yet about mind or the power to think; it seems to be a widely different kind of soul, differing as what is eternal from what is perishable; it alone is capable of existence in isolation from all other psychic powers. All the other parts of soul, it is evident from what we have said, are, in spite of certain statements to the contrary, incapable of separate existence though, of course, distinguishable by definition. If opining is distinct from perceiving, to be capable of opining and to be capable of perceiving must be distinct, and so with all the other forms of living above enumerated. Further, some animals possess all these parts of soul, some certain of them only, others one only (this is what enables us to classify
414ᵃ   animals); the cause must be considered later. A similar arrangement is found also within the field of the senses; some classes of animals have all

the senses, some only certain of them, others only one, the most indispensable, touch.

Since the expression "that whereby we live and perceive" has two meanings, just like the expression "that whereby we know"—that may mean either (a) knowledge or (b) the soul, for we can speak of knowing by or *with* either, and similarly that whereby we are in health may be either (a) health or (b) the body or some part of the body; and since of the two terms thus contrasted knowledge or health is the name of a form, essence, or ratio, or if we so express it an actuality of a recipient matter—knowledge of what is capable of knowing, health of what is capable of being made healthy (for the operation of that which is capable of originating change terminates and has its seat in what is changed or altered); further, since it is the soul by or with which primarily we live, perceive, and think:—it follows that the soul must be a ratio or formulable essence, not a matter or subject. For, as we said, the word substance has three meanings —form, matter, and the complex of both—and of these three what is called matter is potentiality, what is called form actuality. Since then the complex here is the living thing, the body cannot be the actuality of the soul; it is the soul which is the actuality of a certain kind of body. Hence the rightness of the view that the soul cannot be without a body, while it cannot *be* a body; it is not a body but something relative to a body. That is why it is *in* a body, and a body of a definite kind. It was a mistake, therefore, to do as former thinkers did, merely to fit it into a body without adding a definite specification of the kind or character of that body. Reflection confirms the observed fact; the actuality of any given thing can only be realized in what is already potentially that thing, i.e. in a matter of its own appropriate to it. From all this it follows that soul is an actuality or formulable essence of something that possesses a potentiality of being besouled.

FACULTIES OR FUNCTIONS OF SOUL

3   Of the psychic powers above enumerated some kinds of living things, as we have said, possess all, some less than all, others one only. Those we have mentioned are the nutritive, the appetitive, the sensory, the locomotive, and the power of thinking. Plants have none but the first, the nutritive, while another order of living things has this *plus* the sensory. If any order of living things has the sensory, it must also have the appetitive; for appetite is the genus of which desire, passion, and wish are the species; now all animals have one sense at least, viz. touch, and whatever has a sense has the capacity for pleasure and pain and therefore has pleasant and painful objects present to it, and wherever these are present, there is desire, for desire is just appetition of what is pleasant. Further, all animals have the sense for food (for touch is the sense for food); the food of all living things consists of what is dry, moist, hot, cold, and these are the qualities appre-

414ᵇ

hended by touch; all other sensible qualities are apprehended by touch only indirectly. Sounds, colours, and odours contribute nothing to nutriment; flavours fall within the field of tangible qualities. Hunger and thirst are forms of desire, hunger a desire for what is dry and hot, thirst a desire for what is cold and moist; flavour is a sort of seasoning added to both. We must later clear up these points, but at present it may be enough to say that all animals that possess the sense of touch have also appetition. The case of imagination is obscure; we must examine it later. Certain kinds of animals possess in addition the power of locomotion, and still another order of animate beings, i.e. man and possibly another order like man or superior to him, the power of thinking, i.e. mind. It is now evident that a single definition can be given of soul only in the same sense as one can be given of figure. For, as in that case there is no figure distinguishable and apart from triangle, &c., so here there is no soul apart from the forms of soul just enumerated. It is true that a highly general definition can be given for figure which will fit all figures without expressing the peculiar nature of any figure. So here in the case of soul and its specific forms. Hence it is absurd in this and similar cases to demand an absolutely general definition, which will fail to express the peculiar nature of anything that *is,* or again, omitting this, to look for separate definitions corresponding to each *infima species.* The cases of figure and soul are exactly parallel; for the particulars subsumed under the common name in both cases—figures and living beings—constitute a series, each successive term of which potentially contains its predecessor, e.g. the square the triangle, the sensory power the self-nutritive. Hence we must ask in the case of each order of living things, What is its soul, i.e. What is the soul of plant, animal, man? Why the terms are related in this serial way must form the subject of later examination. But the facts are that the power of perception is never found apart from the power of self-nutrition, while—in plants—the latter is found isolated from the former. Again, no sense is found apart from that of touch, while touch *is* found by itself; many animals have neither sight, hearing, nor smell. Again, among living things that possess sense some have the power of locomotion, some not. Lastly, certain living beings—a small minority—possess calculation and thought, for (among mortal beings) those which possess calculation have all the other powers above mentioned, while the converse does not hold—indeed some live by imagination alone, while others have not even imagination. The mind that knows with immediate intuition presents a different problem.

415ᵃ

It is evident that the way to give the most adequate definition of soul is to seek in the case of *each* of its forms for the most appropriate definition.

4   It is necessary for the student of these forms of soul first to find a definition of each, expressive of what it is, and then to investigate its derivative properties, &c. But if we are to express what each is, viz. what the thinking power is, or the perceptive, or the nutritive, we must go farther

back and first give an account of thinking or perceiving, for in the order of investigation the question of what an agent does precedes the question, what enables it to do what it does. If this is correct, we must on the same ground go yet another step farther back and have some clear view of the objects of each; thus we must *start* with these objects, e.g. with food, with what is perceptible, or with what is intelligible.

NUTRITION AND REPRODUCTION

It follows that first of all we must treat of nutrition and reproduction,[15] for the nutritive soul is found along with all the others and is the most primitive and widely distributed power of soul, being indeed that one in virtue of which all are said to have life. The acts in which it manifests itself are reproduction and the use of food—reproduction, I say, because for any living thing that has reached its normal development and which is unmutilated, and whose mode of generation is not spontaneous, the most natural act is the production of another like itself, an animal producing an animal, a plant a plant, in order that, as far as its nature allows, it may partake in the eternal and divine. That is the goal towards which all things   415^b strive, that for the sake of which they do whatsoever their nature renders possible. The phrase "for the sake of which" is ambiguous; it may mean either (*a*) the end to achieve which, or (*b*) the being in whose interest, the act is done. Since then no living thing is able to partake in what is eternal and divine by uninterrupted continuance (for nothing perishable can for ever remain one and the same), it tries to achieve that end in the only way possible to it, and success is possible in varying degrees; so it remains not indeed as the self-same individual but continues its existence in something *like* itself—not numerically but specifically one.[16]

The soul is the cause or source of the living body. The terms cause and source have many senses. But the soul is the cause of its body alike in all three senses which we explicitly recognize. It is (*a*) the source or origin of movement, it is (*b*) the end, it is (*c*) the essence of the whole living body.

That it is the last, is clear; for in everything the essence is identical with the ground of its being, and here, in the case of living things, their being is to live, and of their being and their living the soul in them is the cause or source. Further, the actuality of whatever is potential is identical with its formulable essence.

It is manifest that the soul is also the final cause of its body. For Nature, like mind, always does whatever it does for the sake of something, which something is its end. To that something corresponds in the case of animals the soul and in this it follows the order of nature; all natural bodies are organs of the soul. This is true of those that enter into the constitution

---

[15] *Sc.* "which we shall see to be inseparable from nutrition." [R. MC K.]

[16] There is an unbroken current of the same specific life flowing through a discontinuous series of individual beings of the same species united by descent. [R. MC K.]

of plants as well as of those which enter into that of animals. This shows that that for the sake of which they are is soul. We must here recall the two senses of "that for the sake of which," viz. (*a*) the end to achieve which, and (*b*) the being in whose interest, anything is or is done.

We must maintain, further, that the soul is also the cause of the living body as the original source of local movement. The power of locomotion is not found, however, in all living things. But change of quality and change of quantity are also due to the soul. Sensation is held to be a qualitative alteration, and nothing except what has soul in it is capable of sensation. The same holds of the quantitative changes which constitute growth and decay; nothing grows or decays naturally [17] except what feeds itself, and nothing feeds itself except what has a share of soul in it.

416ᵇ

· · ·

SENSATION

5 Having made these distinctions let us now speak of sensation in the widest sense. Sensation depends, as we have said, on a process of movement or affection from without, for it is held to be some sort of change of quality. Now some thinkers assert that like is affected only by like; in what sense this is possible and in what sense impossible, we have explained in our general discussion of acting and being acted upon.

417ᵃ

Here arises a problem: why do we not perceive the senses themselves as well as the external objects of sense, or why without the stimulation of external objects do they not produce sensation, seeing that they contain in themselves fire, earth, and all the other elements, which are the direct or indirect objects of sense? It is clear that what is sensitive is so only potentially, not actually. The power of sense is parallel to what is combustible, for that never ignites itself spontaneously, but requires an agent which has the power of starting ignition; otherwise it could have set itself on fire, and would not have needed actual fire to set it ablaze.

In reply we must recall that we use the word "perceive" in two ways, for we say (*a*) that what has the power to hear or see, "sees" or "hears," even though it is at the moment asleep, and also (*b*) that what is actually seeing or hearing, "sees" or "hears." Hence "sense" too must have two meanings, sense potential, and sense actual. Similarly "to be a sentient" means either (*a*) to have a certain power or (*b*) to manifest a certain activity. To begin with, for a time, let us speak as if there were no difference between (i) being moved or affected, and (ii) being active, for movement is a kind of activity—an imperfect kind, as has elsewhere been explained. Everything that is acted upon or moved is acted upon by an agent which is actually at work. Hence it is that in one sense, as has already been stated, what acts and what is acted upon are like, in another unlike, i.e. prior to and during the change the two factors are unlike, after it like.

---

[17] Of itself. [R. MC K.]

But we must now distinguish not only *between* what is potential and what is actual but also different senses in which things can be said to be potential or actual; up to now we have been speaking as if each of these phrases had only one sense. We can speak of something as "a knower" either (*a*) as when we say that man is a knower, meaning that man falls within the class of beings that know or have knowledge, or (*b*) as when we are speaking of a man who possesses a knowledge of grammar; each of these is so called as having in him a certain potentiality, but there is a difference between their respective potentialities, the one (*a*) being a potential knower, because his kind or matter is such and such, the other (*b*), because he can in the absence of any external counteracting cause realize his knowledge in actual knowing at will. This implies a third meaning of "a knower" (*c*), one who is already realizing his knowledge—he is a knower in actuality and in the most proper sense is knowing, e.g. this A. Both the former are potential knowers, who realize their respective potentialities, the one (*a*) by change of quality, i.e. repeated transitions from one state to its opposite [18] under instruction, the other (*b*) by the transition from the inactive possession of sense or grammar to their active exercise. The two kinds of transition are distinct.   417ᵇ

Also the expression "to be acted upon" has more than one meaning; it may mean either (*a*) the extinction of one of two contraries by the other, or (*b*) the maintenance of what is potential by the agency of what is actual and already like what is acted upon, with such likeness as is compatible with one's being actual and the other potential. For what possesses knowledge becomes an actual knower by a transition which is either not an alteration of it at all (being in reality a development into its true self or actuality) or at least an alteration in a quite different sense from the usual meaning.

Hence it is wrong to speak of a wise man as being "altered" when he uses his wisdom, just as it would be absurd to speak of a builder as being altered when he is using his skill in building a house.

What in the case of knowing or understanding leads from potentiality to actuality ought not to be called teaching but something else. That which starting with the power to know learns or acquires knowledge through the agency of one who actually knows and has the power of teaching either (*a*) ought not to be said "to be acted upon" at all *or* (*b*) we must recognize two senses of alteration, viz. (i) the substitution of one quality for another, the first being the contrary of the second, or (ii) the development of an existent quality from potentiality in the direction of fixity or nature.

In the case of what is to possess sense, the first transition is due to the action of the male parent and takes place before birth so that at birth the living thing is, in respect of sensation, at the stage which corresponds to the *possession* of knowledge. Actual sensation corresponds to the stage of the

[18] Viz. from ignorance or error to knowledge or truth. [R. MC K.]

exercise of knowledge. But between the two cases compared there is a difference; the objects that excite the sensory powers to activity, the seen, the heard, &c., are outside. The ground of this difference is that what actual sensation apprehends is individuals, while what knowledge apprehends is universals, and these are in a sense within the soul. That is why a man can exercise his knowledge when he wishes, but his sensation does not depend upon himself—a sensible object must be there. A similar statement must be made about our *knowledge* of what is sensible—on the same ground, viz. that the sensible objects are individual and external.

A later more appropriate occasion may be found thoroughly to clear up all this. At present it must be enough to recognize the distinctions already drawn; a thing may be said to be potential in either of two senses, (*a*) in the sense in which we might say of a boy that he may become a general or (*b*) in the sense in which we might say the same of an adult, and there are 418ª two corresponding senses of the term "a potential sentient." There are no separate names for the two stages of potentiality; we have pointed out that they are different and how they are different. We cannot help using the incorrect terms "being acted upon or altered" of the two transitions involved. As we have said, what has the power of sensation is potentially like what the perceived object is actually; that is, while at the beginning of the process of its being acted upon the two interacting factors are dissimilar, at the end the one acted upon is assimilated to the other and is identical in quality with it.

DIFFERENT SENSE OBJECTS

6 In dealing with each of the senses we shall have first to speak of the objects which are perceptible by each. The term "object of senses" covers three kinds of objects, two kinds of which are, in our language, directly perceptible, while the remaining one is only incidentally perceptible. Of the first two kinds one (*a*) consists of what is perceptible by a single sense, the other (*b*) of what is perceptible by any and all of the senses. I call by the name of special object of this or that sense that which cannot be perceived by any other sense than that one and in respect of which no error is possible; in this sense colour is the special object of sight, sound of hearing, flavour of taste. Touch, indeed, discriminates more than one set of different qualities. Each sense has one kind of object which it discerns, and never errs in reporting that what is before it is colour or sound (though it may err as to what it is that is coloured or where that is, or what it is that is sounding or where that is). Such objects are what we propose to call the special objects of this or that sense.

"Common sensibles" are movement, rest, number, figure, magnitude; these are not peculiar to any one sense, but are common to all. There are at any rate certain kinds of movement which are perceptible both by touch 424ª and by sight.

SUMMATION OF SENSE THEORY

12   The following results applying to any and every sense may now be, formulated.

(A) By a "sense" is meant what has the power of receiving into itself the sensible forms of things without the matter. This must be conceived of as taking place in the way in which a piece of wax takes on the impress of a signet-ring without the iron or gold; we say that what produces the impression is a signet of bronze or gold, but its particular metallic constitution makes no difference: in a similar way the sense is affected by what is coloured or flavoured or sounding, but it is indifferent what in each case the *substance* is; what alone matters is what *quality* it has, i.e. in what *ratio* its constituents are combined.

(B) By "an organ of sense" is meant that in which ultimately such a power is seated.

The sense and its organ are the same in fact, but their essence is not the same. What perceives is, of course, a spatial magnitude, but we must not admit that either the having the power to perceive or the sense itself is a magnitude; what they are is a certain ratio or power *in* a magnitude. This enables us to explain why objects of sense which possess one of two opposite sensible qualities in a degree largely in excess of the other opposite destroy the organs of sense; if the movement set up by an object is too strong for the organ, the equipoise of contrary qualities in the organ, which just *is* its sensory power, is disturbed; it is precisely as concord and tone are destroyed by too violently twanging the strings of a lyre. This explains also why plants cannot perceive, in spite of their having a portion of soul in them and obviously being affected by tangible objects themselves; for undoubtedly their temperature can be lowered or raised. The explanation is that they have no mean of contrary qualities, and so no principle in them 424ᵇ capable of taking on the forms of sensible objects without their matter; in the case of plants the affection is an affection by form-and-matter together. The problem might be raised: Can what cannot smell be said to be affected by smells or what cannot see by colours, and so on? It might be said that a smell is just what can be smelt, and if it produces any effect it can only be so as to make something smell it, and it might be argued that what cannot smell cannot be affected by smells and further that what can smell can be affected by it only in so far as it has in it the power to smell (similarly with the proper objects of all the other senses).

.   .   .

427ᵃ

BOOK III

.   .   .

3   There are two distinctive peculiarities by reference to which we characterize the soul—(1) local movement and (2) thinking, discriminating,

and perceiving. Thinking, both speculative and practical, is regarded as akin to a form of perceiving; for in the one as well as the other the soul discriminates and is cognizant of something which *is*. Indeed the ancients go so far as to identify thinking and perceiving; e.g. Empedocles says "For 'tis in respect of what is present that man's wit is increased," and again "whence it befalls them from time to time to think diverse thoughts," and Homer's phrase "For suchlike is man's mind" means the same. They all look upon thinking as a bodily process like perceiving, and hold that like is *known* as well as *perceived* by like, as I explained at the beginning of our discussion. Yet they ought at the same time to have accounted for error

427^b also; for it is more intimately connected with animal existence and the soul continues longer in the state of error than in that of truth. They cannot escape the dilemma: either (1) whatever seems is true (and there are some who accept this) or (2) error is contact with the unlike; for that is the opposite of the knowing of like by like.

But it is a received principle that error as well as knowledge in respect to contraries is one and the same.

That perceiving and practical thinking are not identical is therefore obvious; for the former is universal in the animal world, the latter is found in only a small division of it. Further, speculative thinking is also distinct from perceiving—I mean that in which we find rightness and wrongness—rightness in prudence, knowledge, true opinion, wrongness in their opposites; for perception of the special objects of sense is always free from error, and is found in all animals, while it is possible to think falsely as well as truly, and thought is found only where there is discourse of reason as well as sensibility. For imagination is different from either perceiving or discursive thinking, though it is not found without sensation, or judgement without it. That this activity is not the same kind of thinking as judgement is obvious. For imagining lies within our own power whenever we wish (e.g. we can call up a picture, as in the practice of mnemonics by the use of mental images), but in forming opinions we are not free: we cannot escape the alternative of falsehood or truth. Further, when we think something to be fearful or threatening, emotion is immediately produced, and so too with what is encouraging; but when we merely imagine we remain as unaffected as persons who are looking at a painting of some dreadful or encouraging scene. Again within the field of judgement itself we find varieties—knowledge, opinion, prudence, and their opposites; of the differences between these I must speak elsewhere.

IMAGINATION

Thinking is different from perceiving and is held to be in part imagination, in part judgement: we must therefore first mark off the sphere of

428^a imagination and then speak of judgement. If then imagination is that in virtue of which an image arises for us, excluding metaphorical uses of the term, is it a single faculty or disposition relative to images, in virtue of which we discriminate and are either in error or not? The faculties in virtue of which we do this are sense, opinion, science, intelligence.

That imagination is not sense is clear from the following considerations: (1) Sense is either a faculty or an activity, e.g. sight or seeing: imagination takes place in the absence of both, as e.g. in dreams. (2) Again, sense is always present, imagination not. If actual imagination and actual sensation were the same, imagination would be found in all the brutes: this is held not to be the case; e.g. it is not found in ants or bees or grubs. (3) Again, sensations are always true, imaginations are for the most part false. (4) Once more, even in ordinary speech, we do not, when sense functions precisely with regard to its object, say that we imagine it to be a man, but rather when there is some failure of accuracy in its exercise. And (5), as we were saying before, visions appear to us even when our eyes are shut. Neither is imagination *any* of the things that are never in error: e.g. knowledge or intelligence; for imagination may be false.

It remains therefore to see if it is opinion, for opinion may be either true or false.

But opinion involves belief (for without belief in what we opine we cannot have an opinion), and in the brutes though we often find imagination we never find belief. Further, every opinion is accompanied by belief, belief by conviction, and conviction by discourse of reason: while there are some of the brutes in which we find imagination, without discourse of reason. It is clear then that imagination cannot, again, be (1) opinion *plus* sensation, or (2) opinion mediated by sensation, or (3) a blend of opinion and sensation; this is impossible both for these reasons and because the content of the supposed opinion cannot be different from that of the sensation (I mean that imagination must be the blending of the perception of white with the opinion that it is white: it could scarcely be a blend of the opinion that it is good with the perception that it is white): to imagine is therefore (on this view) identical with the thinking of exactly the same as what one in the strictest sense perceives. But what we imagine is sometimes false though our contemporaneous judgement about it is true; e.g. we imagine the sun to be a foot in diameter though we are convinced that it is larger than the inhabited part of the earth, and the following dilemma presents itself. Either (*a*) while the fact has not changed and the observer has neither forgotten nor lost belief in the true opinion which he had, that opinion has disappeared, or (*b*) if he retains it then his opinion is at once true and false. A true opinion, however, becomes false only when the fact alters without being noticed.

Imagination is therefore neither any one of the states enumerated, nor compounded out of them.

But since when one thing has been set in motion another thing may be moved by it, and imagination is held to be a movement and to be impossible without sensation, i.e. to occur in beings that are percipient and to have for its content what can be perceived, and since movement may be pro-

428^b

duced by actual sensation and that movement is necessarily similar in character to the sensation itself, this movement must be (1) necessarily (a) incapable of existing apart from sensation, (b) incapable of existing except when we perceive, (2) such that in virtue of its possession that in which it is found may present various phenomena both active and passive, and (3) such that it may be either true or false.

The reason of the last characteristic is as follows. Perception (1) of the special objects of sense is never in error or admits the least possible amount of falsehood. (2) That of the concomitance of the objects concomitant with the sensible qualities comes next: in this case certainly we may be deceived; for while the perception that there is white before us cannot be false, the perception that what is white is this or that may be false. (3) Third comes the perception of the universal attributes which accompany the concomitant objects to which the special sensibles attach (I mean e.g. of movement and magnitude); it is in respect of these that the greatest amount of sense-illusion is possible.

The motion which is due to the activity of sense in these three modes of its exercise will differ from the activity of sense; (1) the first kind of derived motion is free from error while the sensation is present; (2) and (3) the others may be erroneous whether it is present or absent, especially when the object of perception is far off. If then imagination presents no other features than those enumerated and is what we have described, then imagination must be a movement resulting from an actual exercise of a power of sense.

429ª

As sight is the most highly developed sense, the name *phantasia* (imagination) has been formed from *phaos* (light) because it is not possible to see without light.

And because imaginations remain in the organs of sense and resemble sensations, animals in their actions are largely guided by them, some (i.e. the brutes) because of the non-existence in them of mind, others (i.e. men) because of the temporary eclipse in them of mind by feeling or disease or sleep.

About imagination, what it is and why it exists, let so much suffice.

FACULTY AND OPERATION OF INTELLECT

4 Turning now to the part of the soul with which the soul knows and thinks (whether this is separable from the others in definition only, or spatially as well) we have to inquire (1) what differentiates this part, and (2) how thinking can take place.

If thinking is like perceiving, it must be either a process in which the soul is acted upon by what is capable of being thought, or a process different from but analogous to that. The thinking part of the soul must therefore be, while impassible, capable of receiving the form of an object; that is, must be potentially identical in character with its object without being the object. Mind must be related to what is thinkable, as sense is to what is sensible.

Therefore, since everything is a possible object of thought, mind in order, as Anaxagoras says, to dominate, that is, to know, must be pure from all admixture; for the co-presence of what is alien to its nature is a hindrance and a block: it follows that it too, like the sensitive part, can have no nature of its own, other than that of having a certain capacity. Thus that in the soul which is called mind (by mind I mean that whereby the soul thinks and judges) is, before it thinks, not actually any real thing. For this reason it cannot reasonably be regarded as blended with the body: if so, it would acquire some quality, e.g. warmth or cold, or even have an organ like the sensitive faculty: as it is, it has none. It was a good idea to call the soul "the place of forms," though (1) this description holds only of the intellective soul, and (2) even this is the forms only potentially, not actually.

Observation of the sense-organs and their employment reveals a distinction between the impassibility of the sensitive and that of the intellective faculty. After strong stimulation of a sense we are less able to exercise it than before, as e.g. in the case of a loud sound we cannot hear easily immediately after, or in the case of a bright colour or a powerful odour we cannot see or smell, but in the case of mind, thought about an object that is highly intelligible renders it more and not less able afterwards to think objects that are less intelligible: the reason is that while the faculty of sensation is dependent upon the body, mind is separable from it.

429ᵇ

Once the mind has become each set of its possible objects, as a man of science has, when this phrase is used of one who is actually a man of science (this happens when he is now able to exercise the power on his own initiative), its condition is still one of potentiality, but in a different sense from the potentiality which preceded the acquisition of knowledge by learning or discovery: the mind too is then able to think *itself*.

Since we can distinguish between a spatial magnitude and what it is to be such, and between water and what it is to be water, and so in many other cases (though not in all; for in certain cases the thing and its form are identical), flesh and what it is to be flesh are discriminated either by different faculties, or by the same faculty in two different states: for flesh necessarily involves matter and is like what is snub-nosed, a *this* in a *this*.[19] Now it is by means of the sensitive faculty that we discriminate the hot and the cold, i.e. the factors which combined in a certain ratio constitute flesh: the essential character of flesh is apprehended by something different either wholly separate from the sensitive faculty or related to it as a bent line to the same line when it has been straightened out.

Again in the case of abstract objects what is straight is analogous to

---

[19] A particular form in a particular matter. [R. MC K.]

what is snub-nosed; for it necessarily implies a continuum as its matter: its constitutive essence is different, if we may distinguish between straightness and what is straight: let us take it to be two-ness. It must be apprehended, therefore, by a different power or by the same power in a different state. To sum up, in so far as the realities it knows are capable of being separated from their matter, so it is also with the powers of mind.

The problem might be suggested: if thinking is a passive affection, then if mind is simple and impassible and has nothing in common with anything else, as Anaxagoras says, how can it come to think at all? For interaction between two factors is held to require a precedent community of nature between the factors. Again it might be asked, is mind a possible object of thought to itself? For if mind is thinkable *per se* and what is thinkable is in kind one and the same, then either (*a*) mind will belong to everything, or (b) mind will contain some element common to it with all other realities which makes them all thinkable.

(1) Have not we already disposed of the difficulty about interaction involving a common element, when we said that mind is in a sense potentially whatever is thinkable, though actually it is nothing until it has thought? What it thinks must be in it just as characters may be said to be on a writing-tablet on which as yet nothing actually stands written: this is exactly what happens with mind.

430ᵃ

(2) Mind is itself thinkable in exactly the same way as its objects are. For (*a*) in the case of objects which involve no matter, what thinks and what is thought are identical; for speculative knowledge and its object are identical. (Why mind is not always thinking we must consider later.) [20]

(*b*) In the case of those which contain matter each of the objects of thought is only potentially present. It follows that while *they* will not have mind in them (for mind is a potentiality of them only in so far as they are capable of being disengaged from matter) mind may yet be thinkable.

MIND AS ACTIVE AND AS PASSIVE

5   Since in every class of things, as in nature as a whole, we find two factors involved, (1) a matter which is potentially all the particulars included in the class, (2) a cause which is productive in the sense that it makes them all (the latter standing to the former, as e.g. an art to its material), these distinct elements must likewise be found within the soul.

And in fact mind as we have described it is what it is by virtue of becoming all things, while there is another which is what it is by virtue of making all things: this is a sort of positive state like light; for in a sense light makes potential colours into actual colours.

Mind in this sense of it is separable, impassible, unmixed, since it is in its essential nature activity (for always the active is superior to the passive factor, the originating force to the matter which it forms).

---

[20] Ch. 5. [R. MC K.]

Actual knowledge is identical with its object: in the individual, potential knowledge is in time prior to actual knowledge, but in the universe as a whole it is not prior even in time. Mind is not at one time knowing and at another not. When mind is set free from its present conditions it appears as just what it is and nothing more: this alone is immortal and eternal (we do not, however, remember its former activity because, while mind in this sense is impassible, mind as passive is destructible), and without it nothing thinks.

• • •

431ᵇ

SUMMARY

8 Let us now summarize our results about soul, and repeat that the soul is in a way all existing things; for existing things are either sensible or thinkable, and knowledge is in a way what is knowable, and sensation is in a way what is sensible: in *what* way we must inquire.

Knowledge and sensation are divided to correspond with the realities, potential knowledge and sensation answering to potentialities, actual knowledge and sensation to actualities. Within the soul the faculties of knowledge and sensation are *potentially* these objects, the one what is knowable, the other what is sensible. They must be either the things themselves or their forms. The former alternative is of course impossible: it is not the stone which is present in the soul but its form.

It follows that the soul is analogous to the hand; for as the hand is a   432ᵃ
tool of tools,[21] so the mind is the form of forms and sense the form of sensible things.

Since according to common agreement there is nothing outside and separate in existence from sensible spatial magnitudes, the objects of thought are in the sensible forms, viz. both the abstract objects and all the states and affections of sensible things. Hence (1) no one can learn or understand anything in the absence of sense, and (2) when the mind is actively aware of anything it is necessarily aware of it along with an image; for images are like sensuous contents except in that they contain no matter.

Imagination is different from assertion and denial; for what is true or false involves a synthesis of concepts. In what will the primary concepts differ from images? Must we not say that neither these nor even our other concepts are images, though they necessarily involve them?

9 The soul of animals is characterized by two faculties, (*a*) the faculty of discrimination which is the work of thought and sense, and (*b*) the faculty of originating local movement. Sense and mind we have now sufficiently examined. Let us next consider what it is in the soul which originates movement. Is it a single part of the soul separate either spatially or in definition? Or is it the soul as a whole? If it is a part, is that part different

---

[21] A tool for using tools. [R. MC K.]

from those usually distinguished or already mentioned by us, or is it one of them? The problem at once presents itself, in what sense we are to speak of parts of the soul, or how many we should distinguish. For in a sense there is an infinity of parts: it is not enough to distinguish, with some thinkers, the calculative, the passionate, and the desiderative, or with others the rational and the irrational; for if we take the dividing lines followed by these thinkers we shall find parts far more distinctly separated from one another than these, namely those we have just mentioned: (1) the nutritive, which belongs both to plants and to all animals, and (2) the sensitive, which cannot easily be classed as either irrational or rational; further (3) the imaginative, which is, in its being, different from all, while it is very hard to say with which of the others it is the same or not the same, supposing we determine to posit *separate* parts in the soul; and lastly (4) the appetitive, which would seem to be distinct both in definition and in power from all hitherto enumerated.

432ᵇ

It is absurd to break up the last-mentioned faculty: as these thinkers do, for wish is found in the calculative part and desire and passion in the irrational; [22] and if the soul is tripartite appetite will be found in all three parts. Turning our attention to the present object of discussion, let us ask what that is which originates local movement of the animal.

The movement of growth and decay, being found in all living things, must be attributed to the faculty of reproduction and nutrition, which is common to all: inspiration and expiration, sleep and waking, we must consider later: these too present much difficulty: at present we must consider local movement, asking what it is that originates forward movement in the animal.

That it is not the nutritive faculty is obvious; for this kind of movement is always for an end and is accompanied either by imagination or by appetite; for no animal moves except by compulsion unless it has an impulse towards or away from an object. Further, if it were the nutritive faculty, even plants would have been capable of originating such movement and would have possessed the organs necessary to carry it out. Similarly it cannot be the sensitive faculty either; for there are many animals which have sensibility but remain fast and immovable throughout their lives.

DESIRE

If then Nature never makes anything without a purpose and never leaves out what is necessary (except in the case of mutilated or imperfect growths; and that here we have neither mutilation nor imperfection may be argued from the facts that such animals (*a*) can reproduce their species and (*b*) rise to completeness of nature and decay to an end), it follows that, had they been capable of originating forward movement, they would have possessed the organs necessary for that purpose. Further, neither can

---

[22] All three being forms of appetite. [R. MC K.]

the calculative faculty or what is called "mind" be the cause of such movement; for mind as speculative never thinks what is practicable, it never says anything about an object to be avoided or pursued, while this movement is always in something which is avoiding or pursuing an object. No, not even when it is aware of such an object does it at once enjoin pursuit or avoidance of it; e.g. the mind often thinks of something terrifying or pleasant without enjoining the emotion of fear. It is the heart that is moved (or in the case of a pleasant object some other part). Further, even when the mind does command and thought bids us pursue or avoid something, sometimes no movement is produced; we act in accordance with desire, as in the case of moral weakness. And, generally, we observe that the possessor of medical knowledge is not necessarily healing, which shows that something else is required to produce action in accordance with knowledge; the knowledge alone is not the cause. Lastly, appetite too is incompetent to account fully for movement; for those who successfully resist temptation have appetite and desire and yet follow mind and refuse to enact that for which they have appetite.

433ᵃ

10   These two at all events appear to be sources of movement: appetite and mind (if one may venture to regard imagination as a kind of thinking; for many men follow their imaginations contrary to knowledge, and in all animals other than man there is no thinking or calculation but only imagination).

Both of these then are capable of originating local movement, mind and appetite: (1) mind, that is, which calculates means to an end, i.e. mind practical (it differs from mind speculative in the character of its end); while (2) appetite is in every form of it relative to an end: for that which is the object of appetite is the stimulant of mind practical; and that which is last in the process of thinking is the beginning of the action. It follows that there is a justification for regarding these two as the sources of movement, i.e. appetite and practical thought; for the object of appetite starts a movement and as a result of that thought gives rise to movement, the object of appetite being to it a source of stimulation. So too when imagination originates movement, it necessarily involves appetite.

That which moves therefore is a single faculty and the faculty of appetite; for if there had been two sources of movement—mind and appetite —they would have produced movement in virtue of some common character. As it is, mind is never found producing movement without appetite (for wish is a form of appetite; and when movement is produced according to calculation it is also according to wish), but appetite can originate movement contrary to calculation, for desire is a form of appetite. Now mind is always right, but appetite and imagination may be either right or wrong. That is why, though in any case it is the object of appetite which originates movement, this object may be either the real or the apparent good. To produce movement the object must be more than this: it must be good that can be brought into being by action; and only what can be otherwise than as it is can thus be brought into being. That then such a power in the soul as has been described, i.e. that called appetite, originates movement is clear. Those who distinguish parts in the soul, if they distinguish and divide in accordance with differences of power, find themselves with a very large number of parts, a nutritive, a sensitive, an intellective, a deliberative, and now an appetitive part; for these are more different from one another than the faculties of desire and passion.

433ᵇ

Since appetites run counter to one another, which happens when a principle of reason and a desire are contrary and is possible only in beings with a sense of time (for while mind bids us hold back because of what is future, desire is influenced by what is just at hand: a pleasant object which is just at hand presents itself as both pleasant and good, without condition in either case, because of want of foresight into what is farther away in time), it follows that while that which originates movement must be specifically one, viz. the faculty of appetite as such (or rather farthest back of all the object of that faculty; for it is it that itself remaining unmoved originates the movement by being apprehended in thought or imagination), the things that originate movement are numerically many.

All movement involves three factors, (1) that which originates the movement, (2) that by means of which it originates it, and (3) that which is moved. The expression "that which originates the movement" is ambiguous: it may mean either (*a*) something which itself is unmoved or (*b*) that which at once moves and is moved. Here that which moves without itself being moved is the realizable good, that which at once moves and is moved is the faculty of appetite (for that which is influenced by appetite so far as it is actually so influenced is set in movement, and appetite in the sense of actual appetite *is* a kind of movement), while that which is in motion is the animal. The instrument which appetite employs to produce movement is no longer psychical but bodily: hence the examination of it falls within the province of the functions common to body and soul. To state the matter summarily at present, that which is the instrument in the production of movement is to be found where a beginning and an end coincide as e.g. in a ball and socket joint; for there the convex and the concave sides are respectively an end and a beginning (that is why while the one remains at rest, the other is moved): they are separate in definition but not separable spatially. For everything is moved by pushing and pulling. Hence just as in the case of a wheel, so here there must be a point which remains at rest, and from that point the movement must originate.

To sum up, then, and repeat what I have said, inasmuch as an animal is capable of appetite it is capable of self-movement; it is not capable of appetite without possessing imagination; and all imagination is either (1) calculative or (2) sensitive. In the latter all animals, and not only man, partake.

.   .   .

QUESTIONS FOR STUDY AND DISCUSSION

1. Why is it important to determine whether all activities of man belong to the composite, body and soul, or whether some belong to the soul alone?
2. What is the Aristotelian critique of the theory which views the soul as a harmony?
3. Why does "mind" present a special problem in Aristotle's discussion of the various "faculties" or "powers" of the soul?
4. What is the meaning of Aristotle's first full definition of the soul? What implications follow upon this definition?
5. According to Aristotle, what is the primary, that is, the most basic sensory power of man? Why does he so regard it?
6. Discuss the apparent conflict which results from one's holding that the soul is a form of matter, yet is also immortal?
7. How does Aristotle explain sensation and sensory cognition as taking place?
8. Can a sense err with respect to its "special" or "proper" object? Why or why not?
9. How is *thinking* to be distinguished from *perceiving?*
10. What is meant by the statement that "mind is to what is thinkable as sense is to what is sensible"?
11. What are some of the activities which Aristotle considers proper to "mind"?
12. On the basis of the text, what appears to be Aristotle's position regarding the immortality of the soul?

St. Thomas Aquinas

ST. THOMAS AQUINAS was born in 1225 at Roccasecca near Naples. He joined the newly founded Dominican order and studied at Naples, Cologne, and Paris; St. Albert the Great was one of his mentors. St. Thomas taught at both the University of Paris and in the papal courts in Italy. A theologian and a philosopher, he used Aristotelian thought to explain the nature of the Christian man. This successful synthesis, which incorporates his own original insights, is evidenced in his many theological and philosophical writings.

His career at Paris was a stormy one, for he went against the prevailing trend of intellectual thought which was oriented toward an Augustinian-Platonic synthesis. Certain viewpoints of Aquinas were condemned after his death in 1274; these censures, however, were later removed and the intrinsic value of his great Christian synthesis was recognized and strongly endorsed by the Popes. "Thomism" came to enjoy a preeminent position in the Church.

On the Nature of Man

From *On Spiritual Creatures*

ARTICLE II. Can a spiritual substance be united to a body?

. . .

Answer. It must be said that the difficulty of this question arises from the fact that a spiritual substance is a kind of self-subsistent thing. Now a form must have actual being in something else, that is, in matter, of which it is the act and the perfection. Hence it seems to be contrary to the character of a spiritual substance that it should be the form of the body. And for this reason Gregory of Nyssa[1] in his book *De Anima* [PG[2] XLV, 199] accused Aristotle of asserting that the soul is not self-subsistent, and that it

---

[1] According to the latest scholarship, it was really Nemesius Emesenus' work *De Natura Hominis.* [E.G.S.]

[2] *PG* refers to Migne, *Patrologiae cursus completus Series Graeca*, 162 vols., with Latin translation (Paris: 1857–66). *PG* is short form for *Patrologiae-Series Graeca*, and *PL* for *Patrologiae-Series Latina* (221 vols.; Paris: 1844–64). [E.G.S.]

From St. Thomas Aquinas, *On Spiritual Creatures*, translated by M. C. Fitzpatrick and J. J. Wellmuth. Copyright 1949 by Marquette University Press. Reprinted by permission of the publisher.

is corrupted when the body is corrupted, because he asserted it as the entelechy, that is, as the act or perfection, of the physical body.

But yet, if one carefully studies the matter, it becomes clearly evident that some substance must be the form of the human body. For it is obvious that understanding belongs to "this particular man" (as, for instance, Socrates or Plato). Now no activity belongs to any given thing except through some form which exists in the thing itself, either a substantial or an accidental form, because nothing acts or functions except in consequence of its being actual. Now each individual thing is actual through some form, either substantial or accidental, since a form is an act; thus, for instance, fire is actually fire through "fireness," and actually hot through heat. Accordingly, it must be the case that the principle of that activity which is understanding should be in "this man" in the way of a form. Now the principle of this activity is not a form whose actual being is dependent on matter and tied down to or immersed in matter, because this activity is not effected by means of the body as is proven in *III De Anima* [4, 429a 24]; and hence the principle of this activity possesses an activity that has nothing in common with corporeal matter. Now, the way in which each thing acts is a consequence of its being. Hence the actual being of that principle must be an actual being which is raised above corporeal matter and not dependent on it. Now this is characteristic of a spiritual substance. It is necessary to say, therefore, if the preceding considerations are put together, that some kind of substance is the form of the human body.

But there are some who, while admitting that understanding is the act of a spiritual substance, have denied that such a spiritual substance is united to the body as a form. Among these Averroes asserted that the possible intellect, in its actual being, is separated from the body. He saw nevertheless that unless there were some union of it with "this man," its act could not pertain to "this man." For if there are two substances entirely unconnected, when one is acting or functioning, the other is not said to be functioning. And hence he asserted that such an intellect, which he said was entirely separated from the body in its actual being, is connected with "this man" through phantasms, for this reason, that the intelligible species, which is a perfection of the possible intellect, is based on the phantasms from which it is abstracted. So, therefore, it has a two-fold kind of actual being: one in the possible intellect, of which it is the form, and the other in the phantasms from which it is abstracted. Now the phantasms are in "this man" because the imaginative power is a power within the body; that is, one which has a corporeal organ. The intelligible species itself, therefore, is the medium which joins the possible intellect to "the individual man."

But this connection is in no way sufficient to explain the fact that "this individual man" understands. For, as Aristotle says in his book *III De Anima* [7, 431a 14], the phantasms are related to the possible intellect as color is to the sight. Accordingly, the intelligible species abstracted from the phantasms is in the possible intellect in the same way as the species "color" is in the sense of sight. Now the intelligible species is in the phantasms in the same way as a species which makes seeing possible (*species visibilis*) is in the physical object which is a wall. Now owing to the fact that the species which makes seeing possible, the form "sight," is based on the color of the wall, the act of seeing is not connected with the wall as with a seeing object, but as with a seen object: for by means of it the wall does not see, but is seen; for what constitutes a knower is not the fact that there is in him a form whose image is in some knowing power, but the fact that there is in him the cognitive power itself. And "this man," accordingly, will not be one who understands because of the fact that in him are phantasms whose image, which is an intelligible species, is in the possible intellect; but it does follow because of this fact that his phantasms are understood by him. But the possible intellect itself, which is the understanding power, must be in "this man" in the way of a form, precisely in order that "this man" may understand. He seems to have made a mistake also in regard to the character of connection itself, since the intelligible species is not one with the possible intellect, save insofar as it has been abstracted from the phantasms: for only so is it understood in act, whereas insofar as it is in the phantasms it is understood only in potency. By this fact, then, is proved rather the disconnection of the possible intellect from the phantasms than its connection with them, for it must be the case that two things are entirely disconnected when something cannot be united to one of them unless it has been previously separated from the other.

Setting aside this view then as impossible, we must consider that Plato produced a better result by asserting that "this man" understands, and yet that a spiritual substance is not united to the body as a form. For, as Gregory of Nyssa tells us [*De An. PG* XLV, 216], Plato asserted that the intellectual substance which is called the soul is united to the body by a kind of spiritual contact: and this is understood in the sense in which a thing that moves or acts touches the thing that is moved or is passive, even though it be incorporeal; and for this reason Aristotle says in I *De Generatione* [6, 323a 28] that certain things touch and yet are not touched, because they act and are not passive. And hence Plato used to say, as the aforesaid Gregory relates, that man is not something that is composed of soul and body, but is a soul using a body, so that he is understood to be in a body in somewhat the same way as a sailor is in a ship; and Aristotle seems to be touching upon this in II *De Anima* [1, 413a 8]. Thus, then, "this man" also understands, inasmuch as "this man" is the very spiritual substance which is the soul, whose proper act is understanding, even though, nevertheless, this substance does not exist as the form of the body.

But for the invalidation of this argument the one point suffices which Aristotle brings forward directly against this position in II *De Anima* [1, 412a]. For if the soul were not united to the body as a form, it would follow that the body and its parts would not have specific actual being through the soul; and this is seen to be obviously false: because once the soul departs, one does not say eye or flesh or bone, save equivocally, as one says painted eye or eye of stone. And hence it is obvious that the soul is the form and "the essence of this body," that is, that from which this body has the character of its own species. Exactly how this can be, however, we must proceed to investigate.

Now it must be borne in mind that the more perfect a form is, the more does it surpass corporeal matter. This is clear from induction in regard to the various orders of forms. For the form of an element does not have any activity but the one which takes place through active and passive qualities, which are the dispositions of corporeal matter. But the form "mineral body" has an activity that goes beyond active and passive qualities, and is a consequence of its species by reason of the influence of a heavenly body; for instance, that a magnet attracts iron, and that a sapphire cures an abscess. And further, the vegetative soul (*anima vegetabilis*) has an activity to which the active and passive organic qualities of course contribute; but nevertheless, over and above the power of qualities like these, the soul itself achieves an effect of its own by nurture and growth up to a definite limit, and by carrying on other functions of this sort. And the sensing soul (*anima sensitiva*) has a further activity to which the active and the passive qualities do not extend in any way, save insofar as they are needed for the composition of the organ through which this sort of activity is exercised; such as seeing, hearing, desire, and the like.

But the most perfect of forms, the human soul, which is the end of all natural forms, has an activity that goes entirely beyond matter, and does not take place through a corporeal organ; namely, understanding. And because the actual being of a thing is proportioned to its activity, as has been said, since each thing acts according as it is a being (*ens*), it must be the case that the actual being of the human soul surpasses corporeal matter, and is not totally included in it, but yet in some way is touched upon by it. Inasmuch, then, as it surpasses the actual being of corporeal matter, having of itself the power to subsist and to act, the human soul is a spiritual substance; but inasmuch as it is touched upon by matter and shares its own actual being with matter, it is the form of the body. Now it is touched upon by corporeal matter for this reason, that the highest point of the lowest always touches the lowest point of the highest, as Dionysius makes clear in the seventh chapter [lec. 4] of *De Divinis Nominibus;* and consequently the human soul, which is the lowest in the order of spiritual substances, can communicate its own actual being to the human body, which is the highest in dignity, so that from the soul and the body, as from form and matter, a single being results. But if a spiritual substance were composed of matter and form, it would be impossible for it to be the body's form: because it is essential to matter that it be not in anything else, but that it should itself be the primary subject.

.   .   .

From *The Soul*

ARTICLE I. Whether the soul can be a form and a particular thing?

I answer: "A particular thing," properly speaking, designates an individual in the genus of substance. For the Philosopher [Aristotle] says, in the *Categories,* that first substances undoubtedly signify particular things; second substances, indeed, although they seem to signify particular things, rather signify the specific essence (*quale quid*). Furthermore, an individual in the genus of substance is capable not only of subsisting of itself, but is also a complete entity belonging to a definite species and genus of substance. Wherefore the Philosopher, in the *Categories,* also calls a hand and a foot, and things of this sort, parts of substances rather than first or second substances. For although they do not exist in another as a subject (which is characteristic of a substance), they still do not possess completely the nature of a species. Hence they belong to a species or to a genus only by reduction.

Now some men have denied that the human soul possesses these two real characteristics belonging to a particular thing by its very nature, because they said that the soul is a harmony, as Empedocles did, or a combination [of the elements], as Galen did, or something of this kind. For then the soul will neither be able to subsist of itself, nor will it be a complete thing belonging to a species or genus of substance, but will be a form similar only to other material forms.

But this position is untenable as regards the vegetal soul, whose operations necessarily require some principle surpassing the active and passive qualities [of the elements] which play only an instrumental role in nutrition and growth, as is proved in the *De Anima.* Moreover, a combination and a harmony do not transcend the elemental qualities. This position is likewise untenable as regards the sentient soul, whose operations consist in receiving species separated from matter, as is shown in the *De Anima.* For inasmuch as active and passive qualities are dispositions of matter, they do not transcend matter. Again, this position is even less tenable as regards the rational soul, whose operation consists in understanding, and in abstracting species not only from matter, but from all individuating conditions, this being required for the understanding of universals. However, in the case of the rational soul something of special importance must still be considered, because not only does it receive intelligible species without matter and material conditions, but it is also quite impossible for it, in performing its proper operation, to have anything in common with a bodily organ, as though something corporeal might be an organ of understanding, just as the eye is the organ of sight, as is proved in the *De Anima.* Thus the intellective soul, inasmuch as it performs its proper operation without communicating in any way with the body, must act of itself. And because a thing acts so far as it is actual, the intellective soul must have a complete act of existing in itself, depending in no way on the body. For forms whose act of existing depends on matter or on a subject do not operate of themselves. Heat, for instance, does not act, but something hot.

For this reason the later Greek philosophers came to the conclusion that the intellective part of the soul is a self-subsisting thing. For the Philosopher says, in the *De Anima,* that the intellect is a substance, and is not corrupted. The teaching of Plato, who maintains that the soul is incorruptible and subsists of itself in view of the fact that it moves itself, amounts to the same thing. For he took "motion" in a broad sense to signify every operation; hence he understands that the soul moves itself because it moves itself by itself.

But elsewhere Plato maintained that the human soul not only subsisted of itself, but also had the complete nature of a species. For he held that the complete nature of the [human] species is found in the soul, saying that a man is not a composite of soul and body, but a soul joined to a body in such a way that it is related to the body as a pilot is to a ship, or as one clothed to his clothing. However, this position is untenable, because it is obvious that the soul is the reality which gives life to the body. Moreover, vital activity (*vivere*) is the act of existing (*esse*) of living things. Consequently the soul is that which gives the human body its act of existing. Now a form is of this nature. Therefore the human soul is the form of the body. But if the soul were in the body as a pilot is in a ship, it would give neither the body nor its parts their specific nature. The contrary of this is seen to be true, because, when the soul leaves the body, the body's individual parts retain their original names only in an equivocal sense. For the eye of a dead man, like the eye of a portrait or that of a statue, is called an eye equivocally; and similarly for the other parts of the body. Furthermore, if the soul were in the body as a pilot in a ship, it would follow that the union of soul and body would be an accidental one. Then death, which brings about their separation, would not be a substantial corruption; which is clearly false. So it follows that the soul is a particular thing and that it can subsist of itself, not as a thing having a complete species of its own, but as completing the human species by being the form of the body. Hence it likewise follows that it is both a form and a particular thing.

Indeed, this can be shown from the order of natural forms. For we find among the forms of lower bodies that the higher a form is, the more it resembles and approaches higher principles. This can be seen from the proper operation of forms. For the forms of the elements, being lowest [in the order of forms] and nearest to matter, possess no operation surpassing their active and passive qualities, such as rarefaction and condensation, and the like, which appear to be material dispositions. Over and above these forms are those of the mixed bodies, and these forms have (in addition to the above mentioned operations) a certain activity, consequent upon their species, which they receive from the celestial bodies. The magnet, for instance, attracts iron not because of its heat or its cold or anything of this sort, but because it shares in the powers of the heavens. Again, surpassing these forms are the souls of plants, which resemble not only the forms of earthly bodies but also the movers of the celestial bodies inasmuch as they are principles of a certain motion, themselves being moved. Still higher are brute beasts' forms, which now resemble a substance moving a celestial body not only because of the operation whereby they move bodies, but also because they are capable of knowledge, although their knowledge is concerned merely with material things and belongs to the material order (for which reason they require bodily organs). Again, over and above these forms, and in the highest place, are human souls, which certainly resemble superior substances with respect to the kind of knowledge they possess, because they are capable of knowing immaterial things by their act of intellection. However, human souls differ from superior substances inasmuch as the human soul's intellective power, by its very nature, must acquire its immaterial knowledge from the knowledge of material things attained through the senses.

Consequently the human soul's mode of existing can be known from its operation. For, inasmuch as the human soul has an operation transcending the material order, its act of existing transcends the body and does not depend on the body. Indeed, inasmuch as the soul is naturally capable of acquiring immaterial knowledge from material things, evidently its species can be complete only when it is united to a body. For a thing's species is complete only if it has the things necessary for the proper operation of its species. Consequently, if the human soul, inasmuch as it is united as a form to the body, has an act of existing which transcends the body and does not depend on it, obviously the soul itself is established on the boundary line dividing corporeal from separate substances.

· · ·

ARTICLE II. Whether the human soul, so far as its act of existence is concerned, is separated from the body?

· · ·

I answer: In order to settle this issue we must take into consideration that, whenever a thing is found to be sometimes in potency and sometimes in act, there must be some principle by which it is in potency; just as a man is sometimes actually sensing and sometimes only potentially. Now on account of this it is necessary to maintain that in man there exists a sentient principle which is in potency to sensible things; for if he were always actually sensing, the forms of sensible things would always actually exist in his sentient principle. Similarly, since a man is found sometimes to be actually understanding and sometimes only potentially, it is necessary to maintain that in man there exists an intellective power which is in potency to intelligibles; and the Philosopher, in the *De Anima,* calls this principle the possible intellect. Consequently this possible intellect must be in potency to all things intelligible to man; it must be capable of receiving them and therefore must be devoid of them, because anything capable of receiving other things is in potency to them inasmuch as it lacks them; just as the pupil of the eye, which is capable of receiving all colors, lacks every color. Now man is determined by nature to understand the forms of all sensible things. Therefore, by its very nature the possible intellect must be devoid of all sensible forms and natures, and so also must have no bodily organ. For if it had a bodily organ, it would be limited to some sensible nature, just as the power of vision is limited to the nature of the eye. By means of this proof we exclude the position of the ancient philosophers, who held that the intellect did not differ from the sentient powers, as well as the position of those who maintained that the principle by which a man understands is a certain form or power which is united to the body as other material forms or powers are.

But certain other men avoiding this position, fall into the opposite error. For they think that the possible intellect is devoid of every sensible nature and that it is not present in the body, because it is a certain substance which exists in separation from the body and is in potency to all intelligible forms. But this position cannot be maintained, because we acquire our knowledge of the possible intellect only so far as a man understands by it. Indeed, this is the way Aristotle obtains his knowledge of it, as is evident from what he says in the *De Anima,* when he begins to discuss the possible intellect: "Concerning that part of the soul by which the soul knows and perceives . . . it must be considered . . ."; and in another place he says: "I speak of the possible intellect by which the soul understands." But if the possible intellect were a separate substance, it would be impossible for a man to understand by means of it; because, if a substance performs an operation, that operation cannot belong to any other substance than the one performing it. For although one of two substances can be the cause of the other's operation, as the principal agent is the cause of the activity of the instrument, nevertheless the action of the principal agent is not numerically the same as that of the instrument. For the action of the principal agent consists in moving the instrument, whereas that of the instrument consists in being moved by the principal agent and in moving something else. Consequently, if the possible intellect is a substance existing apart from this or that particular man, it is impossible for the possible intellect's act of intellection to be the act of any particular man. From this it follows that no man understands anything, because the act of intellection is not attributed to any principle in man except the possible intellect. Hence the same manner of arguing is opposed to this position and to those who deny its principles, as is evident from Aristotle's arguments against them in the *Metaphysics.*

Now Averroes, who is a follower of this position, intending to avoid its incongruity maintained that, although the possible intellect existed apart from the body, it must be united to man through the intermediary of phantasms. For phantasms, as the Philosopher says in the *De Anima,* are related to the possible intellect as sensible things are to sense, and colors to sight. Thus an intelligible species has two subjects: one in which it exists with an intelligible mode of existing, and this is the possible intellect: another in which it exists with a real mode of existing, and this subject is the phantasms. Therefore [according to Averroes] there is a certain union of the possible intellect with the phantasms inasmuch as an intelligible species exists in a certain manner in each of these subjects; and a man understands through the [supposedly separate] possible intellect as a result of this union with the phantasms.

However, this union is still not sufficient [to account for man's knowledge], for a thing is capable of knowing, not because intelligible species are present to it, but because it possesses a cognitive power. Now evidently, from what has been said, intelligible species alone will be present to man, whereas the power of understanding, that is, the possible intellect, exists in complete separation from him. Therefore it does not follow from the aforesaid union that a man will have what is necessary for understanding, but only that a species or something in that intellect will be understood. This clearly appears to be the case from the simile introduced above. For if phantasms are related to the intellect as colors are to sight, the union of the [supposedly separate] possible intellect with us through our phantasms, will be the same as that of sight with a wall through its colors. Now it does not follow that a wall sees because it has colors, but only that it is seen. Nor, similarly, does it follow that a man will understand because phantasms are present within him, but only that he will be understood.

Furthermore, a phantasm is not the subject of an intelligible species inasmuch as the latter is actually understood. On the contrary, an intelligible species is made to be actually understood by abstraction from phantasms. Moreover, the possible intellect is the subject of an intelligible species only inasmuch as an intelligible species is now actually understood and abstracted from phantasms. Therefore the species existing in the possible intellect, and that existing in the phantasms, through which the [supposedly separate] possible intellect is united to us, are not one and the same.

Furthermore, if anyone understands through intelligible species only when they are actually understood, it follows, according to the aforesaid position, that we are incapable of understanding anything in any way, for then intelligible species would be present to us only inasmuch as they exist in phantasms, and here they are only potentially understood. Consequently it is evident on the side of our human nature that the above-mentioned position is impossible. This is also apparent from the nature of separate substances. Since these are most perfect, it is impossible for them in their own operations to stand in need of the operations of material things; nor need they be in potency to any things of this kind, for not even the celestial bodies, which are below the separate substances, require things of this sort.

Hence, since the possible intellect is in potency to the species of sensible things, and since its operation may not be completed without phantasms, which depend on our operations, it is impossible and inconceivable for the possible intellect to be one of the separate substances.

Consequently, we must say that the possible intellect is a certain faculty or power of the human soul. For although the human soul is a form united to the body, it is not embraced completely by the body as though immersed in it as other material forms are, but transcends the capacity of the whole of corporeal matter. And so far as the soul transcends corporeal matter, the potentiality for intelligibles exists in the soul and this [potentiality] belongs to the possible intellect. Certainly the soul, so far as it is united to the body, has operations and powers in common with the body; such, for example, are the powers of the nutritive and sentient part. Thus the nature of the possible intellect is as Aristotle proves it to be, for the possible intellect is not a power rooted in any bodily organ. However, a man understands formally by means of it inasmuch as it is rooted in the essence of the human soul, which is the form of man.

. . .

ARTICLE XI. Whether the Rational, Sentient, and Vegetal Soul in man are substantially one and the same?

. . .

Still another incongruity follows. For the form in accordance with which an individual substance receives a generic predication, must be a substantial one, because a genus is a substantial predicate. And thus the sentient soul in virtue of which Socrates is said to be an animal, must be his substantial form, and so must give to the body its act of existing in the absolute sense (*per se*), and make it to be this particular thing (*hoc aliquid*). Therefore, if the rational soul differs substantially from the sentient, it does not make the body to be this particular thing, nor does it give to the body an act of existing in the absolute sense, but only relatively. For in that case a rational form will accrue to a thing already actually subsisting. Consequently it will not be a substantial form but an accidental one, and thus will not make Socrates to be specifically what he is, for a species also is a substantial predicate.

It follows, therefore, that a man's soul, which is rational, sentient, and vegetal, is substantially one only. This is a consequence of the argument given in a preceding article (Art. IX), concerning the order of substantial forms, namely, that no substantial form is united to matter through the medium of another, but that a more perfect form gives to matter whatever an inferior form does, and something over and above. Hence the rational soul gives to the human body everything that the sentient soul gives to the brute and the vegetal soul gives to the plant, and something over and above. For this reason the soul in man is both vegetal, sentient, and rational.

The following example also attests to this, namely, that when the operation of one power is intense, that of another is impeded; and contrariwise, there is an overflowing of one power into another, which would occur only if all the powers were rooted in one and the same essence of the soul.

ARTICLE XIV. Whether the human soul is incorruptible?

I answer: It must necessarily be granted that the human soul is incorruptible. In proof of this we must take into consideration the fact that whatever belongs to a thing in virtue of its very nature (*per se*), cannot be taken away from it; for example, animality cannot be taken away from man, nor can the even and odd be taken away from number. Moreover it is evident that the act of existing in itself is a result of a form, for everything has its act of existing from its proper form; wherefore its act of existing can in no way be separated from its form. Therefore things composed of matter and form are corrupted by losing the form that gives them their act of existing. Moreover a form itself cannot be corrupted in itself (*per se*), but is corrupted accidentally as a result of the disintegration of the composite, inasmuch as the composite, which exists in virtue of its form, ceases to exist as a composite. This, indeed, is the case if the form is one that does not have an act of existing in itself, but is merely that by which a composite exists.

Now if there is a form having an act of existing in itself, then that form must be incorruptible. For a thing having an act of existing (*esse*) does not cease to exist unless its form is separated from it. Hence if the thing having an act of existing is itself a form, it is impossible for its act of existing to be separated from it. Now it is evident that the principle by which a man understands is a form having its act of existing in itself and is not merely that by which something exists. For, as the Philosopher proves in the *De Anima,* intellection is not an act executed by any bodily organ. The main reason why there is no bodily organ capable of receiving the sensible forms of all natural things, is that the recipient must itself be deprived of the nature of the thing received; just as the pupil of the eye does not possess the color that it sees. Now every bodily organ possesses a sensible nature. But the intellect, by which we understand, is capable of apprehending all sensible natures. Therefore its operation, namely, understanding, cannot be carried out by a bodily organ. Thus it is clear that the intellect has an operation of its own in which the body does not share. Now a thing operates in accordance with its nature (*quod est*), for things that exist of themselves have an operation of their own, whereas things that do not exist of themselves have no operation of their own. For example, heat in itself does not produce warmth, but something hot. Consequently it is evident that the intellective principle, by which man understands, has it own mode of existing superior to that of the body and not dependent upon it.

It is also evident that an intellective principle of this sort is not a thing composed of matter and form, because the species of things are received in it in an absolutely immaterial way, as is shown by the fact that the intellect knows universals, which are considered in abstraction from matter and from material conditions. The sole conclusion to be drawn from all this, then, is that the intellective principle, by which man understands, is a form having its act of existing in itself. Therefore this principle must be incorruptible. This indeed agrees with the Philosopher's dictum, that the intellect is something divine and everlasting. Now it was shown in preceding articles (Articles II and V), that the intellective principle, by which man understands, is not a substance existing apart from man but is something formally inhering in him which is either the soul or a part of the soul. Thus, from the foregoing considerations we conclude that the human soul is incorruptible.

Now all those who held that the human soul is corruptible missed some of the points we have already made. Some of these people, holding that the soul is a body, declared that it is not a form in its entirety, but a thing composed of matter and form. Others held that the intellect does not differ from the senses, and so they declared that the intellect does not operate except through a bodily organ; that it does have a higher mode of existence than that of the body, and, therefore, that it is not a form having an act of existing in its own right. Still others held that the intellect, by which man understands, is a separate substance. But the falsity of all these opinions has been demonstrated in preceding articles. It therefore remains that the human soul is incorruptible.

Two additional arguments can be considered as an indication of this: First, respecting the intellect itself, because we see that even those things which are corruptible in themselves are incorruptible so far as they are perceived by the intellect. For the intellect apprehends things in and through universal concepts, and things existing in this [universalized conceptual] mode are not subject to corruption. Secondly, the natural appetite also provides an argument for the incorruptibility of the soul. Natural appetite [desire springing from the nature of man] cannot be frustrated. Now we observe in men the desire for perpetual existence. This desire is grounded in reason. For to exist (*esse*) being desirable in itself, an intelligent being who apprehends existence in the absolute sense, and not merely the here and now, must desire existence in the absolute sense and for all time. Hence it is clear that this desire is not vain, but that man, in virtue of his intellective soul, is incorruptible.

.   .   .

From *Summa Theologica,* Part I

QUESTION 77. ARTICLE 1. Whether the essence of the soul is its power?

· · ·

I answer that, It is impossible to admit that the power of the soul is its essence, although some have maintained it. For the present purpose this may be proved in two ways. First, because, since potency and act divide being and every kind of being, we must refer a potency and its act to the same genus. Therefore, if the act be not in the genus of substance, the potency which is said in relation to that act cannot be in the genus of substance. Now the operation of the soul is not in the genus of substance, for this belongs to God alone, whose operation is His own substance. Therefore the divine potency or power which is the principle of His operation is the divine essence itself. This cannot be true either of the soul or of any creature, as we have said above when speaking of the angels. Secondly, this may be also shown to be impossible in the soul. For the soul by its very essence is an act. Therefore, if the very essence of the soul were the immediate principle of operation, whatever has a soul would always have actual vital actions, as that which has a soul is always an actually living thing. For, as a form, the soul is not an act ordained to a further act; it is rather the ultimate term of generation. Therefore, for it to be in potentiality to another act does not belong to it according to its essence as a form, but according to its power. So the soul itself, as the subject of its power, is called the first act, with a further relation to the second act. Now we observe that what has a soul is not always actual with respect to its vital operations. Hence it is also said in the definition of the soul that it is *the act of a body having life potentially;* which potentiality, however, *does not exclude the soul.* Therefore it follows that the essence of the soul is not its power. For nothing is in potentiality by reason of an act, as act.

· · ·

QUESTION 77. ARTICLE 3. Whether the powers are distinguished by their acts and objects?

· · ·

I answer that, A power as such is directed to an act. Therefore we must derive the nature of a power from the act to which it is directed; and consequently the nature of a power is diversified according as the nature of the act is diversified. Now the nature of an act is diversified according to the various natures of the objects. For every act is either of an active power or of a passive power. Now, the object is to the act of a passive power as the principle and moving cause; for color is the principle of vision, inasmuch as it moves the sight. On the other hand, to the act of an active power the

From St. Thomas Aquinas, *Summa Theologica,* Part I, in *Basic Writings of St. Thomas Aquinas,* vol. I, edited by Anton C. Pegis. Copyright 1945 by Random House, Inc. Reprinted by permission of Random House, Inc., and Burns & Oates Ltd., London.

object is a term and an end; just as the object of the power of growth is perfect quantity, which is the end of growth. Now, from these two things an act receives its species, namely, from its principle, or from its end or term. For the act of heating differs from the act of cooling in this, that the former proceeds from something hot, which is the active principle, to heat; while the latter proceeds from something cold, which is the active principle, to cold. Therefore the powers are of necessity distinguished by their acts and objects.

.   .   .

QUESTION 77. ARTICLE 5. Whether all the powers of the soul are in the soul as their subjects?

.   .   .

I answer that, The subject of operative power is that which is able to operate; for every accident denominates its proper subject. Now it is the same being which is able to operate, and which does operate. Therefore the *subject of power* is of necessity *the subject of operation,* as again the Philosopher says in the beginning of *De Somno et Vigilia.* Now, it is clear from what we have said above that some operations of the soul are performed without a corporeal organ, as to understand and to will. Hence the powers of these operations are in the soul as their subject. But some operations of the soul are performed by means of corporeal organs, as seeing by the eye, and hearing by the ear. And so it is with all the other operations of the nutritive and sensitive parts. Therefore, the powers which are the principles of these operations have their subject in the composite, and not in the soul alone.

.   .   .

QUESTION 77. ARTICLE 8. Whether all the powers remain in the soul when separated from the body?

.   .   .

I answer that, As we have already said, all the powers of the soul belong to the soul alone as their principle. But some powers belong to the soul alone as their subject: such are intellect and will. These powers must remain in the soul, after the destruction of the body. But other powers are in the composite as in their subject; as all the powers of the sensitive and nutritive parts. Now accidents cannot remain after the destruction of the subject. Therefore, when the composite is destroyed, such powers do not remain actually; but they remain virtually in the soul, as in their principle or root.

So it is false that, as some say, these powers remain in the soul even after the corruption of the body. It is much more false that, as they also say, the acts of these powers remain in the separate soul; because these powers have no act apart from a corporeal organ.

QUESTION 78. ARTICLE 4. Whether the interior senses are suitably distinguished?

.   .   .

I answer that, As nature does not fail in necessary things, there must needs be as many actions of the sensitive soul as may suffice for the life of a perfect animal. If any of these actions cannot be reduced to one and the same principle, they must be assigned to diverse powers; since a power of the soul is nothing else than the proximate principle of the soul's operation.

Now we must observe that for the life of a perfect animal, the animal should apprehend a thing not only at the actual time of sensation, but also when it is absent. Otherwise, since animal motion and action follow apprehension, an animal would not be moved to seek something absent; the contrary of which we may observe especially in perfect animals, which are moved by progression, for they are moved towards something apprehended and absent. Therefore, through the sensitive soul an animal must not only receive the species of sensible things, when it is actually affected by them, but it must also retain and preserve them. Now to receive and retain are, in corporeal things, reduced to diverse principles; for moist things are apt to receive, but retain with difficulty, while it is the reverse with dry things. Therefore, since the sensitive power is the act of a corporeal organ, it follows that the power which receives the species of sensible things must be distinct from the power which preserves them.

Again, we must observe that if an animal were moved by pleasing and disagreeable things only as affecting the sense, there would be no need to suppose that an animal has a power besides the apprehension of those forms which the senses perceive, and in which the animal takes pleasure, or from which it shrinks with horror. But the animal needs to seek or to avoid certain things, not only because they are pleasing or otherwise to the senses, but also because of other advantages and uses, or disadvantages; just as the sheep runs away when it sees a wolf, not because of its color or shape, but as a natural enemy. So, too, a bird gathers together straws, not because they are pleasant to the sense, but because they are useful for building its nest. Animals, therefore, need to perceive such intentions, which the exterior sense does not perceive. Now some distinct principle is necessary for this, since the perception of sensible forms comes by an immutation caused by the sensible, which is not the case with the perception of the above intentions.

Thus, therefore, for the reception of sensible forms, the *proper sense* and the *common sense* are appointed. Of their distinction we shall speak later. But for the retention and preservation of these forms, the *phantasy* or *imagination* is appointed, being as it were a storehouse of forms received through the senses. Furthermore, for the apprehension of intentions which are not received through the senses, the *estimative* power is appointed: and for their preservation, the *memorative* power, which is a storehouse of such intentions. A sign of which we have in the fact that the principle of memory in animals is found in some such intention, for instance, that something is harmful or otherwise. And the very character of something as past, which memory observes, is to be reckoned among these intentions.

Now, we must observe that as to sensible forms there is no difference between man and other animals; for they are similarly immuted by external sensibles. But there is a difference as to the above intentions: for other animals perceive these intentions only by some sort of natural instinct, while man perceives them also by means of a certain comparison. Therefore the power which in other animals is called the *natural estimative* in man is called the *cogitative,* which by some sort of comparison discovers these intentions. Therefore it is also called the *particular reason,* to which medical men assign a particular organ, namely, the middle part of the head; for it compares individual intentions, just as the intellectual reason compares universal intentions. As to the memorative power, man has not only memory, as other animals have, in the sudden recollection of the past, but also *reminiscence,* by seeking syllogistically, as it were, for a recollection of the past by the application of individual intentions. Avicenna, however, assigns between the estimative and the imaginative a fifth power, which combines and divides imaginary forms; as when from the imaginary form of gold, and the imaginary form of a mountain, we compose the one form of a golden mountain, which we have never seen. But this operation is not to be found in animals other than man, in whom the imaginative power suffices for this purpose. Averroes also attributes this action to the imagination, in his book *De sensu et sensibilibus.* So there is no need to assign more than four interior powers of the sensitive part—namely, the common sense, the imagination, and the estimative and memorative powers.

. . .

QUESTION 79. ARTICLE 6. Whether memory is in the intellectual part of the soul?

. . .

I answer that, Since it is of the nature of the memory to preserve the species of those things which are not apprehended actually, we must first of all consider whether the intelligible species can thus be preserved in the intellect. For Avicenna held that this was impossible. He admitted that this could happen in the sensitive part, as to some powers, inasmuch as they are acts of corporeal organs, in which certain species may be preserved without actual apprehension; but in the intellect, which has no corporeal organ, nothing but what is intelligible exists. Hence, every thing of which the likeness exists in the intellect must be actually understood. Thus, therefore, according to him, as soon as we cease to understand something actually, the species of that thing ceases to be in our intellect, and if we wish to understand that thing anew, we must turn to the agent intellect, which he held to be a separate substance, in order that the intelligible species may thence flow again into our possible intellect. And from the practice and repetition of turning to the agent intellect there is formed, according to him, a certain aptitude in the possible intellect for turning itself to the agent intellect; which aptitude he calls *the habit of science.* According, therefore, to this supposition, nothing is preserved in the intellectual part that is not actually understood; and hence it would not be possible to admit memory in the intellectual part.

● ● ●

QUESTION 79. ARTICLE 11. Whether the speculative and practical intellects are distinct powers?

● ● ●

I answer that, The speculative and practical intellects are not distinct powers. The reason for this is, as we have said above, that what is accidental to the nature of the object of a power does not differentiate that power; for it is accidental to a colored thing to be a man, or to be great or small. Hence all such things are apprehended by the same power of sight. Now, to a thing apprehended by the intellect, it is accidental whether it be directed to operation or not; but it is according to this that the speculative and practical intellects differ. For it is the speculative intellect which directs what it apprehends, not to operation, but to the sole consideration of truth; while the practical intellect is that which directs what it apprehends to operation. And this is what the Philosopher says, namely, that *the speculative differs from the practical in its end.* Whence each is named from its end: the one speculative, the other practical—i.e., operative.

● ● ●

QUESTION 80. ARTICLE 2. Whether the sensitive and intellectual appetites are distinct powers?

● ● ●

I answer that, We must needs say that the intellectual appetite is a distinct power from the sensitive appetite. For the appetitive power is a passive power, which is naturally moved by the thing apprehended. Therefore *the apprehended appetible is a mover which is not moved, while the appetite is a moved mover,* as the Philosopher says in *De Anima* iii. and in *Metaph.* xii. Now things passive and movable are differentiated according to the distinction of the corresponding active and motive principles, for the motive must be proportionate to the movable, and the active to the passive. Indeed, the passive power itself has its very nature from its relation to its active principle. Therefore, since what is apprehended by the intellect and what is apprehended by sense are generically different, consequently, the intellectual appetite is distinct from the sensitive.

● ● ●

QUESTION 84. ARTICLE 2. Whether the soul understands corporeal things through its essence?

● ● ●

I answer that, The ancient philosophers held that the soul knows bodies through its essence. For it was universally admitted that *like is known by like*. But they thought that the form of the thing known is in the knower in the same way as in the thing known. The Platonists however were of a contrary opinion. For Plato, having observed that the intellectual soul has an immaterial nature, and an immaterial mode of knowing, held that the forms of the things known subsist immaterially. But the earlier natural philosophers, observing that the things known are corporeal and material, held that they must exist materially even in the soul that knows them. And therefore, in order to ascribe to the soul a knowledge of all things, they held that it has the same nature in common with all. And because the nature of an effect is determined by its principles, they ascribed to the soul the nature of a principle. Hence it is that those who thought fire to be the principle of all, held that the soul had the nature of fire, and in like manner as to air and water. Lastly, Empedocles, who held the existence of four material elements and two principles of movement, said that the soul was composed of these. Consequently, since they held that things existed in the soul materially, they maintained that all the soul's knowledge is material, thus failing to distinguish intellect from sense.

But this opinion will not hold. First, because in the material principle of which they were speaking, effects do not exist save in potentiality. But a thing is not known according as it is in potentiality, but only according as it is in act, as is shown in *Metaph*. ix., therefore neither is a power known except through its act. It was therefore insufficient to ascribe to the soul the nature of the principles of things in order to guarantee to the soul a knowledge of all things; it was further necessary to admit in the soul the natures and forms of each individual effect, for instance, of bone, flesh, and the like. Thus does Aristotle argue against Empedocles. Secondly, because if it were necessary for the thing known to exist materially in the knower, there would be no reason why things which have a material existence outside the soul should be devoid of knowledge; why, for instance, if by fire the soul knows fire, that fire also which is outside the soul should not have knowledge of fire.

We must conclude, therefore, that the material things known must needs exist in the knower, not materially, but rather immaterially. The reason for this is that the act of knowledge extends to things outside the knower; for we know even the things that are outside us. Now by matter the form of a thing is determined to some one thing. Therefore it is clear that knowledge is in inverse ratio to materiality. Consequently, things that are not receptive of forms, save materially, have no power of knowledge whatever—such as plants, as the Philosopher says. But the more immaterially a being receives the form of the thing known, the more perfect is its knowledge. Therefore the intellect, which abstracts the species not only from matter, but also from the individuating conditions of matter, knows more perfectly than the senses, which receive the form of the thing known, without matter indeed, but subject to material conditions. Moreover, among the senses themselves, sight has the most perfect knowledge, because it is the least material, as we have remarked above. So, too, among intellects, the more perfect is the more immaterial.

It is therefore clear from the foregoing, that if there be an intellect which knows all things by its essence, then its essence must needs have all things in itself immaterially, much as the early philosophers held that the essence of the soul must be composed actually of the principles of all material things in order to know all things. Now it is proper to God that His essence comprise all things immaterially, as effects pre-exist virtually in their cause. God alone, therefore, understands all things through His essence; but neither the human soul nor the angels can do so.

QUESTION 84. ARTICLE 6. Whether intellectual knowledge is derived from sensible things?

I answer that, On this point the philosophers held three opinions. For Democritus held that *all knowledge is caused by images issuing from the bodies we think of and entering into our souls,* as Augustine says in his letter to Dioscorus. And Aristotle says that Democritus held that knowledge is caused by a *discharge of images.* And the reason for this opinion was that both Democritus and the other early philosophers did not distinguish between intellect and sense, as Aristotle relates. Consequently, since the sense is immuted by the sensible, they thought that all our knowledge is caused merely by an immutation from sensible things. This immutation Democritus held to be caused by a discharge of images.

Plato, on the other hand, held that the intellect differs from sense, and that it is an immaterial power not making use of a corporeal organ for its action. And since the incorporeal cannot be affected by the corporeal, he held that intellectual knowledge is not brought about by sensible things immuting the intellect, but by the participation in separate intelligible forms by the intellect, as we have said above. Moreover he held that sense is a power operating through itself. Consequently not even the sense itself, since it is a spiritual power, affected by sensible things; but the sensible organs are affected by the sensible, with the result that the soul is in a way roused to form within itself the species of the sensible. Augustine seems to touch on this opinion where he says that the *body feels not, but the soul through the body, which it makes use of as a kind of messenger, for reproducing within itself what is announced from without.* Thus according to Plato, neither does intellectual knowledge proceed from sensible knowledge, nor does sensible knowledge itself come entirely from sensible things; but these rouse the sensible soul to sensation, and the senses likewise rouse the intellect to the act of understanding.

Aristotle chose a middle course. For with Plato he agreed that intellect and sense are different. But he held that the sense has not its proper operation without the cooperation of the body; so that *to sense is not an act of the soul alone,* but of the *composite.* And he held the same in regard to all the operations of the sensitive part. Since, therefore, it is not incongruous that the sensible things which are outside the soul should produce some effect in the *composite,* Aristotle agreed with Democritus in this, that the operations of the sensitive part are caused by the impression of the sensible on the sense; not indeed by a discharge, as Democritus said, but by some kind of operation. Democritus, it must be remembered, maintained that every action is by way of a discharge of atoms, as we gather from *De Gener.* i. But Aristotle held that the intellect has an operation in which the body does not share. Now nothing corporeal can make an impression on the incorporeal. And therefore, in order to cause the intellectual operation, according to Aristotle, the impression caused by sensible bodies does not suffice, but something more noble is required, *for the agent is more noble than the patient,* as he says. Not, be it observed, in the sense that the intellectual operation is effected in us by the mere impression of some superior beings, as Plato held; but that the higher and more noble agent which he calls the agent intellect, of which we have spoken above, causes the phantasms received from the senses to be actually intelligible, by a process of abstraction.

According to this opinion, then, on the part of the phantasms, intellectual knowledge is caused by the senses. But since the phantasms cannot of themselves immute the possible intellect, but require to be made actually intelligible by the agent intellect, it cannot be said that sensible knowledge is the total and perfect cause of intellectual knowledge, but rather is in a way the matter of the cause.

· · ·

QUESTION 84. ARTICLE 7. Whether the intellect can understand actually through the intelligible species of which it is possessed, without turning to the phantasms?

· · ·

I answer that, In the state of the present life, in which the soul is united to a corruptible body, it is impossible for our intellect to understand anything actually, except by turning to phantasms. And of this there are two indications. First of all because the intellect, being a power that does not make use of a corporeal organ, would in no way be hindered in its act through the lesion of a corporeal organ, if there were not required for its act the act of some power that does make use of a corporeal organ. Now sense, imagination and the other powers belonging to the sensitive part make use of a corporeal organ. Therefore it is clear that for the intellect to understand actually, not only when it acquires new knowledge, but also when it uses knowledge already acquired, there is need for the act of the imagination and of the other powers. For when the act of the imagination is hindered by a lesion of the corporeal organ, for instance, in a case of frenzy, or when the act of the memory is hindered, as in the case of lethargy, we see that a man is hindered from understanding actually even those things of which he had a previous knowledge. Secondly, anyone can experience this of himself, that when he tries to understand something, he forms certain phantasms to serve him by way of examples, in which as it were he examines what he is desirous of understanding. For this reason it is that when we wish to help someone to understand something, we lay examples before him, from which he can form phantasms for the purpose of understanding.

Now the reason for this is that the power of knowledge is proportioned to the thing known. Therefore the proper object of the angelic intellect, which is entirely separate from a body, is an intelligible substance separate from a body. Whereas the proper object of the human intellect, which is united to a body, is the quiddity or nature existing in corporeal matter; and it is through these natures of visible things that it rises to a certain knowledge of things invisible. Now it belongs to such a nature to exist in some individual, and this cannot be apart from corporeal matter; for instance, it belongs to the nature of a stone to be in an individual stone, and to the nature of a horse to be in an individual horse, and so forth. Therefore the nature of a stone or any material thing cannot be known completely and truly, except in as much as it is known as existing in the individual. Now we apprehend the individual through the sense and the imagination. And, therefore, for the intellect to understand actually its proper object, it must of necessity turn to the phantasms in order to perceive the universal nature existing in the individual. But if the proper object of our intellect were a separate form, or if, as the Platonists say, the natures of sensible things subsisted apart from the individual, there would be no need for the intellect to turn to the phantasms whenever it understands.

. . .

QUESTION 85. ARTICLE 1. Whether our intellect understands corporeal and material things by abstraction from phantasms?

. . .

Reply Obj. 1. Abstraction may occur in two ways. First, by way of composition and division, and thus we may understand that one thing does not exist in some other, or that it is separate from it. Secondly, by way of a simple and absolute consideration; and thus we understand one thing without considering another. Thus, for the intellect to abstract one from another things which are not really abstract from one another, does, in the first mode of abstraction, imply falsehood. But, in the second mode of abstraction, for the intellect to abstract things which are not really abstract from one another, does not involve falsehood, as clearly appears in the case of the senses. For if we said that color is not in a colored body, or that it is separate from it, there would be error in what we thought or said. But if we consider color and its properties, without reference to the apple which is colored, or if we express in word what we thus understand, there is no error in such an opinion or assertion; for an apple is not essential to color, and therefore color can be understood independently of the apple. In the same way, the things which belong to the species of a material thing, such as a stone, or a man, or a horse, can be thought without the individual principles which do not belong to the notion of the species. This is what we mean by abstracting the universal from the particular, or the intelligible species from the phantasm; in other words, this is to consider the nature of the species apart from its individual principles represented by the phantasms. If, therefore, the intellect is said to be false when it understands a thing otherwise than as it is, that is so, if the word *otherwise* refers to the thing understood; for the intellect is false when it understands a thing to be otherwise than as it is. Hence, the intellect would be false if it abstracted the species of a stone from its matter in such a way as to think that the species did not exist in matter, as Plato held. But it is not so, if the word *otherwise* be taken as referring to the one who understands. For it is quite true that the mode of understanding, in one who understands, is not the same as the mode of a thing in being; since the thing understood is immaterially in the one who understands, according to the mode of the intellect, and not materially, according to the mode of a material thing.

QUESTION 85. ARTICLE 2. Whether the intelligible species abstracted from phantasms are related to our intellect as that which is understood?

I answer that, Some have asserted that our intellectual powers know only the impressions made on them; as, for example, that sense is cognizant only of the impression made on its own organ. According to this theory, the intellect understands only its own impressions, namely, the intelligible species which it has received.

This is, however, manifestly false for two reasons. First, because the things we understand are also the objects of science. Therefore, if what we understand is merely the intelligible species in the soul, it would follow that every science would be concerned, not with things outside the soul, but only with the intelligible species within the soul; just as, according to the teaching of the Platonists, all the sciences are about Ideas, which they held to be that which is actually understood. Secondly, it is untrue, because it would lead to the opinion of the ancients who maintained that *whatever seems, is true,* and that consequently contradictories are true simultaneously. For if a power knows only its own impressions, it can judge only of them. Now a thing *seems* according to the impression made on the cognitive power. Consequently the cognitive power will always judge of its own impression as such; and so every judgment will be true. For instance, if taste perceived only its own impression, when anyone with a healthy taste perceives that honey is sweet, he would judge truly, and if anyone with a corrupt taste perceives that honey is bitter, this would be equally true; for each would judge according to the impression on his taste. Thus every opinion, in fact, every sort of apprehension, would be equally true.

Therefore it must be said that the intelligible species is related to the intellect as that by which it understands. Which is proved thus. Now action is twofold, as it is said in *Metaph.* ix: one which remains in the agent (for instance, to see and to understand), and another which passes into an external object (for instance, to heat and to cut). Each of these actions proceeds in virtue of some form. And just as the form from which proceeds an act tending to something external is the likeness of the object of the action, as heat in the heater is a likeness of the thing heated, so the form from which proceeds an action remaining in the agent is a likeness of the object. Hence that by which the sight sees is the likeness of the visible thing; and the likeness of the thing understood, that is, the intelligible species, is the form by which the intellect understands. But since the intellect reflects upon itself, by such reflection it understands both its own act of understanding, and the species by which it understands. Thus the intelligible species is secondarily that which is understood; but that which is primarily understood is the thing, of which the species is the likeness.

This also appears from the opinion of the ancient philosophers, who said that *like is known by like*. For they said that the soul knows the earth outside itself by the earth within itself; and so of the rest. If, therefore, we take the species of the earth instead of the earth, in accord with Aristotle who says *that a stone is not in the soul, but only the likeness of the stone,* it follows that by means of its intelligible species the soul knows the things which are outside it.

• • •

QUESTION 86. ARTICLE 1. Whether our intellect knows singulars?

• • •

I answer that, Our intellect cannot know the singular in material things directly and primarily. The reason for this is that the principle of singularity in material things is individual matter; whereas our intellect, as we have said above, understands by abstracting the intelligible species from such matter. Now what is abstracted from individual matter is universal. Hence our intellect knows directly only universals. But indirectly, however, and as it were by a kind of reflexion, it can know the singular, because, as we have said above, even after abstracting the intelligible species, the intellect, in order to understand actually, needs to turn to the phantasms in which it understands the species, as is said in *De Anima* iii. Therefore it understands the universal directly through the intelligible species, and indirectly the singular represented by the phantasm. And thus it forms the proposition, *Socrates is a man.*

• • •

QUESTION 87. ARTICLE 3. Whether our intellect knows its own act?

• • •

I answer that, As was stated above, a thing is known according as it is in act. Now the ultimate perfection of the intellect consists in its own operation. For this is not an act tending to something else in which lies the perfection of the work accomplished, as building is the perfection of the thing built; but it remains in the agent as its perfection and act, as is said in *Metaph.* ix. Therefore the first thing of the intellect that is understood is its own act of understanding. This occurs in different ways with different intellects. For there is an intellect, namely, the divine, which is its own act of understanding, so that in God the understanding of His understanding and the understanding of His essence are one and the same act, because His essence is His act of understanding. But there is another intellect, the angelic, which is not its own act of understanding, as we have said above; and yet the first object of that act is the angelic essence. Therefore, although there is a logical distinction between the act whereby he understands that he understands, and that whereby he understands his essence, yet he understands both by one and the same act; because to understand his own essence is the proper perfection of his essence, and by one and the same act is a thing, together with its perfection, understood. And there is yet another, namely, the human intellect, which is not its own act of understanding, nor is its own essence the first object of its act of understanding, for this object is the nature of a material thing. And therefore that which is first known by the human intellect is an object of this kind, and that which is known secondarily is the act by which that object is known; and through the act the intellect itself is known, whose perfection is the act itself of understanding. For this reason did the Philosopher assert that objects are known before acts, and acts before powers.

From *Truth*

QUESTION 1. ARTICLE 9. Is truth in sense?

. . .

Reply: Truth is both in intellect and in sense, but not in the same way. It is in intellect as a consequence of the act of the intellect and as known by the intellect. Truth follows the operation of the intellect inasmuch as it belongs to the intellect to judge about a thing as it is. And truth is known by the intellect in view of the fact that the intellect reflects upon its own act—not merely as knowing its own act, but as knowing the proportion of its act to the thing. Now, this proportion cannot be known without knowing the nature of the act; and the nature of the act cannot be known without knowing the nature of the active principle, that is, the intellect itself, to whose nature it belongs to be conformed to things. Consequently, it is because the intellect reflects upon itself that it knows truth.

. . .

QUESTION 1. ARTICLE 12. Is falsity in the intellect?

. . .

Reply: The name *intellect* arises from the intellect's ability to know the

From St. Thomas Aquinas, *Truth*, vol. I, translated by R. W. Mulligan, J. V. McGlynn, and R. W. Schmidt. Copyright 1954 by Henry Regnery Company. Reprinted by permission of the publisher.

most profound elements of a thing; for to understand (*intelligere*) means to read what is inside a thing (*intus legere*). Sense and imagination know only external accidents, but the intellect alone penetrates to the interior, and to the essence of a thing. But even beyond this, the intellect, having perceived essences, operates in different ways by reasoning and inquiring. Hence, *intellect* can be taken in two senses.

First, it can be taken merely according to its relation to that from which it first received its name. We are said to understand, properly speaking, when we apprehend the quiddity of things or when we understand those truths that are immediately known by the intellect, once it knows the quiddities of things. For example, first principles are immediately known when we know their terms, and for this reason intellect or understanding is called "a habit of principles." The proper object of the intellect, however, is the quiddity of a thing. Hence, just as the sensing of proper sensibles is always true, so the intellect is always true in knowing *what a thing is,* as is said in *The Soul.* By accident, however, falsity can occur in this knowing of quiddities, if the intellect falsely joins and separates. This happens in two ways: when it attributes the definition of one thing to another, as would happen were it to conceive that "mortal rational animal" were the definition of an ass; or when it joins together parts of definitions that cannot be joined, as would happen were it to conceive that "irrational, immortal animal" were the definition of an ass. For it is false to say that some irrational animal is immortal. So it is clear that a definition cannot be false except to the extent that it implies a false affirmation. (This twofold mode of falsity is touched upon in the *Metaphysics.*) Similarly, the intellect is not deceived in any way with respect to first principles. It is plain, then, that if intellect is taken in the first sense—according to that action from which it receives the name *intellect*—falsity is not in the intellect.

Intellect can also be taken in a second sense—in general, that is, as extending to all its operations, including opinion and reasoning. In that case, there is falsity in the intellect. But it never occurs if a reduction to first principles is made correctly.

QUESTION 22. ARTICLE 4. In rational beings is will a power distinct from sense appetite?

Reply: The will is a power distinct from sense appetite. It should be noted in this connection that rational appetite is distinguished from that of sense in just the same way as sensitive appetite is distinguished from that of nature—because of a more perfect way of tending. The closer a nature is to God, the more pronounced is the likeness of the divine excellence which is found in it. Now it belongs to the divine excellence to move and incline and direct all things while not being moved, inclined, or directed by any other. Hence the nearer a nature is to God, the less it is inclined by another and the more it is capable of inclining itself.

An insensible nature, therefore, being by reason of its materiality the farthest removed from God, is inclined to an end, to be sure, but has within it nothing which inclines, but only a principle of inclination, as was explained above.

A sensitive nature, however, being closer to God, has within itself something which inclines, i.e., the apprehended object of appetite. Yet this inclination is not within the control of the animal which is inclined but is determined by something else. An animal is not able at the sight of something attractive not to crave it, because animals do not themselves have the mastery over their own inclination. Hence "they do not act but are rather acted upon," as Damascene says. This is because the sensuous appetitive power has a bodily organ and so is nearly in the condition of matter and of corporeal things so as rather to be moved than to move.

But a rational nature, being closest to God, not merely, like inanimate things, has an inclination to something, and, like a sentient nature, a mover of this inclination determined as it were extrinsically, but further so has its inclination within its own power that it does not necessarily incline to anything appetible which is apprehended, but can incline or not incline. And so its inclination is not determined for it by anything else but by itself. This belongs to it inasmuch as it does not use a bodily organ; and so, getting farther away from the nature of what is moved, it approaches that of what moves and acts. It can come about that something determines for itself its inclination to an end only if it knows the end and the bearing of the end upon the means to it. But this belongs to reason alone. Thus such an appetite, which is not determined of necessity by something else, follows the apprehension of reason. Hence, rational appetite, called will, is a power distinct from sense appetite.

.   .   .

QUESTION 22. ARTICLE 5. Does the will will anything necessarily?

.   .   .

Reply: As can be gathered from the words of Augustine, necessity is of two kinds: (1) the necessity of force; and this can by no means apply to the will; and (2) the necessity of natural inclination, as we say that God necessarily lives; and with such necessity the will necessarily wills something.

For an understanding of this it should be noted that among things arranged in an order the first must be included in the second, and in the second must be found not only what belongs to it by its own nature but also what belongs to it according to the nature of the first. Thus it is the lot of man not only to make use of reason, as belongs to him in accordance with his specific difference, *rational;* but also to make use of senses and food, as belongs to him in accordance with his genus, *animal* or *living being.* In like manner we see among the senses that the sense of touch is a sort of foundation for the other senses and that in the organ of each sense there is found not only the distinctive characteristic of the sense whose proper organ it is, but also the characteristics of touch. Thus the eye not only senses white and black as the organ of sight, but also as the organ of touch senses heat and cold and is destroyed by an excess in them.

Now nature and the will stand in such an order that the will itself is a nature, because whatever is found in reality is called a nature. There must accordingly be found in the will not only what is proper to the will but also what is proper to nature. It belongs to any created nature, however, to be ordained by God for good, naturally tending to it. Hence even in the will there is a certain natural appetite for the good corresponding to it. And it has, moreover, the tendency to something according to its own determination and not from necessity. This belongs to it inasmuch as it is the will.

Just as there is an ordination of nature to the will, there is, moreover, a parallel ordination of the things which the will naturally wills to those in regard to which it is determined of itself and not by nature. Thus, just as nature is the foundation of will, similarly the object of natural appetite is the principle and foundation of the other objects of appetite. Now among the objects of appetite the end is the foundation and principle of the means to the end, because the latter, being for the sake of the end, are not desired except by reason of the end. Accordingly what the will necessarily wills, determined to it by a natural inclination, is the last end, happiness, and whatever is included in it: to be, knowledge of truth, and the like. But it is determined to other things, not by a natural inclination, but by so disposing itself without any necessity.

Although the will wills the last end by a certain necessary inclination, it is nevertheless in no way to be granted that it is forced to will it. For force is nothing else but the infliction of some violence. According to the Philosopher that is violent "whose principle is outside it with the being which suffers the violence contributing nothing." The throwing of a stone upward would be an example, because the stone of itself is not at all inclined to that motion. But seeing that the will is an inclination by the fact of its being an appetite, it cannot happen that the will should will anything without having an inclination to it. Thus it is impossible for the will to will anything by force or violently even though it does will something by a natural inclination. It is therefore evident that the will does not will anything necessarily with the necessity of force, yet it does will something necessarily with the necessity of natural inclination.

QUESTION 22. ARTICLE 6. Does the will necessarily will whatever it wills?

Reply: Something is said to be necessary from the fact that it is unchangeably determined to one thing. Since, therefore, the will stands undetermined in regard to many things, it is not under necessity in regard to everything but only in regard to those things to which it is determined by a natural inclination, as has been said. And because everything mobile is reduced to what is immobile as its principle, and everything undetermined, to what is determined, that to which the will is determined must be the principle of tending to the things to which it is not determined; and this is the last end, as has been said. Now there is found to be indetermination of the will in regard to three things: its object, its act, and its ordination to its end.

In regard to its object the will is undetermined as to the means to the end, not as to the last end itself, as has been said. This is so because there are many ways of reaching the last end, and for different people different ways prove suitable. The appetite of the will could not, then, be determined to the means to the end as is the appetite in natural things, which have definite and fixed ways of reaching a definite and fixed end. And so it is evident that natural things not only desire the end necessarily, but also desire the means in the same way, so that there are among the means none to which natural things can either tend or not. The will, however, necessarily desires the last end in such a way that it is unable not to desire it, but it does not necessarily desire any of the means. In their regard, then, it is within the power of the will to desire this or that.

In the second place the will is undetermined in regard to its act, because even concerning a determined object it can perform its act or not perform it when it wishes. It can pass or not pass into the act of willing with regard to anything at all. This is not true of natural things, for something heavy always actually goes down unless something else prevents it. This is the case because inanimate things do not move themselves but are moved by other things. There is in them, then, no ability to be moved or not to be moved. But animate things are their own source of movement. Hence it is that the will can will or not.

A third indetermination of the will is found in regard to its ordination to its end inasmuch as the will can desire what is in truth directed to its appointed end or what is so only in appearance. This indetermination comes from two sources: from the indetermination in regard to its object in the case of the means, and again from the indetermination of our apprehension, which can be correct or not. From a given true principle a false conclusion does not follow unless it is because of some falsity in the reasoning through a false subsumption or the false relating of the principle to the conclusion. In the same way from a correct appetite for the last end the inordinate desire for something could not follow unless reason were to take as referable to the end something which is not so referable. Thus a person who naturally desires happiness with a correct appetite would never be led to desire fornication except in so far as he apprehends it as a good for man, seeing that it is something pleasurable, and as referable to happiness as a sort of copy of it. From this there follows the indetermination of the will by which it can desire good or evil.

Since the will is said to be free inasmuch as it is not necessitated, the freedom of the will can be viewed in three respects: (1) as regards its act, inasmuch as it can will or not will; (2) as regards its object, inasmuch as it can will this or that, even if one is the opposite of the other; and (3) as regards its ordination to the end, inasmuch as it can will good or evil.

In regard to the first of these three there is freedom in the will in any state of nature with reference to any object, for the act of any will is in its power as regards any object. The second of these is had with reference to some objects, the means and not the end itself. This too holds for any state of nature. The third is not with reference to all objects but only certain ones, the means to the end, and not with reference to any state of nature but only that in which nature can fail. Where there is no failure in apprehending and comparing, there can be no willing of evil even when there is question of means, as is clear among the blessed. For this reason it is said that to will evil is not freedom or any part of it, though it is a sign of freedom.

QUESTION 22. ARTICLE 11. Is the will a higher power than the intellect, or is the opposite true?

Reply: A thing can be said to be more eminent than another either simply or in a certain respect. For something to be shown to be simply better than another the comparison must be made on the basis of what is essential to them and not on that of accidentals. In the latter case one thing would be shown to stand out over another merely in a certain respect. Thus if a man were to be compared to a lion on the basis of essential differences, he would be found to be simply nobler inasmuch as the man is a rational animal, the lion irrational. But if a lion is compared to a man on the basis of physical strength, he surpasses the man. But this is to be nobler only in a certain respect. To see, then, which of these two powers, the will or the intellect, is better without qualification, we must consider the matter from their essential differences.

The perfection and dignity of the intellect consists in this, that the species of the thing which is understood is in the intellect itself, since in this way it actually understands, and from this its whole dignity is seen. The nobility of the will and of its act, however, consists in this, that the soul is directed to some noble thing in the very existence which that thing has in itself. Now it is more perfect, simply and absolutely speaking, to have within oneself the nobility of another thing than to be related to a noble thing outside oneself. Hence, if the will and the intellect are considered absolutely, and not with reference to this or that particular thing, they have this order, that the intellect is simply more excellent than the will.

But it may happen that to be related in some way to some noble thing is more excellent than to have its nobility within oneself. This is the case, for instance, when the nobility of that thing is possessed in a way much inferior to that in which the thing has it within itself. But if the nobility of one thing is in another just as nobly or more nobly than it is in the thing to which it belongs, then without doubt that which has the nobility of that thing within itself is nobler than that which is related in any way whatsoever to that noble thing. Now the intellect takes on the forms of things superior to the soul in a way inferior to that which they have in the things themselves; for the intellect receives things after its own fashion, as is said in *The Causes*. And for the same reason the forms of things inferior to the soul, such as corporeal things, are more noble in the soul than in the things themselves.

The intellect can accordingly be compared to the will in three ways: (1) Absolutely and in general, without any reference to this or that particular thing. In this way the intellect is more excellent than the will, just as it is more perfect to possess what there is of dignity in a thing than merely to be related to its nobility. (2) With regard to material and sensible things. In this way again the intellect is simply nobler than the will. For example, to know a stone intellectually is nobler than to will it, because the form of the stone is in the intellect, inasmuch as it is known by the intellect, in a nobler way than it is in itself as desired by the will. (3) With reference to divine things, which are superior to the soul. In this way to will is more excellent than to understand, as to will God or to love Him is more excellent than to know Him. This is because the divine goodness itself is more perfectly in God Himself as He is desired by the will than the participated goodness is in us as known by the intellect.

QUESTION 22. ARTICLE 12. Does the will move the intellect and the other powers of the soul?

Reply: In a way the intellect moves the will, and in a way the will moves the intellect and the other powers. For the clarification of this it should be noted that both an end and an efficient cause are said to move, but in different ways. Two things are to be taken into account in any action, the agent and the reason for acting. In heating, the agent is fire and the reason for acting is heat. Similarly in moving, the end is said to move as the reason for moving, but the efficient cause, as the one producing the movement, that is, the one which brings the subject of the motion from potency to act.

The reason for acting is the form of the agent by which it acts. It must accordingly be in the agent for it to act. It is not there, however, according to its perfect act of being; for when that is had the motion comes to rest. But it is in the agent by way of an intention, for the end is prior in intention but posterior in being. Thus the end pre-exists in the mover in a proper sense intellectually (for it belongs to intellect to receive something by way of an intention) and not according to its real existence. Hence the intellect moves the will in the way in which an end is said to move—by conceiving beforehand the reason for acting and proposing it to the will.

To move in the manner of an efficient cause, however, belongs to the will and not to the intellect; for the will is referred to things as they are in themselves, whereas the intellect is referred to them as existing spiritually in the soul. Now to act and to move pertain to things according to their own act of being by which they subsist in themselves, not according as they exist in the soul in the manner of an intention. It is not heat in the soul which heats, but that which is in fire. Thus the will is referred to things as subject to motion, but not the intellect. Furthermore the act of the will is an inclination to something, but not that of the intellect. But an inclination is the disposition of something that moves other things as an efficient cause moves. It is accordingly evident that the will has the function of moving in the manner of an agent cause; not, however, the intellect.

The higher powers of the soul, because immaterial, are capable of reflecting upon themselves. Both the will and the intellect, therefore, reflect upon themselves, upon each other, upon the essence of the soul, and upon all its powers. The intellect understands itself and the will and the essence of the soul and all the soul's powers. Similarly the will wills that it will, that the intellect understand, that the soul be, and so of the other powers. Now when one power is brought to bear upon another, it is referred to that other according to what is proper to itself. When the intellect understands that the will is willing, it receives within itself the intelligible character of willing. When the will is brought to bear upon the other powers of the soul, it is directed to them as things to which motion and operation belong, and it inclines each to its own operation. Thus the will moves in the manner of an efficient cause not only external things but also the very powers of the soul.

· · ·

QUESTION 24. ARTICLE 1. Is man endowed with free choice?

· · ·

Reply: Without any doubt it must be affirmed that man is endowed with free choice. The faith obliges us to this, since without free choice there cannot be merit and demerit, or just punishment and reward. Clear indications, from which it appears that man freely chooses one thing and refuses another, also lead us to this. Evident reasoning also forces us to this conclusion. Tracing out by its means the origin of free choice for the purposes of our investigation, we shall proceed as follows.

Among things which are moved or which act in any way, this difference is found. Some have within themselves the principle of their motion or operation; and some have it outside themselves, as is the case with those which are moved violently, "in which the principle is outside and the being subjected to the violence contributes nothing," as the Philosopher teaches. We cannot hold free choice to be in the latter inasmuch as they are not the cause of their own motion, whereas a free being is "that which is for its own sake," as the Philosopher teaches.

Among the things whose principle of motion is within themselves some are such as to move themselves, as animals, but there are some which do not move themselves even though they do have within themselves some principle of their motion, as heavy and light things. These do not move themselves because they cannot be distinguished into two parts, of which one does the moving and the other is moved. This double principle is verified in animals. Their motion is consequent upon a principle within them, their form. Because they have this from the being which generated them, they are said to be moved essentially by their genitor and accidentally by that which removes an obstacle, according to the Philosopher. These are moved by means of themselves but not by themselves. Hence free choice is not found in these either, because they are not their own cause of acting and moving but are set to acting or moving by something which they have received from another.

Among those beings which are moved by themselves, the motions of some come from a rational judgment; those of others, from a natural judgment. Men act and are moved by a rational judgment, for they deliberate about what is to be done. But all brutes act and are moved by a natural judgment. This is evident from the fact that all brutes of the same species work in the same way, as all swallows build their nests alike. It is also evident from the fact that they have judgment in regard to some definite action, but not in regard to all. Thus bees have skill at making nothing but honeycombs; and the same is true of other animals.

It is accordingly apparent to anyone who considers the matter aright that judgment about what is to be done is attributed to brute animals in the same way as motion and action are attributed to inanimate natural bodies. Just as heavy and light bodies do not move themselves so as to be by that fact the cause of their own motion, so too brutes do not judge about their own judgment but follow the judgment implanted in them by God. Thus they are not the cause of their own decision nor do they have freedom of choice. But man, judging about his course of action by the power of reason, can also judge about his own decision inasmuch as he knows the meaning of an end and of a means to an end, and the relationship of the one with reference to the other. Thus he is his own cause not only in moving but also in judging. He is therefore endowed with free choice—that is to say, with a free judgment about acting or not acting.

QUESTION 22. ARTICLE 15. Is choice an act of will?

Reply: Choice contains something of the will and something of reason. But the Philosopher seems to leave in doubt whether it is properly an act of the will or of reason, when he says that choice is an act either of the intellective appetite (that is, of appetite as subordinated to the intellect) or of the appetitive intellect (that is, of the intellect in subordination to appetite). The first, that it is an act of the will in subordination to reason, is the truer.

That it is directly an act of the will is clear from two considerations: (1) From the formality of its object. The proper object of choice is the means to an end, and this belongs to the formality of good, which is the object of the will. For both the end, such as the honorable or the pleasurable, and the means, namely, the useful, are called good. (2) From the formality of the act itself. Choice is the final acceptance of something to be carried out. This is not the business of reason but of will; for, however much reason puts one ahead of the other, there is not yet the acceptance of one in preference to the other as something to be done until the will inclines to the one rather than to the other. The will does not of necessity follow reason. Choice is nevertheless not an act of the will taken absolutely but in its relation to reason, because there appears in choice what is proper to reason: the comparing of one with the other or the putting of one before the other. This is, of course, found in the act of the will from the influence of reason: reason proposes something to the will, not as useful simply, but as the more useful to an end.

It is accordingly clear that the act of the will is to will, to choose, and to intend. It is to will in so far as reason proposes to the will something good absolutely, whether it is something to be chosen for itself, as an end, or because of something else, as a means. In either case we are said to will it. In so far as reason proposes to the will a good as the more useful to an end, the act is to choose. It is to intend in so far as reason proposes to the will a good as an end to be attained through a means.

QUESTIONS FOR STUDY AND DISCUSSION

1. What is Aquinas' reasoning behind his position that the soul is substantially united to matter in man?
2. What does Aquinas mean when he says that understanding does not take place through a bodily organ? How does he establish his point?
3. Show the various ways in which man's soul is different from the vital principle of either the brute or the plant.
4. Why cannot the intellect exist apart from man and be the same one for all mankind?
5. What powers will remain in the separated soul? Why will the other powers not be present?
6. List four internal senses of man and distinguish their respective activities.
7. Summarize Aquinas' explanation of how sensory and intellectual knowledge come about.
8. Explain Aquinas' understanding of freedom.
9. Discuss the reciprocal relationship between the intellect and will in man.
10. Summarize the principal argument Aquinas employs to prove that the human soul is immortal.

TOPICS FOR DISCUSSION AND TERM PAPERS

A.

1. How do Plato and Aristotle differ in their understanding of "the body"?
2. How do Plato and Aquinas differ in their understanding of the nature of the union between body and soul?
3. Discuss the following statement, defending, rejecting, or clarifying it: "Neither Plato, Aristotle, nor Aquinas established personal immortality for man, for each spoke only of the soul (or some aspect of it) as being immortal."
4. Discuss the following statement, defending, rejecting, or clarifying it: "Plato, a pagan, seems to present man in a more spiritual light than Aquinas, a Christian and a saint."
5. In what major areas in the philosophy of man do Plato, Aristotle, and Aquinas agree? Disagree? Explain.
6. List two problems in which Aquinas, while remaining true to Aristotle, nonetheless develops and extends Aristotle's viewpoints by adding new insights.
7. What are the greatest strengths and weaknesses in:

    a) the Platonic philosophy of man
    b) the Aristotelian philosophy of man
    c) the Thomistic philosophy of man

B.

1. What are the principal causes which give rise to the differing philosophies of man represented in this volume?
2. What are the major points of agreement in the philosophy of man between the classical and Christian tradition and:

    a) Marxism
    b) Naturalism
    c) Positivism
    d) Existentialism

3. What aspects or problems in a philosophy of man are highlighted in one of the five traditions, but not stressed in the other four traditions? What accounts for this?
4. Which philosophy of man do you consider most relevant and meaningful for the present era? Give reasons for affirming one position and rejecting others.
5. Which two philosophies of man appear closer to each other and hence more capable of reconciliation than the others?
6. What are the major points in any two philosophies of man which are categorically opposed and irreconcilable?
7. What areas in a philosophy of man require further development in the light of man's increasing understanding of himself? Suggest some outline for this possible development.

RECOMMENDED READINGS

Primary Sources

Aristotle. *De Anima.* Trans. and with Introd. and notes by R. D. Hicks. Cambridge, Eng.: Cambridge University Press, 1907. A standard commentary with a particularly useful introduction.

————. *De Anima.* Ed. by W. D. Ross. Oxford: Clarendon Press, 1961. A definitive text. The Introduction in English is a good statement of Aristotle's philosophy of the soul.

Plato. *Phaedo.* Translated by F. J. Church. New York: Liberal Arts Press, 1951.

————. *Phaedo.* Trans. by R. Hackforth. Cambridge, Eng.: Cambridge University Press, 1955. For a good evaluation of the arguments for immortality, see pp. 11–30.

————. *Phaedo.* Trans. by R. S. Bluck. New York: Liberal Arts Press, 1959. The introduction and commentary are very useful to beginning students, especially the discussion on immortality, pp. 18–33.

St. Thomas Aquinas. *On Spiritual Creatures (Quaestiones Disputatae de Spiritualibus Creaturis).* Trans. and with Introd. by M. C. Fitzpatrick, in collaboration with J. J. Wellmuth. Milwaukee: Marquette University Press, 1949.

————. *The Soul (Quaestiones Disputatae de Anima).* Trans. by J. P. Rowan. St. Louis: B. Herder Book Co., 1959.

————. *Summa Theologica,* Part I, in *Basic Writings of St. Thomas Aquinas.* Ed., annot., and with Introd. by Anton C. Pegis. New York: Random House, 1945. Vol. I. See Qq. 77–79, 80, 84–87.

————. *Truth (Quaestiones Disputatae de Veritate).* 3 vols. Chicago: Henry Regnery Co., 1954. Vol. I (Qq. 1–9), trans. by R. W. Mulligan; vol. II (Qq. 10–20), trans. by J. V. McGlynn; vol. III (Qq. 21–29), trans. by R. W. Schmidt.

Commentaries

Copleston, Frederick C. *Aquinas.* Baltimore: Penguin Books, 1955. See especially pp. 151–234 for an account of Aquinas' philosophy of man. The book is a competent introduction to the philosophy of Aquinas, specifically directed to the beginning student.

————. *A History of Philosophy.* 2 vols. Westminster, Md.: The Newman Press, 1957, 1959. Vol. I, *Greece and Rome.* See chapters on Plato (especially the discussion of Plato's theory of ideas) and Aristotle. Vol. II, *Augustine to Scotus.* See the section on Aquinas for a clear and concise presentation of his psychology.

Crombie, I. M. *An Examination of Plato's Doctrines.* New York: Humanities Press, 1962. Vol. I. Chapter 7 is an excellent presentation of Plato's philosophy of mind.

Demos, Raphael, ed. *The Philosophy of Plato.* New York: Charles Scribner's Sons, 1939. A standard and very helpful introduction to the philosophy of Plato. See Ch. 4, pp. 78–98, for an account of the Platonic theory on the soul.

Gilson, Etienne. *The Christian Philosophy of St. Thomas Aquinas.* Trans. by

L. K. Shook. New York: Random House, 1956. An advanced and definitive account with very useful chapters for the beginning student. Chapters 4, 5, and 6 contain material on life and the soul, as well as other topics relevant to Aquinas' account of the philosophy of man.

———. *Elements of Christian Philosophy.* New York: Doubleday & Co., 1960. Good account of St. Thomas' philosophy of man. See especially Chs. 9–12, pp. 203–80.

Grube, G. M. A. *Plato's Thought.* Boston: Beacon Press, 1958. Chapter 4 is a good presentation of Plato's theory of the soul.

Jaeger, Werner. *Aristotle: Fundamentals of the History of His Development.* Trans. by R. Robinson. Oxford: Oxford University Press, 1934. An important advanced study. Read especially pp. 40–53 on the Aristotelian theory of the soul.

Maritain, Jacques. *St. Thomas Aquinas.* Trans. and rev. by J. W. Evans and P. O'Reilly. New York: Meridian Books, 1958. This account, by one of the leading Thomists today, is an excellent presentation of the psychology of Aquinas for beginning students.

Owens, Joseph. *A History of Ancient Western Philosophy.* New York: Appleton-Century-Crofts, 1959. The section on Greek philosophy, especially that of Plato, is a very good presentation in clear language of the basic theory of ideas that is central to the argument of the *Phaedo.* Read particularly pp. 234–49.

Ross, W. D. *Aristotle.* New York: Meridian Books, 1959. See Ch. 5 on Aristotle's psychological notions.

PART TWO

Introduction

Historical Background

Man: The Hegelian View

Man: The Marxist View

Hegel and the Marxists

Readings

HEGEL: *Knowledge and Consciousness*
Social Self-Consciousness
The Transcendence of the Individual
Man's Freedom Through History

MARX: *Materialism Versus Idealism: Man as a Natural Being*
The Material Determination of Consciousness (with ENGELS)
Man as Alienated
Man's Social Reality

ENGELS: *The Origin of Man*
Determinism in History

SCHAFF: *Modern Marxism and the Individual*

DIALECTICAL THOUGHT:

Hegel
Marx
Engels
Schaff

EDITED BY

Richard T. De George

THE UNIVERSITY OF KANSAS

DIALECTICAL
THOUGHT:
Hegel
Marx
Engels
Schaff

Introduction

Historical Background

Hegelianism and Marxism are philosophies of the nineteenth century, yet their impact on the twentieth century has been and remains considerable. Communism is a political reality of today's world, carrying with it a world view, a theory of society, and a view of man based on the writings of Karl Marx (1818–83) and his close friend and collaborator, Friedrich Engels (1820–95). Though Marx's views were modified to some extent by Lenin, and continue to be modified today, his vision of man and of man's ideal future development still exerts a strong influence on Marxist thought both within and outside of the Soviet Union. Marx's writings are widely read and taught throughout the world, and knowledge of his thought is important for anyone who wishes to understand his own world and his times.

The same can be said of the philosophy of Georg Wilhelm Friedrich Hegel (1770–1831), though his impact is perhaps less obvious. The giant of nineteenth-century philosophy, Hegel influenced not only Marx but Kierkegaard, Nietzsche, the British idealists of the last half of the nineteenth and the first decades of the twentieth centuries, and the present-day existentialists. The British philosopher T. H. Green (1836–82) adapted one version of Hegelianism in defense of individual liberty, the Italian philosopher Giovanni Gentile (1875–1944) adapted another version in defense of Italian Fascism, and both positions can with some justice claim Hegel's rich and varied writings as their source.

Hegel considered his philosophy to be the culmination of Western thought. He attempted to embrace all previous thinkers within his system, and he admitted his debt to them all—from Plato and Aristotle to his immediate predecessors, Immanuel Kant (1724–1804), Johann Gottlieb Fichte (1762–1814), and Friedrich Wilhelm Joseph von Schelling (1775–1854). He was the heir of the French Enlightenment, with its emphasis on reason, and he looked upon the French Revolution as an instance of reason realizing itself in reality.

For Hegel all reality forms a unity, and the whole of reality is ultimately rational. He saw development as an integral part of the world that appears to us in all its variety and complexity. But behind the diversity there is a unity that is manifested through the diversity; the unity is that of reason, which guides the development of the whole. In one sense everything that is, is real; in another, that which embodies reason more fully is more real than that which embodies it less clearly or fully. In this latter sense reason is the touchstone of reality. Hegel summed up his position in the Preface to his *Philosophy of Right:* "The real is rational; and the rational is real."

Hegel's unified view of reality attempts to undercut the historical dichotomy in philosophy between such rationalists as Descartes, Spinoza, and Leibniz on the one hand and such empiricists as Locke, Berkeley, and Hume on the other.

The rationalists emphasized reason and tried to deduce the nature and structure of the world from the nature and structure of their ideas. With respect to man, Descartes believed man to be composed of two substances, a body that is material and extended in space and a mind that is immaterial and so nonspatial. But he was never able to solve the problem of how an immaterial mind is able to act on or be acted upon by a material body. Because he held there are two irreducible realms, the material and the immaterial, he is known as a dualist.

The empiricists emphasized experience instead of reason and sought to hold as true only what could be tested by or found in experience. Hume carried the position of John Locke (1632–1704) to its logical conclusion and ended by denying there was anything that could be called a "self," because he could never find anything in his perceptions that corresponded to it.

Before Hegel, Kant had also tried to overcome the opposition of these conflicting trends. But his solution was far from satisfactory because his thought admitted basic unreconciled oppositions. The first was between the world as it appeared through the senses (which he called phenomenon or world of appearance), and the world as it was independent of man's perceiving it (called by him the real but unknowable thing in itself or noumenon). The second opposition was between man's theoretical activity and his practical or moral activity. For Kant, man as knowing lived in the phenomenal world of appearance, but man as moral agent lived in the noumenal world of the thing in itself. How man straddled both worlds, how his actions could be determined in the realm of sensible experience and yet somehow free in the moral realm remained unresolved in the Kantian system.

Hegel's solution to these dualisms is a monism, or a view in which there is only one basic "stuff" out of which all of reality is made. In Hegel's view there are not two realms, the material and the nonmaterial; rather all of reality is ultimately nonmaterial or spiritual in that all of reality is dependent on and is a manifestation of spirit or mind. This type of monism is called "idealism." Thus in Hegel's "idealistic" view, the essence of man is to be found in his spiritual aspects, and Hegel's study of man focuses primarily on his mind or consciousness.

Hegel's concern for spiritual reality and his monistic view of the world can be seen even in his early essays, which have been collected and translated under the title *Early Theological Writings*. The first important statement of his position, however, is the *Phenomenology of Mind* (1807), a masterly treatise in which he leads his reader from sensual perception to knowledge of reality considered in its totality, which he called the Absolute. In a later work, *Encyclopaedia of the Philosophical Sciences in Outline* (1817), he presented a systematic conspectus of his system in its three main divisions: logic, the philosophy of nature, and the philosophy of mind.

Under logic, Hegel traced the development of concepts. He started with the concept of *being,* which he claimed has no specific content and so is the "emptiest" of concepts. He related this concept to its opposite, *nothing,* and then he related both of them to the concept of *becoming,* which is the passing from nothing to being. The technique employed in passing from one concept to its opposite and from this pair to a third concept is called "dialectics," or the dialectical method. In Hegel's view the third or resulting concept annuls what is negative in each member of the preceding pair of concepts, preserves what is positive in them, and raises or elevates their positive content to a "higher" synthesis. This third concept in its turn is treated as a concept that calls forth its negation or opposite, and so on. Hegel used this method to trace the development of concepts from one to another until he reached the concept of the Absolute, which, since it refers to the totality of reality, is for Hegel the most full or "concrete" concept.

All of reality can thus be conceptualized. But concepts and their logical interrelations do not exhaust reality. Since there are more than concepts in reality, we are dialectically led to this "something more," or to nature. The philosophy of nature forms the second part of Hegel's system. Man is a part of nature, and it is through him that the union or synthesis of logic and nature is achieved. With the appearance of man we find consciousness or spirit in nature. As mankind progresses or develops through the centuries, it forms societies and produces laws, art, culture, religion, and finally philosophy—all of which are products of man's consciousness or, for Hegel, the embodiment or objectification of consciousness or spirit itself.

The third portion of Hegel's system—the synthesis of the two preceding portions—is the philosophy of mind. It contains Hegel's description of the development of spirit in the world and culminates with the whole, or the Absolute, becoming conscious of itself through the philosophy of Hegel.

Hegel's other major works, such as his *Science of Logic* (1812–16), *Philosophy of Right* (1821), and the posthumous *Lectures on the Philosophy of History* (based on his own and his students' notes), develop in detail various portions of his system. We shall return again to his philosophy of history which consists of tracing the chronological development of spirit in the world.

Hegel's followers were numerous and they initially divided into two camps, the Left (also called the Young Hegelians) and the Right Hegelians. In general, the Left Hegelians were unorthodox in religion and radical in politics; in philosophy they emphasized Hegel's method, insisting on the necessity of change, movement, and progress so that reason might develop more and more fully in reality. The Right Hegelians by contrast were orthodox in religion and conservative in politics; they emphasized the content of Hegel's philosophy, insisting on the correctness of his views and the rationality of the status quo.

The transformation of Hegelianism that led to Marx's philosophy started with the Left Hegelian attacks on orthodox religion. David Friedrich Strauss (1808–74), one of the most prominent Left Hegelians, attacked the Gospel stories as myths in his *Life of Jesus* (1835). Another, Bruno Bauer (1809–82), who was a teacher of Marx, denied even the symbolic truth of the Gospels and challenged the historicity of Christ. The attacks that they and others made on orthodox religion paved the way for Marx's attacks on capitalist society.

Most influential of all both on Marx and on Engels was Ludwig Feuerbach (1804–72). Though initially a Left Hegelian, Feuerbach broke with idealism and in its place defended a type of naive materialism. He denied the existence of spirit as such and claimed that matter alone existed. For Feuerbach, man is what he eats. Man's consciousness (which Feuerbach never fully reconciled with his materialism) distinguishes him from other animals since through his consciousness man is aware of himself as part of a species. Feuerbach thus called man a "species-being" and he referred to "species-man," terms Marx adopted in his early essays. In *The Essence of Christianity* (1841) Feuerbach showed how men, because of their psychological make-up, form an idea of God. They then make this idea into an object or an entity separate from and, in Feuerbach's view, alien to themselves. They endow this God with the attributes of man—knowledge, love, life, power—developed to their highest extent. They thus speak of God as all-knowing, all-loving, eternal, and all-powerful. But since the attributes of God are in fact the attributes of humanity, Feuerbach argued, God is really Man or Humanity. True theology (the study of God) is thus seen as equivalent to anthropology (the study of Man), and true religion becomes humanism, or concern with the betterment of the human condition.

It was through the writings of Feuerbach that Marx, who started his philosophical career as a convinced Hegelian with a doctoral dissertation in the Hegelian tradition, was able to free himself from Hegel's idealism.

Marx's debt to Feuerbach is twofold. First, it was through reading Feuerbach's works that Marx arrived at his own materialistic position. But he did not swallow Feuerbach whole, and in his early works he often criticized Feuerbach's materialism as inadequate insofar as it was unable to account satisfactorily either for knowledge or for history. Marx insisted that reality is basically material and that consciousness is a product of matter and essentially dependent on it. In opposition to Hegel's idealistic monism, which claimed that reality was ultimately dependent on mind or spirit, he defended a materialistic monism in which reality consists essentially of matter. But in order to account for knowledge and matter, Marx thought, materialism must be combined with the dialectical method. In Hegel's hands the method was joined to idealism. In Marx's hands it is joined to materialism. The resulting view has come to be known as dialectical materialism.

Marx's second debt to Feuerbach results from the fact that he adopted Feuerbach's analysis of religion, extending it to society. In religion man forms a concept (God) which he separates or alienates from himself and before which he bows down. This constitutes man's religious alienation. But just as man acts this way in religion, Marx argued, he acts in a similar way in society. Man forms a state and institutions that he separates or alienates from himself and before which he bows down; he makes products from which he becomes divorced and that he lets dominate him. He thus lives in and experiences several types of social as well as religious alienation. Moreover, Marx insisted, it is not sufficient merely to make this analysis. One of Feuerbach's mistakes was that he failed to see that philosophers should not merely reinterpret the world; they should change it. If man's alienation is bad, it will not be removed merely by pointing out its origin. Rather, the causes of alienation must be removed. If the present organization of society leads to the alienation of man, then society must be reorganized.

In four early manuscripts known as *The Economic and Philosophical Manuscripts* (written in 1844 but first published in their entirety in 1932) Marx not only attacked Hegel's general philosophical position and his particular view of man, but he presented his own view of man. In 1845–46 Marx collaborated with Engels on *The German Ideology* (which was also first published in 1932). In this work they were critical of the views of Feuerbach and many of the Left Hegelians, but more important they presented their first detailed statement of the materialist view of history, or historical materialism. The moving force of history, they claimed, is not ideas or individuals, but the masses, who are motivated in their action by the economic conditions of their life—what and how they produce. By 1847, when Marx and Engels collaborated to write the *Communist Manifesto,* the Marxist philosophical framework had been established. The way to change man is by changing society; if the driving forces of history are economic, to change society it is necessary to alter its economic structure by eliminating private property, freeing the proletariat from its chains, and establishing communism. It was thus that Karl Marx was led from philosophy to the study of political economy. His most famous work, *Capital* (1867), is an analysis of the economic laws of capitalism.

Engels saw himself as a follower of Marx. He was a devoted friend, coauthor with Marx of several works, and editor of volumes II and III of Marx's *Capital.* He developed no system of his own but he was one of Marx's most faithful and authoritative expositors and interpreters. His writings are considered by Soviet Marxists with as much respect as the writings of Marx. In *Anti-Dühring* (1878) Engels gave his first systematic presentation of Marxism. His *Ludwig Feuerbach* (1888) reviews the development of Marxism from Hegelianism and treats at length some points of dialectical and historical materialism. It is in his posthumous and incomplete *Dialectics of Nature* that he explicitly extended dialectics to the realms of nature and of science. This work also includes the essay "The Part Played by Labour in the Transition from Ape to Man," in which Engels showed how man, by his work, develops both himself and his society.

With the death of Engels, what can be called the "original corpus" of Marxism was closed. But the works of Marx and Engels, often hurriedly written, were not always clear. The ambiguities in the materials led to diverse interpretations. Some of them emphasized Marx's economic determinism and claimed that since communism would eventually triumph no special action by any group was required to bring it about. Others, such as V. I. Lenin (1870–1924), emphasized Marx's dictum that man must take an active part in changing the world. Still others felt that Marx was only partially right in what he wrote and that some of his views must be revised or corrected; they are known as revisionists.

Because of Lenin's political success in the Russian Revolution of 1917 and the subsequent political success of the Soviet Union, Lenin's interpretation of Marx and Engels has become the dominant interpretation, not only in the Soviet Union but throughout the Soviet sphere of influence. Lenin, moreover, not only interpreted Marx and Engels, he also changed or modified their doctrine to suit conditions in Russia, and he added tenets of his own. In philosophy he developed a theory of knowledge that is known as the "copy-theory" of knowledge, since it claims that knowledge is a "copy" in consciousness of material reality. He insisted that consciousness, which is the highest product of matter, is not reducible to matter. Exactly how this is possible is still a much discussed question in the Soviet Union.

In more recent times interest in Marx's writings on man and in Marxist humanism has come to the fore in both Western and Eastern Europe and in the United States. The Soviet writings in this area have not been significant. But in some of the other countries of Eastern Europe, such philosophers as Georg Lukács, Laszek Kolakowski (neither of whom is considered an "orthodox" Marxist by the Soviets), and Adam Schaff (the leading Polish Marxist) have continued the work of Marx. They have also related Marxism to other views of man, especially to the existentialist view. But the writings of Marx and Engels remain the foundation of Marxist thought.

Man: The Hegelian View

The Spiritual Unity of Man

In Hegel's view the search for the essence of man is the search for his genuine reality. He took into account all men in all their diversity and in all their interrelations. Yet amidst the diversity he looked for the basic and ultimate unity. Though Hegel admitted that man is a creature of nature, a physical, corporeal entity, he believed that body or matter is not something distinct from spirit. Nature is spirit spread out in space; nature is a means of spirit's expression, the abstract idea made other and manifest. There is therefore no necessity for Descartes' dualistic separation of man into mind and body. For man in his true reality is a single, unified, basically spiritual being. The search for man's essence is to be pursued not in the physical sciences, not in physics or anatomy or empirical psychology or anthropology; rather it leads to an examination of man as spirit or mind. As Aristotle had seen, man is a living and sentient being, but above all he is a conscious, rational being. Man's reality is the reality of a being who is not only conscious of the world about him, but conscious of himself as well. In his awareness of all of reality, he is able to unify everything that is and to bring to consciousness the truth of this unity. The proper study of man and of his unity is phenomenology, or the study of consciousness itself. It is thus that Hegel undertook his *Phenomenology of Mind.*

Consciousness and Knowledge

What consciousness is is determined by consciousness itself. There is nothing beyond consciousness which could serve as a higher court of appeal or as a further touchstone of truth or reality. For consciousness alone can say what truth or knowledge or reality is. There can consequently be no question of a Kantian unknown and unknowable thing-in-itself beyond its reach which somehow grounds or constitutes it. What consciousness knows and is, is reality. To speak of knowledge is to speak of consciousness's awareness of what is present to it.

OBJECT OF CONSCIOUSNESS. To be an object is precisely to be present to consciousness, to be something *for* consciousnes. It is with the sensuously perceived object of consciousness that Hegel began his analysis in the *Phenomenology of Mind*. We can take any object as it appears to us, a flash of lightning, for instance, and ask, "What is this object?" An analysis of what is present to our consciousness will lead us to say that it is "this," which is "here" and "now," and that it has a certain intensity, color, length, duration. But the terms "here," "now," "bluish-white," and all others we might use to describe the flash of lightning before us will be universal terms, that is, terms which are applicable to more than one entity. Since the flash of lightning is nothing in addition to all its attributes or qualities and since all of these are universals, the lightning is the overlapping or intersection of all the universals which constitute it. There is nothing that makes it up in addition to its qualities. Moreover, not only is the object made up of universals, but to appear as a flash of lightning it must be "mediated" by consciousness; that is, it is an object only if it appears to consciousness, is distinguished by consciousness from that which it is not, and is apprehended by consciousness as being an instance of what are called "flashes of lightning." It is moreover both one and many at the same time and for the same reasons. To understand how this can be, Hegel tells us, we must rise from the level of perception to the higher level of intellect, on which we can grasp the true world of universals, of which the particular objects are instances.

THE LEVEL OF INTELLECT. This higher level of the intellect is the level of science. Scientists search for and study the general laws of nature. They deal with individual instances only insofar as these conform to laws which govern their appearances. Flashes of lightning or flying sparks, for instance, exemplify the laws of electricity; but they are too short-lived to be either grasped or studied or to be a matter of scientific concern, except as they are instances of and follow the laws of electricity. Without the individual instances of it, "electricity" would be an empty concept; but without the general (universal) concept of electricity, the individual instances would be unintelligible.

Thus the sensuous objects of consciousness (such as lightning and sparks) become intelligible only by going beyond what is given in sensible appearance to the nonsensuous universals that stand behind them. But since these universals are not material, physical objects, they belong to the realm of mind. The objects of consciousness are mental in their ultimate reality.

CONSCIOUSNESS AND SELF-CONSCIOUSNESS. If an object is an object *for* consciousness, it is an object only if it is related to a subject (consciousness) from which it is distinguished. Similarly, consciousness is consciousness only if it has an object. To understand further what consciousness is, however, consciousness must become the object of itself. This focusing of consciousness on itself is what constitutes self-consciousness; here consciousness is both *in* and *for* itself. Paradoxically, however, consciousness can achieve true consciousness of itself as subject or mind only through its relation with another self-consciousness. For only in this way can it learn its limits, its dependence, and its constitutive relations with other consciousnesses.

In his famous section describing the master-slave relation, Hegel showed how two consciousnesses are dependent on each other. In seeing the other, each sees itself. There arises between them a dialectical relation similar to that which we saw operating between concepts. Each consciousness finds out what it is in its struggle with the other. The analogy of master and slave operates on several levels. It can be interpreted on the social level as the actual condition of men in society and the social interaction which leads some men to dominate others; it can be interpreted on the historical level as the way mankind came to consciousness of itself; it can be taken abstractly as a discussion of the interplay of consciousnesses in the quest for their true nature.

Both master and slave find they are mutually dependent, for there can be no master without a slave and no slave without a master. While initially the servant feels only anxiety and fear before the master, he soon becomes conscious of himself as a self through the labor he is forced to perform. His consciousness of self is achieved not directly but through working on external reality and expressing himself in his work or activity. In this sense self-consciousness is achieved indirectly or through the *mediation* of objects, through the tools and products of labor.

THE UNITY OF COLLECTIVE CONSCIOUSNESS. But the insight that men or consciousnesses are mutually dependent is only the first step toward true self-knowledge. Hegel's analysis rises above this to the synthesis that emerges from the dialectical relation of master and slave. This synthesis is achieved when consciousness realizes it is not only related to other consciousnesses, but that it is indeed one with them. The analysis takes place in Hegel's discussion of "unhappy" or "contrite" consciousness, where the conscious individual recognizes the division between itself as changing and temporary and the essential unchanging character of consciousness as such. Here consciousness finally arrives at insight into its real, essential nature, which is not particular but universal. Consciousness is essentially one; it has individual instances, but these are unified in the sameness of essential consciousness of which each of the individuals is a part. This means that man is essentially man, not in isolation from other men, not in his individuality, but only insofar as he is together with them. To view each man as a separate, individual consciousness, cut off from other similarly independent and supposedly self-subsistent consciousnesses, is to fail to understand the reality of man. For what makes a man a man is not his peculiarities and idiosyncrasies, but precisely that which is universal and common to all. The essence of man, which lies in his consciousness or reason, is transindividual, and only by going beyond himself to union with all other men does he come to see what he really is. Hegel thus leads us to see that reason or consciousness is one, that individuals are part of a whole, and that their reality consists not in their individuality but in their being parts together of the spirit, which is reality.

The essence of man is not an individual essence, but a collective essence. Just as the intelligibility and truth of a flash of lightning is found in the universal concept of electricity and the laws describing its action, so the intelligibility and truth of man—his essence—are to be found in the universal concept of man and in the sum total of human beings who together manifest the reality of reason or spirit.

Freedom and History

Reason or spirit manifests itself through men and becomes objectified in the world not only through living consciousnesses but also through the embodiments of consciousness in the institutions of society, in culture, and in civilization. Men in a society are interrelated in many ways, and their relations help make them what they are. Moreover, relations as universals transcend individuals. Thus, to take a contemporary example, the office of President of the United States can be defined in terms of certain relations to the citizens of the United States. The President is a citizen elected by other citizens to serve as the chief executive of the country. But the office of the Presidency transcends any individual President and is filled by successive men. To speak of the power of the Presidency is to speak of real powers wielded by different individuals at different times. The office is one created by men; yet as part of the organization of society it is an embodiment of spirit that goes beyond the society's present members. Similarly the culture of a nation transcends its present members. Works of art from past generations are preserved and admired by later generations. The culture of a nation is thus something in addition to the particular individuals in the society, and society at any given moment is more than the sum of the individuals in it.

To understand, then, what man is, it is necessary to study history—to see what men have done and to see how they have expressed themselves in the past. The discipline of history is the investigation of what happened in the past. But in his investigation the historian must know what to look for. Since man is essentially spirit, Hegel considered the study of world history to be the study of the development of spirit in time. And since the essence of spirit is freedom—or rational self-determination—the study of history is the study of the development of freedom. To study history is to study how man has gradually come to realize that he is free. For the Oriental, there was just one man, the despot, who was free; for the Greeks, some men, the citizens, were free. It is only with Christianity and modern history that *all* men were seen to be free. We might add that the concrete implementation of this insight that all men are free because all are parts of the same spirit is still going on today.

Hegel's view of history, however, like his view of man, is concerned not with the particular individuals but with spirit as such in its trans-individual or universal character. Although individual men act from personal interest and from passion, they produce results which extend beyond their knowledge and intent. Spirit utilizes their actions to achieve its own ends. As a consequence there is a direction in history that transcends any individual person's view, but which is discernible nonetheless.

The freedom of man in Hegel's view consists not of the ability to perform capricious acts. For to act capriciously is to be determined by one's passions or inclinations. Freedom is achieved by the individual only when he acts in accordance with reason, only when he rationally determines his actions. Law and morality, provided they are based on and embody reason, are thus expressions of freedom, not restraints on it. Moreover, just as law and morality embody reason, so the State, composed of interrelated individuals, forms a spiritual individual. As parts of a State, citizens are participating members of a structured, corporate whole, of an organic body. Indeed, only the State, and not its members, can be considered a real individual self, for it alone is a *self-subsistent,* spiritual individual.

Hegel's view of the State is not without its ambiguities. It was used by the Right Hegelians to defend the Prussian State and by Gentile to defend Fascism. But the State for Hegel is not just any existing political body; it is a political body whose laws are based on reason and in which the individual is seen as an end in himself insofar as he is part of the universal spirit. The ideal society, in which all men would be free, would be one where all men desired only what was reasonable and acted accordingly. Hegel's view is that throughout history man has been approaching the ideal society more and more.

Hegel's approach to man is concerned primarily with man's conscious activity and with the development of reason, which is trans-individual, in history. His collectivist approach to man and his philosophy of history have exerted great influence on many later philosophers. Not the least of these was Karl Marx who, despite his scathing criticism of Hegel, openly admitted his great debt to him.

Man: The Marxist View

The Material Unity of Man

If for Hegel mankind developed and grew to consciousness of itself historically, it did so no less for Marx; if the essence of man was trans-individual for Hegel, it was no less so for Marx. Yet Hegel was an idealist, emphasizing spirit, and Marx was a materialist, emphasizing matter. So their resulting views, though in many ways similar, were strikingly different.

For Marx, as for Hegel, human nature is not static, fixed, and determined; it is malleable, changeable, and changing. Consequently the essence of man is not eternal but historical, not a priori but a posteriori; that is, the only way to determine man's nature is to see what he is and has become at any given epoch in history. Marx's basic position is succinctly summed up in his sixth Thesis on Feuerbach: [1] "Feuerbach resolves the essence of religion into the essence of *man*. But the essence of man is no abstraction inherent in each separate individual. In its reality it is the *ensemble* of social relations."

According to Marx and Engels, man is a natural being, a part of nature, like all other entities. The way to approach man, therefore, is not through some abstract concept, nor through any given individual. To arrive at the essence of man we must look at how man acts, we must investigate what he does. For, they said, "as individuals express their life, so they are. What they are, therefore, coincides with their production, both with *what* they produce and with *how* they produce. The nature of individuals thus depends on the material conditions determining their production." [2]

As a being acts, so he is. What distinguishes man from the rest of the animal kingdom is the way he expresses his life: he works, he engages in a variety of activities, he changes his environment, and by his activity he produces his means of subsistence. For this reason Marx and Engels claimed that by his work or labor man has produced himself. Unlike other animals whose activities and way of life vary only slightly from generation to generation and age to age, man's life and activity from the early tribal communities to present industrial society have changed quite radically—thus man has changed quite radically. He continues to change as his activity changes. What remains constant is the fact that he alone of the animal kingdom *does* produce his means of subsistence in the variety of ways that he does.

CONSCIOUSNESS.   Whereas Hegel placed great emphasis on consciousness, Marx and Engels considered this emphasis misplaced. They looked at the whole of man, the conscious, physical being interacting with the rest of nature, living by the food he grows and the animals he kills. Man admittedly has consciousness. But Hegel made two mistakes, they claimed, in emphasizing man's consciousness. First, Hegel failed to realize that consciousness itself needed explanation. Consciousness, like man himself, is a historical phenomenon that has grown and developed slowly through time. It did not precede man and it itself has no eternal essence through which man can be understood. Second, and more important, Marx and Engels insisted that consciousness is derived, not primary as Hegel had claimed. Consciousness depends on matter. Man first had to live, to keep himself alive by his work, before he could think. As his work became more and more complicated, man's capabilities developed according to his needs. Man's consciousness, which was primitive in primitive man, thus developed only slowly as man

---

[1] Marx's eleven "Theses on Feuerbach" were written in 1845. They remained unpublished until 1888 when Engels published them as a supplement to his book *Ludwig Feuerbach*.

[2] Mark and Engels, *The German Ideology,* p. 253 of this volume. What people produce is equivalent to "products" of production; how they produce is equivalent to the "means and modes" of production.

faced more complicated tasks. Similarly speech also grew slowly as the need for communication and cooperation among men increased.

Consciousness and speech, therefore, are not abstractions that appeared full blown; they, like man, developed gradually. In the transition from ape to man one can imagine the slow development of speech and the concomitant slow emergence of consciousness. Thus, Marx and Engels claimed, it is a mistake to analyze our present highly developed and civilized consciousness in order to arrive at some abstract concept which we call the essence of consciousness. What we arrive at by this method is perhaps the essence of *our* consciousness or the essence of contemporary civilized man's consciousness. Hegel and others like him generalized from this instance to all men and to all forms and stages of consciousness.

MAN AND NATURE. In searching for the essence of man Marx and Engels looked at the whole individual as he really exists, and they agreed with Hegel that man never exists in isolation. His essence cannot be found in some mysterious way in himself. He acts necessarily on objects which are not himself. He interacts with people other than himself. His essence therefore is not something closed up within him, but it is precisely his relations with what is not himself, that is, with the rest of nature. Paradoxically, then, man's nature is to a large extent outside himself and is a product of his relations to what is outside of him. This is what Marx meant when he said that the essence of man is the ensemble of his social relations.

Among man's social relations, those which Marx and Engels considered most basic are those which are most necessary for the sustenance of life. The essential economic conditions (which Marx and Engels referred to as the *material* conditions) of his life determine man's other social relations—national, political, legal, religious, ideological. For example, a society built on primitive agriculture is obviously different and will produce and support different social customs and relations than a complex industrial society will. The way of life of a twentieth-century American banker is different from that of an Australian bushman. The way they express their lives is different, their social relations are different, and thus their nature is different—though still more similar one to the other than to any other natural being.

HUMAN KNOWLEDGE. Knowledge, like consciousness and speech, develops slowly as man develops. Neither Marx nor Engels presented anything but the embryonic beginnings of a theory of knowledge. For they were concerned not with man's consciousness but with the material conditions of his life. Two points do emerge, however, with respect to knowledge. The first is that knowledge, which is based on the senses, is the conscious reflection of the material world. Secondly, they emphasized the active and practical function of man's thought. Marx in the second Thesis on Feuerbach stated: "In practice man must prove the truth, that is, the reality and power, the this-sidedness of his thinking. The dispute over the reality or non-reality of thinking which is isolated from practice is a purely scholastic question." It is only by uncovering the laws of nature and of social development that man will achieve mastery over nature and be able to intelligently guide his social development.

Man as a Collective Being

Thus far we have seen that the essence of man is to be found in the way he expresses his life and in the social relations that result. It follows from this that it is impossible to define a man in isolation, for in isolation a man is not a man. Here Marx and Engels agreed with Hegel. It is, moreover, from Hegel's discussion of the master and slave that they come to the insight that by their labor men make themselves. Yet this is true only in the collective sense. No man by himself can make himself. Only in society, by joint effort, can men express themselves in the complex ways they do. Consequently man is essentially a social being. Man as man only appears historically with the appearance of society, and only in society is a man a man. To say that the essence of man is the ensemble of his social relations is necessarily to speak of men collectively, not individually. For it is only collectively that men have social relations, it is only collectively that they produce their lives, and so it is only collectively that they are men.

Human reality is thus in a sense derivative; that is, men receive their essence from the society into which they are born. Any man born into a contemporary society finds that society already there. He comes into a world that is already made and receives his essence by being born into it. He inherits his social relations and can at best modify them slightly before handing them on to succeeding generations. What man is, therefore, depends not on any particular individual, but on men taken together. The individual is derivative, secondary, and subordinate to the society of which he is a part. Though man makes himself by his labor, he does so only collectively. He can modify himself not by his individual efforts but by his collective efforts and by changing his society. Moreover, since the legal, political, and other similar relations are dependent on the basic economic relations, to change man or society necessitates changing the economic base of that society.

Hegel had described the alienation of consciousness in his description of the master and slave and of the unhappy consciousness. Marx, inspired in part by these analyses, turned in his *Economic and Philosophical Manuscripts* to an investigation not of consciousness but of nineteenth-century man in industrial societies. Whereas Hegel spoke abstractly of the alienation of consciousness, Marx uncovered the social alienation or separation of the individual from his fellow men. To the descriptive analysis of man he then added an evaluative one. He argued that if the essence of man is the ensemble of his social relations, each man should enjoy or partake of this essence. But because of the structure of capitalist societies, men are divided into haves and have-nots, masters and slaves, capitalists and proletarians. The mass of mankind, he continued, is alienated or separated from the products of its labor (which belong to the manufacturer), from its own productive activity (since men are forced to sell their labor to another), and from other men. Men should express themselves by their labor, as an artist does by his painting. In capitalist society, however, men are like slaves selling their time to the entrepreneurs (who own the means of production) so that they might continue to live. In such a society man does not share himself and his goods with his fellowmen; rather he is separated from them by his property which he safeguards from their grasp. Moreover, instead of expressing himself fully in many different activities, he performs only one task all day long while someone else performs another, and so on—an instance of what Marx called the "division of labor." Private property and the division of labor consequently result in a society in which men are fragmented and alienated from one another and from their social essence. But only insofar as men are united—as they share their common essence—are they truly men.

Consequently, Marx argued, the solution to this unhappy state of man lies in changing the economic base on which society is built. While Hegel overcame alienation through *insight* into the real, universal nature of consciousness, Marx argued that overcoming man's social alienation requires *changing* the real world. By changing the conditions and the relations of production, man can change the social relations that depend upon them as a superstructure does on a base. The way to free man of alienation is to do away with the causes of it—private property and the division of labor. When men are no longer separated by goods, when no man owns another or can buy his time, then man will be man. Only then will man's collective essence be such that it can truly be enjoyed and shared by all the men of the society. Such a society will have achieved what Marx called "communism."

A communist society is one in which, according to Marx, each person will contribute according to his ability and receive according to his need. Each person will be able to develop himself to the greatest extent possible, and he will have the time and the means necessary to do so. When men have what they need, then envy, theft, and other similar traits common to men in a capitalist society will disappear. Man will thus be changed by changing his society and the ensemble of his social relations. Marx emphasized that this golden age of mankind necessitates great wealth and an industrial society capable of producing all that man needs. But he optimistically holds that such a society is possible and can be produced by man's collective labor.

Freedom and History

If the economic conditions of life are basic to what man and society are, they are by no means exhaustive of man's life. Marx and Engels recognized the importance of culture, but they maintained that the cultural world of man is not a world separate unto itself; it depends upon and is a function of the material base of society. Just as man's knowledge is a reflection of the world outside him, so through consciousness man can bring into himself and enjoy the cultural life—the art, the music, the literature—which exists outside of him. A person's interior richness is dependent upon the richness of the culture of his society and upon his own ability to assimilate and enjoy this richness. He can develop his talents and his feelings by work and by mastering what others have already contributed to the cultural life of his society.

Marx and Engels agreed with Hegel that men become conscious of themselves only slowly through history. As Hegel had said, for the Orientals one was free, for the Greeks many were free, and for the enlightened European all are free, at least in theory. Spirit does grow through history, if by spirit we mean the conscious life of men. But, Marx and Engels insisted, the key to history is found in the development of economic conditions. For consciousness is dependent on matter and can only reflect those changes which take place in the material conditions of life. What Hegel said must consequently be understood "materialistically." In primitive societies where the task of producing one's subsistence was a full-time job for all, only the ruler had the leisure to realize himself and the means to do what he wished; in Greek society, based on slavery, the slaves made it possible for the well-to-do citizens to cultivate the arts and pursue knowledge; in capitalist society, though men in theory are said to be free, the actual exercise of the freedom to act is limited for the vast majority by the fact that they must sell themselves to live.

For Marx and Engels freedom consisted of "insight into necessity"; that is, man is free to the extent that he knows the laws of the operation of nature and of society and can act in accord with them in order to produce what he needs and wants. For example, when man learned how to make glass he was then free to do so, provided he had the necessary material. Mankind becomes more and more free in one sense as it grows in knowledge of the laws of nature and of social development and is able to utilize these laws either in the laboratory or in the organization of society for its own ends. In history, therefore, we do see the growth of man's freedom, of his collective freedom in the domination of nature. He acts freely who acts with knowledge and is therefore able to achieve what he intends.

For Hegel freedom consisted of rational self-determination. Man is free when he acts in accordance with reason. If this means that man can act successfully only when he acts with knowledge of the laws of nature, Marx and Engels would agree. But, they felt, Hegel's approach to freedom is too abstract. Freedom must extend not only to consciousness but to the whole man. One must consider not only an individual's self-determination, but whether he has the actual means to carry out his decision. To guarantee all citizens freedom to travel is an empty guarantee for the masses who are too poor to afford the fare. Freedom of the press is not available to those who do not own publishing houses. Most men are in fact not free to do as they choose because they do not have the means to carry through their choices. This aspect of freedom Hegel ignored.

If in one sense the history of mankind shows evidence of a growth of freedom, this is not to be understood in Hegelian fashion. For Hegel the growth of freedom was equivalent to the development of spirit, and this was the driving force of history. Marx and Engels, however, claimed that this growth of freedom is not the driving force but a product of history. The key to history's development lies not in the recognition of spirit or freedom, not in a study of the achievements of world-historical individuals or heroes, but in a study of the masses. The masses make history. To understand their action one must study the forces that motivate them, that is, the material conditions of their lives and their means and modes of production. For Marx and Engels, then, the proper study of history is a study of the economic forces that determine men's motives and ideas. What is important is the economic base, not the political, legal, or cultural superstructure. Thus slavery was abolished not because the philosophers preached that men should be free (even Aristotle taught that some men were born to be slaves) but because it became economically unprofitable. In this sense the study of history must be materialistic, and historical materialism is the only successful approach to understanding and explaining history.

Hegel correctly saw the development of history from age to age. But, according to Marx and Engels, he failed to realize that the development of spirit which he studied was not basic but derivative. As the base develops, so the superstructure develops. Hegel's mistake, they claimed, is that he had history "standing on its head."

Marx and Engels claimed that historically society became divided into classes as different men specialized in doing certain tasks, while others specialized in doing other tasks. This division of labor led to some men dominating others. The interests of the dominating coincided, and they formed the ruling class; the interests of the dominated coincided, and they formed the ruled class. The development of society has been the result of the clash of these groups and their conflicting interests. To uncover the laws governing the actions of these groups, to discover the laws of social development, is to learn the laws of history. History is determined in the sense that what happens on the whole is determined by the economic conditions of society. Man will however rise from the realm of necessity to the kingdom of freedom when he is able to direct the development of his society with knowledge of the laws of social development. But this too, for Marx and Engels, will be fully achieved only when communism has been achieved and when man has truly become man.

The claims of Marx and Engels continue to be echoed and reechoed in the communist world today. The leaders of the Soviet Union are attempting to produce what they call a "new man," a communist man, to live in communist society. But the very fact that they are actively attempting this shows that men are not merely the result of their economic conditions;

otherwise the "new man" would automatically have emerged as socialism replaced capitalism in the Soviet Union. Yet the humanistic goals enunciated by Marx and Engels in their early writings continue to have wide appeal and to be championed by many in the world today. Thus Adam Schaff, in the spirit of Marx, argued against the existentialistic, individualistic view of man championed by Jean-Paul Sartre (b. 1905). But in almost dialectical fashion the encounter with existentialism has forced Schaff to consider the problems of the individual more than Marx or Engels or Lenin had done. In the face of death and human annihilation he emphasizes the meaning of a life devoted to improving society. In the search for happiness he holds that when men are divided, no one can be truly happy.

The teachings of Marx and Engels on man, freedom, and history may certainly be challenged; but there is no doubt that they are still very much alive.

Hegel and the Marxists

The readings which follow are among the most important, influential, and representative of the writings of Hegel, Marx, and Engels on man. Marx and Engels were well acquainted with Hegel's writings and profoundly influenced by them. Though they adopt a materialistic instead of an idealistic position, there are striking similarities between their views and Hegel's. If, as Marx and Engels claimed, they inverted Hegel, taking him off his head and placing him on his feet, the similarities we find should not be too surprising. All three men attempted to account for man in his total reality and in his historical development. Despite the difference of emphasis, they all were faced with similar phenomena for investigation.

In the third section of the *Encyclopaedia,* the philosophy of mind, Hegel outlines his general position with respect to man. Though man is essentially mind or consciousness, Hegel takes into account the empirical aspects of man and the sciences that study him. Still, for Hegel the essence of man is consciousness. The *Phenomenology of Mind* constitutes Hegel's detailed examination of the data of consciousness, especially as they concern self-consciousness. The *Outlines of Hegel's Phenomenology* presents in summary form the content of Hegel's study of consciousness and points up the various stages of development through which consciousness goes. Hegel's analysis leads him to the realization that consciousness as such is universal, not individual, and that consciousness is essentially reason or universal spirit, the Absolute which is equivalent to all of reality. The language and reasoning may seem at first strange and abstract. But a careful reading shows that Hegel does not remain in an esoteric realm. He deals with human reality in many of its most ordinary experiences—man's knowledge of the world of objects, his relations with other men, his self-development through work and other activity, his conflicts with other men despite their mutual dependence. The sections on the master-servant relation and on "contrite consciousness," both of which are given in their entirety in the readings that follow, were especially influential on Marx. He learned a great deal from them and adopted much of the content, though "placing it on its feet."

Marx's *Economic and Philosophical Manuscripts* contain a critique of Hegel, a detailed discussion of alienation, and a description of social man who realizes himself only in a communistic society. The manuscripts are among Marx's early works. His terminology is in part Hegelian and in part Feuerbachian. A careful comparison of these sections with those from Hegel reveal basic similarities despite some obvious differences. Alienation is found in both views, insofar as man is separated from himself, other men, and the world of objects. Hegel's alienation of self and of consciousness becomes in Marx the alienation of man in his labor. But the approach the two writers use and many of the facts they describe are similar. The reader will have to turn to his own experience to test the adequacy of each view and either decide between them, attempt a reconciliation, or pick and choose.

Both positions have implicit in them an ideal view of man in terms of which much of the discussion takes place. The reader should ferret out those views and keep them in mind. He should distinguish those elements that are descriptive of the condition of all men from those that are evaluative or that state how man *should be.* Throughout the readings one must be especially careful of the way in which the term "man" is used. "Man" is a universal term. It sometimes is used to refer to each individual member of mankind, sometimes to refer to mankind as such, sometimes to designate a special portion of mankind, sometimes to designate an ideal. Only by constantly asking what the terms mean can one grasp the Hegelian and Marxist view of man and the full import of the collectivism which is central to both their views.

When we turn to the philosophy of culture and history, we again find basic similarities between Hegel on the one hand and Marx and Engels on the other, despite the fact that Hegel emphasizes the development of spirit and Marx and Engels the development of economic conditions. The extent of their differences should be ascertained and kept in mind while such similarities as the role of the actions of ordinary man in history are noted.

The State for Hegel is extremely important; the parallel in Marx and Engels is the class. Marx and Engels claim to account for all Hegel does and more. But the success with which they accomplish what they claim should be decided by the reader. The two views of freedom and determinism which emerge are in many respects identical. Freedom of the individual is implicit in both views; but for both the individual is free only when he acts in accord not with his passing desire but with the greater whole, be it reason or the demands of mankind. Hegel emphasizes the development of reason, of spirit, and of freedom in history. Marx and Engels handle much of the same phenomena under the form of economic determinism. Their differing meanings of "freedom" and "determinism" should be kept in mind in each of the cases.

The overall view of man that we get from both Hegel and the Marxists is a collectivist view. The individual is considered only as part of a greater whole. Although individuals are obviously necessary to the whole, it is not the individuals as individuals that concern Marx and Hegel. Individual idiosyncracies are quickly dismissed or ignored. Problems of individual psychology, whether in relation to the freedom or determinism of individual acts or to the knowing process, are passed over in silence. The question of personal immortality counts for little when the collective—be it termed State or class, mankind or Absolute—is the central object of concern. Hegel and Marx both defend the value of the individual; but for both the individual's value is derived from the value of the greater whole of which he is a part. This is true also of Schaff's view, though he does explicitly consider the individual and some of his problems. The success with which Schaff formulates the problems of the meaning of life and of individual happiness and with which he defends Marxism against existentialism should be decided by the reader.

The practical implications of views in which the individual has no value in and of himself, in which he has no rights except as part of and derivative from a greater whole, should be carefully considered. That the legal and political systems built on such views easily lead to violence to the individual for the good of the whole has been adequately demonstrated by history in totalitarianisms of both the right and the left. That neither Hegel nor Marx would have sanctioned such regimes as have used their doctrines for a basis or justification should be remembered. But that their views of man have been so used indicates that their doctrines are open to diverse interpretations. The writings of both Hegel and Marx are grand in their sweep, profound in their insights, but often distressingly vague in presentation and expression. Both views are in many instances apparently self-contradictory; both have spawned a variety of interpreters. In reading the selections that follow here, the reader is left to interpret, weigh, and compare for himself two views of man that originated in the nineteenth century and that continue to be important in the world today.

Glossary

(NOTE: Though the definitions which follow are for the most part given in the words of Hegel, Marx, or Engels, the reader should look for changes in shade of meaning and for the variety of connotations the terms take on in different contexts.)

ALIENATION:
A technical term used somewhat differently by Hegel and by Marx. Hegel speaks of alienated (or contrite) consciousness, in which the self experiences itself as divided; and of alienated objects, that is, objects to which one gives up his right or claim. It is also possible to apply the term to some forms of dialectical negation (see *Negation*). Marx speaks primarily of the alienation of man and labor. It consists of the separation of what should be united; for example, when man, who should have the use of the products of his labor, does not, then "the worker is related to the *product of his labor* as to an *alien* object"; or again, as a species-being man should live in harmony with other men, but when some dominate others, man is alienated from man. Alienation also has the connotation of "making external to oneself" and of "setting oneself in opposition to."

ANTITHESIS:
See *Negation*.

BASE:
A technical term in Marxist literature used to designate the sum total of the relations of production and the productive forces that constitute "the economic structure of society, the real foundation, on which rises a legal and political superstructure." (See *Superstructure*.)

COMMUNISM:
Marx defines this differently in different places. In *The Economic and Philosophical Manuscripts* he says: "*Communism* is the *positive* abolition of *private property*, of *human self-alienation*, and thus the real *appropriation* of *human* nature through and for man. . . . It is the *definitive* resolution of the antagonism between man and nature and between man and man." The now classic definition is given in Marx's *Critique of the Gotha Programme*: a society organized according to the principle: "From each according to his ability, to each according to his needs!"

CONSCIOUSNESS:
For Hegel this is "the relation of the Ego and the object to each other"; it is the form of mental activity in which a subject first seeks to comprehend an object; and Hegel sometimes equates it to the pure ego or to the "I" as a subject. Consciousness is the first stage in the development of spirit or mind, and perception and understanding are two of its functions.

inundate – deluge; flood; over flow
                on overwhelm

ogle – to keep looking at with fond
        desire; make eyes at

hoariest – very old; ancient

brush – rash; toohasty; insolent; impudent

CONTRITE CONSCIOUSNESS:
Consciousness that is aware of itself as divided and in conflict with itself.

DIALECTICS:
A method used by Hegel, and later by Marx. For Hegel dialectics also has a content, and the dialectical process is the process of thought and the process of the development of all reality. Hegel maintains that all of reality is both logically interrelated and constantly developing. The logical development follows the laws of dialectics. In general a concept (thesis) leads to its negation (antithesis), and the positive aspects of both are elevated and united in a third concept (synthesis), known as the negation of the negation. This in turn becomes a thesis, which is negated, and so on until one arrives at the all-inclusive concept of the Absolute.

DIVISION OF LABOR:
A term used by Marx and Engels to express "the fact that intellectual and mental activity—enjoyment and labor, production and consumption—devolve on different individuals."

ESTRANGEMENT:
Often used by Hegel and Marx as equivalent to alienation with respect to people, but not with respect to property. (See *Alienation*.)

MEDIATION:
In Hegel "mediate" is the opposite of "immediate." One thing is "mediated" by another if this latter is necessary for the existence of the former or if it relates the former to a third object. Mediation is the process of mediating.

MOMENT:
A technical term used by Hegel (and sometimes by Marx) to indicate an important phase in a movement or element in a process (of thought, history, etc.).

NEGATION:
The second stage or moment in the dialectical process (sometimes called *antithesis*) In the *Science of Logic* Hegel says: "Negation is just as much affirmation as negation for what is self-contradictory resolves itself not into nullity, into abstract nothingness, but essentially only into the negation of its *particular* content. . . . Since what results, the negation, is a definite negation, it has a content. It is a new concept, but a higher, richer concept than that which preceded."

NEGATION OF THE NEGATION:
The third stage or moment in the dialectical process (sometimes called *synthesis*). It negates the negative aspects of the two earlier moments (sometimes called thesis and negation or antithesis) of the dialectical process, preserves their positive aspects, and elevates them into a higher unity.

POLITICAL ECONOMY:
Marx defines this as "the theoretical analysis of modern bourgeois society."

REASON:

For Hegel this is a stage in the development of spirit or mind. "Reason is the conscious certainty of being all reality." Self-consciousness reaches this stage when it realizes that it is not separate and individual. Thus, "Reason is the highest union of consciousness and self-consciousness, or of the knowing of an object and of the knowing of itself."

SELF-CONSCIOUSNESS:

The second stage in the development of consciousness, in which consciousness becomes "conscious of itself in every respect."

SPECIES-BEING:

A term used by Marx (adapted from Feuerbach) to refer to man. For Feuerbach man was a species-being because man alone was conscious, not only of himself as an individual but of his species and of himself as a member of his species. To this notion Marx adds: "It is just in his work upon the objective world that man really proves himself as a species-being. This production is his active species-life." (See *Species-life*.)

SPECIES-LIFE:

A term used by Marx (adapted from Feuerbach) to refer to man's unified social or communal life, that is, the life man leads together with other men with whom he shares in unalienated, productive labor. Alienated labor "transforms the species-life of man into a means of physical existence." (See *Species-being; Alienation*.)

SPIRIT (or MIND):

In the *Phenomenology* Hegel calls spirit "self-contained essential reality"; "the inner being of the world, that which essentially is, and is *per se*"; "the self-supporting absolutely real ultimate being"; "consciousness in general"; and "the self of actual consciousness." Consciousness, self-consciousness, and reason are three stages in the development of mind or spirit. In the *Philosophy of History* spirit, as self-contained existence, is freedom, and develops through time. In the *Encyclopaedia* the philosophy of mind is the synthesis of the logic and the philosophy of nature.

STATE:

For Hegel, "The idea of the State should not denote any particular state." It is a moral, organic whole whose "reality consists in the interest of the whole being realized in particular ends." For Marx and Engels the state is an instrument of oppression in the hands of the ruling class, which will "wither away" with the advent of communism.

SUPERSTRUCTURE:

A technical term in Marxist literature used to designate "the legal, political, religious, aesthetic, or philosophic—in short, ideological forms" of social consciousness and the legal, political, and other institutions corresponding to them that are built upon and are determined by the development of the economic base of society. (See *Base*.)

SYNTHESIS:

See *Negation of the Negation*.

G. W. F. Hegel

GEORG WILHELM FRIEDRICH HEGEL was born in Stuttgart in 1770. He studied at the University of Tübingen and then served briefly as a tutor. He taught at the Universities of Jena, Heidelberg, and finally Berlin, where he occupied the chair of philosophy from 1818 until his death in 1831. He is the most important and influential of the nine-teenth-century idealists. Though his early writings are mainly theo-logical, they are overshadowed by his masterly philosophical system, which remains a landmark in the history of philosophy.

Knowledge and Consciousness

Outlines of Hegel's Phenomenology

INTRODUCTION [1]

1. Our ordinary Knowing has before itself only the object which it knows, but does not at first make an object of itself, i.e. of the Knowing. But the whole which is extant in the act of knowing is not the object alone, but also the Ego that knows, and the relation of the Ego and the object to each other, i.e. Consciousness.

2. In Philosophy, the determinations of the Knowing are not consid-ered exclusively in the phase of determinations of things, but likewise as determinations of the Knowing, to which they belong, although in common likewise to things. In other words: they are not taken merely as objective but also as subjective determinations—or rather as definite species of rela-tion of the object and subject to each other.

---

[1] *In 1840, the Editors of Hegel's works published a small volume with the title, Hegel's Philosophical Propaedeutics. The work, which was edited by Karl Rosenkranz, con-tains substantially the original outline of the Course of Instruction in Philosophy which Hegel gave at the Gymnasium at Nürnberg in 1808-1811, together with sundry additions made from notes taken at the lectures and other sources. We give the entire exposition of the Phenomenology as it occurs in the second year of the course. (The entire course was divided into three years: 1st year, Science of Rights, of Morals, and of Religion; 2nd year, Phenomenology of Spirit and Logic; 3rd year, Science of the Idea and Philosophical Encyclopaedia. The whole is preceded by an admirable preface by the Editor.)* [W.T.H.]

From pp. 68–79 of G. W. F. Hegel, *The Philosophical Propaedeutics*, translated by William T. Harris, in *Outlines of Hegel's Phenomenology*. Copyright 1900 by Charles Scribner's Sons.

3. Since things and their determinations are in the Knowing, it is quite possible, on the one hand, to view the same as in and for themselves outside of Consciousness—as given to the latter in the shape of foreign and already existing material for it;—on the other hand, however, for the reason that Consciousness is essential to the Knowing of these, the view is possible that Consciousness itself posits this world, and produces or modifies the determinations of the same, through its mediating relation and its activity, either wholly or in part. The former mode of view is called "Realism," the latter, "Idealism." Here are to be considered the general determinations of things only as the definite relation of object to the subject.

4. The subject, more definitely seized, is Spirit (the Mind). It is Phenomenal when essentially relating to an existent object; in so far is it Consciousness. The Science of Consciousness is, therefore, called The Phenomenology of Spirit (or Mind).

5. But the Mind, according to its self-activity within itself and in relation to itself independent of all relation to others, is considered in the Science of Mind proper, or "Psychology."

6. Consciousness is in general the knowing of an object, whether external or internal, without regard to whether it presents itself without the help of the Mind, or whether it is produced through this. The Mind is to be considered in its activities in so far as the determinations of its consciousness are ascribed to it.

7. Consciousness is the definite relation of the Ego to an Object. In so far as one regards it from the objective side, it can be said to vary according to the difference of the Objects which it has.

8. At the same time, however, the Object is essentially determined (modified) through the mediating relation to Consciousness. Its diversity is, therefore, to be considered as conversely dependent upon the development of Consciousness. This reciprocity continues through the Phenomenal sphere of Consciousness and leaves the above-mentioned (3) questions undecided.

9. Consciousness has in general three phases, according to the diversity of the object. It (the object) is namely either the object standing in opposition to the Ego, or it is the Ego itself, or something objective which belongs likewise equally to the Ego: Thought. These determinations are not empirically taken up from without, but are moments of Consciousness itself. Hence it is

(1) Consciousness in general;
(2) Self-Consciousness;
(3) Reason.

FIRST PHASE

Consciousness in General

10. Consciousness in general is (1) Sensuous; (2) Perceiving; (3) Understanding.

A. THE SENSUOUS CONSCIOUSNESS

11. The simple sensuous Consciousness is the immediate certitude of an external object. The expression for the immediateness of such an object is that "it is," and moreover a "This," a "Now" according to time, and a "Here" according to space, and different from all other objects and perfectly determined (definite) in itself.

12. This Now and this Here are vanishing somewhats. Now is no more while it is and another Now has entered its place, and this latter Now has likewise vanished. But the Now abides all the same. This abiding Now is the general Now, which is both this and that Now, and is likewise neither of them. This Here which I mean, and point out, has a right and left, an above and a below, a behind and a before, etc., *ad infinitum;* i.e. the Here pointed out is not a simple and hence definite Here, but a unity including many Heres. Therefore, what in truth is extant is not the abstract, sensuous determinateness [the simple "it is"], but the General.

B. PERCEPTION

13. Perception has no longer for object the Sensuous in so far as it is immediate, but in so far as it is general. It is a mingling of sensuous determinations with those of Reflection.

14. The object of this Consciousness is, therefore, the Thing with its Properties. The sensuous properties are (a) *for themselves* immediately in sensation, and likewise determined and mediated through the relation to others; (b) they belong to a thing, and are in this respect, on the one hand, embraced in the individuality of the same; on the other hand, they have generality, according to which they transcend this individual thing, and are at the same time independent of each other.

15. In so far as the Properties are essentially mediated, they have their subsistence in another and are subject to *change*. They are only *accidents*. Things, however, since they subsist in their properties (for the reason that they are distinguished by means of these), perish through the change of those properties, and become an alternation of birth and decay.

16. In this change it is not merely the somewhat that cancels itself and passes over to another, but the other itself changes. But the other of the other, or the change of the changeable, is the Becoming of the Abiding—of the in-and-for-itself Subsisting and Internal.

C. THE UNDERSTANDING

17. The object has now this character: it has (a) a purely accidental side, and (b) also an essentiality and an abiding side. Consciousness, for the reason that the object has for it this character, is the *understanding*— for which the *"things"* of perception pass for mere phenomena, and it (the Understanding) contemplates the "Internal of things."

18. The Internal of things is that in them which, on the one hand, is

free from the Phenomenal manifestation—namely, their multiplicity—which constitutes an External in opposition to it (the Internal); on the other hand, however, it is that which is related to them through its comprehension (ideal totality or "definition"). It is therefore: (1) simple force, which passes over into extantness, its "utterance" (or manifestation).

19. (2) Force remains with this distinction the same in all the sensuous variations of the Phenomenon. The Law of the Phenomenon is its quiet, general image. It is a mediating relation of general abiding determinations whose distinctions are external to the law. The generality and persistence of this mediating relation lead to the necessity of the same; yet without the distinction's being an in-itself-determined or internal one, in which one of the determinations lies immediately in the comprehension (total definition) of the other.

20. This Comprehension—akin to Consciousness itself—gives another phase thereof. Hitherto it was in relation to its object as somewhat alien and indifferent. Since now the distinction in general has become a distinction which at the same time is no distinction, the previous mode of the distinction of Consciousness from its object falls away. It has an object and relates to another, which, however, is at the same time no "other"; in fine, it has itself for object.

21. In other words: the "Internal of things" is the thought or comprehension thereof. While Consciousness has the Internal as object, it has thought, or its own Reflection, or its own form—and, consequently, itself as object.

SECOND PHASE

The Self-Consciousness

22. As Self-Consciousness the Ego intuites itself, and the expression of the same in its purity is Ego = Ego, or: I am I.

23. This proposition of self-consciousness is devoid of all content. The impulse of self-consciousness consists in this: to realize its comprehension ("true nature") and to become conscious of itself in every respect. It is therefore: (1) active in cancelling the otherness (alien-being) of objects, and in positing them like itself; (2) in making itself valid externally, and thus giving itself, through this, objectivity and extantness. These two are one and the same activity. The becoming-determined of self-consciousness is at the same time a self-determining, and conversely. It produces itself as object.

24. Self-Consciousness has in its culture, or movement, three stages: (1) of Desire in so far as it is related to other things: (2) of the Mediating relation of master and slave (dominion and servitude) in so far as it is related to another self-consciousness not identical with itself; (3) of the general Self-Consciousness which recognizes itself in other self-consciousnesses, and is identical with them as well as self-identical.

A. DESIRE

25. Both sides of self-consciousness, the positing and the cancelling, are thus united with each other immediately. Self-Consciousness posits itself through negation of otherness and is *practical* consciousness. If, therefore, in the real consciousness, which also is called the *theoretical,* the determinations of the same and of the object changed or varied of *themselves, now* it happens that this change occurs through the activity of the Consciousness itself and *for* it. It is conscious that this cancelling activity belongs to it. In the comprehension of self-consciousness the not-yet-realized distinction lies as a characteristic. In so far as this distinction makes its appearance, there arises a feeling of otherness (dependence on others) in consciousness—a feeling of negation in itself, or the feeling of deficiency, a *want.*

26. This feeling of its otherness contradicts its identity with itself. The necessity felt to cancel this opposition is Impulse (or appetite). Negation, or otherness, presents itself to the consciousness as an external thing different from it, which however is determined through the self-consciousness (1) as a somewhat suited to gratify the appetency, and (2) as a somewhat in itself negative whose subsistence is to be cancelled by the Self and posited in identity with it (i.e. made identical, or assimilated).

27. The activity of desire thus cancels the otherness (alien element) of the object and its subsistence, and unites it with the subject, and by this means the desire is appeased. This is conditioned thus: (1) through an object existing externally or indifferent to it, or through Consciousness; (2) its activity produces the gratification only through destruction of the object. The self-consciousness arrives through this at its feeling of Self.

28. In Desire, Consciousness stands in relation to itself as individual. It relates to an object devoid of self-hood, which is in and for itself another than the self-consciousness. The latter for this reason only attains self-identity as regards the object through destruction of the latter. Desire is in general (1) destructive, (2) in the gratification of its wants, therefore, it comes to the conscious feeling of its for-itself-being as individual—to the undefined Comprehension of the subject as connected with objectivity.

B. THE RELATION OF MASTER AND SLAVE

29. The comprehension of self-consciousness as Subject which is at the same time object, gives the mediating relation: that *another* self-consciousness exists for the self-consciousness.

30. A self-consciousness which is for another is not as a mere object for it, but as its *other self.* The Ego is no abstract generality in which there is no distinction or determination. Since an Ego is thus the object of the Ego, in this respect there is the same for it as object that it is in itself. It intuites itself in another.

31. This self-intuition of one in another is (1) the abstract moment

204 / G. W. F. HEGEL

of self-sameness. (2) Each has, however, also the peculiarity that it mani-fests itself to the other as an external object, and in so far as an immediate sensuous and concrete existence. (3) Each is absolutely for-itself and in-dividual as opposed to the other, and asserts its right to be such for the other and to pass for such, and to intuite its own freedom as a for-itself-existent in the other and to be recognized by it.

32. In order to make itself valid as a free being and to obtain recogni-tion, self-consciousness must exhibit itself to another as free from natural existence. This moment (i.e. the being-for-another) is as necessary as that of the freedom of self-consciousness *in itself*. The absolute identity of the Ego with itself is essentially not an immediate, but such a one as has been achieved through the cancelling of sensuous immediateness, and the exhibi-tion of the self to another as free and independent from the Sensuous. Thus it shows itself in conformity with its comprehension (ideal), and must be recognized because it gives reality to the Ego.

33. But Independence is freedom not *outside of* and *from* the sensuous immediate extant being, but rather as freedom *in* the same. The one mo-ment is as necessary as the other, but they are not of the same value. For the reason that non-identity enters—that to one of two self-consciousnesses freedom passes for the essential in opposition to sensuous extant being, while with the other the opposite occurs—with the reciprocal demand for recognition there enters into determined actuality the mediating relation (of master and slave) between them; or, in general terms, that of service and submission, in so far as this diversity of independence is extant through the immediate agency of nature.

34. Since of two self-consciousnesses opposed to each other, each must strive to assert and prove itself as an absolute for-itself-existence against and for the other. That one enters into a condition of slavery who prefers life to freedom, and thereby shows that he has not the capacity to abstract from his sensuous extant being by his own might for his inde-pendence.

35. This pure negative Freedom, which consists in the abstraction from natural extant being, does not correspond to the definition (compre-hension) of Freedom, for this latter is the self-identity, even when involved with others: partly the intuition of itself in another self, and partly the free-dom (not *from* the existent, but) *in* the existent, a freedom which itself has extantness. The one who serves is devoid of selfhood and has another self in place of his own, so that for his master he has resigned and cancelled his individual Ego and now views his essential self in another. The master, on the contrary, looks upon the servant (the other Ego) as cancelled and his own individual will as preserved. (History of Robinson and Friday.)

36. The own individual will of the servant, more closely regarded, is cancelled in the fear of the master, and reduced to the internal feeling of its negativity. Its labor for the service of another is a resignation of its own will partly in itself, partly it is at the same time, with the negation of its

own desire, the positive transformation of external things through labor; since through labor the self makes its own determinations the forms of things, and thus views itself as objective in its work. The renunciation of the unessential arbitrary will constitutes the moment of true obedience. (Pisistratus [2] taught the Athenians to obey. Through this he made the Code of Solon an actual power; and after the Athenians had learned this, the dominion of a Ruler over them was superfluous.)

37. This renunciation of individuality as self is the moment (phase) through which self-consciousness makes the transition to the universal will, the transition to positive freedom.

C. UNIVERSALITY OF SELF-CONSCIOUSNESS

38. The universal self-consciousness is the intuition of itself, not as a special existence distinct from others, but an intuition of the self-existent universal self. Thus it recognizes itself and the other self-consciousness in itself, and is in turn recognized by them.

39. Self-consciousness is, according to this its essential universality, only real in so far as it knows its echo (and reflection) in another (I know that another knows me as itself), and as pure spiritual universality (belonging to the family, the native land, &c.) knows itself as essential self. (This self-consciousness is the basis of all virtues, of love, honor, friendship, bravery, all self-sacrifice, all fame, &c.)

THIRD PHASE

Reason

40. Reason is the highest union of consciousness and self-consciousness, or of the knowing of an object and of the knowing of itself. It is the certitude that its determinations are just as much objective, i.e. determinations of the essence of things, as they are subjective thoughts. It (Reason) is just as well the certitude of itself (subjectivity) as being (or objectivity), and this, too, in one and the same thinking activity.

41. Or what we see through the insight of Reason, is: (1) a content which subsists not in our mere subjective notions or thoughts which we make for ourselves, but which contains the in-and-for-itself-existing essence of objects and possesses objective reality; and (2) which is for the Ego no alien somewhat, no somewhat given from without, but throughout penetrated and assimilated by the Ego, and therefore to all intents produced by the Ego.

42. The knowing of Reason is therefore not the mere subjective certitude, but also *Truth,* because Truth consists in the harmony, or rather *unity,* of certitude and Being, or of certitude and objectivity.

---

[2] Pisistratus (*c.* 605–527 B.C.): tyrant of Athens; under him Athens achieved hegemony over the Ionian cities. [R.D.G.]

QUESTIONS FOR STUDY AND DISCUSSION

1. Explain the difference, according to Hegel, between Realism and Idealism.
2. Explain the meaning and significance of the title of Hegel's work, *The Phenomenology of Mind*.
3. Make clear what Hegel means by the "Internal of things."
4. What is the function of Desire in the development of Self-consciousness?
5. What does Hegel mean by Reason?

Social Self-Consciousness

INDEPENDENCE AND DEPENDENCE OF SELF-CONSCIOUSNESS

Master and Servant

Self-consciousness exists in itself and for itself, in that, and by the fact that it exists for another self-consciousness; that is to say, it *is* only by being acknowledged or "recognized." The conception of this its unity in its duplication, of infinitude realizing itself in self-consciousness, has many sides to it and encloses within it elements of varied significance. Thus its moments must on the one hand be strictly kept apart in detailed distinctiveness, and, on the other, in this distinction must, at the same time, also be taken as not distinguished, or must always be accepted and understood in their opposite sense. This double meaning of what is distinguished lies in the nature of self-consciousness: of its being infinite, or directly the opposite of the determinateness in which it is fixed. The detailed exposition of the notion of this spiritual unity in its duplication will bring before us the process of Recognition.

1. [The double self-consciousness.]

Self-consciousness has before it another self-consciousness; it has come outside itself. This has a double significance. First, it has lost its own self, since it finds itself as an *other* being; secondly, it has thereby sublimated that other, for it does not regard the other as essentially real, but sees its own self in the other.

It must suspend this its other self. To do so is to suspend and preserve that first double meaning, and is therefore a second double meaning. First, it must set itself to suspend the other independent being, in order thereby to

---

From pp. 399–410 of G. W. F. Hegel, *Phenomenology of Mind*, translated by J. B. Baillie, in *The Philosophy of Hegel*, edited by Carl J. Friedrich. Copyright 1953 by Random House, Inc. Reprinted by permission of George Allen and Unwin Ltd., London.

become certain of itself as true being; secondly, it thereupon proceeds to suspend its own self, for this other is itself.

This suspension in a double sense of its otherness in a double sense is at the same time a return in a double sense into itself. For, firstly, through suspension, it gets back itself, because it becomes one with itself again through the canceling of *its* otherness; but secondly, it likewise gives otherness back again to the other self-consciousness, for it was aware of being in the other, it cancels this its own being in the other and thus lets the other again go free.

This process of self-consciousness in relation to another self-consciousness has in this manner been represented as the action of one alone. But this action on the part of the one has itself the double significance of being at once its own action and the action of that other as well. For the other is likewise independent, shut up within itself, and there is nothing in it which is not there through itself. The first does not have the object before it in the way that object primarily exists for desire, but as an object existing independently for itself, over which therefore it has no power to do anything for its own behoof, if that object does not *per se* do what the first does to it. The process then is absolutely the double process of both self-consciousness. Each sees the other do the same as itself; each itself does what it demands on the part of the other, and for that reason does what it does, only so far as the other does the same. Action from one side only would be useless, because what is to happen can only be brought about by means of both.

The action has then a *double meaning* not only in the sense that it is an act done to itself as well as to the other, but also inasmuch as it is in its undivided entirety the act of the one as well as of the other.

In this movement we see the process repeated which came before us as the play of forces; in the present case, however, it is found in consciousness. What in the former had effect only for us (contemplating experience), holds here for the terms themselves. The middle term is self-consciousness which breaks itself up into the extremes; and each extreme is this interchange of its own determinateness, and complete transition into the opposite. While *qua* consciousness, it no doubt comes outside itself, still, in being outside itself it is at the same time restrained within itself, it exists for itself, and its self-externalization is for consciousness. *Consciousness* finds that it immediately is and is not another consciousness, as also that this other is for itself only when it cancels itself as existing for itself, and has self-existence only in the self-existence of the other. Each is the mediating term to the other, through which each mediates and unites itself with itself; and each is to itself and to the other an immediate self-existing reality, which, at the same time, exists thus for itself only through this mediation. They recognize themselves as mutually recognizing one another.

This pure conception of recognition, of duplication of self-consciousness within its unity, we must now consider in the way its process appears for self-consciousness. It will, in the first place, present the aspect of the disparity of the two, or the break-up of the middle term into the extremes, which *qua* extremes, are opposed to one another, and of which one is merely recognized, while the other only recognizes.

2. [The conflict of the opposed self-consciousnesses.]

Self-consciousness is primarily simple being-by-itself, self-identity by exclusion of every other from itself. It takes its essential nature and absolute object to be Ego; and in this immediacy, in this bare fact of its self-existence, it is individual. That which for it is the other stands as unessential object, as object with the impress and character of negation. But the other is also a self-consciousness; an individual makes its appearance in antithesis to an individual. Appearing thus in their immediacy, they are for each other in the manner of ordinary objects. They are independent individual forms, modes of consciousness that have not risen above the bare level of life (for the existent object here has been determined as life). They are, moreover, forms of consciousness which have not yet accomplished for one another the process of absolute abstraction, of uprooting all immediate existence, and of being merely the bare, negative fact of self-identical consciousness; or, in other words, have not yet revealed themselves to each other as existing purely for themselves, i.e., as self-consciousness. Each is indeed certain of its own self, but not of the other, and hence its own certainty of itself is still without truth. For its truth would be merely that its own individual existence for itself would be shown to it to be an independent object, or, which is the same thing, that the object would be exhibited as this pure certainty of itself. By the notion of recognition, however, this is not possible, except in the form that as the other is for it, so it is for the other; each in its self through its own action and again through the action of the other achieves this pure abstraction of existence for self.

The presentation of itself, however, as pure abstraction of self-consciousness consists in showing itself as a pure negation of its objective form, or in showing that it is fettered to no determinate existence, that it is not bound at all by the particularity everywhere characteristic of existence as such, and is *not* tied up with life. The process of bringing all this out involves a twofold action—action on the part of the other, and action on the part of itself. In so far as it is the other's action, each aims at the destruction and death of the other. But in this there is implicated also the second kind of action, self-activity; for each implies that it risks its own life. The relation of both self-consciousnesses is in this way so constituted that they prove themselves and each other through a life-and-death struggle. They must enter into this struggle, for they must bring their certainty of themselves, the certainty of being for themselves, to the level of objective truth, and make this a fact both in the case of the other and in their own case as well. And it is solely by risking life, that freedom is obtained; only thus is it tried and proved that the essential nature of self-consciousness is not bare existence, is not the merely immediate form in which it at first make its appearance, is not its mere absorption in the expanse of life. Rather it is thereby guaranteed that there is nothing present but what might be taken as a vanishing moment—that self-consciousness is merely pure self-existence, being-for-self. The individual, who has not staked his life, may, no doubt, be recognized as a person; but he has not attained the truth of this recognition as an independent self-consciousness. In the same way each must aim at the death of the other, as it risks its own life thereby; for that other is to it of no more worth than itself; the other's reality is presented to the former as an external other, as outside itself; it must cancel that externality. The other is a purely existent consciousness and entangled in manifold ways; it must regard its otherness as pure existence for itself or as absolute negation.

This trying and testing, however, by a struggle to the death cancels both the truth which was to result from it, and therewith the certainty of self altogether. For just as life is the natural "position" of consciousness, independence without absolute negativity, so death is the natural "negation" of consciousness, negation without independence, which thus remains without the requisite significance of actual recognition.[1] Through death, doubtless, there has arisen the certainty that both did stake their life, and held it lightly both in their own case and in the case of the other; but that is not for those who underwent this struggle. They cancel their consciousness which had its place in this alien element of natural existence; in other words, they cancel themselves and are sublated, as terms or extremes seeking to have existence on their own account. But along with this there vanishes from the play of change, the essential moment, viz., that of breaking up into extremes with opposite characteristics; and the middle term collapses into a lifeless unity which is broken up into lifeless extremes, merely existent and not opposed. And the two do not mutually give and receive one another back from each other through consciousness; they let one another go quite indifferently, like things. Their act is abstract negation, not the negation characteristic of consciousness, which cancels in such a way that it preserves and maintains what is sublated, and thereby survives its being sublated.

In this experience self-consciousness becomes aware that *life* is as essential to it as pure self-consciousness. In immediate self-consciousness the simple ego is absolute object, which, however, is for us or in itself absolute mediation, and has as its essential moment substantial and solid independence. The dissolution of that simple unity is the result of the first experience; through this there is posited a pure self-consciousness, and a consciousness which is not purely for itself, but for another, i.e., as an existent consciousness, consciousness in the form and shape of thinghood.

---

[1] Death negates consciousness in the sense that an individual's death, according to Hegel, is the end of that individual's consciousness; there is therefore nothing after death that can assert itself. [R.D.G.]

Both moments are essential, since, in the first instance, they are unlike and opposed, and their reflection into unity has not yet come to light, they stand as two opposed forms or modes of consciousness. The one is independent whose essential nature is to be for itself, the other is dependent whose essence is life or existence for another. The former is the Master, or Lord, the latter the Bondsman.

3. [Master and Servant. (a) Rule of the master.]

The master is the consciousness that exists *for itself;* but no longer merely the general notion of existence for the self. Rather, it is consciousness which, while existing on its own account, is mediated with itself through another consciousness, viz., bound up with an independent being or with thinghood in general. The master brings himself into relation to both these moments, to a thing as such, the object of desire, and to the consciousness whose essential character is thinghood, and since the master, *qua* notion of self-consciousness, is (a) an immediate relation of self-existence, but is now moreover at the same time (b) mediation, or a being-for-self which is for itself only through an other—he (the master) stands in relation (a) immediately to both, (b) mediately to each through the other. The master relates himself to the servant mediately through independent existence, for that is precisely what keeps the servant in bond; it is his chain, from which he could not, in the struggle, get away, and for that reason he proves himself dependent, shows that his independence consists in his being a thing. The master, however, is the power controlling this state of existence, for he has shown in the struggle that he holds existence to be merely something negative. Since he is the power dominating the negative nature of existence, while this existence again is the power controlling the other (the servant), the master holds, as a consequence, this other in subordination. In the same way the master relates himself to the thing mediately through the servant. The servant being a self-consciousness in the broad sense, also takes up a negative attitude to things and cancels them; but the thing is, at the same time, independent for him, and, in consequence, he cannot, with all his negating, get so far as to annihilate it outright and be done with it; that is to say, he merely works on it. To the master, on the other hand, by means of this mediating process, belongs the immediate relation, in the sense of the pure negation of it; in other words he gets the enjoyment. What mere desire did not attain, he now succeeds in attaining, viz., to have done with the thing, and find satisfaction in enjoyment. Desire alone did not get the length of this, because of the independence of the thing. The master, however, who has interposed the servant between it and himself, thereby relates himself merely to the dependence of the thing, and enjoys it without qualification and without reserve. The aspect of its independence he leaves to the servant, who labors upon it.

In these two moments, the master gets his recognition through another consciousness, for in them the latter affirms itself as unessential, both by working upon the thing, and, on the other hand, by the fact of being dependent on a determinate existence; in neither case can this other get the mastery over existence, and succeed in absolutely negating it. We have thus here this moment of recognition, viz., that the other consciousness cancels itself as self-existent, and *ipso facto,* itself does what the first does to it. In the same way we have the other moment, that this action on the part of the second is the action proper of the first; for what is done by the servant is properly an action on the part of the master. The latter exists only for himself, that is his essential nature; he is the negative power without qualification, a power to which the thing is nothing, and his is thus the absolutely essential action in this situation, while the servant's is not so, his is an unessential activity. But for recognition proper there is needed the moment that what the master does to the other he should also do to himself, and what the servant does to himself, he should do to the other also. On that account a form of recognition has arisen that is one-sided and unequal.

In all this, the unessential consciousness is, for the master, the object which embodies the truth of his certainty of himself. But it is evident that this object does not correspond to its notion; for, just where the master has effectively achieved rule, he really finds that something has come about quite different from an independent consciousness. It is not an independent, but rather a dependent consciousness that he has achieved. He is thus not assured of self-existence as his truth; he finds that his truth is rather the unessential consciousness, and the fortuitous unessential action of that consciousness.

The truth of the independent consciousness is accordingly the consciousness of the servant. This doubtless appears in the first instance outside it, and not as the truth of self-consciousness. But just as the position of master showed its essential nature to be the reverse of what it wants to be, so, too, the position of servant will, when completed, pass into the opposite of what it immediately is: being a consciousness repressed within itself, it will enter into itself, and change around into real and true independence.

[(b) Anxiety.]

We have seen what the position of servant is only in relation to that of the master. But it is a self-consciousness, and we have now to consider what it is, in this regard, in and for itself. In the first instance, the master is taken to be the essential reality for the state of the servant; hence, for it, the truth is the independent consciousness existing for itself, although this truth is not yet taken as inherent in the servant's position itself. Still, it does in fact contain within itself this truth of pure negativity and self-existence, because it has experienced this reality within it. For this self-consciousness was not in peril and fear for this element or that, nor for this or that moment of time, it was afraid for its entire being; it felt the fear of death, it was in mortal terror of its sovereign master. It has been through that experience melted to its inmost soul, has trembled throughout its every fiber, the stable foundations of its whole being have quaked within it. This complete perturbation of its entire substance, this absolute dissolution of all its stability into fluent continuity, is, however, the simple, ultimate nature of self-consciousness, absolute negativity, pure self-referent existence, which consequently is involved in this type of consciousness. This moment of pure self-existence is moreover a fact for it; for in the master this moment is consciously his object. Further, this servant's consciousness is not only this total dissolution in a general way; in serving and toiling, the servant actually carries this out. By serving he cancels in every particular moment his dependence on and attachment to natural existence, and by his work removes this existence.

[(c) Shaping and fashioning.]

The feeling of absolute power, however, realized both in general and in the particular form of service, is only dissolution implicitly, and albeit the fear of his master is the beginning of wisdom, consciousness is not therein aware of being self-existent. Through work and labor, however, this consciousness of the servant comes to itself. In the moment which corresponds to desire in the case of the master's consciousness, the aspect of the non-essential relation to the thing seemed to fall to the lot of the servant, since the thing there retained its independence. Desire has reserved to itself the pure negating of the object and thereby unalloyed feeling of self. This satisfaction, however, just for that reason is itself only a state of evanescence, for it lacks objectivity or subsistence. Labor, on the other hand, is desire restrained and checked, evanescence delayed and postponed; in other words, labor shapes and fashions the thing. The negative relation to the object passes into the *form* of the object, into something that is permanent and remains; because it is just for the laborer that the object has independence. This negative mediating agency, this activity giving shape and form, is at the same time the individual existence, the pure self-existence of that consciousness, which now in the work it does is externalized and passes into the condition of permanence. The consciousness that toils and serves accordingly comes by this means to view that independent being as its self.

But again, shaping or forming the object has not only the positive significance that the servant becomes thereby aware of himself as factually and objectively self-existent; this type of consciousness has also a negative import, in contrast with its first aspect, the elements of fear. For in shaping the thing it only becomes aware of its own proper negativity, its existence on its own account, as an object, through the fact that it cancels the actual form confronting it. But this objective negative element is precisely the alien, external reality, before which it trembled. Now, however, it destroys this extraneous alien negative, affirms and sets itself up as a negative in the element of permanence, and thereby becomes aware of being objectively for itself. In the master, this self-existence is felt to be an other, is only external; in fear, the self-existence is present implicitly; in fashioning the thing, self-existence comes to be felt explicitly as its own proper being, and it attains the consciousness that itself exists in its own right and on its own account (*an und fuer sich*). By the fact that the form is objectified, it does not become something other than the consciousness molding the thing through work; for just that form is his pure self-existence, which therein becomes truly realized. Thus precisely in labor where there seemed to be merely some outsider's mind and ideas involved, the servant becomes aware, through this rediscovery of himself by himself, of having and being a "mind of his own."

For this reflection of self into self the two moments, fear and service in general, as also that of formative activity, are necessary: and at the same time both must exist in a universal manner. Without the discipline of service and obedience, fear remains formal and does not spread over the whole known reality of existence. Without the formative activity shaping the thing, fear remains inward and mute, and consciousness does not become objective for itself. Should consciousness shape and form the thing without the initial state of absolute fear, then it has merely a vain and futile "mind of its own"; for its form or negativity is not negativity *per se,* and hence its formative activity cannot furnish the consciousness of itself as essentially real. If it has endured not absolute fear, but merely some slight anxiety, the negative reality has remained external to it, its substance has not been through and through infected thereby. Since the entire content of its natural consciousness has not tottered and been shaken, it is still inherently a determinate mode of being; having a "mind of its own" (*der eigene sinn*) is simply stubbornness (*Eigensinn*), a type of freedom which does not get beyond the attitude of the servant. The less the pure form can become its essential nature, the less is that form, as overspreading and controlling particulars, a universal formative activity, an absolute conception; it is rather a piece of cleverness which has power within a certain range, but does not wield universal power and dominate the entire objective reality.

QUESTIONS FOR STUDY AND DISCUSSION

1. In self-consciousness, "being-in" and "being-for" itself are the same. Explain.
2. Why does self-consciousness need another self-consciousness in order to truly know itself?
3. Explain the relationship of "life" to self-consciousness.
4. What is the role of labor in the development of the servant?
5. Hegel's discussion of master and servant is an extended analogy. Point out the terms of the analogy in (a) consciousness, (b) history, and (c) politics.

The Transcendence of the Individual

THE CONTRITE CONSCIOUSNESS

In Scepticism [1] Consciousness learns in truth, that it is divided against itself. And from this experience there is born a new Type of Consciousness, wherein are linked the two thoughts which Scepticism had kept asunder. The thoughtless self-ignorance of Scepticism must pass away; for in fact the two attitudes of Scepticism express One Consciousness. This new Type of Consciousness is therefore explicitly aware of its own doubleness. It regards itself on the one hand as the Deliverer, changeless and self-possessed; on the other hand it regards itself as the absolutely confounded and contrary; and it is the awareness of this its own contradiction. In Stoicism [2] the Self owns itself in the simplicity of freedom. In Scepticism it gives itself embodiment, makes naught of other embodied reality, but, in the very act of so doing, renders itself the rather twofold and is now parted in twain. Hereby the same duplication that was formerly shared between two individuals, the Lord and the Slave, has now entered into the nature of one individual. The differentiation of the Self, which is the essential Law of the Spirit, is already present, but not as constituting an organic unity, and the *Contrite Consciousness* [3] is this awareness of the Self as the Divided Nature, wherein is only conflict.

This Contrite and Broken Consciousness, just because the conflict of its Nature is known as belonging to one person, must forever, in each of its two forms, have the other also present to it. Whenever, in either form, it seems to have come to victory and unity, it finds no rest there, but is forthwith driven over to the other. Its true home-coming, its true reconciliation with itself, will, however, display to us the law of the Spirit, as he will appear when, having come to life, he has entered the world of his manifestation. For it already belongs to the Contrite Consciousness to be one undivided soul in the midst of its doubleness. It is in fact the very gazing of one Self into another; it is both these selves; it has no nature save in so far

---

[1] Scepticism is a philosophical doctrine which claims that valid, certain knowledge is unattainable. Hence in assuming a sceptical attitude, consciousness, which seeks valid, certain knowledge, finds that it is divided against itself. [R.D.G.]

[2] Stoicism is a philosophical doctrine which claims that man should rise above his passions, be unconcerned with joy, grief, or transient cares, and be ruled by reason alone. [R.D.G.]

[3] What Royce translates as "Contrite Consciousness" is often translated by others as "unhappy consciousness," unhappy precisely because it is divided and in conflict with itself. [R.D.G.]

From pp. 614–28 of G. W. F. Hegel, *Phenomenology of Mind*, translated by Josiah Royce, in *Modern Classical Philosophers*, edited by Benjamin Rand. Copyright 1924 by Houghton Mifflin Company. Reprinted by permission of the publisher.

as it unites the two. But thus far it knows not yet this its own real essence; it has not entered into possession of this unity.

For the first, then the Contrite Consciousness is but the unwon unity of the two selves. To its view the two are not one, but are at war together. And accordingly it regards one of them, viz., the simple, the Changeless Consciousness, as the True Self. The other, the multiform and fickle, it regards as the False Self. The Contrite Consciousness finds these two as mutually estranged. For its own part, because it is the awareness of this contradiction, it takes sides with the Changeless Consciousness, and calls itself the False Self. But since it is aware of the Changeless, i.e. of the True Self, its task must be one of self-deliverance, that is, the task of delivering itself from the unreality. For on the one hand it knows itself only as the fickle; and the changeless is far remote from it. And yet the Contrite Consciousness is in its genuine selfhood one with the simple and Changeless Consciousness; for therein lies its own true Self. But yet again it knows that it is not in possession of this true self. So long as the Contrite Consciousness assigns to the two selves this position, they cannot remain indifferent to each other; or, in other words, the Contrite Consciousness cannot itself be indifferent to the Changeless. For the Contrite Consciousness is, as a fact, of both kinds, and knows the relation of the changeless to the fickle as a relation of truth to falsehood. The falsehood must be turned to naught; but since the Contrite Consciousness finds both the false and the true alike necessary to it, and contradictory, there remains to it only the contradictory movement, wherein neither of the opposed elements can find repose in going over to its opponent but must create itself anew in the opponent's very bosom.

To win, then, in this strife against the adversary, is rather to be vanquished. To attain one goal, is rather to lose it in its opposite. The whole life, whatever it be, whatever it do, is aware only of the pain of this being and doing. For this Consciousness has no object besides its opposite, the true Self, and its own nothingness. In aspiration it strives hence towards the Changeless. But this aspiration is itself the Contrite Consciousness, and contains forthwith the knowledge of the opposite, namely of its own individuality. The Changeless, when it enters consciousness, is sicklied o'er with individuality, is present therewith; instead of being lost in the consciousness of Changeless, individuality arises ever afresh therein.

But one thing the Contrite Consciousness thus learns, namely that individuality is made manifest in the Changeless, and that the Changeless is made manifest in individuality. It finds that in general individuality belongs to the changeless true Self, and that in fact its own individuality also belongs thereto. For the outcome of this process is precisely the unity of this twofold consciousness. This unity, then, comes to light, but for the first only as an unity wherein the diversity of the two aspects plays the chief part. For the Contrite Consciousness there thus result three ways in which individuality and the Changeless are linked. First, it rediscovers itself as

216 / G. W. F. HEGEL

again banished into its opposition to the Changeless Self; and it is cast back to the beginning of the strife, which latter still remains the element of the entire relationship. In the second place, the Contrite Consciousness learns that individuality belongs to the very essence of the Changeless, is the incarnation of the Changeless; and the latter hereupon assumes the burden of this whole range of phenomena. In the third place, the Contrite Consciousness discovers itself to be the individual who dwells in the Changeless. In the first stage the Changeless appears to consciousness only as the remote Self, that condemns individuality. In passing through the second stage, consciousness learns that the Changeless is as much an incarnate individual as it is itself; and thus, in the third stage, consciousness reaches the grade of the Spirit, rejoices to find itself in the Spirit, and becomes aware that its individuality is reconciled with the Universal.

What is here set forth as the character and relationship of the Changeless has appeared as the experience that the divided consciousness obtains in its woe. This experience is to be sure not its own one-sided process; for it is itself the Changeless Consciousness, and the latter is also an individual consciousness; so that the process is all the while in the Changeless Consciousness, belonging to the latter quite as much as to the other. For the Changeless Consciousness passes through the three stages, being first the changeless as in general opposed to the individual, then becoming an individual over against another individual, and finally being united with the latter. But this observation, in so far as it is made from our own point of view as observers, is here premature; for thus far we have come to know the Changeless only in so far as consciousness has defined it. Not, as yet, the true Changeless, but the Changeless as modified by the duality of consciousness, has come to our sight; and so we know not how the developed and self-possessed Changeless will behave. What has resulted from the foregoing is only this, that the mentioned characteristics appear, to the consciousness now under consideration, as belonging to the Changeless.

Consequently the Changeless Consciousness itself also preserves even in its incarnate form the character and principle of separation and isolation as against the individual consciousness. From the latter's point of view, the fact that the Changeless takes on the form of individuality appears as something which somehow *comes* to *pass*. The opposition to the Changeless is something, moreover, which the individual consciousness merely finds as a fact. The relation seems to it merely a result of its natural constitution. As for the final reconciliation, the individual consciousness looks upon this as in part of its own deed, the result of its own individuality; but it also regards a part of the unity as due, both in origin and in existence, to the Changeless. The element of opposition thus remains even in the unity. In fact, in taking on its incarnate form, the Changeless has not only retained but actually confirmed its character of remoteness. For although, in assuming a developed and incarnate individuality, it seems on the one hand, to have approached the individual, still, on the other hand, it now stands over against him as an opaque fact of sense, with all the stubborn-ness of the actual about it. The hope that the individual may become one with the Changeless must remain but hope, empty and distant; for between hope and fruition stand now the fatal chance and the lifeless indifference which have resulted from that very incarnation wherein lies the foundation of the hope. Because the Changeless has thus entered the world of facts, has taken on the garments of actuality, it follows necessarily that in the world of time it has vanished, that in space it is far away, and forever far remains.

If at the outset the mere notion of the divided consciousness demanded that it should undertake the destruction of its individuality, and the growth into the Changeless, the present result defines the undertaking thus: That the individual should leave off its relation with the formless ideal, and should come only into relations with the Changeless as incarnate. For it is now the fact of the unity of the individual and the Changeless which has become the truth and the object for consciousness, as before, in the mere notion, only the abstract and disembodied Changeless was the essential ob-ject; and consciousness now finds the total separation of the notion as the relation which is to be forgotten. The thing which has now to be reduced to unity is the still external relation to the embodied Ideal, in so far as the latter is a foreign actuality.

The process whereby the unreal Self seeks to reach this unity is once more threefold, since it will be found to have a threefold relation to its in-carnate but remote Ideal. In the first place it will appear as the Devout Consciousness; in the second place, as an individual, whose relation to the actuality will be one of aspiration and of service; in the third place it will reach the consciousness of self-possession. We must now follow these three states of being, to see how they are involved in the general relation, and are determined thereby.

Taking the first state, that of the Devout Consciousness, one finds in-deed that the incarnate Changeless, as it appears to this consciousness, seems to be present in all the completeness of its being. But as a fact the fashion of the completed being of the Changeless has not yet been devel-oped. Should this completed being be revealed to consciousness, the revela-tion would be, as it were, rather the deed of the Ideal than the work of the Devout Consciousness; and thus the revelation would come from one side alone, would be no full and genuine revelation, but would remain burdened with incompleteness and with duality.

Although the Contrite Consciousness still lacks the presence of its Ideal, it is nevertheless as we see [*also*] beyond the stage of pure thought, whether such thought were the mere abstract thinking of Stoicism, which forgets all individuality, or the merely restless thinking of Scepticism, which in fact embodies individuality in its ignorant contradictions and its ceaseless unrepose. Both of these stages the Contrite Consciousness has transcended. It begins the synthesis of pure thought and of individuality and persists therein. But, it has not yet risen to the thought which is aware of the reconciliation of the conscious individual with the demands of pure thought. The Contrite Consciousness stands between the two extremes, at the place where pure thought and the individual consciousness meet. It is in fact itself this meeting place; it is the unity of pure thought and individuality. It even knows that pure thought, yes the Changeless itself, is essentially individual. But what it does not know is that this its object, the Changeless, which it regards as having necessarily assumed an incarnate individuality, is identical with its own self, with the very individual as he is in consciousness.

Its attitude then, in this first form, in which it appears as the Devout Consciousness, is not one in which it explicitly thinks about its object. It is implicitly indeed the consciousness of a thinking individual, and its object also is a thinking individual. But the relation between these two is still one that defies pure thought. Consciousness accordingly as it were makes but a feint at thinking, and takes the form of Adoration. Such thought as it has remains the mere formless tinkling of an altar bell, or the wreathing of warm incense smoke—a thinking in music, such as never reaches an organized notion, wherein alone an inner objectivity could be attained. This limitless and devout inner Feeling finds indeed its object, but as something uncomprehended, and so as a stranger. Thus comes to pass the inward activity of the devout soul, which is indeed self-conscious, but only in so far as it possesses the mere feeling of its sorrowful disharmony. This activity is one of ceaseless longing. It possesses the assurance that its true Self is just such a pure soul,—pure thought in fact, taking on the form of individuality,—and that this Being, who is the object of the devotion, since he possessed the thought of his own individuality, recognizes and approves the worshipper. But at the same time this Being is the unapproachable and remote. As you seize hold upon him he escapes, or rather he has already gone away. He has already gone away; for he is the Ideal giving himself in thought the form of an individual and therefore consciousness gets without hindrance its self-fulfilment in him,—gets self-fulfilment, but only to learn that it is the very opposite of this Ideal. Instead of seizing hold on the true Self, its mere feeling is all. It sinks back into itself. Unable at the moment of union to escape finding itself as the very opposite of the ideal, it has actually seized hold upon its own untruthfulness, not upon the truth. In the true Self it has sought to find its own fulfilment; but *its own* means only its isolated individual reality. For the same reason it cannot get hold upon the true Self in so far as he is at once an individual and a reality. Where one seeks him, the true Self is not to be found; for by definition he is the remote Self, and so is to be found nowhere. To seek him in so far as he is an individual is not to look for his universal, his ideal individuality, nor for his presence as the law of life but merely to seek him as an individual thing, as a fact amongst facts, as something that sense could touch unhindered. But as such an object the Ideal exists only as a lost object. What consciousness finds is thus only the sepulchre of its true life. But this sepulchre is now the actuality, and, moreover, one that by its nature forbids any biding possession; and the presence of this tomb means only the strife of a search that must be fruitless. But consciousness thus learns that there is no real sepulchre which can contain its true Lord, the Changeless. As Lord who has been taken away he is not the true Lord. The Changeless will no longer be looked for here below, or grasped after as the vanished one. For hereby consciousness learns to look for individuality as a genuine and universal ideal.

In the next place then, the return of the soul to itself is to be defined as its knowledge that in its own individuality it has genuine being. It is the pure heart, which potentially, or from our point of view, has discovered the secret of self-satisfaction. For although in feeling it is sundered from its Ideal, still this feeling is in essence a feeling of self-possession. What has been felt is the Ideal as expressed in terms of pure feeling, and this Ideal is its own very self. It issues from the process then as the feeling of self-possession, and so as an actual and independent being. By this return to itself it has, from our point of view, passed to its second relationship, that of aspiration and service. And in this second stage consciousness confirms itself in the assurance of self-possession (an assurance which we now see it to have attained), by overcoming and feeding upon the true Self, which, in so far as it was an independent thing, was estranged. From the point of view of the Contrite Consciousness, however, all that yet appears is the aspiration and the service. It knows not yet that in finding these it has the assurance of self-possession as the basis of its existence, and that its feeling of the true Self is a self-possessed feeling. Not knowing this, it has still ever within it the fragmentary assurance of itself. Therefore any confirmation which it should receive from the toiling and from communion would still be a fragmentary confirmation. Yes, itself it must destroy even this confirmation also, finding therein indeed a confirmation of something, but only of its isolation and its separation.

The actual world wherein the aspiration and the service find their calling, seems to this consciousness no longer an essentially vain world, that is only to be destroyed and consumed, but rather, like the consciousness itself, a world broken in twain, which is only in one aspect vain, while in another aspect it is a sanctified world, wherein the Changeless is incarnate. For the Changeless has retained the nature of individuality, and being, as changeless, an Universal, its individuality has in general the significance of all actuality.

If consciousness were now aware of its independent personality, and if it regarded the actual world as essentially vain, it would get the feeling of its independence in its service and in its communion, since it would be aware of itself as the victory that overcometh the world. But because the world is regarded by it as an embodiment of the ideal, it may not overcome by its own power. It does indeed attain to conquest over the world and to a feasting thereon, but to this end it is essential that the Changeless should itself give its own body as the food. And in this respect consciousness appears as a mere matter of fact having no part in the deed; but it also appears as inwardly broken in twain, and this doubleness, its division into a Self that stands in a genuine relation to itself and to reality, and a Self whose life is hidden and undeveloped, is now apparent in the contrast between its service and its communion. As in actual relation to the world, consciousness is a doer of works, and knows itself as such, and this side belongs to its individuality. But it has also its undeveloped reality. This is hidden in the true Self, and consists in the talents and virtues of the individual. They are a foreign gift. The Changeless grants them to consciousness that they may be used.

In doing its good works, consciousness is, for the first, parted into a relationship between two extremes. On one side stands the toiler in the world here below; on the other side stands the passive actuality in whose midst he toils. Both are related to each other; both however are also referred to the Changeless as their source, and have their being hidden therein. From each side, then, there is but a shadowy image let free to enter into play with the other. That term of the relationship which is called the Actuality is overcome by the other term, the doer of good works. But the former term, for its part, can only be overcome because its own Changeless Nature overcomes it, divides itself in twain, and gives over the divided part to be the material for deeds. The power that does the deeds appears as the might that overcometh the world. But for this very reason the present Consciousness, which regards its true Self as something foreign, must regard this might also, whereby it works, as a thing remote from itself. Instead of winning self-possession from its good works, and becoming thereby sure of itself, Consciousness relates all this activity back again to the other member of the relationship, which thus proves itself to be the pure Universal, the Absolute Might, whence flows every form of activity, and wherein lies the truth both of the mutually dissolving terms, as they first appeared, and of their interchanging of relationship.

The Changeless Consciousness sacrifices its body, and gives it over to be used. On the other hand the individual consciousness renders thanks for the gift, forbids itself the satisfaction of a sense of independence, and refers all its doings to the Changeless. In these two aspects of the mutual sacrifice made by both the members of the relation, Consciousness does indeed win the sense of its own oneness with the Changeless. But at the same time this oneness is still beladen with the separation, and is divided in itself. This opposition between the Individual and the Universal comes afresh to sight. For Consciousness only *seems* to resign selfish satisfaction. As a fact it gets selfish satisfaction. For it still remains longing, activity, and fulfilment. As Consciousness it has longed, it has acted, it has been filled. In giving thanks, in acknowledging the Other as the true Self, in making naught of itself, it has still been doing its own deed. This deed has repaid the deed of the

Other, has rendered a price for the kindly sacrifice. If the Other has offered its own image as a gift, consciousness, for its part, has made its return in thanks, and has herein done actually more than the Other, since it has offered its All, namely, its good works, while the Other has but parted with its mere image. The entire process returns then back to the side of the individual, and does so not merely in respect of the actual aspiration, service, and communion, but even in respect of the very act of giving thanks, an act that was to attain the opposite result. In giving thanks consciousness is aware of itself as this individual, and refuses to be deceived by its own seeming resignation. What has resulted is only the twofold reference of the process to its two terms; and the result is the renewed division into the conflicting consciousness of the Changeless on the one hand, and, on the other hand, the consciousness of the opposed will, activity, and fulfilment, and even of the very resignation itself; for these constitute in general the separated individuality.

Herewith begins the third phase of the process of this consciousness; which follows from the second as a consciousness that in truth, by will and by deed, has proved its independence. In the first phase it was the mere notion of alive consciousness, an inner life that had not yet attained actuality by service and communion. The second phase was the attainment, as outer activity and communion. Returned from this outer activity, consciousness has now reached the stage where it has experienced its own actuality and power, where it knows in truth that it is fully self-possessed. But now the enemy comes to light in his most genuine form. In the struggle of the inner life the individual had existence only as an abstraction, as "passed in music out of sight." In service and in communion, as the realization of this unreal selfhood, it is able in its immediate experience to forget itself, and its consciousness of its own merit in this actual service is turned to humiliation through the act of thankful acknowledgment. But this humiliation is in truth a return of consciousness to itself, and to itself as the possessor of its own actuality.

This third relationship, wherein this genuine actuality is to be one term, is that relationship of the actuality to the Universal, wherein the actuality is nevertheless to appear as an Unreality; and the process of this relationship is still to be considered.

In the first place, as regards the conflicting relationship of consciousness, wherein its own reality appears to it as an obvious nothingness, the result is that its actual work seems to it a doing of naught, and its satisfaction is but a sense of its misery. Work and satisfaction thus lose all universal content and meaning; for if they had any, then they would involve a full self-possession. Both of them sink to the level of individuality; and consciousness, turning upon this individuality, devotes itself to making naught of it. Consciousness of an actual individual is a consciousness of the mere animal functions of the body. These latter are no longer naïvely carried out as something that is altogether of no moment, and that can have no weight or significance for the spirit; on the contrary, they become the object of earnest concern, and are of the very weightiest moment. The enemy arises anew in his defeat. Consciousness holds him in eye, yet frees itself not from him, but rather dwells upon the sight, and sees constantly its own uncleanness. And because, at the same time, this object of its striving, instead of being significant, is of the most contemptible, instead of being an universal is of the most individual, we therefore behold at this stage only a brooding, unhappy and miserable personality, limited solely to himself and his little deeds.

But all the while this person links both to the sense of his misery and to the worthlessness of his deeds, the consciousness that he is one with the Ideal. For the attempted direct destruction of individuality is determined by the thought of the Ideal, and takes place for the sake of the Ideal. This relation to dependence constitutes the essence of the negative onslaught upon individuality. But the dependence is as such potentially positive, and will bring consciousness to a sense of its own unity.

This determinate dependence is the rational Tie, whereby the individual who at first holds fast by his opposition to the true Self, is still linked to the other term, yet only by means of a third element. This mediating element reveals the true Self to the false Self, which in its turn knows that in the eyes of the true Self it has existence only by virtue of the dependence. It is the dependence then which reveals the two terms of the relationship to one another, and which, as Mediator, takes the part of each one of the terms in presence of the other. The Mediator too is a conscious Being, for its work is the production of this consciousness as such. What it brings to pass is that overcoming of individuality which consciousness is undertaking.

Through the Mediator, then, Consciousness frees itself from regarding its good works and its communion as due to its private merit. It rejects all claim to independence of will. It casts upon the Mediator, the intercessor, the burden of its self-will, its freedom of choice, and its sins. The Mediator, dwelling in the immediate presence of the Ideal, gives counsel as to what is to be done. And what is done, being in submission to the will of another, is no longer one's own act. What is still left to the untrue Self is the objective result of the deed, the fruit of the toil, the satisfaction. But this too it refuses to accept as its own, and resigns not only its self-will, but the actual outcome of its service and its satisfaction. It resigns this outcome, first, because the latter would involve an attainment of self-conscious truth and independence (and this consciousness lives in the thought and the speech of a strange and incomprehensible mystery). Secondly, moreover, it resigns the outcome in so far as the latter consists of worldly goods, and so it abandons, in a measure, whatever it has earned by its labor. Thirdly, it resigns all the satisfaction which has fallen to its lot, forbidding itself such satisfaction through fasting and through penance.

By these characteristics, by the surrender of self-will, of property, and of satisfaction, and by the further and positive characteristic of its undertaking of a mysterious task, consciousness does in truth free itself completely from any sense of inner or outer freedom, from any trust in the reality of its independence. It is sure that it has verily surrendered its Ego, and has reduced its natural self-consciousness to a mere thing, to a fact amongst facts. Only by such a genuine self-surrender could consciousness prove its own resignation. For only thus does there vanish the deceit that lies in the inner offering of thanks with the heart, with the sentiments, with the lips. Such offering does indeed strip from the individual all independent might, and ascribes all the glory to the heavenly Giver. But the individual even when thus stripped, retains his outer self-will, for he abandons not his possessions; and he retains his inner self-will, for he is aware that it is he who undertakes this self-sacrifice, and who has in himself the virtue involved in such an undertaking,—a virtue which he has not exchanged for the mysterious grace that cometh from above.

But in the genuine resignation, when once it has come to pass, consciousness, in laying aside the burden of its own deeds, has also, in effect, laid aside the burden of its grief. Yet that this laying aside has already, in effect, taken place, is due to the deed of the other member of the Tie, namely to the essential Self. The sacrifice of the unreal Self was made not by its own one-sided act, but involved the working of the Other's grace. For the resignation of self-will is only in part negative, and on the other hand involves in its very notion, or in its beginning, the positive transformation of the will, and, in particular, its transformation from an individual into an universal will. Consciousness finds this positive meaning of the denial of self-will to consist in the will of the Changeless, as this will is done, not by consciousness itself, but through the counsel of the Mediator. Consciousness becomes aware, then, that its will is universal and essential, but it does not regard itself as identical with this essential nature. Self-resignation is not seen to be in its very notion identical with the positive work of the universal will. In the same way the abandonment of possession and of satisfaction has only the same negative significance, and the universal that thus comes in sight does not appear to consciousness as its own deed. The unity of truth and of self-possession implied in the notion of this activity, an unity which consciousness accordingly regards as its essence and its reality, is not recognized as implied in this very notion. Nor is the unity recognized by consciousness as its own self-created and immediately possessed object. Rather does consciousness only hear, spoken by the mediator's voice, the still fragile assurance that its own grief is, in the yet hidden truth of the matter, the very reverse, namely the bliss of an activity which rejoices in its tasks, that its own miserable deeds are, in the same hidden truth, the perfect work. And the real meaning of this assurance is that only what is done by an individual is or can be [*ueberhaupt*] a deed. But for consciousness both activity and its own actual deeds remain miserable. Its satisfaction is its sorrow, and the freedom from this sorrow, in a positive joy, it looks for in another world. But this other world, where its activity and its being are to become, even while they remain its own, real activity and being,—what is this world but the image of *Reason*,—of the assurance of Consciousness that in its individuality it is and possesses all Reality?

QUESTIONS FOR STUDY AND DISCUSSION

1. What does Hegel mean by contrite consciousness?
2. Explain the relation of the "true" self to the "false" self.
3. How does contrite consciousness escape from its unhappy state?
4. Is Reason transindividual? Explain.
5. What is the relationship of Spirit to individual consciousness?

Man's Freedom Through History

THE IDEA OF HISTORY AND ITS REALIZATION

The question of how Reason is determined in itself and what its relation is to the world coincides with the question, *What is the ultimate purpose of the world?* This question implies that the purpose is to be actualized and realized. Two things, then, must be considered: first, the content of this ultimate purpose, the determination as such, and, secondly, its realization.

To begin with, we must note that world history goes on within the realm of Spirit. The term "world" includes both physical and psychical nature. Physical nature does play a part in world history, and from the very beginning we shall draw attention to the fundamental natural relations thus involved. But Spirit, and the course of its development, is the substance of history. We must not contemplate nature as a rational system in itself, in its own particular domain, but only in its relation to Spirit.

After the creation of nature appears Man. He constitutes the antithesis to the natural world; he is the being that lifts itself up to the second world. We have in our universal consciousness two realms, the realm of Nature and the realm of Spirit. The realm of Spirit consists in what is produced by man. One may have all sorts of ideas about the Kingdom of God; but it is always a realm of Spirit to be realized and brought about in man.

The realm of Spirit is all-comprehensive; it includes everything that ever has interested or ever will interest man. Man is active in it; whatever he does, he is the creature within which the Spirit works. Hence it is of

From pp. 20–67 of Georg Wilhelm Friedrich Hegel, *Reason in History*, edited by Robert S. Hartman. Copyright 1953 by The Liberal Arts Press, Inc. Reprinted by permission of the Liberal Arts Press Division of The Bobbs-Merrill Company, Inc.

interest, in the course of history, to learn to know spiritual nature in its existence, that is, the point where Spirit and Nature unite, namely, human nature. In speaking of human nature we mean something permanent. The concept of human nature must fit all men and all ages, past and present. This universal concept may suffer infinite modifications; but actually the universal is one and the same essence in its most various modifications. Thinking reflection disregards the variations and adheres to the universal, which under all circumstances is active in the same manner and shows itself in the same interest. The universal type appears even in what seems to deviate from it most strongly; in the most distorted figure we can still discern the human.

. . .

In contemplating world history we must thus consider its ultimate purpose. This ultimate purpose is what is willed in the world itself. We know of God that He is the most perfect; He can will only Himself and what is like Him. God and the nature of His will are one and the same; these we call, philosophically, the *Idea*. Hence, it is the Idea in general, in its manifestation as human spirit, which we have to contemplate. More precisely, it is the idea of human freedom. The purest form in which the Idea manifests itself is Thought itself. In this aspect the Idea is treated in Logic. Another form is that of physical Nature.[1] The third form, finally, is that of Spirit in general. Spirit, on the stage on which we observe it, that of world history, is in its most concrete reality. But nevertheless—or rather in order to understand also the general idea of this concrete existence of Spirit—we must set forth, first, some general definition of the *nature of Spirit*. But this can only be done here as a mere assertion; this is not the place to develop the idea of Spirit through philosophical speculation. As was mentioned above, what can be said in an introduction can be taken only historically—as an assumption to be explained and proved elsewhere or to be verified by the science of history itself.

We have therefore to indicate here:

(1) The abstract characteristics of the nature of Spirit.

(2) The means Spirit uses in order to realize its Idea.

(3) The form which the complete realization of Spirit assumes in existence—the State.

1. THE IDEA OF FREEDOM

The nature of Spirit may be understood by a glance at its direct opposite—Matter. The essence of matter is gravity, the essence of Spirit— its substance—is Freedom. It is immediately plausible to everyone that, among other properties, Spirit also possesses Freedom. But philosophy teaches us that *all* the properties of Spirit exist only through Freedom. All

---

[1] In this aspect the Idea is treated in the Philosophy of Nature. [R.S.H.]

are but means of attaining Freedom; all seek and produce this and this alone. It is an insight of speculative philosophy that Freedom is the sole truth of Spirit. Matter possesses gravity by virtue of its tendency toward a central point; it is essentially composite, consisting of parts that exclude each other. It seeks its unity and thereby its own abolition; it seeks its opposite.[2] If it would attain this it would be matter no longer, but would have perished. It strives toward ideality, for in unity it exists ideally.[3] Spirit, on the contrary, is that which has its center in itself. It does not have unity outside of itself but has found it; it is in itself and with itself. Matter has its substance outside of itself; Spirit is Being-within-itself (self-contained existence). But this, precisely, is Freedom. For when I am dependent, I refer myself to something else which I am not; I cannot exist independently of something external. I am free when I am within myself. This self-contained existence of Spirit is self-consciousness, consciousness of self.

Two things must be distinguished in consciousness, first, *that* I know and, secondly, *what* I know. In self-consciousness the two coincide, for Spirit knows itself. It is the judgment of its own nature and, at the same time, the operation of coming to itself, to produce itself, to make itself (actually) into that which it is in itself (potentially). Following this abstract definition it may be said that world history is the exhibition of spirit striving to attain knowledge of its own nature. As the germ bears in itself the whole nature of the tree, the taste and shape of its fruit, so also the first traces of Spirit virtually contain the whole of history. Orientals do not yet know that Spirit—Man as such—is free. And because they do not know it, they are not free. They only know that *one* is free; but for this very reason such freedom is mere caprice, ferocity, dullness of passion, or, perhaps, softness and tameness of desire—which again is nothing but an accident of nature and thus, again, caprice. This *one* is therefore only a despot, not a free man. The consciousness of freedom first arose among the Greeks, and therefore they were free. But they, and the Romans likewise, only knew that some are free—not man as such. This not even Plato and Aristotle knew. For this reason the Greeks not only had slavery, upon which was based their whole life and the maintenance of their splendid liberty, but their freedom itself was partly an accidental, transient, and limited flowering and partly a severe thralldom of human nature. Only the Germanic peoples came, through Christianity, to realize that man as man is free and the freedom of Spirit is the very essence of man's nature. This realization first arose in religion, in the innermost region of spirit; [4] but to introduce it in the secular world was a further task which could only be solved and ful-

---

[2] See *Encyklopädie der philosophischen Wissenschaften* [*Encyclopaedia of the Philosophical Sciences*], par. 262. [R.S.H.]

[3] Since matter is composed of parts, complete unity is an ideal that matter cannot achieve and that is excluded by its very nature. [R.D.G.]

[4] Of the Jewish people; see *Philosophy of World History*, Part III, Section III, Ch. 2. [R.S.H.]

filled by a long and severe effort of civilization. Thus slavery did not cease immediately with the acceptance of the Christian religion. Liberty did not suddenly predominate in states nor reason in governments and constitutions. The application of the principle to secular conditions, the thorough molding and interpenetration of the secular world by it, is precisely the long process of history. I have already drawn attention to this distinction between a principle as such and its application, its introduction and execution in the actuality of life and spirit. This is a fundamental fact in our science and must be kept constantly in mind. Just as we noted it in the Christian principle of self-consciousness and freedom, so it shows itself in the principle of freedom in general. World history is the progress of the consciousness of freedom—a progress whose necessity we have to investigate.

The preliminary statement given above of the various grades in the consciousness of freedom—that the Orientals knew only that *one* is free, the Greeks and Romans that *some* are free, while we know that *all* men absolutely, that is, as men, are free—is at the same time the natural division of world history and the manner in which we shall treat it. But this is only mentioned in passing; first, we must explain some other concepts.

We have established Spirit's consciousness of its freedom, and thereby the actualization of this Freedom as the final purpose of the world. For the spiritual world is the substance of reality, and the physical world remains subordinate to it, or, in terms of speculative philosophy, has no truth compared with the former. But the term "freedom," without further qualification, is indefinite and infinitely ambiguous. Being the highest concept, it is liable to an infinity of misunderstandings, confusions, and errors and may give rise to all possible kinds of extravagances. All this has never been more clearly known and experienced than today. Yet for the time being we must content ourselves with this general, as yet undefined term. Attention was also drawn to the importance of the infinite difference between the principle, as that which so far is only in itself, and that which is real. At the same time, it is Freedom in itself that comprises within itself the infinite necessity of bringing itself to consciousness and thereby, since knowledge about itself is its very nature, to reality. Freedom is itself its own object of attainment and the sole purpose of Spirit. It is the ultimate purpose toward which all world history has continually aimed. To this end all the sacrifices have been offered on the vast altar of the earth throughout the long lapse of ages. Freedom alone is the purpose which realizes and fulfills itself, the only enduring pole in the change of events and conditions, the only truly efficient principle that pervades the whole. This final aim is God's purpose with the world. But God is the absolutely perfect Being and can, therefore, will nothing but Himself, His own will. The nature of His own will, His own nature, is what we here call the Idea of freedom. Thus we translate the language of religion into that of philosophy. Our next question then is: what are the means the Idea uses for its realization? This is the second point that we have to consider.

228 / G. W. F. HEGEL

2. THE MEANS OF REALIZATION

(a) The Idea and the Individual

The question of the *means* whereby Freedom develops itself into a world leads us directly to the phenomenon of history. Although Freedom as such is primarily an internal idea, the means it uses are the external phenomena which in history present themselves directly before our eyes. The first glance at history convinces us that the actions of men spring from their needs, their passions, their interests, their characters, and their talents. Indeed, it appears as if in this drama of activities these needs, passions, and interests are the sole springs of action and the main efficient cause.[5] It is true that this drama involves also universal purposes, benevolence, or noble patriotism. But such virtues and aims are insignificant on the broad canvas of history. We may, perhaps, see the ideal of Reason actualized in those who adopt such aims and in the spheres of their influence; but their number is small in proportion to the mass of the human race and their influence accordingly limited. Passions, private aims, and the satisfaction of selfish desires are, on the contrary, tremendous springs of action. Their power lies in the fact that they respect none of the limitations which law and morality would impose on them; and that these natural impulses are closer to the core of human nature than the artificial and troublesome discipline that tends toward order, self-restraint, law, and morality.

· · ·

We assert then that nothing has been accomplished without an interest on the part of those who brought it about. And if "interest" be called "passion"—because the whole individuality is concentrating all its desires and powers, with every fiber of volition, to the neglect of all other actual or possible interests and aims, on one object—we may then affirm without qualification that *nothing great in the world* has been accomplished without passion.

Two elements therefore enter into our investigation: first, the Idea, secondly, the complex of human passions; the one the warp, the other the woof of the vast tapestry of world history. Their contact and concrete union constitutes moral liberty in the state. We have already spoken of the Idea of freedom as the essence of Spirit and absolutely final purpose of history. Passion is regarded as something wrong, something more or less evil; man is not supposed to have passions. "Passion," it is true, is not quite the right word for what I wish to express. I mean here nothing more than human activity resulting from private interest, from special or, if you will, self-seeking designs—with this qualification: that the whole energy of will

---

[5] An efficient cause is that which acts as the immediate agency in producing the effect. [R.D.G.]

and character is devoted to the attainment of one aim and that other interests or possible aims, indeed everything else, is sacrificed to this aim. This particular objective is so bound up with the person's will that it alone and entirely determines its direction and is inseparable from it. It is that which makes the person what he is. For a person is a specific existence. He is not man in general—such a thing does not exist—but a particular human being. The term "character" also expresses this uniqueness of will and intelligence. But character comprises all individual features whatever—the way in which a person conducts himself in his private and other relations. It does not connote this individuality itself in its practical and active phase. I shall therefore use the term "passion" to mean the particularity of a character insofar as its individual volitions not only have a particular content but also supply the impelling and actuating force for deeds of universal scope. Passion is thus the subjective and therefore the formal aspect of energy, will, and activity, whose content and aim are at this point still undetermined.[6] And a similar relation exists between individual conviction, insight, and conscience, on the one hand, and their content, on the other. If someone wants to decide whether my conviction and passion are true and substantial, he must consider the *content* of my conviction and the *aim* of my passion. Conversely, if they are true and substantial, they cannot help but attain actual existence.

From this comment on the second essential element in the historical embodiment of an aim, we infer—considering for a moment the institution of the state—that a state is then well constituted and internally vigorous when the private interest of its citizens is one with the common interest of the state, and the one finds gratification and realization in the other—a most important proposition. But in a state many institutions are necessary—inventions, appropriate arrangements, accompanied by long intellectual struggles in order to find out what is really appropriate, as well as struggles with private interests and passions, which must be harmonized in difficult and tedious discipline. When a state reaches this harmony, it has reached the period of its bloom, its excellence, its power and prosperity. But world history does not begin with any conscious aim, as do the *particular* circles of men. Already the simple instinct of living together contains the conscious purpose of securing life and property; once this primal society has been established, the purpose expands. But world history begins its *general* aim—to realize the idea of Spirit—only in an implicit form (*an sich*),[7] namely, as Nature—as an innermost, unconscious instinct. And the whole business of history, as already observed, is to bring it into consciousness.

---

[6] Passion is the individual, personal factor in action. Only a passion directed toward a "true and substantial" aim or object, that is, toward something that is objectively possible and in accordance with the rational development of history, will achieve its aim. [R.D.G.]

[7] *An sich:* in itself. [R.D.G.]

Thus, appearing in the form of nature, of natural will, what we have called the subjective side is immediate, actual existence (*für sich*)[8]: need, instinct, passion, private interest, even opinion and subjective representation. These vast congeries of volitions, interests, and activities constitute the tools and means of the World Spirit for attaining its purpose, bringing it to consciousness, and realizing it. And this purpose is none other than finding itself—coming to itself—and contemplating itself in concrete actuality. But one may indeed question whether those manifestations of vitality on the part of individuals and peoples in which they seek and satisfy their own purposes are, at the same time, the means and tools of a higher and broader purpose of which they know nothing, which they realize unconsciously. This purpose has been questioned, and in every variety of form denied, decried, and denounced as mere dreaming and "philosophy." On this point, however, I announced my view at the very outset, and asserted our hypothesis—which eventually will appear as the result of our investigation—namely, that Reason governs the world and has consequently governed its history. In relation to this Reason, which is universal and substantial, in and for itself, all else is subordinate, subservient, and the means for its actualization. Moreover, this Reason is immanent in historical existence and reaches its own perfection in and through this existence. The union of the abstract universal, existing in and for itself, with the particular or subjective, and the fact that this union alone constitutes truth are a matter of speculative philosophy which, in this general form, is treated in logic. But in its historical development the subjective side, consciousness, is not yet able to know what is the abstract final aim of history, the idea of Spirit, for it is then itself in process and incomplete. The idea of Spirit is not yet its distinct object of desire and interest. Thus desire is still unconscious of its purpose; yet it already exists in the particular purposes and realizes itself through them. The problem concerning the union of the general and the subjective may also be raised under the form of the union of freedom and necessity. We consider the immanent development of the Spirit, existing in and for itself, as necessary, while we refer to freedom the interests contained in men's conscious volitions. Since, as was said, the speculative, that is, the conceptual aspect of this connection belongs to logic, it would be out of place to analyze it here.

· · ·

(b) The Individual as Subject of History

In world history we deal with the Idea as it manifests itself in the element of human will, of human freedom. . . . Objectively seen, the Idea and the particular individual stand in the great opposition of Necessity and Freedom—the struggle of man against fate. But we take necessity not as the external necessity of fate, but as that of the divine Idea. The question

---

[8] *Für sich:* for itself. [R.D.G.]

then is: How is this high Idea to be united with human freedom? The will of the individual is free when it can posit abstractly, absolutely, and in and for itself that which it wills. How then can the universal, the rational in general, be determinant in history? This contradiction cannot be clarified here in complete detail.

. . .

The building of a house is, in the first instance, a subjective aim and design. On the other hand we have, as means, the several substances required for the work—iron, wood, stones. The elements are used in preparing this material: fire to melt the iron, wind to blow the fire, water to set wheels in motion in order to cut the wood, etc. The result is that the wind, which has helped to build the house, is shut out by the house; so also are the violence of rains and floods and the destructive powers of fire, so far as the house is made fire-proof. The stones and beams obey the law of gravity and press downwards so that the high walls are held up. Thus the elements are made use of in accordance with their nature and cooperate for a product by which they become constrained. In a similar way the passions of men satisfy themselves; they develop themselves and their purposes in accordance with their natural destination and produce the edifice of human society. Thus they fortify a structure for law and order *against* themselves.

. . .

This connection implies that human actions in history produce additional results, beyond their immediate purpose and attainment, beyond their immediate knowledge and desire. They gratify their own interests; but something more is thereby accomplished, which is latent in the action though not present in their consciousness and not included in their design. An analogous example is offered in the case of a man who, thirsting for revenge perhaps justly to redress an unjust injury, sets fire to another man's house. The deed immediately establishes a train of circumstances not directly connected with it, taken in itself. In itself it consists in merely presenting a small flame to a small portion of a beam. Events not involved in that simple act follow of themselves. The part of the beam which was set afire is connected with its remote portions; the beam itself is united with the woodwork of the house and this with other houses, and a wide conflagration ensues. It destroys the goods and chattels of many other persons besides those of the original victim and may even cost their lives. This lay neither in the deed itself, nor in the design of the man who committed it. But the action has a further general bearing. In the design of the doer it was only revenge executed against an individual through the destruction of his property. But it is moreover a crime, and that involves punishment. All this may not have been present to the mind of the perpetrator, still less in his intention; but his deed itself, the general principles that it calls into play, its substantial content, entail it. By this example, I wish only to impress on you the consideration that in a simple act something further may be implicated than lies in the intention and consciousness of the agent. The example before us involves, however, this additional consideration, that the substance of the act—consequently we may say the act itself—recoils upon the perpetrator, reacts upon him and destroys him.

This union of the two extremes—the embodiment of a general idea in immediate actuality and the elevation of a particularity into universal truth —comes about under the condition of the diversity and mutual indifference of the two extremes. The human agents have before them limited aims, special interests. But they are also intelligent, thinking beings. Their purposes are interwoven with general and essential considerations of law, the good, duty, etc. For mere desire, volition in its raw and savage form, falls outside the scene and sphere of world history. These general considerations, which at the same time form norms for directing purposes and actions, have a definite content. For such empty abstractions as "good for its own sake" have no place in living actuality. If men are to act, they must not only intend the good but must know whether this or that particular course is good. What special course of action is good or not, right or wrong, is determined, for the ordinary circumstances of private life, by the laws and customs of a state. It is not too difficult to know them.

. . .

In the course of history two factors are important. One is the preservation of a people, a state, of the well-ordered spheres of life. This is the activity of individuals participating in the common effort and helping to bring about its particular manifestations. It is the preservation of ethical life. The other important factor, however, is the decline of a state. The existence of a national spirit is broken when it has used up and exhausted itself. World history, the World Spirit, continues on its course. We cannot deal here with the position of the individuals within the moral whole and their moral conduct and duty. We are concerned with the Spirit's development, its progression and ascent to an ever higher concept of itself. But this development is connected with the degradation, destruction, annihilation of the preceding mode of actuality which the concept of the Spirit had evolved. This is the result, on the one hand, of the inner development of the Idea and, on the other, of the activity of individuals, who are its agents and bring about its actualization. It is at this point that appear those momentous collisions between existing, acknowledged duties, laws, and rights and those possibilities which are adverse to this system, violate it, and even destroy its foundations and existence. Their tenor may nevertheless seem good, on the whole advantageous—yes, even indispensable and necessary. These possibilities now become historical fact; they involve a universal of an order different from that upon which depends the permanence of a people or a state. This universal is an essential phase in the development of the creating Idea, of truth striving and urging toward itself. The historical men, *world-historical individuals,* are those who grasp just such a higher universal, make it their own purpose, and realize this purpose in accordance with the higher law of the spirit.

Caesar was such a man. Before reaching his position of superiority he was in danger of losing his place of equality with the other leaders of Rome. He was about to succumb to those who were just becoming his enemies. These enemies, who at the same time pursued their own personal interests, had on their side the formal constitution of Rome and the power of legal appearance. Caesar fought to keep his position, honor, and safety. But victory over his enemies, who held the power over all the Roman provinces, became at the same time conquest of the entire empire. Thus Caesar, without changing the form of the constitution, became the sole ruler of the state. In accomplishing his originally negative purpose—the autocracy over Rome—he at the same time fulfilled the necessary historical destiny of Rome and the world. Thus he was motivated not only by his own private interest, but acted instinctively to bring to pass that which the times required. It is the same with all great historical individuals: their own particular purposes contain the substantial will of the World Spirit. They must be called "heroes," insofar as they have derived their purpose and vocation not from the calm, regular course of things, sanctioned by the existing order, but from a secret source whose content is still hidden and has not yet broken through into existence. The source of their actions is the inner spirit, still hidden beneath the surface but already knocking against the outer world as against a shell, in order, finally, to burst forth and break it into pieces; for it is a kernel different from that which belongs to the shell. They are men, therefore, who appear to draw the impulses of their lives from themselves. Their deeds have produced a condition of things and a complex of historical relations that appear to be their own interest and their own work.

Such individuals have no consciousness of the Idea as such. They are practical and political men. But at the same time they are thinkers with insight into what is needed and timely. They see the very truth of their age and their world, the next genus, so to speak, which is already formed in the womb of time. It is theirs to know this new universal, the necessary next stage of their world, to make it their own aim and put all their energy into it. The world-historical persons, the heroes of their age, must therefore be recognized as its seers—their words and deeds are the best of the age. Great men have worked for their own satisfaction and not that of others. Whatever prudent designs and well-meant counsels they might have gotten from others would have been limited and inappropriate under the circumstances. For it is they who knew best and from whom the others eventually learned and with whom they agreed or, at least, complied. For Spirit, in taking this new historical step, is the innermost soul of all individuals—but in a state of unconsciousness, which the great men arouse to consciousness. For this reason their fellow men follow these soul-leaders, they stream to their banner. For they feel the irresistible power of their own spirit embodied in them.

Let us now cast a look at the fate of these world-historical individuals. . . . Their whole life was labor and trouble, their whole being was in their passion. Once their objective is attained, they fall off like empty hulls from the kernel. They die early like Alexander, they are murdered like Caesar, transported to Saint Helena like Napoleon.

(c) The Individual as Object of History

We might find it tolerable that individuals, their purposes and gratifications, are thus sacrificed, their happiness abandoned to the realm of natural forces and hence of chance to which it belongs; and that individuals in general are regarded under the category of means. Yet there is one aspect of human individuality that we must refuse to take exclusively in this light even in relation to the highest, an element which is absolutely not subordinate but exists in individuals as essentially eternal and divine. I mean morality,[9] ethics, religion. Already in discussing the role of individuals in the realization of the rational aim we said that the subjective element in them, their interests, cravings, and impulses, their views and judgments had an infinite right to be satisfied, although we regarded these as only the formal aspect of the process. In speaking of means we imagine, first of all, something external to the end which has no share in it. But actually even merely natural things, the most common lifeless objects used as means, must somehow be adapted to their purpose; they must have something in common with it. This bare external relation of mere means is the least relation human beings have to the rational purpose. In the very act of realizing it they make it the occasion of satisfying their personal desires, whose import is different from that purpose. Moreover, they share in the rational purpose itself and for that very reason are ends in themselves—not merely formally, as is the world of other living beings, whose individual life is essentially subordinate to that of man and is properly used up as an instrument. Men, on the contrary, are ends in themselves in regard to the content of the end. This defines those elements which we demand to be exempt from the category of means: morality, ethics, religion.[10]

3. THE STATE

(a) The State as Realization of the Idea

The third point, then, concerns the end to be attained by these means, that is, the form it assumes in the realm of the actual. We have spoken of

---

[9] Hegel here refers to the morality of a reflective person who lives in accordance with reason (which he calls *Moralität*) and not simply customary, unreflective actions of law-abiding persons (which he calls *sittlich*). [R.D.G.]

[10] Hegel later defines the sense in which man is an end in himself: "Man is an end in himself only by virtue of the divine in him—that which we designated at the outset as *Reason*, or, insofar as it has activity and power of self-determination, as *Freedom*." [R.D.G.]

means; but the carrying out of a subjective, limited aim also requires a *material* element, either already present or to be procured or to serve this actualization. Thus the question would arise: What is the material in which the final end of Reason is to be realized? It is first of all the subjective agent itself, human desires, subjectivity in general. In human knowledge and volition, as its material basis, the rational attains existence. We have considered subjective volition with its purpose, namely, the truth of reality, insofar as moved by a great world-historical passion. As a subjective will in limited passions it is dependent; it can gratify its particular desires only within this dependence. But the subjective will has also a substantial life, a reality where it moves in the region of essential being and has the essential itself as the object of its existence. This essential being is the union of the subjective with the rational will; it is the moral whole, the *State*. It is that actuality in which the individual has and enjoys his freedom, but only as knowing, believing, and willing the universal. This must not be understood as if the subjective will of the individual attained its gratification and enjoyment through the common will and the latter were a means for it—as if the individual limited his freedom among the other individuals, so that this common limitation, the mutual constraint of all, might secure a small space of liberty for each. (This would only be negative freedom.) Rather, law, morality, the State, and they alone, are the positive reality and satisfaction of freedom. The caprice of the individual is not freedom. It is this caprice which is being limited, the license of particular desires.

The subjective will, passion, is the force which actualizes and realizes. The Idea is the interior; the State is the externally existing, genuinely moral life. It is the union of the universal and essential with the subjective will, and as such it is *Morality*. The individual who lives in this unity has a moral life, a value which consists in this substantiality alone.[11] Sophocles' Antigone says: "The divine commands are not of yesterday nor of today; no, they have an infinite existence, and no one can say whence they came." [12] The laws of ethics are not accidental, but are rationality itself. It is the end of the State to make the substantial prevail and maintain itself in the actual doings of men and in their convictions. It is the absolute interest of Reason that this moral whole exist; and herein lies the justification and merit of heroes who have founded states, no matter how crude.

.   .   .

The spiritual individual, the people, insofar as it is organized in itself, an organic whole, is what we call the State. This designation is ambiguous in that by "state" and "constitutional law" one usually means the simple political aspect as distinct from religion, science, and art. But when we

---

[11] Man's reflective moral life (which is basically interior) is completed by the establishment of rational, moral (and so public or external) social institutions. Hegel identifies the union of the two with the State. [R.D.G.]

[12] This seems an unfortunate reference, for Antigone *opposes* the eternal laws of the gods to the temporal commands of a state—thus making a point opposed to the one here being made by Hegel. [R.S.H.]

speak of the manifestation of the spiritual we understand the term "state" in a more comprehensive sense, similar to the term *Reich* (empire, realm). For us, then, a people is primarily a spiritual individual. We do not emphasize the external aspects but concentrate on what has been called the spirit of a people. We mean its consciousness of itself, of its own truth, its own essence, the spiritual powers which live and rule in it. The universal which manifests itself in the State and is known in it—the *form* under which everything that is, is subsumed—is that which constitutes the *culture* of a nation. The definite *content* which receives this universal form and is contained in the concrete actuality of the state is the *spirit of the people*. The actual state is animated by this spirit in all its particular affairs, wars, institutions, etc. This spiritual content is something definite, firm, solid, completely exempt from caprice, the particularities, the whims of individuality, of chance. That which is subject to the latter is not the nature of the people: it is like the dust playing over a city or a field, which does not essentially transform it. This spiritual content then constitutes the essence of the individual as well as that of the people. It is the holy bond that ties the men, the spirits together. It is one life in all, a grand object, a great purpose and content on which depend all individual happiness and all private decisions. The state does not exist for the citizens; on the contrary, one could say that the state is the end and they are its means. But the means-end relation is not fitting here. For the state is not the abstract confronting the citizens; they are parts of it, like members of an organic body, where no member is end and none is means. It is the realization of Freedom, of the absolute, final purpose, and exists for its own sake. All the value man has, all spiritual reality, he has only through the state. For his spiritual reality is the knowing presence to him of his own essence, of rationality, of its objective, immediate actuality present in and for him. Only thus is he truly a consciousness, only thus does he partake in morality, in the legal and moral life of the state. For the True is the unity of the universal and particular will. And the universal in the state is in its laws, its universal and rational provisions. The state is the divine Idea as it exists on earth.

Thus the State is the definite object of world history proper. In it freedom achieves its objectivity and lives in the enjoyment of this objectivity. For law is the objectivity of Spirit; it is will in its true form. Only the will that obeys the law is free, for it obeys itself and, being in itself, is free. In so far as the state, our country, constitutes a community of existence, and as the subjective will of man subjects itself to the laws, the antithesis of freedom and necessity disappears. The rational, like the substantial, is necessary. We are free when we recognize it as law and follow it as the substance of our own being. The objective and the subjective will are then reconciled and form one and the same harmonious whole. For the ethos of the state is not of the moral, the reflective kind in which one's own conviction rules supreme. This latter is rather the peculiarity of the modern world. The true and antique morality is rooted in the principle that everybody stands in his place of duty. An Athenian citizen did what was required of him, as it were from instinct. But if I reflect on the object of my activity, I must have the consciousness that my will counts. Morality, however, is the duty, the substantial law, the second nature, as it has been rightly called; for the first nature of man in his immediate animalic existence.

(b) Law as Realization of Freedom

. . .

Freedom as the *ideal* of the original state of nature does not *exist* as original and natural. It must first be acquired and won; and that is possible only through an infinite process of the discipline of knowledge and will power. The state of nature, therefore, is rather the state of injustice, violence, untamed natural impulses, of inhuman deeds and emotions. There is, it is true, a limitation by society and the state, but it is a limitation of the brute emotions and rude instincts, as well as (in a more advanced stage of culture) of self-reflecting caprice and passion. This constraint is part of the process through which is first produced the consciousness of and the desire for freedom in its true, that is, rational and ideal form. The idea of freedom necessarily implies law and morality. These are in and for themselves universal essences, objects, and aims, to be discovered only by the activity of thought, emancipating itself from, and developing itself in opposition to, the merely sensuous; it must be assimilated to and incorporated with the originally sensuous will against its natural inclination. The perpetual misunderstanding of freedom is this: that one knows it only in its formal subjective sense, abstracted from its essential objects and aims. Thus the limitation of impulse, desire, passion—pertaining merely to the particular individual as such—of caprice and willfulness, is taken as a limitation of freedom. On the contrary, such limitation is the very condition leading to liberation; and society and the state are the very conditions in which freedom is realized.

. . .

In summary, the vitality of the State in individuals is what we call Morality.[13] The State, its laws, its institutions are the rights of the citizens; its nature, its soil, its mountains, air, and waters are their land, their country, their external property. The history of the State are their deeds, and what their ancestors have accomplished belongs to them and lives in their memory. Everything is their possession just as they are possessed by it, for it constitutes their substance and being.

Their minds are full of it and their wills are their willing of these laws and of their country. It is this temporal totality which is One Being, the spirit of One People. To it the individuals belong; each individual is the son of his people and, at the same time, insofar as his state is in development,

---

[13] This is a union of reflective, personal morality (*Moralität*) and unreflective, customary social activity (*Sittlichkeit*). [R.D.G.]

the son of his age. No one remains behind it, no one can leap ahead of it. This spiritual being is his—he is one of its representatives—it is that from which he arises and wherein he stands. For the Athenians Athens had a double meaning, the totality of their institutions as well as the goddess which represented the spirit and the unity of the people.

This spirit of a people is a *definite* spirit and, as was just said, is also determined according to the historical state of its development. This spirit, then, is the basis and content of the other forms of consciousness which have been mentioned. For the spirit in its consciousness of itself must be concrete to itself. Its objectivity immediately contains the origin of differences, which in their totality are the various spheres of the objective spirit itself—just as the soul exists only as the organization of its members which constitute it by combining themselves into simple unity. Thus it is one individuality. Its essence is represented, revered, and enjoyed as God, in religion; presented as image and intuition, in art; apprehended cognitively and conceived as thought, in philosophy. Because of the original identity of their substance, their content, and their subject matter with that of the State these products are inseparably united with the spirit of the State. Only with such a religion can there be such a form of the State, and only with such a State such art and such philosophy.

Furthermore, the definite national spirit itself is only one individual in the course of world history. For world history is the manifestation of the Divine, the absolute process of Spirit in its highest forms. It is this development wherein it achieves its truth and the consciousness of itself. The products of its stages are the world-historical national spirits, the definiteness of their moral life, their constitution, art, religion, and science. To realize these stages is the infinite élan of the World Spirit, its irresistible urge; for this differentiation and its realization constitute its concept. World history only shows how the World Spirit gradually attains the consciousness and willing of truth. Dawn rises in the Spirit; it discovers focal points; and finally, it attains full consciousness.

QUESTIONS FOR STUDY AND DISCUSSION

1. What, according to Hegel, is history?
2. What does Hegel mean by "Freedom"?
3. Discuss Hegel's concept of the role of the individual in history.
4. In what sense is the State a spiritual individual?
5. How does the idea of freedom imply law and morality?

Karl Marx

KARL MARX was born in Trier, Prussia, in 1818. He studied at the Universities of Bonn and Berlin, where he wrote a doctoral dissertation in philosophy. He never taught, however, and soon turned to the study of political economy. Expelled from Paris for being a dangerous revolutionary, he went to Brussels where, with Friedrich Engels, he wrote the *Communist Manifesto* (1847). He was then expelled successively from Brussels and Cologne and finally settled in 1849 in London, where he lived in poverty with his family until he died in 1883. He was a prolific writer and the founder and leader of the International Workingman's Association. He is best known as the author of *Capital* (1867) and as the "father of communism."

Materialism Versus Idealism: Man as a Natural Being

Hegel commits a double error. The first appears most clearly in the *Phenomenology,* the birthplace of his philosophy. When Hegel conceives wealth, the power of the state, etc. as entities alienated from the human being, he conceives them only in their thought form. They are entities of thought and thus simply an alienation of *pure* (i.e. abstract) philosophical thought. The whole movement, therefore, ends in absolute knowledge. It is precisely abstract thought from which these objects are alienated, and which they confront with their presumptuous reality. The *philosopher,* himself an abstract form of alienated man, sets himself up as the *measure* of the alienated world. The whole *history of alienation,* and of the retraction of alienation, is, therefore, only the *history of the production* of abstract thought, i.e. of absolute, logical, speculative thought. *Estrangement,* which thus forms the real interest of this alienation and of the supersession of this alienation, is the opposition of *in itself* and *for itself,* of *consciousness* and *self-consciousness,* of *object* and *subject,* i.e. the opposition in thought itself between abstract thought and sensible reality or real sensuous existence. All other contradictions and movements are merely the

From pp. 200–19 of Karl Marx, *The Economic and Philosophical Manuscripts,* in *Karl Marx: Early Writings,* translated and edited by T. B. Bottomore. © 1963 by C. A. Watts and Company Ltd., London. Reprinted by permission of the publisher.

appearance, the *cloak,* the *exoteric* form of these two opposites which are alone important and which constitute the *significance* of the other, profane contradictions. It is not the fact that the human being *objectifies* himself *inhumanly,* in opposition to himself, but that he *objectifies* himself by *distinction* from and in *opposition* to abstract thought, which constitutes alienation as it exists and as it has to be transcended.

[xviii] [1] The appropriation of man's objectified and alienated faculties is thus, in the first place, only an *appropriation* which occurs in *consciousness,* in *pure thought,* i.e. in abstraction. It is the appropriation of these objects as *thoughts* and as *movements of thought.* For this reason, despite its thoroughly negative and critical appearance, and despite the genuine criticism which it contains and which often anticipates later developments, there is already implicit in the *Phenomenology,* as a germ, as a potentiality and a secret, the uncritical positivism and uncritical idealism of Hegel's later works—the philosophical dissolution and restoration of the existing empirical world. *Secondly,* the vindication of the objective world for man (for example, the recognition that *sense* perception is not *abstract* sense perception but *human* sense perception, that religion, wealth, etc. are only the alienated reality of *human* objectification, of *human* faculties put to work, and are, therefore, a *way* to genuine *human* reality), this appropriation, or the insight into this process, appears in Hegel as the recognition of *sensuousness, religion,* state power, etc. as *mental* phenomena, for *mind* alone is the *true* essence of man, and the true form of mind is thinking mind, the logical, speculative mind. The *human character* of nature, of historically produced nature, of man's products, is shown by their being *products* of abstract mind, and thus phases of *mind, entities of thought.* The *Phenomenology* is a concealed, unclear and mystifying criticism, but in so far as it grasps the *alienation* of man (even though man appears only as mind) *all* the elements of criticism are contained in it, and are often *presented* and *worked out* in a manner which goes far beyond Hegel's own point of view. The sections devoted to the "unhappy consciousness," the "honest consciousness," the struggle between the "noble" and the "base" consciousness, etc., etc. contain the *critical* elements (though still in an alienated form) of whole areas such as religion, the state, civil life, etc.[2] Just as the *entity,* the *object,* appears as an entity of thought, so also the *subject* is always *consciousness* or *self-consciousness;* or rather, the object appears only as *abstract* consciousness and man as *self-consciousness.* Thus the distinctive forms of alienation which are manifested are only different forms of consciousness and self-consciousness. Since abstract consciousness (the form in which the object is conceived) is in *itself* merely a distinctive moment of self-consciousness, the outcome of the movement is the identity of self-consciousness and consciousness—absolute knowledge

[1] The bracketed Roman numerals indicate the original pagination by Marx of his manuscripts. [R.D.G.]
[2] See pp. 214–24 of this volume. [R.D.G.]

—the movement of abstract thought not directed outwards but proceeding within itself; i.e. the dialectic of pure thought is the result.

[xxiii] The outstanding achievement of Hegel's *Phenomenology*—the dialectic of negativity as the moving and creating principle—is, first, that Hegel grasps the self-creation of man as a process, objectification as loss of the object, as alienation and transcendence of this alienation, and that he, therefore, grasps the nature of *labour,* and conceives objective man (true, because real man) as the result of his *own labour.* The *real,* active orientation of man to himself as a species-being, or the affirmation of himself as a real species-being (i.e. as a human being) is only possible so far as he really brings forth all his *species-powers* (which is only possible through the co-operative endeavours of mankind and as an outcome of history) and treats these powers as objects, which can only be done at first in the form of alienation.

We shall next show in detail Hegel's one-sidedness and limitations, as revealed in the final chapter of the *Phenomenology,* on absolute knowledge; a chapter which contains the concentrated spirit of the *Phenomenology,* its relation to the dialectic, and also Hegel's *consciousness* of both and of their interrelations.

For the present, let us make these preliminary observations: Hegel's standpoint is that of modern political economy. He conceives *labour* as the *essence,* the self-confirming essence of man; he observes only the positive side of labour, not its negative side. Labour is *man's coming to be for himself* within *alienation,* or as an *alienated man.* Labour as Hegel understands and recognizes it is *abstract mental* labour. Thus, that which above all constitutes the *essence* of philosophy, the *alienation of man knowing himself,* or *alienated* science *thinking* itself, Hegel grasps as its essence. Consequently, he is able to bring together the separate elements of earlier philosophy and to present his own as the philosophy. What other philosophers did, that is, to conceive separate elements of nature and of human life as phases of self-consciousness and indeed of abstract self-consciousness, Hegel *knows* by *doing* philosophy; therefore, his science is absolute.

Let us now turn to our subject.

ABSOLUTE KNOWLEDGE
(The final chapter of the *Phenomenology*)

The main point is that the *object of consciousness* is nothing else but *self-consciousness,* that the object is only *objectified* self-consciousness, self-consciousness as an object. (Positing man = self-consciousness.)[3]

It is necessary, therefore, to surmount the *object of consciousness.* Objectivity as such is regarded as an alienated human relationship which does not correspond with the *essence of man,* self-consciousness. The reappro-

---

[3] For Hegel man is essentially self-consciousness. Marx proceeds to refute this position. [R.D.G.]

242 / KARL MARX

priation of the objective essence of man, which was produced as something
alien and determined by alienation, signifies the supersession not only of
alienation but also of *objectivity*; that is, man is regarded as a *non-objective, spiritual* being.

The process of *overcoming the object of consciousness* is described by
Hegel as follows: The *object* does not reveal itself only as *returning* into
the Self (according to Hegel that is a *one-sided* conception of the movement, considering only one aspect). Man is equated with self. The Self,
however, is only man conceived *abstractly* and produced by abstraction.
Man is self-referring. His eye, his ear, etc. are *self-referring*; every one of
his faculties has this quality of *self*-reference. But it is entirely false to say
on that account, *"Self-consciousness* has eyes, ears, faculties." Self-
consciousness is rather a quality of human nature, of the human eye, etc.;
human nature is not a quality of [XXIV] *self-consciousness.*

The Self, abstracted and determined for itself, is man as an *abstract
egoist,* purely abstract *egoism* raised to the level of thought. (We shall return to this point later.)

For Hegel, *human life, man,* is equivalent to *self-consciousness.* All
alienation of human life is, therefore, *nothing* but *alienation of self-
consciousness.* The alienation of self-consciousness is not regarded as the
expression, reflected in knowledge and thought, of the *real* alienation of
human life. Instead, *actual* alienation, that which appears real, is in its *innermost* hidden nature (which philosophy first discloses) only the *phenomenal being* of the alienation of real human life, of *self-consciousness.*
The science which comprehends this is therefore called *Phenomenology.*
All reappropriation of alienated objective life appears, therefore, as an incorporation in self-consciousness. The person who takes possession of his
being is only the self-consciousness which takes possession of objective
being; the return of the object into the Self is, therefore, the reappropriation of the object.

Expressed in a *more comprehensive way* the *supersession of the object
of consciousness* means: [4] (1) that the object as such presents itself to
consciousness as something disappearing; (2) that it is the alienation of
self-consciousness which establishes "thinghood"; (3) that this alienation
has *positive* as well as *negative* significance; (4) that it has this significance not only *for us* or in itself, but also *for self-consciousness itself;*
(5) that for *self-consciousness* the negative of the object, its self-
supersession, has *positive* significance, or self-consciousness *knows* thereby
the nullity of the object in that self-consciousness alienates itself, for in this
alienation it establishes *itself* as object or, for the sake of the indivisible
unity of *being-for-itself,* establishes the object as itself; (6) that, on the

---

[4] The paragraph which follows is taken directly from the last section of Hegel's
Phenomenology of Mind. Marx's critique of each of Hegel's eight points follows,
though only the first six are referred to directly. [R.D.G.]

other hand, this other "moment" is equally present, that self-consciousness has superseded and reabsorbed this alienation and objectivity, and is thus *at home* in its other being as such; (7) that this is the movement of consciousness and consciousness is, therefore, the totality of its "moments"; (8) that similarly, consciousness must have related itself to the object in all its determinations, and have conceived it in terms of each of them. This totality of determinations makes the object *intrinsically* a *spiritual being,* and it becomes truly so for consciousness by the apprehension of every one of these determinations as the Self, or by what was called earlier the *spiritual* attitude towards them.

ad 1. That the object as such presents itself to consciousness as something disappearing is the above-mentioned *return of the object into the Self.*

ad 2. *The alienation of self-consciousness* establishes *"thinghood."* Because man equals self-consciousness, his alienated objective being or *"thinghood"* is equivalent to *alienated self-consciousness,* and "thinghood" is established by this alienation. ("Thinghood" is that which is *an object for him,* and an object for him is really only that which is an essential object, consequently his *objective* essence. And since it is not the *real man,* nor *nature*—man being *human nature*—who becomes as such a subject, but only an abstraction of man, self-consciousness, "thinghood" can only be *alienated self-consciousness.*) It is quite understandable that a living, natural being endowed with objective (i.e. material) faculties should have *real natural objects* of its being, and equally that its self-alienation should be the establishment of a *real,* objective world, but in the form of *externality,* as a world which does not belong to, and dominates, its being. There is nothing incomprehensible or mysterious about this. The converse, rather, would be mysterious. But it is equally clear that a self-consciousness, i.e. its alienation, can only establish *"thinghood,"* i.e. only an abstract thing, a thing created by abstraction and not a real thing. It is [xxvi] clear, moreover, that "thinghood" is totally lacking in *independence,* in *being, vis-à-vis* self-consciousness; it is a mere *construct* established by self-consciousness. And what is established is not self-confirming; it is the confirmation of the act of establishing, which for an instant, but only for an instant, fixes its energy as a product and *apparently* confers upon it the role of an independent, real being.

When real, corporeal *man,* with his feet firmly planted on the solid ground, inhaling and exhaling all the powers of nature, *posits* his real objective faculties, as a result of his alienation, as alien objects, the *positing* is not the subject of this act but the subjectivity of *objective* faculties whose action must also, therefore, be *objective.* An objective being acts objectively, and it would not act objectively if objectivity were not part of its essential being. It creates and establishes *only objects, because* it is established by objects, and because it is fundamentally *natural.* In the act of establishing it does not descend from its "pure activity" to the *creation of objects;* its *objective* product simply confirms its *objective* activity, its activity as an objective, natural being.

We see here how consistent naturalism [5] or humanism is distinguished from both idealism and materialism, and at the same time constitutes their unifying truth. We see also that only naturalism is able to comprehend the process of world history.

Man is directly a *natural being.* As a natural being, and as a living natural being he is, on the one hand, endowed with *natural powers* and *faculties,* which exist in him as tendencies and abilities, as *drives.* On the other hand, as a natural, embodied, sentient, objective being he is a *suffering,* conditioned and limited being, like animals and plants. The *objects* of his drives exist outside himself as *objects* independent of him, yet they are *objects* of his *needs,* essential *objects* which are indispensable to the exercise and confirmation of his faculties. The fact that man is an *embodied,* living, real, sentient, objective being with natural powers, means that he has *real, sensuous objects* as the objects of his being, or that he can only express his being in real, sensuous objects. *To be* objective, natural, sentient and at the same time to have object, nature and sense outside oneself, or to be oneself object, nature and sense for a third person, is the same thing. Hunger is a natural *need;* it requires, therefore, a *nature* outside itself, an *object* outside itself, in order to be satisfied and stilled. Hunger is the objective need of a body for an *object* which exists outside itself and which is essential for its integration and the expression of its nature. The sun is an *object,* a necessary and life-assuring object, for the plant, just as the plant is an object for the sun, an *expression* of the sun's life-giving power and *objective* essential powers.

A being which does not have its nature outside itself is not a *natural* being and does not share in the being of nature. A being which has no object outside itself is not an objective being. A being which is not itself an object for a third being has no being for its *object,* i.e. it is not objectively related and its being is not objective.

[XXVII] A non-objective being is a *non-being.* Suppose a being which neither is an object itself nor has an object. In the first place, such a being would be the *only* being; no other being would exist outside itself and it would be solitary and alone. For as soon as there exists objects outside myself, as soon as I am not *alone,* I am *another, another reality* from the object outside me. For this third object I am thus an *other reality* than itself, i.e. *its object.* To suppose a being which is not the object of another being would be to suppose that *no* objective being exists. As soon as I have an object, this object has me for its object. But a *non-objective* being is an unreal, non-sensuous, merely conceived being; i.e. a merely imagined being,

---

[5] Marx uses "naturalism" to refer to his own position that man is a natural being. For the sense in which he unifies the truth of idealism (Hegel) and materialism (Feuerbach), see the Introduction to this section. [R.D.G.]

an abstraction. To be *sensuous,* i.e. real, is to be an object of sense or *sensuous* object, and thus to have sensuous objects outside oneself, objects of one's sensations. To be sentient is to *suffer* (to experience).

Man as an objective sentient being is a *suffering* being, and since he feels his suffering, a *passionate* being. Passion is man's faculties striving to attain their object.

But man is not merely a natural being; he is a *human* natural being. He is a being for himself, and, therefore, a *species-being;* and as such he has to express and authenticate himself in being as well as in thought. Consequently, *human* objects are not natural objects as they present themselves directly, nor is *human sense,* as it is immediately and objectively *given,* *human* sensibility and human objectivity. Neither objective nature nor subjective nature is directly presented in a form adequate to the *human* being. And as everything natural must have its *origin* so *man* has his process of genesis, *history,* which is for him, however, a conscious process and thus one which is consciously self-transcending. (We shall return to this point later.)

Thirdly, since this establishment of "thinghood" is itself only an appearance, an act which contradicts the nature of pure activity, it has to be annulled again and "thinghood" has to be denied.

ad 3, 4, 5, 6. (3) This alienation of consciousness has not only negative but also a positive significance, and (4) it has this positive significance not only *for us* or in itself, but for consciousness itself. (5) For *consciousness* the negation of the object, or its annulling of itself by that means, has positive significance; it *knows* the nullity of the object by the fact that it alienates *itself,* for in this alienation it *knows* itself as the object or, for the sake of the indivisible unit of *being-for self,* knows the object as itself. (6) On the other hand, this other "moment" is equally present, but consciousness has superseded and reabsorbed this alienation and objectivity and is thus *at home in its other being as such.*

We have already seen that the appropriation of alienated objective being, or the supersession of objectivity in the form of *alienation* (which has to develop from indifferent otherness to real antagonistic alienation), signifies for Hegel also, or primarily, the supersession of *objectivity,* since it is not the determinate character of the object but its *objective* character which is the scandal of alienation for self-consciousness. The object is therefore negative, self-annulling, a *nullity.* This nullity of the object has a positive significance because it *knows* this nullity, objective being, as its *self-alienation,* and knows that this nullity exists only through its self-alienation. . . .

The way in which consciousness is, and in which something is for it, is *knowing.* Knowing is its only act. Thus something comes to exist for consciousness so far as it *knows* this *something.* Knowing is its only objective relation. It knows, then, the nullity of the object (i.e. knows the non-existence of the distinction between itself and the object, the non-existence of the object for it) because it knows the object as its *self-alienation*. That is to say, it knows itself (knows knowing as an object), because the object is only the *semblance* of an object, a deception, which is intrinsically nothing but knowing itself which has confronted itself with itself, has established in face of itself a *nullity*, a "something" which has *no* objective existence outside the knowing itself. Knowing knows that in relating itself to an object it is only *outside* itself, alienates itself, and that *it* only *appears* to itself as an object; or in other words, that that which appears to it as an object is only itself.

On the other hand, Hegel says, this other "moment" is present at the same time; namely, that consciousness has equally superseded and reabsorbed this alienation and objectivity, and consequently is *at home in its other being as such.*

In this discussion all the illusions of speculation are assembled.

First, consciousness—self-consciousness—is *at home in its other being as such.* It is, therefore—if we abstract from Hegel's abstraction and substitute the self-consciousness of man for self-consciousness—*at home in its other being as such.* This implies, first, that consciousness (knowing as knowing, thinking as thinking) claims to be directly the *other* of itself, the sensuous world, reality, life; it is thought over-reaching itself in thought (Feuerbach). This aspect is contained in it, in so far as consciousness as mere consciousness is offended not by the alienated objectivity but by *objectivity as such.*

Secondly, it implies that self-conscious man, in so far as he has recognized and superseded the spiritual world (or the universal spiritual mode of existence of his world) then confirms it again in this alienated form and presents it as his true existence; he re-establishes it and claims to *be at home in his other being.* Thus, for example, after superseding religion, when he has recognized religion as a product of self-alienation, he then finds a confirmation of himself in *religion as religion. This is* the root of Hegel's *false* positivism, or of his merely *apparent* criticism; what Feuerbach calls the positing, negation and re-establishment of religion or theology, but which has to be conceived in a more general way. Thus reason is at home in unreason as such. Man, who has recognized that he leads an alienated life in law, politics, etc. leads his true human life in this alienated life as such. Self-affirmation, in contradiction with itself, with the knowledge and the nature of the object, is thus the true *knowledge* and *life.*

There can no longer be any question about Hegel's compromise with religion, the state, etc., for this falsehood is the falsehood of his whole argument.

[XXIX] If I *know* religion as *alienated* human self-consciousness what I know in it as religion is not my self-consciousness but my alienated self-consciousness confirmed in it. Thus my own self, and the self-consciousness which is its essence, is not confirmed in *religion* but in the *abolition* and *supersession* of religion.

In Hegel, therefore, the negation of the negation is not the confirmation of true being by the negation of illusory being. It is the confirmation of illusory being, or of self-alienating being in its denial; or the denial of this illusory being as an objective being existing outside man and independently of him, and its transformation into a subject.

The act of *supersession* plays a strange part in which *denial* and preservation, denial and affirmation, are linked together. Thus, for example, in Hegel's *Philosophy of Right, private right* superseded equals *morality,* morality superseded equals *the family,* the family superseded equals *civil society,* civil society superseded equals the *state,* and the state superseded equals *world history.* But in *actuality* private right, morality, the family, civil society, the state, etc. remain; only they have become "moments," modes of existence of man, which have no validity in isolation but which mutually dissolve and engender one another. *They are "moments" of the movement.*

In their actual existence this *mobile* nature is concealed. It is first revealed in thought, in philosophy; consequently, my true religious existence is my existence in the *philosophy of religion,* my true political existence is my existence in the *philosophy of right,* my true natural existence is my existence in the *philosophy of nature,* my true artistic existence is my existence in the *philosophy of art,* and my true human existence is my existence in *philosophy.* In the same way, the true existence of religion, the state, nature and art, is the *philosophy* of religion, of the state, of nature, and of art. But if the philosophy of religion is the only true existence of religion I am only truly religious as a *philosopher of religion,* and I deny *actual* religious sentiment and the actual *religious* man. At the same time, however, I *confirm* them, partly in my own existence or in the alien existence with which I confront them (for this *is* only their philosophical expression), and partly in their own original form, since they are for me the merely *apparent* other being, allegories, the lineaments of their own true existence (i.e. of my *philosophical* existence) concealed by sensuous draperies.

In the same way, *quality* superseded equals *quantity,* quantity superseded equals *measure,* measure superseded equals *being,* being superseded equals *phenomenal being,* phenomenal being superseded equals *actuality,* actuality superseded equals the *concept,* the concept superseded equals *objectivity,* objectivity superseded equals the *absolute idea,* the absolute idea superseded equals *nature,* nature superseded equals *subjective* spirit, subjective spirit superseded equals *ethical* objective spirit, *ethical* spirit superseded equals *art,* art superseded equals *religion,* and religion superseded equals *absolute knowledge.*

On the other hand, this supersession is supersession of an entity of thought; thus, private property *as thought* is superseded in the *thought* of morality. And since thought imagines itself to be, without mediation, the other aspect of itself, namely *sensuous reality,* and takes its own action for *real, sensuous action,* this supersession in thought, which leaves its object in existence in the real world, believes itself to have really overcome it. On the other hand, since the object has now become for it a "moment" of thought, it is regarded in its real existence as a confirmation of thought, of self-consciousness, of abstraction.

[xxx] From the one aspect the existent which Hegel *supersedes* in philosophy is not therefore the *actual* religion, state or nature, but religion itself as an object of knowledge, i.e. *dogmatics;* and similarly with *jurisprudence, political science* and *natural science.* From this aspect, therefore, he stands in opposition both to the actual being and to the direct, non-philosophical science (or the non-philosophical *concepts*) of this being. Thus he contradicts the conventional conceptions.

From the other aspect, the religious man, etc. can find in Hegel his ultimate confirmation.

We have now to consider the *positive* moments of Hegel's dialectic, within the condition of alienation.

(*a*) *Supersession* as an objective movement which *reabsorbs* alienation into itself. This is the insight, expressed within alienation, into the *appropriation* of the objective being through the supersession of its alienation. It is the alienated insight into the *real objectification* of man, into the real appropriation of his objective being by the destruction of the *alienated* character of the objective world, by the annulment of its alienated mode of existence. In the same way, atheism as the annulment of God is the emergence of theoretical humanism, and communism as the annulment of private property is the vindication of real human life as man's property. The latter is also the emergence of practical humanism, for atheism is humanism mediated to itself by the annulment of religion, while communism is humanism mediated to itself by the annulment of private property. It is only by the supersession of this mediation (which is, however, a necessary precondition) that the self-originating *positive* humanism can appear.

But atheism and communism are not flight or abstraction from, nor loss of, the objective world which men have created by the objectification of their faculties. They are not an impoverished return to unnatural, primitive simplicity. They are rather the first real emergence, the genuine actualization, of man's nature as something real.

Thus Hegel, in so far as he sees the *positive* significance of the self-referring negation (though in an alienated mode) conceives man's self-estrangement, alienation of being, loss of objectivity and reality, as self-discovery, change of nature, objectification and realization. In short, Hegel conceives labour as man's *act of self-creation* (though in abstract terms); he grasps man's relation to himself as an alien being and the emergence of *species-consciousness* and *species-life* as the demonstration of his alien being.

(*b*) But in Hegel, apart from, or rather as a consequence of, the inversion we have already described, this act of genesis appears, in the first place, as one which is merely *formal,* because it is abstract, and because human nature itself is treated as merely *abstract, thinking nature,* as self-consciousness.

Secondly, because the conception is *formal* and *abstract* the annulment of alienation becomes a confirmation of alienation. For Hegel, this movement of *self-creation* and *self-objectification* in the form of *self-estrangement* is the *absolute* and hence final *expression of human life,* which has its end in itself, is at peace with itself and at one with its own nature.

This movement, in its abstract [XXXI] form as dialectic, is regarded therefore as *truly human life,* and since it is nevertheless an abstraction, an alienation of human life, it is regarded as a *divine process* and thus as the divine process of mankind; it is a process which man's abstract, pure, absolute being, as distinguished from himself, traverses.

Thirdly, this process must have a bearer, a subject; but the subject first emerges as a result. This result, the subject knowing itself as absolute self-consciousness, is therefore *God, absolute spirit, the self-knowing and self-manifesting idea.* Real man and real nature become mere predicates, symbols of this concealed unreal man and unreal nature. Subject and predicate have, therefore, an inverted relation to each other; a *mystical subject-object,* or a *subjectivity reaching beyond the object,* the *absolute subject* as a process of self-alienation and of return from alienation into itself, and at the same time of reabsorption of this alienation, the *subject* as this process; pure, *unceasing* revolving within itself.

First, the formal and abstract conception of man's act of self-creation or self-objectification.

Since Hegel equates man with self-consciousness, the alienated object, the alienated real being of man, is simply *consciousness,* merely the thought of alienation, its abstract and hence vacuous and unreal expression, the *negation.* The annulment of alienation is also, therefore, merely an abstract and vacuous annulment of this empty abstraction, the *negation of the negation.* The replete, living, sensuous, concrete activity of self-objectification is, therefore, reduced to a mere abstraction, *absolute negativity,* an abstraction which is then crystallized as such and is conceived as an independent activity, as activity itself. Since this so-called negativity is merely the *abstract, vacuous* form of that real living act, its content can only be a *formal* content produced by abstraction from all content. They are, therefore, general, abstract *forms of abstraction* which refer to any content and are thus neutral towards, and valid for, any content; forms of thought, logical forms which are detached from *real* spirit and *real* nature. (We shall expound later the *logical* content of absolute negativity.)

Hegel's positive achievement in his speculative logic is to show that the *determinate concepts,* the universal *fixed thought-forms,* in their independence from nature and spirit, are a necessary result of the general alienation of human nature and also of human thought; and to depict them as a whole as moments in the process of abstraction. For example, being superseded is essence, essence superseded is concept, the concept superseded is . . . the absolute idea. But what is the absolute idea? It must supersede itself if it does not want to traverse the whole process of abstraction again from the beginning and to rest content with being a totality of abstractions or a self-comprehending abstraction. But the self-comprehending abstraction knows itself to be nothing; it must abandon itself, the abstraction, and so arrives at an entity which is its exact opposite, *nature*. The whole *Logic* is therefore, a demonstration that abstract thought is nothing for itself, that the absolute idea is nothing for itself, that only *nature* is something.

[XXXII] The absolute idea, the *abstract* idea which *"regarded* from the aspect of its unity with itself, is *intuition"* (Hegel's *Encyclopaedia,* 3rd ed., p. 222), and which "in its own absolute truth *resolves* to let the moment of its particularity or of initial determination and other-being, the *immediate idea,* as its reflection, *emerge freely from itself as nature"* (ibid.); this whole idea which behaves in such a strange and fanciful way and which has given the Hegelians such terrible headaches is throughout nothing but *abstraction,* i.e. the abstract thinker. It is abstraction which, made wise by experience and enlightened about its own truth, resolves under various (false and still abstract) conditions to *abandon* itself, and to establish its other being, the particular, the determinate, in place of its self-absorption, non-being, universality and indeterminateness; and which resolves to let nature, which it concealed within itself only as an abstraction, as an entity of thought, *emerge freely from itself.* That is, it decides to forsake abstraction and to observe nature *free* from abstraction. The abstract idea, which without mediation becomes *intuition,* is nothing but abstract thought which abandons itself and decides for *intuition.* This whole transition from logic to the philosophy of nature is simply the transition from *abstracting* to *intuiting,* a transition which is extremely difficult for the abstract thinker to accomplish and which he therefore describes in such strange terms. The *mystical feeling* which drives the philosopher from abstract thinking to intuition is *ennui,* the longing for a content.

(Man alienated from himself is also the thinker alienated from his *being,* i.e. from his natural and human life. His thoughts are consequently spirits existing outside nature and man. In his *Logic* Hegel has imprisoned all these spirits together, and has conceived each of them first as negation, i.e. as *alienation of human* thought, and secondly as negation of the negation, i.e. as the supersession of this alienation and as the real expression of human thought. But since this negation of the negation is itself still confined within the alienation, it is in part a restoration of these fixed spiritual forms in their alienation, in part an immobilization in the final act, the act of self-reference, as the true being of these spiritual forms.[6] Further, in so

---

[6] That is, Hegel substitutes the act of abstraction revolving within itself, for these fixed abstractions. In so doing, he has first of all the merit of having indicated the source of all these inappropriate concepts which originally belonged to different philosophies, and of having brought them together and established the comprehensive range of abstractions, instead of some particular abstraction, as the object of criti-

far as this abstraction conceives itself, and experiences an increasing weariness of itself, there appears in Hegel an abandonment of abstract thought which moves solely in the sphere of thought, devoid of eyes, ears, teeth, everything, and a resolve to recognize *nature* as being and to go over to intuition.)

[XXXIII] But *nature* too, taken abstractly, for itself, and rigidly separated from man, is *nothing* for man. It goes without saying that the abstract thinker who has committed himself to intuition, intuits nature abstractly. As nature lay enclosed in the thinker in a form which was obscure and mysterious even to himself, as absolute idea, as an entity of thought, so in truth, when he let it emerge from himself it was still only *abstract nature,* nature as an *entity of thought,* but now with the significance that it is the other-being of thought, is real, intuited nature, distinguished from abstract thought. Or, to speak in human language, the abstract thinker discovers from intuiting nature that the entities which he thought to create out of nothing, out of pure abstraction, to create in the divine dialectic as the pure products of thought endlessly shuttling back and forth in itself and never regarding external reality, are simply *abstractions* from *natural characteristics.* The whole of nature, therefore, reiterates to him the logical abstractions, but in a sensuous, external form. He *analyses* nature and these abstractions again. His intuition of nature is, therefore, simply the act of confirmation of his abstraction from the intuition of nature; his conscious re-enactment of the process of generating his abstraction. Thus, for example, Time equals Negativity which refers to itself (loc. cit., p. 238). In the natural form, superseded Movement as Matter corresponds to superseded Becoming as Being. In the *natural* form Light is *Reflection-in itself.* Body as *Moon* and *Comet* is the natural form of the antithesis which, according to the *Logic,* is on the one hand the *positive grounded upon itself,* and on the other hand, the *negative grounded upon itself.* The Earth is the *natural* form of the logical *ground,* as the negative unity of the antithesis, etc.[7]

Nature as nature, i.e. so far as it is sensuously distinguished from that secret sense concealed within it, nature separated and distinguished from these abstractions is *nothing* (a *nullity demonstrating its nullity*), is *devoid of sense,* or has only the sense of an external thing which has been superseded.

"In the finite-*teleological* view is to be found the correct premise that nature does not contain within itself the absolute purpose" (loc. cit., p.

---

cism. We shall see later why Hegel separates thought from the *subject.* It is already clear, however, that if man is not human the expression of his nature cannot be human, and consequently thought itself could not be conceived as an expression of man's nature, as the expression of a human and natural subject, with eyes, ears, etc. living in society, in the world, and in nature. [K.M.]

[7] References to Time, Matter, Body, etc., are found in Hegel's philosophy of nature. There he treats the concepts of nature dialectically; that is, he applies to them the dialectical development of concepts which we find in his *Logic.* See the Introduction to this section. [R.D.G.]

225). Its purpose is the confirmation of abstraction. "Nature has shown itself to be the idea in the *form* of *other-being*. Since the idea is in this form the negative of itself, or *external to itself,* nature is not just relatively external *vis-à-vis* this idea, but *externality* constitutes the form in which it exists as nature" (loc. cit., p. 227).

Externality should not be understood here as the *self-externalizing world of sense,* open to the light and to man's senses. It has to be taken here in the sense of alienation, as error, a defect, that which ought not to be. For that which is true is still the idea. Nature is merely the form of its other-being. And since abstract thought is *being,* that which is external to it is by its nature a merely *external thing.* The abstract thinker recognizes at the same time that *sensuousness, externality* in contrast to thought which shuttles back and forth *within itself,* is the essence of nature. But at the same time he expresses this antithesis in such a way that this *externality* of nature, and its *contrast* with thought, appears as a deficiency, and that nature distinguished from abstraction appears as a deficient being. [XXXIV] A being which is deficient, not simply for me or in my eyes, but in itself, has something outside itself which it lacks. That is to say, its being is something other than itself. For the abstract thinker, nature must therefore supersede itself, because it is already posited by him as a potentially *superseded* being.

"*For us,* spirit has *nature as its premise,* being the *truth* of nature and thereby its *absolute primus.* In this truth nature has *vanished,* and spirit has surrendered itself as the idea which has attained being-for-itself, whose *object,* as well as the *subject,* is the *concept.* This identity is *absolute negativity,* for whereas in nature the concept has its perfect external objectivity, here its alienation has been superseded and the concept has become identical with itself. It is this identity only so far as it is a return from nature" (loc. cit., p. 392).

"*Revelation,* as the *abstract* idea, is unmediated transition to, the *coming-to-be* of, nature; as the revelation of the spirit, which is free, it is the *establishment* of nature as *its own* world, an establishment which, as reflection, is simultaneously the *presupposition* of the world as independently existing nature. Revelation in conception is the creation of nature as spirit's own being, in which it acquires the *affirmation* and *truth* of its freedom." "*The absolute is spirit;* this is the highest definition of the absolute."

QUESTIONS FOR STUDY AND DISCUSSION

1. What, according to Marx, is Hegel's double error?
2. What does Marx mean when he says that man has his nature outside of himself?
3. Explain the role of consciousness in Marx's view of man.
4. In what does Marx's humanism consist?
5. Are there any aspects of Hegel's discussion of man that Marx considers valid? Explain.

The Material Determination
of Consciousness

The premises from which we begin are not arbitrary ones, not dogmas, but real premises from which abstraction can only be made in the imagination. They are the real individuals, their activity and the material conditions under which they live, both those which they find already existing and those produced by their activity. These premises can thus be verified in a purely empirical way.

The first premise of all human history is, of course, the existence of living human individuals.[1] Thus the first fact to be established is the physical organisation of these individuals and their consequent relation to the rest of nature. Of course, we cannot here go either into the actual physical nature of man, or into the natural conditions in which man finds himself—geological, orohydrographical, climatic and so on.[2] The writing of history must always set out from these natural bases and their modification in the course of history through the action of men.

Men can be distinguished from animals by consciousness, by religion or anything else you like. They themselves begin to distinguish themselves from animals as soon as they begin to *produce* their means of subsistence, a step which is conditioned by their physical organisation. By producing their means of subsistence men are indirectly producing their actual material life.

The way in which men produce their means of subsistence depends first of all on the nature of the actual means of subsistence they find in existence and have to reproduce. This mode of production must not be considered simply as being the reproduction of the physical existence of the individuals. Rather it is a definite form of activity of these individuals, a definite form of expressing their life, a definite *mode of life* on their part. As individuals express their life, so they are. What they are, therefore, coincides with their production, both with *what* they produce and with *how* they produce. The nature of individuals thus depends on the material conditions determining their production.

---

[1] [The following passage is crossed out in the manuscript:] The first *historical* act of these individuals distinguishing them from animals is not that they think, but that they begin to *produce their means of subsistence*. [S.R.]

[2] [The following passage is crossed out in the manuscript:] Not only the original, spontaneous organisation of men, especially racial differences, depends on these conditions but also the entire further development, or lack of development, of men up to the present time. [S.R.]

From pp. 31–39 of Karl Marx and Friedrich Engels, *The German Ideology,* edited by S. Ryazanskaya. Copyright 1964 by Progress Publishers, Moscow. Reprinted by permission of the publisher.

This production only makes its appearance with the *increase of population*. In its turn this presupposes the *intercourse* [*Verkehr*] [3] of individuals with one another. The form of this intercourse is again determined by production.

The relations of different nations among themselves depend upon the extent to which each has developed its productive forces, the division of labour and internal intercourse. This statement is generally recognised. But not only the relation of one nation to others, but also the whole internal structure of the nation itself depends on the stage of development reached by its production and its internal and external intercourse. How far the productive forces of a nation are developed is shown most manifestly by the degree to which the division of labour has been carried. Each new productive force, insofar as it is not merely a quantitative extension of productive forces already known (for instance the bringing into cultivation of fresh land), causes a further development of the division of labour.

The division of labour inside a nation leads at first to the separation of industrial and commercial from agricultural labour, and hence to the separation of *town* and *country* and to the conflict of their interests Its further development leads to the separation of commercial from industrial labour. At the same time through the divison of labour inside these various branches there develop various divisions among the individuals co-operating in definite kinds of labour. The relative position of these individual groups is determined by the methods employed in agriculture, industry and commerce (patriarchalism, slavery, estates, classes). These same conditions are to be seen (given a more developed intercourse) in the relations of different nations to one another.

The various stages of development in the division of labour are just so many different forms of ownership, i.e., the existing stage in the division of labour determines also the relations of individuals to one another with reference to the material, instrument, and product of labour.

The first form of ownership is tribal [*Stammeigentum*] [4] ownership. It

---

[3] In *The German Ideology* the word *"Verkehr"* is used in a very wide sense, encompassing the material and spiritual intercourse of separate individuals, social groups and entire countries. Marx and Engels show that material intercourse, and above all the intercourse of men with each other in the production process, is the basis of every other form of intercourse.

The terms *"Verkehrsform"* (form of intercourse), *"Verkehrsweise"* (mode of intercourse) and *"Verkehrsverhältnisse"* (relations, or conditions, of intercourse) which we encounter in *The German Ideology* are used by Marx and Engels to express the concept "relations of production" which during that period was taking shape in their mind.

The ordinary dictionary meanings of *"Verkehr"* are traffic, intercourse, commerce. In this translation the word *"Verkehr"* has been mostly rendered as "intercourse" and occasionally as "association" or "commerce". [INSTITUTE OF MARXISM-LENINISM]

[4] The term *"Stamm"*—rendered in the present volume by the word "tribe"—played a considerably greater part in historical works written during the forties of the last century, than it does at present. It was used to denote a community of people descended from a common ancestor, and comprised the modern concepts of "gens" and "tribe". The first to define and differentiate these concepts was Lewis Henry

corresponds to the undeveloped stage of production, at which a people lives by hunting and fishing, by the rearing of beasts or, in the highest stage, agriculture. In the latter case it presupposes a great mass of uncultivated stretches of land. The division of labour is at this stage still very elementary and is confined to a further extension of the natural division of labour existing in the family. The social structure is, therefore, limited to an extension of the family; patriarchal family chieftains, below them the members of the tribe, finally slaves. The slavery latent in the family only develops gradually with the increase of population, the growth of wants, and with the extension of external relations, both of war and of barter.

The second form is the ancient communal and State ownership which proceeds especially from the union of several tribes into a *city* by agreement or by conquest, and which is still accompanied by slavery. Beside communal ownership we already find movable, and later also immovable, private property developing, but as an abnormal form subordinate to communal ownership. The citizens hold power over their labouring slaves only in their community, and on this account alone, therefore, they are bound to the form of communal ownership. It is the communal private property which compels the active citizens to remain in this spontaneously derived form of association over against their slaves. For this reason the whole structure of society based on this communal ownership, and with it the power of the people, decays in the same measure as, in particular, immovable private property evolves. The division of labour is already more developed. We already find the antagonism of town and country; later the antagonism between those states which represent town interests and those which represent country interests, and inside the towns themselves the antagonism between industry and maritime commerce. The class relation between citizens and slaves is now completely developed.

This whole interpretation of history appears to be contradicted by the fact of conquest. Up till now violence, war, pillage, murder and robbery, etc., have been accepted as the driving force of history. Here we must limit ourselves to the chief points and take, therefore, only the most striking example—the destruction of an old civilisation by a barbarous people and the resulting formation of an entirely new organisation of society. (Rome and the barbarians; feudalism and Gaul; the Byzantine Empire and the Turks.) With the conquering barbarian people war itself is still, as indicated above, a regular form of intercourse, which is the more eagerly exploited as the increase in population together with the traditional and, for

Morgan in his work *Ancient Society; or, Researches in the Lines of Human Progress from Savagery Through Barbarism to Civilisation*, London, 1877. This outstanding American ethnographer and historian showed for the first time the significance of the gens as the nucleus of the primitive communal system and thereby laid the scientific foundations for the history of primitive society as a whole. Engels drew the general conclusions from Morgan's discoveries and made a comprehensive analysis of the meaning of the concepts "gens" and "tribe" in his work *The Origin of the Family, Private Property and the State* (1884). [INSTITUTE OF MARXISM-LENINISM.]

it, the only possible, crude mode of production gives rise to the need for new means of production. In Italy, on the other hand, the concentration of landed property (caused not only by buying-up and indebtedness but also by inheritance, since loose living being rife and marriage rare, the old families gradually died out and their possessions fell into the hands of a few) and its conversion into grazing-land (caused not only by the usual economic forces still operative today but by the importation of plundered and tribute-corn and the resultant lack of demand for Italian corn) brought about the almost total disappearance of the free population. The very slaves died out again and again, and had constantly to be replaced by new ones. Slavery remained the basis of the whole productive system. The plebeians, midway between freemen and slaves, never succeeded in becoming more than a proletarian rabble. Rome indeed never became more than a city; its connection with the provinces was almost exclusively political and could, therefore, easily be broken again by political events.

With the development of private property, we find here for the first time the same conditions which we shall find again, only on a more extensive scale, with modern private property. On the one hand, the concentration of private property, which began very early in Rome (as the Licinian agrarian law proves [5]) and proceeded very rapidly from the time of the civil wars and especially under the Emperors; on the other hand, coupled with this, the transformation of the plebeian small peasantry into a proletariat, which, however, owing to its intermediate position between propertied citizens and slaves, never achieved an independent development.

The third form of ownership is feudal or estate property. If antiquity started out from the *town* and its little territory, the Middle Ages started out from the *country*. This different starting-point was determined by the sparseness of the population at that time, which was scattered over a large area and which received no large increase from the conquerors. In contrast to Greece and Rome, feudal development at the outset, therefore, extends over a much wider territory, prepared by the Roman conquests and the spread of agriculture at first associated with it. The last centuries of the declining Roman Empire and its conquest by the barbarians destroyed a number of productive forces; agriculture had declined, industry had decayed for want of a market, trade had died out or been violently suspended, the rural and urban population had decreased. From these conditions and the mode of organisation of the conquest determined by them, feudal property developed under the influence of the Germanic military constitution. Like tribal and communal ownership, it is based again on a community; but the directly producing class standing over against it is not,

---

[5] The *Licinian agrarian law*—the agrarian law of Licinius and Sextius, Roman tribunes of the people, passed in 367 B.C. as a result of the struggle which the plebeians waged against the patricians. According to this law a Roman citizen could not hold more than 500 Yugera (approximately 309 acres) of common land (*ager publicus*). [INSTITUTE OF MARXISM-LENINISM.]

as in the case of the ancient community, the slaves, but the enserfed small peasantry. As soon as feudalism is fully developed, there also arises antagonism to the towns. The hierarchical structure of landownership, and the armed bodies of retainers associated with it, gave the nobility power over the serfs. This feudal organisation was, just as much as the ancient communal ownership, an association against a subjected producing class; but the form of association and the relation to the direct producers were different because of the different conditions of production.

This feudal system of landownership had its counterpart in the *towns* in the shape of corporative property, the feudal organisation of trades. Here property consisted chiefly in the labour of each individual person. The necessity for association against the organised robber-nobility, the need for communal covered markets in an age when the industrialist was at the same time a merchant, the growing competition of the escaped serfs swarming into the rising towns, the feudal structure of the whole country: these combined to bring about the *guilds*. The gradually accumulated small capital of individual craftsmen and their stable numbers, as against the growing population, evolved the relation of journeyman and apprentice, which brought into being in the towns a hierarchy similar to that in the country.

Thus the chief form of property during the feudal epoch consisted on the one hand of landed property with serf labour chained to it, and on the other of the labour of the individual with small capital commanding the labour of journeymen. The organisation of both was determined by the restricted conditions of production—the small-scale and primitive cultivation of the land, and the craft type of industry. There was little division of labour in the heyday of feudalism. Each country bore in itself the antithesis of town and country; the division into estates was certainly strongly marked; but apart from the differentiation of princes, nobility, clergy and peasants in the country, and masters, journeymen, apprentices and soon also the rabble of casual labourers in the towns, no division of importance took place. In agriculture it was rendered difficult by the strip-system, beside which the cottage industry of the peasants themselves emerged. In industry there was no division of labour at all in the individual trades themselves, and very little between them. The separation of industry and commerce was found already in existence in older towns; in the newer it only developed later, when the towns entered into mutual relations.

The grouping of larger territories into feudal kingdoms was a necessity for the landed nobility as for the towns. The organisation of the ruling class, the nobility, had, therefore, everywhere a monarch at its head.

The fact is, therefore, that definite individuals who are productively active in a definite way enter into these definite social and political relations. Empirical observation must in each separate instance bring out empirically, and without any mystification and speculation, the connection of the social and political structure with production. The social structure and the State

258 / KARL MARX

are continually evolving out of the life-process of definite individuals, but of individuals, not as they may appear in their own or other people's imagination, but as they *really* are; i.e., as they operate, produce materially, and hence as they work under definite material limits, presuppositions and conditions independent of their will.[6]

The production of ideas, of conceptions, of consciousness, is at first directly interwoven with the material activity and the material intercourse of men, the language of real life. Conceiving, thinking, the mental intercourse of men, appear at this stage as the direct efflux of their material behaviour. The same applies to mental production as expressed in the language of politics, laws, morality, religion, metaphysics, etc., of a people. Men are the producers of their conceptions, ideas, etc.—real, active men, as they are conditioned by a definite development of their productive forces and of the intercourse corresponding to these, up to its furthest forms. Consciousness can never be anything else than conscious existence, and the existence of men is their actual life-process. If in all ideology men and their circumstances appear upside-down as in a *camera obscura*,[7] this phenomenon arises just as much from their historical life-process as the inversion of objects on the retina does from their physical life-process.

In direct contrast to German philosophy which descends from heaven to earth, here we ascend from earth to heaven. That is to say, we do not set out from what men say, imagine, conceive, nor from men as narrated, thought of, imagined, conceived, in order to arrive at men in the flesh. We set out from real, active men, and on the basis of their real life-process we demonstrate the development of the ideological reflexes and echoes of this life-process. The phantoms formed in the human brain are also, necessarily, sublimates of their material life-process, which is empirically verifiable and bound to material premises. Morality, religion, metaphysics, all the rest of ideology and their corresponding forms of consciousness, thus no longer retain the semblance of independence. They have no history, no development; but men, developing their material production and their material intercourse, alter, along with this their real existence, their thinking and the products of their thinking. Life is not determined by consciousness, but

---

[6] [The following passage is crossed out in the manuscript:] The ideas which these individuals form are ideas either about their relation to nature or about their mutual relations or about their own nature. It is evident that in all these cases their ideas are the conscious expression—real or illusory—of their relationships and activities, of their production and intercourse and of their social and political organisation. The opposite assumption is only possible if in addition to the spirit of the real, materially evolved individuals a separate spirit is presupposed. If the conscious expression of the real relations of these individuals is illusory, if in their imagination they turn reality upside-down, then this in its turn is the result of their limited material mode of activity and their limited social relations arising from it. [S.R.]

[7] *Camera obscura:* a darkened room or enclosure with an aperture through which light from external objects enters to form a reversed image of the object on the opposite surface. [R.D.G.]

consciousness by life. In the first method of approach the starting-point is consciousness taken as the living individual; in the second method, which conforms to real life, it is the real living individuals themselves, and consciousness is considered solely as *their* consciousness.

This method of approach is not devoid of premises. It starts out from the real premises and does not abandon them for a moment. Its premises are men, not in any fantastic isolation and rigidity, but in their actual, empirically perceptible process of development under definite conditions. As soon as this active life-process is described, history ceases to be a collection of dead facts as it is with the empiricists (themselves still abstract), or an imagined activity of imagined subjects, as with the idealists.

Where speculation ends—in real life—there real, positive science begins: the representation of the practical activity, of the practical process of development of men. Empty talk about consciousness ceases, and real knowledge has to take its place. When reality is depicted, philosophy as an independent branch of knowledge loses its medium of existence. At the best its place can only be taken by a summing-up of the most general results, abstractions which arise from the observation of the historical development of men. Viewed apart from real history, these abstractions have in themselves no value whatsoever. They can only serve to facilitate the arrangement of historical material, to indicate the sequence of its separate strata. But they by no means afford a recipe or schema, as does philosophy, for neatly trimming the epochs of history. On the contrary, our difficulties begin only when we set about the observation and the arrangement—the real depiction—of our historical material, whether of a past epoch or of the present. The removal of these difficulties is governed by premises which it is quite impossible to state here, but which only the study of the actual life-process and the activity of the individuals of each epoch will make evident. We shall select here some of these abstractions, which we use in contradistinction to the ideologists, and shall illustrate them by historical examples.

QUESTIONS FOR STUDY AND DISCUSSION

1. Explain what Marx means when he says: "The nature of individuals thus depends on the material conditions determining their production."
2. Define the term "division of labor."
3. Explain the relationship of the search for man's nature and Marx's discussion of different forms of ownership.
4. According to Marx, what is "ideology" and how is it determined?
5. Can Marx successfully defend himself against the charge that his own writings, like those of his predecessors, are determined by his life and so are no more true than theirs? Explain.

Man as Alienated

[xxii] We have begun from the presuppositions of political economy. We have accepted its terminology and its laws. We presupposed private property; the separation of labour, capital and land, as also of wages, profit and rent; the division of labour; competition; the concept of exchange value, etc. From political economy itself, in its own words, we have shown that the worker sinks to the level of a commodity, and to a most miserable commodity; that the misery of the worker increases with the power and volume of his production; that the necessary result of competition is the accumulation of capital in a few hands, and thus a restoration of monopoly in a more terrible form; and finally that the distinction between capitalist and landlord, and between agricultural labourer and industrial worker, must disappear, and the whole of society divide into the two classes of property *owners* and *propertyless* workers.

Political economy begins with the fact of private property; it does not explain it. It conceives the *material* process of private property, as this occurs in reality, in general and abstract formulas which then serve it as laws. It does not *comprehend* these laws; that is, it does not show how they arise out of the nature of private property. Political economy provides no explanation of the basis for the distinction of labour from capital, of capital from land. When, for example, the relation of wages to profits is defined, this is explained in terms of the interests of capitalists; in other words, what should be explained is assumed. Similarly, competition is referred to at every point and is explained in terms of external conditions. Political economy tells us nothing about the extent to which these external and apparently accidental conditions are simply the expression of a necessary development. We have seen how exchange itself seems an accidental fact. The only motive forces which political economy recognizes are *avarice* and the *war between the avaricious, competition*.

Just because political economy fails to understand the interconnexions within this movement it was possible to oppose the doctrine of competition to that of monopoly, the doctrine of freedom of the crafts to that of the guilds, the doctrine of the division of landed property to that of the great estates; for competition, freedom of crafts, and the division of landed property were conceived only as accidental consequences brought about by will and force, rather than as necessary, inevitable and natural consequences of monopoly, the guild system and feudal property.

From pp. 120–34 of Karl Marx, *The Economic and Philosophical Manuscripts*, in *Karl Marx: Early Writings*, translated and edited by T. B. Bottomore. © 1963 by C. A. Watts and Company Ltd., London. Reprinted by permission of the publisher.

Thus we have now to grasp the real connexion between this whole system of alienation—private property, acquisitiveness, the separation of labour, capital and land, exchange and competition, value and the devaluation of man, monopoly and competition—and the system of *money.*

Let us not begin our explanation, as does the economist, from a legendary primordial condition. Such a primordial condition does not explain anything; it merely removes the question into a grey and nebulous distance. It asserts as a fact or event what it should deduce, namely, the necessary relation between two things; for example, between the division of labour and exchange. In the same way theology explains the origin of evil by the fall of man; that is, it asserts as a historical fact what it should explain.

We shall begin from a *contemporary* economic fact. The worker becomes poorer the more wealth he produces and the more his production increases in power and extent. The worker becomes an ever cheaper commodity the more goods he creates. The *devaluation* of the human world increases in direct relation with the *increase in value* of the world of things. Labour does not only create goods; it also produces itself and the worker as a *commodity,* and indeed in the same proportion as it produces goods.

This fact simply implies that the object produced by labour, its product, now stands opposed to it as an *alien being,* as a *power independent* of the producer. The product of labour is labour which has been embodied in an object and turned into a physical thing; this product is an *objectification* of labour. The performance of work is at the same time its objectification. The performance of work appears in the sphere of political economy as a *vitiation* of the worker, objectification as a *loss* and as *servitude to the object,* and appropriation as *alienation.*

So much does the performance of work appear as vitiation that the worker is vitiated to the point of starvation. So much does objectification appear as loss of the object that the worker is deprived of the most essential things not only of life but also of work. Labour itself becomes an object which he can acquire only by the greatest effort and with unpredictable interruptions. So much does the appropriation of the object appear as alienation that the more objects the worker produces the fewer he can possess and the more he falls under the domination of his product, of capital.

All these consequences follow from the fact that the worker is related to the *product of his labour* as to an *alien* object. For it is clear on this presupposition that the more the worker expends himself in work the more powerful becomes the world of objects which he creates in face of himself, the poorer he becomes in his inner life, and the less he belongs to himself. It is just the same as in religion. The more of himself man attributes to God the less he has left in himself. The worker puts his life into the object, and his life then belongs no longer to himself but to the object. The greater his activity, therefore, the less he possesses. What is embodied in the product of his labour is no longer his own. The greater this product is, therefore, the more he is diminished. The *alienation* of the worker in his product means not only that his labour becomes an object, assumes an *external* existence, but that it exists independently, *outside himself,* and alien to him, and that it stands opposed to him as an autonomous power. The life which he has given to the object sets itself against him as an alien and hostile force.

[XXIII] Let us now examine more closely the phenomenon of *objectification;* the worker's production and the *alienation* and *loss* of the object it produces, which is involved in it. The worker can create nothing without *nature,* without the *sensuous external world.* The latter is the material in which his labour is realized, in which it is active, out of which and through which it produces things.

But just as nature affords the *means of existence* of labour, in the sense that labour cannot *live* without objects upon which it can be exercised, so also it provides the *means of existence* in a narrower sense; namely the means of physical existence for the *worker* himself. Thus, the more the worker *appropriates* the external world of sensuous nature by his labour the more he deprives himself of *means of existence,* in two respects: first, that the sensuous external world becomes progressively less an object belonging to his labour or a means of existence of his labour, and secondly, that it becomes progressively less a means of existence in the direct sense, a means for the physical subsistence of the worker.

In both respects, therefore, the worker becomes a slave of the object; first, in that he receives an *object of work,* i.e. receives *work,* and secondly, in that he receives *means of subsistence.* Thus the object enables him to exist, first as a *worker* and secondly, as a *physical subject.* The culmination of this enslavement is that he can only maintain himself as a *physical subject* so far as he is a *worker,* and that it is only as a *physical subject* that he is a worker.

(The alienation of the worker in his object is expressed as follows in the laws of political economy: the more the worker produces the less he has to consume; the more value he creates the more worthless he becomes; the more refined his product the more crude and misshapen the worker; the more civilized the product the more barbarous the worker; the more powerful the work the more feeble the worker; the more the work manifests intelligence the more the worker declines in intelligence and becomes a slave of nature.)

Political economy conceals the alienation in the nature of labour in so far as it does not examine the direct relationship between the worker (work) and production. Labour certainly produces marvels for the rich but it produces privation for the worker. It produces palaces, but hovels for the worker. It produces beauty, but deformity for the worker. It replaces labour by machinery, but it casts some of the workers back into a barbarous kind of work and turns the others into machines. It produces intelligence, but also stupidity and cretinism for the workers.

The direct relationship of labour to its products is the relationship of the worker to the objects of his production. The relationship of property owners to the objects of production and to production itself is merely a *consequence* of this first relationship and confirms it. We shall consider this second aspect later.

Thus, when we ask what is the important relationship of labour, we are concerned with the relationship of the *worker* to production.

So far we have considered the alienation of the worker only from one aspect; namely, *his relationship with the products of his labour.* However, alienation appears not merely in the result but also in the *process of production,* within *productive activity* itself. How could the worker stand in an alien relationship to the product of his activity if he did not alienate himself in the act of production itself? The product is indeed only the *résumé* of activity, of production. Consequently, if the product of labour is alienation, production itself must be active alienation—the alienation of activity and the activity of alienation. The alienation of the object of labour merely summarizes the alienation in the work activity itself.

What constitutes the alienation of labour? First, that the work is *external* to the worker, that it is not part of his nature; and that, consequently, he does not fulfil himself in his work but denies himself, has a feeling of misery rather than well-being, does not develop freely his mental and physical energies but is physically exhausted and mentally debased. The worker, therefore, feels himself at home only during his leisure time, whereas at work he feels homeless. His work is not voluntary but imposed, *forced labour.* It is not the satisfaction of a need, but only a *means* for satisfying other needs. Its alien character is clearly shown by the fact that as soon as there is no physical or other compulsion it is avoided like the plague. External labour, labour in which man alienates himself, is a labour of self-sacrifice, of mortification. Finally, the external character of work for the worker is shown by the fact that it is not his own work but work for someone else, that in work he does not belong to himself but to another person.

Just as in religion the spontaneous activity of human fantasy, of the human brain and heart, reacts independently as an alien activity of gods or devils upon the individual, so the activity of the worker is not his own spontaneous activity. It is another's activity and a loss of his own spontaneity.

We arrive at the result that man (the worker) feels himself to be freely active only in his animal functions—eating, drinking and procreating, or at most also in his dwelling and in personal adornment—while in his human functions he is reduced to an animal. The animal becomes human and the human becomes animal.

Eating, drinking and procreating are of course also genuine human functions. But abstractly considered, apart from the environment of human activities, and turned into final and sole ends, they are animal functions.

We have now considered the act of alienation of practical human activity, labour, from two aspects: (1) the relationship of the worker to the *product of labour* as an alien object which dominates him. This relationship is at the same time the relationship to the sensuous external world, to natural objects, as an alien and hostile world; (2) the relationship of labour to the *act of production* within *labour*. This is the relationship of the worker to his own activity as something alien and not belonging to him, activity as suffering (passivity), strength as powerlessness, creation as emasculation, the *personal* physical and mental energy of the worker, his personal life (for what is life but activity?), as an activity which is directed against himself, independent of him and not belonging to him. This is *self-alienation* as against the above-mentioned alienation of the *thing*.

[XXIV] We have now to infer a third characteristic of *alienated labour* from the two we have considered.

Man is a species-being not only in the sense that he makes the community (his own as well as those of other things) his object both practically and theoretically, but also (and this is simply another expression for the same thing) in the sense that he treats himself as the present, living species, as a *universal* and consequently free being.[1]

Species-life, for man as for animals, has its physical basis in the fact that man (like animals) lives from inorganic nature, and since man is more universal than an animal so the range of inorganic nature from which he lives is more universal. Plants, animals, minerals, air, light, etc. constitute, from the theoretical aspect, a part of human consciousness as objects of natural science and art; they are man's spiritual inorganic nature, his intellectual means of life, which he must first prepare for enjoyment and perpetuation. So also, from the practical aspect, they form a part of human life and activity. In practice man lives only from these natural products, whether in the form of food, heating, clothing, housing, etc. The universality of man appears in practice in the universality which makes the whole of nature into his inorganic body: (1) as a direct means of life; and equally (2) as the material object and instrument of his life activity. Nature is the inorganic body of man; that is to say nature, excluding the human body itself. To say that man *lives* from nature means that nature is his *body* with which he must remain in a continuous interchange in order not to die. The statement that the physical and mental life of man, and nature, are interdependent means simply that nature is interdependent with itself, for man is a part of nature.

Since alienated labour: (1) alienates nature from man; and (2) alienates man from himself, from his own active function, his life activity; so it alienates him from the species. It makes *species-life* into a means of individual life. In the first place it alienates species-life and individual life,

---

[1] In this passage Marx reproduces Feuerbach's argument in *Das Wesen des Christentums* [*The Essence of Christianity*]. [T.B.B.]

and secondly, it turns the latter, as an abstraction, into the purpose of the former, also in its abstract and alienated form.

For labour, *life activity, productive life,* now appear to man only as *means* for the satisfaction of a need, the need to maintain his physical existence. Productive life is, however, species-life. It is life creating life. In the type of life activity resides the whole character of a species, its species-character; and free, conscious activity is the species-character of human beings. Life itself appears only as a *means of life.*

The animal is one with its life activity. It does not distinguish the activity from itself. It is *its activity.* But man makes his life activity itself an object of his will and consciousness. He has a conscious life activity. It is not a determination with which he is completely identified. Conscious life activity distinguishes man from the life activity of animals. Only for this reason is he a species-being. Or rather, he is only a self-conscious being, i.e. his own life is an object for him, because he is a species-being. Only for this reason is his activity free activity. Alienated labour reverses the relationship, in that man because he is a self-conscious being makes his life activity, his *being,* only a means for his *existence.*

The practical construction of an *objective world,* the *manipulation* of inorganic nature, is the confirmation of man as a conscious species-being, i.e. a being who treats the species as his own being or himself as a species-being. Of course, animals also produce. They construct nests, dwellings, as in the case of bees, beavers, ants, etc. But they only produce what is strictly necessary for themselves or their young. They produce only in a single direction, while man produces universally. They produce only under the compulsion of direct physical needs, while man produces when he is free from physical need and only truly produces in freedom from such need. Animals produce only themselves, while man reproduces the whole of nature. The products of animal production belong directly to their physical bodies, while man is free in face of his product. Animals construct only in accordance with the standards and needs of the species to which they belong, while man knows how to produce in accordance with the standards of every species and knows how to apply the appropriate standard to the object. Thus man constructs also in accordance with the laws of beauty.

It is just in his work upon the objective world that man really proves himself as a *species-being.* This production is his active species-life. By means of it nature appears as *his* work and his reality. The object of labour is, therefore, the *objectification of man's species-life;* for he no longer reproduces himself merely intellectually, as in consciousness, but actively and in a real sense, and he sees his own reflection in a world which he has constructed. While, therefore, alienated labour takes away the object of production from man, it also takes away his *species-life,* his real objectivity as a species-being, and changes his advantage over animals into a disadvantage in so far as his inorganic body, nature, is taken from him.

Just as alienated labour transforms free and self-directed activity into a means, so it transforms the species-life of man into a means of physical existence.

Consciousness, which man has from his species, is transformed through alienation so that species-life becomes only a means for him. (3) Thus alienated labour turns the *species-life of man,* and also nature as his mental species-property, into an *alien* being and into a *means* for his *individual existence.* It alienates from man his own body, external nature, his mental life and his *human* life. (4) A direct consequence of the alienation of man from the product of his labour, from his life activity and from his species-life, is that *man is alienated* from other *men.* When man confronts himself he also confronts *other* men. What is true of man's relationship to his work, to the product of his work and to himself, is also true of his relationship to other men, to their labour and to the objects of their labour.

In general, the statement that man is alienated from his species-life means that each man is alienated from others, and that each of the others is likewise alienated from human life.

Human alienation, and above all the relation of man to himself, is first realized and expressed in the relationship between each man and other men. Thus in the relationship of alienated labour every man regards other men according to the standards and relationships in which he finds himself placed as a worker.

[xxv] We began with an economic fact, the alienation of the worker and his production. We have expressed this fact in conceptual terms as *alienated labour,* and in analysing the concept we have merely analysed an economic fact.

Let us now examine further how this concept of alienated labour must express and reveal itself in reality. If the product of labour is alien to me and confronts me as an alien power, to whom does it belong? If my own activity does not belong to me but is an alien, forced activity, to whom does it belong? To a being *other* than myself. And who is this being? The *gods?* It is apparent in the earliest stages of advanced production, e.g. temple building, etc. in Egypt, India, Mexico, and in the service rendered to gods, that the product belonged to the gods. But the gods alone were never the lords of labour. And no more was *nature.* What a contradiction it would be if the more man subjugates nature by his labour, and the more the marvels of the gods are rendered superfluous by the marvels of industry, the more he should abstain from his joy in producing and his enjoyment of the product for love of these powers.

The *alien* being to whom labour and the product of labour belong, to whose service labour is devoted, and to whose enjoyment the product of labour goes, can only be *man* himself. If the product of labour does not belong to the worker, but confronts him as an alien power, this can only be because it belongs to *a man other than the worker.* If his activity is a torment to him it must be a source of *enjoyment* and pleasure to another. Not the gods, nor nature, but only man himself can be this alien power over men.

Consider the earlier statement that the relation of man to himself is first *realized, objectified,* through his relation to other men. If he is related to the product of his labour, his objectified labour, as to an *alien,* hostile, powerful and independent object, he is related in such a way that another alien, hostile, powerful and independent man is the lord of this object. If he is related to his own activity as to unfree activity, then he is related to it as activity in the service, and under the domination, coercion and yoke, of another man.

Every self-alienation of man, from himself and from nature, appears in the relation which he postulates between other men and himself and nature. Thus religious self-alienation is necessarily exemplified in the relation between laity and priest, or, since it is here a question of the spiritual world, between the laity and a mediator. In the real world of practice this self-alienation can only be expressed in the real, practical relation of man to his fellow men. The medium through which alienation occurs is itself a *practical* one. Through alienated labour, therefore, man not only produces his relation to the object and to the process of production as to alien and hostile men; he also produces the relation of other men to his production and his product, and the relation between himself and other men. Just as he creates his own production as a vitiation, a punishment, and his own product as a loss, as a product which does not belong to him, so he creates the domination of the non-producer over production and its product. As he alienates his own activity, so he bestows upon the stranger an activity which is not his own.

We have so far considered this relation only from the side of the worker, and later on we shall consider it also from the side of the non-worker.

Thus, through alienated labour the worker creates the relation of another man, who does not work and is outside the work process, to this labour. The relation of the worker to work also produces the relation of the capitalist (or whatever one likes to call the lord of labour) to work. *Private property* is, therefore, the product, the necessary result, of *alienated labour,* of the external relation of the worker to nature and to himself.

Private property is thus derived from the analysis of the concept of *alienated labour;* that is, alienated man, alienated labour, alienated life, and estranged man.

We have, of course, derived the concept of *alienated labour* (*alienated life*) from political economy, from an analysis of the *movement of private property*. But the analysis of this concept shows that although private property appears to be the basis and cause of alienated labour, it is rather a consequence of the latter, just as the gods are *fundamentally* not the cause but the product of confusions of human reason. At a later stage, however, there is a reciprocal influence.

Only in the final stage of the development of private property is its secret revealed, namely, that it is on one hand the *product* of alienated labour, and on the other hand the *means* by which labour is alienated, *the realization of this alienation.*

This elucidation throws light upon several unresolved controversies—

1. Political economy begins with labour as the real soul of production and then goes on to attribute nothing to labour and everything to private property. Proudhon,[2] faced by this contradiction, has decided in favour of labour against private property. We perceive, however, that this apparent contradiction is the contradiction of *alienated labour* with itself and that political economy has merely formulated the laws of alienated labour.

We also observe, therefore, that *wages* and *private property* are identical, for wages, like the product or object of labour, labour itself remunerated, are only a necessary consequence of the alienation of labour. In the wage system labour appears not as an end in itself but as the servant of wages. We shall develop this point later on and here only bring out some of the [XXVI] consequences.

An enforced *increase in wages* (disregarding the other difficulties, and especially that such an anomaly could only be maintained by force) would be nothing more than a *better remuneration of slaves,* and would not restore, either to the worker or to the work, their human significance and worth.

Even the *equality of incomes* which Proudhon demands would only change the relation of the present-day worker to his work into a relation of all men to work. Society would then be conceived as an abstract capitalist.

2. From the relation of alienated labour to private property it also follows that the emancipation of society from private property, from servitude, takes the political form of the *emancipation of the workers;* not in the sense that only the latter's emancipation is involved, but because this emancipation includes the emancipation of humanity as a whole. For all human servitude is involved in the relation of the worker to production, and all the types of servitude are only modifications or consequences of this relation.

As we have discovered the concept of *private property* by an *analysis* of the concept of *alienated labour,* so with the aid of these two factors we can evolve all the *categories* of political economy, and in every category, e.g. trade, competition, capital, money, we shall discover only a particular and developed expression of these fundamental elements.

However, before considering this structure let us attempt to solve two problems.

---

[2] Pierre Joseph Proudhon (1809–65): French economist and social theorist, most famous for his pamphlet *What Is Property?* His book *The Philosophy of Poverty* was bitingly criticized by Marx in *The Poverty of Philosophy.* [R.D.G.]

1. To determine the general nature of *private property* as it has resulted from alienated labour, in its relation to *genuine human and social property*.

2. We have taken as a fact and analysed the *alienation of labour.* How does it happen, we may ask, that *man alienates his labour?* How is this alienation founded in the nature of human development? We have already done much to solve the problem in so far as we have *transformed* the question concerning the *origin of private property* into a question about the relation between *alienated labour* and the process of development of mankind. For in speaking of private property one believes oneself to be dealing with something external to mankind. But in speaking of labour one deals directly with mankind itself. This new formulation of the problem already contains its solution.

ad 1. *The general nature of private property and its relation to genuine human property.*

We have resolved alienated labour into two parts, which mutually determine each other, or rather, which constitute two different expressions of one and the same relation. *Appropriation* appears as *alienation* and *alienation* as *appropriation,* alienation as genuine acceptance in the community.

We have considered one aspect, *alienated* labour, in its bearing upon the *worker* himself, i.e. *the relation of alienated labour to itself.* And we have found as the necessary consequence of this relation the *property relation* of the *non-worker* to the *worker* and to labour. *Private property* as the material, summarized expression of alienated labour includes both relations; *the relation of the worker to labour, to the product of his labour and to the non-worker,* and the relation of the *non-worker to the worker and to the product of the latter's labour.*

We have already seen that in relation to the worker, who *appropriates* nature by his labour, appropriation appears as alienation, self-activity as activity for another and of another, living as the sacrifice of life, and production of the object as loss of the object to an alien power, an alien man. Let us now consider the relation of this *alien* man to the worker, to labour, and to the object of labour.

It should be noted first that everything which appears to the worker as an *activity of alienation,* appears to the non-worker as a *condition of alienation.* Secondly, the *real, practical* attitude (as a state of mind) of the worker in production and to the product appears to the non-worker who confronts him as a *theoretical* attitude.

[xxvii] Thirdly, the non-worker does everything against the worker which the latter does against himself, but he does not do against himself what he does against the worker.

Let us examine these three relationships more closely.[3]

---

[3] The manuscript breaks off unfinished at this point. [T.B.B.]

QUESTIONS FOR STUDY AND DISCUSSION

1. What does Marx mean by "alienation"?
2. Distinguish the descriptive from the evaluative elements in Marx's discussion of man's alienation.
3. What is the significance, according to Marx, of the fact that man is a "species-being"?
4. How does Marx regard the relationship between private property and alienation?
5. In what does the "human life" from which alienated man is separated consist?

Man's Social Reality

ad page xxxix.[1] But the antithesis between *propertylessness* and *property* is still an indeterminate antithesis, which is not conceived in its *active reference* to its intrinsic relations, not yet conceived as a contradiction, so long as it is not understood as an antithesis between *labour* and *capital*. Even without the advanced development of private property, e.g. in ancient Rome, in Turkey, etc. this antithesis may be expressed in a primitive form. In this form it does not yet *appear* as established by private property itself. But labour, the subjective essence of private property as the exclusion of property, and capital, objective labour as the exclusion of labour, constitute *private property* as the developed relation of the contradiction and thus a dynamic relation which drives towards its resolution.

ad ibidem. The supersession of self-estrangement follows the same course as self-estrangement. *Private property* is first considered only from its objective aspect, but with labour conceived as its essence. Its mode of existence is, therefore, *capital* which it is necessary to abolish "as such" (Proudhon). Or else the *specific form* of labour (labour which is brought to a common level, subdivided, and thus unfree) is regarded as the source of the *nocivity*[2] of private property and of its existence alienated from man. Fourier, in accord with the Physiocrats,[3] regards *agricultural labour*

---

[1] Page referred to is the first page of the Preface to Marx's *Manuscripts*. [R.D.G.]
[2] Harmfulness or perniciousness. [R.D.G.]
[3] Physiocrats: a school or group of French political economists founded in the second half of the eighteenth century by François Quesnay. They advocated a society based on agriculture and lack of governmental restrictions on the economy.

Charles Fourier (1772–1837): a French social philosopher who advocated a social utopia based on small economic units of population.

Saint-Simon (1760–1825): a French social philosopher who advocated the abolition of economic inequalities; his doctrine was a forerunner of socialism. [R.D.G.]

From pp. 152–67 of Karl Marx, *The Economic and Philosophical Manuscripts* in *Karl Marx: Early Writings,* translated and edited by T. B. Bottomore. © 1963 by C. A. Watts and Company Ltd., London. Reprinted by permission of the publisher.

as being at least the exemplary kind of labour. Saint-Simon asserts on the contrary that *industrial labour* as such is the essence of labour, and consequently he desires the *exclusive* rule of the industrialists and an amelioration of the condition of the workers. Finally, *communism* is the positive expression of the abolition of private property, and in the first place of universal private property. In taking this relation in its *universal aspect* [1.] communism is, in its first form, only the generalization and fulfilment of the relation. As such it appears in a double form; the domination of material property looms so large that it aims to destroy everything which is incapable of being possessed by everyone as private property. It wishes to eliminate talent, etc. by *force*. Immediate physical possession seems to it the unique goal of life and existence. The role of *worker* is not abolished, but is extended to all men. The relation of private property remains the relation of the community to the world of things. Finally, this tendency to oppose general private property to private property is expressed in an animal form; *marriage* (which is incontestably a form of *exclusive private property*) is contrasted with the community of women, in which women become communal and common property. One may say that this idea of the *community of women* is the *open secret* of this entirely crude and unreflective communism. Just as women are to pass from marriage to universal prostitution, so the whole world of wealth (i.e. the objective being of man) is to pass from the relation of exclusive marriage with the private owner to the relation of universal prostitution with the community. This communism, which negates the *personality* of man in every sphere, is only the logical expression of private property, which is this negation. Universal *envy* setting itself up as a power is only a camouflaged form of cupidity which re-establishes itself and satisfies itself in a different way. The thoughts of every individual private property are *at least* directed against any *wealthier* private property, in the form of envy and the desire to reduce everything to a common level; so that this envy and levelling in fact constitute the essence of competition. Crude communism is only the culmination of such envy and levelling-down on the basis of a *preconceived* minimum. How little this abolition of private property represents a genuine appropriation is shown by the abstract negation of the whole world of culture and civilization, and the regression to the *unnatural* [IV] simplicity of the poor and wantless individual who has not only not surpassed private property but has not yet even attained to it.

The community is only a community of *work* and of *equality of wages* paid out by the communal capital, by the *community* as universal capitalist. The two sides of the relation are raised to a *supposed* universality; *labour* as a condition in which everyone is placed, and *capital* as the acknowledged universality and power of the community.

In the relationship with *woman,* as the prey and the handmaid of communal lust, is expressed the infinite degradation in which man exists for himself; for the secret of this relationship finds its *unequivocal,* incontestable, *open* and revealed expression in the relation of man to woman and in the way in which the *direct* and *natural* species-relationship is conceived. The immediate, natural and necessary relation of human being to human being is also the *relation* of *man* to *woman*. In this *natural* species-relationship man's relation to nature is directly his relation to man, and his relation to man is directly his relation to nature, to his own *natural* function. Thus, in this relation is *sensuously revealed,* reduced to an observable *fact,* the extent to which human nature has become nature for man and to which nature has become human nature for him. From this relationship man's whole level of development can be assessed. It follows from the character of this relationship how far *man* has become, and has understood himself as, a *species-being,* a *human being.* The relation of man to woman is the *most natural* relation of human being to human being. It indicates, therefore, how far man's *natural* behaviour has become *human,* and how far his *human* essence has become a *natural* essence for him, how far his *human nature* has become *nature* for him. It also shows how far man's needs have become *human* needs, and consequently how far the other person, as a person, has become one of his needs, and to what extent he is in his individual existence at the same time a social being. The first positive annulment of private property, crude communism, is, therefore, only a *phenomenal form* of the infamy of private property representing itself as positive community.

2. Communism [is] (*a*) still political in nature, democratic or despotic; (*b*) with the abolition of the state, yet still incomplete and influenced by private property, that is, by the alienation of man. In both forms communism is already aware of being the reintegration of man, his return to himself, the supersession of man's self-alienation. But since it has not yet grasped the positive nature of private property, or the *human* nature of needs, it is still captured and contaminated by private property. It has well understood the concept, but not the essence.

3. *Communism* is the *positive* abolition of *private property,* of *human self-alienation,* and thus the real *appropriation* of *human* nature through and for man. It is, therefore, the return of man himself as a *social,* i.e. really human, being, a complete and conscious return which assimilates all the wealth of previous development. Communism as a fully developed naturalism is humanism and as a fully developed humanism is naturalism. It is the *definitive* resolution of the antagonism between man and nature, and between man and man. It is the true solution of the conflict between existence and essence, between objectification and self-affirmation, between freedom and necessity, between individual and species. It is the solution of the riddle of history and knows itself to be this solution.

[v] Thus the whole historical development, both the *real* genesis of communism (the birth of its empirical existence) and its thinking consciousness, is its comprehended and conscious process of becoming; whereas the other, still undeveloped, communism seeks in certain historical

forms opposed to private property a *historical* justification founded upon what already exists, and to this end tears out of their context isolated elements of this development (Cabet [4] and Villegardelle [5] are pre-eminent among those who ride this hobby-horse) and asserts them as proofs of its historical pedigree. In doing so, it makes clear that by far the greater part of this development contradicts its own assertions, and that if it has ever existed its past existence refutes its pretension to *essential being*.

It is easy to understand the necessity which leads the whole revolutionary movement to find its empirical, as well its as theoretical, basis in the development of *private property,* and more precisely of the economic system.

This material, directly *perceptible* private property is the material and sensuous expression of *alienated human* life. Its movement—production and consumption—is the *sensuous* manifestation of the movement of all previous production, i.e. the realization or reality of man. Religion, the family, the state, law, morality, science, art, etc. are only *particular* forms of production and come under its general law. The positive supersession of *private property,* as the appropriation of *human* life, is, therefore, the positive supersession of all alienation, and the return of man from religion, the family, the state, etc. to his *human,* i.e. social life. Religious alienation as such occurs only in the sphere of *consciousness,* in the inner life of man, but economic alienation is that of *real life* and its supersession, therefore, affects both aspects. Of course, the development in different nations has a different beginning according to whether the actual and *established* life of the people is more in the realm of mind or more in the external world, is a real or ideal life. Communism begins where atheism begins (Owen),[6] but atheism is at the outset still far from being *communism;* indeed it is still for the most part an abstraction.[7]

Thus the philanthropy of atheism is at first only an abstract *philosophical* philanthropy, whereas that of communism is at once *real* and oriented towards *action.*

We have seen how, on the assumption that private property has been positively superseded, man produces man, himself and then other men; how the object which is the direct activity of his personality is at the same time his existence for other men and their existence for him. Similarly, the material of labour and man himself as a subject are the starting-point as

---

[4] Etienne Cabet (1788–1856): author of *Voyage en Icarie* (1840) and founder of a Utopian Community, Icaria, in Illinois. [T.B.B.]

[5] François Villegardelle (1810–56): French historian and follower of Fourier. He is the author of *History of Social Ideas Before the French Revolution.* [R.D.G.]

[6] Robert Owen (1771–1858): a founder of British socialism. He built a model industrial cooperative town in Scotland. [R.D.G.]

[7] Marx inserted a note here which referred back to his discussion of "crude communism": "Prostitution is only a *specific* expression of the *universal* prostitution of the worker, and since prostitution is a relationship which includes both the one who is prostituted and the one who prostitutes (and the latter is much more base), so the capitalist, etc. comes within this category." [T.B.B.]

well as the result of this movement (and because there must be this starting-point private property is a historical necessity). Therefore, the *social* character is the universal character of the whole movement; *as* society itself produces *man* as *man,* so it is *produced* by him. Activity and mind are social in their content as well as in their *origin;* they are *social* activity and social mind. The *human* significance of nature only exists for *social* man, because only in this case is nature a *bond* with other *men,* the basis of his existence for others and of their existence for him. Only then is nature the *basis* of his own *human* experience and a vital element of human reality. The *natural* existence of man has here become his *human* existence and nature itself has become human for him. Thus *society* is the accomplished union of man with nature, the veritable resurrection of nature, the realized naturalism of man and the realized humanism of nature.

[VI] Social activity and social mind by no means exist *only* in the form of activity or mind which is directly communal. Nevertheless, communal activity and mind, i.e. activity and mind which express and confirm themselves directly in a *real association* with other men, occur everywhere where this direct expression of sociability arises from the content of the activity or corresponds to the nature of mind.

Even when I carry out *scientific* work, etc., an activity which I can seldom conduct in direct association with other men, I perform a *social,* because *human,* act. It is not only the material of my activity—such as the language itself which the thinker uses—which is given to me as a social product. My *own existence* is a social activity. For this reason, what I myself produce I produce for society, and with the consciousness of acting as a social being.

My universal consciousness is only the *theoretical* form of that whose *living* form is the real community, the social entity, although at the present day this universal consciousness is an abstraction from real life and is opposed to it as an enemy. That is why the *activity* of my universal consciousness as such is my *theoretical* existence as a social being.

It is above all necessary to avoid postulating "society" once again as an abstraction confronting the individual. The individual *is* the *social being.* The manifestation of his life—even when it does not appear directly in the form of a communal manifestation, accomplished in association with other men—is, therefore, a manifestation and affirmation of *social life.* Individual human life and species-life are not different things, even though the mode of existence of individual life is necessarily either a more *specific* or a more *general* mode of species-life, or that of species-life a *specific* or more *general* mode of individual life.

In his *species-consciousness* man confirms his real *social life,* and reproduces his real existence in thought; while conversely, species-life confirms itself in species-consciousness and exists for itself in its universality as a thinking being. Though man is a unique individual—and it is just his particularity which makes him an individual, a really *individual* communal being—he is equally the *whole,* the ideal whole, the subjective existence of society as thought and experienced. He exists in reality as the representation and the real mind of social existence, and as the sum of human manifestations of life.

Thought and being are indeed *distinct* but they also form a unity. *Death* seems to be a harsh victory of the species over the individual and to contradict their unity; but the particular individual is only a *determinate species-being* and as such he is mortal.

4. Just as *private property* is only the sensuous expression of the fact that man is at the same time an *objective* fact for himself and becomes an alien and non-human object for himself; just as his manifestation of life is also his alienation of life and his self-realization a loss of reality, the emergence of an *alien* reality; so the positive supersession of private property, i.e. the *sensuous* appropriation of the human essence and of human life, of objective man and of human *creations,* by and for man, should not be taken only in the sense of *immediate,* exclusive *enjoyment,* or only in the sense of *possession* or *having.* Man appropriates his manifold being in an all-inclusive way, and thus as a whole man. All his *human* relations to the world—seeing, hearing, smelling, tasting, touching, thinking, observing, feeling, desiring, acting, loving—in short, all the organs of his individuality, like the organs which are directly communal in form, [VII] are in their objective action (their *action in relation to the object*) the appropriation of this object, the appropriation of human reality. The way in which they react to the object is the confirmation of *human reality.*[8] It is human effectiveness and human *suffering,* for suffering humanly considered is an enjoyment of the self for man.

Private property has made us so stupid and partial that an object is only *ours* when we have it, when it exists for us as capital or when it is directly eaten, drunk, worn, inhabited, etc., in short, *utilized* in some way. But private property itself only conceives these various forms of possession as *means of life,* and the life for which they serve as means is the *life* of *private property*—labour and creation of capital.

Thus *all* the physical and intellectual senses have been replaced by the simple alienation of *all* these senses; the sense of *having.* The human being had to be reduced to this absolute poverty in order to be able to give birth to all his inner wealth. (On the category of *having* see Hess in *Einundzwanzig Bogen.*)[9]

The supersession of private property is, therefore, the complete *emancipation* of all the human qualities and senses. It is such an emancipa-

---

[8] It is, therefore, just as varied as the determinations of human nature and activities are diverse. [K.M.]

[9] *Einundzwanzig Bogen aus der Schweiz* [*Twenty-one Sheets from Switzerland*], p. 329. [K.M.]

Moses Hess (1812–75): chief theoretician of the German movement called "true socialism." [R.D.G.]

tion because these qualities and senses have become *human,* from the subjective as well as the objective point of view. The eye has become a *human* eye when its *object* has become a *human,* social object, created by man and destined for him. The senses have, therefore, become directly theoreticians in practice. They relate themselves to the thing for the sake of the thing, but the thing itself is an *objective human* relation to itself and to man, and vice versa.[10] Need and enjoyment have thus lost their *egoistic* character and nature has lost its mere *utility* by the fact that its utilization has become *human* utilization.

Similarly, the senses and minds of other men have become my *own* appropriation. Thus besides these direct organs, *social* organs are constituted, in the form of society; for example, activity in direct association with others has become an organ for the manifestation of life and a mode of appropriation of *human* life.

It is evident that the human eye appreciates things in a different way from the crude, non-human eye, the human *ear* differently from the crude ear. As we have seen, it is only when the object becomes a *human* object, or objective *humanity,* that man does not become lost in it. This is only possible when man himself becomes a *social* object; when he himself becomes a social being and society becomes a being for him in this object.

On the one hand, it is only when objective reality everywhere becomes for man in society the reality of human faculties, human reality, and thus the reality of his own faculties, that all *objects* become for him the *objectification of himself.* The objects then confirm and realize his individuality, they are *his own* objects, i.e. man himself becomes the object. *The manner in which these objects* become his own depends upon the *nature of the object* and the nature of the corresponding faculty; for it is precisely the *determinate character* of this relation which constitutes the specific *real* mode of affirmation. The object is not the same for the *eye* as for the *ear,* for the ear as for the eye. The *distinctive character* of each faculty is precisely its *characteristic* essence and thus also the characteristic mode of its objectification, of its *objectively real,* living *being.* It is therefore not only in thought, [VIII] but through *all* the senses that man is affirmed in the objective world.

Let us next consider the subjective aspect. Man's musical sense is only awakened by music. The most beautiful music has no meaning for the non-musical ear, is not an object for it, because my object can only be the confirmation of one of my own faculties. It can only be so for me in so far as my faculty exists for itself as a subjective capacity, because the meaning of an object for me extends only as far as the sense extends (only makes sense for an appropriate sense). For this reason, the *senses* of social man are *different* from those of non-social man. It is only through the objectively

---

[10] In practice I can only relate myself in a human way to a thing when the thing is related in a human way to man. [K.M.]

deployed wealth of the human being that the wealth of subjective *human* sensibility (a musical ear, an eye which is sensitive to the beauty of form, in short, senses which are capable of human satisfaction and which confirm themselves as human faculties) is cultivated or created. For it is not only the five senses, but also the so-called spiritual senses, the practical senses (desiring, loving, etc.), in brief, human sensibility and the human character of the senses, which can only come into being through the existence of *its* object, through humanized nature. The cultivation of the five senses is the work of all previous history. Sense which is subservient to crude needs has only a restricted meaning. For a starving man the human form of food does not exist, but only its abstract character as food. It could just as well exist in the most crude form, and it is impossible to say in what way this feeding-activity would differ from that of animals. The needy man, burdened with cares, has no appreciation of the most beautiful spectacle. The dealer in minerals sees only their commercial value, not their beauty or their particular characteristics; he has no mineralogical sense. Thus, the objectification of the human essence, both theoretically and practically is necessary in order to *humanize* man's senses, and also to create the *human senses* corresponding to all the wealth of human and natural being.

Just as society at its beginnings finds, through the development of *private property* with its wealth and poverty (both intellectual and material), the materials necessary for this *cultural development,* so the fully constituted society produces man in all the plenitude of his being, the wealthy man endowed with all the senses, as an enduring reality. It is only in a social context that subjectivism and objectivism, spiritualism and materialism, activity and passivity, cease to be antinomies and thus cease to exist as such antinomies. The resolution of the *theoretical* contradictions is possible *only* through practical means, only through the *practical* energy of man. Their resolution is not by any means, therefore, only a problem of knowledge, but is a *real* problem of life which philosophy was unable to solve precisely because it saw there a purely theoretical problem.

It can be seen that the history of *industry* and industry as it *objectively* exists is an *open* book of the *human faculties,* and a human *psychology* which can be sensuously apprehended. This history has not so far been conceived in relation to human *nature,* but only from a superficial utilitarian point of view, since in the condition of alienation it was only possible to conceive real human faculties and *human* species-action in the form of general human existence, as religion, or as history in its abstract, general aspect as politics, art and literature, etc. *Everyday material industry* (which can be conceived as part of that general development; or equally, the general development can be conceived as a specific part of industry since all human activity up to the present has been labour, i.e. industry, self-alienated activity) shows us, in the form of *sensuous useful objects,* in an alienated form, the *essential human faculties* transformed into objects. No psychology for which this book, i.e. the most tangible and accessible part of history, remains closed, can become a *real* science with a genuine content. What is to be thought of a science which stays aloof from this enormous field of human labour, and which does not feel its own inadequacy even though this great wealth of human activity means nothing to it except perhaps what can be expressed in the single phrase—"need," "common need"?

The *natural sciences* have developed a tremendous activity and have assembled an ever-growing mass of data. But philosophy has remained alien to these sciences just as they have remained alien to philosophy. Their momentary *rapprochement* was only a *fantastic* illusion. There was a desire for union but the power to effect it was lacking. Historiography itself only takes natural science into account incidentally, regarding it as a factor making for enlightenment, for practical utility and for particular great discoveries. But natural science has penetrated all the more *practically* into human life through industry. It has transformed human life and prepared the emancipation of humanity, even though its immediate effect was to accentuate the dehumanization of man. *Industry* is the actual historical relationship of nature, and thus of natural science, to man. If industry is conceived as the *exoteric* manifestation of the essential human *faculties,* the *human* essence of nature and the *natural* essence of man can also be understood. Natural science will then abandon its abstract materialist, or rather idealist, orientation, and will become the basis of a *human* science, just as it has already become—though in an alienated form—the basis of actual human life. One basis for life and another for science is *a priori* a falsehood. Nature, as it develops in human history, in the act of genesis of human society, is the *actual* nature of man; thus nature, as it develops through industry, though in an *alienated* form, is truly *anthropological* nature.

Sense experience (*see* Feuerbach) must be the basis of all science. Science is only genuine science when it proceeds from sense experience, in the two forms of *sense perception* and *sensuous* need; i.e. only when it proceeds from nature. The whole of history is a preparation for "man" to become an object of *sense* perception, and for the development of human needs (the needs of man as such). History itself is a *real* part of *natural history,* of the development of nature into man. Natural science will one day incorporate the science of man, just as the science of man will incorporate natural science; there will be a *single* science.

Man is the direct object of natural science, because directly *perceptible nature* is for man directly human sense experience (an identical expression) in the form of the *other person* who is directly presented to him in a sensuous way. His own sense experience only exists as human sense experience for himself through the *other person.* But *nature* is the direct object of the science of man. The first object for man—man himself—is nature, sense experience; and the particular sensuous human faculties, which can only find objective realization in *natural* objects, can only attain self-knowledge in the science of natural being. The element of thought itself, the element of the living manifestation of thought, language, is sensuous in character. The *social* reality of nature and *human* natural science, or the *natural science of man,* are identical expressions.

It will be seen from this how, in place of the *wealth* and *poverty* of political economy, we have the *wealthy* man and the plenitude of *human* need. The wealthy man is at the same time one who *needs* a complex of human manifestations of life, and whose own self-realization exists as an inner necessity, a *need.* Not only the wealth but also the *poverty* of man acquires, in a socialist perspective, a *human* and thus a social meaning. Poverty is the passive bond which leads man to experience a need for the greatest wealth, the *other* person. The sway of the objective entity within me, the sensuous eruption of my life-activity, is the passion which here becomes the *activity* of my being.

A being does not regard himself as independent unless he is his own master, and he is only his own master when he owes his existence to himself. A man who lives by the favour of another considers himself a dependent being. But I live completely by another person's favour when I owe to him not only the continuance of my life but also *its creation;* when he is its *source.* My life has necessarily such a cause outside itself if it is not my own creation. The idea of *creation* is thus one which it is difficult to eliminate from popular consciousness. This consciousness is *unable to conceive* that nature and man exist on their own account, because such an existence contradicts all the tangible facts of practical life.

The idea of the creation of the *earth* has received a severe blow from the science of geogeny, i.e. from the science which portrays the formation and development of the earth as a process of spontaneous generation. *Generatio aequivoca* (spontaneous generation) is the only practical refutation of the theory of creation.

But it is easy indeed to say to the particular individual what Aristotle said: You are engendered by your father and mother, and consequently it is the coitus of two human beings, a human species-act, which has produced the human being. You see, therefore, that even in a physical sense man owes his existence to man. Consequently, it is not enough to keep in view only one of the two aspects, the *infinite* progression, and to ask further: who engendered my father and my grandfather? You must also keep in mind the *circular movement* which is perceptible in that progression, according to which man, in the act of generation reproduces himself; thus *man* always remains the subject. But you will reply: I grant you this circular movement, but you must in turn concede the progression, which leads ever further to the point where I ask; who created the first man and nature as a whole? I can only reply: your question is itself a product of abstraction. Ask yourself how you arrive at that question. Ask yourself whether your question does not arise from a point of view to which I cannot reply because it is a perverted one. Ask yourself whether that progression exists as such for rational thought. If you ask a question about the creation of nature and man you abstract from nature and man. You suppose them *non-existent* and you want me to demonstrate that they *exist.* I reply: give up your abstraction and at the same time you abandon your question. Or else, if you want to maintain your abstraction, be consistent, and if you think of man and nature as non-existent, [XI] think of yourself too as non-existent, for you are also man and nature. Do not think, do not ask me any questions, for as soon as you think and ask questions your abstraction from the existence of nature and man becomes meaningless. Or are you such an egoist that you conceive everything as non-existent and yet want to exist yourself?

You may reply: I do not want to conceive the nothingness of nature, etc.; I only ask you about the act of its creation, just as I ask the anatomist about the formation of bones, etc.

Since, however, for socialist man, the *whole of what is called world history* is nothing but the creation of man by human labour, and the emergence of nature for man, he, therefore, has the evident and irrefutable proof of his *self-creation,* of his own *origins.* Once the essence of man and of nature, man as a natural being and nature as a human reality, has become evident in practical life, in sense experience, the quest for an *alien* being, a being above man and nature (a quest which is an avowal of the unreality of man and nature) becomes impossible in practice. *Atheism,* as a denial of this unreality, is no longer meaningful, for atheism is a *negation of God* and seeks to assert by this negation the *existence of man.* Socialism no longer requires such a roundabout method; it begins from the *theoretical* and *practical sense perception* of man and nature as essential beings. It is positive human *self-consciousness,* no longer a self-consciousness attained through the negation of religion; just as the *real life* of man is positive and no longer attained through the negation of private property, through *communism.* Communism is the phase of negation of the negation and is, consequently, for the next stage of historical development, a real and necessary factor in the emancipation and rehabilitation of man. Communism is the necessary form and the dynamic principle of the immediate future, but communism is not itself the goal of human development—the form of human society.

QUESTIONS FOR STUDY AND DISCUSSION

1. What does Marx mean by "communism"?
2. In what sense is communism a humanism?
3. How does society produce man as man?
4. Explain the relationship that exists between individual human life and man's species-life.
5. Discuss the status of the individual in Marx's view of man.

Friedrich Engels

FRIEDRICH ENGELS was born in Barmen, Prussia, in 1820. In 1842 he
settled in Manchester where he entered his father's firm. He wrote
a book on the condition of the working class in England, and when he
met Karl Marx in 1844, a close and lifelong friendship began. Engels
collaborated with Marx on a number of early works, helped support
him, and corresponded with him almost daily. He edited volumes II
and III of *Capital* (1885, 1895) after Marx's death and wrote extensively explaining and defending Marxism. He is considered the
most authoritative expositor of Marx's writings. His most significant
original contribution to Marxism consists of his application of dialectics
not only to history but also to natural phenomena and science.

The Origin of Man

THE PART PLAYED BY LABOUR IN THE TRANSITION
FROM APE TO MAN

Labour is the source of all wealth, the political economists assert. And it
really is the source—next to nature, which supplies it with the material that
it converts into wealth. But it is even infinitely more than this. It is the
prime basic condition for all human existence, and this to such an extent
that, in a sense, we have to say that labour created man himself.

Many hundreds of thousands of years ago, during an epoch, not yet
definitely determinable, of that period of the earth's history known to geologists as the Tertiary period, most likely towards the end of it, a particularly highly-developed race of anthropoid apes lived somewhere in the
tropical zone—probably on a great continent that has now sunk to the bottom of the Indian Ocean. Darwin has given us an approximate description
of these ancestors of ours. They were completely covered with hair, they
had beards and pointed ears, and they lived in bands in the trees.

Climbing assigns different functions to the hands and the feet, and
when their mode of life involved locomotion on level ground, these apes

From pp. 172–85 of Friedrich Engels, *Dialectics of Nature,* translated by Clemens
Dutt. Copyright 1964 by Progress Publishers, Moscow. Reprinted by permission of
the publisher.

gradually got out of the habit of using their hands [in walking—*Tr.*] and adopted a more and more erect posture. This was *the decisive step in the transition from ape to man.*

All extant anthropoid apes can stand erect and move about on their feet alone, but only in case of urgent need and in a very clumsy way. Their natural gait is in a half-erect posture and includes the use of the hands. The majority rest the knuckles of the fist on the ground and, with legs drawn up, swing the body through their long arms, much as a cripple moves on crutches. In general, all the transition stages from walking on all fours to walking on two legs are still to be observed among the apes today. The latter gait, however, has never become more than a makeshift for any of them.

It stands to reason that if erect gait among our hairy ancestors became first the rule and then, in time, a necessity, other diverse functions must, in the meantime, have devolved upon the hands. Already among the apes there is some difference in the way the hands and the feet are employed. In climbing, as mentioned above, the hands and feet have different uses. The hands are used mainly for gathering and holding food in the same way as the fore paws of the lower mammals are used. Many apes use their hands to build themselves nests in the trees or even to construct roofs between the branches to protect themselves against the weather, as the chimpanzee, for example, does. With their hands they grasp sticks to defend themselves against enemies, and with their hands they bombard their enemies with fruits and stones. In captivity they use their hands for a number of simple operations copied from human beings. It is in this that one sees the great gulf between the undeveloped hand of even the most man-like apes and the human hand that has been highly perfected by hundreds of thousands of years of labour. The number and general arrangement of the bones and muscles are the same in both hands, but the hand of the lowest savage can perform hundreds of operations that no simian hand can imitate—no simian hand has ever fashioned even the crudest stone knife.

The first operations for which our ancestors gradually learned to adapt their hands during the many thousands of years of transition from ape to man could have been only very simple ones. The lowest savages, even those in whom regression to a more animal-like condition with a simultaneous physical degeneration can be assumed, are nevertheless far superior to these transitional beings. Before the first flint could be fashioned into a knife by human hands, a period of time probably elapsed in comparison with which the historical period known to us appears insignificant. But the decisive step had been taken, *the hand had become free* and could henceforth attain ever greater dexterity; the greater flexibility thus acquired was inherited and increased from generation to generation.

Thus the hand is not only the organ of labour, *it is also the product of labour.* Labour, adaptation to ever new operations, the inheritance of muscles, ligaments, and, over longer periods of time, bones that had undergone special development and the ever-renewed employment of this inherited finesse in new, more and more complicated operations, have given the human hand the high degree of perfection required to conjure into being the pictures of a Raphael, the statues of a Thorwaldsen, the music of a Paganini.

But the hand did not exist alone, it was only one member of an integral, highly complex organism. And what benefited the hand, benefited also the whole body it served; and this in two ways.

In the first place, the body benefited from the law of correlation of growth, as Darwin called it. This law states that the specialised forms of separate parts of an organic being are always bound up with certain forms of other parts that apparently have no connection with them. Thus all animals that have red blood cells without cell nuclei, and in which the head is attached to the first vertebra by means of a double articulation (condyles), also without exception possess lacteal glands for suckling their young. Similarly, cloven hoofs in mammals are regularly associated with the possession of a multiple stomach for rumination. Changes in certain forms involve changes in the form of other parts of the body, although we cannot explain the connection. Perfectly white cats with blue eyes are always, or almost always, deaf. The gradually increasing perfection of the human hand, and the commensurate adaptation of the feet for erect gait, have undoubtedly, by virtue of such correlation, reacted on other parts of the organism. However, this action has not as yet been sufficiently investigated for us to be able to do more here than to state the fact in general terms.

Much more important is the direct, demonstrable influence of the development of the hand on the rest of the organism. It has already been noted that our simian ancestors were gregarious; it is obviously impossible to seek the derivation of man, the most social of all animals, from nongregarious immediate ancestors. Mastery over nature began with the development of the hand, with labour, and widened man's horizon at every new advance. He was continually discovering new, hitherto unknown properties in natural objects. On the other hand, the development of labour necessarily helped to bring the members of society closer together by increasing cases of mutual support and joint activity, and by making clear the advantage of this joint activity to each individual. In short, men in the making arrived at the point where *they had something to say* to each other. Necessity created the organ; the undeveloped larynx of the ape was slowly but surely transformed by modulation to produce constantly more developed modulation, and the organs of the mouth gradually learned to pronounce one articulate sound after another.

Comparison with animals proves that this explanation of the origin of language from and in the process of labour is the only correct one. The little that even the most highly-developed animals need to communicate to each other does not require articulate speech. In a state of nature, no animal feels handicapped by its inability to speak or to understand human speech. It is quite different when it has been tamed by man. The dog and the horse, by association with man, have developed such a good ear for articulate speech that they easily learn to understand any language within their range of concept. Moreover, they have acquired the capacity for feelings such as affection for man, gratitude, etc., which were previously foreign to them. Anyone who has had much to do with such animals will hardly be able to escape the conviction that in many cases they *now* feel their inability to speak as a defect, although, unfortunately, it is one that can no longer be remedied because their vocal organs are too specialised in a definite direction. However, where vocal organs exist, within certain limits even this inability disappears. The buccal organs of birds are as different from those of man as they can be, yet birds are the only animals that can learn to speak; and it is the bird with the most hideous voice, the parrot, that speaks best of all. Let no one object that the parrot does not understand what it says. It is true that for the sheer pleasure of talking and associating with human beings, the parrot will chatter for hours at a stretch, continually repeating its whole vocabulary. But within the limits of its range of concepts it can also learn to understand what it is saying. Teach a parrot swear words in such a way that it gets an idea of their meaning (one of the great amusements of sailors returning from the tropics); tease it and you will soon discover that it knows how to use its swear words just as correctly as a Berlin costermonger. The same is true of begging for titbits.

First labour, after it and then with it speech—these were the two most essential stimuli under the influence of which the brain of the ape gradually changed into that of man, which for all its similarity is far larger and more perfect. Hand in hand with the development of the brain went the development of its most immediate instruments—the senses. Just as the gradual development of speech is inevitably accompanied by a corresponding refinement of the organ of hearing, so the development of the brain as a whole is accompanied by a refinement of all the senses. The eagle sees much farther than man, but the human eye discerns considerably more in things than does the eye of the eagle. The dog has a far keener sense of smell than man, but it does not distinguish a hundredth part of the odours that for man are definite signs denoting different things. And the sense of touch, which the ape hardly possesses in its crudest initial form, has been developed only side by side with the development of the human hand itself, through the medium of labour.

The reaction on labour and speech of the development of the brain and its attendant senses, of the increasing clarity of consciousness, power of abstraction and of conclusion, gave both labour and speech an ever-renewed impulse to further development. This development did not reach its conclusion when man finally became distinct from the ape, but on the whole made further powerful progress, its degree and direction varying among different peoples and at different times, and here and there even being interrupted by local or temporary regression. This further development has been strongly urged forward, on the one hand, and guided along more definite directions, on the other, by a new element which came into play with the appearance of fully-fledged man, namely, *society*.

Hundreds of thousands of years—of no greater significance in the history of the earth than one second in the life of man [1]—certainly elapsed before human society arose out of a troupe of tree-climbing monkeys. Yet it did finally appear. And what do we find once more as the characteristic difference between the troupe of monkeys and human society? *Labour*. The ape herd was satisfied to browse over the feeding area determined for it by geographical conditions or the resistance of neighbouring herds; it undertook migrations and struggles to win new feeding grounds, but it was incapable of extracting from them more than they offered in their natural state, except that it unconsciously fertilised the soil with its own excrement. As soon as all possible feeding grounds were occupied, there could be no further increase in the ape population; the number of animals could at best remain stationary. But all animals waste a great deal of food, and, in addition, destroy in the germ the next generation of the food supply. Unlike the hunter, the wolf does not spare the doe which would provide it with the young the next year; the goats in Greece, that eat away the young bushes before they grow to maturity, have eaten bare all the mountains of the country. This "predatory economy" of animals plays an important part in the gradual transformation of species by forcing them to adapt themselves to other than the usual food, thanks to which their blood acquires a different chemical composition and the whole physical constitution gradually alters, while species that have remained unadapted die out. There is no doubt that this predatory economy contributed powerfully to the transition of our ancestors from ape to man. In a race of apes that far surpassed all others in intelligence and adaptability, this predatory economy must have led to a continual increase in the number of plants used for food and to the consumption of more and more edible parts of food plants. In short, food became more and more varied, as did also the substances entering the body with it, substances that were the chemical premises for the transition to man. But all that was not yet labour in the proper sense of the word. Labour begins with the making of tools. And what are the most ancient tools that we find—the most ancient judging by the heirlooms of prehistoric man that have been discovered, and by the mode of life of the earliest historical peoples and of the rawest of contemporary savages? They are hunting and fishing implements, the former at the same time serving as weapons. But hunting and fishing presuppose the transition from an exclusively vegetable diet to the concomitant use of meat, and this is another important step in the process of transition from ape to man. A *meat diet* contained in an al-

---

[1] A leading authority in this respect, Sir William Thomson, has calculated that *little more than a hundred million years* could have elapsed since the time when the earth had cooled sufficiently for plants and animals to be able to live on it. [F.E.]

most ready state the most essential ingredients required by the organism for its metabolism. By shortening the time required for digestion, it also shortened the other vegetative bodily processes that correspond to those of plant life, and thus gained further time, material and desire for the active manifestation of animal life proper. And the farther man in the making moved from the vegetable kingdom the higher he rose above the animal. Just as becoming accustomed to a vegetable diet side by side with meat converted wild cats and dogs into the servants of man, so also adaptation to a meat diet, side by side with a vegetable diet, greatly contributed towards giving bodily strength and independence to man in the making. The meat diet, however, had its greatest effect on the brain, which now received a far richer flow of the materials necessary for its nourishment and development, and which, therefore, could develop more rapidly and perfectly from generation to generation. With all due respect to the vegetarians man did not come into existence without a meat diet, and if the latter, among all peoples known to us, has led to cannibalism at some time or other (the forefathers of the Berliners, the Weletabians or Wilzians, used to eat their parents as late as the tenth century), that is of no consequence to us today.

The meat diet led to two new advances of decisive importance—the harnessing of fire and the domestication of animals. The first still further shortened the digestive process, as it provided the mouth with food already, as it were, half-digested; the second made meat more copious by opening up a new, more regular source of supply in addition to hunting, and moreover provided, in milk and its products, a new article of food at least as valuable as meat in its composition. Thus both these advances were, in themselves, new means for the emancipation of man. It would lead us too far afield to dwell here in detail on their indirect effects notwithstanding the great importance they have had for the development of man and society.

Just as man learned to consume everything edible, he also learned to live in any climate. He spread over the whole of the habitable world, being the only animal fully able to do so of its own accord. The other animals that have become accustomed to all climates—domestic animals and vermin—did not become so independently, but only in the wake of man. And the transition from the uniformly hot climate of the original home of man to colder regions, where the year was divided into summer and winter, created new requirements—shelter and clothing as protection against cold and damp, and hence new spheres of labour, new forms of activity, which further and further separated man from the animal.

By the combined functioning of hands, speech organs and brain, not only in each individual but also in society, men became capable of executing more and more complicated operations, and were able to set themselves, and achieve, higher and higher aims. The work of each generation itself became different, more perfect and more diversified. Agriculture was added to hunting and cattle raising; then came spinning, weaving, metalworking, pottery and navigation. Along with trade and industry, art and science finally appeared. Tribes developed into nations and states. Law and politics arose, and with them that fantastic reflection of human things in the human mind—religion. In the face of all these images, which appeared in the first place to be products of the mind and seemed to dominate human societies, the more modest productions of the working hand retreated into the background, the more so since the mind that planned the labour was able, at a very early stage in the development of society (for example, already in the primitive family), to have the labour that had been planned carried out by other hands than its own. All merit for the swift advance of civilisation was ascribed to the mind, to the development and activity of the brain. Men became accustomed to explain their actions as arising out of thoughts instead of their needs (which in any case are reflected and perceived in the mind); and so in the course of time there emerged that idealistic world outlook which, especially since the fall of the world of antiquity, has dominated men's minds. It still rules them to such a degree that even the most materialistic natural scientists of the Darwinian school are still unable to form any clear idea of the origin of man, because under this ideological influence they do not recognise the part that has been played therein by labour.

Animals, as has already been pointed out, change the environment by their activities in the same way, even if not to the same extent, as man does, and these changes, as we have seen, in turn react upon and change those who made them. In nature nothing takes place in isolation. Everything affects and is affected by every other thing, and it is mostly because this manifold motion and interaction is forgotten that our natural scientists are prevented from gaining a clear insight into the simplest things. We have seen how goats have prevented the regeneration of forests in Greece; on the island of St. Helena, goats and pigs brought by the first arrivals have succeeded in exterminating its old vegetation almost completely, and so have prepared the ground for the spreading of plants brought by later sailors and colonists. But animals exert a lasting effect on their environment unintentionally and, as far as the animals themselves are concerned, accidentally. The further removed men are from animals, however, the more their effect on nature assumes the character of premeditated, planned action directed towards definite preconceived ends. The animal destroys the vegetation of a locality without realising what it is doing. Man destroys it in order to sow field crops on the soil thus released, or to plant trees or vines which he knows will yield many times the amount planted. He transfers useful plants and domestic animals from one country to another and thus changes the flora and fauna of whole continents. More than this. Through artificial breeding both plants and animals are so changed by the hand of man that they become unrecognisable. The wild plants from which our grain varieties originated are still being sought in vain. There is still some dispute about the wild animals from which our very different breeds of dogs or our equally numerous breeds of horses are descended.

288 / FRIEDRICH ENGELS

It goes without saying that it would not occur to us to dispute the ability of animals to act in a planned, premeditated fashion. On the contrary, a planned mode of action exists in embryo wherever protoplasm, living albumen, exists and reacts, that is, carries out definite, even if extremely simple, movements as a result of definite external stimuli. Such reaction takes place even where there is yet no cell at all, far less a nerve cell. There is something of the planned action in the way insect-eating plants capture their prey, although they do it quite unconsciously. In animals the capacity for conscious, planned action is proportional to the development of the nervous system, and among mammals it attains a fairly high level. While fox-hunting in England one can daily observe how unerringly the fox makes use of its excellent knowledge of the locality in order to elude its pursuers, and how well it knows and turns to account all favourable features of the ground that cause the scent to be lost. Among our domestic animals, more highly developed thanks to association with man, one can constantly observe acts of cunning on exactly the same level as those of children. For, just as the developmental history of the human embryo in the mother's womb is only an abbreviated repetition of the history, extending over millions of years, of the bodily evolution of our animal ancestors, starting from the worm, so the mental development of the human child is only a still more abbreviated repetition of the intellectual development of these same ancestors, at least of the later ones. But all the planned action of all animals has never succeeded in impressing the stamp of their will upon the earth. That was left for man.

In short, the animal merely *uses* his environment, and brings about changes in it simply by his presence; man by his changes makes it serve his ends, *masters* it. This is the final, essential distinction between man and other animals, and once again it is labour that brings about this distinction.

Let us not, however, flatter ourselves overmuch on account of our human victories over nature. For each such victory nature takes its revenge on us. Each victory, it is true, in the first place brings about the results we expected, but in the second and third places it has quite different, unforeseen effects which only too often cancel the first. The people who, in Mesopotamia, Greece, Asia Minor and elsewhere, destroyed the forests to obtain cultivable land, never dreamed that by removing along with the forests the collecting centres and reservoirs of moisture they were laying the basis for the present forlorn state of those countries. When the Italians of the Alps used up the pine forests on the southern slopes, so carefully cherished on the northern slopes, they had no inkling that by doing so they were cutting at the roots of the dairy industry in their region; they had still less inkling that they were thereby depriving their mountain springs of water for the greater part of the year, and making it possible for them to pour still more furious torrents on the plains during the rainy seasons. Those who spread the potato in Europe were not aware that with these farinaceous tubers they were at the same time spreading scrofula. Thus at every step we are reminded that we by no means rule over nature like a conqueror over a foreign people, like someone standing outside nature—but that we, with flesh, blood and brain, belong to nature, and exist in its midst, and that all our mastery of it consists in the fact that we have the advantage over all other creatures of being able to learn its laws and apply them correctly.

And, in fact, with every day that passes we are acquiring a better understanding of these laws and getting to perceive both the more immediate and the more remote consequences of our interference with the traditional course of nature. In particular, after the mighty advances made by the natural sciences in the present century, we are more than ever in a position to realise, and hence to control, even the more remote natural consequences of at least our day-to-day production activities. But the more this progresses the more will men not only feel but also know their oneness with nature, and the more impossible will become the senseless and unnatural idea of a contrast between mind and matter, man and nature, soul and body, such as arose after the decline of classical antiquity in Europe and obtained its highest elaboration in Christianity.

It required the labour of thousands of years for us to learn a little of how to calculate the more remote *natural* effects of our actions in the field of production, but it has been still more difficult in regard to the more remote *social* effects of these actions. We mentioned the potato and the resulting spread of scrofula. But what is scrofula compared to the effect which the reduction of the workers to a potato diet had on the living conditions of the masses of the people in whole countries, or compared to the famine the potato blight brought to Ireland in 1847, which consigned to the grave a million Irishmen, nourished solely or almost exclusively on potatoes, and forced the emigration overseas of two million more? When the Arabs learned to distil spirits, it never entered their heads that by so doing they were creating one of the chief weapons for the annihilation of the aborigines of the then still undiscovered American continent. And when afterwards Columbus discovered this America, he did not know that by doing so he was laying the basis for the Negro slave trade and giving a new lease of life to slavery, which in Europe had long ago been done away with. The men who in the seventeenth and eighteenth centuries laboured to create the steam-engine had no idea that they were preparing the instrument which more than any other was to revolutionise social relations throughout the world. Especially in Europe, by concentrating wealth in the hands of a minority and dispossessing the huge majority, this instrument was destined at first to give social and political domination to the bourgeoisie, but later, to give rise to a class struggle between bourgeoisie and proletariat which can end only in the overthrow of the bourgeoisie and the abolition of all class antagonisms. But in this sphere, too, by long and often cruel experience and by collecting and analysing historical material, we are gradually learning to get a clear view of the indirect, more remote social effects of our production activity, and so are afforded an opportunity to control and regulate these effects as well.

This regulation, however, requires something more than mere knowledge. It requires a complete revolution in our hitherto existing mode of production, and simultaneously a revolution in our whole contemporary social order.

All hitherto existing modes of production have aimed merely at achieving the most immediately and directly useful effect of labour. The further consequences, which appear only later and become effective through gradual repetition and accumulation, were totally neglected. The original common ownership of land corresponded, on the one hand, to a level of development of human beings in which their horizon was restricted in general to what lay immediately available, and presupposed, on the other hand, a certain superfluity of land that would allow some latitude for correcting the possible bad results of this primeval type of economy. When this surplus land was exhausted, common ownership also declined. All higher forms of production, however, led to the division of the population into different classes and thereby to the antagonism of ruling and oppressed classes. Thus the interests of the ruling class became the driving factor of production, since production was no longer restricted to providing the barest means of subsistence for the oppressed people. This has been put into effect most completely in the capitalist mode of production prevailing today in Western Europe. The individual capitalists, who dominate production and exchange, are able to concern themselves only with the most immediate useful effect of their actions. Indeed, even this useful effect— inasmuch as it is a question of the usefulness of the article that is produced or exchanged—retreats far into the background, and the sole incentive becomes the profit to be made on selling.

QUESTIONS FOR STUDY AND DISCUSSION

1. According to Engels, how is man different from the ape?
2. Discuss Engels' explanation of the origin of human speech. Do you consider it a satisfactory explanation? Why or why not?
3. Does Engels believe that man can continue to change himself by his labor? Explain.
4. What, in Engels' view, is the role of consciousness in human development?
5. Is Engels' description of the transition from ape to man compatible with a religious view of man? Explain.

Determinism in History

What is true of nature, which is hereby recognized also as a historical process of development, is also true of the history of society in all its branches and of the totality of all sciences which occupy themselves with things human (and divine). Here, too, the philosophy of history, of law, of religion, etc., has consisted in the substitution of an interconnection fabricated in the mind of the philosopher for the actual interconnection to be demonstrated in the events; and in the comprehension of history as a whole as well as in its separate parts, as the gradual realization of ideas—and, indeed, naturally always the pet ideas of the philosopher himself. According to this, history worked unconsciously but with necessity toward a certain predetermined, ideal goal—as, for example, according to Hegel, towards the realization of his absolute idea—and the unalterable trend towards this absolute idea formed the inner interconnection in the events of history. A new mysterious providence—unconscious or gradually coming into consciousness—was thus put in the place of the real, still unknown interconnection. Here, therefore, just as in the realm of nature, it was necessary to do away with these fabricated, artificial interconnections by the discovery of the real ones; a task which ultimately amounts to the discovery of the general laws of motion which assert themselves as the ruling ones in the history of human society.

In one point, however, the history of the development of society proves to be essentially different from that of nature. In nature—in so far as we ignore man's reactions upon nature—there are only blind unconscious agencies acting upon one another and out of whose interplay the general law comes into operation. Nothing of all that happens—whether in the innumerable apparent accidents observable upon the surface of things, or in the ultimate results which confirm the regularity underlying these accidents—is attained as a consciously desired aim. In the history of society, on the other hand, the actors are all endowed with consciousness, are men acting with deliberation or passion, working towards definite goals; nothing happens without a conscious purpose, without an intended aim. But this distinction, important as it is for historical investigation, particularly of single epochs and events, cannot alter the fact that the course of history is governed by inner general laws. For here, also on the whole, in spite of the consciously desired aims of all individuals, accident apparently reigns on the surface. That which is willed happens but rarely;

in the majority of instances the numerous desired ends cross and conflict with one another, or these ends themselves are from the outset incapable of realization or the means of attaining them are insufficient. Thus the conflict of innumerable individual wills and individual actions in the domain of history produces a state of affairs entirely analogous to that in the realm of unconscious nature. The ends of the actions are intended, but the results which actually follow from these actions are not intended; or when they do seem to correspond to the end intended, they ultimately have consequences quite other than those intended. Historical events thus appear on the whole to be likewise governed by chance. But where on the surface accident holds sway, there actually it is always governed by inner, hidden laws and it is only a matter of discovering these laws.

Men make their own history, whatever its outcome may be, in that each person follows his own consciously desired end, and it is precisely the resultant of these many wills operating in different directions and of their manifold effects upon the outer world that constitutes history. Thus it is also a question of what the many individuals desire. The will is determined by passion or deliberation. But the levers which immediately determine passion or deliberation are of very different kinds. Partly they may be external objects, partly ideal motives, ambition, "enthusiasm for truth and justice," personal hatred or even purely individual whims of all kinds. But, on the one hand, we have seen that the many individual wills active in history for the most part produce results quite other than those they intended —often quite the opposite; their motives therefore in relation to the total result are likewise of only secondary significance. On the other hand, the further question arises: What driving forces in turn stand behind these motives? What are the historical causes which transform themselves into these motives in the brains of the actors?

The old materialism never put this question to itself. Its conception of history, in so far as it has one at all, is therefore essentially pragmatic; it judges everything according to the motives of the action; it divides men in their historical activity into noble and ignoble and then finds that as a rule the noble are defrauded and the ignoble are victorious. Hence it follows for the old materialism that nothing very edifying is to be got from the study of history, and for us, that in the realm of history the old materialism becomes untrue to itself because it takes the ideal driving forces which operate there as ultimate causes, instead of investigating what is behind them, what are the driving forces of these driving forces. The inconsistency does not lie in the fact that *ideal* driving forces are recognized, but in the investigation not being carried further back behind these into their motive causes. On the other hand, the philosophy of history, particularly as represented by Hegel, recognizes that the ostensible and also the really operating motives of men who figure in history are by no means the ultimate causes of historical events; that behind these motives are other motive forces, which have to be discovered. But it does not seek these forces in history itself, it imports them rather from outside, from out of philosophical ideology, into history. Hegel, for example, instead of explaining the history of ancient Greece out of its own inner interconnections, simply maintains that it is nothing more than the working out of "types of beautiful individuality," the realization of a "work of art" as such. He says much in this connection about the old Greeks that is fine and profound but that does not prevent us today from refusing to be put off with such an explanation, which is a mere manner of speech.

When, therefore, it is a question of investigating the driving forces which—consciously or unconsciously, and indeed very often unconsciously —lie behind the motives of men in their historical actions and which constitute the real ultimate driving forces of history, then it is not a question so much of the motives of single individuals, however eminent, as of those motives which set in motion great masses, whole peoples, and again whole classes of the people in each people; and here, too, not the transient flaring up of a straw-fire which quickly dies down, but a lasting action resulting in a great historical transformation. To ascertain the driving causes which here in the minds of acting masses and their leaders—the so-called great men—are reflected as conscious motives, clearly, or unclearly, directly or in ideological, even glorified form—that is the only path which can put us on the track of the laws holding sway both in history as a whole, and at particular periods and in particular lands. Everything which sets men in motion must go through their minds; but what form it will take in the mind will depend very much upon the circumstances. The workers have by no means become reconciled to capitalist machine industry, even though they no longer simply break the machines to pieces as they still did in 1848 on the Rhine.

But while in all earlier periods the investigation of these driving causes of history was almost impossible—on account of the complicated and concealed interconnections between them and their effects—our present period has so far simplified these interconnections that the riddle could be solved. Since the establishment of large-scale industry, *i.e.,* at least since the peace of Europe in 1815, it has been no longer a secret to any man in England that the whole political struggle there has turned on the claims to supremacy of two classes: the landed aristocracy and the middle class. In France, with the return of the Bourbons, the same fact was perceived; the historians of the Restoration period, from Thierry to Guizot, Mignet and Thiers, speak of it everywhere as the key to the understanding of all French history since the Middle Ages. And since 1830 the working class, the proletariat, has been recognized in both countries as a third competitor for power. Conditions had become so simplified that one would have had to close one's eyes deliberately not to see in the fight of these three great classes and in the conflict of their interests the driving force of modern history—at least in the two most advanced countries.

But how did these classes come into existence? If it was possible at first glance still to ascribe the origin of the great, formerly feudal landed property—at least in the first instance—to political causes, to taking possession by force, this could no longer be done in regard to the bourgeoisie and the proletariat. Here the origin and development of two great classes was seen to lie clearly and palpably in purely economic causes. And it was just as clear that in the struggle between landed property and the bourgeoisie, no less than in the struggle between the bourgeoisie and the proletariat, it was a question in the first instance of economic interests, to the furtherance of which political power was intended to serve merely as a means. Bourgeoisie and proletariat both arose in consequence of a transformation of the economic conditions, more precisely, of the mode of production. The transition, first from guild handicrafts to manufacture, and then from manufacture to large-scale industry, with steam and mechanical power, had caused the development of these two classes. At a particular stage the new forces of production set in motion by the bourgeoisie—in the first place the division of labor and the combination of many workers, each producing a particular part, in one complete manufacture—and the conditions and requirements of exchange, developed through these productive forces, became incompatible with the existing order of production historically established and sanctified by law, that is to say, incompatible with the privileges of the guild and the numerous other local and personal privileges (which were only so many fetters to the unprivileged) of the feudal social organization. The forces of production represented by the bourgeoisie rebelled against the order of production represented by the feudal landlords and the guildmasters. The result is known: the feudal fetters were smashed, gradually in England, at one blow in France. In Germany the process is not yet finished. But just as, at a definite stage of its development, manufacture came into conflict with the feudal order of production, so now big industry has already come into conflict with the bourgeois order of production established in its place. Tied down by this order, by the narrow limits of the capitalist mode of production, big industry produces on the one hand an ever increasing proletarianization of the great mass of the people, and on the other hand an ever greater mass of unsalable products. Overproduction and mass misery, each the cause of the other—that is the absurd contradiction which is its outcome, and which of necessity calls for the liberation of the productive forces by means of a change in the mode of production.

In modern history at least it is therefore proved that all political struggles are class struggles, and all class struggles for emancipation in the last resort, despite their necessarily political form—for every class struggle is a political struggle—turn ultimately on the question of economic emancipation. Therefore, here at least, the state—the political order—is the subordinate, and civil society—the realm of economic relations—the decisive element. The traditional conception, to which Hegel, too, pays homage, saw in the state the determining element, and in civil society the element determined by it. Appearances correspond to this. As all the driving forces of the actions of any individual person must pass through his brain, and transform themselves into motives of his will in order to set him into action, so also all the needs of civil society—no matter which class happens to be the ruling one—must pass through the will of the state in order to secure general validity in the form of laws. That is the formal aspect of the matter—the one which is self-evident. The question arises, however, what is the content of this merely formal *will*—of the individual as well as of the state—and whence is this content derived? Why is just this intended and not something else? If we inquire into this we discover that in modern history the will of the state is, on the whole, determined by the changing needs of civil society, by the supremacy of this or that class, in the last resort, by the development of the productive forces and relations of exchange.

But if already in our modern era, with its gigantic means of production and communication, the state is not an independent domain with an independent development, but one whose stock as well as development is to be explained in the last resort by the economic conditions of life of the society, then this must be still more true of earlier times when the production of the material life of man was not carried on with these abundant auxiliary means, and when, therefore, the necessity of such production must necessarily have exercised a still greater mastery over men. If the state today, in the era of big industry and of railways, is on the whole only a reflex, in comprehensive form, of the economic needs of the class controlling production, then this must have been much more so in an epoch when each generation of men was forced to spend a far greater part of its aggregate lifetime in satisfying material needs, and was therefore much more dependent on them than we are today. An examination of the history of earlier periods, as soon as it is seriously undertaken from this angle, most abundantly confirms this. But, of course, this cannot be gone into here.

If the state and public law are determined by economic relations, so, too, of course is private law [1] which indeed in essence sanctions only the existing economic relations between individuals which are normal in the given circumstances. The form in which this happens can, however, vary considerably. It is possible, as happened in England, in harmony with the whole national development, to retain in the main the forms of the old feudal laws while giving them a bourgeois content; in fact, directly giving a bourgeois meaning to the old feudal name. But, also, as happened in Western continental Europe, Roman Law, the first world law of a commodity-producing society, with its unsurpassably acute elaboration of all the essen-

---

[1] The division always made by bourgeois law itself. Public law deals with state institutions, the structure of the administrative apparatus and the political rights of citizens. Civil or private law is mainly concerned with the property rights of citizens (law of property, of debts, of family, of inheritance). [C.D.]

tial legal relations of simple commodity owners (of buyers and sellers, debtors and creditors, contracts, obligations, etc.) can be taken as a foundation. In this case, for the benefit of a still petty-bourgeois and semi-feudal society, it can be adapted to the situation of such a society either simply through every-day legal practice (the common law) or, with the help of allegedly enlightened, moralizing jurists a special law code can be worked out from it to correspond with such social conditions—a code which in these circumstances will also be a bad one from a legal standpoint (*e.g.,* the Prussian *Landrecht*).[2] Whereby again after the great bourgeois revolution, such a classic law code of bourgeois society as the French *Code Civil*[3] can be worked out upon the basis of this same Roman Law. If, therefore, bourgeois legal regulations merely express the economic life-conditions of society in legal form, then this can take place well or ill according to circumstances.

The state presents itself to us as the first ideological power over mankind. Society creates for itself an organ for the safeguarding of its general interests against internal and external attacks. This organ is the state power. Hardly come into being, this organ makes itself independent in regard to society; and, indeed, the more so, the more it becomes the organ of a particular class, the more it directly enforces the supremacy of that class. The fight of the oppressed class against the ruling class becomes necessarily a political fight, a fight first of all against the political dominance of this class. The consciousness of the interconnection between this political struggle and its economic roots becomes dulled and can be lost altogether. While this is not altogether the case with the participants, it almost always happens with the historians. Of the ancient sources on the struggles within the Roman Republic only Appian[4] tells us clearly and distinctly what was at issue in the last resort—namely, landed property.

But once the state has become an independent power in regard to society, it produces forthwith a further ideology. It is indeed only among professional politicians, theorists of constitutional law and jurists of private law, that the connection with economic facts gets completely lost. Since in each particular case the economic facts must assume the form of juristic motives in order to receive legal sanction; and since, in so doing, consideration of course has to be paid to the whole legal system already in operation, the consequence is that the juristic form is made everything and the economic content nothing. Public law and private law are treated as independent spheres, each having its own independent historical development, each

---

[2] *Landrecht:* Prussian "law of the land" concerning rights and obligations connected with land or estates. [R.D.G.]

[3] *Code Civil:* bourgeois law code issued under Napoleon I which became a model for legislation in other countries. [C.D.]

[4] Appian: Roman historian of the second century who wrote mainly about the civil wars of ancient Rome. [C.D.]

being capable of and needing a systematic presentation by the thorough-going elimination of all inner contradictions.

Still higher ideologies, that is, such as are still further removed from the material, economic basis, take the form of philosophy and religion. Here the interconnection between the ideas and their material condition of exist-ence becomes more and more complicated, more and more obscured by in-termediate links. But the interconnection exists. Just as the whole Renais-sance period from the middle of the fifteenth century was an essential product of the towns and therefore of the bourgeoisie so also was the subsequently newly awakened philosophy. Its content was in essence only the philosophical expression of the thoughts corresponding to the develop-ment of the small and middle bourgeoisie into a big bourgeoisie. Among last century's Englishmen and Frenchmen who in many cases were just as much political economists as philosophers, this is clearly evident; and we have proved it above in regard to the Hegelian school.

We will now in addition deal only briefly with religion, since the latter appears to stand furthest away from, and to be the most foreign to, mate-rial life. Religion arose in very primitive times from erroneous and primi-tive ideas of men about their own nature and that of the external world surrounding them. Every ideology, however, once it has arisen, develops in connection with the given concept-material, and develops this material fur-ther; otherwise it would cease to be ideology, that is, occupation with thoughts as with independent entities, developing independently and sub-ject only to their own laws. That the material life conditions of the persons inside whose heads this thought process goes on, in the last resort deter-mine the course of this process, remains of necessity unknown to these persons, for otherwise there would be an end to all ideology. These primi-tive religious notions, therefore, which in the main are common to each group of kindred peoples, develop, after the separation of the group, in a manner peculiar to each people, according to the living conditions falling to their lot. For a number of groups of peoples, and particularly for the Aryans (so-called Indo-Europeans) this process has been shown in detail by comparative mythology. The gods so created by each people were na-tional gods, whose domain extended no farther than the national territory which they were to defend; on the other side of its boundaries other gods held undisputed sway. The idea of them could only continue to exist as long as the nation existed; they fell with its fall. The Roman world empire, the economic conditions of whose origin we do not need to examine here, brought about this downfall of the old nationalities. The old national gods decayed, even those of the Romans, which themselves also were fashioned only to suit the narrow confines of the city of Rome. The need to comple-ment the world empire by means of a world religion was clearly revealed in the attempts made to provide in Rome recognition and altars for all the foreign gods to the slightest degree respectable alongside of the indigenous

298 / FRIEDRICH ENGELS

ones. But a new world religion is not to be made in this fashion, by imperial decree. The new world religion, Christianity, had already quietly come into being, out of a mixture of generalized Oriental, particularly Jewish, theology and vulgarized Greek, particularly Stoic, philosophy. What it originally looked like has to be first laboriously discovered again, since its official form, as it has been handed down to us, is merely that in which it became a state religion, to which purpose it was adapted by the Council of Nicaea. The fact that already after two hundred and fifty years it became a state religion suffices to show that it was a religion in correspondence with the conditions of the time. In the Middle Ages, in the same measure as feudalism developed, it grew into the religious counterpart to it, with a corresponding feudal hierarchy. And as the bourgeoisie arose, there developed within it, in opposition to feudal Catholicism, the Protestant heresy, which first appeared in Southern France, among the Albigenses [5] at the time of the highest flourishing of the cities there. The Middle Ages had attached to theology all the other forms of ideology—philosophy, politics, jurisprudence—and made them sub-divisions of theology. It thereby constrained every social and political movement to take on a theological form. To the masses whose minds were fed with religion to the exclusion of all else, it was necessary to put forward their own interests in a religious guise in order to produce a great agitation. And since the bourgeoisie from the beginning brought into being an appendage of propertyless urban plebeians, day-laborers and servants of all kinds, belonging to no recognized social estate, precursors of the later proletariat, so likewise heresy soon became divided into a bourgeois moderate heresy and a plebeian revolutionary one, the latter an abomination to the bourgeois heretics themselves.

The ineradicability of the Protestant heresy corresponded to the invincibility of the rising bourgeoisie. When the bourgeoisie had become sufficiently strengthened, its struggle against the feudal nobility, which till then had been predominantly local, began to assume national dimensions. The first great action occurred in Germany—the so-called Reformation. The bourgeoisie was neither powerful enough nor sufficiently developed to be able to unite under its banner the rest of the rebellious estates—the plebeians of the towns, the lower nobility and the peasants on the land. At first the nobles were defeated; the peasants rose in a revolt which forms the peak of the whole revolutionary struggle; the cities left them in the lurch, and thus the revolution succumbed to the armies of the secular princes who

---

[5] The Albigenses, Cathari, participated in a movement which covered Southern France during the twelfth and thirteenth centuries. (The name is derived from the town of Albi, in the south of France.) The movement was directed against the exploiting Roman Catholic church headed by the Pope. The urban trading bourgeoisie, the artisans, the city poor and the peasants all took part in the movement. In the beginning of the twelfth century a special crusade was organized by the Pope against the Albigenses resulting in protracted warfare (lasting over 20 years) and ending with the defeat of the Albigenses. [C.D.]

reaped the whole profit.[6] Thenceforward Germany disappears for three centuries from the ranks of countries playing an independent part in history. But besides the German, Luther, appeared the Frenchman, Calvin. With true French acumen he put the bourgeois character of the reformation in the forefront, republicanized and democratized the church. While the Lutheran reformation in Germany degenerated and reduced the country to rack and ruin, the Calvinist reformation served as a banner for the republicans in Geneva, in Holland and in Scotland, freed Holland from Spain and from the German empire and provided the ideological costume for the second act of the bourgeois revolution which took place in England. Here Calvinism justified itself as the true religious disguise of the interests of the bourgeoisie of that time, and on this account did not reach full acceptance, as the revolution was completed in 1689 by a compromise between one part of the nobility and the bourgeoisie. The English state church was re-established; but not in its earlier form of a Catholicism which had the king for its pope, being, instead, strongly Calvinized. The old state church had celebrated the merry Catholic Sabbath and had fought against the dull Calvinist one. The new bourgeois church introduced the latter, which adorns England to this day.

In France, the Calvinist minority was suppressed in 1685 and either Catholicized or driven out of the country. But what was the good? Already at that time the free-thinker Pierre Bayle was at work, and in 1694 Voltaire was born. The forcible measures of Louis XIV only made it easier for the French bourgeoisie to carry through its revolution in the irreligious and exclusively political form which alone was suited to the developed bourgeoisie. Instead of Protestants, free-thinkers took their seats in the national assemblies. Thereby Christianity entered into its final stage. It had become incapable for the future of serving any progressive class as the ideological garb of its aspirations. It became more and more the exclusive possession of the ruling classes and these apply it as a mere means of government, to keep the lower classes within limits. For this each of the different classes uses its own appropriate religion: the landowning class—Catholic Jesuitism or Protestant orthodoxy; the liberal and radical bourgeoisie—rationalism; and it makes little difference whether these gentlemen themselves believe in their respective religions or not.

We see, therefore: religion, once formed, always contains traditional material, just as in all ideological domains tradition forms a great conservative force. But the transformations which this material undergoes spring from class relations, that is to say, out of the economic relations of the persons who execute these transformations. And here that is sufficient.

In the above it could only be a question of giving a general sketch of

---

[6] See Friedrich Engels, *The Peasant War in Germany,* International Publishers, New York. [C.D.]

the Marxist conception of history, at most with a few illustrations as well. The proof is to be found in history itself; and in this regard I may be permitted to say that it has been sufficiently furnished in other writings. This conception, however, puts an end to philosophy in the realm of history, just as the dialectical conception of nature made all natural philosophy both unnecessary and impossible. It is no longer a question anywhere of inventing interconnections from out of our brains, but of discovering them in the facts. For philosophy, which has been expelled from nature and history, there remains only the realm of pure thought (so far as it is left): the theory of the laws of the thought process itself, logic and dialectics.

QUESTIONS FOR STUDY AND DISCUSSION

1. In Engels' view, what is the role of the individual in history?
2. According to Engels, what is the proper object of a historian's study?
3. In what sense do men make their own history?
4. To what sort of proof is the Marxist conception of history susceptible?
5. In what sense is the Marxist conception of history a deterministic one? Explain.

Adam Schaff

ADAM SCHAFF was born in 1913 in Lwow, Poland. He attended the Universities of Lwow and of Paris, and received his Ph.D. in Moscow. In 1948 he assumed his present post of professor of Philosophy at the University of Warsaw. He has written widely on philosophical topics. A member of the Central Committee of the Polish Worker's Communist Party, he is the leading Polish Marxist philosopher.

Modern Marxism and the Individual

I

THE PROBLEM OF THE INDIVIDUAL

In a debate between such contrary philosophies as Marxism and Existentialism—I refer throughout to Sartre's variant which has played so big a role in Poland—it is necessary to go stright to the main point of their differences. This concerns the concept of the individual, which is the central concept of every variety of Existentialism, and around which are grouped all differences of viewpoint between Existentialism and Marxism.

Does the individual create society, by choosing the manner of his behaviour in complete spontaneity and freedom of choice? Or is it society that creates the individual and determines his mode of behaviour?—These questions lie at the heart of the antagonism between Existentialism and Marxism. All others, including the problem of "essence and existence", are consequent upon the way they are answered.

Of course, the different points of departure by no means signify that Existentialism completely rejects the role of society, or Marxism that of the individual. But all varieties of Existentialism—which differ greatly in the areas separating Kierkegaard from Sartre—are united not only by the fact that their central poblems concern the fate and experiences of the individual, but also by—and, indeed, primarily by—their conception of the individual as isolated, lonely and tragic in his senseless struggle with the alien forces of the world around him. Involved here are problems hard to grasp and even harder to express clearly.

From pp. 24–35, 55–62, 82–87 of Adam Schaff, *A Philosophy of Man*. © 1963 by Monthly Review Press. Reprinted by permission of the publisher.

302 / ADAM SCHAFF

This standpoint is ordinarily called subjectivism; and that it actually is, despite the Existentialists' protest against such a designation of their position. Only by taking off from the position of subjectivism can one arrive at such a strange and internally contradictory conception as that of the "sovereign" individual, completely free to make decisions which depend only on himself, who is at the same time defenceless and tragic in his hopeless struggle with malicious fate. The internal contradiction that appears here is that between a voluntarist variety of subjectivism and the concept of an objective fate, independent of human activity.

Sartre's reputation is due to his skillful treatment of the central problem of all varieties of Existentialism, the problem of the individual and his complex relations with the world surrounding him. Sartre's has become the most typical variety of Existentialism. This is due not only to the atmosphere of helplessness and despair with which his whole philosophy is permeated, but to the concept which generates this atmosphere—the asocial concept of the individual who, being isolated and lonely, must determine his behaviour entirely for himself and, with nothing but his own judgment to guide him, grapple with hostile living and non-living forces. This is not a new idea, but it exerts a strong appeal in the conditions of moral chaos of the post-war world, in the conditions of the break up of traditional systems of values while new social values take shape amid conflict and pain. Its appeal is all the greater when expressed by a great writer who is at the same time an excellent psychologist.

But this is only one Sartre. There is another who, in spite of the first, leans towards socialism in his practical activities and towards Marxism in his theoretical work. There is something droll in the fact that Sartre—the Existentialist moving towards Marxism—could in an article specially written for a Polish journal teach something to our Marxists who, moving towards Existentialism, had lost their knowledge of Marxist philosophy and its values. Sartre reminded them that Marxism is the only modern philosophy which has the perspective of further development. I said that there is something amusing in this—but it is at the same time perfectly understandable. When two contrary tendencies—one away from and the other towards Marxism—intersect at a certain point, they by no means come to an agreement there. They are moving in opposite directions, and cannot agree. This is why an Existentialist moving towards Marxism understands Marxism much better than a Marxist who is moving towards Existentialism.

While fully recognising Sartre's stature and talents one should not lose sight of the inner contradictions of his views, which do not decrease but rather increase with the development of his views. There is a contradiction between the Sartre who clings to traditional Existentialism and the Sartre who pays tribute to the philosophy of Marxism. This contradiction can be overcome only by abandoning one or other of the two antagonistic views he now holds. And it is concentrated mainly in his conception of the individual.

The young Marx, whom certain of his "admirers" in Poland wish violently to transform into an Existentialist, wrote in his famous *Theses on Feuerbach:* "The human essence is no abstraction inherent in each single individual. In its reality it is the ensemble of the social relations." This statement, aphoristic in form, was directed against Feuerbach, who in Marx's opinion did not understand the social individual and so committed a double sin: (1) against the *historical* conditioning of the individual, whom Feuerbach conceived abstractly as an isolated being; (2) against his *social* conditioning, which Feuerbach conceived in a naturalistic way in terms of the bonds uniting the individual members of a species.

Referring to Feuerbach's views on the individual's religious beliefs, Marx further wrote: "Feuerbach consequently does not see that the 'religious sentiment' is itself a social product, and that the abstract individual whom he analyses belongs in reality to a particular form of society."

It requires no special keenness of mind to realise that what Marx said hits not only at Feuerbach but strikes with equal force at the mistaken approach to the individual of both modern naturalism and Existentialism.

Marx states that "the human essence is no abstraction inherent in each individual. In its reality it is the ensemble of the social relations." This statement goes to the heart of the problem—if we discount the fact that this would not be today the ordinary way of phrasing this thought. The human being, as an individual, is "the ensemble of the social relations," in the sense that his origin and development can be understood only in the social and historical context, in the sense that he is the *product* of social life. This social and therefore historical approach to the investigation of the spiritual life of man and his works is the indisputable and tremendously important theoretical content of Marxism, freeing it from the limitations of both naturalism and Existentialist subjectivism in the analysis of human affairs.

It is important to emphasise this point not only in opposition to Existentialism but also to the vulgarised interpretation of the position held by the young Marx. I have already referred to the causes which led our latest revisionists to plagiarise Existentialism. The same causes led indirectly to the distortion and Existentialist vulgarisation of the young Marx. The great enthusiasm of some of our intellectuals for the themes treated by the young Marx—and this is, moreover, a broader phenomenon of international significance—can be explained by their quest for answers to their pervasive question about human affairs, their desire to "humanise" the problems posed by Marxist theory, to saturate these problems with a humanist content, to connect them with the fate of the individual. That theme and its inspiration are, of course, comprised in the works of the young Marx. It is important to deepen one's analysis of this theme, making use of the further development of Marx's thought. But that is a task by no means connected only with the immediate social stimuli which actually propelled the theme to the fore.

The very social causes and spiritual shocks which caused the defection of some intellectuals, formerly connected with Marxism, to Existentialism led to their misrepresenting the tenets of the young Marx in the spirit of Existentialism. When, in contradiction with historical facts, they vulgarised their interpretation of the views of the young Marx, it was by no means with them a question of an objective investigation. It is in this light that one may understand the ignorant attempts, made with such boastfulness and aplomb by our revisionists, to counterpose the young Marx not only to Engels but also to the older Marx. For such enthusiasts, Marx was finished somewhere around 1846.

And yet it is precisely in the teachings of the young Marx that we find a firm and decisive refutation of Existentialist views on the problems of the individual. The views expressed by Marx on these problems, already expounded in the *Theses on Feuerbach,* and developed in his later theoretical works, constitute a rejection of the theoretical foundations of Existentialism—subjectivism, the a-social and a-historical conception of the individual.

The internal contradictions of Sartre's views are related precisely to this question. It is not possible simultaneously to pay tribute to the tenets of both Existentialism and Marxism on philosophical problems in general and the problem of the individual in particular, without falling into eclecticism and toleration of contradictions. If one approaches the problem of the individual in a Marxist way, that is, historically and socially, one must abandon the idealist, subjectivist foundations of Existentialism. One must reject the thesis that because the individual must make independent decisions in situations of moral conflict—true, a real problem is involved here —he is condemned to loneliness and consequently to helplessness and despair. On the contrary, Marxism shows that the individual, in making independent decisions and, in a certain sense, choosing between given attitudes and activities, always does so socially, in the sense of the social conditioning of his personality. Marxism teaches that the individual's attitudes are social products, and that, in adopting the attitudes he does, the individual "belongs in reality to a particular form of society." In this light, the "philosophy of despair" has its basis only in the attitudes of certain social classes who lose their so-called "eternal" philosophical truths at turning points of history. There is a fundamental contradiction between Marxism and Existentialism. It is possible to choose between these two alternative points of view; what is not possible is to combine them into one consistent system of thought.

We may note here that even atheistic Existentialism is much closer to the tenets of religion on the problems of the obligations and destiny of individuals than would appear at first sight. This is the price of departing from the social and historical analysis of human affairs.

I have already pointed out that Existentialism contains a contradiction between the postulate of the "sovereignty" of the individual, who is supposedly the independent creator of his own destiny (in the deepest sense, this is the thesis that "existence" is prior to "essence"), and the whole content of the "philosophy of despair." For that philosophy proclaims that man is a mere pawn in the hands of fate. As Sartre indicates primarily in his plays, evil triumphs regardless of human choosing (this conception perhaps finds its sharpest expression in Sartre's play *The Devil and the Good God*). But this is precisely the antinomy of religious moralists, especially those who derive their morality from the Mosaic religion, of which Christianity is a copy. The Judaic Jehovah and the Existentialist Fate are the one as spiteful as the other: they truly create man "in their own image." They give him, cunningly enough, the power to recognise good and evil, but only so that they may condemn him. This miserable worm, with such means of knowledge at his command as the Ten Commandments, racks his brains as to what to do in life's conflicting situations and lives in a state of discord and fear, only to earn condemnation at the end. And yet this miserable and helpless creature, worthy of both pity and contempt, is in the light of religion the sovereign individual, God's highest creation! Atheistic and religious Existentialism alike repeat the tale of the cruelty and maliciousness of the old Jehovah. They create their individual as supposedly sovereign in order to make him lonely. They condemn to helplessness and despair the wretched puppets who are the sport of malicious fate while wearing the hollow crown of "sovereignty." For it is clear that the separation of the individual from society does not give him any sovereignty. On the contrary, it deprives him of all real independence. This cannot be doubted if one reads Kafka's *Trial* and *The Castle,* or sees on the stage the fate of Sartre's hero in *The Devil and the Good God*. The "philosophy of despair" is humanism inside-out; it is in essence amoral morality, dehumanised humanism.

But enough of that. What most concerns us here is that it is actually possible to choose between Marxism and Existentialism, but impossible to combine them into one. Sartre himself will, sooner or later, have to make such a choice. It is impossible to complement Marxism with Existentialism. This does not mean, however, that to be a Marxist one must give up the *subject matter* of Existentialism.

In his article on *Marxism and Existentialism* Sartre stated that his Existentialism only fills in the gap which now exists in Marxism, and that the moment this is accomplished Existentialism loses all reason for existence as an independent current of thought.

It all depends on how the above statement is to be understood. If it is a matter of "completing" Marxism with the theory and methodology of Existentialism, then Sartre's proposition is very doubtful, since fire cannot complete water. But if it is a matter of Marxism undertaking, on the basis of the Marxist method, a more thorough investigation of the problems of the individual, which it has tended to neglect and which have been monopolised by Existentialism, then we have here an important proposal.

If it is true that Existentialism has raised questions which profoundly affect people and we have neglected them, and if it is true that this neglect has had political consequences, then it becomes important to get clear, in the first place, about exactly what questions are involved.

The usual answer is: Marxism has neglected the problems of ethics, and so it is necessary to undertake a comprehensive study of the broad principles of morality. This is true; but it is a truth of the kind that says little. What exactly is the object of a comprehensive study of the principles of morality, and how is it to be done? When it comes to the point, little remains for such studies but fine phrases.

A serious analysis of what amongst the problems posed by Existentialism is of most concern to people today brings two complexes of problems to the fore:

1. the problems of personal responsibility for one's actions, including political action and particularly in situations involving conflicts between opposing moral standards;
2. the problems of the individual's place and role in the world, which have been rather hazily expressed as "the problem of the meaning of life."

These are not single problems, but complexes of problems. They belong to the sphere of the science of morality, broadly conceived; but unhappily they were not in evidence when the traditional themes of Marxist ethics were developed. Because of that, the demand for the general "development of Marxist ethics" cannot be considered satisfactory. For the whole difficulty lies precisely in the question of how the subject is to be understood, i.e. what is the range of the problems of this ethics. By picking on particular problems we shall not, of course, develop a whole theory of ethics; but we may at least say something definite.

When an Existentialist raises problems of the individual's responsibility he does so in a rhetorical and abstract manner. And this he cannot help. For by removing the problem of the freedom of choice and responsibility of the individual from its social and historical context he cannot but treat the individual and his responsibility as abstractions. Sartre understands very well the conflicting character of situations in real life which present the individual with a choice as to how he will behave—he has expressed this in his work L'Existentialisme est un Humanisme, and in his literary works; but he considers this choice as the free act of the individual. We cannot accept this abstract way of posing the problem of the individual's responsibility.

How has this problem actually presented itself to us, arising from recent experiences? The problem of responsibility for one's deeds did not present itself to us in a purely theoretical and abstract form, but in a most living and practical way in conflict between party discipline and one's conscience, and in judgment of those who, not motivated by any personal considerations, were guilty of evil deeds under the conviction that they were fulfilling their social obligations.

Existentialism cannot answer problems posed in this concrete way. Its abstract and subjectivist outlook is useless in relation to such problems. To deal with them requires the development of a whole complex of theories, and first of all the sociological theory of *the individual in society* and, connected with this, the dialectics of personal freedom and the necessities flowing from social determinism. Here we find already a firm theoretical foundation in Marxism. But there arise also a number of more neglected questions, of which the chief is that of the definition of responsibility in its sociological, psychological and moral aspects. Finally, there arises the difficult problem of conflicting situations and the definition of responsibility in relation to them.

Standard theories of ethics tend to overlook the fact that in real life moral judgments often relate to conflicting situations. So standard ethics simplifies its tasks and promulgates *absolute* solutions of moral problems independently of time, place and social circumstances. All religious systems and most so-called lay codes of morals attempt to do this.

All absolute ethical systems, so called, erected on the basis of supposedly eternal and immutable moral truths, are helpless before the problems occurring most often in life, namely, situations of conflict in which doing what is thought to be right brings about evil consequences. Uncertainty here does not arise because the so-called sinner is ignorant of the moral norm obligatory for him in the given situation; the moralist may come forward with his pompous commandments and prohibitions, but that does not help, because the situation is connected with a clash of contradictory standards and the poor sinner cannot decide which has priority. This may be called an "Orestes" situation. Such situations confound all "absolute" moral systems, religious or lay. Existentialism has the merit of having been aware of the problem, although it cannot solve it. Marxism has the best equipment for solving it, but has so far remained somewhat aloof.

The second main complex of problems relates to questions which are only reluctantly mentioned by philosophies pretending to the name of science. These problems, it is said, are so hazy and so burdened with tradition, that they should be regarded as belonging to the spheres of religion, mysticism or poetry rather than science. Such, indeed, is the opinion of the Neo-Positivists, who class them among "pseudo-problems." But as I have already pointed out, to call a problem a "pseudo-problem" does not abolish it; it merely hands the problem over to those least equipped to tackle it seriously. The traditional mystification of a problem does not abolish either the problem or the possibility of its scientific analysis. "What is the meaning of life?" "What is man's place in the universe?" It seems difficult to express oneself scientifically on such hazy topics. And yet if one should assert ten times over that these are typical pseudo-problems, problems would remain. Let us therefore consider what is behind the haze.

"Vanity, vanity, all is vanity!" These words, repeated in various forms in all philosophies of the East, seem to appeal to many who in old age begin to reflect on life and death. It is possible to shrug this off with a compassionate smile as nonsense. And yet the words echo a problem which cannot simply be ignored. Nor can the questions "Why?" "What for?" which force their way to the lips of people tired of the adversities and delusions of life. This applies all the more to the compulsive questions which come from reflection on death—why all this effort to stay alive if we are going to die anyway? It is difficult to evade the feeling that death is senseless—avoidable, accidental death especially. Of course, we can ask: senseless from what point of view? From the point of view of the progression of nature death is entirely sensible. But from the point of view of a given individual, death is senseless and places in doubt everything he does. Religion has tried to counter this feeling of senselessness. The old and very wise religions of the East pointed to *nirvana* as the final goal, thus giving death a clear meaning. Other, more primitive, religions instil faith in a life after death. But what is to be done when religious belief itself loses all sense?

Attempts to ridicule all this do not help at all. The fact alone of some agnostics undergoing deathbed conversions gives much food for thought. Philosophy must take the place of religion here. It must tackle a number of diverse questions which have remained from the wreck of the religious view of life—the senselessness of suffering, of broken lives, of death, and many, many other questions relating to the fate of living, struggling, suffering and dying individuals. Can this be done scientifically, that is, in a way that is communicable and subject to some form of verification? It certainly can. True, not by following the same methods as in physics or chemistry—for this is not a matter of physics or chemistry. This is why the Neo-Positivists are wrong in their sweeping verdict that these are empty pseudo-problems. And so are those Marxists who fail just as dismally to express themselves on these questions, and who cover their scornful silence by concentrating attention exclusively on great social processes and their laws of development. These are undoubtedly very important and socially decisive matters. But they do not provide automatic solutions to problems relating to individuals.

II

THE MEANING OF LIFE

Faced with such a hazy question as "What is the meaning of life?" it is necessary first of all to try to make the question more precise. There are perhaps two main interpretations of this question. He who asks about the meaning of life questions first of all the value of life: is life worth living? And secondly, he questions the aim of life.

"Is life worth living?" is a common question, whether the questioner seriously proposes to draw practical conclusions from a negative answer, or whether he asks in the hope of cheering himself up. The Stoics maintained that it is not necessary to console people over the inevitability of death; on the contrary, they must be persuaded that it is worth while to go on living.

However that may be, death—the threat of one's own death and the death of near ones—is often the chief incentive for reflections on the meaning of life. For besides peoples' dread of dying, they experience the tragedy of separation in the actual deaths of those close to them. People fear dying as a possibility, and experience the death of someone near to them as an actuality. We are only sometimes reminded of the inevitable approach of our own death; if it were otherwise, if people lived with the continual consciousness of death inevitably approaching, they would surely go mad. We feel the passage of time, like the flow of blood in the veins, only occasionally. Nikolaj Kuzmicz, in Rilke's *Laurid Brigge's Malta Notebook,* could live no longer once he became conscious of the passage of time.

But the question "Is life worth living?" is suggested not only by death. Physical as well as moral suffering—particularly when it seems undeserved—prompts the same question. How can such a question be answered? And how can we explain our answer to others?

We would like to answer: although death is inevitable, although suffering is unavoidable, life is still worth while, life has a meaning. But why? We are obliged to say why, if we are to convince anyone and if our answer is to express anything more than an individual opinion.

The ground we are moving on now becomes excessively slippery, and a different mode of approach is needed from that adopted towards problems in the exact or empirical sciences, or towards epistemological and ontological problems arising from the sciences. We can speak of certainties in deductive sciences and probabilities in empirical sciences which differ in degree but are always based on hard data. This also applies, though in a different way, to propositions of the philosophy of science. But with the questions we are now discussing it is not a matter of ascertaining the truth or falsity of propositions, but of assessing, evaluating. It is doubtful whether there can ever be a valid transition from description to evaluation. It is doubtful whether a description of life, however true and well founded, would automatically justify any evaluation of life.

At this point a Neo-Positivist may interject that evaluations cannot express facts and cannot be verified, so that all evaluation is subjective. He would undoubtedly be right. But he would at the same time be wrong if he concluded that questions of evaluation were pseudo-questions and so refused to deal with them. In that case he would simply be assuming what has to be proved; he would be assuming a criterion of meaningfulness and scientific character which would prejudge the problem from the start.

Actually, in examining questions such as the meaning of life, the philosopher must proceed quite differently from any procedure of the natural sciences. He must proceed differently because the subject that interests him demands a different procedure. But it does not follow that his method is impermissible, or necessarily unscientific. He, too, generalises from the facts of experience; he too bases himself on the findings of specific sciences, such as sociology or psychology. But he proceeds differently, because he does not simply describe but assesses, evaluates. And where an assessment or evaluation is being made, some scale of assessment, some chosen system of values, enters into his calculations. Of course, the selection of this scale or system is not made arbitrarily: it is socially conditioned. But social conditioning is not the only factor. Other factors come into play as well, both psychological and physiological, which belongs to the individual's own personality. In one way or another such factors will always make themselves felt whenever there is a question of choice, including choice of a world view. And not only intellectual factors are involved here, but emotional factors. Hence subjectivity does play its part.

Consequently, the process of generalisation is also different. The gap between established empirical facts and their philosophical generalisation is greater; and therefore the possibility of varied interpretation is also greater. In this field the philosopher resembles the ancient sage musing over human life, rather than the experimental natural scientist. This is so, simply because the procedures of the natural scientist are useless here. The philosopher who devotes himself to questioning the meaning of life is not proceeding scientifically—but that does not imply that he is unscientific. The alternative "scientific-unscientific" does not apply here, and to call the philosopher "unscientific" would, logically, be like concluding that love is not rectangular from a negative answer to the question whether love is rectangular.

A wise man is not the same as a scholar, though scholarship and wisdom may often go together. A scholar is one who possesses a fund of knowledge in some field; he is erudite in that field. But one is wise to the extent that he is intelligent and experienced, particularly in his dealings with others. Some people are scholars in some special field but are not wise, either in the sense of general intelligence or of experience of life and knowledge of how to get on with other people. And vice versa, some people are wise without possessing erudition. The philosophy of one who engages in the problems we are concerned with should be classed as "wise" or "unwise," as suitable or unsuitable, but not as "scientific" or "unscientific." In certain situations it is a person wise in the ways of life who is most needed. So a philosopher should be not only a scholar but a wise man too. This does not contradict the requirement that he should be scientific. Scientific knowledge, the scientific approach, helps with reflections on human life and with defining an attitude towards life. The answer proposed to problems such as "What is the meaning of life?" depends, as we have seen, on various factors, but primarily on the world view of the person reflecting on the question; and such a world view may be scientific or unscientific.

For the religious believer, the question whether life has a meaning and is worth living is answered very simply, because even suffering, pain and death are in accord with the will of a higher being, who has prepared rewards in the hereafter for the faithful and punishment for transgressors. For the believer, the most difficult problems appear very simple. But a high price has to be paid for this convenience; it is bought only at the cost of a scientific attitude.

It is not possible from a lay standpoint to provide any kind of categorical and universal answer to the question whether life is worth while. Whether it is worth while or not for a given individual depends upon his actual conditions and perspectives of life—and the individual concerned has the last word here. He can draw up a kind of balance sheet, recalling everything in his life which he evaluates positively, and reminding himself of what he may easily forget under emotional strain—that he lives only once, that time alleviates suffering, that he has responsibilities to those close to him and to society, and so on. But only he can sum up the balance. For if one does not accept absolute standards, which are in essence religious, one cannot prejudge the answers for each individual. That would mean making a choice for him, which only he can make.

But he who asks whether life is worth while asks at the same time about the aim of life. What do we live for? This question is put by everyone harassed by the problem of how he should live. For our behaviour, especially in situations of conflict, depends on what we consider to be the aim of life. This remains true whether we have consciously formulated for ourselves an aim of life or not; for an idea of the aim of life, induced by education in the broadest sense of the word, is implicit in human behaviour. This applies alike to the hero who dedicates his life to the defense of some ideal, the traitor who collaborates with the enemy for money, the conscientious man who sacrifices his own interests to what he considers to be right, or the opportunist who accommodates himself to his superiors despite his own convictions.

From a religious standpoint the question of the aim of life is answered very simply. Man is subject to an external purpose, that of God, which he should obey. The only problem is to find out what this purpose is—which is done by study of the scriptures or other records of revelation. The argument against this standpoint must seek to demonstrate scientifically the human origin of these revelations, to show that God does not create man but man creates God in his own image. But of course, there can be no argument against a believer who will not accept the canons of scientific demonstration.

Lay answers to the question of the aim of life are various, and have long since been classified within the history of philosophy. So far as general approach is concerned, it is now difficult to think of anything new, except for new names. It is an "eternal question," concerning the answers to which we may feel inclined to agree that "there is nothing new under the sun." Yet the moment we stop limiting ourselves to merely abstract and general characterisation of views, and begin to penetrate deeply into the social conditions required for realising one or another aim of our activity, the situation changes. Marxist theory, like several very different ontological and epistemological theories, leads to the general position that may be called "social hedonism"—the view that the aim of human life is to secure the maximum happiness for the broadest masses of the people, and that only within the compass of this aim can personal happiness be realised. But taking into account the social conditions required to realise this aim, the Marxist avows socialist humanism as his supreme principle. Socialist humanism is indeed a variety of "social hedonism." But it is a concretised conception so closely connected with all the other tenets of Marxism that its admission implies the acknowledgement of the whole system.

The propositions of socialist humanism and its precepts for behaviour flow from the theory of Historical Materialism, and in particular: (1) the specific understanding of the individual as a social product—as a product of "the totality of social relations," of which we shall say more later; (2) the specific understanding of the relation of the individual to society on the basis of the historical materialist conception of social development; (3) the recognition that ideals can be realised only under given social conditions, without which recognition they degenerate into utopias. All this leads, not to abstract ideals, but to scientifically based concepts from which flow definite and practical conclusions in the form of precepts for behaviour.

The socialist humanist is persuaded that he can find personal happiness only through the happiness of society. For only broader horizons for personal development and enlarged possibilities for the satisfaction of human desires on a social scale create the necessary foundations for realising personal aspirations. He does not limit himself to seeking relations of friendship or love with those near him—although that is closest to his heart. He understands that the realisation of his aspirations demands struggle, that the cause he serves is socially conditioned and requires definite changes in social relations. In a society based on social antagonism he understands that the realisation of his aspirations demands changes in property relations and in the class relations based on them. He advocates the class struggle in the name of the love of near ones and of universal friendship, and he proclaims his hatred of the exploitation of man by man in the name of love of man.

The socialist humanist knows that man is the product of social conditions, but he also knows that these conditions were created by man. He is a dialectician, and, precisely because of that, fights while proclaiming peace.

His ideal of socialism is at one with his humanism. As an ideal, socialism is the consistent expression of humanism; at the same time, socialism is the material realisation of the ideal of humanism. For this cause, the socialist humanist is ready to make the greatest sacrifices, and to appeal to others to do the same. He accepts the precept of "love thy neighbour," and has only contempt for those who proclaim this beautiful precept in words and betray it in deeds. For socialist humanism not only proclaims certain ideals but calls for struggle to implement them in life, and to convince other people of the necessity of joining this struggle.

III

FOUNDATIONS OF A MARXIST PHILOSOPHY OF MAN

We may now return to the general problem of the need, task and place of a philosophy of man within the general system of human thought. But we return enriched with certain considerations in the field of the philosophy of man, which I have tried to indicate rather than to finalise. We can, however, perhaps grasp the problem differently now. It is now no longer a question of whether man may be the legitimate subject of philosophy, but of the range and possible directions of such philosophy.

What problems enter into the field of investigation of a philosophy of man? And what are the lines of demarcation between this philosophy and the humanist sciences, such as anthropology, sociology, individual and social psychology? I have already indicated some of the problems; and I should say at once that, in my opinion, there can be no rigid demarcation here between what is philosophical and what strictly pertains to one or other of the empirical sciences. In general, a philosophy of man differs from any of the special sciences of man by applying itself to its subject in a different manner. The central axis of the philosophical investigation of man is the definition of the essence of the individual's role in his relations with society as a whole and with other individuals within society. Around this central axis revolve a wide range of problems concerning the destinies of individuals in their relations with the external world, and the social obligations and moral responsibilities of individuals.

So understood, the philosophy of man absorbs the problems of traditional ethics, creating a foundation for their analysis and solution. In my opinion, the demand for "a Marxist ethics" will not be realised until that ethics is developed in the spirit of a broadly understood philosophy of man.

This demand is often confused with the demand for some kind of Marxist code of morals, a substitute for the Ten Commandments. Such confusion is understandable. For what is more understandable than the illusion that the difficulties, including the moral difficulties, of a period of social transformation may be overcome by some kind of new moral code, and that it is only a matter of laying down the rules? However, it remains an illusion. For a Marxist should know, in the first place, that moral codes arise from life as specific reflections in human consciousness of existing social relations, and so cannot be composed or decreed at will. And in the second place, a Marxist should know that the traditional type of code was always formulated in the belief that moral standards were imposed on man somehow from outside, and because of that had a religious character even when they had an outwardly lay appearance. If it is agreed that man is the master of his own destiny, as the whole of modern knowledge demonstrates, and if the creative character of social and individual human practice is made the basis of our whole conception of the individual, society and history, then the idea of laying down moral standards from above in the traditional way becomes impossible.

Hence the philosophy of man includes ethics, but not the codification of morals. Historical materialism provides the theoretical basis for such a philosophy. It lays the basis for the social understanding of the individual, for setting the individual man against his social background, preserving his social essence, without losing what is personal in man.

Classical German idealist philosophy, by disclosing the active factor of human endeavour in man's relations with the external world, undoubtedly contributed to overcoming belief in the merely external determination of human behaviour. But so long as that thesis was tied to idealism it was impossible completely to overcome illusions of the external determination of human affairs. This task fell to the lot of Marxism, which shifted the problem of the active role of the individual onto a materialist foundation. Marxism thus created the premises for a materialist philosophy of man, which it further developed in its teachings on alienation and socialist humanism. But historical materialism is the premise for such a philosophy not the philosophy itself. The further development of a philosophy of man has today become a burning necessity for Marxism.

A philosophy of man can start off from two opposite principles:

1. That man's existence is the realisation of some superhuman conception or plan, external to man.
2. That man's existence is the creation of man himself—man makes himself, and the starting point of all considerations about man should be that he is autonomous.

These principles express respectively the religious conception that essence is prior to existence, and the lay conception that existence is prior and that what we call "essence" must be deduced from existence. The thesis of atheistic Existentialism, that existence is prior to essence, is a clear negation of the Thomist thesis that man's existence is participation in the essence and existence of God—or, to put it more simply, is decreed by Providence and not made what it is by the activity of man himself. In this general sense of opposition to the religious conception of the external determination of human destiny, every materialist, including the Marxist materialist, approves the Existentialist thesis. For the materialist also recognises human existence as the true point of departure for the investigation of human affairs. But the problem only begins where the Existentialist supposes it ends.

The whole findings of a philosophy of man depend on how one understands human existence.

In speaking of existence as contrasted to essence we refer to the real life of man, and not to the idea of what it should be. But if our interest lies in real human life, we may still approach the matter from two different aspects,

1. from the aspect of men acting in society and on nature, that is, of the material life of man,
2. from the aspect of the spiritual life of man, the spiritual activity of the human subject.

In the last analysis, the whole philosophy of man will depend on which of these aspects we select as fundamental for the interpretation of human existence. Merely to speak of "existence" does not prejudge whether we shall regard this existence from its subjective or its objective, material aspect. Marxism adopts the latter stand-point. But Existentialism cannot adopt it if it wishes to remain faithful to its own teachings.

To be an Existentialist it is not enough, as some believe, only to say that existence is prior to essence. As we have seen, materialism, from which Existentialism so energetically separates itself, says this too. In order to be an Existentialist it is necessary to say that the individual is "lonely," "condemned to freedom," and the rest of it. An Existentialist believes that the individual possesses absolute freedom of choice, and is himself alone and in isolation responsible for his choice and deeds. He must therefore renounce all determinism and historical necessity. And this imposes upon Existentialism a subjectivist conception of the individual and his existence. Existentialism is a closed subjectivist system: it cannot choose at will between different interpretations of existence, unless it is prepared to contradict its own teachings. Jean Hyppolite, who claims to be a supporter of Sartre's version of Existentialism, told us in Warsaw that Existentialism maintains "the unity of subjective and objective" in the real stream of events of human life. But Sartre's Existentialism implies a subjective interpretation of human existence, and Hyppolite is mistaken in thinking that Existentialism can adopt a realist interpretation, and survive—just as Sartre is mistaken in thinking it possible to patch together Marxism and Existentialism.

The problem of the creative historical role of the human individual has to be understood against this same background. Not only the individual's existence but his creative role, and his status in the world of things and people surrounding him, can be understood in two ways.

Understood in one way—in a realist way, from the aspect of the material life of man—man's creative possibilities, which are related to the nature of his freedom, are not unlimited. Man acts on the material world and, by transforming it, creates new conditions of his own existence. Man is the product of material conditions, of his natural and social environment, and at the same time shapes those conditions. "The educator must himself be educated," as Marx said: the conditions shaping man must in turn be shaped by him. But this does not signify that man can do whatever he likes. Man always confronts the real material world with its objective laws, and does not by his action annul those laws. His freedom does not consist in annulling necessity but in recognising and making use of it.

But there is another interpretation of human creativeness arising from the subjectivist interpretation of human existence. With this, the objective factors disappear, natural and social realities dissolve in the subject and his "creative activity." Man takes the place of God and, indeed, surpasses God—in as much as the latter created the material world and its laws only once, while man is supposed to be its creator in permanence.

Although Existentialism modestly pretends to be only a philosophy of man it nevertheless implies, as we now see, a complete idealist metaphysic.

We thus find ourselves again at the crossroads, which proves how differently a philosophy of man may be constructed by taking off from supposedly similar assumptions. Obviously, there is a connection between a philosophy of man and a general world outlook. A Marxist philosophy of man is explicitly based on materialism.

QUESTIONS FOR STUDY AND DISCUSSION

1. Why does Schaff call the conception of a "sovereign" individual contradictory?
2. How does Schaff characterize the essence of the dispute between the existentialists and the Marxists?
3. How does Schaff suggest the question "What is the meaning of life?" be approached?
4. Of what does "socialist humanism" consist?
5. What does Schaff mean when he says, "A Marxist philosophy of man is explicitly based on materialism"?

TOPICS FOR DISCUSSION AND TERM PAPERS

A.

1. How successful is Hegel's treatment of the physical aspects of man? How successful is the treatment of man's consciousness that is presented by Marx and Engels? Explain.
2. Marx criticizes Hegel's view of man. Consider the arguments he presents against Hegel's position. Are the arguments valid and conclusive? Discuss.
3. Both Hegel and Marx reject a static view of man and of his nature. Is it possible to speak of man's nature if it is constantly changing? Explain.
4. In Hegel's view consciousness and reason are essential to man. Does this mean that someone in an unconscious state is no longer a man? Does it mean that there might be different degrees of being a man (e.g., that if one person is more rational than another, he is more a man)? Explain.
5. What does Hegel mean by "freedom"? What do Marx and Engels mean by "freedom"? Are the Hegelian and the Marxist views compatible? Explain.
6. Both Hegel and Marx have an ideal view of what man can and should be. State their views and then compare and contrast them.
7. According to Marx the essence of man is the ensemble of his social relations. Make clear what he means by this.
8. Both Marx and Hegel speak of the alienation of man. Explain what each of them means by this and where their views differ. According to either view, is it possible for man to overcome his alienation completely? Explain.
9. Explain the basis in Hegel and in Marx and Engels for their collectivist views of man. In what sense are they opposed to an individualistic view of man?
10. Is a collectivist view of man compatible with a doctrine of individual inalienable rights? Discuss.

B.

1. Compare and contrast Aquinas' discussion of the spiritual aspects of man with Hegel's treatment of the spirit. Are the two compatible? Explain.
2. Both the pragmatists and Marx emphasize the continuity between man and the rest of nature. Compare the pragmatic and the Marxist approaches to man, making clear both similarities and differences.
3. Moore and Russell reacted against the idealism of their predecessors. Is their treatment of consciousness more satisfactory than Hegel's? Discuss.
4. Both Sartre and Schaff hold that man in some sense makes himself. Yet Sartre is a champion of individualism and Schaff of collectivism. How do you account for this difference in the light of their seeming initial agreement?
5. Must one choose between an individualistic or a collectivistic view of man? If so, which is preferable and why? If not, what other alternative is there?

RECOMMENDED READINGS

Primary Sources

Bradley, F. H. *Ethical Studies.* New York: Liberal Arts Press, 1951. The early part of the essay "My Station and Its Duties" presents a persuasive argument by a distinguished British idealist against individualism and for an organic view of society.

Hegel, G. W. F. *Early Theological Writings.* Trans. by T. M. Knox. New York: Harper & Row, 1961. Paperback. The two essays "Love" and "Fragment of a System" are an early account of Hegel's view of the unity of men and of man with God and nature.

————. *Philosophy of Mind.* Trans. from the *Encyclopaedia of the Philosophical Sciences* by William Wallace. Oxford: Clarendon Press, 1894. Section I, Subsection C (Psychology) presents Hegel's view of the theoretical (intuition, recollection, imagination, memory, thinking) and the practical (impulse, choice) aspects of mind.

Lenin, V. I. *Materialism and Empirio-Criticism.* Moscow: Foreign Languages Publishing House. This work contains Lenin's "copy" theory of knowledge. Chapters 1, 2, and 3 are especially important, though the work as a whole is still assiduously studied by students in the Soviet Union.

Marx, Karl, and Friedrich Engels. *Basic Writings on Politics and Philosophy.* Ed. by Lewis Feuer. New York: Doubleday & Co., 1959. This is a useful paperback collection of the most important works of Marx and Engels. The excerpt from Marx's *A Contribution to the Critique of Political Economy,* pp. 42–46, gives a concise statement of the doctrine of historical materialism; Engels' *Socialism: Utopian and Scientific,* pp. 68–111, presents the Marxist view of the evolution of communism; and the *Communist Manifesto,* pp. 1–41, is a classic in which the revolutionary aspects of Marxism are strongly stated.

Plekhanov, George. *The Role of the Individual in History.* New York: International Publishers, 1940. This short essay by a prominent early Russian Marxist remains the most extended discussion of this topic in the Marxist literature.

Schaff, Adam. *A Philosophy of Man.* New York: Monthly Review Press, 1963. Part III of this book contains a statement of a contemporary Marxist humanism, built upon Schaff's general philosophy of man.

Commentaries

De George, Richard T. "The Soviet Concept of Man," *Studies in Soviet Thought,* IV (1964), 261–76. A critical analysis of the Soviet Marxist view of man.

Dupré, Louis. *The Philosophical Foundations of Marxism.* New York: Harcourt, Brace & World, 1966. A direct introduction to Marx's own texts, this analytic commentary familiarizes the reader with Marx's technical language and method of thinking. Chapters 1 and 2 contain a historical introduction to Hegel's social philosophy and a detailed discussion of the *Philosophy of Right.*

Findlay, J. N. *Hegel: A Reexamination.* New York: Collier Books, 1962. A clear presentation of Hegel's philosophy, which interprets Hegel as an empiricist. Chapters 4 and 5 summarize the *Phenomenology of Mind;* Ch. 10 presents Hegel's psychology.

Fromm, Erich. *Marx's Concept of Man.* New York: Frederick Ungar Publishing Co., 1961. A controversial presentation of Marx's early writings with an existentialist twist. This volume, in addition to Fromm's essay, also contains some of Marx's most pertinent writings on man.

Hook, Sidney. *From Hegel to Marx: Studies in the Intellectual Development of Karl Marx.* Ann Arbor, Mich.: University of Michigan Press, 1962. The first chapters point up some of the differences between Hegel and Marx. The volume is the best exposition of Marx's relations with the Young Hegelians.

Marcuse, Herbert. *Reason and Revolution: Hegel and the Rise of Social Theory.* Boston: Beacon Press, 1960. The Introductions to Parts I and II are good, brief presentations of the setting from which Hegel's and Marx's thoughts arose. The volume as a whole is a valuable discussion of the social and political influence of Hegelianism and Marxism.

Royce, Josiah. *Lectures on Modern Idealism.* New Haven: Yale University Press, 1964. The chapters on Hegel by Royce, one of America's most famous idealists, remain classic expositions of Hegel's doctrine.

Sartre, Jean-Paul. *Literary and Philosophical Essays.* New York: Macmillan Co., 1962. Sartre's essay on Marxism presents a critique of Soviet Marxism. The issues of individualism and collectivism and the notion of freedom receive fairly full treatment.

Stace, W. T. *The Philosophy of Hegel: A Systematic Exposition.* New York: Dover Publications, 1955. Part IV, first division, presents Hegel's doctrine of the Subjective Spirit (anthropology, consciousness, psychology). Stace interprets Hegel as an absolute idealist.

PART THREE

Introduction

The American Milieu: A Prologue

Naturalism: Historical Background

Pragmatism as the Art of Making Ideas Clear: Historical Background

Peirce: Man as Knower

James: Man as Committed and Free

Dewey: Man as Unified Organism

Santayana: Man in a Changing Environment

Readings

PEIRCE: *How to Make Our Ideas Clear*

JAMES: *What Pragmatism Means*
The Will to Believe

DEWEY: *The Influence of Darwinism*
The Supremacy of Method

SANTAYANA: *Flux and Constancy in Human Nature*

AMERICAN PRAGMATIC-NATURALIST THOUGHT:

Peirce
James
Dewey
Santayana

EDITED BY

Robert J. Kreyche

ROCKHURST COLLEGE

AMERICAN
PRAGMATIC-NATURALIST
THOUGHT:
Peirce
James
Dewey
Santayana

Introduction

The American Milieu: A Prologue (introduction)

surrounding or environment

At the very beginning of this essay we want to stress the importance of understanding the motivations of a given philosophy as a means of discovering both its limitations and its positive worth. It is in the concrete historical light of conflicting movements within American culture at large that the real meaning of naturalism and pragmatism come to the fore. Why, for example, have naturalists (as part of the American scene) reacted in such vigorous fashion to many of the forms of traditional religion in spite of the fact that it was, by and large, men of religious ideals who forged "the American dream"? Questions of this sort admit of no easy answer. Yet it is certainly relevant to suggest that the religious commitment in this country both before and after the Revolutionary War was dominated by the Puritan ethic—an ethic that for the most part tended to denigrate the value of human existence by placing man simply as a tool in the hands of an angry God. Unfortunately, then, the exaggerations of Calvinism, together with the philosophic justification of it in terms of a Berkeleian mentalism, could only have the effect of producing a reaction in the other extreme—and the "other extreme" was an intense reaction on the part of some of the founding fathers against all forms of supernatural religion. The spirit of the times immediately following the decline of Puritanism as a theology was the spirit of a naturalistic deism—such as we find expressed in the writings of Jefferson, Paine, and Franklin. As against the Calvinistic doctrine of predestination we find, for example, Benjamin Franklin insisting that "the Lord helps those who help themselves."

Further, under the impact of Darwinism the rise of the new secularistic spirit was given a fresh impetus—especially against the background of the reactionary, defensive posture of the ministers of religion who rejected evolutionism in the name of theology. It was under the impact of the Darwinian revolution that the biological, naturalistic point of view began to prevail—not as an antireligion, but as a secularism that tended to regard all forms of religion as superfluous and, except possibly for women and children, as irrelevant to the building of empires in the workaday world of business, politics, and law.[1]

James K. Feibleman (b. 1904) assesses the inner and still unresolved conflict that prevails in American society at large as a conflict between pragmatism (not so much as a philosophic theory but as a way of life) and a form of religious idealism, such as we find in the tradition of Edwards, Emerson, and Royce.[2]

Though historically related, naturalism and pragmatism are not synonymous terms. Naturalism signifies what might be called, in the terms of traditional philosophy, a "philosophy of being"—a world view or, in a more restricted fashion, a method or approach to reality. It implies a certain way of looking at the world that excludes any reality outside the universe at large, outside the cosmos. Yet it must be clearly understood at the outset that not all naturalists are agreed among themselves as to whether naturalism is chiefly a world view or primarily, if not exclusively, a method of examining reality. Although most naturalists do agree that their philosophy is a kind of metaphysics, there are others who stringently deny that this is so. Note, for example, the following statement:

> The naturalistic principle may be stated as the resolution to pursue inquiry into any set of phenomena by means of methods which administer the checks of intelligent experiential verification in accordance with contemporary criteria of objectivity. The significance of this principle does not lie in the advocation of empirical methods, but in the conception of the regions where that method is to be employed. That scientific analysis must not be restricted in any quarter, that its extension to any field, to any special set of phenomena, must

---

[1] Historically, perhaps, it was impossible for American naturalists as philosophers to appreciate what John Herman Randall, Jr., called the "inner core" of Christianity. Their own critique of the tradition of "supernatural religion" was too heavily laden with the image of ministers of the gospel who had no taste for science and who preached a Christianity that had little appreciation for or love of the values of this world. Culturally and historically, then, a sharp dichotomy arose between religious and secular values, and it has been the point of view of the naturalist to show that secular values alone are of any ultimate worth. As Santayana expressed it: "Every ideal has a natural basis and everything natural has an ideal fulfillment." While traditional theists would agree with the first part of this statement, they would deny that the ideal fulfillment of natural values is adequately insured within the natural process itself—insofar as in their view man has a final end outside of nature that gives a transcendent and ultimate meaning to the whole of his natural life.

[2] See "The Hidden Philosophy of Americans," *The Saturday Review*, XLV (March 10, 1962), 15–16.

not be curtailed—this is the nerve of the naturalistic principle. "Continuity" of analysis can thus mean only that all analysis must be scientific analysis.[3]

Pragmatism, by contrast, is not a world view at all, but rather a theory of cognition that, according to Charles Sanders Peirce (1839–1914), aims to get at the meaning of things by making our ideas clear. In this introductory essay, however, the immediate concern is not to get into a technical elaboration of either naturalism or pragmatism as a philosophy but to indicate that these terms—though related—are different.

Naturalism: Historical Background

One of the best ways of coming to know a philosophy is to get at the motivations that inspired it. To study a philosophy in purely abstract terms—out of its historical context—is to fail to appreciate the particular point of view that its authors had in mind.

In order to have an accurate understanding of the doctrines themselves, it is necessary to examine the historical background of naturalism as a philosophy.

The origins of naturalism can be found in the very first school of philosophy, that of the early Greek naturalists from Thales (c. 624–546 B.C.) through Heraclitus (c. 540–475 B.C.). These men were "naturalists" in the sense that they attempted to seek out the causes of nature *within nature itself*. Their central problem was to discover for themselves the underlying cause of *all* that is—whether in the end they identified this reality with water, air, earth, or fire. In no sense, however, should it be assumed that the early Greek cosmologists were dogmatic naturalists or materialists. They simply took the world as they found it, hoping to give the best explanation they could of what they assumed to be its underlying substratum, that is, the principle of unity that lay at the basis of all the multiplicity in the universe. Such a view represents the first attempt at the development of an independent philosophy, an attempt that was in no way characterized, as naturalism today is characterized, by a *denial* of the necessity of some other world or reality outside nature. It simply did not occur to the earliest naturalists that anything outside of nature did or could exist. Only at a later stage of the development of Greek philosophy did some philosophers find it necessary to posit something outside of and distinct from nature, like the *Nous* of Anaxagoras (c. 500–428 B.C.), thus accounting both for its origin and for the orderly line of its teleological development.

Although naturalism goes back to the earliest Greek "schools" of phi-

---

[3] Thelma Z. Lavine, "Naturalism and the Sociological Analysis of Knowledge," in *Naturalism and the Human Spirit*, ed. by Yervant H. Krikorian (New York: Columbia University Press, 1944), pp. 184–85.

losophy, it was not until the days of Epicurus (341–270 B.C.) and Lucretius (*c.* 96–55 B.C.) that we find a much more explicit development of
naturalism as a philosophy of man and as a philosophy of human life itself.
In a sense, Democritus (*c.* 460–370 B.C.) and Leucippus (*fl.* 460 B.C.)
were naturalists, but the real flavor of naturalism as a kind of humanism
came to the fore in the exuberant praise given Mother Nature by men like
Epicurus and Lucretius. For these men the present life, that is, man's life
on earth, embraces the whole of things, and there is no immortality save
that which in some cosmic sense is to be found *within* nature itself.

In accordance with this spirit, it is not surprising to discover that Epicurus was the enemy of the "supernaturalists" of his time. The "supernaturalists, in Epicurus' opinion, were those men who, because they were
ignorant of the causes of nature, adhered to a complicated system of non-
verifiable gods. From a more positive viewpoint he advocated as the supreme
end of human existence a life of pleasure—pleasure understood mainly in
those things, such as serenity of soul, that bring permanent satisfaction to
the human psyche. Epicurus' system of values is a happiness-on-earth
formula, which in naturalistic fashion disavows all abject subservience to
what he regarded as an imagined world of the unknown. Man must release
himself from his hidden fears and to do so he must appreciate the world as
he finds it and for all that it is.

The classical and poetical expression of naturalism in its ancient form
is found in the celebrated poem of the Roman Lucretius, *De Rerum
Natura.* Dedicating himself to Epicurus, whom he regarded as the greatest of
all philosophers, Lucretius set forth a naturalistic credo that is unequalled
in the clarity of its thought and the beauty of its expression. Historically,
Lucretius is significant for being the prototype for the naturalist philosophers to come; the spirit of his naturalism is not too radically different
from the naturalism of the present day, even though present-day naturalism leans far more in the direction of science than it does in the direction
of poetry.

It was Francis Bacon (1561–1626) who, centuries later, "rediscovered" ancient naturalism and praised the early Greek cosmology for not
seeking after unknown causes in the manner of Aristotle.[4] Indeed, the new
era of naturalism that issued forth with the dawn of modern science and of
which Francis Bacon was at least the prophet, differed little from that of its

[4] That Bacon took none too kindly to Aristotle may be gathered from the following
quotation: "[Aristotle] was always more solicitous to provide an answer to the
question and affirm something in positive words than about the inner truth of things;
a failing best shown when his philosophy is compared with other systems of note
among the Greeks. For the *homaeoromera* of Anaxagoras; the atoms of Leucippus
and Democritus; . . . Heraclitus' doctrine how bodies are resolved into the indifferent nature of fire . . . have all of them some taste of the natural philosopher—
some savor of the nature of things." (Francis Bacon, *Novum Organum,* Aphorism
LXIII, in *The English Philosophers from Bacon to Mill,* ed. by Edwin A. Burtt
[New York: Random House, 1939], p. 43.)

ancient predecessors—insofar as it was still fundamentally based on a mechanistic view of the world.

Only in more recent times, with the repudiation of the mechanistic view of the world for one that is evolutionary in scope and character, have any radical changes been brought about in the development of naturalism as a philosophy. Naturalism as it exists today, for example, in the works of John Dewey (1859–1952) and Roy Wood Sellars (b. 1880), rejects the view that nature is a mechanism and espouses the doctrine that it is an evolutionary system of development. Contemporary naturalism is in harmony with the latest developments of modern science, not with the view that men had of the universe in the sixteenth century. This point of the difference is of crucial importance; however, we must first examine the mechanistic view that at one time prevailed.

The mechanistic view of the universe, of which Thomas Hobbes (1588–1679) is a prime exponent, attempts to reduce the complexities of nature and life to a few basic principles. The materialism of Hobbes recognizes only two ultimate principles, matter and motion. All that exists for Hobbes is matter and motion and *matter in motion*. It was in the tradition of Hobbes that David Hume (1711–76) and many other thinkers in Britain did what they could to retrace the problems of man and of human knowledge to their source on the level of a mechanistic type of analysis. The psychological laws of association themselves as anticipated by Hume and developed by John Stuart Mill (1806–73) and others were an attempt to get at the key to human nature. The fundamental hope of the mechanists was to provide a "science" of human nature itself that would parallel in the simplicity of its explanation the Newtonian laws of motion. In other words, the science of nature as embodied in the discoveries of Newton and others was taken both as a paradigm and as a prediction: the hope of the mechanists was that some day man could "solve" the problem of man in the way that science is "solving" the problem of nature at large. In the light of such naive hopes as these, it is not surprising that William James (1842–1910) toward the end of the nineteenth century characterized the doctrine of Mill as having reached the heights of "paroxysmal unintelligibility."

But what was the reason, what was the turn of events that brought about such a fundamental change of outlook? Without question the most important single event in the history of contemporary naturalism was the publication in 1859 (1860 in America) of Darwin's *Origin of Species*.[5] In it Darwin introduced a whole new concept of the evolutionary development of nature and of man within the context of nature. Prior to Darwin it had been assumed (according to the old mechanistic philosophy) that there was really "nothing new under the sun." Changes took place in man and in nature, but once man had discovered the key it would always be possible to predict the course of these changes. As in the older mechanistic philosophies

---

[5] See Harold A. Larrabee, "Naturalism in America," in Krikorian, pp. 347 ff.

of the Greeks, the new mechanism was simply a rearrangement (in somewhat different patterns) of the old; the secret of success was to have discovered (by means of a few simple laws) the frequency and regularity of these patterns.

Evolutionism, however, changed all that, and the development of naturalism in its more modern setting has come to mean a recognition of *qualitative* differences in man and of man *in* nature. This latter point too is of crucial importance. According to contemporary naturalists, the older philosophies, including the classical forms of modern philosophy, failed, even when they attempted to do so, to regard man *within* the context of nature. Their mistake was to imagine that man could, as it were, pull himself up by his own bootstraps to solve the riddle of the universe. Needless to say, no such pretensions exist among the naturalists of today: man in the contemporary view is too much part of the universe to stand completely above it. More important than the attainment of any overall view of the world is the matter of man's adjusting to the world and learning how to control nature for his own ends.[6]

After Darwin it was no longer possible to reduce man to just a few simple laws. There was, therefore, the need (in the language of James) for the development of a "radical empiricism"—an empiricism that is open to the development of new pathways for man and for his understanding of nature. What some of these new pathways are will be made evident in the course of our readings, but the main point to know is that naturalism, especially as it applies to man, is not all of one piece, and the chief characteristic of naturalism since the days of Darwin is its fundamentally *evolutionary* outlook on the nature of man. There is no modern naturalist who is not in some way influenced—and profoundly so—by the fundamental inspiration of the Darwinian hypothesis.

As a case in point, it is impossible to understand the thought of John Dewey except against the background of an evolutionary concept of nature and of man. Man, in other words, is a part of nature, an emergent product of it; just as the course of nature itself has only a limited range of predictability, so it is with reference to man. Man himself is in a constant process of development, and the role of human intelligence is somehow to get *inside* this process to discover what it can, not about the "nature" of man as an abstract entity but about the actual development of man in relation to a future that remains as yet unknown.

The spirit, then, of American naturalism is a spirit of "openness" to the condition of man. It is a spirit characterized by a "radical empiricism," which makes no presupposition as to any fundamental nature that man might have. It is a spirit, moreover, that is characterized by the rejection of any traditional type of philosophy, including materialism itself, that would attempt to reduce man to one or to a few basic principles. In method and

---

[6] See the discussion later in this essay of the thought of John Dewey, pp. 337–40.

structure or appearance,
having similar or identical

object it is a spirit of openness and inquiry which, in the language of Roy Wood Sellars, is isomorphic with the methods of science. However much naturalists may differ among themselves, they are all in fundamental agreement on the point that man is a part of nature and must accordingly be viewed within the evolutionary context of nature. Man, in other words, is part of a continuum, and it is impossible for him to understand himself if he ever loses sight of this fundamental fact.

a thing whose parts can't be separated

Not all naturalists will agree with the following statement by Dewey, but it sums up the typically naturalistic approach to the "problem of man":

> To see the organism *in* nature, the nervous system in the organism, the brain in the nervous system, the cortex in the brain is the answer to the problems which haunt philosophy. And when thus seen they will be seen to be *in,* not as marbles are in a box but as events are in history, in a moving, growing never finished process.[7]

To an outlook such as this, one is tempted to ask as a point of critical inquiry whether modern naturalism is any less reductive in its approach to the problem of man than naturalisms of the past. Yet any criticism of a man's position (prior to a thorough examination of it) is premature, and the point here is merely to illustrate the fact that an ingrained part of American naturalism, as we know it, is to regard man in continuity with the rest of nature. Expressed in more basic philosophic terms, for the naturalist, and certainly for Dewey, man is immanently one with nature and any attempt to see whether or not man transcends nature must be viewed against the background of this fundamental point of veiw.

Résumé

living remaining or operating in
inherent (basic, inborn)

At this point the reader has at least a working idea of the meaning of naturalism as it relates to the philosophy of man. He has seen that the dominant motive of naturalist psychology (at least in its typically modern and American setting) is to stress the fundamental continuity between man and the rest of nature. Contemporary naturalism represents a vigorous protest against any attempt to "bifurcate" [8] either man himself or to bifurcate him from the rest of nature. In the naturalistic view, one bifurcates man himself by positing a fundamental dualism in man, like the alleged dualism between body and soul, and from this point of view most naturalists would prefer to speak of man simply as an organism. On the other hand, one bifurcates man from the rest of nature whenever he likens man in some fashion to a kind of transcendental spirit whose body is little more than an appendage. Historically and doctrinally, naturalism is opposed to any "transcendentalist" view of man that (like that of Ralph Waldo Emer-

---

[7] John Dewey, *Experience and Nature* (New York: Dover Publications, 1958), p. 295.
[8] This is one of the favorite expressions of naturalists themselves. To bifurcate means to establish a split, a radical discontinuity, a dualism between one thing (or a part of one thing) and another.

son) tends to separate man *from* nature and to establish in some metaphysical sense man's superiority *over* nature. To the contemporary naturalist, man simply is an evolved product *of* nature, and it is in this context that we must view his accomplishments, including the phenomenon of human knowledge itself.

Pragmatism as the Art of Making Ideas Clear: Historical Background

To this point we have traced out the backgrounds of American naturalistic thought, and we have seen that naturalism in its broader perspective is not so much a theory of knowledge as it is an overall view of reality. This is not to suggest, of course, that the naturalist is uninterested in the problem of knowledge, but it is not the kind of problem in which he specializes except in relation to the purposes of life. Knowledge to the naturalist is itself a natural phenomenon and must accordingly be regarded within the context of nature. As Dewey remarked, human knowledge is a function of the organism and therefore its primary purpose is not contemplation but control. At this point, however, the naturalist may or may not become a pragmatist, but if he does, the examination of such problems as the meaning of truth, falsity, and error will subsequently be a matter of central concern. This is not to deny that most naturalists are pragmatists, which indeed they are, but merely to affirm that the direction of pragmatism as an epistemological theory is less toward the problems of ontology than toward the problem of knowledge as such. Accordingly, although naturalism and pragmatism are intimately related to each other, and therefore complementary aspects of the same basic coin, they are nonetheless different insofar as there is a division of labor between them; the main concern of the pragmatist is not any overall view of the universe, but the actual conditions under which the progress of human knowledge takes place. As part of our study, then, of the backgrounds of pragmatism in America, we turn immediately to the pragmatism of Charles Sanders Peirce.

Peirce is the founder of pragmatism in America. His essay "How to Make Ideas Clear," the first selection in the readings, is important for a basic understanding of pragmatism. The title gives the reader a clue to the meaning of pragmatism that was intended by its founder; pragmatism is not so much an abstract theory of knowledge (though it includes such a theory) as it is a method for "making ideas clear." How we make ideas clear will be taken up subsequently, but first it is necessary to know why pragmatism developed and what was the central motivation behind the movement.

Peirce wrote his essay considerably before the turn of the twentieth century; one of his chief desires was to extricate philosophy from the epistemological knots into which it had bound itself over the past two or three hundred years. To appreciate what pragmatism is as a movement, we must see it against the historical background of René Descartes (1596–1650), of the British empirical movement, and of Immanuel Kant (1724–1804).

Modern philosophy (in its classical sense) began with Descartes' attempt to counteract the scepticism that prevailed during the first half of the seventeenth century. Descartes, the "father of modern philosophy," sought to establish philosophy on a new footing, to secure for philosophy the rate of progress that marked the development of the physical sciences. This attempt represented a significant departure both from the scholasticism of his day, which had become overripe, and from Montaigne's scepticism.

The Cartesian method is introspective; that is, certainty is looked for within the consciousness of the thinking subject. It is typified by the famous underlying principle *Cogito, ergo sum* (I think, therefore I am). Descartes' method for making ideas clear begins not from the outer world of experience but from within the domain of the consciousness of the individual. Peirce expressed this point as follows:

> When Descartes set about the reconstruction of philosophy, his first step was to (theoretically) permit scepticism and to discard the practice of the schoolmen of looking to authority as the ultimate source of truth. That done, he sought a more natural foundation of true principles, and professed to find it in the human mind; thus passing . . . from the method of authority to that of apriority . . . . *Self-consciousness* was to furnish us with our fundamental truths, and to decide what was *agreeable to reason*. But since, evidently, not all ideas are true, he was led to note, as the first condition of infallibility, that they must be *clear*.[9] [Italics added.]

Obviously Peirce was in sympathy with Descartes in the rejection of the "method of authority"—but not with Descartes' method of introspective analysis. As we shall see, to the pragmatist both the truth and the meaning of ideas are to be gathered from their relatedness to the outside world. Even so, it is important to note the basic continuity between the Cartesian desire to clarify ideas and the subsequent desire of pragmatists like Peirce to do the same thing, though in a radically different way.[10]

In reaction to what Peirce has called the "apriority"[11] of Descartes, the epistemologists of the British school (Locke, Berkeley, and Hume) commonly rejected the attempt to accept any idea that does not have its basis in experience. Their problem then was to trace all ideas back to their source

---

[9] From "How to Make Ideas Clear," originally published in *Popular Science Monthly*, XII (Jan., 1878), p. 287.

[10] The methods of pragmatism are closely related to the desire to find the ultimate source of "clarity" not in the *ideas themselves*, but in the mode of their applicability and the force of their relevance to the outside world insofar as it is subject to human prediction and control.

[11] Apriority may be defined as a preconceived method of approaching reality according to the inclination of the mind itself (in contrast to the evidence of the world outside the mind).

in experience. Their method for making ideas clear was the alleged empirical method of attempting to determine whether these same ideas represent to a certain extent the contents of our sensible experience. If they do, we can in a limited fashion accept these ideas; if not, we can assume that the source of a given idea lies within the subject himself. The central objection of the pragmatist to the classical British approach to the problem of knowledge is: *British empiricism is not "radical" enough;* it is, so to speak, only a halfway house, and as such falls far short of the mark of what true empiricism should be. From the point of view of the pragmatist, the Achilles' heel of classical British philosophy is the supposition (taken over unwittingly from Descartes) that ideas themselves, and not what exists in the world, are the direct object of knowledge.

For example, if we begin with the doctrine that the very contents of knowledge are the ideas (and sensations) that exist in our mind, we can never be sure that these ideas truly represent the things in the external world that they are supposed to represent. From such a view we become involved in all the difficulties of classical modern idealism, whose chief characteristic is the assumption that the mind of man is detached, as it were, from the very world to which it is supposed to be essentially related.

One further point: Why should anyone suppose, as the British empiricists did, that sensations and ideas are meant to be copies of reality in the first place? Is it really the function of knowledge to represent? To the mind of the pragmatist no such presupposition is necessary, for, as Dewey explained, *ideas* have served their purpose if they serve only as *instruments* for action and reaction, for prediction and control. In other words, to the pragmatists there is no need to ask, as the earlier empiricists had asked, if ideas conform to reality; it is sufficient to know if they harmonize and get into working contact with the realm of our experience.

In summary, ideas to the pragmatists are means, instruments, or tools of action for getting in contact with the world; they are not "copies," "representations," or, least of all, "intuitions" of the world itself. In this view it is irrelevant to ask whether we can "know" reality because knowledge is not something static, it is not something apart from the ongoing process of life itself, but an integral part, as Dewey attempted to establish, of the biological continuum. Man is part of nature, and human knowledge is integrally related to the purposes of human life.

The overall purpose of pragmatism is to reinterpret knowledge as *function.* Insofar as the pragmatists helped to get the knower outside of himself and his ideas, they made a clean break from the position of modern classical idealism and introduced in its place a form of realism that gets man in contact with the outside world of his experience. In so doing they made a decision in the right direction by rejecting the assumption that the mind is confined, as it were, to its own mental states.

So far we have examined some points of comparison and contrast between pragmatism and Cartesian rationalism and between pragmatism and

British empiricism. It remains for us now to complete this historical background by making some reference to the philosophy of Immanuel Kant. Kant was a German philosopher who according to his own testimony had been awakened from his "dogmatic slumbers" by the pan-phenomenalism of David Hume, which reduced everything to the level of appearances. Kant, like Descartes, wanted to get human knowledge off on another footing. Philosophy had reached an impasse in the culminating influence of the scepticism of Hume, and Kant wanted to restore it in a way that would transcend the limits of both Descartes' classical rationalism and modern British empiricism. How was he to accomplish his task?

Kant set out with the presupposition that knowledge is the result of two factors, one external, the other internal. The external factor—the element of the "given"—is provided for by the phenomena of the outside world, which for him is the world of external appearances. This world of appearances provides man with the empirical basis of his ideas. Even so, the external world, as we encounter it, is a discrete, disorganized mass of details. To give order to the phenomenal contents of our experience, it is necessary for us to superimpose on these data a double set of a priori forms: both the forms of sense intuition, time and space, and of understanding, such as being, substance, and cause—elements that give meaning to the world of our experience, even though their source lies within the knowing subject. To understand what these forms meant to Kant, we must keep in mind that they are "categories" either of sense intuition or of understanding. A category for Kant is not what it was for Aristotle—an item of knowledge that is based on experience. For Kant, a category (taken as a priori form) is something *prior to* experience that we *superimpose* upon experience.

The distinguishing mark of Kant's noetics (his theory of knowledge) is that, unlike the British empiricists, he made no attempt to trace our ideas back to experience. Ideas themselves are underived and prior to all experience; it is sufficient that they merely serve to help us organize our experience. Further, ideas are not passively impressed on the mind but are the active ingredients of our knowledge. They play a dominant role in giving meaning to the disorganized contents of our experience.

Can any point of comparison be drawn between Kant and the pragmatists? Offhand, no two schools of thought could seem to be farther apart, if only because pragmatic empiricism is of one mind in rejecting anything that even remotely resembles a doctrine of a priori forms. However, one further point should be noted: Kant, more effectively than anyone who preceded him, undermined, for good or for ill, the speculative basis of all philosophic realism, and in so doing relegated it to the category of dogmatism. Realism here means any philosophic theory that holds that the human mind is naturally equipped to get authentic insight into the nature or essence of things as they exist outside the mind. From the time of Kant onward (and in this sense pragmatism is a direct offshoot of Kantianism), metaphysics in its traditional sense had been ruled out of court. What the pragmatists accepted from Kant therefore was the common rejection of a realistic metaphysics in the sense of a theory of knowledge that could produce a genuine understanding or insight into the nature of being itself. Both to Kant and the pragmatists the thing in itself or noumenon is completely hidden from the view of the intellect of man.

This point is of crucial importance: A realistic metaphysics is one that regards being (or reality) as having a fundamental intelligibility of its own. This means that in the traditional, pre-Kantian view the source of intelligibility lies not within the mind as Kant believed, but in being. Thus, according to traditional realists the role of the mind is not to superimpose itself on the contents of experience but to derive from experience whatever intelligible significance it implicitly contains. This doctrine was rejected by Kant and, what is more important for our purposes, it was rejected in an implicit fashion by the pragmatists.

The point of affinity between the Kantian noetic and pragmatism as a method for making ideas clear lies in the fact that both stress the fundamentally active role of the mind, which is not to abstract the intelligible contents of experience but to give meaning to the contents of experience, which of themselves are disorganized, discrete, and ephemeral. But wherein lies the source of this meaning? To Kant the source of meaning lies in the forms themselves, that is, in a set of a priori forms. To the pragmatists the source of meaning lies not in any set of a priori forms but in the needs, interests, and vital concerns of the knower himself. Thus in pragmatism it is the knower who gives focus, direction, and meaning to the whole enterprise that is known as knowledge. As Dewey frequently reminded us, knowledge is relative to the knower and cannot be divorced from the purposes that govern his life.

Résumé

Such, then, are the basic presuppositions underlying pragmatism as a theory of knowledge, viewed against the background of its historical antecedents. In the spirit of Descartes (though by totally different methods), the pragmatists intended to make ideas clear, not by a mental or introspective process but by testing them against the background of experience. In the spirit of the British empiricists, the pragmatists desired to relate human knowledge to experience. However, the pragmatic conceptions of what experience is and how the mind is related to experience are totally different from those of the British empiricists. For the empiricists the fundamental role of the mind is to represent passively the contents of our sensible impressions; for the pragmatists the mind is essentially active. This last point indicates a fundamental likeness between pragmatic thought and the noetics of Kant. The distinguishing mark of pragmatism, however, is: The activity of the mind is related in a radically empirical fashion (and not by the method of a priori forms) to real events in the outside world. It is the needs of the inquirer, whether personal or scientific, that determine how the knower will relate himself noetically and biologically to the outside world.[12]

Peirce: Man as Knower

We have already made several references to Peirce's essay "How to Make Ideas Clear." Basically, it is the intent of the author to show that "the action of thought is excited by the irritation of doubt." In other words, the beginning of all human inquiry is not an artificial doubt, as had been supposed by Descartes, but a real doubt. Furthermore, in Peirce's view, the action of thought ceases once inquiry leads to belief.

What then is the nature of belief? Peirce gives a much broader application to this term than we customarily attach to it in analyzing three of its basic properties: (1) it is something we are consciously aware of; (2) it appeases the irritation of doubt; (3) it involves the establishment in our nature of a rule of action or of what Peirce calls a habit. He considers the essence of belief itself to be the establishment of a habit and different beliefs are distinguished by the different modes of action to which they give rise.

Fundamental to the pragmatism of Peirce is the doctrine that ideas and beliefs are differentiated, not by the supposed differences of their internal meanings but by the sum total of their practical consequences, whether the fulfillment of these consequences be actual or merely possible. Accordingly, no matter how much people may quibble about the differences in their beliefs, these differences are purely fictitious unless they lead to a difference in practice. Suppose, for example, that two persons believe an object to be hard; if both persons on the basis of their belief expect the same consequences, then their idea of hardness is identical. Thus, no matter how much your idea of hardness as an abstract quality may differ from mine, your idea is identical with mine if we both expect the same consequences, such as the consequence of a head-on collision when two cars are moving toward each other in the same lane.

This consideration is important to the understanding of Peirce: he is no mere subjectivist. Truth to Peirce is not merely what you and I make a situation to be; it is the result of public knowledge and investigation. As he stresses near the end of his essay, the truth is ultimately that upon which the community of investigators agree; it is not the private opinion of one man,

---

[12] It was no mere historical accident that Peirce on his own testimony spent two hours a day for a period of three years reading Kant. Indeed, the affinity between pragmatism and the noetics of Kant is deep-seated, since the underlying assumption of all pragmatic noetics is the fundamental Kantian doctrine of the mind itself being the determining source of its own activity. However, the pragmatists criticize Kant (and rightly so) for both his doctrine of a priori forms and his failure to relate the activity of the mind to the rest of our human experiences.

nor least of all a kind of emotional response. As the reader will gather from his essay, the dominant interests of Peirce are in the direction of logic and science. He is, as it were, logician and physicist turned philosopher.

James: Man as Committed and Free

Next in the readings is a set of two essays from the writings of William James. The dominant interest of James, as is manifest in the essays, is not logic and science but problems more closely related to human interests as such, especially in the areas of psychology and religion. In fact, it was James who popularized the overall idea of pragmatism, a popularization that Peirce later rejected.

The most outstanding feature of James's philosophy is that it is alive, that it is, to use a modern term, existential—replete with an awareness of man and his situation in the world. James is at once a radical empiricist, a pragmatist, an intense student of religion and psychology, and also, as Santayana rightly claimed, a romanticist. Few persons have ever lived philosophy as deeply as did William James.[13] In fact, it is sometimes said that just as Henry James, his brother, wrote novels as if he were a psychologist, so William James wrote psychology like a novelist.[14] With respect to certain points of his doctrine, especially the source of unity in man, this claim may unfortunately be true, in the sense that James's theory of the stream of consciousness, taken as a substitute for the theory of a substantial self, is a pure work of fiction. Yet whether this point of criticism is valid or not, few thinkers before or after James have manifested a more penetrating understanding of human nature. James's position as a great classical psychologist is secure.

In reading James, the student will see that the spirit of James's personality is revealed in his writing. He will discover that James's interpretation of pragmatism is concise and to the point. For example, note the following from "What Pragmatism Means":

---

[13] Note, too, the remarkably fine words of George Herbert Mead concerning James: "His mental and moral citizenship was in America. . . . He condemned the crudity, the political corruption, the materialism of American life, but he condemned it as an American. . . . His philosophy was a native American growth. . . . If any man's culture has been a part of himself, this was true of James." ("The Philosophies of Royce, James, and Dewey in Their American Setting," in *The Development of American Philosophy,* ed. by Walter G. Meulder *et al.* [New York: Houghton Mifflin Co., 1960], p. 357.)

[14] The following quotation from Roy Wood Sellars helps to corroborate this point: "[James] wanted to be concrete in his thinking, to keep abstract ideas in touch with perceptual experience. Sometimes his phrasing was a little too concrete, as when he spoke of the cash value of ideas. At such times, his desire for a vivid style got the better of him. But such lapses were rare. Good writing ran in the James family. His father was a brilliant conversationalist and his brother Henry was a master of prose." ("Existentialism, Realistic Empiricism, and Materialism," *Philosophy and Phenomenological Research,* XXV, 3 [March, 1965], 319–20.)

> To attain perfect clearness in our thoughts of an object, we need only consider what conceivable effects of a practical kind the object may involve—what sensations we are to expect from it, and what reactions we must prepare. *Our conception of these effects, whether immediate or remote, is then for us the whole of our conception of the object.* [Italics added.]

As is clear from the selection "What Pragmatism Means," William James does not have a monistic view of the universe, or even a set of propositions about it, but rather thinks of pragmatism as a method and a spirit of inquiry that constantly leads one on to the discovery of new truths. Thus in the pragmatic interpretation of philosophy,

> The whole function of philosophy ought to be what definite difference it will make to you and to me . . . if this world formula or that would be the true one . . . at the outset, at least, [philosophy] stands for no particular results. It has no dogmas, and no doctrines save its methods.

Should we try to discover from James what the exact nature of this method might be, it is likely that we would find more than one source of ambiguity in his answer. The point is, however, that James had no tolerance for world systems as such, least of all for the kind of philosophy that the absolute idealism of Hegel represents.[15]

Expressed in its simplest terms, the main thesis of the second James reading, "The Will to Believe," is: Life is an ongoing affair and is filled with many uncertainties. Faced with life as you find it, you can, before saying "yes" to a challenge or a situation, either wait until you have fully understood it or commit yourself whether you fully understand it or not. To withhold consent on the grounds that you don't understand is to let life pass you by, and to fail to make the kind of decision that life demands. The question of having moral beliefs at all or of not having them "is decided by our will. . . . How can your pure intellect decide? If your heart does not *want* a world of moral reality, your head will never assuredly make you believe in one."

Truth, in the sense in which it matters most and in which it directly affects our lives, is not something for us to discover full-blown; *truth is what we make it to be,* and a decision is true if the commitment we make renders our lives richer and more meaningful. Thus, only if a proposition is such as to reach into our lives in some significant way can we say that it is a "live" hypothesis. There is no point, as James sees it, in quarreling over meaningless issues or items of past concern.

Difficult as it is to make a summary evaluation of "The Will to Believe," this much can be said: There is a profound element of truth in James's position, and the need for commitment is a discovery that James

---

[15] James's protest against Hegel is equally as vigorous as that of Kierkegaard. Hegel, in James's view, is the "great de-realizer of the only world we feel at home in."

made considerably before the development of existentialism as we know it today. Even so, James had his critics, like Santayana, and their principal complaint was that once James had gotten hold of a truth, he had the habit of stretching it to the breaking point. It is against this background of criticism that the reader, however prepared he might be to accept the positive insights of James, might do well to detach from them whatever exaggeration they contain.[16]

Dewey: Man as Unified Organism

Although James holds an important position in the development of American philosophy, John Dewey, despite his recent vintage, is generally acknowledged as the greatest classical figure in American thought. The following readings include two of Dewey's essays, which represent only a fragment of his total work but are typical of his overall point of view.

The leading characteristic of Dewey's *Weltanschauung* is its radically evolutionary emphasis. In fact, a substantial measure of Dewey's criticism is directed against the "older" traditional metaphysics that in Dewey's understanding of it is based on a static conception of both man and the universe. The role of the human intelligence is not to construct "wholesale" types of philosophies, but to get man into a working relationship with his environment. The human intelligence is too much a part of the evolutionary process to enable man by means of his intelligence to transcend it. The following paragraph by Sellars expertly sums up this aspect of Dewey's thought:

> John Dewey, who was to exert such a prolonged influence on American thought, was early trained in Kant and Hegel and only slowly departed from them, partly under the stimulus of William James and partly because of the impact of Darwinian thought. He began to emphasize the role of reflection and of problem-solving. He became persuaded that the job of human thought was not to reproduce a cosmic pattern in a constitutive way but to handle situations as these confronted man. Ideas, he came to hold, were instruments in such adjustments. Experience was something to be *reconstituted*. There was nothing beyond experience, nothing transcendental to be mirrored in thought. Thinking was forward-looking, an affair of plans and projects. Clearly, this is a form of activism and it did agree with the American temperament. American culture is usually regarded

---

[16] Take, for example, James's contention that God exists for me as long as the ideal of God makes a real difference in my life. The question still remains: Does God really exist or not, that is, independently of any commitment that I or anyone else makes or fails to make? In spite of the bold assertions of James's pragmatism, metaphysical questions like this are unavoidable, and perhaps not nearly as meaningless as both Peirce and James often assert them to be.

as pragmatic; and James and Dewey are considered its spokesmen. And there is a great deal of truth in this assumption.[17]

Any attempt, therefore, to produce a "spectator" view of reality—of the sort that would disregard man's role as a participant in the evolutionary process—is both futile and irrelevant.

As James has already pointed out, man's work is cut out for him insofar as he should occupy himself in the construction of fruitful or, in James's terminology, live hypotheses, not of idle speculations, regardless of their value from a purely esthetic point of view. Only live hypotheses are relevant because they relate to the ongoing flow of life, to those purposes that are meaningful to man. The purposes themselves, according to Dewey, should not be mistaken for goals that are prescribed from above and without, nor are they a built-in feature of the nature of man himself.[18] Rather the goals of life are nothing less than those that man, living in society, prescribes for himself. This means that every society should, through the instrumentality of its own experience, determine which kind of purposes it will serve. Man for Dewey is an organism constantly interacting with other organisms in his environment to direct both the organisms and the environment to his own ends.

Lest it be thought that Dewey is an old-fashioned individualist of the laissez-faire school (like the political economists Thomas Robert Malthus, David Ricardo, and Adam Smith), we point to the radically social nature of Dewey's philosophy, which is, above all else, a philosophy of social reconstruction, not a metaphysics in the classical sense of the term. On this point I would like to suggest that a strong similarity exists between Dewey and Marx. Marx had said at one time that prior to his own contribution the philosophers of the world had only *theorized* about reality, instead of changing it. Much the same insistence is to be found in Dewey; although for him philosophy is definitely not an instrument of propaganda, it is an instrument for social reconstruction and reform. The philosopher, rather than remaining transcendentally aloof in a preserve of his own, can serve society in a pragmatic way by giving direction to the work of social reform.[19]

---

[17] Sellars, p. 320.

[18] On this point one can clearly see a radical point of contrast between Dewey's position and that of scholastic realism. In the realism of the perennial philosophy, which stems from the positions of Aristotle and Aquinas, there is a fundamental element of stability within human nature, a stability that is characterized by a recognition of man's having a common nature, a common end, and a common ability to know something about this nature through the power of abstraction and judgment. Both the evolutionary naturalism of Dewey and modern existentialism are oriented in the direction of a denial of these fundamental claims. For Dewey no common ends exist other than those that men in society agree upon for themselves.

[19] Thus, "Philosophy must in time become a method of locating and interpreting the more serious of the conflicts that occur in life, and a method of projecting ways for dealing with them: *a method of moral and political diagnosis.*" ("The Influence of Darwinism." Italics added.)

In the light of all this, it is understandable that Dewey should have dedicated himself thoroughly to the work of educational reform. Education in Dewey's opinion is the prime instrument for bringing about those changes necessary for the progress of mankind, whether they be in economics, politics, law, or other realms. So that society will not perpetuate the mistakes of the past, it must provide enlightened guidance for its youth, and this can only be accomplished by a constant spirit of educational reform.

The spirit of change and flux that characterizes Dewey's entire outlook on man is forcefully presented in the essay entitled "The Influence of Darwinism." Even a casual reading of this essay will leave no doubt in the mind of the reader that Dewey is on the side of Darwin, and not of Aristotle. The entire first part of the essay is a polemic against any view of man that would regard him as a static essence, as though human nature were in no significant way subject to radical modification and change. To Dewey man is not a "species" but an organism that develops its ends and goals. Dewey rejects any attempt on the part of traditional philosophy to prescribe for man any overall purpose of life, or to say that all men have the same final goal. All goals are tentative, and man, in the course of the evolutionary changes he undergoes, prescribes his own goals. Evolution need not be mechanistic; however, it would be wrong to imagine from Dewey's point of view that it is teleological in the classical sense of the term. Purpose, like intelligence, is an outgrowth of nature, not a part of its original equipment.

Dewey believed that the methods of philosophy should parallel in every important respect the methods of the physical and biological sciences; this is the whole burden of the second essay, "The Supremacy of Method." Dewey makes it clear that man can successfully liberate himself from his prejudices and superstitions if he becomes empirically minded, like the scientists. Nature is regarded less with an attitude of wonder (in the Aristotelian sense) than with one of inquiry, and natural phenomena no longer take on the characteristic of ends but of means—means for human control. They become *instrumental* (in the way that human intelligence is instrumental) to the purpose of subjugating nature in its raw state to distinctively human ends. There is, as Dewey expresses it, "a change from knowing as an esthetic enjoyment of . . . nature regarded as a work of divine nature, to knowing as a means of secular control."

The reader is invited to examine whatever element of truth, falsity, or exaggeration is latent in Dewey's pragmatic interpretation of knowledge, as shown in the above paragraph. For example, he may very well be tempted to ask whether it is the *failure* of modern man to enjoy nature and—more importantly—his fellow man for what they are in themselves that has led to an attitude of mind that we might call pan-pragmatism. Perhaps Dewey is too quick to dismiss the value of a contemplative kind of knowledge— precisely, the art of knowing and loving things and persons for their intrinsic worth, not for any utilitarian end. Further, much of the protest of modern existentialism is against the idea of regarding things from the standpoint of the scientist. It is questions and issues of this sort that the reader must examine in order to make a proper assessment of the overall value of Dewey's pragmatism and his social instrumentalism. All philosophy must ultimately involve a personal evaluation on the part of the individual who learns it.

Santayana: Man in a Changing Environment

Our last reading selection is by George Santayana (1863–1952). Taken from *The Life of Reason,* it deals with the problem of flux and constancy in human nature. To appreciate this essay or any other significant aspect of Santayana's work, one must understand something of both his personal background and his leading philosophical ideas. Let it be said first of all that the classification of Santayana as an American philosopher is in need of serious qualifications, which Santayana made as follows:

> The limitations of my Americanism are easily told. I have no American or English blood; I was not born in the United States; I have never become an American citizen; as soon as I was my own master I spent every free winter and almost every summer in Europe; I never married or kept house or expected to end my days in America. This sense of belonging elsewhere, or rather of not belonging where I lived, was nothing anomalous or unpleasant to me but, as it were, hereditary. My father had done his lifework in a remote colony; my mother had had no home as a child, her first husband had been of one nationality and her second husband of another, and she had always been a stranger, like me, wherever she was. *This is rather consonant with my philosophy and may have helped to form it.* It is not a thing I regret. So that my intentional detachability from America is balanced by my equal detachability from every other place. . . . Yet as this book shows, my intellectual relations and labors still unite me closely with America; and *it is as an American writer that I must be counted, if I am counted at all.*[20] [Italics added.]

Santayana regards himself as a naturalist, but he is not either by temperamental affinity or doctrine a pragmatist. In fact, the element of pragmatism in the thought of both James and Dewey occasioned several attacks from him. Pragmatism, both as a habit of mind and as a philosophical doctrine, was directly contrary to what he regards as the "life of reason."

Even the proposition that Santayana is a naturalist is one that must be carefully explained lest we be led to think that the naturalism of Santayana is of one accord with that of Dewey. Both thinkers share the basic postulate of all strictly naturalistic belief that nothing outside the realm of nature

---

[20] George Santayana, "Apologia Pro Mente Sua," in *The Philosophy of George Santayana,* ed. by Paul Schilpp (Evanston, Ill.: Northwestern University Press, 1940), pp. 602–03.

exists. As evident in his essay "Flux and Constancy in Human Nature," Santayana holds in common with Dewey a fundamental commitment to an evolutionism in which man is totally the result of natural changes. Neither Dewey nor Santayana would admit that there is a higher principle in man, such as the soul, that is the result of some principle outside the evolutionary flux.

Beyond this point, however, the contrast between Dewey's naturalism and Santayana's becomes very sharp. Perhaps the sharpest point of contrast is Dewey's preoccupation with the scientific and the practical, and Santayana's with the literary, the poetic, and the esthetic. If there is any characteristic that most aptly sets off Santayana's naturalism from any other form, it is precisely his insistence upon the reality of "essences" that man through his esthetic faculties can contemplate and enjoy. By essences Santayana has in mind *anything* that the mind or imagination can propose to itself and that can function either as an ideal or as an object of contemplation. Strange as it appears, this seemingly idealistic bent of Santayana's philosophy is to be construed within the framework of a materialism that recognizes matter in motion to be the only existential principle of reality. This is to say that matter alone exists or that existence is a property of matter. The other and complementary side of Santayana's philosophy is his doctrine that values belong to essence. This latter claim is not to be taken as a denial of values, especially moral, spiritual, and esthetic ones, but rather an attempt to locate them within nature, not as physical objects but as contemplated essences within the mind of man. Such in its basic perspective is Santayana's doctrine of essence.

In summary, Santayana's naturalism is very close to idealism, but to an idealism that differs from that of any philosophers for whom there exists outside of nature a distinct and independent ontological reality, such as the reality of God. All "realities" that are the object of reason and imagination "exist," but they exist, as we would say now, phenomenologically as essences. In other words, they are constructions of reason and imagination, though Santayana would forbid us to say mere construction, since it is the essence that gives life its meaning and provides man with the basic ideals he seeks.

A sharp contrast exists between Santayana's doctrine of essence and any form of existentialism or realism that would require the object of human values to have a basis in something other than the construction of the mind or the imagination. In the area of religion, to which Santayana devotes a good measure of his writing, it is a mistake to take as real, that is, beyond the realm of essence, the object of one's religious belief. It is enough that the object exist in the mind or heart of the believer as an essence. To a realist, on the contrary, the object of religious belief must, to save it from becoming an illusion, exist independent of the mind and intention of the believer. In this latter view, the object of belief is not constituted by the intention of the believer but rather by the objective existence of the reality in which one believes, and it is precisely this understanding of the nature of religious belief that Santayana denies.

According to Santayana everything that is ideal has a natural basis, and everything natural has an ideal fulfillment. In the realm of morals, ideals, and spiritual values—whatever pertains to the life of reason—everything finds its matrix in the content of nature and in no other source. Beyond this, however, nature as reinterpreted by the mind and emotions of man, that is, nature beyond its raw physical status, has a higher fulfillment in the realm of essence. No doubt many critics would question whether fulfillment in the realm of essence is real fulfillment, but that question would take us beyond an expository analysis of Santayana's position.

The point, then, of Santayana's essay, "Flux and Constancy in Human Nature," is to show how the life of reason can thrive within the context of evolutionary materialism, as Santayana interprets this term. To him it is a mistake to suppose that human nature is an unaltered species. It is equally wrong to imagine that reason should be at odds with itself in a world of universal change, "since human nature has for its core the substance of nature at large."

Perhaps no single statement better epitomizes Santayana's overall view of man and his place in nature than the following from his essay:

> [Human nature] varies indefinitely in its historical manifestation and fades into what, as a matter of natural history, might no longer be termed human. At each moment it has its fixed and determinate entelechy, the ideal of that being's life, based on his instincts, summed up in his character, brought to a focus in his reflection, and shared by all who have attained or may inherit his organization. His perceptive and reasoning faculties are parts of human nature, as embodied in him; all objects of belief or desire, with all standards of justice and duty which he can possibly acknowledge, are transcripts of it, conditioned by it, and justifiable only as expressions of its inherent tendencies.

Conclusion

The purpose of this essay has been largely restricted (1) to an examination of the historical background of pragmatism and naturalism in America, and (2) to an expository analysis of the central doctrines of each of the men in relation to the readings provided in the text. Of necessity, such an analysis is incomplete and leaves open the need for a critical examination of each of the positions outlined. I use the term "critical" in the Greek sense, meaning the need to judge and evaluate the comparative points of strength and of weakness with reference to a given doctrine. While criticism in this sense would take us beyond the scope of this essay, the need for such criticism should not escape the attention of the reader as the role of philosophy is to understand and to evaluate. Regardless of any position taken by any one philosopher, the ultimate concern of the student should be the discovery of truth for its own sake.

Glossary

BELIEF:
In Peirce's doctrine, anything that appeases the irritation of doubt and establishes a guideline for action.

CLASSICAL, MODERN IDEALISM:
Position held by those thinkers from Descartes on who assume that ideas and sensations (rather than objects) are the direct and immediate object of experience.

NATURALISM:
Basic position that holds that nature as a spatiotemporal system is the whole of reality and that man himself is totally the result of the development of an evolutionary process in nature.

PRAGMATISM:
Theory of knowledge in which the meaning or truth of an idea is equivalent to the consequences (actual or possible) to which that idea leads.

RADICAL EMPIRICISM:
Term used by James to designate his own position as one that insists on fidelity to the immediate source of experience in contrast to the empiricism of classic British thought such as that of Locke and Hume.

REALISM:
In its traditional sense any theory of knowledge that insists on the objective basis in the outside world for the human understanding both of essence and existence.

SCIENTIFIC METHOD:
Any means of developing knowledge through the use of observation and experiment.

TELEOLOGY:
Doctrine held by the scholastics and denied by Dewey that natural entities are possessed of certain fixed ends or goals.

THINKING:
In Dewey's philosophy any activity of the mind that is a response to the doubtful as such.

WILL TO BELIEVE:
James's term for the inherent tendency and need in human nature to adopt a belief even in the absence of any compelling evidence for its acceptance.

Charles Sanders Peirce

CHARLES SANDERS PEIRCE, the founder of American pragmatism, was born in Cambridge, Massachusetts, in 1839. In his youth he had the benefit of personal contact with William James, Oliver Wendell Holmes, and other important figures. He received his formal training at Harvard University in mathematics and physics. He held one academic position as an instructor in logic at Johns Hopkins from 1879 to 1884, but spent most of his years as a physicist for the U.S. Coastal and Geodetic Survey. In 1890 he retired to Milford, Pennsylvania, where he devoted his time to philosophy. His works are contained in the *Collected Papers of Charles Sanders Peirce* (8 vols., 1931–58), edited by Charles Hartshorne, Paul Weiss, and Arthur W. Burks. He died at Cambridge in 1914.

How to Make Our Ideas Clear

I

Whoever has looked into a modern treatise on logic of the common sort, will doubtless remember the two distinctions between *clear* and *obscure* conceptions, and between *distinct* and *confused* conceptions. They have lain in the books now for nigh two centuries, unimproved and unmodified, and are generally reckoned by logicians as among the gems of their doctrine.

A clear idea is defined as one which is so apprehended that it will be recognized wherever it is met with, and so that no other will be mistaken for it. If it fails of this clearness, it is said to be obscure.

This is rather a neat bit of philosophical terminology; yet, since it is clearness that they were defining, I wish the logicians had made their definition a little more plain. Never to fail to recognize an idea, and under no circumstances to mistake another for it, let it come in how recondite a form it may, would indeed imply such prodigious force and clearness of intellect

From Charles Sanders Peirce, "How to Make Our Ideas Clear," *Popular Science Monthly,* XII (1878). It is the second of the six papers Peirce published in that periodical during 1877 and 1878 under the general title "Illustrations of the Logic of Science." The paper has been reprinted many times and is included in the *Collected Papers of Charles Sanders Peirce, 1931–58.*

as is seldom met in this world. On the other hand, merely to have such an acquaintance with the idea as to have become familiar with it, and to have lost all hesitancy in recognizing it in ordinary cases, hardly seems to deserve the name of clearness of apprehension, since after all it only amounts to a subjective feeling of mastery which may be entirely mistaken. I take it, however, that when the logicians speak of "clearness," they mean nothing more than such a familiarity with an idea, since they regard the quality as but a small merit, which needs to be supplemented by another, which they call *distinctness*.

A distinct idea is defined as one which contains nothing which is not clear. This is technical language; by the *contents* of an idea logicians understand whatever is contained in its definition. So that an idea is *distinctly* apprehended, according to them, when we can give a precise definition of it, in abstract terms. Here the professional logicians leave the subject; and I would not have troubled the reader with what they have to say, if it were not such a striking example of how they have been slumbering through ages of intellectual activity, listlessly disregarding the enginery of modern thought, and never dreaming of applying its lessons to the improvement of logic. It is easy to show that the doctrine that familiar use and abstract distinctness make the perfection of apprehension has its only true place in philosophies which have long been extinct; and it is now time to formulate the method of attaining to a more perfect clearness of thought, such as we see and admire in the thinkers of our own time.

When Descartes set about the reconstruction of philosophy, his first step was to (theoretically) permit skepticism and to discard the practice of the schoolmen of looking to authority as the ultimate source of truth. That done, he sought a more natural fountain of true principles, and professed to find it in the human mind; thus passing, in the directest way, from the method of authority to that of apriority, as described in my first paper. Self-consciousness was to furnish us with our fundamental truths, and to decide what was agreeable to reason. But since, evidently, not all ideas are true, he was led to note, as the first condition of infallibility, that they must be clear. The distinction between an idea *seeming* clear and really being so, never occurred to him. Trusting to introspection, as he did, even for a knowledge of external things, why should he question its testimony in respect to the contents of our own minds? But then, I suppose, seeing men, who seemed to be quite clear and positive, holding opposite opinions upon fundamental principles, he was further led to say that clearness of ideas is not sufficient, but that they need also to be distinct, i.e., to have nothing unclear about them. What he probably meant by this (for he did not explain himself with precision) was, that they must sustain the test of dialectical examination; that they must not only seem clear at the outset, but that discussion must never be able to bring to light points of obscurity connected with them.

Such was the distinction of Descartes, and one sees that it was precisely on the level of his philosophy. It was somewhat developed by Leibnitz. This great and singular genius was as remarkable for what he failed to see as for what he saw. That a piece of mechanism could not do work perpetually without beng fed with power in some form, was a thing perfectly apparent to him; yet he did not understand that the machinery of the mind can only transform knowledge, but never originate it, unless it be fed with facts of observation. He thus missed the most essential point of the Cartesian philosophy, which is, that to accept propositions which seem perfectly evident to us is a thing which, whether it be logical or illogical, we cannot help doing. Instead of regarding the matter in this way, he sought to reduce the first principles of science to formulas which cannot be denied without self-contradiction, and was apparently unaware of the great difference between his position and that of Descartes. So he reverted to the old formalities of logic, and, above all, abstract definitions played a great part in his philosophy. It was quite natural, therefore, that on observing that the method of Descartes labored under the difficulty that we may seem to ourselves to have clear apprehensions of ideas which in truth are very hazy, no better remedy occurred to him than to require an abstract definition of every important term. Accordingly, in adopting the distinction of *clear* and *distinct* notions, he described the latter quality as the clear apprehension of everything contained in the definition; and the books have ever since copied his words. There is no danger that his chimerical scheme will ever again be overvalued. Nothing new can ever be learned by analyzing definitions. Nevertheless, our existing beliefs can be set in order by this process, and order is an essential element of intellectual economy, as of every other. It may be acknowledged, therefore, that the books are right in making familiarity with a notion the first step toward clearness of apprehension, and the defining of it the second. But in omitting all mention of any higher perspicuity of thought, they simply mirror a philosophy which was exploded a hundred years ago. That much-admired "ornament of logic"—the doctrine of clearness and distinctness—may be pretty enough, but it is high time to relegate to our cabinet of curiosities the antique *bijou,* and to wear about us something better adapted to modern uses.

The very first lesson that we have a right to demand that logic shall teach us is, how to make our ideas clear; and a most important one it is, depreciated only by minds who stand in need of it. To know what we think, to be masters of our own meaning, will make a solid foundation for great and weighty thought. It is most easily learned by those whose ideas are meagre and restricted; and far happier they than such as wallow helplessly in a rich mud of conceptions. A nation, it is true, may, in the course of generations, overcome the disadvantage of an excessive wealth of language and its natural concomitant, a vast, unfathomable deep of ideas. We may see it in history, slowly perfecting its literary forms, sloughing at length its metaphysics, and, by virtue of the untirable patience which is often a compensation, attaining great excellence in every branch of mental acquirement. The page of history is not yet unrolled which is to tell us whether such a people will or will not in the long run prevail over one whose ideas (like the words of their language) are few, but which possesses a wonderful mastery over those which it has. For an individual, however, there can be no question that a few clear ideas are worth more than many confused ones. A young man would hardly be persuaded to sacrifice the greater part of his thoughts to save the rest; and the muddled head is the least apt to see the necessity of such a sacrifice. Him we can usually only commiserate, as a person with a congenital defect. Time will help him, but intellectual maturity with regard to clearness comes rather late, an unfortunate arrangement of Nature, inasmuch as clearness is of less use to a man settled in life, whose errors have in great measure had their effect, than it would be to one whose path lies before him. It is terrible to see how a single unclear idea, a single formula without meaning, lurking in a young man's head, will sometimes act like an obstruction of inert matter in an artery, hindering the nutrition of the brain, and condemning its victim to pine away in the fullness of his intellectual vigor and in the midst of intellectual plenty. Many a man has cherished for years as his hobby some vague shadow of an idea, too meaningless to be positively false; he has, nevertheless, passionately loved it, has made it his companion by day and by night, and has given to it his strength and his life, leaving all other occupations for its sake, and in short has lived with it and for it, until it has become, as it were, flesh of his flesh and bone of his bone; and then he has waked up some bright morning to find it gone, clean vanished away like the beautiful Melusina of the fable, and the essence of his life gone with it. I have myself known such a man; and who can tell how many histories of circle-squarers, metaphysicians, astrologers, and what not, may not be told in the old German story?

II

The principles set forth in the first of these papers lead, at once, to a method of reaching a clearness of thought of a far higher grade than the "distinctness" of the logicians. We have there found that the action of thought is excited by the irritation of doubt, and ceases when belief is attained; so that the production of belief is the sole function of thought. All these words, however, are too strong for my purpose. It is as if I had described the phenomena as they appear under a mental microscope. Doubt and Belief, as the words are commonly employed, relate to religious or other grave discussions. But here I use them to designate the starting of any question, no matter how small or how great, and the resolution of it. If, for instance, in a horse-car, I pull out my purse and find a five-cent nickel and five coppers, I decide, while my hand is going to the purse, in which way I will pay my fare. To call such a question Doubt, and my decision Belief, is certainly to use words very disproportionate to the occasion. To speak of such a doubt as causing an irritation which needs to be appeased, suggests a temper which is uncomfortable to the verge of insanity. Yet, looking at the matter minutely, it must be admitted that, if there is the least hesitation as to whether I shall pay the five coppers or the nickel (as there will be sure to be, unless I act from some previously contracted habit in the matter), though irritation is too strong a word, yet I am excited to such small mental activity as may be necessary to deciding how I shall act. Most frequently doubts arise from some indecision, however momentary, in our action. Sometimes it is not so. I have, for example, to wait in a railway-station, and to pass the time I read the advertisements on the walls, I compare the advantages of different trains and different routes which I never expect to take, merely fancying myself to be in a state of hesitancy, because I am bored with having nothing to trouble me. Feigned hesitancy, whether feigned for mere amusement or with a lofty purpose, plays a great part in the production of scientific inquiry. However the doubt may originate, it stimulates the mind to an activity which may be slight or energetic, calm or turbulent. Images pass rapidly through consciousness, one incessantly melting into another, until at last, when all is over—it may be in a fraction of a second, in an hour, or after long years—we find ourselves decided as to how we should act under such circumstances as those which occasioned our hesitation. In other words, we have attained belief.

In this process we observe two sorts of elements of consciousness, the distinction between which may best be made clear by means of an illustration. In a piece of music there are the separate notes, and there is the air. A single tone may be prolonged for an hour or a day, and it exists as perfectly in each second of that time as in the whole taken together; so that, as long as it is sounding, it might be present to a sense from which everything in the past was as completely absent as the future itself. But it is different with the air, the performance of which occupies a certain time, during the portions of which only portions of it are played. It consists in an orderliness in the succession of sounds which strike the ear at different times; and to perceive it there must be some continuity of consciousness which makes the events of a lapse of time present to us. We certainly only perceive the air by hearing the separate notes; yet we cannot be said to directly hear it, for we hear only what is present at the instant, and an orderliness of succession cannot exist in an instant. These two sorts of objects, what we are *immediately* conscious of and what we are *mediately* conscious of, are found in all consciousness. Some elements (the sensations) are completely present at every instant so long as they last, while others (like thought) are actions having beginning, middle, and end, and consist in a congruence in the succession of sensations which flow through the mind. They cannot be immediately present to us, but must cover some portion of the past or future. Thought is a thread of melody running through the succession of our sensations.

We may add that just as a piece of music may be written in parts, each part having its own air, so various systems of relationship of succession subsist together between the same sensations. These different systems are distinguished by having different motives, ideas, or functions. Thought is only one such system, for its sole motive, idea, and function, is to produce belief, and whatever does not concern that purpose belongs to some other system of relations. The action of thinking may incidentally have other results; it may serve to amuse us, for example, and among *dillettanti* it is not rare to find those who have so perverted thought to the purposes of pleasure that it seems to vex them to think that the questions upon which they delight to exercise it may ever get finally settled; and a positive discovery which takes a favorite subject out of the arena of literary debate is met with ill-concealed dislike. This disposition is the very debauchery of thought. But the soul and meaning of thought, abstracted from the other elements which accompany it, though it may be voluntarily thwarted, can never be made to direct itself toward anything but the production of belief. Thought in action has for its only possible motive the attainment of thought at rest; and whatever does not refer to belief is no part of the thought itself.

And what, then, is belief? It is the demi-cadence which closes a musical phrase in the symphony of our intellectual life. We have seen that it has just three properties: First, it is something that we are aware of; second, it appeases the irritation of doubt; and, third it involves the establishment in our nature of a rule of action, or, say, for short, a *habit*. As it appeases the irritation of doubt, which is the motive for thinking, thought relaxes, and comes to rest for a moment when belief is reached. But, since belief is a rule for action, the application of which involves further doubt and further thought, at the same time that it is a stopping-place, it is also a new starting-place for thought. That is why I have permitted myself to call it thought at rest, although thought is essentially an action. The *final* upshot of thinking is the exercise of volition, and of this thought no longer forms a part; but belief is only a stadium of mental action, an effect upon our nature due to thought, which will influence future thinking.

The essence of belief is the establishment of a habit, and different beliefs are distinguished by the different modes of action to which they give rise. If beliefs do not differ in this respect, if they appease the same doubt by producing the same rule of action, then no mere differences in the manner of consciousness of them can make them different beliefs, any more than playing a tune in different keys is playing different tunes. Imaginary distinctions are often drawn between beliefs which differ only in their mode of expression;—the wrangling which ensues is real enough, however. To believe that any objects are arranged as in Fig. 1, and to believe that they are arranged [as] in Fig. 2, are one and the same belief; yet it is conceivable that a man should assert one proposition and deny the other. Such false distinctions do as much harm as the confusion of beliefs really different, and are among the pitfalls of which we ought constantly to beware, especially when we are upon metaphysical ground. One singular deception of this sort, which often occurs, is to mistake the sensation produced by our own unclearness of thought for a character of the object we are thinking. Instead of perceiving that the obscurity is purely subjective, we fancy that we contemplate a quality of the object which is essentially mysterious; and if our conception be afterward presented to us in a clear form we do not recognize it as the same, owing to the absence of the feeling of unintelligibility. So long as this deception lasts, it obviously puts an impassable barrier in the way of perspicuous thinking; so that it equally inter-

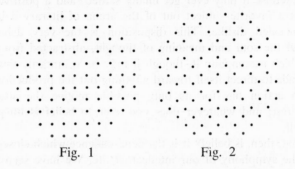

Fig. 1   Fig. 2

ests the opponents of rational thought to perpetuate it, and its adherents to guard against it.

Another such deception is to mistake a mere difference in the grammatical construction of two words for a distinction between the ideas they express. In this pedantic age, when the general mob of writers attend so much more to words than to things, this error is common enough. When I just said that thought is an *action,* and that it consists in a *relation,* although a person performs an action but not a relation, which can only be the result of an action, yet there was no inconsistency in what I said, but only a grammatical vagueness.

From all these sophisms we shall be perfectly safe so long as we reflect that the whole function of thought is to produce habits of action; and that whatever there is connected with a thought, but irrelevant to its purpose, is an accretion to it, but no part of it. If there be a unity among our sensations which has no reference to how we shall act on a given occasion, as when we listen to a piece of music, why we do not call that thinking. To develop its meaning, we have, therefore, simply to determine what habits it produces, for what a thing means is simply what habits it involves. Now, the identity of a habit depends on how it might lead us to act, not merely under such circumstances as are likely to arise, but under such as might possibly occur, no matter how improbable they may be. What the habit is depends on *when* and *how* it causes us to act. As for the *when,* every stimulus to action is derived from perception; as for the *how,* every purpose of action is to produce some sensible result. Thus, we come down to what is tangible and practical, as the root of every real distinction of thought, no matter how subtle it may be; and there is no distinction of meaning so fine as to consist in anything but a possible difference of practice.

. . .

It appears, then, that the rule for attaining the third grade of clearness of apprehension is as follows: Consider what effects, which might conceivably have practical bearings, we conceive the object of our conception to have. Then, our conception of these effects is the whole of our conception of the object.

III

Let us illustrate this rule by some examples; and, to begin with the simplest one possible, let us ask what we mean by calling a thing *hard*. Evidently that it will not be scratched by many other substances. The whole conception of this quality, as of every other, lies in its conceived effects. There is absolutely no difference between a hard thing and a soft thing so long as they are not brought to the test. Suppose, then, that a diamond could be crystallized in the midst of a cushion of soft cotton, and should remain there until it was finally burned up. Would it be false to say that that diamond was soft? This seems a foolish question, and would be so, in fact, except in the realm of logic. There such questions are often of the greatest utility as serving to bring logical principles into sharper relief than real discussions ever could. In studying logic we must not put them aside with hasty answers, but must consider them with attentive care, in order to make out the principles involved. We may, in the present case, modify our question, and ask what prevents us from saying that all hard bodies remain perfectly soft until they are touched, when their hardness increases with the pressure until they are scratched. Reflection will show that the reply is this: where would be no *falsity* in such modes of speech. They would involve a modification of our present usage of speech with regard to the words hard and soft, but not of their meanings. For they represent no fact to be different from what it is; only they involve arrangements of facts which would be exceedingly maladroit. This leads us to remark that the question of what would occur under circumstances which do not actually arise is not a question of fact, but only of the most perspicuous arrangement of them. For example, the question of free-will and fate in its simplest form, stripped of verbiage, is something like this; I have done something of which I am ashamed; could I, by an effort of the will, have resisted the temptation, and done otherwise? The philosophical reply is, that this is not a question of fact, but only of the arrangement of facts. Arranging them so as to exhibit what is particularly pertinent to my question—namely, that I ought to blame myself for having done wrong—it is perfectly true to say that, if I had willed to do otherwise than I did, I should have done otherwise. On the other hand, arranging the facts so as to exhibit another important consideration, it is equally true that, when a temptation has once been allowed to work, it will, if it has a certain force, produce its effect, let me struggle how I may. There is no objection to a contradiction in what would result from a false supposition. The *reductio ad absurdum* consists in showing that contradictory results would follow from a hypothesis which is consequently judged to be false. Many questions are involved in the free-will discussion, and I am far from desiring to say that both sides are equally right. On the contrary, I am of opinion that one side denies important facts, and that the other does not. But what I do say is, that the above single question was the origin of the whole doubt; that, had it not been for this question, the controversy would never have arisen; and that this question is perfectly solved in the manner which I have indicated.

. . .

IV

Let us now approach the subject of logic, and consider a conception which particularly concerns it, that of *reality*. Taking clearness in the sense of familiarity, no idea could be clearer than this. Every child uses it with perfect confidence, never dreaming that he does not understand it. As for clearness in its second grade, however, it would probably puzzle most men, even among those of a reflective turn of mind, to give an abstract definition of the real. Yet such definition may perhaps be reached by considering the points of difference between reality and its opposite, fiction. A figment is a product of somebody's imagination; it has such characters as his thought impresses upon it. That whose characters are independent of how you or I think is an external reality. There are, however, phenomena within our own minds, dependent upon our thought, which are at the same time real in the sense that we really think them. But though their characters depend on how we think, they do not depend on what we think those characters to be. Thus, a dream has a real existence as a mental phenomenon, if somebody has really dreamt it; that he dreamt so and so, does not depend on what anybody thinks was dreamt, but is completely independent of all opinion on the subject. On the other hand, considering, not the fact of dreaming, but the thing dreamt, it retains its peculiarities by virtue of no other fact than that it was dreamt to possess them. Thus we may define the real as that whose characters are independent of what anybody may think them to be.

But, however satisfactory such a definition may be found, it would be a great mistake to suppose that it makes the idea of reality perfectly clear. Here, then, let us apply our rules. According to them, reality, like every other quality, consists in the peculiar sensible effects which things partaking of it produce. The only effect which real things have is to cause belief, for all the sensations which they excite emerge into consciousness in the form of beliefs. The question therefore is, how is true belief (or belief in the real) distinguished from false belief (or belief in fiction). Now, as we have seen in the former paper, the ideas of truth and falsehood, in their full development, appertain exclusively to the scientific method of settling opinion. A person who arbitrarily chooses the propositions which he will adopt can use the word truth only to emphasize the expression of his determination to hold on to his choice.

. . .

Different minds may set out with the most antagonistic views, but the progress of investigation carries them by a force outside of themselves to one and the same conclusion. This activity of thought by which we are carried, not where we wish, but to a foreordained goal, is like the operation of destiny. No modification of the point of view taken, no selection of other facts for study, no natural bent of mind even, can enable a man to escape the predestinate opinion. This great law is embodied in the conception of truth and reality. The opinion which is fated [1] to be ultimately agreed to by all who investigate, is what we mean by the truth, and the object represented in this opinion is the real. That is the way I would explain reality.

But it may be said that this view is directly opposed to the abstract definition which we have given of reality, inasmuch as it makes the characters of the real to depend on what is ultimately thought about them. But the answer to this is that, on the one hand, reality is independent, not necessarily of thought in general, but only of what you or I or any finite number of men may think about it; and that, on the other hand, though the object of the final opinion depends on what that opinion is, yet what that opinion is does not depend on what you or I or any man thinks. Our perversity and that of others may indefinitely postpone the settlement of opinion; it might even conceivably cause an arbitrary proposition to be universally accepted as long as the human race should last. Yet even that would not change the nature of the belief, whch alone could be the result of investigation carried sufficiently far; and if, after the extinction of our race, another should arise with faculties and disposition for investigation, that true opinion must be the one which they would ultimately come to. "Truth crushed to earth shall rise again," and the opinion which would finally result from investigation does not depend on how anybody may actually think. But the reality of that which is real does depend on the real fact that investigation is destined to lead, at last, if continued long enough, to a belief in it.

But I may be asked what I have to say to all the minute facts of history, forgotten never to be recovered, to the lost books of the ancients, to the buried secrets.

> Full many a gem of purest ray serene
> The dark, unfathomed caves of ocean bear;
> Full many a flower is born to blush unseen,
> And waste its sweetness on the desert air.

---

[1] Fate means merely that which is sure to come true, and can nohow be avoided. It is a superstition to suppose that a certain sort of events are ever fated, and it is another to suppose that the word fate can never be freed from its superstitious taint. We are all fated to die. [C.S.P.]

Do these things not really exist because they are hopelessly beyond the reach of our knowledge? And then, after the universe is dead (according to the prediction of some scientists), and all life has ceased forever, will not the shock of atoms continue though there will be no mind to know it? To this I reply that, though in no possible state of knowledge can any number be great enough to express the relation between the amount of what rests unknown and the amount of the known, yet it is unphilosophical to suppose that, with regard to any given question (which has any clear meaning), investigation would not bring forth a solution of it, if it were carried far enough. Who would have said, a few years ago, that we could ever know of what substances stars are made whose light may have been longer in reaching us than the human race has existed? Who can be sure of what we shall not know in a few hundred years? Who can guess what would be the result of continuing the pursuit of science for ten thousand years, with the activity of the last hundred? And if it were to go on for a million, or a billion, or any number of years you please, how is it possible to say that there is any question which might not ultimately be solved?

But it may be objected, "Why make so much of these remote considerations, especially when it is your principle that only practical distinctions have a meaning?" Well, I must confess that it makes very little difference whether we say that a stone on the bottom of the ocean, in complete darkness, is brilliant or not—that is to say, that it *probably* makes no difference, remembering always that that stone *may* be fished up tomorrow. But that there are gems at the bottom of the sea, flowers in the untraveled desert, etc., are propositions which, like that about a diamond being hard when it is not pressed, concern much more the arrangement of our language than they do the meaning of our ideas.

It seems to me, however, that we have, by the application of our rule, reached so clear an apprehension of what we mean by reality, and of the fact which the idea rests on, that we should not, perhaps, be making a pretension so presumptuous as it would be singular, if we were to offer a metaphysical theory of existence for universal acceptance among those who employ the scientific method of fixing belief. However, as metaphysics is a subject much more curious than useful, the knowledge of which, like that of a sunken reef, serves chiefly to enable us to keep clear of it, I will not trouble the reader with any more Ontology at this moment. I have already been led much further into that path than I should have desired; and I have given the reader such a dose of mathematics, psychology, and all that is most abstruse, that I fear he may already have left me, and that what I am now writing is for the compositor and proof-reader exclusively. I trusted to the importance of the subject. There is no royal road to logic, and really valuable ideas can only be had at the price of close attention. But I know that in the matter of ideas the public prefer the cheap and nasty; and in my next paper I am going to return to the easily intelligible, and not wander from it again. The reader who has been at the pains of wading through this month's paper, shall be rewarded in the next one by seeing how beautifully what has been developed in this tedious way can be applied to the ascertainment of the rules of scientific reasoning.

We have, hitherto, not crossed the threshold of scientific logic. It is certainly important to know how to make our ideas clear, but they may be ever so clear without being true. How to make them so, we have next to study. How to give birth to those vital and procreative ideas which multiply into a thousand forms and diffuse themselves everywhere, advancing civilization and making the dignity of man, is an art not yet reduced to rules, but of the secret of which the history of science affords some hints.

QUESTIONS FOR STUDY AND DISCUSSION

1. Discuss and examine Peirce's account of Descartes' method of making ideas clear.
2. Discuss and examine the following statement of Peirce: "The action of thought is excited by the irritation of doubt, and ceases when belief is attained; so that the production of belief is the sole function of thought."
3. Explain Peirce's doctrine that different beliefs are distinguished by the different modes of action to which they give rise.
4. Do you agree with the author's position that the whole function of thought is to produce habits of action? Examine and discuss.
5. On the basis of Peirce's pragmatism, what is the criterion for differentiating one kind of philosophy from another?

William James

WILLIAM JAMES was born in New York City in 1842. Born into a distinguished family and brother of novelist Henry James, he was educated in England and on the Continent, as well as in the United States. James studied painting, chemistry, and comparative anatomy, and received a medical degree from Harvard in 1869. He also developed a strong interest in psychology and in 1876 organized the first laboratory of psychological research in the United States. In 1877 he began lecturing in philosophy and thirteen years later he published the famous *Principles of Psychology*. In 1902 James published his now famous *Varieties of Religious Experience*. His most noted work, *Pragmatism,* appeared in 1907, and his Hibbert Lectures at Oxford in 1908 were published under the title *A Pluralistic Universe* in 1909. James died at Chocorua, New Hampshire, in 1910.

What Pragmatism Means

Some years ago, being with a camping party in the mountains, I returned from a solitary ramble to find every one engaged in a ferocious metaphysical dispute. The *corpus* of the dispute was a squirrel—a live squirrel supposed to be clinging to one side of a tree-trunk; while over against the tree's opposite side a human being was imagined to stand. This human witness tries to get sight of the squirrel by moving rapidly round the tree, but no matter how fast he goes, the squirrel moves as fast in the opposite direction, and always keeps the tree between himself and the man, so that never a glimpse of him is caught. The resultant metaphysical problem now is this: *Does the man go round the squirrel or not?* He goes round the tree, sure enough, and the squirrel is on the tree; but does he go round the squirrel? In the unlimited leisure of the wilderness, discussion had been worn threadbare. Every one had taken sides, and was obstinate; and the numbers on both sides were even. Each side, when I appeared therefore appealed to me to make it a majority. Mindful of the scholastic adage that whenever you meet a contradiction you must make a distinction, I immediately sought and found one, as follows: "Which party is right," I said, "depends on what you *practically mean* by 'going round' the squirrel. If you mean passing from the north of him to the east, then to the south, then to the west, and then to the north of him again, obviously the man does go round him, for he occupies these successive positions. But if on the contrary you mean being first in front of him, then on the right of him, then behind him, then on his left, and finally in front again, it is quite as obvious that the man fails to go round him, for by the compensating movements the squirrel makes, he keeps his belly turned towards the man all the time, and his back turned away. Make the distinction, and there is no occasion for any farther dispute. You are both right and both wrong according as you conceive the verb 'to go round' in one practical fashion or the other."

Although one or two of the hotter disputants called my speech a shuffling evasion, saying they wanted no quibbling or scholastic hairsplitting, but meant just plain honest English 'round,' the majority seemed to think that the distinction had assuaged the dispute.

I tell this trivial anecdote because it is a peculiarly simple example of what I wish now to speak of as *the pragmatic method*. The pragmatic method is primarily a method of settling metaphysical disputes that otherwise might be interminable. Is the world one or many?—fated or free? —material or spiritual?—here are notions either of which may or may not hold good of the world; and disputes over such notions are unending. The pragmatic method in such cases is to try to interpret each notion by tracing its respective practical consequences. What difference would it practically make to any one if this notion rather than that notion were true? If no practical difference whatever can be traced, then the alternatives mean practically the same thing, and all dispute is idle. Whenever a dispute is serious, we ought to be able to show some practical difference that must follow from one side or the other's being right.

A glance at the history of the idea will show you still better what pragmatism means. The term is derived from the same Greek word *pragma,* meaning action, from which our words "practice" and "practical" come. It was first introduced into philosophy by Mr. Charles Peirce in 1878. In an article entitled "How to Make Our Ideas Clear" in the *Popular Science Monthly* for January of that year, Mr. Peirce, after pointing out that our beliefs are really rules for action, said that, to develop a thought's meaning, we need only determine what conduct it is fitted to produce: that conduct is for us its sole significance. And the tangible fact at the root of all our thought-distinctions, however subtle, is that there is no one of them so fine as to consist in anything but a possible difference of practice. To attain perfect clearness in our thoughts of an object, then, we need only consider what conceivable effects of a practical kind the object may involve—what sensations we are to expect from it, and what reactions we must prepare. Our conception of these effects, whether immediate or remote, is then for us the whole of our conception of the object, so far as that conception has positive significance at all.

This is the principle of Peirce, the principle of pragmatism. It lay entirely unnoticed by any one for twenty years, until I, in an address before Professor Howison's philosophical union at the University of California, brought it forward again and made a special application of it to religion. By that date (1898) the times seemed ripe for its reception. The word "pragmatism" spread, and at present it fairly spots the pages of the philosophic journals. On all hands we find the "pragmatic movement" spoken of, sometimes with respect, sometimes with contumely, seldom with clear understanding. It is evident that the term applies itself conveniently to a number of tendencies that hitherto have lacked a collective name, and that it has "come to stay."

To take in the importance of Peirce's principle, one must get accustomed to applying it to concrete cases. I found a few years ago that Ostwald, the illustrious Leipzig chemist, had been making perfectly distinct use of the principle of pragmatism in his lectures on the philosophy of science, though he had not called it by that name.

"All realities influence our practice," he wrote me, "and that influence is their meaning for us. I am accustomed to put questions to my classes in this way: In what respects would the world be different if this alternative or that were true? If I can find nothing that would become different, then the alternative has no sense."

That is, the rival views mean practically the same thing, and meaning, other than practical, there is for us none. Ostwald in a published lecture gives this example of what he means. Chemists have long wrangled over the inner constitution of certain bodies called "tautomerous." Their properties seemed equally consistent with the notion that an instable hydrogen atom oscillates inside of them, or that they are instable mixtures of two bodies. Controversy raged, but never was decided. "It would never have begun," says Ostwald, "if the combatants had asked themselves what particular experimental fact could have been made different by one or the other view being correct. For it would then have appeared that no difference of fact could possibly ensue; and the quarrel was as unreal as if, theorizing in primitive times about the raising of dough by yeast, one party should have invoked a 'brownie,' while another insisted on an 'elf' as the true cause of the phenomenon." [1]

It is astonishing to see how many philosophical disputes collapse into insignificance the moment you subject them to this simple test of tracing a concrete consequence. There can *be* no difference anywhere that doesn't *make* a difference elsewhere—no difference in abstract truth that doesn't express itself in a difference in concrete fact and in conduct consequent

---

[1] I find a still more radical pragmatism than Ostwald's in an address by Professor W. S. Franklin: "I think that the sickliest notion of physics, even if a student gets it, is that it is 'the science of masses, molecules, and the ether.' And I think that the healthiest notion, even if a student does not wholly get it, is that physics is the science of the ways of taking hold of bodies and pushing them!" (*Science*, January 2, 1903.) [W.J.]

upon the fact, imposed on somebody, somehow, somewhere, and somewhen. The whole function of philosophy ought to be to find out what definite difference it will make to you and me, at definite instants of our life, if this world-formula or that world-formula be the true one.

There is absolutely nothing new in the pragmatic method. Socrates was an adept at it. Aristotle used it methodically. Locke, Berkeley, and Hume made momentous contributions to truth by its means. Shadworth Hodgson keeps insisting that realities are only what they are "known as." But these forerunners of pragmatism used it in fragments: they were preluders only. Not until in our times has it generalized itself, become conscious of a universal mission, pretended to a conquering destiny. I believe in that destiny, and I hope I may end by inspiring you with my belief.

Pragmatism represents a perfectly familiar attitude in philosophy, the empiricist attitude, but it represents it, as it seems to me, both in a more radical and in a less objectionable form than it has ever yet assumed. A pragmatist turns his back resolutely and once for all upon a lot of inveterate habits dear to professional philosophers. He turns away from abstraction and insufficiency, from verbal solutions, from bad *a priori* reasons, from fixed principles, closed systems, and pretended absolutes and origins. He turns towards concreteness and adequacy, towards facts, towards action and towards power. That means the empiricist temper regnant and the rationalist temper sincerely given up. It means the open air and possibilities of nature, as against dogma, artificiality, and the pretense of finality in truth.

At the same time it does not stand for any special results. It is a method only. But the general triumph of that method would mean an enormous change in what I called in my last lecture the "temperament" of philosophy. Teachers of the ultra-rationalistic type would be frozen out, much as the courtier type is frozen out in republics, as the ultramontane type of priest is frozen out in protestant lands. Science and metaphysics would come much nearer together, would in fact work absolutely hand in hand.

Metaphysics has usually followed a very primitive kind of quest. You know how men have always hankered after unlawful magic, and you know what a great part in magic *words* have always played. If you have his name, or the formula of incantation that binds him, you can control the spirit, genie, afrite, or whatever the power may be. Solomon knew the names of all the spirits, and having their names, he held them subject to his will. So the universe has always appeared to the natural mind as a kind of enigma, of which the key must be sought in the shape of some illuminating or power-bringing word or name. That word names the universe's *principle,* and to possess it is after a fashion to possess the universe itself. "God," "Matter," "Reason," "the Absolute," "Energy," are so many solving names. You can rest when you have them. You are at the end of your metaphysical quest.

But if you follow the pragmatic method, you cannot look on any such word as closing your quest. You must bring out of each word its practical cash-value, set it at work within the stream of your experience. It appears less as a solution, then, than as a program for more work, and more particularly as an indication of the ways in which existing realities may be *changed*.

Theories thus become instruments, not answers to enigmas, in which we can rest. We don't lie back upon them, we move forward, and, on occasion, make nature over again by their aid. Pragmatism unstiffens all our theories, limbers them up and sets each one at work. Being nothing essentially new, it harmonizes with many ancient philosophic tendencies. It agrees with nominalism for instance, in always appealing to particulars; with utilitarianism in emphasizing practical aspects; with positivism in its disdain for verbal solutions, useless questions and metaphysical abstractions.

All these, you see, are *anti-intellectualist* tendencies. Against rationalism as a pretension and a method pragmatism is fully armed and militant. But, at the outset, at least, it stands for no particular results. It has no dogmas, and no doctrines save its method. As the young Italian pragmatist Papini has well said, it lies in the midst of our theories, like a corridor in a hotel. Innumerable chambers open out of it. In one you may find a man writing an atheistic volume; in the next some one on his knees praying for faith and strength; in a third a chemist investigating a body's properties. In a fourth a system of idealistic metaphysics is being excogitated; in a fifth the impossibility of metaphysics is being shown. But they all own the corridor, and all must pass through it if they want a practicable way of getting into or out of their respective rooms.

No particular results then, so far, but only an attitude of orientation, is what the pragmatic method means. *The attitude of looking away from first things, principles, "categories," supposed necessities; and of looking towards last things, fruits, consequences, facts.*

So much for the pragmatic method! You may say that I have been praising it rather than explaining it to you, but I shall presently explain it abundantly enough by showing how it works on some familiar problems. Meanwhile the word pragmatism has come to be used in a still wider sense, as meaning also a certain *theory of truth*. I mean to give a whole lecture to the statement of that theory, after first paving the way, so I can be very brief now. But brevity is hard to follow, so I ask for your redoubled attention for a quarter of an hour. If much remains obscure, I hope to make it clearer in the later lectures.

One of the most successfully cultivated branches of philosophy in our time is what is called inductive logic, the study of the conditions under which our sciences have evolved. Writers on this subject have begun to show a singular unanimity as to what the laws of nature and elements of fact mean, when formulated by mathematicians, physicists and chemists. When the first mathematical, logical, and natural uniformities, the first *laws,* were discovered, men were so carried away by the clearness, beauty and simplification that resulted, that they believed themselves to have deciphered authentically the eternal thoughts of the Almighty. His mind also thundered and reverberated in syllogisms. He also thought in conic sections, squares and roots and ratios, and geometrized like Euclid. He made Kepler's laws for the planets to follow; he made velocity increase proportionally to the time in falling bodies, he made the law of the sines for light to obey when refracted; he established the classes, orders, families and genera of plants and animals, and fixed the distances between them. He thought the archetypes of all things, and devised their variations; and when we rediscover any one of these his wondrous institutions, we seize his mind in its very literal intention.

But as the sciences have developed farther, the notion has gained ground that most, perhaps all, of our laws are only approximations. The laws themselves, moreover, have grown so numerous that there is no counting them; and so many rival formulations are proposed in all the branches of science that investigators have become accustomed to the notion that no theory is absolutely a transcript of reality, but that any one of them may from some point of view be useful. Their great use is to summarize old facts and to lead to new ones. They are only a man-made language, a conceptual shorthand, as some one calls them, in which we write our reports of nature; and languages, as is well known, tolerate much choice of expression and many dialects.

Thus human arbitrariness has driven divine necessity from scientific logic. If I mention the names of Sigwart, Mach, Ostwald, Pearson, Milhaud, Poincaré, Duhem, Ruyssen, those of you who are students will easily identify the tendency I speak of, and will think of additional names.

Riding now on the front of this wave of scientific logic Messrs. Schiller and Dewey appear with their pragmatistic account of what truth everywhere signifies. Everywhere, these teachers say, "truth" in our ideas and beliefs means the same thing that it means in science. It means, they say, nothing but this, *that ideas (which themselves are but parts of our experience) become true just in so far as they help us to get into satisfactory relation with other parts of our experience,* to summarize them and get about among them by conceptual shortcuts instead of following the interminable succession of particular phenomena. Any idea upon which we can ride, so to speak; any idea that will carry us prosperously from any one part of our experience to any other part, linking things satisfactorily, working securely, simplifying, saving labor; is true for just so much, true in so far forth, true *instrumentally.* This is the "instrumental" view of truth taught so successfully at Chicago, the view that truth in our ideas means their power to "work," promulgated so brilliantly at Oxford.

Messrs. Dewey, Schiller and their allies, in reaching this general conception of all truth, have only followed the example of geologists, biologists and philologists. In the establishment of these other sciences, the successful stroke was always to take some simple process actually observable in operation—as denudation by weather, say, or variation from parental type, or change of dialect by incorporation of new words and pronunciations —and then to generalize it, making it apply to all times, and produce great results by summating its effects through the ages.

The observable process which Schiller and Dewey particularly singled out for generalization is the familiar one by which any individual settles into *new opinions*. The process here is always the same. The individual has a stock of old opinions already, but he meets a new experience that puts them to a strain. Somebody contradicts them; or in a reflective moment he discovers that they contradict each other; or he hears of facts with which they are incompatible; or desires arise in him which they cease to satisfy. The result is an inward trouble to which his mind till then had been a stranger, and from which he seeks to escape by modifying his previous mass of opinions. He saves as much of it as he can, for in this matter of belief we are all extreme conservatives. So he tries to change first this opinion, and then that (for they resist change very variously), until at last some new idea comes up which he can graft upon the ancient stock with a minimum of disturbance of the latter, some idea that mediates between the stock and the new experience and runs them into one another most felicitously and expediently.

This new idea is then adopted as the true one. It preserves the older stock of truths with a minimum of modification, stretching them just enough to make them admit the novelty, but conceiving that in ways as familiar as the case leaves possible. An *outrée* explanation, violating all our preconceptions, would never pass for a true account of a novelty. We should scratch round industriously till we found something less eccentric. The most violent revolutions in an individual's beliefs leave most of his old order standing. Time and space, cause and effect, nature and history, and one's own biography remain untouched. New truth is always a go-between, a smoother-over of transitions. It marries old opinion to new fact so as ever to show a minimum of jolt, a maximum of continuity. We hold a theory true just in proportion to its success in solving this "problem of maxima and minima." But success in solving this problem is eminently a matter of approximation. We say this theory solves it on the whole more satisfactorily than that theory; but that means more satisfactorily to ourselves, and individuals will emphasize their points of satisfaction differently. To a certain degree, therefore, everything here is plastic.

The point I now urge you to observe particularly is the part played by the older truths. Failure to take account of it is the source of much of the unjust criticism levelled against pragmatism. Their influence is absolutely controlling. Loyalty to them is the first principle—in most cases it is the only principle; for by far the most usual way of handling phenomena so novel that they would make for a serious re-arrangement of our preconception is to ignore them altogether, or to abuse those who bear witness for them.

You doubtless wish examples of this process of truth's growth, and the only trouble is their superabundance. The simplest case of new truth is of course the mere numerical addition of new kinds of facts, or of new single facts of old kinds, to our experience—an addition that involves no alteration in the old beliefs. Day follows day, and its contents are simply added. The new contents themselves are not true, they simply *come* and *are*. Truth is *what we say about them,* and when we say that they have come, truth is satisfied by the plain additive formula.

But often the day's contents oblige a re-arrangement. If I should now utter piercing shrieks and act like a maniac on this platform, it would make many of you revise your ideas as to the probable worth of my philosophy. "Radium" came the other day as part of the day's content, and seemed for a moment to contradict our ideas of the whole order of nature, that order having come to be identified with what is called the conservation of energy. The mere sight of radium paying heat away indefinitely out of its own pocket seemed to violate that conservation. What to think? If the radiations from it were nothing but an escape of unsuspected "potential" energy, pre-existent inside of the atoms, the principle of conservation would be saved. The discovery of "helium" as the radiation's outcome, opened a way to this belief. So Ramsay's view is generally held to be true, because, although it extends our old ideas of energy it causes a minimum of alteration in their nature.

I need not multiply instances. A new opinion counts as "true" just in proportion as it gratifies the individual's desire to assimilate the novel in his experience to his beliefs in stock. It must both lean on old truths and grasp new fact; and its success (as I said a moment ago) in doing this, is a matter for the individual's appreciation. When old truth grows, then, by new truth's addition, it is for subjective reasons. We are in the process and obey the reasons. That new idea is truest which performs most felicitously its function of satisfying our double urgency. It makes itself true, gets itself classed as true, by the way it works; grafting itself then upon the ancient body of truth, which thus grows much as a tree grows by the activity of a new layer of cambium.

Now Dewey and Schiller proceed to generalize this observation and to apply it to the most ancient parts of truth. They also once were plastic. They also were called true for human reasons. They also mediated between still earlier truths and what in those days were novel observations. Purely objective truth, truth in whose establishment the function of giving human satisfaction in marrying previous parts of experience with newer parts played no role whatever, is nowhere to be found. The reason why we call things true is the reason why they *are* true, for "to be true" *means* only to perform this marriage-function.

The trail of the human serpent is thus over everything. Truth independent; truth that we *find* merely; truth no longer malleable to human need; truth incorrigible, in a word; such truth exists indeed superabundantly—or is supposed to exist by rationalistically minded thinkers; but then it means only the dead heart of the living tree, and its being there means only that truth also has its paleontology, and its "prescription," and may grow stiff with years of veteran service and petrified in men's regard by sheer antiquity. But how plastic even the oldest truths nevertheless really are has been vividly shown in our day by the transformation of logical and mathematical ideas, a transformation which seems even to be invading physics. The ancient formulas are reinterpreted as special expressions of much wider principles, principles that our ancestors never got a glimpse of in their present shape and formulation. . . .

The Will to Believe

I

Let us give the name of *hypothesis* to anything that may be proposed to our belief; and just as the electricians speak of live and dead wires, let us speak of any hypothesis as either *live* or *dead*. A live hypothesis is one which appeals as a real possibility to him to whom it is proposed. If I ask you to believe in the Mahdi, the notion makes no electric connection with your nature—it refuses to scintillate with any credibility at all. As an hypothesis it is completely dead. To an Arab, however (even if he be not one of the Mahdi's followers), the hypothesis is among the mind's possibilities: it is alive. This shows that deadness and liveness in an hypothesis are not intrinsic properties, but relations to the individual thinker. They are measured by his willingness to act. The maximum of liveness in an hypothesis means willingness to act irrevocably. Practically, that means belief; but there is some believing tendency wherever there is willingness to act at all.

Next, let us call the decision between two hypotheses an *option*. Options may be of several kinds. They may be—1, *living* or *dead;* 2, *forced* or *avoidable;* 3, *momentous* or *trivial,* and for our purposes we may call an option a *genuine* option when it is of the forced, living, and momentous kind.

1. A living option is one in which both hypotheses are live ones. If I say to you: "Be a theosophist or be a Mohammedan," it is probably a dead option, because for you neither hypothesis is likely to be alive. But if I say:

From pp. 2–30 of William James, *The Will to Believe, and Other Essays in Popular Philosophy.* Copyright 1897 by William James.

"Be an agnostic or be a Christian," it is otherwise: trained as you are, each hypothesis makes some appeal, however small, to your belief.

2. Next, if I say to you: "Choose between going out with your umbrella or without it," I do not offer you a genuine option, for it is not forced. You can easily avoid it by not going out at all. Similarly, if I say, "Either love me or hate me," "Either call my theory true or call it false," your option is avoidable. You may remain indifferent to me, neither loving nor hating, and you may decline to offer any judgment as to my theory. But if I say, "Either accept this truth or go without it," I put on you a forced option, for there is no standing place outside of the alternative. Every dilemma based on a complete logical disjunction, with no possibility of not choosing, is an option of this forced kind.

3. Finally, if I were Dr. Nansen and proposed to you to join my North Pole expedition, your option would be momentous; for this would probably be your only similar opportunity, and your choice now would either exclude you from the North Pole sort of immortality altogether or put at least the chance of it into your hands. He who refuses to embrace a unique opportunity loses the prize as surely as if he tried and failed. *Per contra,* the option is trivial when the opportunity is not unique, when the stake is insignificant, or when the decision is reversible if it later prove unwise. Such trivial options abound in the scientific life. A chemist finds an hypothesis live enough to spend a year in its verification: he believes in it to that extent. But if his experiments prove inconclusive either way, he is quit for his loss of time, no vital harm being done.

It will facilitate our discussion if we keep all these distinctions well in mind.

II

The next matter to consider is the actual psychology of human opinion. When we look at certain facts, it seems as if our passional and volitional nature lay at the root of all our convictions. When we look at others, it seems as if they could do nothing when the intellect had once said its say. Let us take the latter facts up first.

Does it not seem preposterous on the very face of it to talk of our opinions being modifiable at will? Can our will either help or hinder our intellect in its perceptions of truth? Can we, by just willing it, believe that Abraham Lincoln's existence is a myth, and that the portraits of him in *McClure's Magazine* are all of some one else? Can we, by any effort of our will, or by any strength of wish that it were true, believe ourselves well and about when we are roaring with rheumatism in bed, or feel certain that the sum of the two one-dollar bills in our pocket must be a hundred dollars? We can *say* any of these things, but we are absolutely impotent to believe them; and of just such things is the whole fabric of the truths that we do believe in made up—matters of fact, immediate or remote, as Hume said, and relations between ideas, which are either there or not there for us if we see them so, and which if not there cannot be put there by any action of our own.

In Pascal's *Thoughts* there is a celebrated passage known in literature as Pascal's wager. In it he tries to force us into Christianity by reasoning as if our concern with truth resembled our concern with the stakes in a game of chance. Translated freely his words are these: You must either believe or not believe that God is—which will you do? Your human reason cannot say. A game is going on between you and the nature of things which at the day of judgment will bring out either heads or tails. Weigh what your gains and your losses would be if you should stake all you have on heads, or God's existence: if you win in such case, you gain eternal beatitude; if you lose, you lose nothing at all. If there were an infinity of chances, and only one for God in this wager, still you ought to stake your all on God; for though you surely risk a finite loss by this procedure, and finite loss is reasonable, even a certain one is reasonable, if there is but the possibility of infinite gain. . . .

You probably feel that when religious faith expresses itself thus, in the language of the gaming-table, it is put to its last trumps. Surely Pascal's own personal belief in masses and holy water had far other springs; and this celebrated page of his is but an argument for others, a last desperate snatch at a weapon against the hardness of the unbelieving heart. We feel that a faith in masses and holy water adopted wilfully after such a mechanical calculation would lack the inner soul of faith's reality; and if we were ourselves in the place of the Deity, we should probably take particular pleasure in cutting off believers of this pattern from their infinite reward. It is evident that unless there be some pre-existing tendency to believe in masses and holy water, the option offered to the will by Pascal is not a living option. Certainly no Turk ever took to masses and holy water on its account; and even to us Protestants these means of salvation seem such foregone impossibilities that Pascal's logic, invoked for them specifically, leaves us unmoved. As well might the Mahdi write to us, saying, "I am the Expected One whom God has created in his effulgence. You shall be infinitely happy if you confess me; otherwise you shall be cut off from the light of the sun. Weigh, then, your infinite gain if I am genuine against your finite sacrifice if I am not!" His logic would be that of Pascal; but he would vainly use it on us, for the hypothesis he offers us is dead. No tendency to act on it exists in us to any degree.

The talk of believing by our volition seems, then, from one point of view, simply silly. From another point of view it is worse than silly, it is vile. When one turns to the magnificent edifice of the physical sciences, and sees how it was reared; what thousands of disinterested moral lives of men lie buried in its mere foundations; what patience and postponement, what choking down of preference, what submission to the icy laws of outer fact are wrought into its very stones and mortar; how absolutely impersonal it stands in its vast augustness—then how besotted and contemptible seems every little sentimentalist who comes blowing his voluntary smoke-wreaths, and pretending to decide things from out of his private dream! Can we wonder if those bred in the rugged and manly school of science should feel like spewing such subjectivism out of their mouths? The whole system of loyalties which grow up in the schools of science go dead against its toleration; so that it is only natural that those who have caught the scientific fever should pass over to the opposite extreme, and write sometimes as if the incorruptibly truthful intellect ought positively to prefer bitterness and unacceptableness to the heart in its cup.

> It fortifies my soul to know
> That, though I perish, Truth is so—

sings Clough, while Huxley exclaims: "My only consolation lies in the reflection that, however bad our posterity may become, so far as they hold by the plain rule of not pretending to believe what they have no reason to believe, because it may be to their advantage so to pretend [the word "pretend" is surely here redundant], they will not have reached the lowest depth of immorality." And that delicious *enfant terrible* Clifford writes: "Belief is desecrated when given to unproved and unquestioned statements for the solace and private pleasure of the believer. . . . Whoso would deserve well of his fellows in this matter will guard the purity of his belief with a very fanaticism of jealous care, lest at any time it should rest on an unworthy object, and catch a stain which can never be wiped away. . . . If [a] belief has been accepted on insufficient evidence [even though the belief be true, as Clifford on the same page explains] the pleasure is a stolen one. . . . It is sinful because it is stolen in defiance of our duty to mankind. That duty is to guard ourselves from such beliefs as from a pestilence which may shortly master our own body and then spread to the rest of the town. . . . It is wrong always, everywhere, and for every one, to believe anything upon insufficient evidence."

III

All this strikes one as healthy, even when expressed, as by Clifford, with somewhat too much of robustious pathos in the voice. Free-will and simple wishing do seem, in the matter of our credences, to be only fifth wheels to the coach. Yet if any one should hereupon assume that intellectual insight is what remains after wish and will and sentimental preference have taken wing, or that pure reason is what then settles our opinions, he would fly quite as directly in the teeth of the facts.

It is only our already dead hypotheses that our willing nature is unable to bring to life again. But what has made them dead for us is for the most part a previous action of our willing nature of an antagonistic kind. When I say "willing nature," I do not mean only such deliberate volitions as may have set up habits of belief that we cannot now escape from—I mean all such factors of belief as fear and hope, prejudice and passion, imitation and partisanship, the circumpressure of our caste and set. As a matter of fact we find ourselves believing, we hardly know how or why. Mr. Balfour gives the name of "authority" to all those influences, born of the intellectual climate, that make hypotheses possible or impossible for us, alive or dead. Here in this room, we all of us believe in molecules and the conservation of energy, in democracy and necessary progress, in Protestant Christianity, and the duty of fighting for "the doctrine of the immortal Monroe," all for no reasons worthy of the name. We see into these matters with no more inner clearness, and probably with much less, than any disbeliever in them might possess. His unconventionality would probably have some grounds to show for its conclusions; but for us, not insight, but the *prestige* of the opinions, is what makes the spark shoot from them and light up our sleeping magazines of faith. Our reason is quite satisfied, in nine hundred and ninety-nine cases out of every thousand of us, if it can find a few arguments that will do to recite in case our credulity is criticized by some one else. Our faith is faith in some one else's faith, and in the greatest matters this is most the case. Our belief in truth itself, for instance, that there is a truth, and that our minds and it are made for each other—what is it but a passionate affirmation of desire, in which our social system backs us up? We want to have a truth; we want to believe that our experiments and studies and discussions must put us in a continually better and better position towards it; and on this line we agree to fight out our thinking lives. But if a pyrrhonistic sceptic asks us *how we know* all this, can our logic find a reply? No! certainly it cannot. It is just one volition against another—we willing to go in for life upon a trust or assumption which he, for his part, does not care to make.

As a rule we disbelieve all facts and theories for which we have no use. Clifford's cosmic emotions find no use for Christian feeling. Huxley belabors the bishops because there is no use for sacerdotalism in his scheme of life. Newman, on the contrary, goes over to Romanism, and finds all sorts of reasons good for staying there, because a priestly system is for him an organic need and delight. Why do so few "scientists" even look at the evidence for telepathy, so called? Because they think, as a leading biologist, now dead, once said to me, that even if such a thing were true, scientists ought to band together to keep it suppressed and concealed. It would undo the uniformity of Nature and all sorts of other things without which scientists cannot carry on their pursuits. But if this very man had been shown something which as a scientist he might *do* with telepathy, he might not only have examined the evidence, but even have found it good enough. This very law which the logicians would impose upon us—if I may give the name of logicians to those who would rule out our willing nature here—is based on nothing but their own natural wish to exclude all elements for which they, in their professional quality of logicians, can find no use.

Evidently, then, our non-intellectual nature does influence our convictions. There are passional tendencies and volitions which run before and others which come after belief, and it is only the latter that are too late for the fair; and they are not too late when the previous passional work has been already in their own direction. Pascal's argument, instead of being powerless, then seems a regular clincher, and is the last stroke needed to make our faith in masses and holy water complete. The state of things is evidently far from simple; and pure insight and logic, whatever they might do ideally, are not the only things that really do produce our creeds.

IV

Our next duty, having recognized this mixed-up state of affairs, is to ask whether it be simply reprehensible and pathological, or whether, on the contrary, we must treat it as a normal element in making up our minds. The thesis I defend is, briefly stated, this: *Our passional nature not only lawfully may, but must, decide an option between propositions, whenever it is a genuine option that cannot by its nature be decided on intellectual grounds; for to say, under such circumstances, "Do not decide, but leave the question open," is itself a passional decision—just like deciding yes or no—and is attended with the same risk of losing the truth.* The thesis thus abstractly expressed will, I trust, soon become quite clear. But I must first indulge in a bit more of preliminary work.

V

It will be observed that for the purposes of this discussion we are on "dogmatic" ground—ground, I mean, which leaves systematic philosophical scepticism altogether out of account. The postulate that there is truth, and that it is the destiny of our minds to attain it, we are deliberately resolving to make, though the sceptic will not make it. We part company with him, therefore, absolutely, at this point. But the faith that truth exists, and that our minds can find it, may be held in two ways. We may talk of the *empiricist* way and of the *absolutist* way of believing in truth. The absolutists in this matter say that we not only can attain to knowing truth, but we can *know when* we have attained to knowing it; while the empiricists think that although we may attain it, we cannot infallibly know when. To *know* is one thing, and to know for certain *that* we know is another. One may hold to the first being possible without the second; hence the empircists and the absolutists, although neither of them is a sceptic in the usual philosophic sense of the term, show very different degrees of dogmatism in their lives.

If we look at the history of opinions, we see that the empiricist tendency has largely prevailed in science, while in philosophy the absolutist tendency has had everything its own way. The characteristic sort of happiness, indeed, which philosophies yield has mainly consisted in the conviction felt by each successive school or system that by it bottom-certitude has been attained. "Other philosophies are collections of opinions, mostly false; *my* philosophy gives standing-ground forever"—who does not recognize in this the key-note of every system worthy of the name? A system, to be a system at all, must come as a *closed* system, reversible in this or that detail, perchance, but in its essential features never!

Scholastic orthodoxy, to which one must always go when one wishes to find perfectly clear statement, has beautifully elaborated this absolutist conviction in a doctrine which it calls that of "objective evidence." If, for example, I am unable to doubt that I now exist before you, that two is less than three, or that if all men are mortal then I am mortal too, it is because these things illumine my intellect irresistibly. The final ground of this objective evidence possessed by certain propositions is the *adæquatio intellectûs nostri cum rê.*[1] The certitude it brings involves an *aptitudinem ad extorquendum certum assensum* [2] on the part of the truth envisaged, and on the side of the subject a *quietem in cognitione,*[3] when once the object is mentally received, that leaves no possibility of doubt behind; and in the whole transaction nothing operates but the *entitas ipsa* [4] of the object and the *entitas ipsa* of the mind. We slouchy modern thinkers dislike to talk in Latin—indeed, we dislike to talk in set terms at all; but at bottom our own state of mind is very much like this whenever we uncritically abandon ourselves: You believe in objective evidence, and I do. Of some things we feel that we are certain: we know and we know that we know. There is something that gives a click inside of us, a bell that strikes twelve, when the hands of our mental clock have swept the dial and meet over the meridian hour. The greatest empiricists among us are only empiricists on reflection: when left to their instincts, they dogmatize like infallible popes. When the Cliffords tell us how sinful it is to be Christians on such "insufficient evidence," insufficiency is really the last thing they have in mind. For them the evidence is absolutely sufficient, only it makes the other way. They believe so completely in an anti-Christian order of the universe that there is no living option: Christianity is a dead hypotheses from the start.

VI

But now, since we are all such absolutists by instinct, what in our quality of students of philosophy ought we to do about the fact? Shall we espouse and indorse it? Or shall we treat it as a weakness of our nature from which we must free ourselves, if we can?

I sincerely believe that the latter course is the only one we can follow as reflective men. Objective evidence and certitude are doubtless very fine ideals to play with, but where on this moonlit and dream-visited planet are they found? I am, therefore, myself a complete empiricist so far as my theory of human knowledge goes. I live, to be sure, by the practical faith

---

[1] *Adæquatio intellectûs nostri cum rê:* the conformity of our intellect with the thing or object. [R.J.K.]

[2] *Aptitudinem ad extorquendum certum assensum:* an aptitude for producing a certain type of assent. [R.J.K.]

[3] *Quietem in cognitione:* at rest in knowledge. [R.J.K.]

[4] *Entitas ipsa:* the being itself. [R.J.K.]

that we must go on experiencing and thinking over our experience, for only thus can our opinions grow more true; but to hold any one of them—I absolutely do not care which—as if it never could be reinterpretable or corrigible, I believe to be a tremendously mistaken attitude, and I think that the whole history of philosophy will bear me out. There is but one indefectibly certain truth, and that is the truth that Pyrrhonistic scepticism itself leaves standing—the truth that the present phenomenon of consciousness exists. That, however, is the bare starting-point of knowledge, the mere admission of a stuff to be philosophized about. The various philosophies are but so many attempts at expressing what this stuff really is. And if we repair to our libraries what disagreement do we discover! Where is a certainly true answer found? Apart from abstract propositions of comparison (such as two and two are the same as four), propositions which tell us nothing by themselves about concrete reality, we find no proposition ever regarded by any one as evidently certain that has not either been called a falsehood, or at least had its truth sincerely questioned by some one else. The transcending of the axioms of geometry, not in play but in earnest, by certain of our contemporaries (as Zöllner and Charles H. Hinton), and the rejection of the whole Aristotelian logic by the Hegelians, are striking instances in point.

No concrete test of what is really true has ever been agreed upon. Some make the criterion external to the moment of perception, putting it either in revelation, the *consensus gentium,* the instincts of the heart, or the systematized experience of the race. Others make the perceptive moment its own test—Descartes, for instance, with his clear and distinct ideas guaranteed by the veracity of God; Reid with his "common-sense"; and Kant with his forms of synthetic judgment *a priori*. The inconceivability of the opposite; the capacity to be verified by sense; the possession of complete organic unity or self-relation, realized when a thing is its own other—are standards which, in turn, have been used. The much lauded objective evidence is never triumphantly there; it is a mere aspiration or *Grenzbegriff,* marking the infinitely remote ideal of our thinking life. To claim that certain truths now possess it, is simply to say that when you think them true and they *are* true, then their evidence is objective, otherwise it is not. But practically one's conviction that the evidence one goes by is of the real objective brand, is only one more subjective opinion added to the lot. For what a contradictory array of opinions have objective evidence and absolute certitude been claimed! The world is rational through and through—its existence is an ultimate brute fact; there is a personal God—a personal God is inconceivable; there is an extra-mental physical world immediately known—the mind can only know its own ideas; a moral imperative exists —obligation is only the resultant of desires; a permanent spiritual principle is in every one—there are only shifting states of mind; there is an endless chain of causes—there is an absolute first cause; an eternal necessity—a freedom; a purpose—no purpose; a primal One—a primal Many; a universal continuity—an essential discontinuity in things; an infinity—no infinity. There is this—there is that; there is indeed nothing which some one has not thought absolutely true, while his neighbor deemed it absolutely false; and not an absolutist among them seems ever to have considered that the trouble may all the time be essential, and that the intellect, even with truth directly in its grasp, may have no infallible signal for knowing whether it be truth or no. . . .

But please observe, now, that when as empiricists we give up the doctrine of objective certitude, we do not thereby give up the quest or hope of truth itself. We still pin our faith on its existence, and still believe that we gain an ever better position towards it by systematically continuing to roll up experiences and think. Our great difference from the scholastic lies in the way we face. The strength of his system lies in the principles, the origin, the *terminus a quo* of his thought; for us the strength is in the outcome, the upshot, the *terminus ad quem*. Not where it comes from but what it leads to is to decide. It matters not to an empiricist from what quarter an hypothesis may come to him; he may have acquired it by fair means or by foul; passion may have whispered or accident suggested it; but if the total drift of thinking continues to confirm it, that is what he means by its being true.

VII

One more point, small but important, and our preliminaries are done. There are two ways of looking at our duty in the matter of opinion—ways entirely different, and yet ways about whose difference the theory of knowledge seems hitherto to have shown very little concern. *We must know the truth;* and *we must avoid error*—these are our first and great commandments as would-be knowers; but they are not two ways of stating an identical commandment, they are two separable laws. Although it may indeed happen that when we believe the truth *A,* we escape as an incidental consequence from believing the falsehood *B,* it hardly ever happens that by merely disbelieving *B* we necessarily believe *A.* We may in escaping *B* fall into believing other falsehoods, *C* or *D,* just as bad as *B;* or we may escape *B* by not believing anything at all, not even *A.*

Believe truth! Shun error!—these, we see, are two materially different laws; and by choosing between them we may end by coloring differently our whole intellectual life. We may regard the chase for truth as paramount, and the avoidance of error as secondary; or we may, on the other hand, treat the avoidance of error as more imperative, and let truth take its chance. Clifford, in the instructive passage which I have quoted, exhorts us to the latter course. Believe nothing, he tells us, keep your mind in suspense forever, rather than by closing it on insufficient evidence incur the awful risk of believing lies. You, on the other hand, may think that the risk of being in error is a very small matter when compared with the blessings of real knowledge, and be ready to be duped many times in your investigation rather than postpone indefinitely the chance of guessing true. I myself find it impossible to go with Clifford. We must remember that these feelings of our duty about either truth or error are in any case only expressions of our passional life. Biologically considered, our minds are as ready to grind out falsehood as veracity, and he who says, "Better go without belief forever than believe a lie!" merely shows his own preponderant private horror of becoming a dupe. He may be critical of many of his desires and fears, but this fear he slavishly obeys. He cannot imagine any one questioning its binding force. For my own part, I have also a horror of being duped; but I can believe that worse things than being duped may happen to a man in this world; so Clifford's exhortation has to my ears a thoroughly fantastic sound. It is like a general informing his soldiers that it is better to keep out of battle forever than to risk a single wound. Not so are victories either over enemies or over nature gained. Our errors are surely not such awfully solemn things. In a world where we are so certain to incur them in spite of all our caution, a certain lightness of heart seems healthier than this excessive nervousness on their behalf. At any rate, it seems the fittest thing for the empiricist philosopher.

VIII

And now, after all this introduction, let us go straight at our question. I have said, and now repeat it, that not only as a matter of fact do we find our passional nature influencing us in our opinions, but that there are some options between opinions in which this influence must be regarded both as an inevitable and as a lawful determinant of our choice.

I fear here that some of you my hearers will begin to scent danger, and lend an inhospitable ear. Two first steps of passion you have indeed had to admit as necessary—we must think so as to avoid dupery, and we must think so as to gain truth; but the surest path to those ideal consummations, you will probably consider, is from now onwards to take no further passional step.

Well, of course, I agree as far as the facts will allow. Wherever the option between losing truth and gaining it is not momentous, we can throw the chance of *gaining truth* away, and at any rate save ourselves from any chance of *believing falsehood,* by not making up our minds at all till objective evidence has come. In scientific questions, this is almost always the case; and even in human affairs in general, the need of acting is seldom so urgent that a false belief to act on is better than no belief at all. Law courts, indeed, have to decide on the best evidence attainable for the moment, because a judge's duty is to make law as well as to ascertain it, and (as a learned judge once said to me) few cases are worth spending much time over; the great thing is to have them decided on *any* acceptable principle, and got out of the way. But in our dealings with objective nature we obviously are recorders, not makes, of the truth; and decisions for the mere sake of deciding promptly and getting on to the next business would be wholly out of place. Throughout the breadth of physical nature facts are what they are quite independently of us, and seldom is there any such hurry about them that the risks of being duped by believing a premature theory need be faced. The questions here are always trivial options, the hypotheses are hardly living (at any rate not living for us spectators), the choice between believing truth or falsehood is seldom forced. The attitude of sceptical balance is therefore the absolutely wise one if we would escape mistakes. What difference, indeed, does it make to most of us whether we have or have not a theory of the Röntgen rays, whether we believe or not in mind-stuff, or have a conviction about the causality of conscious states? It makes no difference. Such options are not forced on us. On every account it is better not to make them, but still keep weighing reasons *pro et contra* with an indifferent hand.

I speak, of course, here of the purely judging mind. For purposes of discovery such indifference is to be less highly recommended, and science would be far less advanced than she is if the passionate desires of individuals to get their own faiths confirmed had been kept out of the game. See for example the sagacity which Spencer and Weismann now display. On the other hand, if you want an absolute duffer in an investigation, you must, after all, take the man who has no interest whatever in its results; he is the warranted incapable, the positive fool. The most useful investigator, because the most sensitive observer, is always he whose eager interest in one side of the question is balanced by an equally keen nervousness lest he become deceived. Science has organized this nervousness into a regular *technique,* her so-called method of verification; and she has fallen so deeply in love with the method that one may even say she has ceased to care for truth by itself at all. It is only truth as technically verified that interests her. The truth of truths might come in merely affirmative form, and she would decline to touch it. Such truth as that, she might repeat with Clifford, would be stolen in defiance of her duty to mankind. Human passions, however, are stronger than technical rules. *"Le coeur a ses raisons,"* as Pascal says, *"que la raison ne connaît pas";* and however indifferent to all but the bare rules of the game the umpire, the abstract intellect, may be, the concrete players who furnish him the materials to judge of are usually, each one of them, in love with some pet "live hypothesis" of his own. Let us agree, however, that wherever there is no forced option, the dispassionately judicial intellect with no pet hypothesis, saving us, as it does, from dupery at any rate, ought to be our ideal.

The question next arises: Are there not somewhere forced options in our speculative questions, and can we (as men who may be interested at least as much in positively gaining truth as in merely escaping dupery) always wait with impunity till the coercive evidence shall have arrived? It seems *a priori* improbable that the truth should be so nicely adjusted to our needs and powers as that. In the great boarding-house of nature, the cakes and the butter and the syrup seldom come out so even and leave the plates so clean. Indeed, we should view them with scientific suspicion if they did.

IX

Moral questions immediately present themselves as questions whose solution cannot wait for sensible proof. A moral question is a question not of what sensibly exists, but of what is good, or would be good if it did exist. Science can tell us what exists; but to compare the *worths,* both of what exists and of what does not exist, we must consult not science, but what Pascal calls our heart. Science herself consults her heart when she lays it down that the infinite ascertainment of fact and correction of false belief are the supreme goods for man. Challenge the statement, and science can only repeat it oracularly, or else prove it by showing that such ascertainment and correction bring man all sorts of other goods which man's heart in turn declares. The question of having moral beliefs at all or not having them is decided by our will. Are our moral preferences true or false, or are they only odd biological phenomena, making things good or bad for *us,* but in themselves indifferent? How can your pure intellect decide? If your heart does not *want* a world of moral reality, your head will assuredly never make you believe in one. Mephistophelian scepticism, indeed, will satisfy the head's play-instincts much better than any rigorous idealism can. Some men (even at the student age) are so naturally cool-hearted that the moralistic hypothesis never has for them any pungent life, and in their supercilious presence the hot young moralist always feels strangely ill at ease. The appearance of knowingness is on their side, of *naïveté* and gullibility on his. Yet, in the inarticulate heart of him, he clings to it that he is not a dupe, and that there is a realm in which (as Emerson says) all their wit and intellectual superiority is no better than the cunning of a fox. Moral scepticism can no more be refuted or proved by logic than intellectual scepticism can. When we stick to it that there *is* truth (be it of either kind), we do so with our whole nature, and resolve to stand or fall by the results. The sceptic with his whole nature adopts the doubting attitude; but which of us is the wiser, Omniscience only knows.

Turn now from these wide questions of good to a certain class of questions of fact, questions concerning personal relations, states of mind between one man and another. *Do you like me or not?*—for example. Whether you do or not depends, in countless instances, on whether I meet you half-way, am willing to assume that you must like me, and show you trust and expectation. The previous faith on my part in your liking's existence is in such cases what makes your liking come. But if I stand aloof, and refuse to budge an inch until I have objective evidence, until you shall have done something apt, as the absolutists say, *ad extorquendum assensum meum,*[5] ten to one your liking never comes. How many women's hearts are vanquished by the mere sanguine insistence of some man that they *must* love him! he will not consent to the hypothesis that they cannot. The desire for a certain kind of truth here brings about that special truth's existence; and so it is in innumerable cases of other sorts. Who gains promotions, boons, appointments, but the man in whose life they are seen to play the part of live hypotheses, who discounts them, sacrifices other things for their sake before they have come, and takes risks for them in advance? His faith acts on the powers above him as a claim, and creates its own verification.

A social organism of any sort whatever, large or small, is what it is because each member proceeds to his own duty with a trust that the other members will simultaneously do theirs. Wherever a desired result is achieved by the coöperation of many independent persons, its existence as a fact is a pure consequence of the precursive faith in one another of those immediately concerned. A government, an army, a commercial system, a ship, a college, an athletic team, all exist on this condition, without which not only is nothing achieved, but nothing is even attempted. A whole train of passengers (individually brave enough) will be looted by a few highwaymen, simply because the latter can count on one another, while each passenger fears that if he makes a movement of resistance, he will be shot before any one else backs him up. If we believed that the whole car-full would rise at once with us, we should each severally rise, and train-robbing would never even be attempted. There are, then, cases where a fact cannot come at all unless a preliminary faith exists in its coming. *And where faith in a fact can help create the fact,* that would be an insane logic which should say that faith running ahead of scientific evidence is the "lowest kind of immorality" into which a thinking being can fall. Yet such is the logic by which our scientific absolutists pretend to regulate our lives!

X

In truths dependent on our personal action, then, faith based on desire is certainly a lawful and possibly an indispensable thing.

But now, it will be said, these are all childish human cases, and have nothing to do with great cosmical matters, like the question of religious faith. Let us then pass on to that! Religions differ so much in their accidents that in discussing the religious question we must make it very generic and broad. What then do we now mean by the religious hypothesis? Science says things are; morality says some things are better than other things; and religion says essentially two things.

First, she says that the best things are the more eternal things, the overlapping things, the things in the universe that throw the last stone, so to speak, and say the final word. "Perfection is eternal"—this phrase of

---

[5] *Ad extorquendum assensum meum:* for producing my assent. [R.J.K.]

Charles Secrétan seems a good way of putting this first affirmation of religion, an affirmation which obviously cannot yet be verified scientifically at all.

The second affirmation of religion is that we are better off even now if we believe her first affirmation to be true.

Now, let us consider what the logical elements of this situation are *in case the religious hypothesis in both its branches be really true.* (Of course, we must admit that possibility at the outset. If we are to discuss the question at all, it must involve a living option. If for any of you religion be a hypothesis that cannot by any living possibility be true, then you need go no farther. I speak to the "saving remnant" alone.) So proceeding, we see, first, that religion offers itself as a *momentous* option. We are supposed to gain, even now, by our belief, and to lose by our non-belief, a certain vital good. Secondly, religion is a *forced* option, so far as that good goes. We cannot escape the issue by remaining sceptical and waiting for more light, because, although we do avoid error in that way *if religion be untrue,* we lose the good, *if it be true,* just as certainly as if we positively chose to disbelieve. It is as if a man should hesitate indefinitely to ask a certain woman to marry him because he was not perfectly sure that she would prove an angel after he brought her home. Would he not cut himself off from that particular angel-possibility as decisively as if he went and married some one else? Scepticism, then, is not avoidance of option; it is option of a certain particular kind of risk. *Better risk loss of truth than chance of error—* that is your faith-vetoer's exact position. He is actively playing his stake as much as the believer is; he is backing the field against the religious hypothesis, just as the believer is backing the religious hypothesis against the field. To preach scepticism to us as a duty until "sufficient evidence" for religion be found, is tantamount therefore to telling us, when in presence of the religious hypothesis, that to yield to our fear of its being error is wiser and better than to yield to our hope that it may be true. It is not intellect against all passions, then; it is only intellect with one passion laying down its law. And by what, forsooth, is the supreme wisdom of this passion warranted? Dupery for dupery, what proof is there that dupery through hope is so much worse than dupery through fear? I, for one, can see no proof; and I simply refuse obedience to the scientist's command to imitate his kind of option, in a case where my own stake is important enough to give me the right to choose my own form of risk. If religion be true and the evidence for it be still insufficient, I do not wish, by putting your extinguisher upon my nature (which feels to me as if it had after all some business in this matter), to forfeit my sole chance in life of getting upon the winning side—that chance depending, of course, on my willingness to run the risk of acting as if my passional need of taking the world religiously might be prophetic and right.

All this is on the supposition that it really may be prophetic and right, and that, even to us who are discussing the matter, religion is a live hypothesis which may be true. Now, to most of us religion comes in a still further way that makes a veto on our active faith even more illogical. The more perfect and more eternal aspect of the universe is represented in our religions as having personal form. The universe is no longer a mere *It* to us, but a *Thou,* if we are religious; and any relation that may be possible from person to person might be possible here. For instance, although in one sense we are passive portions of the universe, in another we show a curious autonomy, as if we were small active centres on our own account. We feel, too, as if the appeal of religion to us were made to our own active good-will, as if evidence might be forever withheld from us unless we met the hypothesis halfway. To take a trivial illustration: just as a man who in a company of gentlemen made no advances, asked a warrant for every concession, and believed no one's word without proof, would cut himself off by such churlishness from all the social rewards that a more trusting spirit would earn—so here, one who should shut himself up in snarling logicality and try to make the gods extort his recognition willy-nilly, or not get it at all, might cut himself off forever from his only opportunity of making the gods' acquaintance. This feeling, forced on us we know not whence, that by obstinately believing that there are gods (although not to do so would be so easy both for our logic and our life) we are doing the universe the deepest service we can, seems part of the living essence of the religious hypothesis. If the hypothesis *were* true in all its parts, including this one, then pure intellectualism, with its veto on our making willing advances, would be an absurdity; and some participation of our sympathetic nature would be logically required. I, therefore, for one, cannot see my way to accepting the agnostic rules for truth-seeking, or wilfully agree to keep my willing nature out of the game. I cannot do so for this plain reason, that *a rule of thinking which would absolutely prevent me from acknowledging certain kinds of truth if those kinds of truth were really there, would be an irrational rule.* That for me is the long and short of the formal logic of the situation, no matter what the kinds of truth might materially be.

I confess I do not see how this logic can be escaped. But sad experience makes me fear that some of you may still shrink from radically saying with me, *in abstracto,* that we have the right to believe at our own risk any hypothesis that is live enough to tempt our will. I suspect, however, that if this is so, it is because you have got away from the abstract logical point of view altogether, and are thinking (perhaps without realizing it) of some particular religious hypothesis which for you is dead. The freedom to "believe what we will" you apply to the case of some patent superstition; and the faith you think of is the faith defined by the schoolboy when he said, "Faith is when you believe something that you know ain't true." I can only repeat that this is misapprehension. *In concreto,* the freedom to believe can only cover living options which the intellect of the individual cannot by itself resolve; and living options never seem absurdities to him who has them to consider. When I look at the religious question as it really puts itself to concrete men, and when I think of all the possibilities which both practically and theoretically it involves, then this command that we shall put a stopper on our heart, instincts, and courage, and *wait*—acting of course meanwhile more or less as if religion were *not* true [6] —till doomsday, or till such time as our intellect and senses working together may have raked in evidence enough—this command, I say, seems to me the queerest idol ever manufactured in the philosophic cave. Were we scholastic absolutists, there might be more excuse. If we had an infallible intellect with its objective certitudes, we might feel ourselves disloyal to such a perfect organ of knowledge in not trusting to it exclusively, in not waiting for its releasing word. But if we are empiricists, if we believe that no bell in us tolls to let us know for certain when truth is in our grasp, then it seems a piece of idle fantasticality to preach so solemnly our duty of waiting for the bell. Indeed we *may* wait if we will—I hope you do not think that I am denying that— but if we do so, we do so at our peril as much as if we believed. In either case we *act,* taking our life in our hands. No one of us ought to issue vetoes to the other, nor should we bandy words of abuse. We ought, on the contrary, delicately and profoundly to respect one another's mental freedom: then only shall we bring about the intellectual republic; then only shall we have that spirit of inner tolerance without which all our outer tolerance is soulless, and which is empiricism's glory; then only shall we live and let live, in speculative as well as in practical things. . . .

QUESTIONS FOR STUDY AND DISCUSSION

1. James regards the pragmatic method as a method of settling disputes. How is this accomplished? Give examples.
2. In what way does James associate pragmatism with empiricism? What is James's attitude toward philosophers of the past?
3. What in the author's view is an "option" and how does he classify "options"?
4. According to James we are frequently required to make a choice in matters that cannot be decided by the intellect alone. What are the author's reasons for maintaining this position?
5. What is James's outlook regarding the value of "objective evidence"? Is such evidence in his view attainable? If so, under what conditions? What is his view of different and opposed philosophical positions?
6. Outline some of James's chief observations concerning morality and religion. Would you characterize James as an agnostic? Explain.

---

[6] Since belief is measured by action, he who forbids us to believe religion to be true, necessarily also forbids us to act as we should if we did believe it to be true. The whole defense of religious faith hinges upon action. If the action required or inspired by the religious hypothesis is in no way different from that dictated by the naturalistic hypothesis, then religious faith is a pure superfluity, better pruned away, and controversy about its legitimacy is a piece of idle trifling, unworthy of serious minds. I myself believe, of course, that the religious hypothesis gives to the world an expression which specifically determines our reactions, and makes them in a large part unlike what they might be on a purely naturalistic scheme of belief. [W.J.]

John Dewey

JOHN DEWEY was born in Burlington, Vermont, in 1859. After earning his doctorate at the Johns Hopkins University (1884), he received honorary degrees from the Universities of Wisconsin, Oslo, Paris, and others. He served as professor of Philosophy at the University of Michigan, the University of Chicago, and Columbia University, retiring from Columbia in 1930. Dewey was a prolific writer, and among some of his most important works are: *Democracy and Education* (1916); *Human Nature and Conduct* (1922); *Experience and Nature* (1925); *The Quest for Certainty* (1929); and *Education Today* (1940). Dewey traveled widely and studied the educational systems of a variety of countries, including Japan, Russia, and England; many of these experiences were incorporated into his books on education. He died in New York City in 1952.

The Influence of Darwinism

That the publication of the "Origin of Species" marked an epoch in the development of the natural sciences is well known to the layman. That the combination of the very words origin and species embodied an intellectual revolt and introduced a new intellectual temper is easily overlooked by the expert. The conceptions that had reigned in the philosophy of nature and knowledge for two thousand years, the conceptions that had become the familiar furniture of the mind, rested on the assumption of the superiority of the fixed and final; they rested upon treating change and origin as signs of defect and unreality. In laying hands upon the sacred ark of absolute permanency, in treating the forms that had been regarded as types of fixity and perfection as originating and passing away, the "Origin of Species" introduced a mode of thinking that in the end was bound to transform the logic of knowledge, and hence the treatment of morals, politics, and religion.

No wonder, then, that the publication of Darwin's book, a half century

From pp. 336–44 of John Dewey, *The Influence of Darwin on Philosophy, and Other Essays.* Copyright 1910 by Henry Holt and Company; 1938 by John Dewey. Used by permission of Holt, Rinehart and Winston, Inc.

ago, precipitated a crisis. The true nature of the controversy is easily concealed from us, however, by the theological clamor that attended it. The
vivid and popular features of the anti-Darwinian row tended to leave the
impression that the issue was between science on one side and theology on
the other. Such was not the case—the issue lay primarily within science itself, as Darwin himself early recognized. The theological outcry he dis-
counted from the start, hardly noticing it save as it bore upon the "feelings
of his female relatives." But for two decades before final publication he
contemplated the possibility of being put down by his scientific peers as a
fool or as crazy; and he set, as the measure of his success, the degree in
which he should affect three men of science: Lyell in geology, Hooker in
botany, and Huxley in zoölogy.

Religious considerations lent fervor to the controversy, but they did not
provoke it. Intellectually, religious emotions are not creative but conservative. They attach themselves readily to the current view of the world and
consecrate it. They steep and dye intellectual fabrics in the seething vat of
emotions; they do not form their warp and woof. There is not, I think, an
instance of any large idea about the world being independently generated
by religion. Although the ideas that rose up like armed men against Darwinism owed their intensity to religious associations, their origin and meaning are to be sought in science and philosophy, not in religion.

II

Few words in our language foreshorten intellectual history as much as does
the word species. The Greeks, in initiating the intellectual life of Europe,
were impressed by characteristic traits of the life of plants and animals; so
impressed indeed that they made these traits the key to defining nature and
to explaining mind and society. And truly, life is so wonderful that a seemingly successful reading of its mystery might well lead men to believe that
the key to the secrets of heaven and earth was in their hands. The Greek
rendering of this mystery, the Greek formulation of the aim and standard
of knowledge, was in the course of time embodied in the word species, and
it controlled philosophy for two thousand years. To understand the intellectual face-about expressed in the phrase "Origin and Species," we must,
then, understand the long dominant idea against which it is a protest.

Consider how men were impressed by the facts of life. Their eyes fell
upon certain things slight in bulk, and frail in structure. To every appearance, these perceived things were inert and passive. Suddenly, under certain
circumstances, these things—henceforth known as seeds or eggs or germs
—begin to change, to change rapidly in size, form, and qualities. Rapid
and extensive changes occur, however, in many things—as when wood is
touched by fire. But the changes in the living thing are orderly; they are
cumulative; they tend constantly in one direction; they do not, like other
changes, destroy or consume, or pass fruitless into wandering flux; they
realize and fulfil. Each successive stage, no matter how unlike its predeces-

382 / JOHN DEWEY

sor, preserves its net effect and also prepares the way for a fuller activity on the part of its successor. In living beings, changes do not happen as they seem to happen elsewhere, any which way; the earlier changes are regulated in view of later results. This progressive organization does not cease till there is achieved a true final term, a *telos,* a completed, perfected end. This final form exercises in turn a plentitude of functions, not the least noteworthy of which is production of germs like those from which it took its own origin, germs capable of the same cycle of self-fulfilling activity.

But the whole miraculous tale is not yet told. The same drama is enacted to the same destiny in countless myriads of individuals so sundered in time, so severed in space, that they have no opportunity for mutual consultation and no means of interaction. As an old writer quaintly said, "things of the same kind go through the same formalities"—celebrate, as it were, the same ceremonial rites.

This formal activity which operates throughout a series of changes and holds them to a single course; which subordinates their aimless flux to its own perfect manifestation; which, leaping the boundaries of space and time, keeps individuals distant in space and remote in time to a uniform type of structure and function: this principle seemed to give insight into the very nature of reality itself. To it Aristotle gave the name, *eidos.* This term the scholastics translated as *species.*

The force of this term was deepened by its application to everything in the universe that observes order in flux and manifests constancy through change. From the casual drift of daily weather, through the uneven recurrence of seasons and unequal return of seed time and harvest, up to the majestic sweep of the heavens—the image of eternity in time—and from this to the unchanging pure and contemplative intelligence beyond nature lies one unbroken fulfilment of ends. Nature as a whole is a progressive realization of purpose strictly comparable to the realization of purpose in any single plant or animal.

The conception of *eidos,* species, a fixed form and final cause, was the central principle of knowledge as well as of nature. Upon it rested the logic of science. Change as change is mere flux and lapse; it insults intelligence. Genuinely to know is to grasp a permanent end that realizes itself through changes, holding them thereby within the metes and bounds of fixed truth. Completely to know is to relate all special forms to their one single end and good: pure contemplative intelligence. Since, however, the scene of nature which directly confronts us is in change, nature as directly and practically experienced does not satisfy the conditions of knowledge. Human experience is in flux, and hence the instrumentalities of sense-perception and of inference based upon observation are condemned in advance. Science is compelled to aim at realities lying behind and beyond the processes of nature, and to carry on its search for these realities by means of rational forms transcending ordinary modes of perception and inference.

There are, indeed, but two alternative courses. We must either find the appropriate objects and organs of knowledge in the mutual interactions of changing things; or else, to escape the infection of change, we *must* seek them in some transcendent and supernal region. The human mind, deliberately as it were, exhausted the logic of the changeless, the final, and the transcendent, before it essayed adventure on the pathless wastes of generation and transformation. We dispose all too easily of the efforts of the schoolmen to interpret nature and mind in terms of real essences, hidden forms, and occult faculties, forgetful of the seriousness and dignity of the ideas that lay behind. We dispose of them by laughing at the famous gentleman who accounted for the fact that opium put people to sleep on the ground it had a dormitive faculty. But the doctrine, held in our own day, that knowledge of the plant that yields the poppy consists in referring the peculiarities of an individual to a type, to a universal form, a doctrine so firmly established that any other method of knowing was conceived to be unphilosophical and unscientific, is a survival of precisely the same logic. This identity of conception in the scholastic and anti-Darwinian theory may well suggest greater sympathy for what has become unfamiliar as well as greater humility regarding the further unfamiliarities that history has in store.

Darwin was not, of course, the first to question the classic philosophy of nature and of knowledge. The beginnings of the revolution are in the physical science of the sixteenth and seventeenth centuries. When Galileo said: "It is my opinion that the earth is very noble and admirable by reason of so many and so different alterations and generations which are incessantly made therein," he expressed the changed temper that was coming over the world; the transfer of interest from the permanent to the changing. When Descartes said: "The nature of physical things is much more easily conceived when they are beheld coming gradually into existence, than when they are only considered as produced at once in a finished and perfect state," the modern world became self-conscious of the logic that was henceforth to control it, the logic of which Darwin's "Origin of Species" is the latest scientific achievement. Without the methods of Copernicus, Kepler, Galileo, and their successors in astronomy, physics, and chemistry, Darwin would have been helpless in the organic sciences. But prior to Darwin the impact of the new scientific method upon life, mind, and politics, had been arrested, because between these ideal or moral interests and the inorganic world intervened the kingdom of plants and animals. The gates of the garden of life were barred to the new ideas; and only through this garden was there access to mind and politics. The influence of Darwin upon philosophy resides in his having conquered the phenomena of life for the principle of transition, and thereby freed the new logic for application to mind and morals and life. When he said of species what Galileo had said of the earth, *e pur se muove,*[1] he emancipated, once for all, genetic and

---

[1] *E pur se muove:* and yet it moves. [R.J.K.]

experimental ideas as an organon of asking questions and looking for explanations.

III

The exact bearings upon philosophy of the new logical outlook are, of course, as yet, uncertain and inchoate. We live in the twilight of intellectual transition. One must add the rashness of the prophet to the stubbornness of the partizan to venture a systematic exposition of the influence upon philosophy of the Darwinian method. At best, we can but inquire as to its general bearing—the effect upon mental temper and complexion, upon that body of half-conscious, half-instinctive intellectual aversions and preferences which determine, after all, our more deliberate intellectual enterprises. In this vague inquiry there happens to exist as a kind of touchstone a problem of long historic currency that has also been much discussed in Darwinian literature. I refer to the old problem of design *versus* chance, mind *versus* matter, as the causal explanation, first or final, of things.

As we have already seen, the classic notion of species carried with it the idea of purpose. In all living forms, a specific type is present directing the earlier stages of growth to the realization of its own perfection. Since this purposive regulative principle is not visible to the senses, it follows that it must be an ideal or rational force. Since, however, the perfect form is gradually approximated through the sensible changes, it also follows that in and through a sensible realm a rational ideal force is working out its own ultimate manifestation. These inferences were extended to nature: (a) She does nothing in vain; but all for an ulterior purpose. (b) Within natural sensible events there is therefore contained a spiritual causal force, which as spiritual escapes perception, but is apprehended by an enlightened reason. (c) The manifestation of this principle brings about a subordination of matter and sense to its own realization, and this ultimate fulfilment is the goal of nature and man. The design argument thus operated in two directions. Purposefulness accounted for the intelligibility of nature and the possibility of science, while the absolute or cosmic character of this purposefulness gave sanction and worth to the moral and religious endeavors of man. Science was underpinned and morals authorized by one and the same principle, and their mutual agreement was eternally guaranteed.

This philosophy remained, in spite of sceptical and polemic outbursts, the official and the regnant philosophy of Europe for over two thousand years. The expulsion of fixed first and final causes from astronomy, physics, and chemistry had indeed given the doctrine something of a shock. But, on the other hand, increased acquaintance with the details of plant and animal life operated as a counterbalance and perhaps even strengthened the argument from design. The marvelous adaptations of organisms to their environment, of organs to the organism, of unlike parts of a complex organ—like the eye—to the organ itself; the foreshadowing by lower forms of the higher; the preparation in earlier stages of growth for organs that only later had their functioning—these things were increasingly recognized with the progress of botany, zoölogy, paleontology, and embryology. Together, they added such prestige to the design argument that by the late eighteenth century it was, as approved by the sciences of organic life, the central point of theistic and idealistic philosophy.

The Darwinian principle of natural selection cut straight under this philosophy. If all organic adaptations are due simply to constant variation and the elimination of those variations which are harmful in the struggle for existence that is brought about by excessive reproduction, there is no call for a prior intelligent causal force to plan and preordain them. Hostile critics charged Darwin with materialism and with making chance the cause of the universe.

Some naturalists, like Asa Gray, favored the Darwinian principle and attempted to reconcile it with design. Gray held to what may be called design on the installment plan. If we conceive the "stream of variations" to be itself intended, we may suppose that each successive variation was designed from the first to be selected. In that case, variation, struggle and selection simply define the mechanism of "secondary causes" through which the "first cause" acts; and the doctrine of design is none the worse off because we know more of its *modus operandi*.

Darwin could not accept this mediating proposal. He admits or rather he asserts that it is "impossible to conceive this immense and wonderful universe including man with his capacity of looking far backwards and far into futurity as the result of blind chance or necessity." [2] But nevertheless he holds that since variations are in useless as well as useful directions, and since the latter are sifted out simply by the stress of the conditions of struggle for existence, the design argument as applied to living beings is unjustifiable; and its lack of support there deprives it of scientific value as applied to nature in general. If the variations of the pigeon, which under artificial selection give the pouter pigeon, are not preordained for the sake of the breeder, by what logic do we argue that variations resulting in natural species are pre-designed? [3]

IV

So much for some of the more obvious facts of the discussion of design *versus* chance, as causal principles of nature and of life as a whole. We brought up this discussion, you recall, as a crucial instance. What does our touchstone indicate as to the bearing of Darwinian ideas upon philosophy? In the first place, the new logic outlaws, flanks, dismisses—what you will —one type of problems and substitutes for it another type. Philosophy forswears inquiry after absolute origins and absolute finalities in order to explore specific values and the specific conditions that generate them.

---

[2] "Life and Letters," Vol. I, p. 282; *cf*. 285. [J.D.]
[3] "Life and Letters," Vol. II, pp. 146, 170, 245; Vol. I, pp. 283–84. See also the closing portion of his "Variations of Animals and Plants under Domestication." [J.D.]

Darwin concluded that the impossibility of assigning the world to chance as a whole and to design in its parts indicated the insolubility of the question. Two radically different reasons, however, may be given as to why a problem is insoluble. One reason is that the problem is too high for intelligence; the other is that the question in its very asking makes assumptions that render the question meaningless. The latter alternative is unerringly pointed to in the celebrated case of design *versus* chance. Once admit that the sole verifiable or fruitful object of knowledge is the particular set of changes that generate the object of study together with the consequences that then flow from it, and no intelligible question can be asked about what, by assumption, lies outside. To assert—as is often asserted—that specific values of particular truth, social bonds and forms of beauty, if they can be shown to be generated by concretely knowable conditions, are meaningless and in vain; to assert that they are justified only when they and their particular causes and effects have all at once been gathered up into some inclusive first cause and some exhaustive final goal, is intellectual atavism. Such argumentation is reversion to the logic that explained the extinction of fire by water through the formal essence of aqueousness and the quenching of thirst by water through the final cause of aqueousness. Whether used in the case of the special event or that of life as a while, such logic only abstracts some aspect of the existing course of events in order to reduplicate it as a petrified eternal principle by which to explain the very changes of which it is the formalization.

When Henry Sidgwick casually remarked in a letter that as he grew older his interest in what or who made the world was altering into interest in what kind of a world it is anyway, his voicing of a common experience of our own day illustrates also the nature of that intellectual transformation effected by the Darwinian logic. Interest shifts from the wholesale essence back of special changes to the question of how special changes serve and defeat concrete purposes; shifts from an intelligence that shaped things once for all to the particular intelligences which things are even now shaping; shifts from an ultimate goal of good to the direct increments of justice and happiness that intelligent administration of existent conditions may beget and that present carelessness or stupidity will destroy or forego.

In the second place, the classic type of logic inevitably set philosophy upon proving that life *must* have certain qualities and values—no matter how experience presents the matter—because of some remote cause and eventual goal. The duty of wholesale justification inevitably accompanies all thinking that makes the meaning of special occurrences depend upon something that once and for all lies behind them. The habit of derogating from present meanings and uses prevents our looking the facts of experience in the face; it prevents serious acknowledgment of the evils they present and serious concern with the goods they promise but do not as yet fulfil. It turns thought to the business of finding a wholesale transcendent remedy for the one and guarantee for the other. One is reminded of the way many moralists and theologians greeted Herbert Spencer's recognition of an unknowable energy from which welled up the phenomenal physical processes without and the conscious operations within. Merely because Spencer labeled his unknowable energy "God," this faded piece of metaphysical goods was greeted as an important and grateful concession to the reality of the spiritual realm. Were it not for the deep hold of the habit of seeking justification for ideal values in the remote and transcendent, surely this reference of them to an unknowable absolute would be despised in comparison with the demonstrations of experience that knowable energies are daily generating about us precious values.

The displacing of this wholesale type of philosophy will doubtless not arrive by sheer logical disproof, but rather by growing recognition of its futility. Were it a thousand times true that opium produces sleep because of its dormitive energy, yet the inducing of sleep in the tired, and the recovery to waking life of the poisoned, would not be thereby one least step forwarded. And were it a thousand times dialectically demonstrated that life as a whole is regulated by a transcendent principle to a final inclusive goal, none the less truth and error, health and disease, good and evil, hope and fear in the concrete, would remain just what and where they now are. To improve our education, to ameliorate our manners, to advance our politics, we must have recourse to specific conditions of generation.

Finally, the new logic introduces responsibility into the intellectual life. To idealize and rationalize the universe at large is after all a confession of inability to master the courses of things that specifically concern us. As long as mankind suffered from this impotency, it naturally shifted a burden of responsibility that it could not carry over to the more competent shoulders of the transcendent cause. But if insight into specific conditions of value and into specific consequences of ideas is possible, philosophy must in time become a method of locating and interpreting the more serious of the conflicts that occur in life, and a method of projecting ways for dealing with them: a method of moral and political diagnosis and prognosis.

The claim to formulate *a priori* the legislative constitution of the universe is by its nature a claim that may lead to elaborate dialectic developments. But it is also one that removes these very conclusions from subjection to experimental test, for, by definition, these results make no differences in the detailed course of events. But a philosophy that humbles its pretensions to the work of projecting hypotheses for the education and conduct of mind, individual and social, is thereby subjected to test by the way in which the ideas it propounds work out in practice. In having modesty forced upon it, philosophy also acquires responsibility.

Doubtless I seem to have violated the implied promise of my earlier remarks and to have turned both prophet and partizan. But in anticipating the direction of the transformations in philosophy to be wrought by the Darwinian genetic and experimental logic, I do not profess to speak for any save those who yield themselves consciously or unconsciously to this logic.

No one can fairly deny that at present there are two effects of the Darwinian mode of thinking. On the one hand they are making many sincere and vital efforts to revise our traditional philosophic conceptions in accordance with its demands. On the other hand, there is as definitely a recrudescence of absolutistic philosophies; an assertion of a type of philosophic knowing distinct from that of the sciences, one which opens to us another kind of reality from that to which the sciences give access; an appeal through experience to something that essentially goes beyond experience. This reaction affects popular creeds and religious movements as well as technical philosophies. The very conquest of the biological sciences by the new ideas has led many to proclaim an explicit and rigid separation of philosophy from science.

Old ideas give way slowly; for they are more than abstract logical forms and categories. They are habits, predispositions, deeply engrained attitudes of aversion and preference. Moreover, the conviction persists—though history shows it to be a hallucination—that all the questions that the human mind has asked are questions that can be answered in terms of the alternatives that the questions themselves present. But in fact intellectual progress usually occurs through sheer abandonment of questions together with both of the alternatives they assume—an abandonment that results from their decreasing vitality and a change of urgent interest. We do not solve them: we get over them. Old questions are solved by disappearing, evaporating, while new questions corresponding to the changed attitude of endeavor and preference take their place. Doubtless the greatest dissolvent in contemporary thought of old questions, the greatest precipitant of new methods, new intentions, new problems, is the one effected by the scientific revolution that found its climax in the "Origin of Species."

The Supremacy of Method

Uncertainty is primarily a practical matter. It signifies uncertainty of the *issue* of present experiences; these are fraught with future peril as well as inherently objectionable. Action to get rid of the objectionable has no warrant of success and is itself perilous. The intrinsic troublesome and uncertain quality of situations lies in the fact that they hold outcomes in suspense; they move to evil or to good fortune. The natural tendency of man is to do something at once; there is impatience with suspense, and lust for immediate action. When action lacks means for control of external conditions, it takes the form of acts which are the prototypes of rite and cult. Intelligence signifies that direct action has become indirect. It continues to be overt, but it is directed into channels of examination of conditions, and doings that are tentative and preparatory. Instead of rushing to "do something about it," action centers upon finding out something about obstacles and resources and upon projecting inchoate later modes of definite response. Thinking has been well called deferred action. But not all action is deferred; only that which is final and in so far productive of irretrievable consequences. Deferred action is present exploratory action.

The first and most obvious effect of this change in the quality of action is that the dubious or problematic situation becomes *a* problem. The risky character that pervades a situation as a whole is translated into an object of inquiry that locates what the trouble is, and hence facilitates projection of methods and means of dealing with it. Only after expertness has been gained in special fields of inquiry does the mind set out at once from problems: even then in novel cases, there is a preliminary period of groping through a situation which is characterized throughout by confusion, instead of presenting a clear-cut problem for investigation.

Many definitions of mind and thinking have been given. I know of but one that goes to the heart of the matter:—response to the doubtful as such. No inanimate thing reacts to things *as* problematic. Its behavior to other things is capable of description in terms of what is determinately there. Under given conditions, it just reacts or does not react. Its reactions merely enstate a new set of conditions, in which reactions continue without regard to the nature of their outcome. It makes no difference, so to say, to a stone what are the results of its interactions with other things. It enjoys the advantage that it makes no difference how it reacts, even if the effect is its own pulverization. It requires no argument to show that the case is different with a living organism. To live signifies that a connected continuity of acts is effected in which preceding ones prepare the conditions under which later ones occur. There is a chain of cause and effects, of course, in what happens with inanimate things. But for living creatures, the chain has a particular cumulative continuity, or else death ensues.

As organisms become more complex in structure and thus related to a more complex environment, the importance of a particular act in establishing conditions favorable to subsequent acts that sustain the continuity of the life process, becomes at once more difficult and more imperative. A juncture may be so critical that the right or wrong present move signifies life or death. Conditions of the environment become more ambivalent: it is more uncertain what sort of action they call for in the interests of living. Behavior is thus compelled to become more hesitant and wary, more expectant and preparatory. In the degree that responses take place to the doubtful *as* the doubtful, they acquire *mental* quality. If they are such as to have a directed tendency to change the precarious and problematic into the secure and resolved, they are *intellectual* as well as mental. Acts are then relatively more instrumental and less consummatory or final; even the latter are haunted by a sense of what may issue from them.

This conception of the mental brings to unity various modes of response; emotional, volitional and intellectual. It is usual to say that there is no fundamental difference among these activities—that they are all different phases or aspects of a common action of mind. But I know of but one way of making this assertion good: that in which they are seen to be distinctive modes of response to the uncertain. The emotional aspect of responsive behavior is its *immediate* quality. When we are confronted with the precarious, an ebb and flow of emotion marks a disturbance of the even tenor of existence. Emotions are conditioned by the indeterminateness of present situations with respect to their issue. Fear and hope, joy and sorrow, aversion and desire, as perturbations, are qualities of a divided response. They involve concern, solicitude, for what the present situation may *become*. "Care" signifies two quite different things: fret, worry and anxiety, and cherishing attention to that in whose potentialities we are interested. These two meanings represent different poles of reactive behavior to a present having a future which is ambiguous. Elation and depression, moreover, manifest themselves only under conditions wherein not everything from start to finish is completely determined and certain. They may occur at a final moment of triumph or defeat, but this moment is one of victory or frustration in connection with a previous course of affairs whose issue was in suspense. Love for a Being so perfect and complete that our regard for it can make no difference to it is not so much affection as (a fact which the scholastics saw) it is concern for the destiny of our own souls. Hate that is sheer antagonism without any element of uncertainty is not an emotion, but is an energy devoted to ruthless destruction. Aversion is a state of affectivity only in connection with an obstruction offered by the disliked object or person to an end made uncertain by it.

The volitional phase of mental life is notoriously connected with the emotional. The only difference is that the latter is the immediate, the cross-sectional, aspect of response to the uncertain and precarious, while the volitional phase is the tendency of the reaction to modify indeterminate, ambiguous conditions in the direction of a preferred and favored outcome; to actualize one of its possibilities rather than another. Emotion is a hindrance or an aid to resolute will according as it is overwhelming in its immediacy or as it marks a gathering together of energy to deal with the situation whose issue is in doubt. Desire, purpose, planning, choice, have no meaning save in conditions where something is at stake, and where action in one direction rather than another may eventuate in bringing into existence a new situation which fulfills a need.

The intellectual phase of mental action is identical with an *indirect* mode of response, one whose purpose is to locate the nature of the trouble and form an idea of how it may be dealt with—so that operations may be directed in view of an intended solution. Take any incident of experience you choose, seeing a color, reading a book, listening to conversation, manipulating apparatus, studying a lesson, and it has or has not intellectual, cognitive, quality according as there is deliberative endeavor to deal with the indeterminate so as to dispose of it, to settle it. Anything that may be called knowledge, or a known object, marks a question answered, a difficulty disposed of, a confusion cleared up, an inconsistency reduced to coherence, a perplexity mastered. Without reference to this mediating element, what is called knowledge is but direct and unswerving action or else a possessive enjoyment. Similarly, thinking is the actual transition from the problematic to the secure, as far as that is intentionally guided. There is no separate "mind" gifted in and of itself with a faculty of thought; such a conception of thought ends in postulating the mystery of a power outside of nature and yet able to intervene within it. Thinking is objectively discoverable as that mode of serial responsive behavior to a problematic situation in which transition to the relatively settled and clear is effected.

The concrete pathologies of belief, its failures and perversions, whether of defect or excess, spring from failure to observe and adhere to the principle that knowledge is the completed resolution of the inherently indeterminate or doubtful. The commonest fallacy is to suppose that since the state of doubt is accompanied by a feeling of uncertainty, knowledge arises when this feeling gives way to one of assurance. Thinking then ceases to be an effort to effect change in the objective situation and is replaced by various devices which generate a change in feeling or "consciousness." Tendency to premature judgment, jumping at conclusions, excessive love of simplicity, making over of evidence to suit desire, taking the familiar for the clear, etc., all spring from confusing the feeling of certitude with a certified situation. Thought hastens toward the settled and is only too likely to force the pace. The natural man dislikes the dis-ease which accompanies the doubtful and is ready to take almost any means to end it. Uncertainty is got rid of by fair means or foul. Long exposure to danger breeds an overpowering love of security. Love for security, translated into a desire not to be disturbed and unsettled, leads to dogmatism, to acceptance of beliefs upon authority, to intolerance and fanaticism on one side and to irresponsible dependence and sloth on the other.

Here is where ordinary thinking and thinking that is scrupulous diverge from each other. The natural man is impatient with doubt and suspense: he impatiently hurries to be shut of it. A disciplined mind takes delight in the problematic, and cherishes it until a way out is found that approves itself upon examination. The questionable becomes an active questioning, a search; desire for the emotion of certitude gives place to quest for the objects by which the obscure and unsettled may be developed into the stable and clear. The scientific attitude may almost be defined as that which is capable of enjoying the doubtful; scientific method is, in one aspect, a technique for making a productive use of doubt by converting it into operations of definite inquiry. . . .

. . . Just what did the new experimental method do to the qualitative objects of ordinary experience? Forget the conclusions of Greek philosophy, put out of the mind all theories about knowledge and about reality. Take the simple direct facts: Here are the colored, resounding, fragrant, lovable, attractive, beautiful things of nature which we enjoy, and which we suffer when they are hateful, ugly, disgusting. Just what is the effect upon them wrought by physical science?

If we consent for the time being to denude the mind of philosophical and metaphysical presuppositions, and take the matter in the most simple and naïve way possible, I think our answer, stated in technical terms, will be that it *substitutes data for objects.* (It is not meant that this outcome is the whole effect of the experimental method; that as we saw at the outset is complex; but that the first effect as far as stripping away qualities is concerned is of this nature.) That Greek science operated with *objects* in the sense of the stars, rocks, trees, rain, warm and cold days of ordinary experience is evident enough. What is signified by saying that the first effect of experimentation was to reduce these things from the status of objects to that of data may not be so clear.[1] By data is signified subject-matter for *further* interpretation; something to be thought about. *Objects* are finalities; they are complete, finished; they call for thought only in the way of definition, classification, logical arrangement, subsumption in syllogisms, etc. But data signify "material to serve"; they are indications, evidence, signs, clues to and of something still to be reached; they are intermediate, not ultimate; means, not finalities.

In a less technical way the matter may be stated as follows: The subject-matter which had been taken as satisfying the demands of knowledge, as the material with which to frame solutions, became something which set *problems.* Hot and cold, wet and dry, light and heavy, instead of being self-evident matters with which to explain phenomena, were things to be investigated; they were "effects," not causal principles; they set question marks instead of supplying answers. The differences between the earth, the region of the planets, and the heavenly ether, instead of supplying ultimate principles which could be used to mark off and classify things, were something to be explained and to bring under identical principles. Greek and medieval science formed an art of accepting things as they are enjoyed and suffered. Modern experimental science is an art of control.

The remarkable difference between the attitude which accepts the objects of ordinary perception, use and enjoyment as final, as culminations of natural processes and that which takes them as starting points for reflection and investigation, is one which reaches far beyond the technicalities of science. It marks a revolution in the whole spirit of life, in the entire attitude taken toward whatever is found in existence. When the things which exist

---

[1] For this shift from objects to data see G. H. Mead's essay in the volume entitled *Creative Intelligence* (New York, 1917). [J.D.]

around us, which we touch, see, hear and taste are regarded as interrogations for which an answer must be sought (and must be sought by means of deliberate introduction of changes till they are reshaped into something different), nature as it already exists ceases to be something which must be accepted and submitted to, endured or enjoyed, just as it is. It is now something to be modified, to be intentionally controlled. It is material to act upon so as to transform it into new objects which better answer our needs. Nature as it exists at any particular time is a challenge, rather than a completion; it provides possible starting points and opportunities rather than final ends.

In short, there is a change from knowing as an esthetic enjoyment of the properties of nature regarded as a work of divine art, to knowing as a means of secular control—that is, a method of purposefully introducing changes which will alter the direction of the course of events. Nature as it exists at a given time is material for arts to be brought to bear upon it to reshape it, rather than already a finished work of art. Thus the changed attitude toward change to which reference was made has a much wider meaning than that which the new science offered as a technical pursuit. When correlations of changes are made the goal of knowledge, the fulfillment of its aim in discovery of these correlations, is equivalent to placing in our hands an instrument of control. When one change is given, and we know with measured accuracy its connection with another change, we have the potential means of producing or averting that other event. The esthetic attitude of necessity directed to what is already there; to what is finished, complete. The attitude of control looks to the future, to production.

The same point is stated in another way in saying that the reduction of given objects to data for a knowing or an investigation still to be undertaken liberates man from subjection to the past. The scientific attitude, as an attitude of interest in change instead of interest in isolated and complete fixities, is necessarily alert for problems; every new question is an opportunity for further experimental inquiries—for effecting more directed change. There is nothing which a scientific mind would more regret than reaching a condition in which there were no more problems. That state would be the death of science, not its perfected life. We have only to contrast this disposition with that which prevails in morals and politics to realize the difference which has already been made, as well as to appreciate how limited its development still is. For in higher practical matters we still live in dread of change and of problems. Like men of olden time—with respect to natural phenomena—we prefer to accept and endure or to enjoy—as the case may happen to be—what is, what we find in possession of the field, and at most, to arrange it under concepts, and thus give it the form of rationality.

Before the rise of experimental method, change was simply an inevitable evil; the world of phenomenal existence, that is of change, while an inferior realm compared with the changeless, was nevertheless there and had to be accepted practically as it happened to occur. The wise man if he were sufficiently endowed by fortune would have as little to do with such things as possible, turning away from them to the rational realm. Qualitative forms and complete ends determined by nature are not amenable to human control. They are grateful when they happen to be enjoyed, but for human purposes nature means fortune, and fortune is the contrary of art. A good that happens is welcome. Goods, however, can be made secure in existence only through regulation of processes of change, a regulation dependent upon knowledge of their relations. While the abolition of fixed tendencies toward definite ends has been mourned by many as if it involved a despiritualization of nature, it is in fact a precondition of the projection of new ends and of the possibility of realizing them through intentional activity. Objects which are not fixed goals of nature and which have no inherent defining forms become candidates for receiving new qualities; means for serving new purposes. Until natural objects were denuded of determinate ends which were regarded as the proper outcome of the intrinsic tendency of nature's own operations, nature could not become a plastic material of human desires and purposes.

Such considerations as these are implicit in that changed attitude which by experimental analysis reduces objects to data: the aim of science becomes discovery of constant relations among changes in place of definition of objects immutable beyond the possibility of alteration. It is interested in the mechanism of occurrences instead of in final causes. In dealing with the proximate instead of with the ultimate, knowledge deals with the world in which we live, the world which is experienced, instead of attempting through the intellect to escape to a higher realm. Experimental knowledge is a mode of doing, and like all doing takes place at a time, in a place, and under specifiable conditions in connection with a definite problem.

The notion that the findings of science are a disclosure of the inherent properties of the ultimate real, of existence at large, is a survival of the older metaphysics. It is because of injection of an irrelevant philosophy into interpretation of the conclusions of science that the latter are thought to eliminate qualities and values from nature. Thus is created the standing problem of modern philosophy:—the relation of science to the things we prize and love and which have authority in the direction of conduct. The same injection, in treating the results of mathematical-mechanistic science as a definition of natural reality in its own intrinsic nature, accounts for the antagonism shown to naturalism, and for the feeling that it is the business of philosophy to demonstrate the being of a realm beyond nature, one not subject to the conditions which mark all natural objects. Drop the conception that knowledge is knowledge only when it is a disclosure and definition of the properties of fixed and antecedent reality; interpret the aim and test of knowing by what happens in the actual procedures of scientific inquiry, and the supposed need and problem vanish.

For scientific inquiry always starts from things of the environment experienced in our everyday life, with things we see, handle, use, enjoy and suffer from. This is the ordinary qualitative world. But instead of accepting the qualities and values—the ends and forms—of this world as providing the objects of knowledge, subject to their being given a certain logical arrangement, experimental inquiry treats them as offering a challenge to thought. They are the materials of problems not of solutions. They are *to be* known, rather than objects of knowledge. The first step in knowing is to locate the problems which need solution. This step is performed by altering obvious and given qualities. These are effects; they are things *to be* understood, and they are understood in terms of their generation. The search for "efficient causes" instead of for final causes, for extrinsic relations instead of intrinsic forms, constitutes the aim of science. But the search does not signify a quest for reality in contrast with experience of the unreal and phenomenal. It signifies a search for those relations upon which the *occurrence* of real qualities and values depends, by means of which we can regulate their occurrence. To call existences as they are directly and qualitatively experienced "phenomena" is not to assign to them a metaphysical status. It is to indicate that they set the problem of ascertaining the relations of interaction upon which their occurrence depends. . . .

We have seen that situations are precarious and perilous because the persistence of life-activity depends upon the influence which present acts have upon future acts. The continuity of a life-process is secured only as acts performed render the environment favorable to subsequent organic acts. The formal generalized statement of this fact is as follows: The occurrence of problematic and unsettled situations is due to the *characteristic union of the discrete or individual and the continuous or relational*. All perceived objects are individualized. They are, as such, wholes complete in themselves. Everything directly experienced is qualitatively unique; it has its own focus about which subject-matter is arranged, and this focus never exactly recurs. While every such situation shades off indefinitely, or is not sharply marked off from others, yet the pattern of arrangement of content is never exactly twice alike.

If the interactions involved in having such an individualized situation in experience were wholly final or consummatory, there would be no such thing as a situation which is problematic. In being individual and complete in itself, just what it is and nothing else, it would be discrete in the sense in which discreteness signifies complete isolation. Obscurity, for example, would be a final quality, like any other quality and as good as any other— just as the dusk of twilight is enjoyed instead of being troublesome until we need to see something the dusk interferes with seeing. Every situation has vagueness attending it, as it shades off from a sharper focus into what is indefinite; for vagueness is added quality and not something objectionable except as it obstructs gaining an eventual object.

There are situations in which self-enclosed, discrete, individualized characters dominate. They constitute the subject-matter of esthetic experience; and every experience is esthetic in as far as it is final or arouses no search for some other experience. When this complete quality is conspicuous the experience is denominated esthetic. The fine arts have as their purpose the construction of objects of just such experiences; and under some conditions the completeness of the object enjoyed gives the experience a quality so intense that it is justly termed religious. Peace and harmony suffuse the entire universe gathered up into the situation having a particular focus and pattern. These qualities mark any experience in as far as its final character dominates; in so far a mystic experience is simply an accentuated intensification of a quality of experience repeatedly had in the rhythm of experiences.

Interactions, however, are not isolated. No experienced situation can retain indefinitely its character of finality, for the interrelations that constitute it are, because they are interactions, themselves changing. They produce a change in what is experienced. The effort to maintain directly a consummatory experience or to repeat it exactly is the source of unreal sentimentality and of insincerity. In the continuous ongoing of life, objects part with something of their final character and become conditions of subsequent experiences. There is regulation of the change in the degree in which a causal character is rendered preparatory and instrumental.

In other words, all experienced objects have a double status. They are individualized, consummatory, whether in the way of enjoyment or of suffering. They are also involved in a continuity of interactions and changes, and hence are causes and potential means of later experiences. Because of this dual capacity, they become problematic. Immediately and directly they are just what they are; but as transitions to and possibilities of later experiences they are uncertain. There is a divided response; part of the organic activity is directed to them for what they immediately are, and part to them as transitive means of other experienced objects. We react to them both as finalities and in preparatory ways, and the two reactions do not harmonize.

This two-fold character of experienced objects is the source of their problematic character. Each of us can recall many occasions when he has been perplexed by disagreement between things directly present and their potential value as signs and means; when he has been torn between absorption in what is now enjoyed and the need of altering it so as to prepare for something likely to come. If we state the point in a formal way, it is signified that there is an incompatibility between the traits of an object in its direct individual and unique nature and those traits that belong to it in its relations or continuities. This incompatibility can be removed only by actions which temporarily reconstruct what is given and constitute a new object having both individuality and the internal coherence of continuity in a series.

Previous discussion has been a statement of the chief factors that operate in bringing about this reconstruction—of resolving a problematic situation: Acts of analytic reduction of the gross total situation to determine data—qualities that locate the nature of the problem; formation of ideas or hypotheses to direct further operations that reveal new material; deductions and calculations that organize the new and old subject-matter together; operations that finally determine the existence of a new integrated situation with added meaning, and in so doing test or prove the ideas that have been employed.

Without retraversing that discussion, I wish to add a few words on one point involved in it. Nothing is more familiar than the standardized objects of reference designated by common nouns. Their distinction from proper names shows that they are not singular or individual, not existing things. Yet *"the* table" is both more familiar and seemingly more substantial than *this* table, the individual. "This" undergoes change all the time. It is interacting with other things and with me, who are not exactly the same person as when I last wrote upon it. "This" is an indefinitely multiple and varied series of "thises."

But save in extreme cases, these changes are indifferent, negligible, from the standpoint of means for consequences. *The* table is precisely the constancy among the serial "thises" of whatever serves as an instrument for a single end. *Knowledge* is concerned wholly with this constant, this standardized and averaged set of properties and relations:—just as esthetic perception is occupied with "this" in its individuality, irrespective of value in use. In the degree in which reactions are inchoate and unformed, "this" tends to be the buzzing, blooming confusion of which James wrote. As habits form, action is stereotyped into a fairly constant series of acts having a common end in view; *the* table serves a single use, in spite of individual variations. A group of properties is set aside, corresponding to the abiding end and single mode of use which form *the* object, in distinction from "this" of unique experiences. *The* object is an abstraction, but unless it is hypostatized it is not a vicious abstraction. It designates selected relations of things which, with respect to their mode of operation, are constant within the limits practically important. Moreover, the abstracted object has a consequence *in* the individualized experiences, one that is immediate and not merely instrumental to them. It marks an ordering and organizing of responses in a single focused way in virtue of which the original blur is definitized and rendered significant. Without habits dealing with recurrent and constant uses of things for abiding purposes, immediate esthetic perception would have neither rich nor clear meanings immanent within it.

The scientific or physical object marks an extension of the same sort of operation. *The* table, as *not* a table but as a swarm of molecules in motions of specified velocities and accelerations, corresponds to a liberated generalization of the purposes which *the* object may serve. "Table" signifies a definite but restricted set of uses; stated in the physical terms of science it is thought of in a wider environment and free from any specified set of uses; out of relation to any particular individualized experience. The abstraction is as legitimate as is that which gives rise to the idea of *the* table, for it consists of standardized relations or interactions. It is even more useful or more widely instrumental. For it has connection with an indefinite variety of unspecified but possible consummatory individual observations and enjoyments. It waits like a servant, idle for a time, but ready to be called upon as special occasion arises. When this standardized constant, the result of series of operations and expressing an indefinite multitude of possible relations among concrete things, is treated as the reality of nature, an instrument made for a purpose is hypostatized into a substance complete and self-sufficient in isolation. Then the fullness of qualities present in individual situations have to be treated as subjective impressions mysteriously produced in mind by the real object or else as products of a mysterious creative faculty of consciousness.

The bearing of the conclusion upon the qualitative values of experienced objects is evident. Interactions of things with the organism eventuate in objects perceived to be colored and sonorous. They also result in qualities that make the object hateful or delightful. All these qualities, taken as directly perceived or enjoyed, are terminal effects of natural interactions. They are individualized culminations that give static quality to a network of changes. Thus "tertiary" qualities (as they have been happily termed by Mr. Santayana), those which, in psychological analysis, we call affectional and emotional, are as much products of the doings of nature as are color, sound, pressure, perceived size and distance. But their very consummatory quality stands in the way of using the things they qualify as signs of other things. Intellectually they are even more in the way than are "secondary" qualities. With respect to preparatory acts they are useless; when they are treated as signs and means they work injury to thought and discovery. When not experienced, they are projected in thought as ends to be reached and in that dependence upon thought they are felt to be peculiarly mental. But only if *the* object, the physical object, instrumental in character, is supposed to define "the real" in an exhaustive way, do they cease to be for the philosopher what they are for the common man:—real qualities of natural objects. This view forms the only complete and unadulterated realism.

The problem which is supposed to exist between two tables, one that of direct perception and use and the other that of physics (to take the favorite illustration of recent discussion) is thus illusory. The perceived and used table is the only table, for it alone has both individuality of form—without which nothing can exist or be perceived, and also includes within itself a continuum of relations or interactions brought to a focus. We may perhaps employ more instructively an illustration derived from the supposed contrast between an object experienced in perception as it is rendered by a poet and the same object described by a physicist. There is the instance of a body of water where the movement of the wind over its surface is reflected in sunlight. As an object of science, it is reported as follows: "Etherial vibrations of various wave lengths, reflected at different angles from the disturbed interface between air and water, reached our eyes and by photo-electric action caused appropriate stimuli to travel along optic nerves to a brain center." Such a statement, however, includes ordinary objects of individual perceptions; water, air, brain and nerves. Consequently, it must be reduced still further; when so reduced it consists of mathematical functions between certain physical constants having no counterpart in ordinary perception.[2]

It is worth while at this point to recur to the metric character of the physical object. Defining metric traits are reached by a series of operations of which they express the statistically constant outcome; they are not the result of a single act. Hence the physical object cannot be taken to be a single or individual thing in existence. Metric definitions are also, in large measure, reached by indirect measurements, by calculation. In other words, the conception of the physical object is, in considerable degree, the outcome of complex operations of comparison and translation. In consequence, while the physical object is *not* any one of the things compared, it enables things qualitatively unlike and individual to be treated as if they were members of a comprehensive, homogeneous, or non-qualitative system. The possibility of control of the *occurrence* of individualized objects is thereby increased. At the same time, the latter gain added meaning, for the import of the scheme of continuity of relationships with other things is incorporated within them. The procedure of physics itself, not any metaphysical or epistemological theory, discloses that physical objects cannot be individual existential objects. In consequence, it is absurd to put them in opposition to the qualitatively individual objects of concrete experience.

The vogue of the philosophy that identifies the object of knowledge as such with the reality of the subject-matter of experience makes it advisable to carry the discussion further. Physical science submits the things of ordinary experience to specifiable operations. The result are objects of thought stated in numbers, where the numbers in question permit inclusion within complex systems of equations and other mathematical functions. In the physical object everything is ignored but the relations expressed by these numbers. It is safe to assert that no physicist *while at work* ever thought of denying the full reality of the things of ordinary, coarse experience. He pays no attention to their qualities except as they are signs of operations to be performed and of inference to relations to be drawn. But in these capacities he has to admit their full reality on pain of having, logically, to deny reality to the conclusions of his operative inferences. He takes the instruments he employs, including his own sensory-motor organs and measuring instruments, to be real in the ordinary sense of the word. If he denied

---

[2] The illustration is borrowed from Eddington, *The Nature of the Physical World;* see pp. 316–319. It is indicative of the hold which the older tradition of knowledge as the exclusive revelation of reality has obtained, that Eddington finds no way to combine this account with the poetic account, save to suppose that while the scientific statement describes reality as it is "in itself," the creative activity of mind adds to this skeleton the qualities characterizing an object in direct experience. [J.D.]

the reality of these things as they are had in ordinary non-cognitive perceptual experience, the conclusions reached by them would be equally discredited. Moreover, the numbers which define his metric object are themselves results of noting interactions or connections among perceived things. It would be the height of absurdity to assert the reality of these relations while denying the reality of the things between which they hold. If the latter are "subjective" what becomes of the former? Finally, observation is resorted to for verification. It is a strange world in which the conception of the real has to be corroborated by reference to that the reality of which is made dubious by the conception. To common sense these comments may seem wholly superfluous. But since common sense may also hold the doctrine from which flow the conclusions to which the critical comments are apposite, common sense should first ask whether it holds that knowledge is a disclosure of the antecedently real? If it entertains this belief, then the dismissal by science of the experienced object to a limbo of unreality, or subjectivity or the phenomenal—whatever terms be used—results logically from his own position.

Our discussion involves a summary as well as some repetition of points previously made. Its significance lies in the liberation which comes when knowing, in all its phases, conditions and organs, is understood after the pattern provided by experimental inquiry, instead of upon the groundwork of ideas framed before such knowing had a systematic career opened to it. For according to the pattern set by the practice of knowing, knowledge is the fruit of the undertakings that transform a problematic situation into a resolved one. Its procedure is public, a part and partner of the Nature in which all interactions exist. But experienced situations come about in two ways and are of two distinct types. Some take place with only a minimum of regulation, with little foresight, preparation and intent. Others occur because, in part, of the prior occurrence of intelligent action. Both kinds are *had;* they are undergone, enjoyed or suffered. The first are not known; they are not understood; they are dispensations of fortune or providence. The second have, as they are experienced, meanings that present the funded outcome of operations that substitute definite continuity for experienced discontinuity and for the fragmentary quality due to isolation. Dream, insanity and fantasy are natural products, as "real" as anything else in the world. The acts of intentional regulation which constitute thinking are also natural developments, and so are the experienced things in which they eventuate. But the latter are resolutions of the problems set by objects experienced without intent and purpose; hence they have a security and fullness of meaning the first lack. Nothing happens, as Aristotle and the scholastics said, without an end—without a terminal effectuation. *Every* experienced object is, in some sense, such a closing and consummatory closing episode: alike the doubtful and secure, the trivial and significant, the true and mistaken, the confused and ordered. Only when the ends are closing termini of *intelligent operations* of thinking are they ends in the honorific sense. We always experience individual objects, but only the individual things which are fruits of intelligent action have in them intrinsic order and fullness of qualities.

The conditions and processes of nature generate uncertainty and its risks as truly as nature affords security and means of insurance against perils. Nature is characterized by a constant mixture of the precarious and the stable. This mixture gives poignancy to existence. If existence were either completely necessary or completely contingent, there would be neither comedy nor tragedy in life, nor need of the will to live. The significance of morals and politics, of the arts both technical and fine, of religion and of science itself as inquiry and discovery, all have their source and meaning in the union in Nature of the settled and the unsettled, the stable and the hazardous. Apart from this union, there are no such things as "ends," either as consummations or as those ends-in-view we call purposes. There is only a block universe, either something ended and admitting of no change, or else a predestined march of events. There is no such thing as fulfillment where there is no risk of failure, and no defeat where there is no promise of possible achievement. . . .

Physical inquiry has been taken as typical of the nature of knowing. The selection is justified because the operations of physical knowledge are so perfected and its scheme of symbols so well devised. But it would be misinterpreted if it were taken to mean that science is the only valid kind of knowledge; it is just an intensified form of knowing in which are written large the essential characters of any knowing. It is in addition the most powerful tool we possess for developing other modes of knowledge. But we know with respect to any subject-matter whatsoever in the degree in which we are able deliberately to transform doubtful situations into resolved ones. Physical knowledge has the advantage of its specialized character, its wholehearted devotion to a single purpose. The attitude involved in it, its method, has not as yet gone far beyond its own precincts. Beliefs current in morals, politics and religion, are marked by dread of change and by the feeling that order and regulative authority can be had only through reference to fixed standards accepted as finalities, because referring to fixed antecedent realities. Outside of physical inquiry, we shy from problems; we dislike uncovering serious difficulties in their full depth and reach; we prefer to accept what is and muddle along. Hence our social and moral "sciences" consist largely in putting facts as they are into conceptual systems framed at large. Our logic in social and humane subjects is still largely that of definition and classification as until the seventeenth century it was in natural science. For the most part the lesson of experimental inquiry has still to be learned in the things of chief concern.

We are, socially, in a condition of division and confusion because our best authenticated knowledge is obtained by directed practice, while this method is still limited to things aloof from man or concerning him only in the technologies of industries. The rest of our practice in matters that come home to us most closely and deeply is regulated not by intelligent operations, but by tradition, self-interest and accidental circumstance. The most significant phase of physical science, that which concerns its method, is unapplied in social practice, while its technical results are utilized by those in positions of privileged advantage to serve their own private or class ends. Of the many consequences that result, the state of education is perhaps the most significant. As the means of the general institution of intelligent action, it holds the key to orderly social reconstruction. But inculcation of fixed conclusions rather than development of intelligence as a method of action still dominates its processes. Devotion to training in technical and mechanical skills on one hand and to laying in a store of abstract information on the other is to one who has the power to read the scene an almost perfect illustration of the significance of the historic separation of knowledge and action, theory and practice. As long as the isolation of knowledge and practice holds sway, this division of aims and dissipation of energy, of which the state of education is typical, will persist. The effective condition of the integration of all divided purposes and conflicts of belief is the realization that intelligent action is the sole ultimate resource of mankind in every field whatsoever.

It is not claimed, therefore, that there is *no* philosophical problem of the relation of physical science to the things of ordinary experience. It is asserted that the problem *in the form* in which it has chiefly occupied modern philosophy is an artificial one, due to the continued assumption of premises formed in an earlier period of history and now having no relevancy to the state of physical inquiry. Clearing the ground of this unreal problem, however, only imposes upon philosophy the consideration of a problem which is urgently practical, growing out of the conditions of contemporary life. What revisions and surrenders of current beliefs about authoritative ends and values are demanded by the method and conclusions of natural science? What possibilities of controlled transformation of the content of present belief and practice in human institutions and associations are indicated by the control of natural energies which natural science has effected? These questions are as genuine and imperative as the traditional problem is artificial and futile.

QUESTIONS FOR STUDY AND DISCUSSION

1. Recapitulate various points of criticism raised by Dewey against belief in "fixed" laws and species in the universe.
2. Evaluate Dewey's criticism of the traditional philosophy, especially in its insistence on the evidence of purpose in the universe. Do you think an evolutionary view of the universe excludes a doctrine of finality concerning man and the universe?
3. Set forth what you consider to be the main features of Dewey's approach to the development of a new kind of philosophy. Cite quotations from "The

Influence of Darwinism" and "The Supremacy of Method" to illustrate his point of view.

4. What are some of the implications of Dewey's acceptance of the definition that thinking is "response to the doubtful as such"? How does he proceed to develop this doctrine?

5. Briefly explain Dewey's doctrine regarding the three following modes of response: (1) emotional, (2) volitional, and (3) intellectual.

6. What distinction does Dewey make between "objects" and "data"? Evaluate this distinction.

7. What does the author mean when he states that "experimental knowledge is a mode of being"?

8. What is Dewey's position concerning the extension of the methods of science to the problems of philosophy?

George Santayana

GEORGE SANTAYANA was born in Avila, Spain, in 1863 and was brought to the United States when he was eight to attend the Boston Latin School. He received his higher education as an undergraduate at Harvard, 1882–86. From 1886 to 1888 he did graduate work in Berlin, but he returned to the United States in 1889 to complete his doctoral work at Harvard, where he received his Ph.D. Except for some time spent in England, Santayana taught at Harvard from 1889 until 1912. After that he returned to England for four years (1914–18) and then spent the rest of his days in Paris and Rome. He died in Rome in 1952. His outstanding works are *The Life of Reason* (5 vols., 1905–06), *Scepticism and Animal Faith* (1923), *Realms of Being* (4 vols., 1927–40). Though a Spaniard by birth, Santayana is classified as an American philosopher and so wished to be remembered. He was the most famous pupil both of Royce and of James at Harvard.

Flux and Constancy in Human Nature

A conception of something called human nature arises not unnaturally on observing the passions of men, passions which under various disguises seem to reappear in all ages and countries. The tendency of Greek philosophy, with its insistence on general concepts, was to define this idea of human nature still further and to encourage the belief that a single and identical essence, present in all men, determined their powers and ideal destiny. Christianity, while it transposed the human ideal and dwelt on the superhuman affinities of man, did not abandon the notion of a specific humanity. On the contrary, such a notion was implied in the Fall and Redemption, in the Sacraments, and in the universal validity of Christian doctrine and precept. For if human nature were not one, there would be no propriety in requiring all men to preserve unanimity in faith or conformity in conduct. Human nature was likewise the entity which the English psychologists set themselves to describe; and Kant was so entirely dominated by the notion of a fixed and universal human nature that its constancy, in his opinion, was the source of all natural as well as moral laws. Had he doubted for a moment the stability of human nature, the foundations of his system would have fallen out; the forms of perception and thought would at once have lost their boasted necessity, since tomorrow might dawn upon new categories and a modified *a priori* intuition of space or time; and the avenue would also have been closed by which man was led, through his unalterable moral sentiments, to assumptions about metaphysical truths.

The force of this long tradition has been broken, however, by two influences of great weight in recent times, the theory of evolution and the revival of pantheism. The first has reintroduced flux into the conception of existence and the second into the conception of values. If natural species are fluid and pass into one another, human nature is merely a name for a group of qualities found by chance in certain tribes of animals, a group to which new qualities are constantly tending to attach themselves while other faculties become extinct, now in whole races, now in sporadic individuals. Human nature is therefore a variable, and its ideal cannot have a greater constancy than the demands to which it gives expression. Nor can the ideal of one man or one age have any authority over another, since the harmony existing in their nature and interests is accidental and each is a transitional phase in an indefinite evolution. The crystallisation of moral forces at any moment is consequently to be explained by universal, not by human, laws; the philosopher's interest cannot be to trace the implications of present and unstable desires, but rather to discover the mechanical law by which these desires have been generated and will be transformed, so that they will change irrevocably both their basis and their objects.

To this picture of physical instability furnished by popular science are to be added the mystical self-denials involved in pantheism. These come to reinforce the doctrine that human nature is a shifting thing with the sentiment that it is a finite and unworthy one: for every determination of being, it is said, has its significance as well as its origin in the infinite continuum of which it is a part. Forms are limitations, and limitations, according to this philosophy, would be defects, so that man's only goal would be to escape humanity and lose himself in the divine nebula that has produced and must invalidate each of his thoughts and ideals. As there would be but one spirit in the world, and that infinite, so there would be but one ideal and that omnivorous. The despair which the naturalist's view of human instability might tend to produce is turned by this mystical initiation into a sort of ecstasy; and the deluge of conformity suddenly submerges that Life of Reason which science seemed to condemn to gradual extinction.

Reason is a human function. Though the name of reason has been applied to various alleged principles of cosmic life, vital or dialectical, these principles all lack the essence of rationality, in that they are not conscious movements toward satisfaction, not, in other words, moral and beneficent principles at all. Be the instability of human nature what it may, therefore, the instability of reason is not less, since reason is but a function of human nature. However relative and subordinate, in a physical sense, human ideals may be, these ideals remain the only possible moral standards for man, the only tests which he can apply for value or authority in any other quarter. And among unstable and relative ideals none is more relative and unstable than that which transports all value to a universal law, itself indifferent to good and evil, and worships it as a deity. Such an idolatry would indeed be impossible if it were not partial and veiled, arrived at in following out some human interest and clung to by force of moral inertia and the ambiguity of words. In truth mystics do not practise so entire a renunciation of reason as they preach; eternal validity and the capacity to deal with absolute reality are still assumed by them to belong to thought or at least to feeling. Only they overlook in their description of human nature just that faculty which they exercise in their speculation; their map leaves out the ground on which they stand. The rest, which they are not identified with for the moment, they proceed to regard *de haut en bas* and to discredit as a momentary manifestation of universal laws, physical or divine. They forget that this faith in law, this absorption in the blank reality, this enthusiasm for the ultimate thought, are mere human passions like the rest; that they endure them as they might a fever and that the animal instincts are patent on which those spiritual yearnings repose.

This last fact would be nothing against the feelings in question, if they were not made vehicles for absolute revelations. On the contrary, such a relativity in instincts is the source of their importance. In virtue of this relativity they have some basis and function in the world; for did they not repose on human nature they could never express or transform it. Religion and philosophy are not always beneficent or important, but when they are it is precisely because they help to develop human faculty and to enrich human life. To imagine that by means of them we can escape from human nature and survey it from without is an ostrich-like illusion obvious to all but to the victim of it. Such a pretension may cause admiration in the schools, where self-hypnotisation is easy, but in the world it makes its professors ridiculous. For in their eagerness to empty their mind of human prejudices they reduce its rational burden to a minimum, and if they still continue to dogmatise, it is sport for the satirist to observe what forgotten accident of language or training has survived the crash of the universe and made the one demonstrable path to Absolute Truth.

Neither the path of abstraction followed by the mystics, nor that of direct and, as it avers, unbiassed observation followed by the naturalists, can lead beyond that region of common experience, traditional feeling, and conventional thought which all minds enter at birth and can elude only at the risk of inward collapse and extinction. The fact that observation involves the senses, and the senses their organs, is one which a naturalist can hardly overlook; and when we add that logical habits, sanctioned by utility, are needed to interpret the data of sense, the humanity of science and all its constructions becomes clearer than day. Superstition itself could not be more human. The path of unbiassed observation is not a path away from conventional life; it is a progress in conventions. It improves human belief by increasing the proportion of two of its ingredients, attentive perception and relevant calculus. The whole resulting vision, as it is sustained from moment to moment by present experience and instinct, has no value apart from actual ideals. And if it proves human nature to be unstable, it can build that proof on nothing more stable than human faculty as at the moment it happens to be.

Nor is abstraction a less human process, as if by becoming very abstruse indeed we could hope to become divine. Is it not a commonplace of the schools that to form abstract ideas is the prerogative of man's reason? Is not abstraction a method by which mortal intelligence makes haste? Is it not the makeshift of a mind overloaded with its experience, the trick of an eye that cannot master a profuse and ever-changing world? Shall these diagrams drawn in fancy, this system of signals in thought, be the Absolute Truth dwelling within us? Do we attain reality by making a silhouette of our dreams? If the scientific world be a product of human faculties, the metaphysical world must be doubly so; for the material there given to human understanding is here worked over again by human art. This constitutes the dignity and value of dialectic, that in spite of appearances it is so human; it bears to experience a relation similar to that which the arts bear to the same, where sensible images, selected by the artist's genius and already coloured by his aesthetic bias, are redyed in the process of reproduction whenever he has a great style, and saturated anew with his mind.

There can be no question, then, of eluding human nature or of conceiving it and its environment in such a way as to stop its operation. We may take up our position in one region of experience or in another, we may, in unconsciousness of the interests and assumptions that support us, criticise the truth or value of results obtained elsewhere. Our criticism will be solid in proportion to the solidity of the unnamed convictions that inspire it, that is, in proportion to the deep roots and fruitful ramifications which those convictions may have in human life. Ultimate truth and ultimate value will be reasonably attributed to those ideas and possessions which can give human nature, as it is, the highest satisfaction. We may admit that human nature is variable; but that admission, if justified, will be justified by the satisfaction which it gives human nature to make it. We might even admit that human ideals are vain but only if they were worth nothing for the attainment of the veritable human ideal.

The given constitution of reason, with whatever a dialectical philosophy might elicit from it, obviously determines nothing about the causes that may have brought reason to its present pass or the phases that may have preceded its appearance. Certain notions about physics might no doubt suggest themsleves to the moralist, who never can be the whole man; he might suspect, for instance, that the transitive intent of intellect and will pointed to their vital basis. Transcendence in operation might seem appropriate only to a being with a history and with an organism subject to external influences, whose mind should thus come to represent not merely its momentary state but also its constitutive past and its eventual fortunes. Such suggestions, however, would be extraneous to dialectical self-knowledge. They would be tentative only, and human nature would be freely admitted to be as variable, as relative, and as transitory as the natural history of the universe might make it.

The error, however, would be profound and the contradiction hopeless if we should deny the ideal authority over ourselves of human nature because we had discovered its origin and conditions. Nature and evolution, let us say, have brought life to the present form; but this life lives, these organs have determinate functions, and human nature, here and now, in relation to the ideal energies it unfolds, is a fundamental source. As the structure of the steam-engine has varied greatly since its first invention, and its attributions have increased, so the structure of human nature has undoubtedly varied since man first appeared upon the earth; but as in each steam-engine at each moment there must be limit of mobility, a unity of function and a clear determination of parts and tensions, so in human nature, as found at any time in any man, there is a definite scope by virtue of which alone he can have a reliable memory, a recognisable character, a faculty of connected thought and speech, a social utility, and a moral ideal.

Thinkers of different experience and organisation have *pro tanto* different logics and different moral laws. There are limits to communication even among beings of the same race, and the faculties and ideals of one intelligence are not transferable without change to any other. If this historic diversity in minds were complete, so that each lived in its own moral world, a science of each of these moral worlds would still be possible provided some inner fixity or constancy existed in its meaning. In every human thought together with an immortal intent there is a mortal and irrecoverable perception: something in it perishes instantly. Unanimity in thought involves identity of functions and similarity in organs. These conditions mark off the sphere of rational communication and society; where they fail altogether there is no mutual intelligence, no conversation, no moral solidarity.

The inner authority of reason, however is no more destroyed because it has limits in physical expression or because irrational things exist, than the grammar of a given language is invalidated because other languages do not share it, or because some people break its rules and others are dumb altogether. Innumerable madmen make no difference to the laws of thought, which borrow their authority from the inward intent and cogency of each rational mind. Reason, like beauty, is its own excuse for being.

The true philosopher, who is not one chiefly by profession, must be prepared to tread the winepress alone. He may indeed flourish like the bay-tree in a grateful environment, but more often he will rather resemble a reed shaken by the wind. Whether starved or fed by the accidents of fortune he must find his essential life in his own ideal. In spiritual life, heteronomy is suicide. That universal soul sometimes spoken of, which is to harmonise and correct individual demands, if it were a will and an intelligence in act, would itself be an individual like the others; while if it possessed no will and no intelligence, such as individuals may have, it would be a physical force or law, a dynamic system without moral authority and with a merely potential or represented existence. For to be actual and self-existent is to be individual. The living mind cannot surrender its rights to any physical power or subordinate itself to any figment of its own art without falling into manifest idolatry.

Human nature, in the sense in which it is the transcendental foundation of all science and morals, is a functional unity in each man; it is no general or abstract essence, the average of all men's characters, nor even the complex of the qualities common to all men. It is the entelechy of the living individual, be he typical or singular. That his type should be odd or common is merely a physical accident. If he can know himself by expressing the entelechy of his own nature in the form of a consistent ideal, he is a rational creature after his own kind, even if, like the angels of Saint Thomas, he be the only individual of his species. What the majority of human animals may tend to, or what the past or future variations of a race may be, has nothing to do with determining the ideal of human nature in a living man, or in an ideal society of men bound together by spiritual kinship. Otherwise Plato could not have reasoned well about the republic without adjusting himself to the politics of Buddha or Rousseau, and we should not be able to determine our own morality without making concessions to the cannibals or giving a vote to the ants. Within the field of an anthropology that tests humanity by the skull's shape, there might be room for any number of independent moralities, and although, as we shall see, there is actually a similar foundation in all human and even in all animal natures, which supports a rudimentary morality common to all, yet a perfect morality is not really common to any two men nor to any two phases of the same man's life.

The distribution of reason, though a subject irrelevant to pure logic or morals, is one naturally interesting to a rational man, for he is concerned to know how far beings exist with a congenial structure and an ideal akin to his own. That circumstance will largely influence his happiness if, being a man, he is a gregarious and sympathetic animal. His moral idealism itself will crave support from others, if not to give it direction, at least to give it warmth and courage. The best part of wealth is to have worthy heirs, and mind can be transmitted only to a kindred mind. Hostile natures cannot be brought together by mutual invective nor harmonised by the brute destruction and disappearance of either party. But when one or both parties have actually disappeared, and the combat has ceased for lack of combatants, natures not hostile to one another can fill the vacant places. In proportion to their inbred unanimity these will cultivate a similar ideal and rejoice together in its embodiment.

This has happened to some extent in the whole world, on account of natural conditions which limit the forms of life possible in one region; for nature is intolerant in her laxity and punishes too great originality and heresy with death. Such moral integration has occurred very markedly in every good race and society whose members, by adapting themselves to the same external forces, have created and discovered their common soul. Spiritual unity is a natural product. There are those who see a great mystery in the presence of eternal values and impersonal ideals in a moving and animal world, and think to solve that dualism, as they call it, by denying that nature can have spiritual functions or spirit a natural cause; but nothing can be simpler if we make, as we should, existence the test of possibility. *Ab esse ad posse valet illatio.* Nature is a perfect garden of ideals, and passion is the perpetual and fertile soil for poetry, myth, and speculation. Nor is this origin merely imputed to ideas by a late and cynical observer: it is manifest in the ideals themselves, by their subject matter and intent. For what are ideals about, what do they idealise, except natural existence and natural passions? That would be a miserable and superfluous ideal indeed that was nobody's ideal of nothing. The pertinence of ideals binds them to nature, and it is only the worst and flimsiest ideals, the ideals of a sick soul, that elude nature's limits and belie her potentialities. Ideals are forerunners or heralds of nature's successes, not always followed, indeed, by their fulfilment, for nature is but nature and has to feel her way; but they are an earnest, at least, of an achieved organisation, an incipient accomplishment, that tends to maintain and root itself in the world.

To speak of nature's successes is, of course, to impute success retroactively; but the expression may be allowed when we consider that the same functional equilibrium which is looked back upon as a good by the soul it serves, first creates individual being and with it creates the possibility of preference and the whole moral world; and it is more than a metaphor to call that achievement a success which has made a sense of success possible and actual. That nature cannot intend or previously esteem those formations which are the condition of value or intention existing at all, is a truth too obvious to demand repetition; but when those formations arise they determine estimation, and fix the direction of preference, so that the evolution which produced them, when looked back upon from the vantage-ground thus gained, cannot help seeming to have been directed toward the good now distinguished and partly attained. For this reason creation is regarded as a work of love, and the power that brought order out of chaos is called intelligence.

These natural formations, tending to generate and realise each its ideal, are, as it were, eddies in the universal flux, produced no less normally, doubtless, than the onward current, yet seeming to arrest or to reverse it. Inheritance arrests the flux by repeating a series of phases with a recognisable rhythm; memory reverses it by modifying this rhythm itself by the integration of earlier phases into those that supervene. Inheritance and memory make human stability. This stability is relative, being still a mode of flux, and consists fundamentally in repetition. Repetition marks some progress on mere continuity, since it preserves form and disregards time and matter. Inheritance is repetition on a larger scale, not excluding spontaneous variations; while habit and memory are a sort of heredity within the individual, since here an old perception reappears, by way of atavism, in the midst of a forward march. Life is thus enriched and reaction adapted to a wider field; much as a note is enriched by its overtones, and by the tensions, inherited from the preceding notes, which give it a new setting.

Progress, far from consisting in change, depends on retentiveness. When change is absolute there remains no being to improve and no direction is set for possible improvement: and when experience is not retained, as among savages, infancy is perpetual. Those who cannot remember the past are condemned to repeat it. In the first stage of life the mind is frivolous and easily distracted; it misses progress by failing in consecutiveness and persistence. This is the condition of children and barbarians, in whom instinct has learned nothing from experience. In a second stage men are docile to events, plastic to new habits and suggestions, yet able to graft them on original instincts, which they thus bring to fuller satisfaction. This is the plane of manhood and true progress. Last comes a stage when retentiveness is exhausted and all that happens is at once forgotten; a vain, because unpractical, repetition of the past takes the place of plasticity and fertile readaptation. In a moving world readaptation is the price of longevity. The hard shell, far from protecting the vital principle, condemns it to die down slowly and be gradually chilled; immortality in such a case must have been secured earlier, by giving birth to a generation plastic to the contemporary world and able to retain its lessons. Thus old age is as forgetful as youth, and more incorrigible; it displays the same inattentiveness to conditions; its memory becomes self-repeating and degenerates into an instinctive reaction, like a bird's chirp.

Not all readaptation, however, is progress, for ideal identity must not be lost. The Latin language did not progress when it passed into Italian. It died. Its amiable heirs may console us for its departure, but do not remove the fact that their parent is extinct. So every individual, nation, and religion has its limit of adaptation; so long as the increment it receives is digestible, so long as the organisation already attained is extended and elaborated without being surrendered, growth goes on; but when the foundation itself shifts, when what is gained at the periphery is lost at the centre, the flux appears again and progress is not real. Thus a succession of generations or languages or religions constitutes no progress unless some ideal present at the beginning is transmitted to the end and reaches a better expression there; without this stability at the core no common standard exists and all comparison of value with value must be external and arbitrary. Retentiveness, we must repeat, is the condition of progress.

The variation human nature is open to is not, then, variation in any direction. There are transformations that would destroy it. So long as it endures it must retain all that constitutes it now, all that it has so far gathered and worked into its substance. The genealogy of progress is like that of man, who can never repudiate a single ancestor. It starts, so to speak, from a single point, free as yet to take any direction. When once, however, evolution has taken a single step, say in the direction of vertebrates, that step cannot be retraced without extinction of the species. Such extinction may take place while progress in other lines is continued. All that preceded the forking of the dead and the living branch will be as well represented and as legitimately continued by the surviving radiates as it could have been by the vertebrates that are no more; but the invertebrate ideal is lost for ever, and no more progress is possible along that line.

The future of moral evolution is accordingly infinite, but its character is more and more determinate at every step. Mankind can never, without perishing, surrender its animal nature, its need to eat and drink, its sexual method of reproduction, its vision of nature, its faculty of speech, its arts of music, poetry, and building. Particular races cannot subsist if they renounce their savage instincts, but die, like wild animals, in captivity; and particular individuals die when not suffered any longer to retain their memories, their bodies, or even their master passions. Thus human nature survives amid a continual fluctuation of its embodiments. At every step twigs and leaves are thrown out that last but one season; but the underlying stem may have meantime grown stronger and more luxuriant. Whole branches sometimes wither, but others may continue to bloom. Spiritual unity runs, like sap, from the common root to every uttermost flower; but at each forking in the growth the branches part company, and what happens in one is no direct concern of the others. The products of one age and nation may well be unintelligible to another; the elements of humanity common to both may lie lower down. So that the highest things are communicable to the fewest persons, and yet, among these few, are the most perfectly communicable. The more elaborate and determinate a man's heritage and genius are, the more he has in common with his next of kin, and the more he can transmit and implant in his posterity for ever. Civilisation is cumulative. The farther it goes the intenser it is, substituting articulate interests for animal fumes and for enigmatic passions. Such articulate interests can be shared; and the infinite vistas they open up can be pursued for ever with the knowledge that a work long ago begun is being perfected and that an ideal is being embodied which need never be outworn.

So long as external conditions remain constant it is obvious that the greater organisation a being possesses the greater strength he will have. If indeed primary conditions varied, the finer creatures would die first; for their adaptation is more exquisite and the irreversible core of their being much larger relatively; but in a constant environment their equipment makes them irresistible and secures their permanence and multiplication. Now man is a part of nature and her organisation may be regarded as the foundation of his own; the word nature is therefore less equivocal than it seems, for every nature is Nature herself in one of her more specific and better articulated forms. Man therefore represents the universe that sustains him; his existence is a proof that the cosmic equilibrium that fostered his life is a natural equilibrium, capable of being long maintained. Some of the ancients thought it eternal; physics now suggests a different opinion. But even if this equilibrium, by which the stars are kept in their courses and human progress is allowed to proceed, is fundamentally unstable, it shows what relative stability nature may attain. Could this balance be preserved indefinitely, no one knows what wonderful adaptations might occur within it, and to what excellence human nature in particular might advance. Nor is it unlikely that before the cataclysm comes time will be afforded for more improvement than moral philosophy has ever dreamed of. For it is remarkable how inane and unimaginative Utopias have generally been. This possibility is not uninspiring and may help to console those who think the natural conditions of life are not conditions that a good life can be lived in. The possibility of essential progress is bound up with the tragic possibility that progress and human life should some day end together. If the present equilibrium of forces were eternal all adaptations to it would have already taken place and, while no essential catastrophe would need to be dreaded, no essential improvement could be hoped for in all eternity. I am not sure that a humanity such as we know, were it destined to exist for ever, would offer a more exhilarating prospect than a humanity having indefinite elasticity together with a precarious tenure of life. Mortality has its compensations: one is that all evils are transitory, another that better times may come.

Human nature, then, has for its core the substance of nature at large, and is one of its more complex formations. Its determination is progressive. It varies indefinitely in its historic manifestations and fades into what, as a matter of natural history, might no longer be termed human. At each moment it has its fixed and determinate entelechy, the ideal of that being's life, based on his instincts, summed up in his character, brought to a focus in his reflection, and shared by all who have attained or may inherit his organisation. His perceptive and reasoning faculties are parts of human nature, as embodied in him; all objects of belief or desire, with all standards of justice and duty which he can possibly acknowledge, are transcripts of it, conditioned by it, and justifiable only as expressions of its inherent tendencies.

This definition of human nature, clear as it may be in itself and true to the facts, will perhaps hardly make sufficiently plain how the Life of Reason, having a natural basis, has in the ideal world a creative and absolute authority. A more concrete description of human nature may accordingly not come amiss, especially as the important practical question touching the extension of a given moral authority over times and places depends on the degree of kinship found among the creatures inhabiting those regions. To give a general picture of human nature and its rational functions will be the task of the following pages. The truth of a description which must be largely historical may not be indifferent to the reader, and I shall study to avoid bias in the presentation, in so far as is compatible with frankness and brevity; yet even if some bias should manifest itself and if the picture were historically false, the rational principles we shall be trying to illustrate will not thereby be invalidated. Illustrations might have been sought in some fictitious world, if imagination had not seemed so much less interesting than reality, which besides enforces with unapproachable eloquence the main principle in view, namely, that nature carries its ideal with it and that the progressive organisation of irrational impulses makes a rational life.

QUESTIONS FOR STUDY AND DISCUSSION

1. According to Santayana the theory of evolutionism has reintroduced flux into the conception of existence. What are the implications of this view as developed in Santayana's theory?
2. Discuss Santayana's ideas concerning the nature and role of abstraction.
3. On the basis of your reading of this entire essay, what is your interpretation of Santayana's views as to the role of ideals and moral standards in human life? Are they relative or absolute? Are they purely subjective or do they have an objective basis?
4. What do you think are some of the implications of the statement: "Nature is a perfect garden of ideals, and passion is the perpetual and fertile soil for poetry, myth, and speculation"?
5. Comment on Santayana's statement: "Progress, far from consisting in change, depends on retentiveness."
6. To what extent in your view does Santayana insist on constancy in human nature?
7. Is Santayana a complete naturalist in making the following type of statement: "Human nature, then, has for its core the substance of nature at large, and is one of its more complex formations."?

TOPICS FOR DISCUSSION AND TERM PAPERS

A.

1. Trace the origins of naturalism in classical Greek and Roman thought. Identify some of the leading thinkers.
2. Contrast the mechanistic and evolutionary view of the universe and explain the importance of the development of evolutionary thought for the understanding of naturalism as it is professed today.
3. Evaluate the aim of naturalistic thinkers who insist on establishing what they regard as the fundamental continuity between man and the rest of nature. Does "continuity" in your understanding rule out "transcendence"? Explain.
4. Trace some of the historical background of pragmatism. What is the significance of Descartes, Hume, and Kant in relation to the subsequent development of pragmatism?
5. Contrast the position of pragmatists who regard ideas as instruments of action with the position of earlier empiricists who regarded them as copies or representations of qualities in the external world.
6. Show one basic point of affinity between the fundamental position of Kant and that of the pragmatists. Show one basic point of difference.
7. What are some of the relations in American philosophy between pragmatism and naturalism? Can you name any naturalists who were not committed to pragmatism or vice versa?
8. How would you contrast the tenor of Peirce, James, Dewey, and Santayana? Bring out points of similarity where they exist and points of difference.
9. Thoroughly examine what you regard as fundamental points of strength and possible points of weakness within pragmatism as a theory of knowledge.
10. Thoroughly examine what you regard as fundamental points of strength and possible points of weakness within naturalism as a view of the universe.

B.

1. James and Dewey both place a great deal of insistence on human freedom. In your view does their doctrine as pragmatists provide an adequate theoretical basis for human freedom? Compare with other schools of thought discussed in this volume.
2. Is there any significant difference between the Marxist view of man as a product of nature and that of American naturalists? If not, how would you account for the fact of the divergence between these two schools of thought in the area of social, economic, and political philosophy?
3. Set forth what you consider to be significant points of similarity and contrast between pragmatic realism and the realism of the Thomistic Aristotelian tradition. As theories of knowledge are these schools of philosophy incompatible with each other?
4. Do you think there are strong reasons for regarding William James as an existentialist? Clarify the meaning of terms in your discussion.
5. Compare various aspects of Santayana's doctrine of essences with the insistence on the part of phenomenologists upon the "bracketing of existence."

RECOMMENDED READINGS

Primary Sources

Dewey, John. *Logic: The Theory of Inquiry.* New York: Henry Holt and Co., 1938. In this volume Dewey sets forth his view concerning the nature of logic as it relates to the purposes of life and as it is founded on the basis of induction. The reader is invited to sample various parts of this work to discover Dewey's central point of view.

―――. *Reconstruction in Philosophy.* Boston: Beacon Press, 1957. This volume, originally published in 1920, is intended to show that the role of philosophy is to establish tools for the advancement of human happiness through social reconstruction, especially through education. Chapter 1 of this work is helpful to an understanding of Dewey's basic approach to philosophy. See "Changing Conceptions of Philosophy," pp. 1–27.

James, William. *Pragmatism and Other Essays.* New York: Washington Square Press, 1963. This collection of essays represents the basic thought of William James. Especially recommended are "Pragmatism and Common Sense," pp. 73–86, and "The Moral Philosopher and the Moral Life," pp. 214–35.

―――. *Radical Empiricism* and *A Pluralistic Universe.* New York: Longmans, Green & Co., 1943. These works are published in a single volume and the reader is invited to examine portions of each to catch the essential flavor of James's philosophy of experience.

―――. *The Varieties of Religious Experience.* New York: The New American Library, 1964. This volume is the product of James's Gifford Lectures delivered in 1901–02 that acquired for James a reputation as a philosopher beyond the one he had already achieved as a psychologist. One of the central theses of this volume is that religion performs a function in our lives that no other portion of our nature can fulfill. See, for example, his Lectures XI, XII, and XIII on "Saintliness," pp. 207–55.

Peirce, Charles Sanders. *Collected Papers of Charles Sanders Peirce.* 8 vols. Ed. by Charles Hartshorne and Paul Weiss (vols. I–VI) and Arthur W. Burks (vols. VII–VIII). Cambridge, Mass.: Harvard University Press, 1931–58. These volumes contain Peirce's complete writings.

―――. *Philosophical Writings.* Ed. by J. Buchler. New York: Dover Publications, 1940. This anthology contains a representative portion of the writings of Peirce in paperback form. Of special interest to the student should be Ch. 21, "Pragmatism in Retrospect: A Last Formulation," pp. 269–89.

Santayana, George. "Apologia Pro Mente Sua," in *The Philosophy of George Santayana.* Ed. by Paul Schilpp. Evanston, Ill.: Northwestern University Press, 1940. This essay, comprising pp. 497–605 of the volume, is a major summary by Santayana of his own philosophy. In the early section of the essay Santayana makes many interesting statements on his relationship to Royce and James during his early years at Harvard University. The last section, entitled "Personalities and Personal Remarks," pp. 595–605, is particularly readable and interesting.

―――. "The Genteel Tradition in American Philosophy," in *The Development of American Philosophy.* Ed. by Walter G. Muelder *et al.* New

York: Houghton Mifflin Co., 1960. Pp. 171–81. This is one of the greatest essays written by Santayana. In it the author traces the puritan origins of American thought. He presents a penetrating analysis of certain fundamental aspects of some of America's leading philosophers, including Emerson and James.

————. *The Philosophy of Santayana.* Ed. by Irwin Edman. New York: Charles Scribner's Sons, 1953. This volume contains selections from all the major works of Santayana. The ordering of selections is chronological, dating from 1896 to the time of Santayana's death. The student reader will find the section on "Scepticism and Animal Faith," pp. 368–441, a good introduction to Santayana's view on the nature of human knowledge.

Commentaries

Barry, Robert M. "Direction of American Philosophy: A Bibliographical Review," *The American Benedictine Review,* XV (June, 1964), 215–36. This article is an excellent summary both of some of the highlights in American philosophy and of some of the current literature in the field.

Fisch, Max H., *et al.,* eds. *Classic American Philosophers.* New York: Appleton-Century-Crofts, 1951. Especially recommended in this volume are the introductory essays to Peirce, James, and Dewey.

Krikorian, Yervant H., ed. *Naturalism and the Human Spirit.* New York: Columbia University Press, 1944. This volume comprises fifteen essays on a variety of topics by different naturalists from Dewey to Randall. The last two essays of the book are especially recommended to the general reader: Harold A. Larrabee, Ch. 14, "Naturalism in America," pp. 319–53; and John Herman Randall, Jr., "Epilogue: The Nature of Naturalism," pp. 354–83.

Moore, Edward C. *American Pragmatism: Peirce, James, and Dewey.* New York: Columbia University Press, 1961. This book is a good basic presentation of the men mentioned in the title of the work.

Muelder, Walter G., *et al.,* eds. *The Development of American Philosophy.* New York: Houghton Mifflin Co., 1960. The volume contains many excellent essays and reading selections in American philosophy. Of particular value is the following: George Herbert Mead, "The Philosophy of Royce, James, and Dewey in Their American Setting," pp. 351–60.

Ratner, Joseph, ed. *Intelligence in the Modern World: John Dewey's Philosophy.* New York: Random House, 1939. A thorough introduction to Dewey's philosophy together with substantial selections from various parts of his works.

Roth, Robert J. "The Challenge of American Naturalism," *Thought,* XXXIX, 155 (Winter, 1964), 559–84. This article is an excellent presentation of the need to study American naturalism, especially that of Dewey, as a means of confronting some of the leading problems of contemporary man.

PART FOUR

Introduction

The Task of Philosophy

Historical Background

Development of Linguistic Philosophy

Notes on the Readings

Summary: The Challenge of Analysis

Readings

HUME: *On Personal Identity*

CARNAP: *Psychology in Physical Language*

RUSSELL: *Mind and Matter*

AYER: *Freedom and Necessity*
Personal Identity

RYLE: *Descartes' Myth*
The Self

WITTGENSTEIN: *The Will, Death, Immortality, and Other*
"Unspeakables"

MOORE: *Wittgenstein's Lectures in 1930–1933, Parts I and III*

STRAWSON: *Persons*

HAMPSHIRE: *Self-Knowledge and the Will*

ANALYTIC-POSITIVIST THOUGHT:

Hume

Carnap

Russell

Ayer

Ryle

Wittgenstein

Moore

Strawson

Hampshire

EDITED BY

Margaret Gorman, R.S.C.J.

NEWTON COLLEGE OF THE SACRED HEART

ANALYTIC-POSITIVIST THOUGHT:

- Hume
- Carnap
- Russell
- Ayer
- Ryle
- Wittgenstein
- Moore
- Strawson
- Hampshire

[handwritten annotations: "verification principle"; "meaning of a word lies in its use, phil of ordinary language as opposed to therapeutic phi"; "common language, very precise & systematic"]

Introduction

The Task of Philosophy

Analytic philosophy, now dominant in Great Britain and well entrenched in the United States, Australia, and Scandinavia, seems to have a special attraction for the Anglo-Saxon temperament. Its origin is clearly visible in the reaction to the excessive idealism of the neo-Hegelians at Oxford at the end of the nineteenth century—an idealism that held that the only reality lies in one's ideas, not in external events. The reaction was first expressed in the work of George Edward Moore (1873–1958), but the questions analytic philosophy raises and the attitude of mind it fosters have recurred often in the development of philosophical thought.

The note common to all philosophers in the analytic tradition (there is no school as such) is their conception of the task of philosophy. The task of philosophy, they hold, is to *dis*solve (not solve) the problems or puzzles that arise through the misunderstanding of the logic of our language. Such a task demands piecemeal analysis of different words or concepts to show that the confusion is unnecessary. The dissolution of the problem would not mean that any clear position would be taken with regard to that problem or to the nature of reality as a whole. Analytic philosophers either

420

deny the meaningfulness of metaphysics or take no position with regard to ultimates. For example, an analysis by Gilbert Ryle (b. 1900) of the mind-body problem, raised by René Descartes (1596–1650) in an acute form and plaguing man since the beginning of philosophical thought, leads not to a solution but to a dissolution of the problem. The problem no longer exists. There is no difficulty about the relation of mind to body, for these are not different things but one. It is by the use of the words *mind* and *body* that we split man into two different things. Therefore, the analytic philosophers held that the question of their relationship is caused by the use of inadequate language. The following statements from Ludwig Wittgenstein (1889–1951), generally considered to be the greatest analytic philosopher, also illustrates their readiness to shift their views as they continue to analyze philosophical problems. Wittgenstein wrote the first statement as part of the preface of the *Tractatus Logico-Philosophicus* in 1921. The second, from the preface of *Philosophical Investigations* (published posthumously in 1953), shows both his honesty and his desire to inspire others to an honest rethinking of problems:

> . . . the truth of the thoughts that are here set forth seems to me unassailable and definitive. I therefore believe myself to have found, on all essential points, the final solution of the problems. And if I am not mistaken in this belief, then, the second thing in which the value of this work consists is that it shows how little is achieved when these problems are solved.[1]

> For since beginning to occupy myself with philosophy again, sixteen years ago, I have been forced to recognize grave mistakes in what I wrote in that first book . . . .
> I should not like my writing to spare other people the trouble of thinking. But, if possible to stimulate someone to thoughts of his own.[2]

The method of philosophical analysis, in general, is either to explore the various uses of a word in ordinary language or to translate philosophical problems into linguistic or grammatical terms. For example, the medieval problem of universals ("Do they exist in themselves or are they mere names—*flatus vocis,* words, or sounds without any real referents?") is expressed by the analyst in grammatical terms ("do abstract words, such as dog, cat, and goodness, function as proper names—which names cannot be defined or analyzed further, but can only denote or point to?"). Or again, an ethical problem, formerly expressed as "is this to be done or avoided?" is translated by the analyst into the grammatical problem: "is it a prescriptive or imperative sentence?" We see here the problem of the relation of

---

[1] Ludwig Wittgenstein, *Tractatus Logico-Philosophicus,* trans. by D. F. Pears and B. F. McGuinness (New York: Humanities Press, 1961), p. 5.

[2] Wittgenstein, *Philosophical Investigations,* 2nd ed., trans. by G. E. M. Anscombe (Oxford: Oxford University Press, 1963), p. viii.

word to thought and of thought to thing and perhaps an implicit admission that our language reflects not only our thought but the world. To clarify our language would mean to clarify our thought; to clarify our thought is to get at reality more directly. When we know more about the way in which man's thought relates to or reflects reality we know more about man.

Key Problems in a Philosophy of Man

In this volume on the philosophy of man, we are interested in analytical philosophers largely because of their discussion of man as knower and communicator. In their analysis of man's use of language they also touch on the other problems under consideration: the unity of man, his freedom, his immortality.

Each tradition represented in this book has a decidedly different perspective on these key problems. The classical and scholastic philosophers indicated that their philosophizing was "getting at" the way man knows, or rather at his powers of knowing and choosing, as well as at the essential structure common to all men that makes man both one and immortal. Dialectic philosophers presented a view of man as reached by thought and as a part of a highly systematized structure of reality conceived by the mind. The American philosophers were interested more in the functioning of free will and knowing, and in the consequences of these functions, than in describing their essential structure or in fitting them into a system. The existentialists and phenomenologists look at these problems, not from the common or universal objective elements in men, but in the concrete experiences of freedom and unity that each individual person has in his own concrete situation.

The analytic philosophers approach man from another perspective. Views of man as he knows himself and others can be clarified, they hold, by analyzing man's *statements* about these functions. Certainly when we consider as Wittgenstein does (in Moore's descriptions of his lectures) the sentences "I have a toothache" and "He has a toothache," we see that man knows these two facts differently. Our consciousness of *our own* experience, such as a toothache, is quite different from our knowledge of *another*'s toothache. The analytic philosophers then do not study man's powers of knowing nor his experiences of knowing but his statements about his knowledge of his own mind and other minds.

The same is true about the problem of the unity of man. The article by Hume raises the question: What do we mean by "self?" David Hume (1711–76) had already indicated that "cause" is merely a word put on a phenomenon that recurs often—the following of one event by another. "Self" also could be merely the word applied to the perceptions of which we are aware. By analyzing cause and self we bring words back from their philosophical to their actual everyday usage, to their use in the language, which is their original home. As Wittgenstein showed, the nature of philosophical investigation compels a man to go over a wide range of the uses of a word (for example, self), approaching it from many different directions, inventing intermediate cases, and rearranging these views so that in surveying the word "self" we may get insights into the problem of the unity of man.

Implicit here is a view that such an investigation will not unearth new facts but present new ways of looking at and organizing truths already possessed. The selection by Rudolf Carnap (b. 1891), the logical positivist,[3] reveals an interest in language but it does not show the multiple approach to the uses of a word that is characteristic of analytic philosophers. Another discussion of man's unity is developed as these philosophers discuss the so-called mind-body problem.

Stuart Hampshire (b. 1914) treats free will in a similar way. He looks at the uses of the words connected with freedom, such as responsibility, choice, and decision. For the analytic philosopher believes that one of the best ways to see a problem is to see how the concept or word would function in a variety of circumstances, imaginary and real. Language has many uses—artistic, ethical, emotional, literary, religious, metaphysical. By seeing a word in its various contexts the philosopher clarifies our view of the reality that this word can describe, suggest, or signify, but never fully encompass. The important thing to remember is that the analytic philosopher does not believe that there is a one-to-one correspondence between the word and the thing, or its referent. The words "self," "free will," "knowledge," and the realities they point to are not identical. By seeing the words in many different uses we may more closely approach these realities, but we must remember that these are *approaches* and not detailed photographs.

As yet none of the great analytic philosophers has discussed immortality at length and in depth. The analytic method, though, could well and fruitfully be applied to this problem. The logical positivist would not recognize it as a meaningful problem since it lies beyond the realm of the senses. The only selection from Wittgenstein in this volume shows how he was grappling with the problem (6.431–6.432) and felt that it is beyond natural science, beyond words: "These problems of life remain completely untouched" and are both mystical and a mystery. Peter Frederick Strawson (b. 1919) indirectly discusses immortality in trying to analyze what we mean by it when we speak about our body and its relationship to consciousness or the self or person.

Historical Background

How and why did this emphasis on language arise? A philosophical approach never occurs in a vacuum. It always has its roots in other attempts

---

[3] Logical positivists maintain that the only reality is that grasped by the senses.

to probe the mystery or mysteries of reality, usually as a reaction against some extreme philosophical position or method.

Throughout the development of philosophy two trends on a continuum can be noted, concerning both content and method. With reference to content, the empirical-sensist trend gradually lessens its emphasis on experience as it meets the idealist, intuitive, or rationalist trend. With reference to method, there is the systematic, precise approach as opposed to the conversational use of inexact, even mythical expressions in face of the ineffable. The analysts, for the most part, belong to the empirical-sensist group and many prefer precise formal language. Ludwig Wittgenstein combines both trends.

The desire to reduce all philosophical problems to their simplest components is a classic aim of philosophy. Thales (*c.* 624–546 B.C.), the first Western philosopher, argued that all things are really just water; Descartes tried to reduce complex propositions to the most simple; Gottfried Wilhelm Leibniz (1646–1716) talked of concepts so primitive that they cannot be resolved into others; John Locke (1632–1704) thought that all ideas could be reduced to simple ones, mere names which could not be defined. Wittgenstein himself quotes Plato's *Theaetetus:* "In consequence it is impossible to give an account of any primary element; for it, nothing is possible but the bare name; its name is all it has." [4]

Pre-Kantian Insights

This relation of thought to word or name was also discussed in the days of Heraclitus (*c.* 540–475 B.C.), who thought the relationship was a natural one, and Democritus (*c.* 460–370 B.C.), who thought words were attached to their meanings merely by convention. In the first half of the fifth century B.C., the Sophists invented grammar and, with Protagoras (480–410 B.C.), they were the first to classify parts of speech. This enabled Aristotle (384–322 B.C.) to systematize thought and to establish the rules of logic. The relationship between words and thought was centered in the great nominalist struggle in the twelfth and thirteenth centuries. To the nominalist, language is thought or thought is language. The nominalist believes that our forms of thought are not given to us by the structure of the world nor are they found in our minds. They are human contrivances open to change and to breakdown. Three medieval English philosophers, Roger Bacon (1214–94), Duns Scotus (1265–1308), and William of Ockham (*c.* 1280–1349), were critically interested in language. The interest was revived by the English empiricist philosophers of the seventeenth century— Francis Bacon (1561–1626), Thomas Hobbes (1588–1679), and John Locke. It was Locke who devoted Book III, "On Words," of his chief work, *Essay Concerning Human Understanding* (1690), to the signification and right use of words. Hume challenged the existence of nonempirical

---

[4] *Investigations*, Sect. 46, p. 21. The passage is taken from *Theaetetus* 201D–202B.

entities—essences, concepts, meanings, causality, ideas. In his famous effort to discover in himself a self, he had to admit that all he could experience was a bundle of perceptions, although through his intuition he felt there was a personal identity.

Here is manifest a phenomenon in philosophy that occurs again and again. As the philosopher intuits, he apprehends reality; as he tries to express or even to systematize his intuition, the insight becomes lifeless, orderly but sterile. So Descartes intuited himself as "Cogito," that is, as existing and thinking, but then immediately he classified himself as a thinking substance precisely cut off from any nonthinking part. And Hume, with *scientific* rigor, could analytically find only "a bundle of perceptions," but *intuitively* he admitted that he felt he had an identity both inexpressible and unanalyzable.

Kant and the Categories of Understanding

Immanuel Kant (1724–1804) accentuated this split in man's knowledge between the cognitional and the intuitive. In fact, with Kant we begin to see more types of knowledge than merely the sense or empirical intuition of the empiricists or the cognition of rationalists. He informed us that there are also pure intuitions (immediate awareness of the a priori), in particular, intuitions of space and of time.

Kant's division of all knowledge into noumena (things in themselves) and phenomena (things as they appear), his classification of judgments into a priori and a posteriori, analytic and synthetic, and his new view of the role of categories influenced all philosophers who came after him. Kant wished to show the limits and functions of theoretical knowledge. The Procrustean myth may help to clarify his theory: just as Procrustes chopped off the head or limbs of anyone too large for his iron bed and stretched those too small for it, so Kant viewed man as chopping off the manifold of sensation (or stretching it) in order to fit it into the categories of preconceived size. "Categories are concepts which prescribe laws a priori to appearances and therefore to nature, the sum of all appearances." [5] Thus our knowledge is ordered or regulated with a kind of vicious precision by a priori categories, but that there are metaphysical realities behind the categories, such as substance or causality, cannot be known.

A priori judgments are those that are absolutely independent of all experience. For example, mathematical statements (such as two and three are five) are independent of experience since they are not about objects actually experienced here and now. Logical independence is required here. If a judgment is thought to be necessary or universal, then it is a priori. No set of statements about experienced objects can contradict mathematical statements; all we need is mastery of the language in which these state-

---

[5] Immanuel Kant, *Critique of Pure Reason*, 2nd ed., trans. by Norman Kemp Smith (London: St. Martin's Press, 1963), B 163.

ments are made. If we think that these statements are independent of experience, then the judgment is a priori.

The analytic-synthetic distinction is based on the relation of the subject to the predicate. If the predicate is contained in the meaning of the subject, then the judgment is analytic, or the statement is a tautology. An example would be: A bachelor is an unmarried man. If new knowledge is added by the predicate, the judgment is synthetic. For example: Christmas falls on Monday this year. In the four types of judgment—analytic a priori, synthetic a priori, analytic a posteriori, synthetic a posteriori—the first gives no new knowledge. A priori judgments are the only certain ones; therefore for Kant the only judgments that give knowledge primarily are synthetic a priori judgments. They give knowledge because they are synthetic (the result of experience); they are certain because they are a priori (independent of experience, though perhaps "gradually realized" by each man).

According to Kant, synthetic a priori judgments are to be found in mathematics, natural science, legitimate mathematics, and ethical theory. In answer to his question about how synthetic a priori judgments are possible, he states that there are two components in human experience, one emanating from our sensations and therefore empirical and a posteriori (after experience), the other emanating from our theoretical reason and a priori (before experience). The sensations must be put in order, in a framework of space and time. Space and time then are the a priori forms of perception. The perceptions must be ordered within a conceptual framework, within categories that are a priori. The form or perception could be such frameworks (for example, the law of causality) that are in us prior to experience as experience. The task of theoretical philosophy is to make transcendental deductions concerning the limits of theoretical discourse, not to speculate what transcends this limit and cannot be theoretically known.

The transcendent includes the *Ding an sich,* the noumenon or thing in itself, which exists independently of experience. Principles of practical reason can only be postulated as necessary conditions for the moral order of the world; these principles cannot be known or intuited, only postulated. Our experience therefore has a form or category, founded on theoretical reason, into which the content must fit, that is, the content from our sensa- tions. Transcendent propositions such as propositions on God, the immortal soul, or free will, cannot be known to be true by theoretical reason but can only be *postulated* to be true by *practical* reason.

Post-Kantian Views of Knowledge and Language

Whether or not Kant's view of knowledge as consisting primarily of synthetic a priori judgments is valid, or even possible, does not concern us here, except insofar as his respect for the certainty of mathematics is inherited by the analytic philosophers and his view of analytic statements is taken over by the logical positivists. His notion of categories of thought as regulating the manifold of experience is transformed by the analysts into the view that language orders our experiences. But language to them is not like an a priori category. It is rather like the language of mathematics— chosen by man arbitrarily. Just as the mathematician says, "Let x equal 2," so we say, "Let rose designate such and such a plant."

In a sense, Kant's critique of pure reason wherein he showed that any theoretical knowledge of the thing in itself is impossible and that ordered thought is an imposition of "hypothetical constructs" on the manifold of sensation is transformed by Wittgenstein into a critique of pure language. In an analogous way Wittgenstein shows that language orders our thought but does not get to the essence, to the unsayable, to the thing itself.

In fact, it is largely to the metaphysical agnosticism of Kant and the notion of man's knowledge as *constitutive* rather than *regulative* of experience that the logical positivists can trace their rejection of metaphysics as unthinkable. The extreme nominalism of Ockham and the metaphysical agnosticism of Kant were developed further in John Stuart Mill's (1806–73) theory of meaning as given in *System of Logic* (1843). Finally with Charles Sanders Peirce (1839–1914) we find a very penetrating account of language. He developed Locke's view that logic is the same as semiotics, or the theory of signs.

The Influence of Mathematics and Science

The linguistic theory maintains that language and thought grow to- gether as inseparable human achievements. Accordingly, a necessary truth does not tell us how the world must be but rather how we describe it, given our decisions about the meaning of words. All necessary truths are found in the truths of logic, mathematics, and philosophy. Necessity is a generalization of Kant's idea of analyticity. An analytic statement is one whose truth depends solely on the meaning of terms. We do not *discover* the meaning so much or its necessity, but we *decide* on the meaning by choosing the words to be used in a certain way.

The analyst's method emphasizes the analysis of language. This is a re- jection of psychologism, which is an analysis of *how* we think more than of *what* we think. It was practiced by Locke, Hume, and Mill; with them philosophy seemed to result in a psychology of thinking. The analysts turned from a consideration of consciousness to a study of *discourse,* preferably of very concrete language. They were repelled by the abstract subjective speculations of the neo-Hegelians. They wished to make philosophy as respectable as science, especially after the development in the nineteenth century of formal logic and the philosophy of mathematics. To the hardheaded analytic philosopher, knowledge is science and science is not psychological; it is a body of statements about objective facts. At this point we must distinguish between methodological linguistic analysis and the metaphysical version of philosophical analysis. The philosopher, using only the method, says that there are good practical reasons for philosophers to study thought by confining themselves to the study of its expression in language; the metaphysical analyst says that it is just in language that thought consists.

Traditionally, no one had thought there was a problem in investigating thought directly; to think was merely to manipulate abstract essences, ideas, and meanings. Confusion in language could be removed by comparing words with thoughts. Those in the Platonic tradition saw ideas as corresponding to objective abstractions, to fixed meanings that were waiting for us to grasp them with our concepts and to express them in our language.

As mathematics became more refined and Aristotelian logic more debased, the violent explosion of George Boole's logical algebra, Peirce's logic of relations, and Gottlob Frege's theory of quantification completed the destruction of the debased Aristotelian logic. The first model of analytic procedure was the *Principia Mathematica* (1910–13) of Alfred North Whitehead (1861–1947) and Bertrand Russell (b. 1872). They, or at least Russell, hoped that mathematics could be reduced to logic; the final goal of philosophical analysis was fixed by them as a comprehensive systematization of the whole of our conceptual apparatus in which methods of formal logic would be used to reduce all concepts to their empirical foundation.

Wittgenstein actually marks the starting point of linguistic analysis in his account of the analytic nature of logical and mathematical truth. With Russell he developed the philosophy of logical atomism (later repudiated by both) in which the logical structure of human knowledge was discussed according to the new method. This, together with the indirect influence of such philosophically minded scientists as Ernest Mach, Jules Henri Poincaré, and Percy W. Bridgman, was to influence the formalists in the direction of logical positivism. This group has been described as "the more Russellian, positivistically inclined formalists," while the other group has been named "the more Moorean philosophers of language." [6]

The second group derives from the violent reaction of George Edward Moore and other English philosophers to the "intellectual slovenliness and self-indulgent edification of much of the British Hegelianism of the late Victorian period." [7] Moore wished only to examine minutely the sense of such words as "know" and "good," in order to reveal the systematic misuses of the speculative philosophers. He was the initiator of the Oxford revolt against extreme subjective and speculative Hegelianism; under the influence of Bertrand Russell, his essay in 1903, *The Refutation of Idealism,* was the first intimation of its collapse.

Moore appealed to common sense, urged the analysis of statements, and stressed the importance of ordinary language although admitting that reference to ordinary language is not the infallible test. He wished to distinguish between analytic and synthetic statements. Norman Malcolm (b.

---

[6] Anthony Quinton, "Linguistic Analysis," in *Philosophy in the Mid-Century,* ed. by Raymond Klibansky (Florence: La Nuova Italia Editrice, 1961), p. 158.
[7] *Ibid.*

1911) says that the essence of Moore's technique of refuting statements consists in showing that they go against ordinary language. Moore himself admits that he has never been confined to mere language but that he analyzes the concept or proposition (the thought) behind the statement. The fact that his work is philosophically inconclusive—one formulation of a satisfactory analysis—is the result of his method. The very neutrality of his philosophy causes the lack of criterion by which to judge the adequacy of an analysis. He can show the errors and confusion of a man's thought but he cannot cure the confusion. His influence on English philosophy has been slight, for no one has accepted in their entirety his concepts of common sense or analyticity. However, as a concrete example of a new kind of philosophical inquiry—painstaking, minute, unsystematic—his influence is great. John Wisdom (b. 1904) was to say that Moore perhaps did more than any other man to show that philosophy really is logic.

The line of thought that flowed from Moore converged with the positivistically inclined formalists in the person of Bertrand Russell, only to diverge again later. The convergence is expressed in Wittgenstein's *Tractatus;* the beginning of linguistic analysis and of philosophical analysis is produced through Russell's influence on Wittgenstein.

Development of Linguistic Philosophy

With the publication of the *Tractatus* in 1921, the movement of philosophical analysis was officially launched. Wittgenstein proposed in this work the picture theory of meaning, which accorded with the view of the world now called logical atomism. The world is a plurality of logically independent facts. To think is to form pictures of these facts, and language is the most important of the many ways in which facts can be depicted. The meaning of a statement is the fact it points to, or that which it pictures. If the fact is in reality, the statement is true. Elementary facts can be combined into assemblages, and the truth function of the assemblages depends on the truth or falsity of the elements, as the *Principia Mathematica* had set out. However, necessary statements are true, regardless of their components, since the conclusion is contained in the premises. In an ideal language where meanings of statements must be clear immediately, necessary truths are indispensable. But ethical and religious statements and those of traditional metaphysics are senseless because they do not picture even possible facts. Yet as Wittgenstein said in the preface,

> The whole sense of the book might be summed up in the following words: what can be said at all can be said clearly, and what we cannot talk about we must pass over in silence.
>   Thus the aim of the book is to set a limit to thought or rather—not to thought but to the expression of thoughts.

> It will therefore only be in language that the limit can be set and what lies on the other side of the limit will simply be nonsense.[8]

This passage as well as that of 6.54 in the *Tractatus* seems to imply that Wittgenstein held that metaphysical statements are nonsense. He even went on to say:

> My propositions serve as elucidations in the following way:
> Anyone who understands me eventually recognizes them as nonsensical, when he has used them as steps to climb up beyond them. (He must, so to speak throw away the ladder after he has climbed up it.)
> He must transcend these propositions and then he will see the world aright.[9]

From these statements, it might be easy to conclude that the way to deal with metaphysical propositions is merely to ask what sense-observation would verify or falsify them. This was, in fact, the development of thought by the Vienna Circle and in England by A. J. Ayer (b. 1910)—the so-called school of logical positivism.

Although the logical positivists *could* develop their principle of verification from the ideas implicit in the *Tractatus,* Wittgenstein avows that this is not his intention. In a letter to Bertrand Russell he said:

> Now I'm afraid you haven't really got hold of my main contention, to which the whole business of logical propositions is only corollary. The main point is the theory of what can be expressed (*gesagt*) by propositions—i.e., by language (and, what comes to the same, what can be thought) and what cannot be expressed by propositions, but only shown (*gezeigt*); which, I believe, is the cardinal problem of philosophy.[10]

G. E. M. Anscombe, in fact, maintains that Wittgenstein did not intend the principle of verification by sense experience to be a general method of criticizing sentences. He was trying to break the influence of the psychologism of Locke and Hume and their preoccupation with sensation, perception, and experience by concentrating on the philosophy of logic.

It is maintained that the *Tractatus* in many respects generated logical postivism, even though logical positivism was never accepted as a part of analytic philosophy. In fact, the two philosophies are incompatible.[11] Moritz Schlick's (1882–1936) "Meaning and Verification" shows the transition from Wittgenstein's statement to his view of the ostensive definition (or the experience that can verify this), that is, Wittgenstein's "I determine

---

[8] *Tractatus,* p. 3.
[9] *Ibid.,* p. 151.
[10] G. E. M. Anscombe, *An Introduction to Wittgenstein's Tractatus,* 2nd ed. (London: Hutchison University Library, 1963), p. 161.
[11] *Ibid.,* p. 152.

the sense of a proposition by determining in what circumstances the sentence 'p' is true" becomes for Schlick, "what experience verifies this?" If no experience verifies this, "p" is meaningless. This verification principle that a statement is true only if verified in experience supplants Wittgenstein's account of the pictorial relation between language and the world. Philosophy is led back to the realm of the significantly expressible by the leaders of the Vienna Circle, Rudolf Carnap and Alfred Tarski (b. 1902), who viewed statements as either analytic (Carnap) or semantic (Tarski).

The Vienna Circle, formed in the early 1920s, was most active for the next ten years through their publication, *Erkenntnis*. The right wing, led by Schlick, consisted of fairly orthodox followers of Wittgenstein and laid down complete verifiability as a condition of significance. Carnap, aware that scientific theories are not verifiable *as theories,* chose an intersubjective basis for knowledge. His doctrine of physicalism is a behavioristic philosophy of mind and a claim that science could be unified because all meaningful utterance could be translated into the language of physical things.

In the formalist-positivist tradition are two groups. The old European group, led by Carnap, includes Carl Hempel, Gustav Bergmann, Herbert Feigl, Hans Reichenbach, and Arthur Pap. The younger group owes much to the interaction with American pragmatism and a few independents such as Roy Wood Sellars, Roderick Chisholm, and Joseph Church. Because they are interested in problems peripheral to a philosophy of man (problems about meaning, conditionals, the analytic-synthetic distinction), their works will not be considered here.

Meanwhile, in Great Britain a different form of linguistic analysis arose following Moore's interest in ordinary language. Wittgenstein was soon to develop from the picture theory of language the theory that the meaning of a word lies in its use, and that the task of philosophy is therapeutic in nature, alleviating the intellectual strains that arise from the metaphysical misuse of words.[12] In fact, John Wisdom likened the intellectual therapy of philosophy to the emotional therapy of psychoanalysis. Since 1945, in turn, these ideas have been developed by Ryle, John Austin, James Urmson, Antony Flew, and Strawson, the philosophers of ordinary language. Yet they have none of Moore's hesitation and neutrality and none of Wittgenstein's suspicion of definite results. They have looked into the use of daily language more literally than Wittgenstein ever did. Analytic philosophers in England can thus be divided into those stressing therapeutic analysis such as Wisdom and Anscombe at Cambridge (Malcolm and Morris Lazerowitz in the United States), and those stressing the philosophy of ordinary language such as Ryle, Austin, and Strawson at Oxford. Their views are a reflection more of Wittgenstein's *Philosophical Investigations* than of his earlier *Tractatus*.

---

[12] This theory is presented in Wittgenstein's *Investigations*.

To understand the development of Wittgenstein's thinking, we must show how some of the ideas expressed first in the *Tractatus* are modified in the *Philosophical Investigations*. The *Philosophical Investigations* may be said to translate the ideas of the *Tractatus* into a new key, to present his ideas in a new context and apply them in a new way. The following schema illustrates this:

Tractatus	*Philosophical Investigations*
1. language in general becomes	1. language games in particular
2. limits of language become in general	2. limits of particular language games
3. what cannot be said becomes	3. rules or paradigms of specific games
4. sense and nonsense are conceived univocally	4. but vary in language games
5. meaning is the object denoted by the word	5. meaning is defined in the role it plays in the language game—*its use*

We must accept particular language games as they are with their rules; they are significant because they simply function in fact. Ordinary language, that is, language before it is justified or corrected by philosophical reflection, is significant, and the Russellian notion of the need for an ideal language implying that it is the task of philosophy to correct or reform ordinary everyday language is rejected. What is said of language in *Tractatus* is said of languages in *Philosophical Investigations*. Philosophy to Wittgenstein is a battle against the bewitchment of our intelligence by means of language. Philosophy simply puts everything before us, and neither explains nor deduces anything. Things will then show themselves. We see here a coincidence or similarity between Wittgenstein's ideas regarding philosophy as pure description and the ideas of the phenomenologists, particularly Martin Heidegger's (b. 1889) idea of truth as a revelation or unveiling.

In the *Philosophical Investigations* the world is no longer granular or atomistic, and language seems to have many more functions than that of giving a cool and neutral description of the world. The world is what we think it is in our most ordinary moments, and the meaning of words is to be found in their use, in rules that govern their employment and not in some relation between them and facts or objects of which the world is composed. The object of philosophy is no longer analysis in the old sense, the revelation of the hidden structure of language that it must share with an ideal language. It is, rather, to draw our attention to the way in which language actually works and, by doing so, to overcome the fascination that our forms of expression have for us, such as those analogies that seduce us into metaphysical perplexity. There is no final analysis of our linguistic forms, no perfect language into which our ordinary discourse can be translated. Philosophy describes in detail the workings of language as it actually is. The object of this description is therapeutic—relief of those intellectual strains whose characteristic symptom is metaphysics, that is, large paradoxical assertions about the world. Metaphysical utterances do not disclose an insight into the nature of things but a deep-seated conceptual confusion. From construction of an ideal language, Wittgenstein turns to construction of language games: simplified models of parts of our actual language that can bring out the multiplicity of its functions and lay bare the complexities of its operation. There are no stable philosophical results. Philosophy is an activity, an illumination of conceptually confused and noncommunicable theses.

Besides his inquiries into the nature of language and philosophy, the main topic of Wittgenstein's work is philosophical psychology, or the philosophy of the mind. This started with a consideration of the problem of "other minds," in which the question is raised as to how we can ever claim to have knowledge about the minds of others. We never have the kind of direct acquaintance with these minds that their owners have; we have only an awareness of the behavior accompanying their thoughts. Wittgenstein, Wisdom, and Ryle all wished to show that it is a mistake to suppose that there is some uncrossable abyss separating mental processes from behavior.

In this respect, Ryle is most definite. He identifies mental processes with behavior, actual and potential. To say one is angry is a hypothetical statement about what one is likely to do. There are not two worlds, the physical and mental, but two ways of speaking, *categorical discourse* about what we observe and *hypothetical discourse* about the dispositions others have to behave in a certain way. There is symmetry between the actions of myself and others. What I can find out about myself is the same as what I discover about other people. The methods of discovery are much the same. For Ryle, all statements about the mind, whether autobiographical or not, are similar. They can be conveyed in terms of what is as accessible to one observer as to another, namely, in terms of the overt performances. He attacks Cartesian intellectualism; he says knowledge is as much a matter of skills (knowing how) as of information (knowing that). Thinking is not a private interior process that lies behind its expression in language, but, with certain reservations, it is identical with that expression and with comparable skilled performances.

The account Wittgenstein gave of language and meaning leads naturally into an examination of the idea of understanding. He considered that it is not some kind of inner experience; rather, the only way to find out whether someone has understood something is to see how he applies something he claims to have understood. He did not deny, as Ryle does, the existence of accompanying experiences, but insisted that in using psychological words we are not primarily describing or reporting such experiences. There is no such thing as private language.

The main similarity between Ryle and Wittgenstein is their common conviction that psychological words derive their significance from the surroundings of their application and not from a correlation with some isolable immediate occurrence. Wittgenstein admitted "I am in pain" functions very differently from "He is in pain." Ryle does not admit this. Wittgenstein saw "I am in pain" not as the report of a private experience but as an extension of the ordinary natural expression of pain, as a kind of conventionalized cry or grimace and more as an exclamation than a statement. He then examined the whole gamut of psychological notions—the relations of thought and language, the concept of introspection and intention and will as well as ethics, and the concepts of free will, motive, desire, choice, and decision. The emotive theory of ethics has been formulated largely by the analytic philosophers. On the problem of free will, there is much disagreement.

Wittgenstein's Mysticism

A word can be said in regard to Wittgenstein's mysticism, which has been deprecated by some and misunderstood by many. As Kant had already pointed out, there is a difference between a direct awareness of something without intermediaries and a form of knowledge requiring symbolism. Intuition is the direct, nonsymbolic awareness of or insight into reality. Arthur Schopenhauer (1788–1860) and Henri Bergson (1859–1941) described it as a direct apprehension of reality. In the symbolic kind of knowledge called rationalism or cognition, we use parts of our experience to represent other parts. Cognition must include the two-termed relation of sign and signified. We cognize by means of our own signs, interpreted according to our own rules of symbolism. Thus language or symbols help us to cognize, but to cognize only that which can be put into symbols. What can be put into symbols can be expressed; what can be expressed can be communicated. Since we use parts of experience to represent other parts, there is danger of distortion if the first experiences are inadequate representations. It also follows, however, that what cannot be put into symbols cannot be expressed; what cannot be expressed cannot be communicated. Therefore Wittgenstein's last sentence in the *Tractatus*—"What we cannot speak about, we must pass over in silence"—need not be and most probably is not a denial of metaphysics, but a statement that some things are inexpressible or beyond expression.

"These are indeed called things that cannot be put into words. They make themselves manifest. They are what is mystical." (6.522)

Similarly, in a lecture on Ethics he said:

> If I want to fix my mind on what I mean by absolute or ethical value, it always happens that one particular experience presents itself to me which is therefore in a sense my experience for excellence. . . . the best way of describing it is to say that when I have it I wonder at the existence of the world.[13]

In each of these instances Wittgenstein went beyond the tenets of analytic philosophy and shared with us his own intuitions. It is in this way, too, that

[13] Anscombe, *Introduction*, p. 173.

his view of the "I" and the "self" must be considered. He has been accused of solipsism—the theory that reality is only as he sees it and that the only thing he can know is his own thoughts as he thinks them. The traditional solipsist says there are only two things that exist: 1) the thinking, knowing, experiencing self, the subject of experiences; 2) that which the self experiences. Wittgenstein had other views. The self, (1), the subject, must be rejected. Only the experiences, (2), exist. "The thought is the thinker," as James said. Although Hume and Kant had expressed this earlier, Wittgenstein, most critics believe, received the idea from Schopenhauer's *World as Will and Idea,* written in 1819.

In the development of analytic philosophy then, some definite trends emerge:

1. the beginnings with Moore (a reaction against Hegel and a search for a philosophy of common sense) and Russell (emphasis on the need for an ideal language similar to that of mathematics).

2. a new direction by Wittgenstein giving rise temporarily to logical atomism and the picture theory of language.

3. the offshoot and deviation of logical positivism as seen in A. J. Ayer's attempt to combine what he considered to be the ideas found in Wittgenstein's *Tractatus* with those of the Vienna Circle.

4. the return of Wittgenstein to philosophy, his rejection of the picture theory of language and of logical postivism, and his proposal of the theory of language games, that is, the theory that the meaning of a word lies in its use.

5. the resumption of or continuation of Moore's emphasis on ordinary language by the therapeutic analysts such as Wisdom at Cambridge.

6. the present position of the Oxford philosophers of ordinary language—Ryle, Austin, Strawson.

Notes on the Readings

Since the analytic philosophers have claimed that philosophy is an *activity* rather than a body of knowledge, our final consideration must be according to their criteria. It is true that some problems are caused by misuse of language. In fact, Plato had indicated this in the *Sophist.*[14] Moreover, at least Wittgenstein has indicated also that reality is more than that which can be expressed or discussed. No philosopher can ever claim to present a complete view of reality. Although in the *Tractatus* Wittgenstein (and later those of his followers who adopted this spirit) aimed at finding a final remedy for the philosophical disease, he admitted in the *Philosophical In-*

---

[14] "They cross-examine a man's words, when he thinks he is saying something and is really saying nothing, and easily convict him of inconsistencies in his opinions . . . he must be purged of his prejudices first and made to think that he knows only what he knows, and no more." (*Sophist* 230.)

vestigations: "There is not a philosophical method, but there are indeed methods, like different therapies." [15] No answers are given by the analysts, but some very good questions, as will be seen in the readings that follow, are raised and faced.

David Hume, for example, continues the methodical doubt begun by Descartes and challenges the notion of self as substance, since this notion is not empirically verifiable. He says there is a "fictitious ascription of identity," and later Wisdom will call this a myth and will admit its usefulness. In the selection from the Appendix of *A Treatise of Human Nature,* Hume admits that his philosophical principles of scepticism conflict with his strong feeling of identity. The same problem is taken up by Ayer, Wittgenstein, Ryle, Strawson, and Wisdom. Indeed, the problem of the self is of concern to existentialists, to many psychologists, and even to "ordinary people."

Rudolf Carnap was one of the most famous of the logical positivists and, with Moritz Schlick, the founder of the Vienna Circle. He admits that the earlier positivistic view that sense data is the only reality has been largely abandoned; no longer is it held that there is a rock-bottom basis of knowledge. He claims there is indeed no basic difference between the conception of the logical positivists today and any scientist's view, but he holds that the logical positivists differ in important matters with those members of the traditional philosophical schools who look for absolute knowledge.[16] In the selection "Psychology in Physical Language," Carnap argues that the laws of psychology can be translated into physical language. The reader should follow the line of reasoning closely to see if this means to Carnap that man is an object of the science of physics—that is, inanimate matter. Although first published in volume III of *Erkenntnis,* Carnap allowed its publication in 1957 after adding some remarks at the end.

Bertrand Russell was the first of those in the analytical tradition to accept and state clearly that there is no fundamental difference between mind and matter. He explains that we think of mental and physical events as different because of the differences between the laws of psychology and those of physics. Carnap, Ryle, Wittgenstein, and Strawson also consider this problem, each with a different emphasis but each implying that the difference is more verbal than metaphysical. In the selection from *The Analysis of Mind,* Russell criticizes Carnap's theory of physicalism, that is, the effort to describe psychological behavior in terms of physics only.

A. J. Ayer's selection, "Freedom and Necessity," is an example of what people mean by "freedom of the will." It is an exercise in logical or philosophical analysis, meant to clarify the issue rather than to solve it. The second selection, taken from *The Problem of Knowledge,* shows Ayer's view

---

[15] Sect. 133, p. 51.
[16] Paul A. Schlipp, ed., *The Philosophy of Rudolf Carnap* (La Salle, Ill.: Open Court Publishing Co., 1963), p. 38.

of the nature of philosophical inquiry. He maintains that philosophy is distinguished from the other branches of knowledge by its methods, not by its subject matter. In *The Problem of Knowledge,* published some twenty years after he first enunciated the famous verification principle in 1936 (and then modified it in 1946 in the second edition of *Language, Truth, and Logic*), Ayer admits that a philosophical proof is not, or is only very seldom, like the proof of a mathematical statement. He intends, in a detailed analysis of some philosophical problems (specifically, in this selection, the problem of personal identity and the knowledge of others), merely to clear the way for their solution.

It was Gilbert Ryle's book, *The Concept of Mind,* that practically put an end to the philosophical discussion of the relation of the mind to the body. He showed that the split was in our minds and resulted from the way we spoke about ourselves, and that the myth (Descartes' Myth) of the machine run by the mind did not correspond to reality. He also took up the problem raised by Hume concerning the "I" and in true analytic fashion examined all the ways in which we use the word. He refers to higher-order thinking. For example, in the article entitled "Self-Knowledge" he will show that speaking of my laughing about my mistake is a third-order reference, since my words are two steps removed from the first action of making the mistake. His concluding reference to the "I" as similar to "my own shadow" is reminiscent of Hume's insight into the "I"; Ryle admits that the constancy of the shadow "I" seems to endow the "I" with a "mystifying uniqueness and adhesiveness." Here and elsewhere the analytic philosophers have flashes of insight into the problem of the unity of man but they hesitate to make any clear-cut statements about a solution.

Ludwig Wittgenstein, by far the greatest and most original of the analytic philosophers, wrote the two books, *Tractatus Logico-Philosophicus* and *Philosophical Investigations,* that, as we have seen, gave voice to the two trends in the movement. A short selection from the *Tractatus* is included, and some familiarity with the later Wittgenstein [17] may be acquired from reading the reports of his lectures during the years 1930–33, as noted by George Edward Moore. This period is contemporary with *The Blue and Brown Books* (notes Wittgenstein had dictated to a small number of his students and which were published in 1958). The lectures show the trend of his thinking before *Philosophical Investigations,* his masterpiece. Of particular interest is his discussion of the difference between our knowledge as indicated by "I have toothache" and "He has toothache"—which becomes in the *Investigations* "I am in pain" and "He is in pain."

Peter Frederick Strawson's selection, taken from his best-known work,

---

[17] Because the executors of his literary estate did not grant permission to reproduce any of the writings of Ludwig Wittgenstein published after his death, we are unable to present selections from *Philosophical Investigations* (1953), *The Blue and Brown Books* (1958), or *Notebooks, 1914–1916* (1961).

Individuals, is an example of the philosophy of ordinary language. Straw-son maintains that *revisionary* metaphysics, as exemplified by the systems of Descartes and Leibniz, attempts to *construct* a Reality behind Appear-ance. He prefers *descriptive* metaphysics, which attempts merely to *dis-close* the latent structure of our thought and thinking about the world and man in the world. In this selection he analyzes our thinking about man, the mind-body problem, and our thoughts on immortality. This should be com-pared with the discussions on the same topic by Russell, Carnap, Ryle, and Wittgenstein.

The concluding selection, Stuart Hampshire's "Self-Knowledge," is an excellent example of the philosophy of ordinary language as developed from Wittgenstein's theory of language games. We understand a statement by seeing how the word or statement is used, and Hampshire applies this method to the will and to words associated with the will. It should be noted that his aim is only to clarify the term and its use—it is not to prove any-thing or to make absolute statements about the nature of the will.

Thus the selections taken from the analytic philosophers discuss not so much the reality behind the four great problems in any philosophy of man as the *way men speak* about these problems. In what sense, on what occa-sion, or in what language games do we use the words freedom, knowledge or consciousness, immortality, a person, a mind-body unity? Once the ap-proach of the analytic philosopher is accepted, the reader can realize the purpose of philosophy as stated by Wittgenstein: "to say what is sayable so that what is unsayable can be shown."

Summary: The Challenge of Analysis

Both the traditional philosopher and the analytic philosopher wish to re-move whatever clouds our vision of reality. The traditional philosopher may say that the clouds are due to the *appearance* of things; the analytic philosopher says they are due to *language*. Both agree that philosophy is not so much a process of *explanation* as of *explication,* of things implicit in daily experiences.

It is good to be alerted by the analysts that no one approach to reality is complete. The danger is that since man cannot know ultimate reality *totally* and since a fixed static position is wrong, he may conclude that whatever he cannot or does not know simply does not exist. If, instead, he is led to "wonder at the existence of the world" [18] and, standing on a position he has chosen that is at once flexible and firm, if he goes on in his quest to know man in himself and in his world, then the *destructive* chal-lenge of analysis will be only of the scaffolding and ladders, a destruction that is necessary on the way to greater and wider visions.

---

[18] Wittgenstein, in Anscombe, *Introduction,* p. 173.

The challenge of analysis, then, will be *constructive* of a brighter showing forth of the intelligible mysteries of man's experience. We will, or we must, "so to speak, throw away the ladder after [we] have climbed it." Then we "will see the world aright." [19]

Glossary

A PRIORI STATEMENTS:

Statements such as mathematical or logical definitions that are not grounded in empirical facts. For example, "the square root of 9 is 3" or "a father is a male parent." These are contrasted with "empirical statements," whose truth or falsehood can be determined only by referring to the order of experience. For example, "this oven is hot."

COHERENCE THEORY OF TRUTH:

Criterion by which a statement is determined to be true, not because of correspondence with fact, but because of its consistency with other statements. Held by the Vienna Circle of logical positivists. (See *Protocol Statements*.)

CONCEPTS:

Apparatus of our thinking, that is, the sensory and intellectual images or representations found in human consciousness.

EMPIRICISM:

Philosophical position that holds in extreme form that all knowledge is derived from and reducible to sense experience exclusively. This position denies the ability of the intellect to abstract from or to transcend sensory data in the quest for further knowledge. Hume's empiricism analyzed only *ideas* to their experiential counterparts. Russell's empiricism analyzes *propositions* to their experiential counterparts and hence is characterized as a logical empiricism (atomism).

FACTS:

According to Wittgenstein, a fact is an existing combination of objects. The world is the totality of atomic facts, or situations. The situation is a "concatenation of simple objects which hang in one another like the links of a chain" (Wittgenstein).

IDEAL LANGUAGE:

A context-free language, such as is found in science or mathematics, with no emotional overtones, containing only particular statements and no general statements. Russell and the logical positivists hoped to achieve such a language.

LANGUAGE GAMES:

Since Wittgenstein thought that words have no unitary or fixed meaning and do not designate essences, we can be free from philosophical bewilderment

---

[19] Wittgenstein, *Tractatus*, 6.54, p. 151.

once we free ourselves from the belief in an essence corresponding to each word we utter. He therefore investigated the different uses of one word. He called these speech activities language games and, by playing them for a philosophically confusing word such as " pain" or "I," he hoped to dispel confusion.

LOGICAL ATOMISM:

A metaphysical view of the world based on the structure of Russell's mathematical logic. The world consists of independent, externally connected facts; just as logic defines and makes superfluous complex concepts of mathematics, the same techniques would also simplify the view of the world by analyzing it into its atomic facts.

LOGICAL POSITIVISM:

Philosophical tradition, held most strongly by the Vienna Circle, that rejects metaphysics as factually meaningless. It accepts only statements that can be empirically or directly observed or are logically noncontradictory. Sometimes known as "logical empiricism."

MEANING:

The meaning of a name is the object it denotes. A name can have no meaning if there is no object corresponding to it. A proposition has sense, not meaning. The sense of a proposition is the situation it describes. In Wittgenstein's view, the understanding of the meaning of a proposition is independent of its truth or falsity. (See *Sense*.)

OSTENSIVE DEFINITION:

Meaning of a word given by pointing to the object it denotes. Strictly speaking, only names can be so defined.

PHENOMENALIST:

One who holds that the only reality is that available from objects as known by the senses. There is no reality behind the appearances or, if there is, it cannot be known.

PHYSICALISM:

Thesis that the language of physics interpreted as containing any sentences used to describe *physical events* (not just those belonging to the science of physics) is universal language. All statements can and should be translated into this language. This is a modern form of materialism.

PICTURE THEORY OF LANGUAGE:

Just as music scores have a structure similar to the structure of the actual music, so language has a structure similar to the structure of fact. Although it was accepted by the Vienna Circle, most analytic philosophers do not accept this theory because it would be effective only if our language were perfect.

PRINCIPLE OF VERIFICATION:

Held by the logical positivists as formulated largely by A. J. Ayer, this principle states that the meaning of a statement is determined by the way it is verified; its verification consists in being tested by direct observation or by logical analysis.

PROPER NAME:

According to Russell, the only kind of word that is theoretically capable of standing for a particular is a logically proper name. Ordinary proper names are abbreviated descriptions. A logically proper name stands for an object here and now without ascribing any characteristics; it denotes but does not connote anything.

PROPOSITION:

A complete unit of thought expressed in statements or sentences. For example, "the young lady was in a hurry." A "proposition" is opposed to individual "terms," such as "baby" or "father." Terms are a part of propositions.

PROTOCOL STATEMENTS:

Basic reports of direct observations by reference to which the truth of all other empirical statements are supposed to be tested.

SENSE:

Wittgenstein holds that names only have meaning or reference. Propositions only have sense. Propositions describe situations. The sense of a proposition is the situation it describes. (See *Meaning*.)

SOLIPSISM:

Theory that only one's own private experience can verify a statement. It implies that we cannot know the experience of others; only what "I know is real" (Wittgenstein).

TAUTOLOGY:

Statement or sentence in which the predicate simply clarifies the information already contained in the subject and reveals nothing new about the subject. For example, "a bachelor is an unmarried man." Since all tautologies are true by definition (being reducible to the statement "A is A"), they apply universally to all possible situations. Sometimes called "a priori" statement or "analytic" statement.

THERAPEUTIC ANALYSIS:

Attempts to remove the confusion among philosophers by an analysis of their language which has caused the confusion of thought.

TRUTH FUNCTION:

Process by which the logician is able to derive the truth or falsity of a statement solely on the basis of its components. For example, the truth function of the two categorical propositions, "he is young" and "he is healthy," gives the copulative proposition, "he is young and healthy."

TRUTH VALUE:

Truth or falsehood of a proposition as determined by the truth function (see above) of its components.

David Hume

DAVID HUME was born in 1711 in Edinburgh, Scotland. His principal interests were in the study of law, philosophy, and history, and for a short time he held the post of Undersecretary of State for Scotland. Hume's keenly analytical mind is revealed in his many literary works, particularly in those bearing on philosophy and history. In 1739 he published his philosophical masterpiece, *A Treatise of Human Nature,* which, however, "fell dead born from the press," as he admitted himself. He expressed the chief ideas of the *Treatise* in another work, *Philosophical Essays Concerning Human Understanding* (1748), and achieved fame as a smasher of idols with *An Enquiry Concerning the Principles of Morals* (1751) and *Dialogues upon Natural Religion* (1779), published three years after his death in 1776. Contemporary analysts have rediscovered Hume and acknowledge that many of their ideas have their origin in his works.

On Personal Identity

But what have I here said, that reflexions very refined and metaphysical have little or no influence upon us? This opinion I can scarce forbear retracting and condemning from my present feeling and experience. The *intense* view of these manifold contradictions and imperfections in human reason has so wrought upon me, and heated my brain, that I am ready to reject all belief and reasoning, and can look upon no opinion even as more probable or likely than another. Where am I, or what? From what causes do I derive my existence, and to what condition shall I return? Whose favour shall I court, and whose anger must I dread? What beings surround me? and on whom have I any influence, or who have any influence on me? I am confounded with all these questions, and begin to fancy myself in the most deplorable condition imaginable, environed with the deepest darkness, and utterly deprived of the use of every member and faculty.

Most fortunately it happens that, since reason is incapable of dispelling these clouds, nature herself suffices to that purpose, and cures me of this philosophical melancholy and delirium, either by relaxing this bent of mind, or by some avocation, and lively impression of my senses, which

From David Hume, *A Treatise of Human Nature,* first published in 1739.

obliterate all these chimeras. I dine, I play a game of backgammon, I converse, and am merry with my friends; and when, after three or four hours' amusement, I would return to these speculations, they appear so cold, and strained, and ridiculous, that I cannot find in my heart to enter into them any farther.

Here, then, I find myself absolutely and necessarily determined to live, and talk, and act, like other people in the common affairs of life. But notwithstanding that my natural propensity, and the course of my animal spirits and passions, reduce me to this indolent belief in the general maxims of the world. I still feel such remains of my former disposition that I am ready to throw all my books and papers into the fire, and resolve never more to renounce the pleasures of life for the sake of reasoning and philosophy. For those are my sentiments in that splenetic humour which governs me at present. I may, nay I must, yield to the current of nature, in submitting to my senses and understanding; and in this blind submission I show most perfectly my sceptical disposition and principles. But does it follow that I must strive against the current of nature, which leads me to indolence and pleasure; that I must seclude myself, in some measure, from the commerce and society of men, which is so agreeable; and that I must torture my brain with subtilities and sophistries, at the very time that I cannot satisfy myself concerning the reasonableness of so painful an application, nor have any tolerable prospect of arriving by its means at truth and certainty? Under what obligation do I lie of making such an abuse of time? And to what end can it serve, either for the service of mankind, or for my own private interest? No: If I must be a fool, as all those who reason or believe any thing *certainly* are, my follies shall at least be natural and agreeable. Where I strive against my inclination I shall have a good reason for my resistance; and will no more be led a wandering into such dreary solitudes, and rough passages, as I have hitherto met with. . . .

An Appendix on the Treatise

I had entertained some hopes that, however deficient our theory of the intellectual world might be, it would be free from those contradictions and absurdities which seem to attend every explication that human reason can give of the material world. But upon a more strict review of the section concerning *personal identity,* I find myself involved in such a labyrinth that, I must confess, I neither know how to correct my former opinions, nor how to render them consistent. If this be not a good *general* reason for scepticism it is at least a sufficient one (if I were not already abundantly supplied) for me to entertain a diffidence and modesty in all my decisions. I shall propose the arguments on both sides, beginning with those that induced me to deny the strict and proper identity and simplicity of a self or thinking being.

When we talk of *self* or *substance,* we must have an idea annexed to these terms, otherwise they are altogether unintelligible. Every idea is derived from preceding impressions; and we have no impression of self or substance as something simple and individual. We have, therefore, no idea of them in that sense.

Whatever is distinct, is distinguishable; and whatever is distinguishable, is separable by the thought or imagination. All perceptions are distinct. They are, therefore, distinguishable and separable, and may be conceived as separately existent, and may exist separately, without any contradiction or absurdity.

When I view this table and that chimney, nothing is present to me but particular perceptions, which are of a like nature with all the other perceptions. This is the doctrine of philosophers. But this table, which is present to me, and that chimney, may and do exist separately. This is the doctrine of the vulgar, and implies no contradiction. There is no contradiction, therefore, in extending the same doctrine to all the perceptions.

In general, the following reasoning seems satisfactory. All ideas are borrowed from preceding perceptions. Our ideas of objects, therefore, are derived from that source. Consequently no proposition can be intelligible or consistent with regard to objects, which is not so with regard to perceptions. But it is intelligible and consistent to say that objects exist distinct and independent, without any common *simple* substance or subject of inhesion. This proposition, therefore, can never be absurd with regard to perceptions.

When I turn my reflection on *myself,* I never can perceive this *self* without some one or more perceptions; nor can I ever perceive any thing but the perceptions. It is the composition of these, therefore, which forms the self.

We can conceive a thinking being to have either many or few perceptions. Suppose the mind to be reduced even below the life of an oyster. Suppose it to have only one perception, as of thirst or hunger. Consider it in that situation. Do you conceive any thing but merely that perception? Have you any notion of *self* or *substance?* If not, the addition of other perceptions can never give you that notion.

The annihilation, which some people suppose to follow upon death, and which entirely destroys this self, is nothing but an extinction of all particular perceptions; love and hatred, pain and pleasure, thought and sensation. These therefore must be the same with self; since the one cannot survive the other.

Is *self* the same with *substance?* If it be, how can that question have place, concerning the subsistence of self under a change of substance? If they be distinct, what is the difference betwixt them? For my part, I have a notion of neither, when conceived distinct from particular perceptions.

Philosophers begin to be reconciled to the principle, *that we have no idea of external substance, distinct from the ideas of particular qualities.* This must pave the way for a like principle with regard to the mind, *that we have no notion of it, distinct from the particular perceptions.*

So far I seem to be attended with sufficient evidence. But having thus loosened all our particular perceptions, when I proceed to explain the principle of connexion which binds them together, and makes us attribute to them a real simplicity and identity; I am sensible that my account is very defective, and that nothing but the seeming evidence of the precedent reasonings could have induced me to receive it. If perceptions are distinct existences, they form a whole only by being connected together. But no connexions among distinct existences are ever discoverable by human understanding. We only *feel* a connexion or determination of the thought to pass from one object to another. It follows, therefore, that the thought alone finds personal identity, when reflecting on the train of past perceptions that compose a mind; the ideas of them are felt to be connected together, and naturally introduce each other. However extraordinary this conclusion may seem, it need not surprise us. Most philosophers seem inclined to think that personal identity *arises* from consciousness; and consciousness is nothing but a reflected thought or perception. The present philosophy, therefore, has so far a promising aspect. But all my hopes vanish when I come to explain the principles that unite our successive perceptions in our thought or consciousness. I cannot discover any theory which gives me satisfaction on this head.

In short, there are two principles, which I cannot render consistent; nor is it in my power to renounce either of them; viz., *that all our distinct perceptions are distinct existences, and that the mind never perceives any real connexion among distinct existences.* Did our perceptions either inhere in something simple and individual, or did the mind perceive some real connexion among them, there would be no difficulty in the case. For my part, I must plead the privilege of a sceptic, and confess that this difficulty is too hard for my understanding. I pretend not, however, to pronounce it absolutely insuperable. Others perhaps, or myself upon more mature reflexions, may discover some hypothesis, that will reconcile those contradictions.

QUESTIONS FOR STUDY AND DISCUSSION

1. What arguments induced Hume to deny the strict identity of a self or thinking being?
2. What does Hume mean when he says that all ideas are *borrowed* from preceding perceptions?
3. How does he reach the conclusion that the self is a composition of perceptions?
4. Hume has been called an empiricist, that is, one who relies only on the evidence of the senses. Does he contradict himself when he says that no connections among distinct existences are ever discoverable by the *human understanding*?
5. Why does Hume say it is not his power to renounce either of his two principles when considering the human person? Answer by analyzing Hume's presentation of his position.

Rudolf Carnap

RUDOLF CARNAP, the most famous logical positivist living today, was born in Wuppertal, Germany, in 1891. Educated at Jena, he taught at Vienna and Prague from 1926 to 1935, and was in Vienna when Wittgenstein was there. Together with Moritz Schlick, Herbert Feigl, and others, he was a member of the Vienna Circle, a group of early positivist philosophers. Carnap assigned to philosophy its present predominant role as investigator of the language of the factual sciences; his best-known work, *The Logical Syntax of Language* (1937), details such an investigation. Carnap came to the United States in 1935 and became a naturalized American citizen in 1941. After teaching for many years at the University of Chicago, since 1954 he has been asociated with the University of California at Los Angeles. In recent years, Carnap's interests have broadened, leading him to make both syntactical and semantical investigations.

Psychology in Physical Language

INTRODUCTION. PHYSICAL LANGUAGE AND PROTOCOL LANGUAGE

In what follows, we intend to explain and to establish the thesis that *every sentence of psychology may be formulated in physical language.* To express this in the material mode of speech: *all sentences of psychology describe physical occurrences, namely, the physical behavior of humans and other animals.* This is a sub-thesis of the general thesis of *physicalism* to the effect that *physical language is a universal language,* that is, a language into which every sentence may be translated. The general thesis has been discussed in an earlier article, whose position shall here serve as our point of departure. Let us first briefly review some of the conclusions of the earlier study.

In meta-linguistic [1] discussion we distinguish the customary *material mode of speech* (e.g. "The sentences of this language speak of this and that object.") from the more correct *formal mode of speech* (e.g. "The sentences of this language contain this and that word and are constructed in

---

[1] Pertains to study *about* the uses of language rather than study *of* language. [M.G.]

From pp. 165–68, 181–94, and 197–98 of Rudolf Carnap, *Psychology in Physical Language,* translated by George Schick, in *Logical Positivism,* edited by A. J. Ayer. © 1959 by The Free Press. The selection originally appeared in *Erkenntnis,* 1932–33. Reprinted by permission of Rudolf Carnap.

this and that manner."). In using the material mode of speech we run the risk of introducing confusions and pseudo-problems. If, because of its being more easily understood, we occasionally do use it in what follows, we do so only as a paraphrase of the formal mode of speech.

Of first importance for epistemological analyses are the *protocol language,* in which the primitive protocol sentences [2] (in the material mode of speech: the sentences about the immediately given) of a particular person are formulated, and the *system language,* in which the sentences of the system of science are formulated. A person S *tests* (verifies) a system-sentence by deducing from it sentences of his own protocol language, and comparing these sentences with those of his actual protocol. The possibility of such a deduction of protocol sentences constitutes the *content* of a sentence. If a sentence permits no such deductions, it has no content, and is meaningless. If the same sentences may be deduced from two sentences, the latter two sentences have the same content. They say the same thing, and may be translated into one another.

To every sentence of the system language there corresponds some sentence of the physical language [3] such that the two sentences are inter-translatable. It is the purpose of this article to show that this is the case for the sentences of psychology. Moreover, every sentence of the protocol language of some specific person is inter-translatable with some sentence of physical language, namely, with a sentence about the physical state of the person in question. The various protocol languages thus become sub-languages of the physical language. The *physical language is universal and inter-subjective.* This is the thesis of physicalism.

If the physical language, on the grounds of its universality, were adopted as the system language of science, all science would become physics. Metaphysics would be discarded as meaningless. The various domains of science would become parts of unified science. In the material mode of speech: there would, basically, be only one kind of object—physical occurrences, in whose realm law would be all-encompassing.

Physicalism ought not to be understood as requiring psychology to concern itself only with physically describable situations. The thesis, rather, is that psychology may deal with whatever it pleases, it may formulate its sentences as it pleases—these sentences will, in every case, be translatable into physical language.

We say of a sentence P that it is *translatable* (more precisely, that it is reciprocally translatable) into a sentence Q if there are rules, independent of space and time, in accordance with which Q may be deduced from P and

---

[2] Sentences about basic sense experiences which, according to Carnap, can be completely verifiable. These sentences are about events that cannot be doubted since they are experienced by the senses. Anything not evident to the senses cannot be expressed and is meaningless. [M.G.]

[3] Language about material sense data. All languages, according to Carnap, should be put into physical language to free them from vagueness. [M.G.]

P from Q; to use the material mode of speech, P and Q describe the same state of affairs; epistemologically speaking, every protocol sentence which confirms P also confirms Q and *vice versa*. The definition of an expression "a" by means of expressions "b," "c" . . . , represents a translation-rule with the help of which any sentence in which "a" occurs may be translated into a sentence in which "a" does not occur, but "b," "c," . . . do, and *vice versa*. The translatability of all the sentences of language L_1 into a (completely or partially) different language L_2 is assured if, for every expression of L_1, a definition is presented which directly or indirectly (i.e., with the help of other definitions) derives that expression from expressions of L_2. Our thesis thus states that a definition may be constructed for every psychological concept (i.e. expression) which directly or indirectly derives that concept from physical concepts. We are not demanding that psychology formulate each of its sentences in physical terminology. For its own purposes psychology may, as heretofore, utilize its own terminology. All that we are demanding is the production of the definitions through which psychological language is linked with physical language. We maintain that these definitions can be produced, since, implicitly, they already underlie psychological practice.

If our thesis is correct, the generalized sentences of psychology, the *laws* of psychology, are also translatable into the physical language. They are thus physical laws. Whether or not these physical laws are deducible from those holding in inorganic physics, remains, however, an open question. This question of the deducibility of the laws is completely independent of the question of the definability of concepts. We have already considered this matter in our discussion of biology. As soon as one realizes that the sentences of psychology belong to the physical language, and also overcomes the emotional obstacles to the acceptance of this provable thesis, one will, indeed, incline to the conjecture, which cannot as yet be proved, that the laws of psychology are special cases of physical laws holding in inorganic physics as well. But we are not concerned with this conjecture here.

Let us permit ourselves a brief remark—apart from our principal point —concerning the emotional resistance to the thesis of physicalism. Such resistance is always exerted against any thesis when an Idol is being dethroned by it, when we are asked to discard an idea with which dignity and grandeur are associated. As a result of Copernicus' work, man lost the distinction of a central position in the universe; as a result of Darwin's, he was deprived of the dignity of a special supra-animal existence; as a result of Marx's, the factors by means of which history can be causally explained were degraded from the realm of ideas to that of material events; as a result of Nietzsche's, the origins of morals were stripped of their halo; as a result of Freud's, the factors by means of which the ideas and actions of men can be causally explained were located in the darkest depths, in man's nether regions. The extent to which the sober, objective examination of these theories was obstructed by emotional opposition is well known. Now it is proposed that psychology, which has hitherto been robed in majesty as the theory of spiritual events, be degraded to the status of a part of physics. Doubtless, many will consider this an offensive presumption. Perhaps we may therefore express the request that the reader make a special effort in this case to retain the objectivity and openness of mind always requisite to the testing of a scientific thesis.

. . .

BEHAVIORISM AND "INTUITIVE" PSYCHOLOGY

The position we are advocating here coincides in its broad outlines with the psychological movement known as "behaviorism" [4]—when, that it, its epistemological principles rather than its special methods are considered. We have not linked our exposition with a statement of behaviorism since our only concern is with epistemological foundations while behaviorism is above all else interested in a specific method of research and in specific concept formations.

The advocates of behaviorism were led to their position through their concern with animal psychology. In this domain, when the material given to observation does not include statements but only inarticulate behavior, it is most easy to arrive at the correct method of approach. This approach leads one to the correct interpretation of the statements of human experimental subjects, for it suggests that these statements are to be conceived as acts of verbalizing behavior, basically no different from other behavior.

Behaviorism is confronted with views, more influential in Germany than in the United States, which uphold the thesis that psychology's concern is not with behavior in its physical aspect, but rather, with *meaningful behavior*. For the comprehension of meaningful behavior the special method known as "intuitive understanding" ("Verstehen") is said to be required. Physics allegedly knows nothing of this method. Neither meaningful behavior considered collectively nor the individual instances of such behavior which psychology investigates can possibly—so it is maintained —be characterized in terms of physical concepts.

In intuitive psychology this view is generally linked with the view that beside physical behavior there is yet another, psychical event, which constitutes the true subject-matter of psychology, and to which intuitive understanding leads. We do not want to consider this idea any further here, since we have already thoroughly examined it.

But even after one puts this idea aside, intuitive psychology poses the following objection to physicalism.

---

[4] Concept that the matter for psychological study is external behavior, the only behavior that can be observed and measured in physical terms. Since consciousness cannot be so measured it does not exist, at least, so extreme behaviorists such as B. F. Skinner maintain. [M.G.]

Objection based on the occurrence of "meaningful behavior." "When psychology considers the behavior of living creatures (we disregard here the question whether it deals only with such behavior), it is interested in it as meaningful behavior. This aspect of behavior cannot, however, be grasped in terms of physical concepts, but only by means of the method of intuitive understanding. And this is why psychological sentences cannot be translated into physical sentences."

Rebuttal. Let us recall a previous example of the *physicalization* of an intuitive impression, i.e. of a qualitative designation in the protocol language. We there showed that it is possible by investigating optical state-coordinates, to determine the entirety of those physical conditions which correspond to "green of this specific sort" and to subsume them under laws. The same is the case here. It simply depends on the physical nature of an act—say, of an arm-movement—whether I can intuitively understand it —as, say, a beckoning-motion—or not. Consequently, physicalization is possible here too. The class of arm-movements to which the protocol-designation "beckoning motion" corresponds can be determined, and then described in terms of physical concepts. But perhaps doubts may be raised as to whether the classification of arm-movements as intelligible or unintelligible, and, further, the classification of intelligible arm-movements as beckoning motions or others really depends, as our thesis claims, solely on the physical constitution of the arms, the rest of the body, and the environment. Such doubts are readily removed if, for instance, one thinks of films. We understand the *meaning* of the action on the movie screen. And our understanding would doubtless be the same if, instead of the film presented, another which resembled it in every physical particular were shown. Thus one can see that both our understanding of meaning and the particular forms it takes are, in effect, completely determined by the physical processes impinging on our sense-organs (in the film-example, those impinging on our optic and auditory sense-organs).

The problem of physicalization in this area, that is, the problem of the characterization of *understandable* behavior as such and of the various kinds of such behavior by means of concepts of systematized physics, is not as yet solved. But does not then our basic thesis rest on air? It states that all psychological sentences can be translated into physical sentences. One may well ask to what extent such a translation is possible, given the present state of our knowledge. Even today every sentence of psychology *can* be translated into a sentence which refers to the physical behavior of living creatures. In such a physical characterization terms do indeed occur which have not yet been physicalized, i.e. reduced to the concepts of physical science. Nevertheless, the concepts used *are* physical concepts, though of a primitive sort—just as "warm" and "green" (applied to bodies) were physical concepts before one could express them in terms of physical state-coordinates (temperature and electromagnetic field, respectively).

[Comparison of mechanical detectors and living detectors]

We should like, again, to make the matter clear by using a *physical example*. Let us suppose that we have found a substance whose electrical conductivity is noticeably raised when it is irradiated by various types of electro-magnetic radiation. We do not yet, however, know the internal structure of this substance and so cannot yet explain its behavior. We want to call such a substance a "detector" for radiation of the sort involved. Let us suppose, further, that we have not yet systematically determined to what sorts of radiation the detector reacts. We now discover that the sorts of radiation to which it responds share still another characteristic, say, that they accelerate specific chemical reactions. Now suppose that we are interested in the photo-chemical effects of various sorts of radiation, but that the determination of these effects, in the case of a specific sort of radiation, is difficult and time-consuming, while the determination of the detector's reaction to it is easy and quickly accomplished; then we shall find it useful to adopt the detector as a test-instrument. With its aid we can determine for any particular sort of radiation whether or not it is likely to have the desired photo-chemical effect. This practical application will not be impeded by our ignorance of the detector's micro-structure and our inability to explain its reaction in physical terms. In spite of our ignorance, we can certainly say that the detector isolates a certain physically specified class of rays. The objection that this is not a physical class since we cannot characterize it by a specification of optical state-coordinates but only by the behavior of the detector will not stand. For to begin with, we know that if we carried out a careful empirical investigation of the electro-magnetic spectrum, we could identify the class of rays to which the detector responds. On the basis of this identification we could then physicalize the characterization of the rays in terms of detector-reactions, by substituting for it a characterization in terms of systematic physical concepts. But even our present way of characterizing the radiation in terms of the detector-test is a physical characterization, though an indirect one. It is distinguished from the direct characterization which is our goal only through being more circumstantial. There is no difference of kind between the two characterizations, only one of degree, though the difference of degree is indeed sufficiently great to give us a motive for pursuing the empirical investigations which might bring the direct physical characterization within our grasp.

Whether *the detector is organic or inorganic* is irrelevant to the epistemological issue involved. The function of the detector is basically the same whether we are dealing with a physical detector of specific sorts of radiation or with a tree-frog as a detector of certain meteorological states of affairs or (if one may believe the newspapers) with a sniffing dog as a detector of certain human diseases. People take a practical interest in meteorological forecasts. Where barometers are not available they may, consequently, use a tree-frog for the same purpose. But let us be clear about the fact that this method does not determine the state of the tree-frog's soul, but a physically specified weather condition, even if one cannot describe this condition in terms of the concepts of systematized physics. People, likewise, have a practical interest in medical diagnoses. When the directly determinable symptoms do not suffice, they may, consequently, enlist a dog's delicate sense of smell for the purpose. It is clear to the doctor that, in doing so, he is not determining the state of the dog's soul, but a physically specified condition of his patient's body. The doctor may not be able, given the present state of physiological knowledge, to characterize the diseased condition in question in terms of the concepts of systematic physics. Nonetheless, he knows that his diagnosis—whether it is based on the symptoms he himself has directly observed or on the reactions of the diagnostic dog—determines nothing and can determine nothing but the physical condition of his patient. Even apart from this, the physiologist acknowledges the need for physicalization. This would here consist in describing the bodily condition in question, i.e. defining the disease involved in purely physiological terms (thus eliminating any mention of the dog's reaction). A further task would be to trace these back to chemical terms, and these, in turn, to physical ones.

The case with *intuitive psychology* is precisely analogous. The situation here happens to be complicated for epistemological analysis (though for psychological practice it is simplified) by the fact that in the examination of an experimental subject the intuitive psychologist is both the observer and detector. The doctor here is his own diagnostic dog; which, indeed, is also often the case in medical diagnoses—in their intuitive phases. The psychologist calls the behavior of the experimental subject "understandable" or, in a special case, for instance, "a nod of affirmation," when his detector responds to it, or—in our special case—when it results in his protocols registering "A nods affirmatively." Science is not a system of experiences, but of sentences; it does not include the psychologist's experience of understanding, but rather, his protocol sentence. The utterance of the psychologist's protocol sentence is a reaction whose epistemological function is analogous to the tree-frog's climbing and to the barking of the diagnostic dog. To be sure, the psychologist far surpasses these animals in the variety of his reactions. As a result, he is certainly very valuable to the pursuit of science. But this constitutes only a difference of degree, not a difference of kind.

In the light of these considerations, two demands are to be made of the psychologist. First, we shall expect him (as we expect the doctor) to be clear about the fact that, in spite of his complicated diagnostic reaction, he establishes nothing but the existence of some specific physical condition of the experimental subject, though a condition which can be characterized only indirectly—by his own diagnostic reaction. Secondly, he must acknowledge (as the physiologist does) that it is a task of scientific research to find a way of physicalizing the indirect characterization. Psychology must determine what are the physical conditions to which people's detector-reactions correspond. When this is carried out for every reaction of this sort, i.e. for every result of intuitive understanding, psychological concept formation can be physicalized. The indirect definitions based on detector-reactions will be replaced by direct definitions in terms of the concepts of systematized physics. Psychology, like the other sciences, must and will reach the level of development at which it can replace the tree-frog by the barometer. But even in the tree-frog stage psychology already uses physical language, though of a primitive sort.

. . .

SENTENCES ABOUT ONE'S OWN MIND; "INTROSPECTIVE PSYCHOLOGY"

Our argument has shown that a sentence about other minds refers to physical processes in the body of the person in question. On any other interpretation the sentence becomes untestable in principle, and thus meaningless. The situation is the same with sentences about one's own mind, though here the emotional obstacles to a physical interpretation are considerably greater. The relationship of a sentence about one's own mind to one about someone else's may most readily be seen with respect to a sentence about some *past state* of one's own mind, e.g. P_1: "I was excited yesterday." The testing of this sentence involves either a *rational* inference from protocol sentences of the form of p_1—which refer to presently perceived script, photographs, films, etc. originating with me yesterday; or it involves an *intuitive* method, e.g. utilizing the protocol sentence p_2, "I recall having been excited yesterday." The content of P_1 exceeds both that of the protocol sentence p_1 and that of the protocol sentence p_2, as is most clearly indicated by the possibility of error and disavowal where P_1 is concerned. P_1 can only be progressively better confirmed by sets of protocol sentences of the form of p_1 and p_2. The very same protocol sentences, however, also confirm the physical sentence P_2: "My body was yesterday in that physical condition which one tends to call 'excitement.' " P_1 has, consequently, the same content as the physical sentence P_2.

In the case of a sentence about the *present state* of one's own mind, *e.g.* P_1: "I now am excited" one must clearly distinguish between the system sentence P_1 and the protocol sentence p_2, which, likewise, may read "I now am excited." The difference rests in the fact that the system sentence P_1 may, under certain circumstances, be disavowed, whereas a protocol sentence, being an epistemological point of departure, cannot be rejected. The protocol sentences p_1 which rationally support P_1 have here some such form as "I feel my hands trembling," "I see my hands trembling," "I hear my voice quavering," etc. Here too, the content of P_1 exceeds that of both p_1 and P_2, in that it subsumes all the possible sentences of this sort. P_1 has the same content as the physical sentence P_2, "My body is now in that condition which, both under my own observation and that of others, exhibits such and such characteristics of excitement," the characteristics in question being those which are mentioned both in my own protocol sentences of the sort of p_1 and p_2 and in other people's protocol sentences of corresponding sorts (discussed above in our example of sentences about other minds).

THE PHYSICALISTIC INTERPRETATION OF PSYCHOLOGICAL SENTENCES

	1. *Sentence about* *the Wooden Support* *(As an Analogy)*
System sentence P_1: a) *rationally* derived from protocol sentence p_1:	"The support is firm"
	"The support has such and such a color and shape"
or	
b) *intuitively* derived from protocol sentence p_2:	"The support looks firm"
P_1 has the same content as the *physical sentence* P_2:	"The support is physically firm"
The physical term: is hereby defined as a disposition to react under certain circumstances in a specified way:	"physically firm"
	"Under such and such a load, such and such a distortion occurs; under such and such a load, breakage occurs"

The table opposite shows the analogous application of the physicalist thesis to the three cases we have discussed by exhibiting the parallelism of sentences about other minds, sentences about some past condition of one's own mind, and sentences about the present condition of one's own mind, with the physical sentence about the wooden support.

Objection from introspective psychology: "When the psychologist is not investigating other experimental subjects, but pursues self-observation, or "introspection," instead, he grasps, in a direct manner, something non-physical—and this is the proper subject-matter of psychology."

Rebuttal. We must distinguish between a question of the justification of the use of some prevalent practical method of inquiry and a question of the justification of some prevalent interpretation of the results of that method.

Every method of inquiry is justified; disputes can arise only over the question of the purpose and fruitfulness of a given method, which is a question our problem does not involve. We may apply any method we choose; we cannot, however, interpret the obtained sentences as we choose. The meaning of a sentence, no matter how obtained, can unequivocally be deter-

2. *Sentence about the State of Someone Else's Mind*	3. *Sentence about the State of One's Own Mind at Some Time in the Past*	4. *Sentence about the Present State of One's Own Mind*
"A is excited"	"I was excited yesterday"	"I am now excited"
"A has such and such an expression"	"These letters (written by me yesterday) have such and such a shape"	"My hands are now trembling"
"A is excited (A looks excited)"	"Now a recollection of excitement"	"Now excited"
"A's body is physically excited"	"My body was physically excited yesterday."	"My body is now physically excited"

"physically excited"

"Under such and such circumstances, such and such gestures, expressions, actions, and words occur."

mined by a logical analysis of the way in which it is derived and tested. A psychologist who adopts the method of what is called "introspection" does not thereby expose himself to criticism. Such a psychologist admits sentences of the form "I have experienced such and such events of consciousness" into his experiment-protocol and then arrives at general conclusions of his own by means of inductive generalization, the construction of hypotheses, and, finally, a comparison of his hypotheses with the conclusions of other persons. But again we must conclude, both on logical and epistemological grounds, that the singular as well as the general sentences must be interpreted physically. Let us say that psychologist A writes sentence p_2: "(I am) now excited" into his protocol. An earlier investigation has shown that the view which holds that protocol sentences cannot be physically interpreted, that, on the contrary, they refer to something non-physical (something "psychical," some "experience-content," some "datum of consciousness," etc.) leads directly to the consequence that every protocol sentence is meaningful only to its author. If A's protocol sentence p_2 were not subject to a physical interpretation, it could not be tested by B, and would, thus, be meaningless to B. On the previous occasion in question we showed, further, that the non-physical interpretation leads one into insoluble contradictions. Finally, we found that every protocol sentence has the same content as some physical sentence, and that this physical translation does not presuppose an accurate knowledge of the physiology of the central nervous system, but is feasible even at present. Sentences about one's own mind—whether one takes these to be inter-subjective system sentences or so-called introspective protocol sentences—are thus in every case translatable into sentences of the physical language.

.   .   .

SUMMARY

So-called psychological sentences—whether they are concrete sentences about other minds, or about some past condition of one's own mind, or about the present condition of one's own mind, or, finally, general sentences—are always translatable into physical language. Specifically, every psychological sentence refers to physical occurrences in the body of the person (or persons) in question. On these grounds, psychology is a part of the domain of unified science based on physics. By "physics" we wish to mean, not the system of currently known physical laws, but rather the science characterized by a mode of concept formation which traces every concept back to state-coordinates, that is, to systematic assignments of numbers to space-time points. Understanding "physics" in this way, we can rephrase our thesis—a particular thesis of physicalism—as follows: *psychology is a branch of physics.*

Remarks by the Author (1957)

While I would still maintain the essential content of the main thesis of this article, I would today modify some special points. Perhaps the most important of them is the following. In the article I regarded a psychological term, say "excited," as designating a state characterized by the disposition to react to certain stimuli with overt behavior of certain kinds. This may be admissible for the psychological concepts of everyday language. But at least for those of scientific psychology, as also of other fields of science, it seems to me more in line with the actual procedure of scientists, to introduce them not as disposition concepts, but rather as theoretical concepts (sometimes called "hypothetical constructs"). This means that they are introduced as primitives by the postulates of a theory, and are connected with the terms of the observation language, which designate observable properties, by so-called rules of correspondence. This method is explained and discussed in detail in my article "The Methodological Character of Theoretical Concepts," in H. Feigl and M. Scriven, eds., *Minnesota Studies in the Philosophy of Science,* Vol. I.

The main thesis of physicalism remains the same as before. It says that psychological statements, both those of everyday life and of scientific psychology, say something about the physical state of the person in question. It is different from the corresponding statements in terms of microphysiology or micro-physics (which at the present stage of scientific development are not yet known, comp. § 4A above) by using the conceptual framework of psychology instead of those of the two other fields. To find the specific features of the correspondence will be an empirical task (comp. § 6, the third part of the procedure of physicalization). Once known, the correspondence can be expressed by empirical laws or, according to our present view, by theoretical postulates. Our present conception of physicalism, the arguments for it, and the development which led to it, are represented in the following two articles by Herbert Feigl: (1) "Physicalism, Unity of Science and the Foundations of Psychology," in: P. A. Schilpp, editor, *The Philosophy of Rudolf Carnap* (Library of Living Philosophers); see also my reply to Feigl in the same volume; (2) "The 'Mental' and the 'Physical,' " in Vol. II of *Minnesota Studies in Philosophy of Science.*

QUESTIONS FOR STUDY AND DISCUSSION

1. If an event can be translated into physical language, does it follow that that event is physical? What does Carnap think?
2. If Carnap considers that psychology is a branch of physics, what do you consider is his concept of man?
3. Do you agree with Carnap's reasoning that intuitive psychology is precisely analogous to the case of a living detector of weather? Discuss Carnap's position and your own.
4. How does Carnap show that the statement, "The wood is firm," is analogous to "I was excited yesterday," even though the latter may be considered to be an introspective statement? Refer specifically to his argument that the way the statement is learned clarifies this analogy.
5. Is Carnap talking about the language of psychology or about its subject—man? Is this a development of Hume's effort to describe only what he observed?
6. Has he radically changed his position by his remarks at the end of the essay?
7. Do you agree that psychology is a branch of physics? Discuss.

Bertrand Russell

BERTRAND RUSSELL was born in England in 1872. He studied mathematics and philosophy at Cambridge University and, for a time, served as lecturer at Trinity College, Cambridge. He was dismissed from the University and imprisoned during World War I because of his pacifist activities. Since then his penchant for assuming unpopular political and ethical views has frequently brought him into conflict with the authorities. Russell's philosophical positions have run from idealism to logical atomism, yet throughout he has revealed a predilection for analysis. Lord Russell helped to shape modern mathematical logic with the *Principia Mathematica* (3 vols., 1910–13), written in conjunction with Alfred North Whitehead. A prolific and talented writer, he was awarded the Nobel prize for literature in 1950.

Mind and Matter

At the end of our journey it is time to return to the question from which we set out, namely: What is it that characterizes mind as opposed to matter? Or, to state the same question in other terms: How is psychology to be distinguished from physics? The answer provisionally suggested at the outset of our inquiry was that psychology and physics are distinguished by the nature of their causal laws, not by their subject matter. At the same time we held that there is a certain subject matter, namely images, to which only psychological causal laws are applicable; this subject matter, therefore, we assigned exclusively to psychology. But we found no way of defining images except through their causation; in their intrinsic character they appeared to have no universal mark by which they could be distinguished from sensations.

In this last lecture I propose to pass in review various suggested methods of distinguishing mind from matter. I shall then briefly sketch the nature of that fundamental science which I believe to be the true metaphysic, in which mind and matter alike are seen to be constructed out of a neutral stuff, whose causal laws have no such duality as that of psychology, but form the basis upon which both physics and psychology are built.

In search for the definition of "mental phenomena," let us begin with "consciousness," which is often thought to be the essence of mind. In the first lecture I gave various arguments against the view that consciousness is fundamental, but I did not attempt to say what consciousness is. We must find a definition of it, if we are to feel secure in deciding that it is not fundamental. It is for the sake of the proof that it is not fundamental that we must now endeavour to decide what it is.

"Consciousness," by those who regard it as fundamental, is taken to be a character diffused throughout our mental life, distinct from sensations and images, memories, beliefs and desires, but present in all of them. Dr. Henry Head, in an article which I quoted in Lecture III, distinguishing sensations from purely physiological occurrences, says: "Sensation, in the strict sense of the term, demands the existence of consciousness" (p. 184). This statement, at first sight, is one to which we feel inclined to assent, but I believe we are mistaken if we do so. Sensation is the sort of thing of which we *may* be conscious, but not a thing of which we *must* be conscious. We have been led, in the course of our inquiry, to admit unconscious beliefs and unconscious desires. There is, so far as I can see, no class of mental or other occurrences of which we are always conscious whenever they happen.

The first thing to notice is that consciousness must be *of* something. In view of this, I should define "consciousness" in terms of that relation of an image or a word to an object which we defined, in Lecture XI, as "meaning." When a sensation is followed by an image which is a "copy" of it, I think it may be said that the existence of the image constitutes consciousness of the sensation, provided it is accompanied by that sort of belief which, when we reflect upon it, makes us feel that the image is a "sign" of something other than itself. This is the sort of belief which, in the case of memory, we expressed in the words "this occurred"; or which, in the case of a judgment of perception, makes us believe in qualities correlated with present sensations, as e.g., tactile and visual qualities are correlated. The addition of some element of belief seems required, since mere imagination does not involve consciousness of anything, and there can be no consciousness which is not of something. If images alone constituted consciousness of their prototypes, such imagination-images as in fact have prototypes would involve consciousness of them; since this is not the case, an element of belief must be added to the images in defining consciousness. The belief must be of that sort that constitutes objective reference, past or present. An image, together with a belief of this sort concerning it, constitutes, according to our definition, consciousness of the prototype of the image.

But when we pass from consciousness of sensations to consciousness of objects of perception, certain further points arise which demand an addition to our definition. A judgment of perception, we may say, consists of a core of sensation, together with associated images, with belief in the present existence of an object to which sensation and images are referred in a way which is difficult to analyse. Perhaps we might say that the belief is not fundamentally in any *present* existence, but is of the nature of an expectation: for example, when we see an object, we expect certain sensations to result if we proceed to touch it. Perception, then, will consist of a present sensation together with expectations of future sensations. (This, of course, is a reflective analysis, not an account of the way perception appears to unchecked introspection.) But all such expectations are liable to be erroneous, since they are based upon correlations which are usual but not invariable. Any such correlation may mislead us in a particular case, for example, if we try to touch a reflection in a looking-glass under the impression that it is "real." Since memory is fallible, a similar difficulty arises as regards consciousness of past objects. It would seem odd to say that we can be "conscious" of a thing which does not or did not exist. The only way to avoid this awkwardness is to add to our definition the proviso that the beliefs involved in consciousness must be *true*.

In the second place, the question arises as to whether we can be conscious of images. If we apply our definition to this case, it seems to demand images of images. In order, for example, to be conscious of an image of a cat, we shall require, according to the letter of the definition, an image which is a copy of our image of the cat, and has this image for its prototype. Now, it hardly seems probable, as a matter of observation, that there are images of images, as opposed to images of sensations. We may meet this difficulty in two ways, either by boldly denying consciousness of images, or by finding a sense in which, by means of a different accompanying belief, an image, instead of meaning its prototype, can mean another image of the same prototype.

The first alternative, which denies consciousness of images, has already been discussed when we were dealing with Introspection in Lecture VI. We then decided that there must be, in some sense, consciousness of images. We are therefore left with the second suggested way of dealing with knowledge and images. According to this second hypothesis, there may be two images of the same prototype, such that one of them means the other, instead of meaning the prototype. It will be remembered that we defined meaning by association: a word or image means an object, we said, when it has the same associations as the object. But this definition must not be interpreted too absolutely: a word or image will not have *all* the same associations as the object which it means. The word "cat" may be associated with the word "mat," but it would not happen except by accident that a cat would be associated with a mat. And in like manner an image may have certain associations which its prototype will not have, e.g. an association with the word "image." When these associations are active, an image means an image, instead of meaning its prototype. If I have had images of a given prototype many times, I can mean one of these, as opposed to the rest, by recollecting the time and place or any other distinctive association of that one occasion. This happens, for example, when a place recalls to us some thought we previously had in that place, so that we remember a thought as opposed to the occurrence to which it referred. Thus we may say that we think of an image A when we have a similar image B associated with recollections of circumstances connected with A, but not with its prototype or with other images of the same prototype. In this way we become aware of images without the need of any new store of mental contents, merely by the help of new associations. This theory, so far as I can see, solves the problems of introspective knowledge, without requiring heroic measures such as those proposed by Knight Dunlap, whose views we discussed in Lecture VI.

According to what we have been saying, sensation itself is not an instance of consciousness, though the immediate memory by which it is apt to be succeeded is so. A sensation which is remembered becomes an object of consciousness as soon as it begins to be remembered, which will normally be almost immediately after its occurrence (if at all); but while it exists it is not an object of consciousness. If, however, it is part of a perception, say of some familiar person, we may say that the person perceived is an object of consciousness. For in this case the sensation is a *sign* of the perceived object in much the same way in which a memory-image is a sign of a remembered object. The essential practical function of "consciousness" and "thought" is that they enable us to act with reference to what is distant in time or space, even though it is not at present stimulating our senses. This reference to absent objects is possible through association and habit. Actual sensations, in themselves, are not cases of consciousness, because they do not bring in this reference to what is absent. But their connection with consciousness is very close, both through immediate memory, and through the correlations which turn sensations into perceptions.

Enough has, I hope, been said to show that consciousness is far too complex and accidental to be taken as the fundamental characteristic of mind. We have seen that belief and images both enter into it. Belief itself, as we saw in an earlier lecture, is complex. Therefore, if any definition of mind is suggested by our analysis of consciousness, images are what would naturally suggest themselves. But since we found that images can only be defined causally, we cannot deal with this suggestion, except in connection with the difference between physical and psychological causal laws.

I come next to those characteristics of mental phenomena which arise out of mnemic causation.[1] The possibility of action with reference to what is not sensibly present is one of the things that might be held to characterize mind. Let us take first a very elementary example. Suppose you are in a familiar room at night, and suddenly the light goes out. You will be able to find your way to the door without much difficulty by means of the picture of the room which you have in your mind. In this case vis-

---

[1] The action of the memory by which, through association, other thoughts in the mind are aroused. [M.G.]

ual images serve, somewhat imperfectly it is true, the purpose which visual sensations would otherwise serve. The stimulus to the production of visual images is the desire to get out of the room, which, according to what we found in Lecture III, consists essentially of present sensations and motor impulses caused by them. Again, words heard or read enable you to act with reference to the matters about which they give information; here, again, a present sensible stimulus, in virtue of habits formed in the past, enables you to act in a manner appropriate to an object which is not sensibly present. The whole essence of the practical efficiency of "thought" consists in sensitiveness to *signs:* the sensible presence of A, which is a sign of the present or future existence of B, enables us to act in a manner appropriate to B. Of this, words are the supreme example, since their effects as signs are prodigious, while their intrinsic interest as sensible occurrences on their own account is usually very slight.

The operation of signs may or may not be accompanied by consciousness. If a sensible stimulus A calls up an image of B, and we then act with reference to B, we have what may be called consciousness of B. But habit may enable us to act in a manner appropriate to B as soon as A appears, without ever having an image of B. In that case, although A operates as a sign, it operates without the help of consciousness. Broadly speaking, a very familiar sign tends to operate directly in this manner, and the intervention of consciousness marks an imperfectly established habit.

The power of acquiring experience, which characterizes men and animals, is an example of the general law that, in mnemic causation, the causal unit is not one event at one time, but two or more events at two or more times. A burnt child fears the fire, that is to say, the neighbourhood of fire has a different effect upon a child which has had the sensations of burning than upon one which has not. More correctly, the observed effect, when a child which has been burnt is put near a fire, has for its cause, not merely the neighbourhood of the fire, but this together with the previous burning. The general formula, when an animal has acquired experience through some event A, is that, when B occurs at some future time, the animal to which A has happened acts differently from an animal which A has not happened. Thus A and B together, not either separately, must be regarded as the cause of the animal's behaviour, unless we take account of the effect which A has had in altering the animal's nervous tissue, which is a matter not patent to external observation except under very special circumstances. With this possibility, we are brought back to causal laws, and to the suggestion that many things which seem essentially mental are really neural. Perhaps it is the nerves that acquire experience rather than the mind. If so, the possibility of acquiring experience cannot be used to define mind.

Very similar considerations apply to memory, if taken as the essence of mind. A recollection is aroused by something which is happening now, but is different from the effect which the present occurrence would have produced if the recollected event had not occurred. This may be accounted for by the physical effect of the past event on the brain, making it a different instrument from that which would have resulted from a different experience. The causal peculiarities of memory *may,* therefore, have a physiological explanation. With every special class of mental phenomena this possibility meets us afresh. If psychology is to be a separate science at all, we must seek a wider ground for its separateness than any that we have been considering hitherto.

We have found that "consciousness" is too narrow to characterize mental phenomena, and that mnemic causation is too wide. I come now to a characteristic which, though difficult to define, comes much nearer to what we require, namely subjectivity.

Subjectivity, as a characteristic of mental phenomena, was considered in Lecture VII, in connection with the definition of perception. We there decided that those particulars which constitute the physical world can be collected into sets in two ways, one of which makes a bundle of all those particulars that are appearances of a given thing from different places, while the other makes a bundle of all those particulars which are appearances of different things from a given place. A bundle of this latter sort, at a given time, is called a "perspective"; taken throughout a period of time, it is called a "biography." Subjectivity is the characteristic of perspectives and biographies, the characteristic of giving the view of the world from a certain place. We saw in Lecture VII that this characteristic involves none of the other characteristics that are commonly associated with mental phenomena, such as consciousness, experience and memory. We found in fact that it is exhibited by a photographic plate, and, strictly speaking, by any particular taken in conjunction with those which have the same "passive" place in the sense defined in Lecture VII. The particulars forming one perspective are connected together primarily by simultaneity; those forming one biography, primarily by the existence of direct time-relations between them. To these are to be added relations derivable from the laws of perspective. In all this we are clearly not in the region of psychology, as commonly understood; yet we are also hardly in the region of physics. And the definition of perspectives and biographies, though it does not yet yield anything that would be commonly called "mental," is presupposed in mental phenomena, for example in mnemic causation: the causal unit in mnemic causation, which gives rise to Semon's engram,[2] is the whole of one perspective—not of *any* perspective, but of a perspective in a place where there is nervous tissue, or at any rate living tissue of some sort. Perception also, as we saw, can only be defined in terms of perspectives. Thus the conception of subjectivity, i.e. of the "passive" place of a

---

[2] A hypothesized, permanently altered state of living tissue resulting from temporary excitation; synonomous with memory trace. [M.G.]

particular, though not alone sufficient to define mind, is clearly an essential element in the definition.

I have maintained throughout these lectures that the data of psychology do not differ in their intrinsic character from the data of physics. I have maintained that sensations are data for psychology and physics equally, while images, which may be in some sense exclusively psychological data, can only be distinguished from sensations by their correlations, not by what they are in themselves. It is now necessary, however, to examine the notion of a "datum," and to obtain, if possible, a definition of this notion.

The notion of "data" is familiar throughout science, and is usually treated by men of science as though it were perfectly clear. Psychologists, on the other hand, find great difficulty in the conception. "Data" are naturally defined in terms of theory of knowledge: they are those propositions of which the truth is known without demonstration, so that they may be used as premises in proving other propositions. Further, when a proposition which is a datum asserts the existence of something, we say that the something is a datum, as well as the proposition asserting its existence. Thus those objects of whose existence we become certain through perception are said to be data.

There is some difficulty in connecting this epistemological definition of "data" with our psychological analysis of knowledge; but until such a connection has been effected, we have no right to use the conception "data."

It is clear, in the first place, that there can be no datum apart from a belief. A sensation which merely comes and goes is not a datum; it only becomes a datum when it is remembered. Similarly, in perception, we do not have a datum unless we have a *judgment* of perception. In the sense in which objects (as opposed to propositions) are data, it would seem natural to say that those objects of which we are conscious are data. But consciousness, as we have seen, is a complex notion, involving beliefs, as well as mnemic phenomena such as are required for perception and memory. It follows that no datum is theoretically indubitable, since no belief is infallible; it follows also that every datum has a greater or less degree of vagueness, since there is always some vagueness in memory and the meaning of images.

Data are not those things of which our consciousness is earliest in time. At every period of life, after we have become capable of thought, some of our beliefs are obtained by inference, while others are not. A belief may pass from either of these classes into the other, and may therefore become, or cease to be, a belief giving a datum. When, in what follows, I speak of data, I do not mean the things of which we feel sure before scientific study begins, but the things which, when a science is well advanced, appear as affording grounds for other parts of the science, without themselves being believed on any ground except observation. I assume, that is to say, a trained observer, with an analytic attention, knowing the sort of thing to look for, and the sort of thing that will be important. What he observes is, at the stage of science which he has reached, a datum for his science. It is just as sophisticated and elaborate as the theories which he bases upon it, since only trained habits and much practice enable a man to make the kind of observation that will be scientifically illuminating. Nevertheless, when once it has been observed, belief in it is not based on inference and reasoning, but merely upon its having been seen. In this way its logical status differs from that of the theories which are proved by its means.

In any science other than psychology the datum is primarily a perception, in which only the sensational core is ultimately and theoretically a datum, though some such accretions as turn the sensation into a perception are practically unavoidable. But if we postulate an ideal observer, he will be able to isolate the sensation, and treat this alone as datum. There is, therefore, an important sense in which we may say that, if we analyse as much as we ought, our data, outside psychology, consist of sensations, which include within themselves certain spatial and temporal relations.

Applying this remark to physiology, we see that the nerves and brain as physical objects are not truly data; they are to be replaced, in the ideal structure of science, by the sensations through which the physiologist is said to perceive them. The passage from these sensations to nerves and brain as physical objects belongs really to the initial stage in the theory of physics, and ought to be placed in the reasoned part, not in the part supposed to be observed. To say we see the nerves is like saying we hear the nightingale; both are convenient but inaccurate expressions. We hear a sound which we believe to be causally connected with the nightingale, and we see a sight which we believe to be causally connected with a nerve. But in each case it is only the sensation that ought, in strictness, to be called a datum. Now, sensations are certainly among the data of psychology. Therefore all the data of the physical sciences are also psychological data. It remains to inquire whether all the data of psychology are also data of physical science, and especially of physiology.

If we have been right in our analysis of mind, the ultimate data of psychology are only sensations and images and their relations. Beliefs, desires, volitions, and so on, appeared to us to be complex phenomena consisting of sensations and images variously interrelated. Thus (apart from certain relations) the occurrences which seem most distinctively mental, and furthest removed from physics, are, like physical objects, constructed or inferred, not part of the original stock of data in the perfected science. From both ends, therefore, the difference between physical and psychological data is diminished. Is there ultimately no difference, or do images remain as irreducibly and exclusively psychological? In view of the causal definition of the difference between images and sensations, this brings us to a new question, namely: Are the causal laws of psychology different from those of any other science, or are they really physiological?

Certain ambiguities must be removed before this question can be adequately discussed.

First, there is the distinction between rough approximate laws and such as appear to be precise and general. I shall return to the former presently; it is the latter that I wish to discuss now.

Matter, as defined at the end of Lecture V, is a logical fiction, invented because it gives a convenient way of stating causal laws. Except in cases of perfect regularity in appearances (of which we can have no experience), the actual appearances of a piece of matter are not members of that ideal system of regular appearances which is defined as being the matter in question. But the matter is, after all, inferred from its appearances, which are used to *verify* physical laws. Thus, in so far as physics is an empirical and verifiable science, it must assume or prove that the inference from appearances to matter is, in general, legitimate, and it must be able to tell us, more or less, what appearances to expect. It is through this question of verifiability and empirical applicability to experience that we are led to a theory of matter such as I advocate. From the consideration of this question it results that physics, in so far as it is an empirical science, not a logical phantasy, is concerned with particulars of just the same sort as those which psychology considers under the name of sensations. The causal laws of physics, so interpreted, differ from those of psychology only by the fact that they connect a particular with other appearances in the same piece of matter, rather than with other appearances in the same perspective. That is to say, they group together particulars having the same "active" place, while psychology groups together those having the same "passive" place. Some particulars, such as images, have no "active" place, and therefore belong exclusively to psychology.

We can now understand the distinction between physics and psychology. The nerves and brain are matter: our visual sensations when we look at them may be, and I think are, members of the system constituting irregular appearances of this matter, but are not the whole of the system. Psychology is concerned, *inter alia,* with our sensations when we see a piece of matter, as opposed to the matter which we see. Assuming, as we must, that our sensations have physical causes, their causal laws are nevertheless radically different from the laws of physics, since the consideration of a single sensation requires the breaking up of the group of which it is a member. When a sensation is used to verify physics, it is used merely as a sign of a certain material phenomenon, i.e. of a group of particulars of which it is a member. But when it is studied by psychology, it is taken away from that group and put into quite a different context, where it causes images or voluntary movements. It is primarily this different grouping that is characteristic of psychology as opposed to all the physical sciences, including physiology; a secondary difference is that images, which belong to psychology, are not easily to be included among the aspects which constitute a physical thing or piece of matter.

I think, however, on grounds of the theory of matter explained in Lectures V and VII, that an ultimate scientific account of what goes on in the world, if it were ascertainable, would resemble psychology rather than physics in what we found to be the decisive difference between them. I think, that is to say, that such an account would not be content to speak, even formally, as though matter, which is a logical fiction, were the ultimate reality. I think that, if our scientific knowledge were adequate to the task, which it neither is nor is likely to become, it would exhibit the laws of correlation of the particulars constituting a momentary condition of a material unit, and would state the causal laws [3] of the world in terms of these particulars, not in terms of matter. Causal laws so stated would, I believe, be applicable to psychology and physics equally; the science in which they were stated would succeed in achieving what metaphysics has vainly attempted, namely a unified account of what really happens, wholly true even if not the whole of truth, and free from all convenient fictions or unwarrantable assumptions of metaphysical entities. A causal law applicable to particulars would count as a law of physics if it could be stated in terms of those fictitious systems of regular appearances which are matter; if this were not the case, it would count as a law of psychology if one of the particulars were a sensation or an image, i.e. were subject to mnemic causation. I believe that the realization of the complexity of a material unit, and its analysis into constituents analogous to sensations, is of the utmost importance to philosophy, and vital for any understanding of the relations between mind and matter, between our perceptions and the world which they perceive. It is in this direction, I am convinced, that we must look for the solution of many ancient perplexities.

It is probable that the whole science of mental occurrences, especially where its initial definitions are concerned, could be simplified by the development of the fundamental unifying science in which the causal laws of particulars are sought, rather than the causal laws of those systems of particulars that constitute the material units of physics. This fundamental science would cause physics to become derivative, in the sort of way in which theories of the constitution of the atom make chemistry derivative from physics; it would also cause psychology to appear less singular and isolated among sciences. If we are right in this, it is a wrong philosophy of matter which has caused many of the difficulties in the philosophy of mind —difficulties which a right philosophy of matter would cause to disappear.

The conclusions at which we have arrived may be summed up as follows:

1. Physics and psychology are not distinguished by their material. Mind and matter alike are logical constructions; the particulars out of

---

[3] In a perfected science, causal laws will take the form of differential equations—or of finite-difference equations, if the theory of quanta should prove correct. [B.R.]

which they are constructed, or from which they are inferred, have various relations, some of which are studied by physics, others by psychology. Broadly speaking, physics group particulars by their active places, psychology by their passive places.

2. The two most essential characteristics of the causal laws which would naturally be called psychological are *subjectivity* and *mnemic causation;* these are not unconnected, since the causal unit in mnemic causation is the group of particulars having a given passive place at a given time, and it is by this manner of grouping that subjectivity is defined.

3. Habit, memory and thought are all developments of mnemic causation. It is probable, though not certain, that mnemic causation is derivative from ordinary physical causation in nervous (and other) tissue.

4. Consciousness is a complex and far from universal characteristic of mental phenomena.

5. Mind is a matter of degree, chiefly exemplified in number and complexity of habits.

6. All our data, both in physics and psychology, are subject to psychological causal laws; but physical causal laws, at least in traditional physics, can only be stated in terms of matter, which is both inferred and constructed, never a datum. In this respect psychology is nearer to what actually exists.

QUESTIONS FOR STUDY AND DISCUSSION

1. Why does Russell reject the definition of sensation which demands the existence of consciousness?
2. What line of reasoning leads Russell to propose tentatively that many things that seem essentially mental are really neural?
3. Why does he select subjectivity as an essential element of mind?
4. Does Russell think that matter is a reality?
5. What does he think is the difference between physics and psychology?
6. What difference does he think lies in the notion of a causal law in physics and a causal law in psychology?

A. J. Ayer

ALFRED JULES AYER, perhaps the leading exponent of the modified form of logical positivism, was born in 1910 and was educated at Eton and Oxford. He was a professor at the University of London from 1946 until 1959, when he went to Oxford as Wykeham Professor of Logic. His major work, *Language, Truth, and Logic* (1936), reveals his supreme confidence in philosophical analysis. His thought has undergone some modification in recent years, but he remains one of the more controversial figures in the movement.

Freedom and Necessity

When I am said to have done something of my own free will it is implied that I could have acted otherwise; and it is only when it is believed that I could have acted otherwise that I am held to be morally responsible for what I have done. For a man is not thought to be morally responsible for an action that it was not in his power to avoid. But if human behaviour is entirely governed by causal laws, it is not clear how any action that is done could ever have been avoided. It may be said of the agent that he would have acted otherwise if the causes of his action had been different, but they being what they were, it seems to follow that he was bound to act as he did. Now it is commonly assumed both that men are capable of acting freely, in the sense that is required to make them morally responsible, and that human behaviour is entirely governed by causal laws: and it is the apparent conflict between these two assumptions that gives rise to the philosophical problem of the freedom of the will.

Confronted with this problem, many people will be inclined to agree with Dr. Johnson: "Sir, we *know* our will is free, and *there's* an end on't." But, while this does very well for those who accept Dr. Johnson's premiss, it would hardly convince anyone who denied the freedom of the will. Certainly, if we do know that our wills are free, it follows that they are so. But the logical reply to this might be that since our wills are not free, it follows that no one can know that they are: so that if anyone claims, like Dr.

From pp. 271–84 of A. J. Ayer, *Philosophical Essays*. Copyright 1954 by The Macmillan Company. Reprinted by permission of St. Martin's Press, Inc., The Macmillan Company of Canada Ltd., and Macmillan and Company Ltd., London.

Johnson, to know that they are, he must be mistaken. What is evident, indeed, is that people often believe themselves to be acting freely; and it is to this "feeling" of freedom that some philosophers appeal when they wish, in the supposed interests of morality, to prove that not all human action is causally determined. But if these philosophers are right in their assumption that a man cannot be acting freely if his action is causally determined, then the fact that someone feels free to do, or not to do, a certain action does not prove that he really is so. It may prove that the agent does not himself know what it is that makes him act in one way rather than another: but from the fact that a man is unaware of the causes of his action, it does not follow that no such causes exist.

So much may be allowed to the determinist;[1] but his belief that all human actions are subservient to causal laws still remains to be justified. If indeed, it is necessary that every event should have a cause, then the rule must apply to human behaviour as much as to anything else. But why should it be supposed that every event must have a cause? The contrary is not unthinkable. Nor is the law of universal causation a necessary presupposition of scientific thought. The scientist may try to discover causal laws, and in many cases he succeeds; but sometimes he has to be content with statistical laws, and sometimes he comes upon events which, in the present state of his knowledge, he is not able to subsume under any law at all. In the case of these events he assumes that if he knew more he would be able to discover some law, whether causal or statistical, which would enable him to account for them. And this assumption cannot be disproved. For however far he may have carried his investigation, it is always open to him to carry it further; and it is always conceivable that if he carried it further he would discover the connection which had hitherto escaped him. Nevertheless, it is also conceivable that the events with which he is concerned are not systematically connected with any others: so that the reason why he does not discover the sort of laws that he requires is simply that they do not obtain.

Now in the case of human conduct the search for explanations has not in fact been altogether fruitless. Certain scientific laws have been established; and with the help of these laws we do make a number of successful predictions about the ways in which different people will behave. But these predictions do not always cover every detail. We may be able to predict that in certain circumstances a particular man will be angry, without being able to prescribe the precise form that the expression of his anger will take. We may be reasonably sure that he will shout, but not sure how loud his shout will be, or exactly what words he will use. And it is only a small proportion of human actions that we are able to forecast even so precisely as this. But that, it may be said, is because we have not carried our investi-

---

[1] One who holds that man has no free will and must act according to inner impulses or outer pressures. [M.G.]

gations very far. The science of psychology is still in its infancy and, as it is developed, not only will more human actions be explained, but the explanations will go into greater detail. The ideal of complete explanation may never in fact be attained: but it is theoretically attainable. Well, this may be so: and certainly it is impossible to show *a priori* that it is not so: but equally it cannot be shown that it is. This will not, however, discourage the scientist who, in the field of human behaviour, as elsewhere, will continue to formulate theories and test them by the facts. And in this he is justified. For since he has no reason *a priori* to admit that there is a limit to what he can discover, the fact that he also cannot be sure that there is no limit does not make it unreasonable for him to devise theories, nor, having devised them, to try constantly to improve them.

But now suppose it to be claimed that, so far as men's actions are concerned, there is a limit: and that this limit is set by the fact of human freedom. An obvious objection is that in many cases in which a person feels himself to be free to do, or not to do, a certain action, we are even now able to explain, in causal terms, why it is that he acts as he does. But it might be argued that even if men are sometimes mistaken in believing that they act freely, it does not follow that they are always so mistaken. For it is not always the case that when a man believes that he has acted freely we are in fact able to account for his action in causal terms. A determinist would say that we should be able to account for it if we had more knowledge of the circumstances, and had been able to discover the appropriate natural laws. But until those discoveries have been made, this remains only a pious hope. And may it not be true that, in some cases at least, the reason why we can give no causal explanation is that no causal explanation is available; and that this is because the agent's choice was literally free, as he himself felt it to be?

The answer is that this may indeed be true, inasmuch as it is open to anyone to hold that no explanation is possible until some explanation is actually found. But even so it does not give the moralist what he wants. For he is anxious to show that men are capable of acting freely in order to infer that they can be morally responsible for what they do. But if it is a matter of pure chance that a man should act in one way rather than another, he may be free but he can hardly be responsible. And indeed when a man's actions seem to us quite unpredictable, when, as we say, there is no knowing what he will do, we do not look upon him as a moral agent. We look upon him rather as a lunatic.

To this it may be objected that we are not dealing fairly with the moralist. For when he makes it a condition of my being morally responsible that I should act freely, he does not wish to imply that it is purely a matter of chance that I act as I do. What he wishes to imply is that my actions are the result of my own free choice: and it is because they are the result of my own free choice that I am held to be morally responsible for them.

But now we must ask how it is that I come to make my choice. Either it is an accident that I choose to act as I do or it is not. If it is an accident, then it is merely a matter of chance that I did not choose otherwise; and if it is merely a matter of chance that I did not choose otherwise, it is surely irrational to hold me morally responsible for choosing as I did. But if it is not an accident that I choose to do one thing rather than another, then presumably there is some causal explanation of my choice: and in that case we are led back to determinism.

Again, the objection may be raised that we are not doing justice to the moralist's case. His view is not that it is a matter of chance that I choose to act as I do, but rather that my choice depends upon my character. Nevertheless he holds that I can still be free in the sense that he requires; for it is I who am responsible for my character. But in what way am I responsible for my character? Only, surely, in the sense that there is a causal connection between what I do now and what I have done in the past. It is only this that justifies the statement that I have made myself what I am: and even so this is an over-simplification, since it takes no account of the external influences to which I have been subjected. But, ignoring the external influences, let us assume that it is in fact the case that I have made myself what I am. Then it is still legitimate to ask how it is that I have come to make myself one sort of person rather than another. And if it be answered that it is a matter of my strength of will, we can put the same question in another form by asking how it is that my will has the strength that it has and not some other degree of strength. Once more, either it is an accident or it is not. If it is an accident, then by the same argument as before, I am not morally responsible, and if it is not an accident we are led back to determinism.

Furthermore, to say that my actions proceed from my character, or, more colloquially, that I act in character, is to say that my behaviour is consistent and to that extent predictable: and since it is, above all, for the actions that I perform in character that I am held to be morally responsible, it looks as if the admission of moral responsiblity, so far from being incompatible with determinism, tends rather to presuppose it. But how can this be so if it is a necessary condition of moral responsibility that the person who is held responsible should have acted freely? It seems that if we are to retain this idea of moral responsibility, we must either show that men can be held responsible for actions which they do not do freely, or else find some way of reconciling determinism with the freedom of the will.

It is no doubt with the object of effecting this reconciliation that some philosophers have defined freedom as the consciousness of necessity. And by so doing they are able to say not only that a man can be acting freely when his action is causally determined, but even that his action must be causally determined for it to be possible for him to be acting freely. Nevertheless this definition has the serious disadvantage that it gives to the word "freedom" a meaning quite different from any that it ordinarily bears. It is indeed obvious that if we are allowed to give the word "freedom" any meaning that we please, we can find a meaning that will reconcile it with determinism: but this is no more a solution of our present problem than the fact that the word "horse" could be arbitrarily used to mean what is ordinarily meant by "sparrow" is a proof that horses have wings. For suppose that I am compelled by another person to do something "against my will." In that case, as the word "freedom" is ordinarily used, I should not be said to be acting freely: and the fact that I am fully aware of the constraint to which I am subjected makes no difference to the matter. I do not become free by becoming conscious that I am not. It may, indeed, be possible to show that my being aware that my action is causally determined is not incompatible with my acting freely: but it by no means follows that it is in this that my freedom consists. Moreover, I suspect that one of the reasons why people are inclined to define freedom as the consciousness of necessity is that they think that if one is conscious of necessity one may somehow be able to master it. But this is a fallacy. It is like someone's saying that he wishes he could see into the future, because if he did he would know what calamities lay in wait for him and so would be able to avoid them. But if he avoids the calamities then they don't lie in the future and it is not true that he foresees them. And similarly if I am able to master necessity, in the sense of escaping the operation of a necessary law, then the law in question is not necessary. And if the law is not necessary, then neither my freedom nor anything else can consist in my knowing that it is.

Let it be granted, then, that when we speak of reconciling freedom with determinism we are using the word "freedom" in an ordinary sense. It still remains for us to make this usage clear: and perhaps the best way to make it clear is to show what it is that freedom, in this sense, is contrasted with. Now we began with the assumption that freedom is contrasted with causality: so that a man cannot be said to be acting freely if his action is causally determined. But this assumption has led us into difficulties and I now wish to suggest that it is mistaken. For it is not, I think, causality that freedom is to be contrasted with, but constraint. And while it is true that being constrained to do an action entails being caused to do it, I shall try to show that the converse does not hold. I shall try to show that from the fact that my action is causally determined it does not necessarily follow that I am constrained to do it: and this is equivalent to saying that it does not necessarily follow that I am not free.

If I am constrained, I do not act freely. But in what circumstances can I legitimately be said to be constrained? An obvious instance is the case in which I am compelled by another person to do what he wants. In a case of this sort the compulsion need not be such as to deprive one of the power of choice. It is not required that the other person should have hypnotized me, or that he should make it physically impossible for me to go against his will. It is enough that he should induce me to do what he wants by making it clear to me that, if I do not, he will bring about some situation that I regard as even more undesirable than the consequences of the action that he wishes me to do. Thus, if the man points a pistol at my head I may still choose to disobey him: but this does not prevent its being true that if I do fall in with his wishes he can legitimately be said to have compelled me. And if the circumstances are such that no reasonable person would be expected to choose the other alternative, then the action that I am made to do is not one for which I am held to be morally responsible.

A similar, but still somewhat different, case is that in which another person has obtained an habitual ascendancy over me. Where this is so, there may be no question of my being induced to act as the other person wishes by being confronted with a still more disagreeable alternative: for if I am sufficiently under his influence this special stimulus will not be necessary. Nevertheless I do not act freely, for the reason that I have been deprived of the power of choice. And this means that I have acquired so strong a habit of obedience that I no longer go through any process of deciding whether or not to do what the other person wants. About other matters I may still deliberate; but as regards the fulfilment of this other person's wishes, my own deliberations have ceased to be a causal factor in my behaviour. And it is in this sense that I may be said to be constrained. It is not, however, necessary that such constraint should take the form of subservience to another person. A kleptomaniac is not a free agent, in respect of his stealing, because he does not go through any process of deciding whether or not to steal. Or rather, if he does go through such a process, it is irrelevant to his behaviour. Whatever he resolved to do, he would steal all the same. And it is this that distinguishes him from the ordinary thief.

But now it may be asked whether there is any essential difference between these cases and those in which the agent is commonly thought to be free. No doubt the ordinary thief does go through a process of deciding whether or not to steal, and no doubt it does affect his behaviour. If he resolved to refrain from stealing, he could carry his resolution out. But if it be allowed that his making or not making this resolution is causally determined, then how can he be any more free than the kleptomaniac? It may be true that unlike the kleptomaniac he could refrain from stealing if he chose: but if there is a cause, or set of causes, which necessitate his choosing as he does, how can he be said to have the power of choice? Again, it may be true that no one now compels me to get up and walk across the room: but if my doing so can be causally explained in terms of my history or my environment, or whatever it may be, then how am I any more free than if some other person had compelled me? I do not have the feeling of constraint that I have when a pistol is manifestly pointed at my head; but the chains of causation by which I am bound are no less effective for being invisible.

The answer to this is that the cases I have mentioned as examples of constraint do differ from the others: and they differ just in the ways that I have tried to bring out. If I suffered from a compulsion neurosis, so that I got up and walked across the room, whether I wanted to or not, or if I did so because somebody else compelled me, then I should not be acting freely. But if I do it now, I shall be acting freely, just because these conditions do not obtain; and the fact that my action may nevertheless have a cause is, from this point of view, irrelevant. For it is not when my action has any cause at all, but only when it has a special sort of cause, that it is reckoned not to be free.

But here it may be objected that, even if this distinction corresponds to ordinary usage, it is still very irrational. For why should we distinguish, with regard to a person's freedom, between the operations of one sort of cause and those of another? Do not all causes equally necessitate? And is it not therefore arbitrary to say that a person is free when he is necessitated in one fashion but not when he is necessitated in another?

That all causes equally necessitate is indeed a tautology, if the word "necessitate" is taken merely as equivalent to "cause": but if, as the objection requires, it is taken as equivalent to "constrain" or "compel," then I do not think that this proposition is true. For all that is needed for one event to be the cause of another is that, in the given circumstances, the event which is said to be the effect would not have occurred if it had not been for the occurrence of the event which is said to be the cause, or *vice versa,* according as causes are interpreted as necessary, or sufficient, conditions: and this fact is usually deducible from some causal law which states that whenever an event of the one kind occurs then, given suitable conditions, an event of the other kind will occur in a certain temporal or spatio-temporal relationship to it. In short, there is an invariable concomitance between the two classes of events; but there is no compulsion, in any but a metaphorical sense. Suppose, for example, that a psycho-analyst is able to account for some respect of my behaviour by referring it to some lesion that I suffered in my childhood. In that case, it may be said that my childhood experience, together with certain other events, necessitates my behaving as I do. But all that this involves is that it is found to be true in general that when people have had certain experiences as children, they subsequently behave in certain specifiable ways; and my case is just another instance of this general law. It is in this way indeed that my behaviour is explained. But from the fact that my behaviour is capable of being explained, in the sense that it can be subsumed under some natural law, it does not follow that I am acting under constraint.

If this is correct, to say that I could have acted otherwise is to say, first, that I should have acted otherwise if I had so chosen; secondly, that my action was voluntary in the sense in which the actions, say, of the kleptomaniac are not; and thirdly, that nobody compelled me to choose as I did: and these three conditions may very well be fulfilled. When they are fulfilled, I may be said to have acted freely. But this is not to say that it was a matter of chance that I acted as I did, or, in other words, that my action could not be explained. And that my actions should be capable of being explained is all that is required by the postulate of determinism.

If more than this seems to be required it is, I think, because the use of the very word "determinism" is in some degree misleading. For it tends to suggest that one event is somehow in the power of another, whereas the truth is merely that they are factually correlated. And the same applies to the use, in this context of the word "necessity" and even of the word "cause" itself. Moreover, there are various reasons for this. One is the tendency to confuse causal with logical necessitation, and so to infer mistakenly that the effect is contained in the cause. Another is the uncritical use of a concept of force which is derived from primitive experiences of pushing and striking. A third is the survival of an animistic conception of causality, in which all causal relationships are modelled on the example of one person's exercising authority over another. As a result we tend to form an imaginative picture of an unhappy effect trying vainly to escape from the clutches of an overmastering cause. But, I repeat, the fact is simply that when an event of one type occurs, an event of another type occurs also, in a certain temporal or spatio-temporal relation to the first. The rest is only metaphor. And it is because of the metaphor, and not because of the fact, that we come to think that there is an antithesis between causality and freedom.

Nevertheless, it may be said, if the postulate of determinism is valid, then the future can be explained in terms of the past: and this means that if one knew enough about the past one would be able to predict the future. But in that case what will happen in the future is already decided. And how then can I be said to be free? What is going to happen is going to happen and nothing that I do can prevent it. If the determinist is right, I am the helpless prisoner of fate.

But what is meant by saying that the future course of events is already decided? If the implication is that some person has arranged it, then the proposition is false. But if all that is meant is that it is possible, in principle, to deduce it from a set of particular facts about the past, together with the appropriate general laws, then, even if this is true, it does not in the least entail that I am the helpless prisoner of fate. It does not even entail that my actions make no difference to the future: for they are causes as well as effects; so that if they were different their consequences would be different also. What it does entail is that my behaviour can be predicted: but to say that my behaviour can be predicted is not to say that I am acting under constraint. It is indeed true that I cannot escape my destiny if this is taken to mean no more than that I shall do what I shall do. But this is a tautology, just as it is a tautology that what is going to happen is going to happen. And such tautologies as these prove nothing whatsoever about the freedom of the will.

1. Because of our inability to discover all the causes of man's behavior, Ayer implies that freedom consists solely in our concept of it. Discuss.
2. Ayer believes that if we do not discover the cause of a man's action, then the action is by chance rather than by choice. How does he answer those philosophers who claim that freedom is consciousness of necessity?
3. Why does he reject the term "freedom from causality" and accept "freedom from constraint"?

Personal Identity

• • •

To the question what makes a person the person that he is we can, then, answer that certain properties are after all essential; the property of having some human characteristics, perhaps also the property of occupying some position or other in space and time. But if such properties are essential, it is because the possession of them is necessary to one's being a person at all: they do not serve to differentiate one person from another. And when we come to properties which do individuate, properties such as that of being at a certain place at a certain time, or having such and such physical traits, or being the author of such and such a work, which are in fact uniquely characteristic of the person in question, we find that they are not essential. Any one of them can be denied to their owner without self-contradiction. Nevertheless, if too many are denied the reference to the owner may be lost.

To identify me is, then, to say, not what, but who I am. It is to list some of the descriptions that I satisfy, and preferably those that I satisfy uniquely. But if I alone do satisfy them, it is as a matter of empirical fact, not of logical necessity. Logically, they might apply to others as well; or they might not apply to me. In this sense, I could be a different, even a very different person; but not an utterly different person. At a certain point, what might pass for a misdescription of me ceases to be a description, even a misdescription, of *me* at all: it is no longer I that is identified. The difficulty is that there appear to be no rules for determining when this point is reached.

A view which I have not considered is that people are differentiated from one another, not by the possession of any special properties, but by being different spiritual substances, or souls. And the reason why I have not considered it is that I do not find it intelligible. I do not see by what criterion it could possibly be decided whether any such spiritual substances existed. How are we to tell, for example, whether the same soul inhabits different bodies, simultaneously or successively? Does it ever happen that two souls get into a single body? Can there be an exchange of souls from one living body to another? There might, indeed, be phenomena which would lead us to consider the possibilities of co-consciousness or reincarnation; we might be induced to admit exceptions to the rule of one body, one person. But then it is the phenomena in question that would supply us with our new criteria on personal identity. We should still have no warrant for interpreting them in terms of the concentration, or dispersal, or transmigration of souls: we should not have given any meaning to talk of this kind, except as a way of restating what we already express more clearly by talking abut persons. But the reference to souls is intended to account for a person's being the person that he is, not merely to record the fact that one has somehow been identified.

If it is thought to provide an explanation, the reason may be that the process of identifying by description seems inadequate: it catches the person whom it is used to identify but it does not pin him down sufficiently. The fact that I answer to certain descriptions may enable me in practice to be recognized; but, as we have seen, it is a contingent fact; I might not have answered to them, even though I do. One may, therefore, be tempted to infer that *I* must be something different; a substance that merely happens to have the properties so described. Furthermore it does not seem necessary that two different people should always be descriptively distinguishable. If, for example, history were cyclical, I should have my exact counterpart in every cycle: assuming that the whole process had no beginning or end, so that we were not differently related to a uniquely describable point of origin or termination, every description that I satisfied would also be satisfied by my counterparts; merely by the use of predicates there would be no way of differentiating between us. Even so, we should not be identical: the very posing of the question implies that we are not. If it were contradictory to speak of different things as being descriptively indistinguishable, the suggestion that history might be cyclical could not significantly be made. But while it is a fanciful suggestion, which has no likelihood at all of being true, it does not seem to be unintelligible. That I should have such counterparts would appear to be logically possible. But in that case it will follow that people can differ otherwise than through their properties. And what, then, remains but to say that they differ in substance? Since the argument applies not only to people, but to any individual thing, it does not, indeed, establish the existence of the soul; but the proof, if it were valid, that one was at least a substance would be an important contributory step.

Now what this argument does prove is that we are not restricted to individuating by description. We can discriminate further by the use of demonstratives, taken in their actual contexts. That I differ from my hypo-thetical counterparts is shown by the fact that in using the word "I" I point to *this,* while they do not. In the same way I, along among us, am living *here* and *now.* Descriptions of time and place will not divide us: for *ex hypothesi* each of us will stand in the same spatial relations to objects of exactly the same kind and in the same temporal relations to exactly similar events. It will be true of each of us also that he says that his use of the word "I" points to what he indicates by saying "this." But the reference will be different in every case. It is a difference which defies description, just because it is not a difference of properties, not even of spatio-temporal properties unless these are made to include a reference to some point which is demonstratively identified. The use of a demonstrative on a given occa-sion *shows* what is being referred to: but if we are asked to say *what* is being referred to, we can reply only by giving a description; a description which normally does individuate but conceivably might not.

But does this give us any warrant for talking about substances? I do not think that it does. It seems to me, on the contrary, that philosophers have fallen here into the mistake of supposing that because referential expres-sions are not used to describe properties they must be used to describe something else; and substances are then brought in to fill the gap. But the truth is that they do not owe their meaning to their describing anything at all. I call them referential expressions just because their use is demonstra-tive and not descriptive. In an actual context, one can, as it were, produce what they refer to: but if we have to identify it by description, then we can do no more than instance some of its properties; for there is nothing else to be described. But what is it that has the properties? Surely it must be some-thing, even if there is nothing that one can say about it; so that one is re-duced, like Locke, to speaking of it as "something we know not what." [1] But what is the sense of this question? What possible ways could there be of answering it? In favourable circumstances one can produce the object that one is referring to; and that is one form of answer. Or one can give a description of it, which is necessarily a listing of its properties. No other possibility remains.

GENERAL CRITERIA OF PERSONAL IDENTITY. MUST THEY BE PHYSICAL?

At this point it may be objected that since various descriptions apply to the same thing, or person, there must be something that, as it were, holds them all together. It was one and the same man, Napoleon Bonaparte, who won the Battle of Austerlitz and lost the Battle of Waterloo. But in what sense was he the same? What is it that makes a set of descriptions, which are logically independent of one another, into descriptions of the same person?

This is a different question from that which we have so far been con-sidering. We have found that, apart from the contingent fact that certain

---

[1] *Essay Concerning Human Understanding,* Book II, Ch. 23. [A.J.A.]

things may be true of him alone, there is nothing that especially makes a person the person that he is. But it remains possible that there are general criteria of personal identity, criteria that must be satisfied if we are to be entitled to say of any two events that they are events in the same person's history. Indeed, it would seem that there have to be such criteria if our talk of persons is to have any meaning at all. And if we can discover them, we can also give an answer of a sort to our original question. For having picked out, by one method or another, an event in which some person uniquely figures, or a characteristic which he alone possesses, we can say that his being the person that he is consists in his being the same person as is concerned in the event or owns the characteristic in question: the fact that we have given an account of what it is to be the same person will free the definition from circularity. It will remain contingent, a matter of good fortune, that our original point of reference does identify him; but this we have seen to be inescapable. And if the event or characteristic which we have chosen is not sufficiently discriminating, we can always select another one instead.

Now it would seem that the best way to discover the general criteria of personal identity would be to consider what criteria are actually applied. How do we in fact succeed in recognizing people? What makes me say, for example, that a man whom I can now see is the same man as I saw a week ago? Perhaps only that he looks the same; that there is, in other words, a fairly close resemblance between the appearance of this man and the appearance, as I remember it, of the man I saw last week. This does not imply, of course, that I consciously compare them. My remembering how the man looked last week may just consist in my recognizing this as the same man. But I assume that my recollection would not operate in this way unless the appearances were similar. The fact that people's physical characteristics tend to be distinctive, and that many constant features commonly persist throughout what is only a gradual process of change, makes this, as we have noted, a practical method of identification. As a criterion, it is however, neither necessary nor sufficient. People can look very different indeed at different periods of their lives, and different people can look very much alike. But suppose that I were able to trace the movements of the man I saw a week ago from the moment at which I saw him, and that I found that the series of positions which he successively occupied from that time to this terminated in the position which was occupied by the man now before me. In that case I should have a conclusive reason for saying that it was the same man. This criterion of spatio-temporal continuity is not, indeed, sufficient by itself. In the example given, it has been assumed that the man continues to look much the same; or, if speaking of *the* man be thought to beg the question of identity, that each of the series of positions is occupied by a body of roughly similar appearance. If these appearances had changed at any point to a very considerable extent, I might be entitled to conclude that it was not the same man; one must allow for the possibility that a man, like any other object, alters his identity, that he is, as it were, replaced by something else. Men die, and their death does not at once destroy the identity of their bodies; but after a certain time at least, one ceases to identify the man with whatever remains of his corpse, even though the criterion of spatio-temporal continuity is still fulfilled. But when it is reinforced by other factors, such as the persistence of the appropriate physical characteristics, then I think that this criterion is sufficient.

The first thing to be noticed about it is that it applies equally to persons and to things: the proof that this is the same carpet as I saw in this room a week ago follows the same lines as the proof that this is the same man. In this sense, the identity of a person is founded on the identity of his body. But is this the only sense in which we can significantly speak of a person's remaining the same, that is, of his being the same individual? Many philosophers would say that it was. They would maintain that, whatever might be said about the union or dissociation of personalities, it was contradictory, or meaningless, to speak of a person's inhabiting different bodies at the same or different times, or of there being more than one person in the same body, or of the separation of persons from their bodies, their survival in a disembodied state. The procedure of deriving the identity of persons from the identity of their bodies is, in their view, the only one that can be significantly applied; so long, at least, as we are using words in any ordinary sense.

If this view were shown to be correct, we should have, among other things, to re-examine the question of phenomenalism. For, as we have seen, the phenomenalist is bound to hold that the identity of any physical body is subject to analysis in terms of sense-data. Roughly speaking, it would turn on the possibility of there being a series of successive sense-fields in which corresponding positions were occupied by similar sense-data: one might hope in this way to reformulate the essential condition of spatio-temporal continuity. But so far we have allowed ourselves to talk of sense-data only as a means of expressing how things seem to people. And if sense-data have to be defined in terms of persons, and the identity of persons is itself derived from the identity of their bodies, then the analysis of physical identity in terms of relations between sense-data would appear to create a vicious circle. Failing a wholly different account of personal identity, the only way of escape would be to deny that sense-data have to be defined in terms of persons. Thus it might be argued that, even if one finds it necessary to refer to persons in order to explain what is meant by a sense-datum, there is no need to bring them into its definition. It would, indeed, be a mistake, at least for a phenomenalist, to offer any definition of sense-data at all. The concept of a sense-datum is taken by him as basic; everything else, including the concept of a person, is to be analysed in terms of it: and it is therefore not to be expected that it should itself be analysable in terms of anything else. But even if the concept of a sense-datum need not be defined, it must at least be shown to be intelligible: and while there may, as we have seen, be a use for it in the analysis of perception, it is not at all clear that it remains intelligible when its customary attachments are removed. For example, if the existence of a given person is made to depend upon certain relations obtaining between sense-data, these relations must presumably be factual. That is to say, it must be a contingent and not a necessary fact that the sense-data in question are related to each other in the appropriate ways. It is conceivable that they should not have been. But this suggests that it is at any rate logically possible for there to be sense-data which are, so to speak, personally independent. The relations which they have to other sense-data would not be such as would be required to constitute a person, or any other living thing: just as, in the case of a hallucination, there may be sense-data which are not the appearances of any physical object, so, on this view of their nature, there may be actual sense-data which do not enter into the experience of any sentient being. It is obvious that if there were sense-data of this kind, nobody would in fact know of their existence. It is, at best, a logical possibility; but is it even that? I confess that I am very doubtful whether this conception of unowned sense-data has any significance at all.

The same difficulty arises if, as an alternative or supplement to the criterion of bodily identity, one tries to make "being the same person" consist in a relation between experiences. This is the Humean view that the self is "a bundle of perceptions"; [2] many empiricists have held it, in one form or another. But whatever the relations between experiences may be that are taken to constitute self-identity—and we shall see that they are hard to discover—they must again be factual. Each experience is, on this view, a distinct occurrence; there can therefore be no logical connection between them; the existence of any one of them is not deducible from the existence of any other. But this suggests that it is logically conceivable that there should be experiences which were not the experiences of any person; experiences which were not owned by anything at all. For their having an owner would depend upon their being related in a certain way to other experiences; and they might in fact not be so related. This notion of an unowned experience is not, indeed, wholly unfamiliar to philosophers: but that is not to say that it is meaningful.

But if there cannot be experiences without someone to have them, then it would seem that any attempt to analyse personal identity in terms of relations between experiences must again involve us in a vicious circle. And since recourse to the idea of a spiritual substance does not provide an answer, we would appear to have no alternative but to make people's identities depend upon the identity of their bodies, at the same time forgoing any attempt to analyse bodily identity in terms of sense-data. But the consequences of this position are not very easy to accept. I agree, for example, that, in view of the dependence of conscious processes upon the condition

---

[2] *A Treatise of Human Nature,* Book I, Section vi. [A.J.A.]

of one's body, there are very good reasons for supposing that people do not survive their death. But this is not to say that the notion of survival is self-contradictory, or meaningless. On the contrary, unless the hypothesis at least made sense, one would not be entitled to say that it was highly improbable; for only what is possible can be false. But if a person's identity depends upon the identity of his body, it must be logically impossible that he should exist in a disembodied state. If the hypothesis of survival can be entertained at all, it must be taken as implying the re-animation of the body. It is for this reason, perhaps, that in some forms of religion it is orthodox to believe in a physical resurrection. But what is sometimes overlooked is that this would require the preservation of spatio-temporal continuity. Otherwise, it would not be the same body. On this view, the dissolution of the body destroys the person, no matter what subsequently happens.

Even so, many people do believe, or say that they believe, in the existence of disembodied spirits: and, however little chance such beliefs may have of being true, it is at least not obvious that they are meaningless. Could one not imagine circumstances in which there would be reason to say that one existed without a body? Suppose, for example, that, after a period of unconsciousness, one awoke to find things appearing much as they did before, except only that one's body seemed to have vanished from the scene. One would not perceive it in any way at all, and other people, whom one would still be able to observe, although one could not make one's presence known to them, would show by their behaviour that they did not perceive it either: one would observe that they acted as if one were dead. Would it not be reasonable in such a case to conclude that one had somehow survived one's death? Such a story is indeed a fantasy. That one should continue to see and hear without sense-organs is causally impossible. But, as a fantasy, it seems to be intelligible. And, if it is even intelligible, we must be able to form a concept of personal identity which does not depend for its application upon the identity of one's body.

But, granting that there could be such a concept, by what criteria would its use be governed? How, in our fanciful example, would it be determined that one was still the same person? The only answer that there seems any hope in offering is that it would be necessary that one should remember the experiences that one had had before one's death. In the same way, the only means by which it seems possible to give any sense to such a hypothesis as that of reincarnation is to make it imply some continuity of memory. Suppose, for example, that someone now living claimed to be Julius Caesar. Our first reaction, of course, would be to dismiss him as a lunatic. Even if his character and abilities were similar to those that historians attribute to Caesar, we should not be in the least inclined to allow that he really could be Caesar. But suppose that he claimed to remember Caesar's experiences, and that not only did his description of them agree with all the known facts, but new discoveries were made which confirmed his account

484 / A. J. AYER

of events in Caesar's life that were hitherto unknown to us. In that case we should hardly know what to say. Since the circumstances do not in fact arise, our language is not adapted to meet them. But if they did frequently arise, we should have to come to a decision. We might still refuse to allow the possibility of the same person's inhabiting more than one body, or of his leading a series of lives with intervals of time between them, and in that case we should have to find another way of accounting for the facts. As has already been remarked, we might decide to make it possible to remember experiences that one had never had. But we might instead prefer to say, in such a case as I have described, that the man really was Julius Caesar after all. This would not, indeed, be an explanation of the facts, in any scientific sense, but simply a redescription of them. The man's *really* being Julius Caesar would just consist in his having these powers of memory, and perhaps also in his behaving in certain other ways that we chose to consider relevant. It would be a matter of fact that he satisfied the criteria which we had laid down: but, given that he satisfied them, to go on to ask whether he really was the person that he claimed to be would not be to raise a question of fact. It would be, at this stage, a demand for a ruling. We should have simply to decide whether we thought it useful so to extend the usage of "being the same person" that it covered cases of this sort.

This question of the possibility of reincarnation is comparatively straightforward. It is assumed that we are confronted with someone who satisfies the ordinary physical criteria of personal identity, and our problem is then only to consider whether we shall allow the continuity of memory to make him the same person as one who, if we went by the physical criteria alone, would be reckoned to be someone else. But when it comes to the possibility of a person's continuing to exist in a disembodied state, a much greater difficulty arises. For here we have to find a criterion not only for our subject's being the same person as one who is physically identified, but for his being a person at all. We have to make sense of saying that someone exists without a body, before we can raise the question whether he is the same person as one who existed with a body. And for this, continuity of memory, though it may be necessary, will not be sufficient. Assuming for the moment that it is meaningful to speak of a series of experiences, without the implication that they are the experiences of any person, we may try to thread them together by supposing that later experiences consist partly in recollections of their predecessors. If we want to enlist every member of the series, we shall have to assume that each of them is related to at least one of the others either actively or passively with respect to memory. For if memory is to be the only link between them, an experience which contained no recollection of any previous member of the series, and was not itself recollected at any later stage in it, would fall outside the series altogether. On the face of it, it would seem possible for people to have such experiences; but this possibility is removed when personal identity is made to depend solely upon memory. Furthermore, unless we assume that every detail of every experience is subsequently recollected, there will be elements that make their way into the series only because they are accompanied by memories, or by other elements which are remembered. But what is this relation of accompanying? We may say that it is the relation that holds between two items of experience if and only if they are parts of the same total experience at any given moment. But what is meant here by a total experience is just the experience of one and the same person. We can hold that the relation between its parts is *sui generis,* but then we can also hold that the relation between the successive experiences of the same person is *sui generis:* and in that case we do not need to bring in memory at all.

A further objection is that to remember an experience entails claiming it as an experience of one's own: from which it would seem to follow that personal identity cannot be founded on this type of memory since it is already presupposed by it. But here the circle may be only apparent. To claim an experience as one's own may consist in nothing more than a disposition to use first person language in describing it. It may, indeed, be argued that the use of first person language itself presupposes the notion of personal identity, but I am not sure that this is so. I think that one can, for example, come to use the word "I" correctly and intelligently, without necessarily thinking of the series of one's own experiences as being in any way related; it seems to me possible even that the use of the word should be learned by someone who was not self-conscious at all. And this is borne out by the fact that to ask "Is this experience mine?" is not to raise a serious question. Neither is this just a peculiarity of the employment of the present tense. It is rather that to refer to an experience demonstratively is to preclude any doubt about its ownership; there can be no question whose it is. The inference which I wish to draw from this is that in using the first person, one need not be raising the question whether any criteria of personal identity are satisfied; otherwise, it would always be sensible to ask of any experience whether it was one's own. Admittedly, the experience in question will not in fact be one's own, unless the criteria are satisfied: but I suggest that it does not follow that one need actually be stating that they are satisfied when one claims an experience by the use of first person language. I conclude, therefore, with some hesitation, that if the other obstacles to founding personal identity upon memory were overcome, this charge of circularity could be met.

This is, however, only a subsidiary question. The major objection on the score of circularity still remains. I find myself here in the sort of dilemma that frequently arises in philosophy. On the one hand, I am inclined to hold that personal identity can be constituted by the presence of a certain factual relation between experiences. On the other hand, I doubt if it is meaningful to talk of experiences except as the experiences of a person; or at least of an animate creature of some kind. As I have already remarked, these views appear to be inconsistent with each other, but I think it possible that they can be reconciled. In saying that the relations between experiences which are supposed to constitute personal identity are factual, I am implying that it is never necessary that any two experiences should be related by them. Either one of the experiences in question might occur, even if the other did not. But while it follows from this that there are no experiences in particular to which any given experience need be so related, it does not follow that it could fail to stand in any such relation to any experiences at all. It does not follow that the experience could exist entirely on its own. And indeed the suggestion that there are experiences which so exist is one that I do find nonsensical; there would seem to be no conceivable way in which its truth or falsehood could be tested. But if it is nonsensical, we cannot talk of experiences without implying that they have owners. And then we seem to involve ourselves in a circle when we make the existence of persons consist only in a certain relationship between experiences. But I do not think that this circle is vicious. It shows that we could not understand what is meant by an experience unless we already understood what was meant by being a person; but, as we have already seen in other instances, to understand what is meant by an expression does not entail that one can give a satisfactory analysis of its use. So even if the existence of an experience entails the existence of a person, an analysis of personal identity in terms of experiences could still be informative. What is disturbing is the implication that the relations between experiences, which would furnish such an analysis, must be logically necessary. But they will be necessary only in the sense that from the fact that an experience occurs it will follow, on this view, that there are some other experiences to which it bears the relations in question. But the other experiences are not specified. Any statement to the effect that two given experiences are so related will remain contingent. Thus, of the two principles which Hume admitted that he could neither renounce nor reconcile—"that all our distinct perceptions are distinct existences" and "that the mind never perceives any real connection among distinct existences" [3]—we must, I think, renounce or at least reinterpret the first. Distinct perceptions are distinct existences inasmuch as, given any set of perceptions, $A, B, C, \ldots$, the existence of any one of them is compatible with the non-existence of any of the others. But if it does not make sense to talk of perceptions without a percipient, then, on the Humean view that the self is "a bundle of perceptions," the existence of any one perception A must entail the existence of some other. It is consistent with the existence of A that $B, C \ldots$ should not have existed, but it is implied that if they had not existed some other perceptions would have taken their place. And the same applies to sense-data, which are indeed to be counted as perceptions, in Hume's sense. Their existence may be made to depend upon the existence of physical objects, or of other sense-data, but no sense-datum can exist entirely on its own. We have seen,

---

[3] *A Treatise of Human Nature,* Appendix. [A.J.A.]

however, that this alone does not exclude the possibility of giving a phenomenalist account of the self.

None of this proves, of course, that there are any other criteria of personal identity than those that depend upon the identity of the body. We have not succeeded in discovering any relation by which the constituents of Hume's bundles could be adequately held together. Some continuity of memory is necessary, but not, I think, sufficient. It needs to be backed by some other relation of which, perhaps, nothing more illuminating can be said than that it is the relation that holds between experiences when they are constituents of the same consciousness. The alternative is to regard it as a necessary proposition that a person's existence is tied to the existence of his body. But I am not convinced that this proposition is necessary, though I believe that it is true.

QUESTIONS FOR STUDY AND DISCUSSION

1. What is Ayer's approach to the refusal to accept the "I" as a substance? How does he use the demonstrative pronoun "I" to support his approach? Does he change his position later on as to the force of the proof of personal identity from the use of the pronoun "I"?
2. What difficulties does Ayer say arise when one tries to derive the identity of the person from the identity of his body?
3. How does he criticize the Humean view that the self is a bundle of perceptions?
4. What does Ayer say of the immortality of the soul and how does he apply to the question the dictum that "only what is possible can be false" in this discussion? What is the role of memory in a sense of personal identity after death?
5. How does Ayer formulate the problem of the freedom of the will?

Gilbert Ryle

GILBERT RYLE, born in 1900, is at present professor of Metaphysical Philosophy at Oxford, where he has taught since 1924. Ryle's thought is closer to the philosophy of Wittgenstein than to most of the other contemporary thinkers. He succeeded George Edward Moore as editor of *Mind* in 1948. Greatly interested in the problem that the views of Descartes pose for a philosophy of mind, Ryle is best known for his work on the mind-body problem as set forth in *The Concept of Mind* (1949).

Descartes' Myth

THE OFFICIAL DOCTRINE

There is a doctrine about the nature and place of minds which is so prevalent among theorists and even among laymen that it deserves to be described as the official theory. Most philosophers, psychologists and religious teachers subscribe, with minor reservations, to its main articles and, although they admit certain theoretical difficulties in it, they tend to assume that these can be overcome without serious modifications being made to the architecture of the theory. It will be argued here that the central principles of the doctrine are unsound and conflict with the whole body of what we know about minds when we are not speculating about them.

The official doctrine, which hails chiefly from Descartes, is something like this. With the doubtful exceptions of idiots and infants in arms every human being has both a body and a mind. Some would prefer to say that every human being is both a body and a mind. His body and his mind are ordinarily harnessed together, but after the death of the body his mind may continue to exist and function.

Human bodies are in space and are subject to the mechanical laws which govern all other bodies in space. Bodily processes and states can be inspected by external observers. So a man's bodily life is as much a public affair as the lives of animals and reptiles and even as the careers of trees, crystals and planets.

But minds are not in space, nor are their operations subject to mechan-

From pp. 11–18 and 23–24 of Gilbert Ryle, *The Concept of Mind*. Copyright 1949 by Barnes and Noble, Inc. Reprinted by permission of the publisher.

ical laws. The workings of one mind are not witnessable by other observers; its career is private. Only I can take direct cognisance of the states and processes of my own mind. A person therefore lives through two collateral histories, one consisting of what happens in and to his body, the other consisting of what happens in and to his mind. The first is public, the second private. The events in the first history are events in the physical world, those in the second are events in the mental world.

It has been disputed whether a person does or can directly monitor all or only some of the episodes of his own private history; but, according to the official doctrine, of at least some of these episodes he has direct and unchallengeable cognisance. In consciousness, self-consciousness and introspection he is directly and authentically apprised of the present states and operations of his mind. He may have great or small uncertainties about concurrent and adjacent episodes in the physical world, but he can have none about at least part of what is momentarily occupying his mind.

It is customary to express this bifurcation of his two lives and of his two worlds by saying that the things and events which belong to the physical world, including his own body, are external, while the workings of his own mind are internal. This antithesis of outer and inner is of course meant to be construed as a metaphor, since minds, not being in space, could not be described as being spatially inside anything else, or as having things going on spatially inside themselves. But relapses from this good intention are common and theorists are found speculating how stimuli, the physical sources of which are yards or miles outside a person's skin, can generate mental responses inside his skull, or how decisions framed inside his cranium can get going movements of his extremities.

Even when "inner" and "outer" are construed as metaphors, the problem how a person's mind and body influence one another is notoriously charged with theoretical difficulties. What the mind wills, the legs, arms and the tongue execute; what affects the ear and the eye has something to do with what the mind perceives; grimaces and smiles betray the mind's moods and bodily castigations lead, it is hoped, to moral improvement. But the actual transactions between the episodes of the private history and those of the public history remain mysterious, since by definition they can belong to neither series. They could not be reported among the happenings described in a person's autobiography of his inner life, but nor could they be reported among those described in some one else's biography of that person's overt career. They can be inspected neither by introspection nor by laboratory experiment. They are theoretical shuttlecocks which are forever being bandied from the physiologist back to the psychologist and from the psychologist back to the physiologist.

Underlying this partly metaphorical representation of the bifurcation of a person's two lives there is a seemingly more profound and philosophical assumption. It is assumed that there are two different kinds of existence or status. What exists or happens may have the status of physical existence, or it may have the status of mental existence. Somewhat as the faces of coins are either heads or tails, or somewhat as living creatures are either male or female, so, it is supposed, some existing is physical existing, other existing is mental existing. It is a necessary feature of what has physical existence that it is in space and time, it is a necessary feature of what has mental existence that it is in time but not in space. What has physical existence is composed of matter, or else is a function of matter; what has mental existence consists of consciousness, or else is a function of consciousness.

There is thus a polar opposition between mind and matter, an opposition which is often brought out as follows. Material objects are situated in a common field, known as "space," and what happens to one body in one part of space is mechanically connected with what happens to other bodies in other parts of space. But mental happenings occur in insulated fields, known as "minds," and there is, apart maybe from telepathy, no direct causal connection between what happens in one mind and what happens in another. Only through the medium of the public physical world can the mind of one person make a difference to the mind of another. The mind is its own place and in his inner life each of us lives the life of a ghostly Robinson Crusoe. People can see, hear and jolt one another's bodies, but they are irremediably blind and deaf to the workings of one another's minds and inoperative upon them.

What sort of knowledge can be secured of the workings of a mind? On the one side, according to the official theory, a person has direct knowledge of the best imaginable kind of the workings of his own mind. Mental states and processes are (or are normally) conscious states and processes, and the consciousness which irradiates them can engender no illusions and leaves the door open for no doubts. A person's present thinkings, feelings and willings, his perceivings, rememberings and imaginings are intrinsically "phosphorescent"; their existence and their nature are inevitably betrayed to their owner. The inner life is a stream of consciousness of such a sort that it would be absurd to suggest that the mind whose life is that stream might be unaware of what is passing down it.

True, the evidence adduced recently by Freud seems to show that there exist channels tributary to this stream, which run hidden from their owner. People are actuated by impulses the existence of which they vigorously disavow; some of their thoughts differ from the thoughts which they acknowledge; and some of the actions which they think they will to perform they do not really will. They are thoroughly gulled by some of their own hypocrisies and they successfully ignore facts about their mental lives which on the official theory ought to be patent to them. Holders of the official theory tend, however, to maintain that anyhow in normal circumstances a person must be directly and authentically seized of the present state and workings of his own mind.

Besides being currently supplied with these alleged immediate data of consciousness, a person is also generally supposed to be able to exercise from time to time a special kind of perception, namely inner perception, or introspection. He can take a (non-optical) "look" at what is passing in his mind. Not only can he view and scrutinize a flower through his sense of sight and listen to and discriminte the notes of a bell through his sense of hearing; he can also reflectively or introspectively watch, without any bodily organ of sense, the current episodes of his inner life. This self-observation is also commonly supposed to be immune from illusion, confusion or doubt. A mind's reports of its own affairs have a certainty superior to the best that is possessed by its reports of matters in the physical world. Sense-perceptions can, but consciousness and introspection cannot, be mistaken or confused.

On the other side, one person has no direct access of any sort to the events of the inner life of another. He cannot do better than make problematic inferences from the observed behaviour of the other person's body to the states of mind which, by analogy from his own conduct, he supposes to be signalised by that behaviour. Direct access to the workings of a mind is the privilege of that mind itself; in default of such privileged access, the workings of one mind are inevitably occult to everyone else. For the supposed arguments from bodily movements similar to their own to mental workings similar to their own would lack any possibility of observational corroboration. Not unnaturally, therefore, an adherent of the official theory finds it difficult to resist this consequence of his premises, that he has no good reason to believe that there do exist minds other than his own. Even if he prefers to believe that to other human bodies there are harnessed minds not unlike his own, he cannot claim to be able to discover their individual characteristics, or the particular things that they undergo and do. Absolute solitude is on this showing the ineluctable destiny of the soul. Only our bodies can meet.

As a necessary corollary of this general scheme there is implicitly prescribed a special way of construing our ordinary concepts of mental powers and operations. The verbs, nouns and adjectives, with which in ordinary life we describe the wits, characters and higher-grade performances of the people with whom we have do, are required to be construed as signifying special episodes in their secret histories, or else as signifying tendencies for such episodes to occur. When someone is described as knowing, believing or guessing something, as hoping, dreading, intending or shirking something, as designing this or being amused at that, these verbs are supposed to denote the occurrence of specific modifications in his (to us) occult stream of consciousness. Only his own privileged access to this stream in direct awareness and introspection could provide authentic testimony that these mental-conduct verbs were correctly or incorrectly applied. The onlooker, be he teacher, critic, biographer or friend, can never assure himself that his comments have any vestige of truth. Yet it was just because we do in fact all know how to make such comments, make them with general correctness and correct them when they turn out to be confused or mistaken, that philosophers found it necessary to construct their theories of the nature and place of minds. Finding mental-conduct concepts being regularly and effectively used, they properly sought to fix their logical geography. But the logical geography officially recommended would entail that there could be no regular or effective use of these mental-conduct concepts in our descriptions of, and prescriptions for, other people's minds.

THE ABSURDITY OF THE OFFICIAL DOCTRINE

Such in outline is the official theory. I shall often speak of it, with deliberate abusiveness, as "the dogma of the Ghost in the Machine." I hope to prove that it is entirely false, and false not in detail but in principle. It is not merely an assemblage of particular mistakes. It is one big mistake and a mistake of a special kind. It is, namely, a category-mistake. It represents the facts of mental life as if they belonged to one logical type or category (or range of types or categories), when they actually belong to another. The dogma is therefore a philosopher's myth. In attempting to explode the myth I shall probably be taken to be denying well-known facts about the mental life of human beings, and my plea that I aim at doing nothing more than rectify the logic of mental-conduct concepts will probably be disallowed as mere subterfuge.

I must first indicate what is meant by the phrase "Category-mistake." This I do in a series of illustrations.

A foreigner visiting Oxford or Cambridge for the first time is shown a number of colleges, libraries, playing fields, museums, scientific departments and administrative offices. He then asks "But where is the University? I have seen where the members of the Colleges live, where the Registrar works, where the scientists experiment and the rest. But I have not yet seen the University in which reside and work the members of your University." It has then to be explained to him that the University is not another collateral institution, some ulterior counterpart to the colleges, laboratories and offices which he has seen. The University is just the way in which all that he has already seen is organized. When they are seen and when their co-ordination is understood, the University has been seen. His mistake lay in his innocent assumption that it was correct to speak of Christ Church, the Bodleian Library, the Ashmolean Museum *and* the University, to speak, that is, as if "the University" stood for an extra member of the class of which these other units are members. He was mistakenly allocating the University to the same category as that to which the other institutions belong.

The same mistake would be made by a child witnessing the march-past of a division, who, having had pointed out to him such and such battalions, batteries, squadrons, etc., asked when the division was going to appear. He would be supposing that a division was a counterpart to the units already seen, partly similar to them and partly unlike them. He would be shown his mistake by being told that in watching the battalions, batteries and squadrons marching past he had been watching the division marching past. The march-past was not a parade of battalions, batteries, squadrons *and* a division; it was a parade of the battalions, batteries and squadrons *of* a division.

One more illustration. A foreigner watching his first game of cricket learns what are the functions of the bowlers, the batsmen, the fielders, the umpires and the scorers. He then says "But there is no one left on the field to contribute the famous element of team-spirit. I see who does the bowling, the batting and the wicket-keeping; but I do not see whose role it is to exercise *esprit de corps.*" Once more, it would have to be explained that he was looking for the wrong type of thing. Team-spirit is not another cricketing-operation supplementary to all of the other special tasks. It is, roughly, the keenness with which each of the special tasks is performed, and performing a task keenly is not performing two tasks. Certainly exhibiting team-spirit is not the same thing as bowling or catching, but nor is it a third thing such that we can say that the bowler first bowls *and* then exhibits team-spirit or that a fielder is at a given moment *either* catching *or* displaying *esprit de corps.*

These illustrations of category-mistakes have a common feature which must be noticed. The mistakes were made by people who did not know how to wield the concepts *University, division* and *team-spirit.* Their puzzles arose from inability to use certain items in the English vocabulary.

The theoretically interesting category-mistakes are those made by people who are perfectly competent to apply concepts, at least in the situations with which they are familiar, but are still liable in their abstract thinking to allocate those concepts to logical types to which they do not belong. An instance of a mistake of this sort would be the following story. A student of politics has learned the main differences between the British, the French and the American Constitutions, and has learned also the differences and connections between the Cabinet, Parliament, the various Ministries, the Judicature and the Church of England. But he still becomes embarrassed when asked questions about the connections between the Church of England, the Home Office and the British Constitution. For while the Church and the Home Office are institutions, the British Constitution is not another institution in the same sense of that noun. So inter-institutional relations which can be asserted or denied to hold between the Church and Home Office cannot be asserted or denied to hold between either of them and the British Constitution. "The British Constitution" is not a term of the same logical type as "the Home Office" and "the Church of England." In a partially similar way, John Doe may be a relative, a friend, an enemy or a stranger to Richard Roe; but he cannot be any of these things to the Average Taxpayer. He knows how to talk sense in certain sorts of discussions about the Average Taxpayer, but he is baffled to say why he could not come across him in the street as he can come across Richard Roe.

It is pertinent to our main subject to notice that, so long as the student of politics continues to think of the British Constitution as a counterpart to the other institutions, he will tend to describe it as a mysteriously occult institution; and so long as John Doe continues to think of the Average Taxpayer as a fellow-citizen, he will tend to think of him as an elusive insubstantial man, a ghost who is everywhere yet nowhere.

My destructive purpose is to show that a family of radical category-mistakes is the source of the double-life theory. The representation of a person as a ghost mysteriously ensconced in a machine derives from this argument. Because, as is true, a person's thinking, feeling and purposive doing cannot be described solely in the idioms of physics, chemistry and physiology, therefore they must be described in counterpart idioms. As the human body is a complex organised unit, so the human mind must be another complex organised unit, though one made of a different sort of stuff and with a different sort of structure. Or, again, as the human body, like any other parcel of matter, is a field of causes and effects, so the mind must be another field of causes and effects, though not (Heaven be praised) mechanical causes and effects.

·   ·   ·

HISTORICAL NOTE

It would not be true to say that the official theory derives solely from Descartes' theories, or even from a more widespread anxiety about the implications of seventeenth century mechanics. Scholastic and Reformation theology had schooled the intellects of the scientists as well as of the laymen, philosophers and clerics of that age. Stoic-Augustinian theories of the will were embedded in the Calvinist doctrines of sin and grace; Platonic and Aristotelian theories of the intellect shaped the orthodox doctrines of the immortality of the soul. Descartes was reformulating already prevalent theological doctrines of the soul in the new syntax of Galileo. The theologian's privacy of conscience became the philosopher's privacy of consciousness, and what had been the bogy of Predestination reappeared as the bogy of Determinism.

It would also not be true to say that the two-worlds myth did no theoretical good. Myths often do a lot of theoretical good, while they are still new. One benefit bestowed by the para-mechanical myth was that it partly superannuated the then prevalent para-political myth. Minds and their Faculties had previously been described by analogies with political superiors and political subordinates. The idioms used were those of ruling, obeying, collaborating and rebelling. They survived and still survive in many ethical and some epistemological discussions. As, in physics, the new myth of occult Forces was a scientific improvement on the old myth of Final Causes, so, in anthropological and psychological theory, the new myth of hidden operations, impulses and agencies was an improvement on the old myth of dictations, deferences and disobediences.

QUESTIONS FOR STUDY AND DISCUSSION

1. Is Ryle's description of the mind-body problem generally taught and accepted? What group of philosophers, if any, hold that the person is a "ghost mysteriously ensconced in a machine"?
2. What is a category-mistake? Give one of Ryle's illustrations and one of your own.
3. What, according to Ryle, is the problem of the freedom of the will?
4. How does Ryle seek to dispel the long-disputed contrast between mind and matter?

The Self

THE SYSTEMATIC ELUSIVENESS OF "I"

We are now in a position to account for the systematic elusiveness of the notion of "I," and the partial non-parallelism between it and the notion of "you" or "he." To concern oneself about oneself in any way, theoretical or practical, is to perform a higher order act, just as it is to concern oneself about anybody else. To try, for example, to describe what one has just done, or is now doing, is to comment upon a step which is not itself, save *per accidens,* one of commenting. But the operation which is the commenting is not, and cannot be, the step on which that commentary is being made. Nor can an act of ridiculing be its own butt. A higher order action cannot be the action upon which it is performed. So my commentary on my performances must always be silent about one performance, namely itself, and this performance can be the target only of another commentary. Self-commentary, self-ridicule and self-admonition are logically condemned to eternal penultimacy. Yet nothing that is left out of any particular commentary or admonition is priviledged thereby to escape comment or admonition for ever. On the contrary it may be the target of the very next comment or rebuke.

The point may be illustrated in this way. A singing-master might criticise the accents or notes of a pupil by mimicking with exaggerations each word that the pupil sang; and if the pupil sang slowly enough, the master could parody each word sung by the pupil before the next came to be uttered. But then, in a mood of humility, the singing-master tries to criticise his own singing in the same way, and more than that to mimic with

From pp. 195–98 of Gilbert Ryle, *The Concept of Mind.* Copyright 1949 by Barnes and Noble, Inc. Reprinted by permission of the publisher.

exaggerations each word that he utters, including those that he utters in self-parody. It is at once clear, first, that he can never get beyond the very earliest word of his song and, second, that at any given moment he has uttered one noise which has yet to be mimicked—and it makes no difference how rapidly he chases his notes with mimicries of them. He can, in principle, never catch more than the coat-tails of the object of his pursuit, since a word cannot be a parody of itself. None the less, there is no word that he sings which remains unparodied; he is always a day late for the fair, but every day he reaches the place of yesterday's fair. He never succeeds in jumping on to the shadow of his own head, yet he is never more than one jump behind.

An ordinary reviewer may review a book, while a second order reviewer criticises reviews of the book. But the second order review is not a criticism of itself. It can only be criticised in a further third order review. Given complete editorial patience, any review of any order could be published, though at no stage would all the reviews have received critical notices. Nor can every act of a diarist be the topic of a record in his diary; for the last entry made in his diary still demands that the making of it should in its turn be chronicled.

This, I think, explains the feeling that my last year's self, or my yesterday's self, could in principle be exhaustively described and accounted for, and that your past or present self could be exhaustively described and accounted for by me, but that my today's self perpetually slips out of any hold of it that I try to take. It also explains the apparent non-parallelism between the notion of "I" and that of "you," without construing the elusive residuum as any kind of ultimate mystery.

There is another thing which it explains. When people consider the problems of the Freedom of the Will and try to imagine their own careers as analogous to those of cocks or water-courses, they tend to boggle at the idea that their own immediate future is already unalterably fixed and predictable. It seems absurd to suppose that what I am just about to think, feel or do is already preappointed, though people are apt to find no such absurdity in the supposition that the futures of other people are so preappointed. The so-called "feeling of spontaneity" is closely connected with this inability to imagine that what I am going to think or do can already be anticipated. On the other hand, when I consider what I thought and did yesterday, there seems to be no absurdity in supposing that that could have been forecast, before I did it. It is only while I am actually trying to predict my own next move that the task feels like that of a swimmer trying to overtake the waves that he sends ahead of himself.

The solution is as before. A prediction of a deed or a thought is a higher order operation, the performance of which cannot be among the things considered in making the prediction. Yet as the state of mind in which I am just before I do something may make some difference to what I do, it follows that I must overlook at least one of the data relevant to my prediction. Similarly, I can give you the fullest possible advice what to do, but I must omit one piece of counsel, since I cannot in the same breath advise you how to take that advice. There is therefore no paradox in saying that while normally I am not at all surprised to find myself doing or thinking what I do, yet when I try most carefully to anticipate what I shall do or think, then the outcome is likely to falsify my expectation. My process of pre-envisaging may divert the course of my ensuing behaviour in a direction and degree of which my prognosis cannot take account. One thing that I cannot prepare myself for is the next thought that I am going to think.

The fact that my immediate future is in this way systematically elusive to me has, of course, no tendency to prove that my career is in principle unpredictable to prophets other than myself, or even that it is inexplicable to myself after the heat of the action. I can point to any other thing with my index-finger, and other people can point at this finger. But it cannot be the object at which it itself is pointing. Nor can a missile be its own target, though anything else may be thrown at it.

This general conclusion that any performance can be the concern of a higher order performance, but cannot be the concern of itself, is connected with what was said earlier about the special functioning of index words, such as "now," "you" and "I." An "I" sentence indicates whom in particular it is about by being itself uttered or written by someone in particular. "I" indicates the person who utters it. So, when a person utters an "I" sentence, his utterance of it may be part of a higher order performance, namely one, perhaps of self-reporting, self-exhortation or self-commiseration, and this performance itself is not dealt with in the operation which it itself is. Even if the person is, for special speculative purposes, momentarily concentrating on the Problem of the Self, he has failed and knows that he has failed to catch more than the flying coat-tails of that which he was pursuing. His quarry was the hunter.

To conclude, there is nothing mysterious or occult about the range of higher order acts and attitudes, which are apt to be inadequately covered by the umbrella-title "self-consciousness." They are the same in kind as the higher order acts and attitudes exhibited in the dealings of people with one another. Indeed the former are only a special application of the latter and are learned first from them. If I perform the third order operation of commenting on a second order act of laughing at myself for a piece of manual awkwardness, I shall indeed use the first personal pronoun in two different ways. I say to myself, or to the company, "I was laughing at myself for being butter-fingered." But so far from this showing that there are two "Mes" in my skin, not to speak, yet, of the third one which is still commenting on them, it shows only that I am applying the public two-pronoun idiom in which we talk of her laughing at him; and I am applying this linguistic idiom, because I am applying the method of inter-personal transaction which the idiom is ordinarily employed to describe.

Before concluding this chapter, it is worth mentioning that there is one influential difference between the first personal pronoun and all the rest. "I," in my use of it, always indicates me and only indicates me. "You," "she" and "they" indicate different people at different times. "I" is like my own shadow; I can never get away from it, as I can get away from your shadow. There is no mystery about this constancy, but I mention it because it seems to endow "I" with a mystifying uniqueness and adhesiveness. "Now" has something of the same besetting feeling.

QUESTIONS FOR STUDY AND DISCUSSION

1. Using Ryle's method of describing second and third order references to the "I," give some examples of your own. Do they help to show that man is not two separate entities (mind and body) but only one?
2. Compare Ryle's and Hume's conclusions on the self.
3. In what way is the ordinary view of the soul similar to Ryle's view of the "I"?

Ludwig Wittgenstein

LUDWIG WITTGENSTEIN was born in Vienna in 1889 and came to Cambridge in 1911, where he met Moore and Russell. He published one book during his lifetime, *Tractatus Logico-Philosophicus* (1921), but it was to serve as a cornerstone for contemporary empiricism. His masterwork, *Philosophical Investigations,* was published posthumously, in 1953, as were *The Blue and Brown Books* (1958) and *Notebooks, 1914–1916* (1961). After spending several years as an obscure village school teacher, Wittgenstein returned to Cambridge in 1929. He retired to Norway in 1947 and later traveled to Ireland and the United States. He died at Cambridge in 1951.

The Will, Death, Immortality, and Other "Unspeakables"

6.4 [1]   All propositions are of equal value.

6.41   The sense of the world must lie outside the world. In the world everything is as it is, and everything happens as it does happen: *in* it no value exists—and if it did exist, it would have no value.

If there is any value that does have value, it must lie outside the whole sphere of what happens and is the case. For all that happens and is the case is accidental.

What makes it non-accidental cannot lie *within* the world, since if it did it would itself be accidental.

It must lie outside the world.

6.42   And so it is impossible for there to be propositions of ethics.

Propositions can express nothing that is higher.

6.421   It is clear that ethics cannot be put into words.

Ethics is transcendental.

(Ethics and aesthetics are one and the same.)

---

[1] Wittgenstein numbers sentences that are linked together with the same whole number. To these whole numbers he adds other numbers to show a subordination of thought. [M.G.]

From pp. 145–51 of Ludwig Wittgenstein, *Tractatus Logico-Philosophicus,* translated by D. F. Pears and B. F. McGuinness. © 1961 by Humanities Press, Inc. Reprinted by permission of Humanities Press, Inc., and Routledge and Kegan Paul Ltd., London.

6.422   When an ethical law of the form, "Thou shalt . . . ," is laid down, one's first thought is, "And what if I do not do it?" It is clear, however, that ethics has nothing to do with punishment and reward in the usual sense of the terms. So our question about the *consequences* of an action must be unimportant.—At least those consequences should not be events. For there must be something right about the question we posed. There must indeed be some kind of ethical reward and ethical punishment, but they must reside in the action itself.

(And it is also clear that the reward must be something pleasant and the punishment something unpleasant.)

6.423   It is impossible to speak about the will in so far as it is the subject of ethical attributes.

And the will as a phenomenon is of interest only to psychology.

6.43   If the good or bad exercise of the will does alter the world, it can alter only the limit of the world, not the facts—not what can be expressed by means of language.

In short the effect must be that it becomes an altogether different world. It must, so to speak, wax and wane as a whole.

The world of the happy man is a different one from that of the unhappy man.

6.431   So too at death the world does not alter, but comes to an end.

6.4311   Death is not an event in life: we do not live to experience death.

If we take eternity to mean not infinite temporal duration but timelessness, then eternal life belongs to those who live in the present.

Our life has no end in just the way in which our visual field has no limits.

6.4312   Not only is there no guarantee of the temporal immortality of the human soul, that is to say of its eternal survival after death; but, in any case, this assumption completely fails to accomplish the purpose for which it has always been intended. Or is some riddle solved by my surviving for ever? Is not this eternal life itself as much of a riddle as our present life? The solution of the riddle of life in space and time lies *outside* space and time.

(It is certainly not the solution of any problems of natural science that is required.)

6.432   *How* things are in the world is a matter of complete indifference for what is higher. God does not reveal himself *in* the world.

6.4321   The facts all contribute only to setting the problem, not to its solution.

6.44   It is not *how* things are in the world that is mystical, but *that* it exists.

6.45   To view the world *sub specie aeterni* is to view it as a whole—a limited whole.

Feeling the world as a limited whole—it is this that is mystical.

6.5   When the answer cannot be put into words, neither can the question be put into words.

The riddle does not exist.

If a question can be framed at all, it is also *possible* to answer it.

6.51   Scepticism is *not* irrefutable, but obviously nonsensical, when it tries to raise doubts where no questions can be asked.

For doubt can exist only where a question exists, a question only where an answer exists, and an answer only where something *can be said.*

6.52   We feel that even when *all possible* scientific questions have been answered, the problems of life remain completely untouched. Of course there are then no questions left, and this itself is the answer.

6.521   The solution of the problem of life is seen in the vanishing of the problem.

(Is not this the reason why those who have found after a long period of doubt that the sense of life became clear to them have then been unable to say what constituted that sense?)

6.522   There are, indeed, things that cannot be put into words. They make themselves manifest. They are what is mystical.

6.53   The correct method in philosophy would really be the following: to say nothing except what can be said, i.e. propositions of natural science—i.e. something that has nothing to do with philosophy—and then, whenever someone else wanted to say something metaphysical, to demonstrate to him that he had failed to give a meaning to certain signs in his propositions. Although it would not be satisfying to the other person—he would not have the feeling that we were teaching him philosophy—*this* method would be the only strictly correct one.

6.54   My propositions serve as elucidations in the following way: anyone who understands me eventually recognizes them as nonsensical, when he has used them—as steps—to climb up beyond them. (He must, so to speak, throw away the ladder after he has climbed up it.)

He must transcend these propositions, and then he will see the world aright.

7   What we cannot speak about we must pass over in silence.

QUESTIONS FOR STUDY AND DISCUSSION

1. Wittgenstein in 6.4 and 6.42 seems to imply that the meaning of the world and even of what is right and wrong, good and bad, lies not in time but above time. In what sense can this be so?

2. In 6.423 and 6.43 he speaks of the will. Earlier he had said that man, the subject, is the limit of the world. Now he says that the will is the limit of the world. In what sense can it be said that you, by a willed decision, can expand or limit the horizons of your world?

3. Can the same objective world be different for a happy man than it is for an unhappy one? What makes the difference? The world or the man?

4. Boethius once defined eternity as simultaneous and perfect possession of endless life. There is no before or after in eternity according to St. Thomas. Does Wittgenstein's statement, "eternal life belongs to those who live in the present," seem to state a similar idea?

5. Is Wittgenstein denying the immortality of the human soul or implying that it is beyond the realm of the natural sciences?

George Edward Moore

GEORGE EDWARD MOORE was born in London in 1873. He spent most of his life at Cambridge University, both as a student and as a professor, and died there in 1958. He is best known as a "philosopher's philosopher" whose chief influence was in directing philosophy in England away from its excessive dependence on Hegelian ideas. His essay, *The Refutation of Idealism,* published in the journal *Mind* in 1903, provided the spearhead for the movement known as British neorealism. His chief work, *Principia Ethica,* was published in the same year. A student of Russell's, Moore influenced Russell—and Wittgenstein—and in turn was influenced by them.

Wittgenstein's Lectures in 1930-1933, Part I

Wittgenstein began to lecture in January 1930, and from the first he adopted a plan to which he adhered, I believe, throughout his lectures at Cambridge.[1] His plan was only to lecture once a week in every week of Full Term, but on a later day in each week to hold a discussion class at which what he had said in that week's lecture could be discussed. At first both lecture and discussion class were held in an ordinary lecture-room in the University Arts School, but very early in the first term Mr. R. E. Priestley (now Sir Raymond Priestley), who was then Secretary General of the Faculties and who occupied a set of Fellows' rooms in the new building of Clare, invited Wittgenstein to hold his discussion classes in these rooms. Later on, I think, both lectures and discussion classes were held in Priestley's rooms, and this continued until, in October 1931, Wittgenstein, being then a Fellow of Trinity, was able to obtain a set of rooms of his own in Trinity which he really liked. These rooms were those which Wittgenstein had occupied in the academic year 1912–13, and which I had occupied the

---

[1] Professor von Wright has subsequently informed me that I was mistaken in believing this: that in 1939, Wittgenstein lectured twice a week and held no discussion class; and that in the Easter Term of 1947, he both gave two lectures a week and also held a discussion class. I have also remembered that at one time (I do not know for how long) he gave, besides his ordinary lectures, a special set of lectures for mathematicians. [G.E.M.]

From *Mind,* vol. LXIII, No. 249. Reprinted by permission of the editor.

year before, and occupied again from October 1913, when Wittgenstein left Cambridge and went to Norway. Of the only two sets which are on the top floor of the gate-way from Whewell's Courts into Sidney Street, they were the set which looks westward over the larger Whewell's Court, and, being so high up, they had a large view of sky and also of Cambridge roofs, including the pinnacles of King's Chapel. Since the rooms were not a Fellow's set, their sitting-room was not large, and for the purpose of his lectures and classes Wittgenstein used to fill it with some twenty plain cane-bottomed chairs, which at other times were stacked on the large landing outside. Nearly from the beginning the discussion classes were liable to last at least two hours, and from the time when the lectures ceased to be given in the Arts School they also commonly lasted at least as long. Wittgenstein always had a blackboard at both lectures and classes and made plenty of use of it.

I attended both lectures and discussion classes in all three terms of 1930 and in the first two terms of 1931. In the Michaelmas Term of 1931 and the Lent term of 1932 I ceased, for some reason which I cannot now remember, to attend the lectures though I still went to the discussion classes; but in May 1932, I resumed the practice of attending the lectures as well, and throughout the academic year 1932–1933 I attended both. At the lectures, though not at the discussion classes, I took what I think were very full notes, scribbled in notebooks of which I have six volumes nearly full. I remember Wittgenstein once saying to me that he was glad I was taking notes, since, if anything were to happen to him, they would contain some record of the results of his thinking.

My lecture-notes may be naturally divided into three groups, to which I will refer as (I), (II), and (III). (I) contains the notes of his lectures in the Lent and May Terms of 1930; (II) those of his lectures in the academic year 1930–1931; and (III) those of lectures which he gave in the May Term of 1932, after I had resumed attending, as well as those of all the lectures he gave in the academic year 1932–1933. The distinction between the three groups is of some importance, since, as will be seen, he sometimes in later lectures corrected what he had said in earlier ones.

The chief topics with which he dealt fall, I think, under the following heads. First of all, in all three periods he dealt (A) with some very general questions about language, (B) with some special questions in the philosophy of Logic, and (C) with some special questions in the philosophy of Mathematics. Next, in (III) and in (III) alone, he dealt at great length, (D) with the difference between the proposition which is expressed by the words "I have got toothache," and those which are expressed by the words "You have got toothache" or "He has got toothache," in which connection he said something about Behaviourism, Solipsism, Idealism, and Realism, and (E) with what he called "the grammar of the word "God" and of ethical and aesthetic statements." And he also dealt, more shortly, in (I) with (F) our use of the term "primary colour"; in (III) with (G) some questions about Time; and in both (II) and (III) with (H) the kind of investigation in which he was himself engaged, and its difference from and relation to what has traditionally been called "philosophy."

I will try to give some account of the chief things he said under all these heads; but I cannot possibly mention nearly everything, and it is possible that some of the things I omit were really more important than those I mention. Also, though I tried to get down in my notes the actual words he used, it is possible that I may sometimes have substituted words of my own which misrepresent his meaning: I certainly did not understand a good many of the things he said. Moreover, I cannot possibly do justice to the extreme richness of illustration and comparison which he used: he was really succeeding in giving what he called a "synoptic" view of things which we all know. Nor can I do justice to the intensity of conviction with which he said everything which he did say, nor to the extreme interest which he excited in his hearers. He, of course, never read his lectures: he had not, in fact, written them out, although he always spent a great deal of time in thinking out what he proposed to say.

(A) He did discuss at very great length, especially in (II), certain very general questions about language; but he said, more than once, that he did not discuss these questions because he thought that language was the subject-matter of philosophy. He did not think that it was. He discussed it only because he thought that particular philosophical errors or "troubles in our thought" were due to false analogies suggested by our actual use of expressions; and he emphasized that it was only necessary for him to discuss those points about language which, as he thought, led to these particular errors or "troubles."

The general things that he had to say about language fall naturally, I think, under two heads, namely (*a*) what he had to say about the meaning of single words, and (*b*) what he had to say about "propositions."

(*a*) About the meaning of single words, the positive points on which he seemed most anxious to insist were, I think, two, namely (*a*) something which he expressed by saying that the meaning of any single word in a language is "defined," "constituted," "determined," or "fixed" (he used all four expressions in different places) by the "grammatical rules" with which it is used in that language, and (*β*) something which he expressed by saying that every significant word or symbol must essentially belong to a "system," and (metaphorically) by saying that the meaning of a word is its "place" in a "grammatical system."

But he said in (III) that the sense of "meaning" of which he held these things to be true, and which was the only sense in which he intended to use the word, was only one of those in which we commonly use it: that there was another which he described as that in which it is used "as a name for a process accompanying our use of a word and our hearing of a word." By the latter he apparently meant that sense of "meaning" in which "to know the meaning" of a word means the same as to "understand" the word; and

I think he was not quite clear as to the relation between this sense of "meaning" and that in which he intended to use it, since he seemed in two different places to suggest two different and incompatible views of this relation, saying in (II) that "the rules applying to negation actually describe my experience in using 'not,' i.e. describe my understanding of the word," and in one place in (III), on the other hand, saying, "perhaps there is a causal connection between the rules and the feeling we have when we hear 'not'." On the former occasion he added that "a logical investigation doesn't teach us anything about the meaning of negation: we can't get any clearer about its meaning. What's difficult is to make the rules explicit."

Still later in (III) he made the rather queer statement that "the idea of meaning is in a way obsolete, except in such phrases as 'this means the same as that' or 'this has no meaning'," having previously said in (III) that "the mere fact that we have the expression 'the meaning' of a word is bound to lead us wrong: we are led to think that the rules are responsible to something not a rule, whereas they are only responsible to rules."

As to (a) although he had said, at least once, that the meaning of a word was "constituted" by the grammatical rules which applied to it, he explained later that he did not mean that the meaning of a word *was* a list of rules; and he said that though a word "carried its meaning with it," it did not carry with it the grammatical rules which applied to it. He said that the student who had asked him whether he meant that the meaning of a word *was* a list of rules would not have been tempted to ask that question but for the false idea (which he held to be a common one) that in the case of a substantive like "the meaning" you have to look for something at which you can point and say "This is the meaning." He seemed to think that Frege and Russell had been misled by the same idea, when they thought they were bound to give an answer to the question "What *is* the number 2?" As for what he meant by saying that the meaning of a word is "determined by" (this was the phrase which he seemed to prefer) the "grammatical rules" in accordance with which it is used, I do not think he explained further what he meant by this phrase.

(β) As to what he meant by saying that, in order that a word or other sign should have meaning, it must belong to a "system," I have not been able to arrive at any clear idea. One point on which he insisted several times in (II) was that if a word which I use is to have meaning, I must "commit myself" by its use. And he explained what he meant by this by saying "If I commit myself, that means that if I use, e.g., 'green' in this case, I have to use it in others," adding "If you commit yourself, there are consequences." Similarly he said a little later, "If a word is to have significance, we must commit ourselves," adding "There is no use in correlating noises to facts, unless we commit ourselves to using the noise in a particular way again—unless the correlation has consequences," and going on to say that it must be possible to be "led by a language." And when he expressly raised, a little later, the question "What is there in this talk of a 'system' to which a symbol must belong?" he answered that we are concerned with the phenomenon of "being guided by." It looked, therefore, as if one use which he was making of the word "system" was such that in order to say that a word or other sign "belonged to a system," it was not only necessary but *sufficient* that it should be used in the same way on several different occasions. And certainly it would be natural to say that a man who habitually used a word in the same way was using it "systematically."

But he certainly also frequently used "system" in such a sense that *different* words or other expressions could be said to belong to the *same* "system"; and where, later on, he gave, as an illustration of what he meant by "Every symbol must essentially belong to a system," the proposition "A crotchet can only give information on what note to play in a system of crotchets," he seemed to imply that for a sign to have significance it is *not* sufficient that we should "commit ourselves" by its use, but that it is also necessary that the sign in question should belong to the same "system" with other signs. Perhaps, however, he only meant, not that for a sign to have *some* meaning, but that for *some* signs to have *the significance which they actually have in a given language,* it is necessary that they should belong to the same "system" with other signs. This word "system" was one which he used very very frequently, and I do not know what conditions he would have held must be satisfied by two different signs in order that they may properly be said to belong to the same "system." He said in one place in (II) that the "system of projection" by which "2 + 3" can be projected into "5" is "in no way inferior" to the "system" by which "11 + 111" can be projected into "11111," and I think one can see, in this case, that "2 + 3 = 5" can be properly said to belong to the same "system" as, e.g., "2 + 2 = 4," and also can properly be said to belong to a different "system" from that to which "11 + 111 = 11111" and "11 + 11 = 1111" both belong, though I have no clear idea as to the sense in which these things can properly be said. Nor do I know whether Wittgenstein would have held, e.g., that in the case of *every* English word, it could not have the significance which it actually has in English unless it belonged to the same "system" as other English words, or whether he would have held that this is only true of *some* English words, e.g. of the words "five" and "four," and of the words "red" and "green."

But besides these two positive things, (α) and (β), which he seemed anxious to say about the meaning of words, he also insisted on three negative things, i.e. that three views which have sometimes been held are mistakes. The first of these mistakes was (γ) the view that the meaning of a word was some image which it calls up by association—a view to which he seemed to refer as the "causal" theory of meaning. He admitted that sometimes you cannot understand a word unless it calls up an image, but insisted that, even where this is the case, the image is just as much a "symbol" as the word is. The second mistake was (δ) the view that, where we can give an "ostensive" definition of a word, the object pointed at is the meaning of the word. Against this view, he said, for one thing, that, in such a case "the gesture of pointing together with the object pointed at can be used *instead* of the word," i.e. is itself something which has meaning and has the same meaning as the word has. In this connection he also pointed out that you may point at a red book, either to show the meaning of "book" or to show the meaning of "red," and that hence in "This is a book" and "This is the colour 'red,' " "this" has quite a different meaning; and he emphasized that, in order to understand the ostensive definition "This is 'red,' " the hearer must already understand what is meant by "colour." And the third mistake was (ε) that a word is related to its meaning in the same way in which a proper name is related to the "bearer" of that name. He gave as a reason for holding that this is false that the bearer of a name can be ill or dead, whereas we cannot possibly say that the meaning of the name is ill or dead. He said more than once that the bearer of a name can be "substituted" for the name, whereas the meaning of a word can never be substituted for that word. He sometimes spoke of this third mistake as the view that words are "representative" of their meanings, and he held that in no case is a word "representative" of its meaning, although a proper name is "representative" of its bearer (if it has one). He added in one place: "The meaning of a word is no longer for us an object corresponding to it."

On the statement "Words, except in propositions, have no meaning" he said that this "is true or false, as you understand it"; and immediately went on to add that, in what he called "language games," single words "have meanings by themselves," and that they may have meaning by themselves even in our ordinary language "if we have provided one." In this connection he said, in (II), that he had made a mistake (I think he meant in the *Tractatus*) in supposing that a proposition must be complex. He said the truth was that we can replace a proposition by a simple sign, but that the simple sign must be "part of a system."

. . .

One chief view about propositions to which he was opposed was a view which he expressed as the view that a proposition is a sort of "shadow" intermediate between the expression which we use in order to assert it and the fact (if any) which "verifies" it. He attributed this view to W. E. Johnson, and he said of it that it was an attempt to make a distinction between a proposition and a sentence. (We have seen that he himself had in (II) made a different attempt to do this.) He said that it regarded the supposed "shadow" as something "similar" to the fact which verifies it, and in that way different from the expression which expresses it, which is not "similar" to the fact in question; and he said that, even if there were such a "shadow" it would not "bring us any nearer to the fact," since "it would be susceptible of different interpretations just as the expression is." He said, "You can't give any picture which can't be misinterpreted" and "No interpolation between a sign and its fulfilment does away with a sign." He added that the only description of an expectation "which is relevant for us" is "the expression of it," and that "the expression of an expectation contains a description of the fact that would fulfil it," pointing out that if I expect to *see a red patch* my expectation is fullfilled if and only I do *see a red patch,* and saying that the words "see a red patch" have the same meaning in both expressions.

Near the beginning of (I) he made the famous statement, "The sense of a proposition is the way in which it is verified"; but in (III) he said this only meant "You can determine the meaning of a proposition by asking how it is verified" and went on to say, "This is necessarily a mere rule of thumb, because 'verification' means different things, and because in some cases the question 'How is that verified?' makes no sense." He gave as an example of a case in which that question "makes no sense" the proposition "I've got toothache," of which he had already said that it makes no sense to ask for a verification of it—to ask "How do you know that you have?" I think that he here meant what he said of "I've got toothache" to apply to all those propositions which he had originally distinguished from "hypotheses" as "what I call propositions"; although in (II) he had distinguished the latter from "hypotheses" by saying that they had "a definite verification or falsification." It would seem, therefore, that in (III) he had arrived at the conclusion that what he had said in (II) was wrong, and that in the case of "what he called propositions," so far from their having "a definite verification," it was senseless to say that they had a verification at all. His "rule of thumb," therefore, could only apply, if at all, to what he called "hypotheses"; and he went on to say that, in many cases, it does not apply even to these, saying that statements in the newspapers could verify the "hypothesis" that Cambridge had won the boat-race, and that yet these statements "only go a very little way towards explaining the meaning of 'boat-race' "; and that similarly "The pavement is wet" may verify the proposition "It has been raining," and that yet "it gives very little of the grammar of 'It has been raining'." He went on to say "Verification determines the meaning of a proposition only where it gives the grammar of the proposition in question"; and in answer to the question "How far is giving a verification of a proposition a grammatical statement about it?" he said that, whereas "When it rains the pavement gets wet" is not a grammatical statement at all, if we say "The fact that the pavement is wet is a *symptom* that it has been raining" this statement is "a matter of grammar."

QUESTIONS FOR STUDY AND DISCUSSION

1. What are the two positive and three negative things that Wittgenstein says about the meaning of words?
2. Why is he against the view that a proposition is a sort of "shadow" between the proposition and the actual fact?
3. How did he change his view of verification?

Wittgenstein's Lectures in 1930-1933, Part III

. . .

(D) He spent, as I have said in the first part of this article . . . a great deal of time on this discussion, and I am very much puzzled as to the meaning of much that he said, and also as to the connection between different things which he said. It seems to me that his discussion was rather incoherent, and my account of it must be incoherent also, because I cannot see the connection between different points which he seemed anxious to make. He said very early in the discussion that the whole subject is "extraordinarily difficult" because "the whole field is full of misleading notations"; and that its difficulty was shown by the fact that the question at issue is the question between Realists, Idealists, and Solipsists. And he also said, more than once, that many of the difficulties are due to the fact that there is a great temptation to confuse what are merely experiential propositions, which might, therefore, not have been true, with propositions which are necessarily true or are, as he once said, "tautological or grammatical statements." He gave, as an instance of a proposition of the latter sort, "I can't feel your toothache," saying that "If you feel it, it isn't mine" is a "matter of grammar," and also that "I can't feel your toothache" means the same as " 'I feel your toothache' has no sense"; and he contrasted this with "I hear my voice coming from somewhere near my eyes," which he said we think to be necessary, but which in fact is not necessary "though it always happens." In this connection he gave the warning "Don't be prejudiced by anything which *is* a fact, but which *might* be otherwise." And he seemed to be quite definite on a point which seems to me certainly true, viz., that I might see without physical eyes, and even without having a body at all; that the connection between seeing and physical eyes is merely a fact learnt by experience, not a necessity at all; though he also said that "the visual field" has certain internal properties, such that you can describe the motion of certain things in it as motions towards or away from "your eye"; but that here "your eye" does not mean your physical eye, nor yet anything whatever which is *in* the visual field. He called "your eye," in this sense, "the eye of the visual field," and said that the distinction between motion towards it and away from it was "on the same level" as "the distinction between 'curved' and 'straight.' "

However, he began the discussion by raising a question, which he said was connected with Behaviourism, namely, the question "When we say 'He

From *Mind*, vol. LXIV, No. 253. Reprinted by permission of the editor.

has toothache' is it correct to say that his toothache is only his behaviour, whereas when I talk about my toothache I am not talking about my behaviour?"; but very soon he introduced a question expressed in different words, which is perhaps not merely a different formulation of the same question, viz., "Is another person's toothache 'toothache' in the same sense as mine?" In trying to find an answer to this question or these questions, he said first that it was clear and admitted that what verifies or is a criterion for "I have toothache" is quite different from what verifies or is a criterion for "He has toothache," and soon added that, since this is so, the *meanings* of "I have toothache" and "He has toothache" must be different. In this connection he said later, first, that the meaning of "verification" is different, when we speak of verifying "I have" from what it is when we speak of verifying "He has," and then, later still, that there is no such thing as a verification for "I have," since the question "How do you know that you have toothache?" is nonsensical. He criticized two answers which might be given to this last question by people who think it is not nonsensical, by saying (1) that the answer "Because I feel it" won't do, because "I feel it" means the same as "I have it," and (2) that the answer "I know it by inspection" also won't do, because it implies that I can "look to see" whether I have it or not, whereas "looking to see whether I have it or not" has no meaning. The fact that it is nonsense to talk of verifying the fact that I have it, puts, he said, "I have it" on "a different level" in grammar from "he has it." And he also expressed his view that the two expressions are on a different grammatical level by saying that they are not both values of a single propositional function "*x* has toothache"; and in favour of this view he gave two definite reasons for saying that they are not, namely, (1) that "I don't know whether I have toothache" is always absurd or nonsense, whereas "I don't know whether he has toothache" is not nonsense, and (2) that "It seems to me that I have toothache" is nonsense, whereas "It seems to me that he has" is not.

He said, that when he said this, people supposed him to be saying that other people never really have what he has, but that, if he did say so, he would be talking nonsense; and he seemed quite definitely to reject the behaviourist view that "he has toothache" means only that "he" is behaving in a particular manner; for he said that "toothache" doesn't in fact only mean a particular kind of behaviour, and implied that when we pity a man for having toothache, we are not pitying hin for putting his hand to his cheek; and, later on, he said that we *conclude* that another person has toothache from his behaviour, and that it is legitimate to conclude this on the analogy of the resemblance of his behaviour to the way in which we behave when we have toothache. It seemed therefore, that just as to his first question he meant to give definitely the answer "No," so to his second question he meant to give definitely the answer "Yes"; the word "toothache" is used in the same sense when we say that he has it (or "you have it") as when we say that I have it, though he never expressly said so; and though he seemed to throw some doubt on whether he meant this by saying "I admit that other people do have toothache—this having *the meaning which we have given it.*"

It seemed, therefore, that he did not think that the difference between "I have toothache" and "He has toothache" was due to the fact that the word "toothache" was used in a different sense in the two sentences. What then was it due to? Much that he said seemed to suggest that his view was that the difference was due to the fact that in "He has toothache" we were necessarily talking of a physical body, whereas in "I have toothache" we were not. As to the first of these two propositions he did not seem quite definite; for though at first he said that "my voice" means "the voice which comes from my mouth," he seemed aferwards to suggest that in "He has toothache" (or "You have") we were not necessarily referring to a *body,* but might be referring only to a *voice,* identified as "his" or "yours" without reference to a body. But as to the second proposition, the one about "I have toothache," the point on which he seemed most anxious to insist was that what we call "having toothache" is what he called a "primary experience" (he once used the phrase "direct experience" as equivalent to this one); and he said that "what characterizes 'primary experience' " is that in its case " 'I' does not denote a possessor." In order to make clear what he meant by this he compared "I have toothache" with "I see a red patch"; and said of what he called "visual sensations" generally, and in particular of what he called "the visual field," that "the idea of a person doesn't enter into the description of it, just as a (physical) eye doesn't enter into the description of what is seen"; and he said that similarly "the idea of a person" doesn't enter into the description of "having toothache." How was he here using the word "person"? He certainly meant to deny that the idea of a physical body enters necessarily into the description; and in one passage he seemed to imply that he used "person" to mean the same as "physical body," since he said "A description of a sensation does not contain a description of a sense-organ, nor, *therefore,* of a person." He was, therefore, still maintaining apparently that one distinction between "I have toothache" and "He has toothache" was due to the fact that the latter necessarily refers to a physical body (or, perhaps, to a voice instead) whereas the former does not. But I think this was not the only distinction which he had in mind, and that he was not always using "person" to mean the same as physical body (or, perhaps, a voice instead). For he said that "Just as no (physical) eye is involved in seeing, so no Ego is involved in thinking or in having toothache"; and he quoted, with apparent approval, Lichtenberg's saying "Instead of 'I think' we ought to say 'It thinks' " ("it" being used, as he said, as "Es" is used in "Es blitzet"); and by saying this he meant, I think, something similar to what he said of "the eye of the visual field" when he said that it is not anything which is *in* the visual field. Like so many other philosophers, in talking of "visual sensations" he seemed not to distinguish between "what I see" and "my seeing of it"; and he did not expressly discuss what appears to be a possibility, namely, that though no person enters into what I see, yet some "person" other than a physical body or a voice, may "enter into" my seeing of it.

In this connection, that in "I have toothache" "I" does not "denote a possessor," he pointed out that, when I talk of "*my* body," the fact that the body in question is "mine" or "belongs to me," cannot be verified by reference to that body itself, thus seeming to imply that when I say "This body belongs to me," "me" is used in the second of the senses which he distinguished for "I," viz., that in which, according to him, it does not "denote a possessor." But he did not seem to be quite sure of this, since he said in one place "*If* there is an ownership such that I possess a body, this isn't verified by reference to a body," i.e., that "This is *my* body" can't possibly mean "This body belongs to this body." He said that, where "I" is replaceable by "this body" "I" and "he" are "on the same (grammatical) level." He was quite definite that the word "I" or "any other word which denotes a subject" is used in "two utterly different ways," one in which it is "on a level with other people," and one in which it is not. This difference, he said, was a difference in "the grammar of our ordinary language." As an instance of one of these two uses, he gave "I've got a matchbox" and I've got a bad tooth," which he said were "on a level" with "Skinner has a match-box" and "Skinner has a bad tooth." He said that in these two cases "I have . . ." and "Skinner has . . ." really were values of the same propositional function, and that "I" and "Skinner" were both "possessors." But in the case of "I have toothache" or "I see a red patch" he held that the use of "I" is utterly different.

In speaking of these two senses of "I" he said, as what he called "a final thing," "In one sense 'I' and 'conscious' are equivalent, but not in another," and he compared this difference to the difference between what can be said of the pictures on a film in a magic lantern and of the picture on the screen; saying that the pictures in the lantern are all "on the same level" but that the picture which is at any given time on the screen is not "on the same level" with any of them, and that if we were to use "conscious" to say of one of the pictures in the lantern that it was at that time being thrown on the screen, it would be meaningless to say of the picture on the screen that it was "conscious." The pictures on the film, he said, "have neighbours," whereas that on the screen has none. And he also compared the "grammatical" difference between the two different uses of "I" with the difference between the meaning of "has blurred edges" as applied to the visual field, and the meaning of the same expression as applied to any drawing you might make of the visual field: your drawing might be imagined to have sharp edges instead of blurred ones, but this is unimaginable in the case of the visual field. The visual field, he said, has no outline or boundary, and he equated this with "It has no sense to say that it has one."

In connection with his statement that "I," in one of its uses, is equivalent to "conscious," he said something abut Freud's use of the terms "conscious" and "unconscious." He said that Freud had really discovered phenomena and connections not previously known, but that he talked as if he had found out that there were in the human mind "unconscious" hatreds, volitions, etc., and that this was very misleading, because we think of the difference between a "conscious" and an "unconscious" hatred as like that between a "seen" and an "unseen" chair. He said that, in fact, the grammar of "felt" and "unfelt" hatred is quite different from that of "seen" and "unseen" chair, just as the grammar of "artificial" flower is quite different from that of "blue" flower. He suggested that "unconscious toothache," if "unconscious" were used as Freud used it, might be necessarily bound up with a physical body, whereas "conscious toothache" is not so bound up."

As regards Solipsism and Idealism he said that he himself had been often tempted to say "All that is real is the experience of the present moment" or "All that is certain is the experience of the present moment"; and that anyone who is at all tempted to hold Idealism or Solipsism knows the temptation to say "The only reality is the present experience" or "The only reality is *my* present experience." Of these two latter statements he said that both were equally absurd, but that, though both were fallacious, "the idea expressed by them is of enormous importance." Both about Solipsism and about Idealism he had insisted earlier that neither of them pretends that what it says is learnt by experience—that the arguments for both are of the form "you can't" or "you must," and that both these expressions "cut (the statement in question) out of our language." Elsewhere he said that both Solipsists and Idealists would say they "couldn't imagine it otherwise," and that, in reply to this, he would say, "If so, your statement has no sense" since "nothing can characterize reality, except as opposed to something else which is not the case." Elsewhere he had said that the Solipsist's statement "Only my experience is real" is absurd "as a statement of fact," but that the Solipsist sees that a person who says "No: my experience is real too" has not really refuted him, just as Dr. Johnson did not refute Berkeley by kicking a stone. Much later he said that Solipsism is right if it merely says that "I have toothache" and "He has toothache" are "on quite a different level," but that "if the Solipsist says that he has something which another hasn't, he is absurd and is making the very mistake of putting the two statements on the same level." In this connection he said that he thought that both the Realist and the Idealist were "talking nonsense" in the particular sense in which "nonsense is produced by trying to express by the use of language what ought to be embodied in the grammar"; and he illustrated this sense by saying that "I can't feel his toothache" means " 'I feel his toothache' has no sense" and therefore does not "express a fact" as "I can't play chess" may do.

(E) He concluded (III) by a long discussion which he introduced by saying "I have always wanted to say something about the grammar of ethical expressions, or, e.g., of the word 'God'." But in fact he said very little about the grammar of such words as "God," and very little also about that of ethical expressions. What he did deal with at length was not Ethics but Aesthetics, saying, however, "Practically everything which I say about 'beautiful' applies in a slightly different way to 'good'." His discussion of Aesthetics, however, was mingled in a curious way with criticism of assumptions which he said were constantly made by Frazer in the *Golden Bough*, and also with criticism of Freud.

About "God" his main point seemed to be that this word is used in many *grammatically* different senses. He said, for instance, that many controversies about God could be settled by saying "I'm not using the word in such a sense that you can say . . . ," and that different religions "treat things as making sense which others treat as nonsense, and don't merely deny some proposition which another religion affirms"; and he illustrated this by saying that if people use "god" to mean something like a human being, then "God has four arms" and "God has two arms" will both have sense, but that others so use "God" that "God has arms" is nonsense— would say "God *can't* have arms." Similarly, he said of the expression "the soul," that sometimes people so use that expression that "the soul is a gaseous human being" has sense, but sometimes so that it has not. To explain what he meant by "grammatically" different senses," he said we wanted terms which are not "comparable," as, e.g., "solid" and "gaseous" are comparable, but which differ as, e.g., "chair" differs from "permission to sit on a chair," or "railway" from "railway accident."

He introduced his whole discussion of Aesthetics by dealing with one problem about the meaning of words, with which he said he had not yet dealt. He illustrated this problem by the example of the word "game," with regard to which he said both (1) that, even if there is something common to all games, it doesn't follow that this is what we mean by calling a particular game a "game," and (2) that the reason why we call so many different activities "games" need not be that there is anything common to them all, but only that there is "a gradual transition" from one use to another, although there may be nothing in common between the two ends of the series. And he seemed to hold definitely that there is nothing in common in our different uses of the word "beautiful," saying that we use it "in a hundred different games"—that, e.g., the beauty of a face is something different from the beauty of a chair or a flower or the binding of a book. And of the word "good" he said similarly that each different way in which one person, A, can convince another, B, that so-and-so is "good" fixes the meaning in which "good" is used in that discussion—"fixes the grammar of that discussion"; but that there will be "gradual transitions," from one of these meanings to another, "which take the place of something in common." In the case of "beauty" he said that a difference of meaning is shown by the fact that "you can say more" in discussing whether the arrangement of flowers in a bed is "beautiful" than in discussing whether the smell of lilac is so.

He went on to say that specific colours in a certain spatial arrangement are not merely "symptoms" that what has them *also* possesses a quality which we call "being beautiful," as they would be, if we meant by "beautiful," e.g., "causing stomach-ache," in which case we could learn by experience whether such an arrangement did always cause stomach-ache or not. In order to discover how we use the word "beautiful" we need, he said, to consider (1) what an actual aesthetic controversy or inquiry is like, and (2) whether such inquiries are in fact psychological inquiries "though they look so very different." And on (1) he said that the actual word "beautiful" is hardly ever used in aesthetic controversies: that we are more apt to use "right," as, e.g., in "That doesn't look quite right yet," or when we say of a proposed accompaniment to a song "That won't do: it isn't right." And on (2) he said that if we say, e.g., of a bass "It is too heavy; it moves too much," we are not saying "If it moved less, it would be more agreeable to me": that, on the contrary, that it should be quieter is an "end in itself," not a means to some other end; and that when we discuss whether a base "will do," we are no more discussing a psychological question than we are discussing psychological questions in Physics; that what we are trying to do is to bring the bass "nearer to an ideal," though we haven't an ideal before us which we are trying to copy; that in order to show what we want, we might point to another tune, which we might say is "perfectly right." He said that in aesthetic investigations "the one thing we are not interested in is causal connections, whereas this is the only thing we are interested in in Psychology." To ask "Why is this beautiful?" is not to ask for a causal explanation: that, e.g., to give a causal explanation in answer to the question "Why is the smell of a rose pleasant?" would not remove our "aesthetic puzzlement."

Against the particular view that "beautiful" means "agreeable" he pointed out that we may refuse to go to a performance of a particular work on such a ground as "I can't stand its greatness," in which case it is disagreeable rather than agreeable; that we may think that a piece of music which we in fact prefer is "just nothing" in comparison to another to which we prefer it; and that the fact that we go to see "King Lear" by no means proves that that experience is agreeable: he said that, even if it is agreeable, that fact "is about the least important thing you can say about it." He said that such a statement as "That bass moves too much" is not a statement about human beings at all, but is more like a piece of Mathematics; and that, if I say of a face which I draw "It smiles too much," this says that it could be brought closer to some "ideal," not that it is not yet agreeable enough, and that to bring it closer to the "ideal" in question would be more like "solving a mathematical problem." Similarly, he said, when a painter tries to improve his picture, he is not making a psychological experiment on himself, and that to say of a door "It is top-heavy" is to say what is wrong with it, *not* what impression it gives you. The question of Aesthetics, he said, was not "Do you like this?" but *"Why* do you like it?"

What Aesthetics tries to do, he said, is to give *reasons,* e. g., for having this word rather than that in a particular place in a poem, or for having this musical phrase rather than that in a particular place in a piece of music. Brahms's *reason* for rejecting Joachim's suggestion that his Fourth Symphony should be opened by two chords was not that that wouldn't produce the feeling he wanted to produce, but something more like "That isn't what I meant." *Reasons,* he said, in Aesthetics, are "of the nature of further descriptions": e.g., you can make a person see what Brahms was driving at by showing him lots of different pieces by Brahms, or by comparing him with a contemporary author; and all that Aesthetics does is "to draw your attention to a thing," to "place things side by side." He said that if, by giving "reasons" of this sort, you make another person "see what you see" but it still "doesn't appeal to him," that is "an end" of the discussion; and that what he, Wittgenstein, had "at the back of his mind" was "the idea that aesthetic discussions were like discussions in a court of law," where you try to "clear up the circumstances" of the action which is being tried, hoping that in the end, what you say will "appeal to the judge." And he said that the same sort of "reasons" were given, not only in Ethics, but also in Philosophy.

As regards Frazer's *Golden Bough,* the chief points on which he seemed to wish to insist were, I think, the three following: (1) That it was a mistake to suppose that there was *only one* "reason," in the sense of "motive," which led people to perform a particular action—to suppose that there was "one motive, which was *the* motive." He gave as an instance of this sort of mistake Frazer's statement, in speaking of Magic, that when primitive people stab an effigy of a particular person, they believe that they have hurt the person in question. He said that primitive people do not *always* entertain this "false scientific belief," though in some cases they may: that they may have quite different reasons for stabbing the effigy. But he said that the tendency to suppose that there is "one motive which is *the* motive" was "enormously strong," giving as an instance that there are theories of play each of which gives *only one* answer to the question "Why do children play?" (2) That it was a mistake to suppose that *the* motive is always "to get something useful." He gave as an instance of this mistake Frazer's supposition that "people at a certain stage thought it useful to kill a person, in order to get a good crop." (3) That it was a mistake to suppose that why, e.g., the account of the Beltane Festival "impresses us so much" is because it has "developed from a festival in which a real man was burnt." He accused Frazer of thinking that this was the reason. He said that our puzzlement as to why it impresses us is not diminished by giving the *causes* from which the festival arose, but is diminished by finding other similar festivals: to find these may make it seem "natural," whereas to give the causes from which it arose cannot do this. In this respect he said that the question "Why does this impress us?" is like the aesthetic questions "Why is this beautiful?" or "Why will this bass not do?"

He said that Darwin, in his "expression of the Emotions," made a mistake similar to Frazer's, e.g., in thinking that "because our ancestors, when angry, wanted to bite" is a sufficient explanation of why we show our teeth when angry. He said you might say that what is satisfactory in Darwin is not such "hypotheses," but his "putting the facts in a system"—helping us to make a "synopsis" of them.

As for Freud, he gave the greater part of two lectures to Freud's investigation of the nature of a "joke" (Witz), which he said was an "aesthetic investigation." He said that Freud's book on this subject was a very good book for looking for philosophical mistakes, and that the same was true of his writings in general, because there are so many cases in which one can ask how far what he says is a "hypothesis" and how far merely a good way of representing a fact—a question as to which he said Freud himself is constantly unclear. He said, for instance, that Freud encouraged a confusion between getting to know the *cause* of your laughter and getting to know the *reason* why you laugh, because what he says sounds as if it were science, when in fact it is only a "wonderful representation." This last point he also expressed by saying "It is all excellent similes, e.g., the comparison of a dream to a rebus." (He had said earlier that all Aesthetics is of the nature of "giving a good simile.") He said that this confusion between *cause* and *reason* had led to the disciples of Freud making "an abominable mess": that Freud did not in fact give any method of analysing dreams which was analogous to the rules which will tell you what are the causes of stomach-ache; that he had genius and therefore might sometimes by psycho-analysis find the *reason* of a certain dream, but that what is most striking about him is "the enormous field of psychical facts which he arranges."

As for what Freud says about jokes, he said first that Freud makes the two mistakes (1) of supposing that there is something common to all jokes, and (2) of supposing that this supposed common character is the meaning of "joke." He said it is not true, as Freud supposed, that *all* jokes enable you to do covertly what it would not be seemly to do openly, but that "joke," like "proposition," "has a rainbow of meanings." But I think the point on which he was most anxious to insist was perhaps that psychoanalysis does not enable you to discover the *cause* but only the *reason* of, e.g., laughter. In support of this statement he asserted that a psychoanalysis is successful only if the patient agrees to the explanation offered by the analyst. He said there is nothing analogous to this in physics; and that what a patient agrees to can't be a *hypothesis* as to the *cause* of his laughter, but only that so-and-so was the *reason* why he laughed. He explained that the patient who agrees did not think of this reason at the moment when he laughed, and that to say that he thought of it "subconsciously" "tells you nothing at to what was happening at the moment when he laughed."

(F) In (I), rather to my surprise, he spent a good deal of time in discussing what would usually be called a question about colours, namely, the question how the four "saturated" colours, pure yellow, pure red, pure blue and pure green, which he called "primary," are distinguished from those "saturated" colours which are not "primary." He drew a circle on the blackboard to represent the arrangement of the saturated colours, with a vertical diameter joining "yellow" at the top to "blue" at the bottom, and a horizontal diameter joining "green" on the left to "red" on the right. And he seemed to be maintaining with regard to these four colours that they are distinguished from the other saturated colours in the two following ways, viz., (1) that the sense in which any purple is "between" pure red and pure blue, and in which any orange is "between" pure yellow and pure red is very different from the sense of "between" in which pure red is "between" any orange and any purple; a difference which he also expressed by saying that whereas an orange can be properly called a "mixture" of yellow and red, red cannot possibly be called a "mixture" of orange and purple; and (2) that whereas pure red can be properly said to be "midway" between pure yellow and pure blue, there is no colour which is "midway" between pure red and pure blue, or "midway" between pure yellow and pure red, etc. He said that, for these reasons, the arrangement of the saturated colours in a square, with the four "primaries" at the four corners, is a better picture of their relations than the arrangement of them in a circle.

I say only that he *seemed* to be making these assertions, because he emphasized from the beginning that "primary" is not an adjective to "colour" in the sense in which "black" may be an adjective to "gown," but that the distinction between "primary" and "not primary" is a "logical" distinction—an expression which he explained later on by saying that, just as sounds are not distinguished from colours by the fact that something is true of the one which is not true of the other, so red, blue, green, and yellow are not distinguished from the other saturated colours by the fact that anything is true of them which is not true of the others. He emphasized to begin with that the sentences "blue is not primary" and "violet is primary" are both of them "nonsense," and I think there is no doubt he held that, since this is so, their contradictories "blue is primary" and "violet is not primary" are also nonsense, though there is a sense in which the two last are true, and the two former false. In other words, I think he certainly held that "blue is primary" is a "necessary proposition"—that we can't imagine its not being true—and that therefore, as he said [in III], it "has no sense." It would seem to follow that if, as he seemed to be, he was really talking about the *colours,* red, blue, green, and yellow, all that he said about them was "nonsense." According to what he said elsewhere, he could only have been talking sense if he was talking, not about the colours, but about certain words used to express them; and accordingly he did actually go on to say that "red is primary" was only a proposition about the use of the English word "red," which, as I said [in II], he cannot seriously have held. The question I am here raising is the question which I discussed at length in the second part of this article, and I have nothing to add except to give one quotation which I ought to have given there. He actually said, in one place in (II), "What corresponds to a necessity in the world must be what in language seems an arbitrary rule." I do not think he had succeeded in getting quite clear as to what relation he wished to assert to hold between what he called "rules of grammar," on the one hand, and "necessary propositions," on the other.

(H) I was a good deal surprised by some of the things he said about the difference between "philosophy" in the sense in which what he was doing might be called "philosophy" (he called this "modern philosophy"), and what has traditionally been called "philosophy." He said that what he was doing was a "new subject," and not merely a stage in a "continuous development"; that there was now, in philosophy, a "kink" in the "development of human thought," comparable to that which occurred when Galileo and his contemporaries invented dynamics; that a "new method" had been discovered, as had happened when "chemistry was developed out of alchemy"; and that it was now possible for the first time that there should be "skilful" philosophers, though of course there had in the past been "great" philosophers.

He went on to say that, though philosophy had now been "reduced to a matter of skill," yet this skill, like other skills, is very difficult to acquire. One difficulty was that it required a "sort of thinking" to which we are not accustomed and to which we have not been trained—a sort of thinking very different from what is required in the sciences. And he said that the required skill could not be acquired merely by hearing lectures: discussion was essential. As regards his own work, he said it did not matter whether his results were true or not: what mattered was that "a method had been found."

In answer to the question why this "new subject" should be called "philosophy" he said in (III) that though what he was doing was certainly different from what, e.g., Plato or Berkeley had done, yet people might feel that it "takes the place of" what they had done—might be inclined to say "This is what I really wanted" and to identify it with what they had done, though it is really different, just as (as I said above [in II]) a person who had been trying to trisect an angle by rule and compasses might, when shown the proof that this is impossible, be inclined to say that this impossible thing was the very thing he had been trying to do, though what he had been trying to do was really different. But in (II) he had also said that the "new subject" did really resemble what had been traditionally called "philosophy" in the three respects that (1) it was very general, (2) it was fundamental both to ordinary life and to the sciences, and (3) it was independent of any special results of science; that therefore the application to it of the word "philosophy" was not purely arbitrary.

He did not expressly try to tell us exactly what the "new method" which had been found was. But he gave some hints as to its nature. He said, in (II), that the "new subject" consisted in "something like putting in order our notions as to what can be said about the world," and compared this to the tidying up of a room where you have to move the same object several times before you can get the room really tidy. He said also that we were "in a muddle about things," which we had to try to clear up; that we had to follow a certain instinct which leads us to ask certain questions, though we don't even understand what these questions mean; that our asking them results from "a vague mental uneasiness," like that which leads children to ask "Why?"; and that this uneasiness can only be cured "either by showing that a particular question is not permitted, or by answering it." He also said that he was not trying to teach us any new facts: that he would only tell us "trivial" things—"things which we all know already"; but that the difficult thing was to get a "synopsis" of these trivialities, and that our "intellectual discomfort" can only be removed by a synopsis of *many* trivialities—that "if we leave out any, we still have the feeling that something is wrong." In this connection he said it was misleading to say that what we wanted was an "analysis," since in science to "analyse" water means to discover some new fact about it, e.g., that it is composed of oxygen and hydrogen, whereas in philosophy "we know at the start all the facts we need to know." I imagine that it was in this respect of needing a "synopsis" of trivialities that he thought that philosophy was similar to Ethics and Aesthetics [in III].

I ought, perhaps, finally to repeat what I said in the first part of this article [in I], namely, that he held that though the "new subject" must say a great deal about language, it was only necessary for it to deal with those points about language which have led, or are likely to lead, to definite philosophical puzzles or errors. I think he certainly thought that some philosophers nowadays have been misled into dealing with linguistic points which have no such bearing, and the discussion of which therefore, in his view, forms no part of the proper business of a philosopher.

QUESTIONS FOR STUDY AND DISCUSSION

1. Does Wittgenstein accept or reject the behavioral view that the sentence "He has a toothache" means only that he is *behaving* in a particular way?
2. Does he think that "He has toothache" refers to possession by a physical body whereas "I have toothache" does not?
3. How does he use Freud's concepts of conscious and unconscious in the discussion of toothache?
4. How does he treat the different uses of the word "God"?

5. Give some of his language games described in his discussion of esthetics. Do you think that these games help to clarify the meaning of esthetics?
6. What is his criticism of Freud's theory of jokes? Is it as a philosopher or as a psychologist that he is criticizing him?
7. How far did Wittgenstein think that philosophy should be concerned with language? Why?

Peter Frederick Strawson

PETER FREDERICK STRAWSON is one of the best known of the younger philosophers in the analytic tradition. Born in 1919, he was educated at Oxford and has been a fellow there since 1948. Although influenced by Wittgenstein and other analysts, Strawson's interests in analysis take on a broader concern. Regarded as an "ordinary language" analyst, Strawson's main effort is directed toward uncovering the way language is actually employed, so that the general features of conceptual structures will be exposed. Rather than attempting to construct an ideal language in the fashion of Carnap and others, Strawson is content to view the examination of the ordinary use of language as a desirable end in its own right. His best known work is *Individuals* (1959).

Persons

1. Each of us distinguishes between himself and states of himself on the one hand, and what is not himself or a state of himself on the other. What are the conditions of our making this distinction, and how are they fulfilled? In what way do we make it, and why do we make it in the way we do? It might appear a misnomer to refer to this group of questions as the issue of solipsism. But I have no qualms about appropriating the name: for that which customarily bears it is not, as we shall see, a genuine issue at all.

In the discussion of this topic, the notion of identification of particulars is once more crucial: primarily in the sense of distinguishing one particular from others in thought, or observation; but also in the original speaker-hearer senses.

Let me recall some of the steps which led to this issue of solipsism. I had argued that, in our actual conceptual scheme, material bodies, in a broad sense of the expression, were basic particulars:[1] that is to say, that material bodies could be identified and reidentified without reference to particulars of other types or categories than their own, whereas the identifi-

---

[1] Individuals—human persons or objects. [M.G.]

From pp. 81–101 and 112–13 of Peter Frederick Strawson, *Individuals: An Essay in Descriptive Metaphysics*. © 1963 by Doubleday and Company, Inc. Reprinted by permission of Methuen and Company Ltd., London.

cation and reidentification of particulars of other categories rested ultimately on the identification of material bodies. I then inquired whether we
could make intelligible to ourselves the idea of a conceptual scheme which
provided for a system of objective particulars, but in which material bodies
were not basic. This led to the construction of a model No-Space world,[2]
in which all the sensory items were auditory, but in which it did seem possible to find a place for the idea of a reidentifiable particular, by exploiting
certain auditory analogues of the idea of spatial distance. The requirement,
however, was for a scheme in which a distinction was made between oneself and what is not oneself. Though it seemed possible that the conditions
for this distinction could be fulfilled in such a world, it was not obvious
how they were to be fulfilled. The introduction of the idea of agency—of a
distinction between changes which were deliberately initiated, and those
that just occurred—seemed inadequate to compel this crucial distinction;
and a final attempt to produce in the auditory world the conditions of a
non-solipsistic consciousness seemed just an attempt to copy indiscrimi-
nately the features of our ordinary human experience in the very restricted
sensory terms available. So, to try to get clearer about what in general
those conditions are, it seemed advisable to inquire how in fact they are
fulfilled in ordinary human experience.

But though I want to ask this question in relation to our ordinary
human experience, yet there is a certain advantage in keeping before our
minds the picture of the purely auditory world, the picture of an experience
very much more restricted than that which we in fact have. For it may help
to sharpen for us the question we are concerned with; it may help to give us
a continuing sense of the strangeness of what we in fact do; and this sense
of strangeness we want to keep alive in order to see that we really meet it
and remove it, and do not just lose or smother it. It helps in this way. We
drew a picture of a purely auditory experience, and elaborated it to a point
at which it seemed that the being whose experience it was—if any such
being were possible at all—might recognize sound-universals and reidentify
sound-particulars and in general form for himself an idea of his auditory
world; but still, it seemed, he would have no place for the idea of himself
as the subject of this experience, would make no distinction between a
special item in his world, namely himself, and the other items in it. Would
it not seem utterly strange to suggest that he might distinguish
himself as one item among others in his auditory world, that is, as a
sound or sequence of sounds? For how could such a thing—a sound—be
also what *had* all those experiences? Yet to have the idea of himself,
must he not have the idea of the subject of the experiences, of that which
has them? So it might begin to look impossible that he should have the
idea of himself—or at any rate the right idea. For to have the idea at all, it

---

[2] Strawson postulates a world without space in order to try to discover what makes
one person different from another, apart from the fact that he occupies a different
part of space and *looks* different. [M.G.]

seems that it must be an idea of some particular thing of which he has experience, and which is set over against or contrasted with other things of which he has experience, but which are not himself. But if it is just an item *within* his experience of which he has this idea, how can it be the idea of that which *has* all of his experiences? And now we seem to have come upon a form of problem which is completely general, which applies as much to the ordinary as to the auditory world. It must, it seems, be soluble for the ordinary world.

Let us now think of some of the ways in which we ordinarily talk of ourselves, of some of the things which we do ordinarily ascribe to ourselves. They are of many kinds. We ascribe to ourselves *actions* and *intentions* (I am doing, did, shall do this); *sensations* (I am warm, in pain); *thoughts* and *feelings* (I think, wonder, want this, am angry, disappointed, contented); *perceptions* and *memories* (I see this, hear the other, remember that). We ascribe to ourselves, in two senses, position: *location* (I am on the sofa) and *attitude* (I am lying down). And of course we ascribe to ourselves not only temporary conditions, states, situations like these, but also relatively enduring characteristics, including physical characteristics like height, colouring, shape and weight. That is to say, among the things we ascribe to ourselves are things of a kind that we also ascribe to material bodies to which we should not dream of ascribing others of the things that we ascribe to ourselves. Now there seems nothing needing explanation in the fact that the particular height, colouring, physical position which we ascribe to ourselves should be ascribed to *something or other;* for that which one calls one's body is, at least, a body, a material thing. It can be picked out from others, identified by ordinary physical criteria and described in ordinary physical terms. But, so long as we keep that for the present indispensable sense of strangeness, it can and must seem to need explanation that one's states of consciousness, one's thoughts and sensations, are ascribed to *the very same thing* to which these physical characteristics, this physical situation, is ascribed. That is, we have not only the question: *Why are one's states of consciousness ascribed to anything at all?* We have also the question: *Why are they ascribed to the very same thing as certain corporeal characteristics, a certain physical situation, &c.?* It is not to be supposed that the answers to these questions will be independent of one another.

[How am I related to my body?]

2. It might indeed be thought that an answer to both of them could be found in the unique role which each person's body plays in his experience, particularly his perceptual experience. All philosophers who have concerned themselves with these questions have referred to the uniqueness of this role. Descartes was well aware of its uniqueness: "I am *not* lodged in my body like a pilot in a vessel." In what does this uniqueness consist? It consists, of course, in a great many things. Consider merely some of the ways in which the character of a person's *perceptual experience* is depend-

ent on facts about his own body. Let us take his visual experience. The dependence is more complicated and many-sided than may at first be obvious. First, there is that group of empirical facts of which the most familiar is that if the eyelids of that body are closed, the person sees nothing. To this group belong all the facts known to ophthalmic surgeons. Second, there is the fact that what falls within his field of vision at any moment depends in part on the *orientation* of his eyes, i.e. on the direction his head is turned in, and on the *orientation* of his eyeballs in their sockets. And, third, there is the fact that *where he sees from*—or what his possible field of vision at any moment is—depends on where his body, and in particular his head, is located. I divide these facts into three groups because I want to emphasize that the fact that visual experience is, in all three ways, dependent on facts about some body or bodies, does not entail that the body should be the same body in each case. It is a contingent fact that it is the same body.

Such points illustrate some of the ways in which each person's body occupies a special position in relation to that person's perceptual experience. We may summarize such facts by saying that for each person there is one body which occupies a certain *causal* position in relation to that person's perceptual experience, a causal position which in various ways is unique in relation to each of the various kinds of perceptual experience he has; and—as a further consequence—that this body is also unique for him as an *object* of the various kinds of perceptual experience which he has. We also noted that this complex uniqueness of the single body appeared to be a contingent matter, or rather a cluster of contingent matters; for it seems that we can imagine many peculiar combinations of dependence and independence of aspects of our perceptual experience on facts about different bodies.

[Why am I attached to one body as mine?]

We reminded ourselves of the special position which a person's body occupies in his experience in the hope that it might help to provide an answer to two questions: viz. (1) Why are one's states of consciousness ascribed to anything at all? and (2) Why are they ascribed to the very same thing as certain corporeal characteristics, a certain physical situation &c.? But now I must say straight away that the facts I have been recalling do not seem to me to provide, by themselves, any answer to our questions at all. Of course, these facts explain something. They provide a good reason why a subject of experience should have a very special regard for just one body, why he should think of it as unique and perhaps more important than any other. They explain—if I may be permitted to put it so—why I feel peculiarly attached to what in fact I call my own body; they even might be said to explain why, granted that I am going to speak of one body as *mine*, I should speak of *this* body as mine. But they do not explain why I should have the concept of *myself* at all, why I should ascribe my thoughts and experiences to *anything*. Moreover, even if we were satisfied with some other explanation of why one's states of consciousness, thoughts and feelings and perceptions, were ascribed to *something,* and satisfied that the facts in question sufficed to explain why the "possession" of a particular body should be ascribed to the *same* thing (i.e. to explain why a particular body should be spoken of as standing in some special relation—called "being possessed by"—to that thing), yet the facts in question still do not explain why we should, as we do, ascribe certain corporeal characteristics not simply to the body standing in this special relation to the thing to which we ascribe thoughts and feelings, &c., but to the thing itself to which we ascribe those thoughts and feelings. For we say *"I* am bald" as well as *"I* am cold," *"I* am lying on the hearthrug" as well as *"I* see a spider on the ceiling." Briefly, the facts in question explain why a subject of experience should pick out one body from others, give it, perhaps, an honoured name and ascribe to it whatever characteristics it has; but they do not explain why the experiences should be ascribed to any subject at all; and they do not explain why, if the experiences are to be ascribed to something, they *and* the corporeal characteristics which might be truly ascribed to the favoured body should be ascribed to the same thing. So the facts in question do not explain the use that we make of the word "I," or how any word has the use that word has. They do not explain the concept we have of a person.

[Why must I say consciousness belongs to a thing?]

3. A possible reaction at this point is to say that the concept we have is wrong or confused, or, if we make it a rule not to say that the concepts we have are confused, that the usage we have, whereby we ascribe, or seem to ascribe, such different kinds of predicate to one and the same thing, is confusing, that it conceals the true nature of the concepts involved, or something of this sort. This reaction can be found in two very important types of view about these matters. The first type of view is Cartesian, the view of Descartes and of others who think like him. Over the attribution of the second type of view I am more hesitant; but there is some evidence that it was held, at one period, by Wittgenstein and possibly also by Schlick. On both of these views, one of the questions we are considering—viz. "Why do we ascribe our states of consciousness to the very same thing as certain corporeal characteristics &c.?"—is a question which does not arise; for, on both views, it is only a linguistic illusion that both kinds of predicate are properly ascribed to one and the same thing, that there is a common owner, or subject, of both types of predicate. On the second of these views, the other question we are considering—viz. "Why do we ascribe our states of consciousness to anything at all?"—is also a question which does not arise; for on this view it is only a linguistic illusion that one ascribes one's states of consciousness at all, that there is any proper subject of these apparent

ascriptions, that states of consciousness belong to, or are states of, anything.

That Descartes held the first of these views is well enough known.[3] When we speak of a person, we are really referring to one or both of two distinct substances, two substances of different types, each of which has its own appropriate types of states and properties; and none of the properties or states of either can be a property or state of the other. States of consciousness belong to one of these substances and not to the other. I shall say no more about the Cartesian view for the moment—what I have to say about it will emerge later on—except to note again that while it escapes one of our questions, it does not escape, but indeed invites, the other: "Why are one's states of consciousness *ascribed* at all, to *any* subject?"

[Does consciousness depend on the body, belong to the body, or differ from the body in any way?]

The second of these views I shall call the "no-ownership" [4] or "no-subject" doctrine of the self. Whether or not anyone has explicitly held this view, it is worth reconstructing, or constructing, in outline.[5] For the errors into which it falls are instructive. The "no-ownership" theorist may be presumed to start his explanation with facts of the sort which illustrate the unique causal position of a certain material body in a person's experience. The theorist maintains that the uniqueness of this body is sufficient to give rise to the idea that one's experiences can be ascribed to some particular, individual thing, can be said to be possessed by, or owned by, that thing.

---

[3] Or at least widely enough supposed to justify our calling it the Cartesian view. [P.F.S.]

[4] The no-ownership doctrine holds that states of consciousness "belong" to no-one. [M.G.]

[5] The evidence that Wittgenstein at one time held such a view is to be found in Moore's articles in *Mind* on "Wittgenstein's Lectures in 1930–33" (*Mind*, Vol. LXIV, pp. 13–14). He is reported to have held that the use of "I" was utterly different in the case of "I have a toothache" or "I see a red patch" from its use in the case of "I've got a bad tooth" or "I've got a matchbox." He thought that there were two uses of "I," and that in one of them "I" was replaceable by "this body." So far the view might be Cartesian. But he also said that in the other use (the use exemplified by "I have a toothache" as opposed to "I have a bad tooth"), the "I" *does not denote a possessor*, and that no Ego is involved in thinking or in having toothache; and referred with apparent approval to Lichtenberg's dictum that, instead of saying "I think," we (or Descartes) ought to say "There is a thought" (i.e. "Es denkt").

The attribution of such a view to Schlick would have to rest on his article, "Meaning and Verification" (see *Readings in Philosophical Analysis,* ed. Feigl and Sellars). Like Wittgenstein, Schlick quotes Lichtenberg, and then goes on to say: "Thus we see that unless we choose to call our body the owner or bearer of the data [the immediate data of experience]—which seems to be a rather misleading expression—we have to say that the data have no owner or bearer." The full import of Schlick's article is, however, obscure to me, and it is quite likely that a false impression is given by the quotation of a single sentence. I shall say merely that I have drawn on Schlick's article in constructing the case of my hypothetical "no-subject" theorist; but shall not claim to be representing his views.

Lichtenberg's anti-Cartesian dictum is, as the subsequent argument will show, one that I endorse, if properly used; but it seems to have been repeated, without being understood, by most of Descartes's critics. (I do not here refer to Wittgenstein and Schlick.) [P.F.S.]

This idea, he thinks, though infelicitously and misleadingly expressed in terms of ownership, would have some validity, would make some sort of sense, so long as we thought of this individual thing, the possessor of the experiences, as the body itself. So long as we thought in this way, then to ascribe a particular state of consciousness to this body, this individual thing, would at least be to say something that might have been false; for the experience in question might have been causally dependent on the state of some other body; in the present admissible, though infelicitous, sense of the word, it might have "belonged" to some other individual thing. But now, the theorist suggests, one becomes confused: one slides from the admissible sense in which one's experiences may be said to belong to, or be possessed by, some particular thing, to a wholly inadmissible and empty sense of these expressions, in which the particular thing is not thought of as a body, but as something else, say an Ego, whose sole function is to provide an owner for experiences. Suppose we call the first type of possession, which is really a certain kind of causal dependence, "having$_1$," and the second type of possession "having$_2$"; and call the individual of the first type "B" and the supposed individual of the second type "E." Then the difference is that while it is genuinely a contingent matter that *all my experiences are had$_1$ by B,* it appears as a necessary truth that *all my experiences are had$_2$ by E.* But the belief in E and the belief in "having$_2$" is an illusion. Only those things whose ownership is logically transferable can be owned at all. So experiences are not owned by anything except in the dubious sense of being causally dependent on the state of a particular body; this is at least a genuine relationship to a thing, in that they might have stood in it to another thing. Since the whole function of E was to own experiences, in a logically non-transferable sense of "own," and since experiences are not owned by anything in this sense, for there is no such sense of "own," E must be eliminated from the picture altogether. It only came in because of a confusion.

I think it must be clear that this account of the matter, though it contains some of the facts, is not coherent. It is not coherent, in that one who holds it is forced to make use of that sense of possession of which he denies the existence, in presenting his case for the denial. When he tries to state the contingent fact, which he thinks gives rise to the illusion of the "ego," he has to state it in some such form as "All *my* experiences are had$_1$ by (i.e. uniquely dependent on the state of) body B." For any attempt to eliminate the *"my,"* or any expression with a similar possessive force, would yield something that was not a contingent fact at all. The proposition that *all* experiences are causally dependent on the state of a single body B, for example, is just false. The theorist means to speak of all the experiences *had by a certain person* being contingently so dependent. And the theorist cannot consistently argue that "all the experiences of person P" *means the same thing* as "all experiences contingently dependent on a certain body B"; for then his proposition would not be contingent, as his theory requires, but analytic. He must mean to be speaking of some class of experiences of the members of which it is in fact contingently true that they are all dependent on body B. The defining characteristic of this class is in fact that they are *"my* experiences" or "the experiences *of* some person," where the idea of possession expressed by "my" and "of" is the one he calls into question.

[Is the ownership of pain non-transferable?]

This internal incoherence is a serious matter when it is a question of denying what *prima facie* is the case: that is, that one does genuinely ascribe one's states of consciousness to something, viz. oneself, and that this kind of ascription is precisely such as the theorist finds unsatisfactory, i.e. is such that it does not seem to make sense to suggest, for example, that the identical pain which was in fact one's own might have been another's. We do not have to seek far in order to understand the place of this logically non-transferable kind of ownership in our general scheme of thought. For if we think, once more, of the requirements of identifying reference in speech to *particular* states of consciousness, or private experiences, we see that such particulars cannot be thus identifyingly referred to except as the states or experiences *of* some identified *person*. States, or experiences, one might say, *owe* their identity as particulars to the identity of the person whose states or experiences they are. From this it follows immediately that if they can be identified as particular states or experiences at all, they must be possessed or ascribable in just that way which the no-ownership theorist ridicules; i.e. in such a way that it is logically impossible that a particular state or experience in fact possessed by someone should have been possessed by anyone else. The requirements of identity rule out logical transferability of ownership. So the theorist could maintain his position only by denying that we could ever refer to particular states or experiences at all; and *this* position is ridiculous.

We may notice, even now, a possible connexion between the no-ownership doctrine and the Cartesian position. The latter is, straightforwardly enough, a dualism of two subjects, or two types of subject. The former could, a little paradoxically, be called a dualism too: a dualism of one subject—the body—and one non-subject. We might surmise that the second dualism, paradoxically so called, arises out of the first dualism, non-paradoxically so called; in other words, that if we try to think of that to which one's states of consciousness are ascribed as something utterly different from that to which certain corporeal characteristics are ascribed, then indeed it becomes difficult to see why states of consciousness should be ascribed to, thought of as belonging to, anything at all. When we think of this possibility, we may also think of another: viz. that both the Cartesian and the no-ownership theorists are profoundly wrong in holding, as each must, that there are two uses of "I," in one of which it denotes something which it does not denote in the other.

[What this no-ownership theory fails to consider]

4. The no-ownership theorist fails to take account of all the facts. He takes account of some of them. He implies, correctly, that the unique position or role of a single body in one's experience is not a sufficient explanation of the fact that one's experiences, or states of consciousness, are ascribed to something which *has* them with that peculiar non-transferable kind of possession which is here in question. It may be a necessary part of the explanation, but is not, by itself, a sufficient explanation. The theorist, as we have seen, goes on to suggest that it is perhaps a sufficient explanation of something else: viz. of our confusedly and mistakenly *thinking* that states of consciousness are to be ascribed to something in this special way. But this, as we have seen, is incoherent: for it involves the denial that someone's states of consciousness are anyone's. We avoid the incoherence of this denial, whilst agreeing that the special role of a single body in someone's experience does not suffice to explain why that experience should be ascribed to anyone. The fact of this special role does not, by itself, give a sufficient reason why what *we* think of as a subject of experience should have any use for the conception of himself as such a subject.

When I say that the no-ownership theorist's account fails through not reckoning with all the facts, I have in mind a very simple, but in this question a very central, thought: viz. that it is a necessary condition of one's ascribing states of consciousness, experiences, to oneself, in the way one does, that one should also ascribe them, or be prepared to ascribe them, to others who are not oneself.[6] This means not less than it says. It means, for example, that the ascribing phrases are used in just the same sense when the subject is another as when the subject is oneself. Of course the thought that this is so gives no trouble to the non-philosopher: the thought, for ex-

---

[6] I can imagine an objection to the unqualified form of this statement, an objection which might be put as follows. Surely the idea of a uniquely applicable predicate, i.e. a predicate which belongs to only one individual, is not absurd. And, if it is not, then surely the most that can be claimed is that a necessary condition of one's ascribing predicates of a certain class to one individual, i.e. oneself, is that one should be prepared, or ready, on appropriate occasions, to ascribe them to other individuals, and hence that one should have a conception of what those appropriate occasions for ascribing them would be; but not, necessarily, that one should actually do so on any occasion.

The shortest way with the objection is to admit it, or at least refrain from disputing it; for the lesser claim is all that the argument strictly requires, though it is slightly simpler to conduct it in terms of the larger claim. But it is well to point out further that we are not speaking of a single predicate, or merely of some group or other of predicates, but of the whole of an enormous class of predicates such that the applicability of those predicates or their negations defines a major logical type or category of individuals. To insist, at this level, on the distinction between the lesser and the larger claim is to carry the distinction over from a level at which it is clearly correct to a level at which it may well appear idle and possibly senseless.

The main point here is a purely logical one: the idea of a predicate is correlative with that of a *range* of distinguishable individuals of which the predicate can be significantly, though not necessarily truly, affirmed. [P.F.S.]

ample, that "in pain" means the same whether one says "I am in pain" or "He is in pain." The dictionaries do not give two sets of meanings for every expression which describes a state of consciousness: a first-person meaning and a second- and third-person meaning. But to the philosopher this thought has given trouble. How could the sense be the same when the method of verification was so different in the two cases—or, rather, when there *was* a method of verification in the one case (the case of others) and not, properly speaking, in the other case (the case of oneself)? Or, again —a more sophisticated scruple—how can it be right to talk of *ascribing* in the case of oneself? For surely there can be a question of ascribing only if there is or could be a question of identifying that to which the ascription is made; and though there may be a question of identifying the one who is in pain when that one is another, how can there be such a question when that one is oneself? But this query answers itself as soon as we remember that we *speak* primarily to others, for the information of others. In one sense, indeed, there is no question of my having to *tell who it is* who is in pain, when I am. In another sense, however, I may have to *tell who it is,* i.e. to let others know who it is.

What I have just said explains, perhaps, how one may properly be said to ascribe states of consciousness to oneself, given that one can ascribe them to others. But how is it that one can ascribe them to others? Now one thing here is certain: that *if* the things one ascribes states of consciousness to, in ascribing them to others, are thought of as a set of Cartesian egos to which only private experiences can, in correct logical grammar, be ascribed, *then* this question is unanswerable and this problem insoluble. If, in identifying the things to which states of consciousness are to be ascribed, private experiences are to be all one has to go on, then, just for the very same reason as that for which there is, from one's own point of view, no question of telling that a private experience is one's own, there is also no question of telling that a private experience is another's. All private experiences, all states of consciousness, will be mine, i.e. no one's. To put it briefly. One can ascribe states of consciousness to oneself only if one can ascribe them to others. One can ascribe them to others only if one can identify other subjects of experience. And one cannot identify others if one can identify them *only* as subjects of experience, possessors of states of consciousness.

[How do I know *my* experiences are mine?]

It might be objected that this way with Cartesianism is too short. After all, there is no difficulty in distinguishing bodies from one another, no difficulty in identifying bodies. Does not this give us an indirect way of identifying subjects of experience, while preserving the Cartesian mode? Can we not identify such a subject as, for example, "the subject that stands to that body in the same special relation as I stand in to this one," or, in other words, "the subject of those experiences which stand in the same unique causal relation to body N as *my* experiences stand in to body M"? But this suggestion is useless. It requires me to have noted that *my* experiences stand in a special relation to body M, when it is just the right to speak of *my* experiences at all that is in question. That is to say, it requires me to have noted that *my* experiences stand in a special relation to body M; but it requires me to have noted this as a condition of being able to identify other subjects of experiences, i.e. as a condition of my having the idea of myself as a subject of experience, i.e. as a condition of thinking of any experiences as *mine*. So long as we persist in talking, in the mode of this explanation, of experiences on the one hand, and bodies on the other, the most I may be allowed to have noted is that experiences, *all* experiences, stand in a special relation to body M, that body M is unique in just this way, that this is what makes body M unique among bodies. (This "most" is perhaps too much—because of the presence of the word "experiences.") The proffered explanation runs: "Another subject of experience is distinguished and identified as the subject of those experiences which stand in the same unique causal relationship to body N as *my* experiences stand in to body M." And the objection is: "But what is the word 'my' doing in the explanation?" It is not as though the explanation could get on without this word. There is a further objection, to which we will recur. It runs: "What right have we, in this explanation, to speak of *the* subject, implying uniqueness? Why should there not be any number of subjects of experience—perhaps qualitatively indistinguishable—each subject and each set of experiences standing in the same unique relation to body N (*or* to body M)? Uniqueness of the body does not guarantee uniqueness of the Cartesian soul."

[What is the primitive concept of person?]

What we have to acknowledge, in order to begin to free ourselves from these difficulties, is the primitiveness of the concept of a person. What I mean by the concept of a person is the concept of a type of entity such that *both* predicates ascribing states of consciousness *and* predicates ascribing corporeal characteristics, a physical situation &c. are equally applicable to a single individual of that single type. What I mean by saying that this concept is primitive can be put in a number of ways. One way is to return to those two questions I asked earlier: viz. (1) why are states of consciousness ascribed to anything at all? and (2) why are they ascribed to the very same thing as certain corporeal characteristics, a certain physical situation &c.? I remarked at the beginning that it was not to be supposed that the answers to these questions were independent of each other. Now I shall say that they are connected in this way: that a necessary condition of states of consciousness being ascribed at all is that they should be ascribed to the *very same things* as certain corporeal characteristics, a certain physical situation &c. That is to say, states of consciousness could not be ascribed at all, *unless* they were ascribed to persons, in the sense I have claimed for this word. We are tempted to think of a person as a sort of compound of two kinds of subjects: a subject of experiences (a pure consciousness, an ego) on the one hand, and a subject of corporeal attributes on the other. Many questions arise when we think in this way. But, in particular, when we ask ourselves how we come to frame, to get a use for, the concept of this compound of two subjects, the picture—if we are honest and careful —is apt to change from the picture of two subjects to the picture of one subject and one non-subject. For it becomes impossible to see how we could come by the idea of different, distinguishable, identifiable subjects of experiences—different consciousnesses—*if this idea is thought of as logically primitive,* as a logical ingredient in the compound-idea of a person, the latter being composed of two subjects. For there could never be any question of assigning an experience, as such, to any subject other than one-self; and therefore never any question of assigning it to oneself either, never any question of ascribing it to a subject at all. So the concept of the pure individual consciousness—the pure ego—is a concept that cannot exist; or, at least, cannot exist as a primary concept in terms of which the concept of a person can be explained or analysed. It can exist only, if at all, as a secondary, non-primitive concept, which itself is to be explained, analysed, in terms of the concept of a person. It was the entity corresponding to this illusory primary concept of the pure consciousness, the ego-substance, for which Hume was seeking, or ironically pretending to seek, when he looked into himself, and complained that he could never discover himself without a perception and could never discover anything but the perception. More seriously—and this time there was no irony, but a confusion, a Nemesis of confusion for Hume—it was this entity of which Hume vainly sought for the principle of unity, confessing himself perplexed and defeated; sought vainly because there is no principle of unity where there is no principle of differentiation. It was this, too, to which Kant, more perspicacious here than Hume, accorded a purely formal ("analytic") unity: the unity of the "I think" that accompanies all my perceptions and therefore might just as well accompany none. Finally it is this, perhaps, of which Wittgenstein spoke, when he said of the subject, first that there is no such thing, and then that it is not a part of the world, but its limit.

So, then, the word "I" never refers to this, the pure subject. But this does not mean, as the no-ownership theorist must think, that "I" in some cases does not refer at all. It refers; because I am a person among others; and the predicates which would, *per impossible* belong to the pure subject if it could be referred to, belong properly to the person to which "I" does refer.

The concept of a person is logically prior to that of an individual consciousness. The concept of a person is not to be analysed as that of an animated body or of an embodied anima. This is not to say that the concept of a pure individual consciousness might not have a logically secondary existence, if one thinks, or finds, it desirable. We speak of a dead person—a body—and in the same secondary way we might at least think of a disembodied person. A person is not an embodied ego, but an ego might be a disembodied person, retaining the logical benefit of individuality from having been a person.

[Does person contain notions of consciousness and corporeal characteristics?]

5. It is important to realize the full extent of the acknowledgement one is making in acknowledging the logical primitiveness of the concept of a person. Let me rehearse briefly the stages of the argument. There would be no question of ascribing one's own states of consciousness, or experiences, to anything, unless one also ascribed, or were ready and able to ascribe, states of consciousness, or experiences, to other individual entities of the same logical type as that thing to which one ascribes one's own states of consciousness. The condition of reckoning oneself as a subject of such predicates is that one should also reckon others as subjects of such predicates. The condition, in turn, of this being possible, is that one should be able to distinguish from one another, to pick out or identify, different subjects of such predicates, i.e. different individuals of the type concerned. The condition, in turn, of this being possible is that the individuals concerned, including oneself, should be of a certain unique type: of a type, namely, such that to each individual of that type there must be ascribed, or ascribable, *both* states of consciousness *and* corporeal characteristics. But this characterization of the type is still very opaque and does not at all clearly bring out what is involved. To bring this out, I must make a rough division, into two, of the kinds of predicates properly applied to individuals of this type. The first kind of predicate consists of those which are also properly applied to material bodies to which we would not dream of applying predicates ascribing states of consciousness. I will call this first kind M-predicates: and they include things like "weighs 10 stone," "is in the drawing-room" and so on. The second kind consists of all the other predicates we apply to persons. These I shall call P-predicates. P-predicates, of course, will be very various. They will include things like "is smiling," "is going for a walk," as well as things like "is in pain," "is thinking hard," "believes in God" and so on.

So far I have said that the concept of a person is to be understood as the concept of a type of entity such that *both* predicates ascribing states of consciousness *and* predicates ascribing corporeal characteristics, a physical situation &c. are equally applicable to an individual entity of that type. All I have said about the meaning of saying that this concept is primitive is that it is not to be analysed in a certain way or ways. We are not, for example, to think of it as a secondary kind of entity in relation to two primary kinds, viz. a particular consciousness and a particular human body. I implied also that the Cartesian error is just a special case of the more general error, present in a different form in theories of the no-ownership type, of thinking of the designations, or apparent designations, of persons as *not* denoting precisely the same thing or entity for all kinds of predicate ascribed to the entity designated. That is, if we are to avoid the general form of this error, we must *not* think of "I" or "Smith" as suffering from type-ambiguity. Indeed, if we want to locate type-ambiguity somewhere, we would do better to locate it in certain predicates like "is in the drawing-room" "was hit by a stone" &c., and say they mean one thing when applied to material objects and another when applied to persons.

[Immortality and the resurrection of the body]

7. Earlier, when I was discussing the concept of a pure individual consciousness, I said that though it could not exist as a primary concept to be used in the explanation of the concept of a person (so that there is no mind-body problem, as traditionally conceived), yet it might have a logically secondary existence. Thus, from within our actual conceptual scheme, each of us can quite intelligibly conceive of his or her individual survival of bodily death. The effort of imagination is not even great. One has simply to think of oneself as having thoughts and memories as at present, visual and auditory experiences largely as at present, even, perhaps—though this involves certain complications—some quasi-tactual and organic sensations as at present, whilst (a) having no perceptions of a body related to one's experience as one's own body is, and (b) having no power of initiating changes in the physical condition of the world, such as one at present does with one's hands, shoulders, feet and vocal chords. Condition (a) must be expanded by adding that no one else exhibits reactions indicating that he perceives a body at the point which one's body would be occupying if one were seeing and hearing in an embodied state from the point from which one is seeing and hearing in a disembodied state. One could, of course, imagine condition (a) being fulfilled, in both its parts, without condition (b) being fulfilled. This would be a rather vulgar fancy, in the class of the table-tapping spirits with familiar voices. But suppose we take disembodiment strictly in the sense that we imagine both (a) and (b) fulfilled. Then two consequences follow, one of which is commonly noted, the other of which is perhaps insufficiently attended to. The first is that the strictly disembodied individual is strictly solitary, and it must remain for him indeed an utterly empty, though not meaningless, speculation, as to whether there are any other members of his class. The other, and less commonly noticed point, is that in order to retain his idea of himself as an individual, he must always think of himself as *dis*embodied, as a *former* person. That is to say, he must contrive still to have the idea of himself as a member of a class or type of entities with whom, however, he is now debarred from entering into any of those transactions the past fact of which was the condition of his having any idea of himself at all. Since then he has, as it were, no personal life of his own to lead, he must live much in the memories of the personal life he did lead; or he might, when this living in the past loses

its appeal, achieve some kind of attenuated vicarious personal existence by taking a certain kind of interest in the human affairs of which he is a mute and invisible witness—much like that kind of spectator at a play who says to himself: "That's what I should have done (or said)" or "If I were he, I should. . . ." In proportion as the memories fade, and this vicarious living palls, to that degree his concept of himself as an individual becomes attenuated. At the limit of attenuation there is, *from the point of view of his survival as an individual,* no difference between the continuance of experience and its cessation. Disembodied survival, on such terms as these, may well seem unattractive. No doubt it is for this reason that the orthodox have wisely insisted on the resurrection of the body.

QUESTIONS FOR STUDY AND DISCUSSION

1. In order to understand the term "persons," Strawson uses language games. List the ones he uses. Is his question at the end of section (1) the same as the question asked by Hume?
2. What are the two questions asked and the two views described?
3. What connection does he show exists between the no-ownership doctrine and the Cartesian position?
4. Why does he say that Hume is confused?
5. Of what does Strawson's concept of person consist?
6. Why does he think that immortality and the resurrection of the body are wisely held by the orthodox?

Stuart Hampshire

STUART HAMPSHIRE was born in 1914. Educated at Oxford University, he received his degree in 1936. Subsequently, he was professor of Philosophy at Oxford and the University of London, except for the few years during World War II when he served in the army. Since 1963 he has been teaching at Princeton University where he is now chairman of the Department of Philosophy. A specialist in the field of ordinary language analysis, he has directed his efforts generally to discovering the actual uses of words and propositions, rather than pronouncing the "object" for which they stand. A frequent contributor to philosophical journals, he is author of *Spinoza* (1951), *Thought and Action* (1959), and *Freedom of the Individual* (1965).

Self-Knowledge and the Will

[The principle of verification]

1. "One understands a statement, if, and only if, one can think of some conditions, however unattainable in fact, in which the statement in question might be known to be true or might be known to be false: and to clarify the meaning of an expression is to specify the conditions in which it could be used with the greatest possible confidence." This formula may be taken as a re-statement of the principle of verification, and (as it seems to me) to preserve its essential insight while avoiding its errors. The insight was that there must be a necessary connection between learning the meaning of an expression and learning what are the standard conditions of its use; secondly, that so-called theories of knowledge are properly interpreted as explanations of the characteristic uses of sentences of different types. To study the conditions for the proper use of "know" and "certain" in conjunction with sentences of different types is to learn how these sentences are typically used. When one is uncertain how some element of the vocabulary is used, one needs to be given some specimens of the standard and most favourable conditions for the use of the expression; and when one can either describe or point to some standard conditions of its use, one has learnt the use of the expression. The mistake of the verificationists was im-

Appeared originally in *Revue Internationale de Philosophie*, No. 25 (1953). Reprinted by permission of *Revue Internationale de Philosophie* and Stuart Hampshire.

possibly to *identify* the meaning of an expression with the standard circumstances of its use, and therefore to suppose that to describe the standard conditions of its use is to analyse (give some equivalent of) the expression itself. To bring out the use of an expression (or what is sometimes misleadingly called "the logic") more clearly, some specimens of the most favourable conditions of its application may be contrasted with specimens of dubious and borderline cases, in which the use of the expression would properly be qualified by "I think" or "probably" or "perhaps" or "maybe." In considering any form of words which may be used to make a statement, we can always point to this contrast between specimens of the optimum conditions of its use and specimens of circumstances in which its use would be dubious. If this is true, it follows that it must be impossible to lay down general conditions for the use of such words as "know," "certain," "probable," "conjecture," "hypothesis": for the conditions for the proper use of such words must vary for every different type of declarative sentence. It must equally be a mistake to pick out a class of propositions, distinguished by their form and topic, and to classify them as certain, or to pick out a class of propositions, distinguished by form and topic, and to classify them as uncertain. If it is the function of the words "known," "certain", "probable," to indicate the conditions, favourable or unfavourable, in which a particular assertion is being made, the phrases "only statements about sense-data are certain" or "general propositions are only probable," must involve an essential misuse of the words "know," "certain," "probable." Given any sentence of any one of these classes, one could always describe conditions of assertion in which the assertor would not have all the assurance he might have that his assertion was true. When a particular statement, or set of statements, is said to be certain or uncertain, it is implied that this statement, or set of statements, has or has not been fully tested and confirmed; and that it has, or has not, been fully tested and confirmed is a matter of fact which lies outside the statement itself.

But these facts of natural history ("People are inscrutable"—"The future is uncertain"), which determine the limits of permissible claims to natural knowledge, may be (and I think sometimes have been) confused with truths of another kind; a philosopher may say "No one can properly claim to be *absolutely* certain about any statement which he makes about the feelings of someone else," or "No one can properly claim to be *absolutely* certain of the truth of any statement about the future"; and he may say this, simply as a way of saying that anyone making a statement about someone else's feelings, or about the future, is never in the best of all possible positions to guarantee the truth of his statement: the designated subject of the statement about feelings, or the contemporary observer of the event predicted, are in a position finally to confirm, or to deny, the statement made; for this reason the assertor cannot claim to be in the best of all possible positions for guaranteeing the truth of what he is saying. And this difference would remain, as a mere matter of logic, in all possible worlds, however unfailingly successful we were in divining the feelings of others. If the form and circumstances of assertion show that a statement is, at the time it is made, subject to confirmation, it always makes sense to ask "How do you know?"; it makes sense to ask for credentials, if it is not shown within the statement itself that the assertor has the best of all possible credentials.

The proper use of the word "know" is not in actual use strictly confined to situations in which the person claiming to know is in the best of all possible positions for guaranteeing the truth of his statement. It is normally sufficient, in justification of a claim to know, to show, firstly, that statements of the kind in question, when made under conditions of this kind and with credentials of this kind, are virtually never shown to be mistaken and are in countless instances maintained or confirmed; and, secondly, that the person claiming to know is, after reflection on the words used, absolutely sure in this particular case of the accuracy of his statement. But if I claim final confirmation in respect of any statement, then I also claim to be in the best possible position for guaranteeing the truth of what I am asserting; I claim that no one could conceivably at any time be in a better position to guarantee the truth of any statement of this type.

2. I have so far mentioned the type of expression which we may use in describing somebody's feelings, dispositions and states of mind. But there is an altogether different type of expression which we use in talking about persons.

Following Hume, many empiricists have written as if the vocabulary of personal disclosure might consist solely of adjectives and nouns used to classify the various feelings, sensations, states of mind which occur to us, the experiences which we undergo. Maine de Biran and William James saw that there was an omission, namely, the essential place of verbs, and of a few active verbs of particular kinds, in any description of the workings of a person's mind. Each of us knows directly in his own case the difference between an idea which simply occurs to him, and an idea which he calls to mind at will, between the gestures and movements which one initiates at will and those which happen of their own accord. "Did you try to remember, or did it just come into your mind?"—only the subject himself can claim to be in the best possible position to answer this question; descriptions of activities and passivities are in this respect comparable with descriptions of feelings and sensations. Closely connected with this distinction, there is the idiom of reflexiveness which we use in making disclosures of our own mental processes; any of our own states of mind, impulses, moods, feelings, may be the objects of our own contemplation; one may survey the conflict of one's own desires or one's own hesitation and apathy. One can—logically can—detach oneself in thought and speech from one's own psychological states and think of them as part of the given material to be coped with. We may in thought present to ourselves, first, the elements of the situation in which we find ourselves, including our own inclinations, fears, and hopes, and then the action which we, distinguished as the ultimate agents, took to meet the situation. We do not attribute this power of self-conscious reflection to very small children or to animals, since reflection in this sense seems inseparable from some use of words. If I say "I was aware at the time of my apathy and indifference," I seem to imply that, in my reflection at that time, I more or less explicitly classified my own condition; or at least I seem to imply that, if I had been asked what I was thinking about, I was ready to answer: "I was thinking that I had become indifferent . . . ." One's awareness of one's own fears, impulses and hesitations is an awareness of them *as* being of a certain character or *as* admitting of a certain description. When one later reports these moments of self-conscious reflection, the indispensable grammar of the language brings with it a distinction between the states and feelings classified, and the indicated subject by whom the classification was made; and so the necessary grammatical form of the sentences may lead one to distinguish the ultimate surveying and acting subject from the succession of states and processes surveyed and acted upon. But it is not true that these reflexive idioms are peculiarly associated with the pronoun "I" and with autobiographical disclosures; in historical or fictional narrative one may equally well say, "He became aware at that moment of a sudden inclination to . . ." We each learn the use of the idiom in interchanging disclosures with others: we each talk to others and about others, as we may each talk to ourselves and about ourselves: every type of personal description admits of conjugation.

Because human beings may represent their own states and impulses to themselves at some moments preceding action, one may accuse them of not having restrained their impulses and of not having exercised their will in the matter; they can be required to direct their thoughts and control their impulses by the exercise of will; they may set themselves to change themselves, and act upon their own states of mind and dispositions. But what is the Will and how do we know of its exercise?

Some small part of the answer (I think) is to be found in the conditions of use of the verbs "try," "choose," "decide."

First "Try."

1. The order "Try to remember what happened" can be expressed by the exactly equivalent form of words, "Remember what happened if you can." Similarly "I did try to remember" is equivalent to "I did all that it was in my power to do towards remembering," and "I am trying to remember" is equivalent to "I am doing all that I can do in order to remember." This is the necessary connection between "try" and "can," between "Will" and "Capacity."

2. To try to do something is not necessarily the same as to make an effort to do something, as William James assumed; the best way to remember might be just *not* to make an effort to remember, but to relax and think about something else. In the essential sense of "try," I have tried to do

something, if and only if, I have not omitted to take the steps known to me as the steps most likely to lead to the required result. In this sense of "try," I have not tried to remember if I have not used those mnemonic devices which are known to me as effective, supposing there are any such known to me; my claim to have tried to do something, whatever it might be, would be refuted by someone saying, "You have not done so-and-so and so-and-so, which you knew to be necessary or effective steps towards this end."

3. It is this sense of "try," which is necessarily connected with "can," as "can" occurs in the formula "ought implies can." An accusation of the form "You could have controlled your panic," is conclusively refuted by the reply, "I tried to control it and failed"; and a defence of this form "I tried to control it and failed" would in its turn be refuted if the accuser pointed to some preliminary steps, which the agent knew to be the first steps in panic-control, and which he had not taken.

4. The tests of whether someone did try to do something necessarily vary with the different kinds of action in question. This variation of the tests may be what is meant by philosophers who deny that there is anything properly called an act of will; they may mean that there is no single experience, always and recognizably, alike, which is called "trying," since what *constitutes* "trying" varies with the nature of the achievement attempted. But there are hosts of verbs of this type in the vocabulary (e.g. "thinking," "working"), and most verbs of human action do not stand for experiences always and recognizably alike; this is no reason for denying that "trying to do X" may stand for a dateable occurrence in a person's history; one may ask "for how long did you try?", and to the question "what have you been doing all this time?" the answer may be, "I have been trying for half an hour to remember his name." But one may also use "try," as most similar verbs, in a dispositional sense, e.g. "He has been trying to achieve this position all his life" (cf. "He has been thinking about this problem all his life").

5. "He could have caught it if he had tried" means the same as "He could have caught it but he did not try"; it is not the same "If . . . then" as "You could have caught it if you had been taller"; his ability to catch it did not depend on his trying; but his ability to catch it did depend on his being taller. Similarly "He could have acted otherwise if he had chosen" does not represent the choosing as the condition of his ability to act otherwise. "He could have done it if he had tried" is an imputation that the failure was specifically a failure of will; "He could have done it if he had chosen to" is an imputation of another kind of failure. It is an imputation of vice rather than of carelessness or weakness.

6. If it is true that "can" and "could," as these are used in discussing human capacities, derive their sense from the possibility of direct falsification by "tried and failed," it follows that there is no sense in saying "I could, or I could not, have tried." For any preliminary steps, which I took

towards controlling my panic, would so far count as trying, providing that I had taken these steps and in the course of taking them had, at a certain stage, failed of my purpose. While I am in conscious possession of my faculties, there are always *some* steps towards the required end which I can take, however ineffectual and remote from the required result; there is always the difference between the exhausted man who takes some steps to counter the effects of exhaustion and the man who acquiesces in his condition and does not attempt the impossible feat. Whenever I am certain that I have seriously tried, I will say "I did all I could towards the proposed end, but it came to nothing; what more could I do?" If anyone says "Why did you not control your panic? You did not try"—I may *know* with absolute certainty that he is being unjust.

"Choose."

1. The word "choose" has both a generic and a specific sense which are often confused in discussions of freedom in ethics. In the imputation "You could have done it if you had chosen," "choose" is used in the generic sense. Used in the specific sense, "to choose" is roughly equivalent to "make a selection"; in this sense of "choose" I may decide, or I may refuse, to choose, i.e. to make a selection between alternatives actually offered to me—e.g. between two candidates for an appointment; "Choose" in this specific sense stands for a definite act which it may be my duty to do, which I may fail to do, and which I may find it difficult to do. But in the generic sense I may be said to have chosen to act in a certain way, whenever I have done something deliberately and knowing what I am doing, even if the action itself was not one which involved making a selection or indicating a preference. "He chose to tell a lie" does not necessarily imply that he went through a process of selecting lying from other alternatives; it implies merely that he lied deliberately (though not necessarily after deliberation), and that he knew what he was doing, and that there was an alternative action open to him.

2. There is no natural sense in which "choosing" in this generic sense can properly be called an act, not even in the sense in which "trying" might be regarded as an act. One cannot say that someone chose to do something unless he actually did it, as one can say that someone tried to do something which he did not actually do; nor can one idiomatically use the continuous present "I am choosing" in analogy with "I am trying," except in the specific sense of "I am making a selection." To say that I chose to do it is to say something about the conditions under which I did it and what kind of action it was; it does not add anything to the history of the sequence of events preceding the action.

3. It follows that there is no sense of "choose to choose," except where the second "choose" is specifically interpreted as "make a selection."

4. It follows also that there is in general no sense in saying either that it was, or was not, in my power to choose, at least as "choose" is used in the phrase "You could have done it if you had chosen"; if it was in my

power to do it, it was also in my power to make that action my choice; I could only escape by arguing that no action under those particular circumstances would have counted as an action done deliberately and with knowledge of what I was doing—i.e. that I was not a free agent in possession of my faculties at the time. Consequently, the question, "Could he have acted otherwise?" does not arise again, and regressively, either in the form of "Could he have tried to act otherwise?" or "Could he have chosen to act otherwise?"

When feeling guilt or exposed to censure, one may say to oneself "It was my fault," and, in support of this, say "I could have avoided the disaster if I had tried," or "if I had chosen"; when one is oneself the subject of such statements, one may sometimes be absolutely certain that they are false, and one may sometimes have good reason to believe that they are true.

"Decide."

1. There is a use of "decide to" in which it means approximately the same as "make up one's mind to." "Decide," and "Make up one's mind," are different from "Try" and "Choose" in that they may naturally be said to represent an act in almost every sense in which this might be denied of "try," and a fortiori denied of "choose." I may decide at exactly 7 p.m. by the clock to do something, and when the time comes to do it, either I may change my mind, or I may be prevented, or I may simply fail to do what I had decided to do; deciding, or making up one's mind, may be difficult, and I may even dramatise the difficulty by saying, absurdly, "I *cannot* make up my mind." "At 11 o'clock I suddenly made up my mind to tell the truth, but an hour later I changed my mind again." This would be a significantly different story from "I made up my mind to do it and yet, when the moment came, I somehow did not do it." The latter represents another kind of failure of will and lays one open to moral imputations of a different kind —not so much "You did not try," or "You did not choose to," but "You were weak and carried away."

2. It seems that "decide to," in this strong sense, is strictly applicable only to symbol-using or language-using creatures. For making up one's mind necessarily involves thinking, in the sense of entertaining proposals, either by the use of words or of images or in some other symbol-using way.

3. When these various stories are told of decisions and changes of mind, and of good intentions which did not emerge in action, it must in general be very difficult for anyone other than the subject himself to judge whether the story is true. The subject himself must assure himself, in answer to a challenge, that, in his story of the events leading up to the actual action, he has not attributed to himself decisions and changes of mind which never in any literal sense occurred; as in description of feelings, he must be accurate, and he can always be asked "Are you sure?"

These are a few only of the types of expression used in describing persons. There is one overriding principle which applies to all forms of self-knowledge: in so far as it is difficult to *discover* the truth about others, it must be difficult to *tell* the truth (to oneself or to others) about oneself, if one uses a common vocabulary; and always, in any matching of words with experience, even if one uses some private and invented idiom of one's own, truth and (above all) accuracy are not easily found; in this domain "Combien ne faut-il pas de précautions pour ne pas mentir?" (*Vie de Henry Brulard*).

QUESTIONS FOR STUDY AND DISCUSSION

1. How does Hampshire's formula preserve the essential insight of the principle of verification and correct its mistakes?
2. Can we, according to Hampshire, be more certain of what we experience than of what others experience?
3. What does Hampshire say is the difference between our inner experience and those of others?
4. Since Hampshire discusses the use of the words "try," "choose," and "decide," do you think that he believes in free will? Or would he take the fact that we use these words as proof of the existence of the will and of its· freedom? Do you think that this is a convincing proof?

TOPICS FOR DISCUSSION AND TERM PAPERS

A.

1. How have the selections illustrated Wittgenstein's view that philosophy is not a source of truth but an activity for clarifying language?
2. Did any one of the selections present any conclusions on the problem discussed? Present these conclusions and evaluate them.
3. Carnap (the logical positivist), Russell (the neutral monist), and Ryle (the philosopher of ordinary language) all seemed to imply that the distinction between mind and body is a false one made by erroneous use of terms or by making concrete what were merely relations. Show how each, in his own way, pointed out the confusion due to language and proposed a solution also in terms of an understanding of the role of language.
4. In the discussion of man, two forms of consciousness and communication inevitably present themselves—consciousness of one's own inner experiences and consciousness of one's outer behavior and of that of others. "I am in pain" reflects one's own experience. "He is in pain" reflects my knowledge of the other's behavior. The philosopher asks:

    a) How is he certain that the other is in pain?
    b) Does his inner experience of his own pain reflected in the statement, "I am in pain," reveal something different than the same external behavior of the other?

    Have the selections discussing this problem helped to solve the problem of man's knowledge of other minds?
5. How far has the use of language games with the word "I" given insight into the nature of personal identity?
6. From these selections and your own readings, in what way do you think analytic philosophy has dissolved, solved, clarified, or perhaps confused any or all of the traditional problems regarding man:

    a) the relation of mind to body
    b) the nature of the self and of personal identity
    c) the difference between our knowledge of our own inner experience and our knowledge of external events
    d) the different kinds of certainty regarding our own inner experience and the experiences of others
    e) the freedom of the will
    f) the immortality of man

7. Can an analysis of how we speak about a man and his behavior and experiences clarify our knowledge about him so that we can get closer to reality?
8. Why do you think that the philosophy of ordinary language triumphed over Russell's philosophy of an ideal language?
9. If we acknowledge that we use myths such as the term "soul" in our language, does this destroy the reality to which the myth refers? To put it

another way, if we speak about the self and admit that such a term is a myth, does this admission on our part *prove* that there *is* or *is not* a self?

10. Does philosophical analysis give genuine philosophical insights into man or does it merely clarify old confusions about man? Does it give *a* philosophy of man or *the* philosophy of man or *no* philosophy of man?

B.

1. Both the phenomenologists and the analytic philosophers rejected the psychologism of Locke and Hume. How far does the phenomenological way of viewing man differ from the analytic piecemeal approach to isolated aspects of man?

2. a) How similar is Merleau-Ponty's view of the body in space to Ryle's view of the mind-body problem?

   b) Is there a similarity between the effort of Ryle to show that there is no dichotomy or absolute split between the body and mind and the view of the existentialists regarding man as a person?

3. Almost all of the philosophers in this book discuss freedom, some accepting it, some denying it. With which position do the analysts agree, or are they neutral?

4. What would the analytic philosopher have to say about the classical philosophers' discussion of freedom and immortality?

5. How would the analytic philosopher approach the dialectic view of man?

6. From your readings you may have concluded that each philosophical approach gives insights into different aspects of man. Once in a while a view of the whole man is briefly unveiled. List below in column form the insights given by the different philosophers into such areas as:

	Classical	Hegelian	Pragmatic	Analytic	Existential
a) Self and personal identity					
b) Decision-free will					
c) Man among others					
Communicating					
Relating					
Separated					
d) Man as aware—of himself					
—of others					
e) Man and the future					
f) Immortality					
g) What is man					
h) Who is man					
i) Where is man going					
j) Why is man					

7. Now in a brief essay give your own philosophy of man, touching if possible most of the problems listed above but presenting a global view of man. Thus, after analyzing various views of man, you will synthesize them into your own coherent picture.

RECOMMENDED READINGS

Primary Sources

Ammerman, Robert R., ed. *Classics of Analytic Philosophy.* New York: McGraw-Hill, 1965. This is an excellent compilation of the representative works of analytic philosophy. Besides the short history of the movement, pp. 1–15, the student will find the selections of C. D. Broad, "The Traditional Problem of Body and Mind," pp. 85–107; G. E. Moore, "Wittgenstein's Lectures in 1930–1933," pp. 233–84; J. Wisdom, "Philosophy and Psycho-analysis," pp. 285–95; and J. Austin, "Other Minds," presenting aspects of the analytic tradition.

Ayer, A. J. *Language, Truth, and Logic,* 2nd ed. New York: Dover Publications, 1946. This second edition is particularly interesting as Ayer in his Introduction admits the error of his extreme position and modifies it somewhat. The Introduction, pp. 5–26, the Preface to the first edition, pp. 31–32, and the chapter on the self, pp. 120–33, are good examples of Ayer's philosophizing.

Gustafson, Donald F., ed. *Essays in Philosophical Psychology.* Garden City, N.Y.: Doubleday & Co., 1964. Although all the essays here are on the philosophy of man in the analytic tradition, the student may especially want to read those selections on identity by B. A. O. Williams, pp. 324–46, and on knowledge of others and other minds by A. J. Ayer and Norman Malcolm, pp. 346–77. The selection from Strawson on "Persons" is the same as that included in this book, except for slight changes and the omission of the last section on immortality.

Russell, Bertrand. *The Basic Writings of Bertrand Russell.* Ed. by Robert E. Egner and Lester E. Denonn. New York: Simon and Schuster, 1961. Pp. 311–45. Here again is Russell discoursing on the nature of mind and matter and on the fact that the distinction between them is outmoded.

———. *My Philosophical Development.* New York: Simon and Schuster, 1959. Pp. 15–27, 110–55. These selections deal with Russell's present philosophical position. It will be seen that even now he feels that the words "consciousness" and "experience" need redefining.

Ryle, Gilbert, *et al. The Revolution in Philosophy.* London: Macmillan Co., 1960. The small book contains lectures, most of which were originally broadcast in Great Britain. The lectures on F. H. Bradley, Russell and Wittgenstein, G. E. Moore, the Vienna Circle, and Wittgenstein are good commentaries on "ordinary language." The lecture by Strawson on "Construction and Analysis" discusses the American school of analysis associated with Carnap and Quine, and the English school associated with Ryle and Austin.

White, Morton, ed. *The Age of Analysis.* New York: The New American Library, 1963. This is an annotated anthology. Selections from G. E. Moore, pp. 21–43, and Russell, Carnap, and Wittgenstein, pp. 189–236, will supplement the readings in the text.

Wisdom, John. *Problems of Mind and Matter.* Cambridge, Eng.: Cambridge University Press, 1963. This contains examples of analytic philosophy. Part I on "Body and Mind" preceded Ryle's *Concept of the Mind,* which really disposed of most of these arguments. The section on "Free Will," pp. 110–31, is also interesting in view of the later positions given in the selections in your text.

Commentaries

Alston, William P. *Philosophy of Language*. Englewood Cliffs, N.J.: Prentice-Hall, 1964. The whole book is a good introduction to the problem of meaning, which is of great concern to the analytic philosophers.

Anscombe, G. E. M. *An Introduction to Wittgenstein's Tractatus*, 2nd ed. London: Hutchison University Library, 1963. Written by the translator of the *Philosophical Investigations*, it gives an authentic approach to the earlier Wittgenstein. The chapters of greatest interest to the student are the Introduction, pp. 11–20, and the last two chapters, pp. 150–72, which discuss Wittgenstein's much disputed "mysticism."

Charlesworth, Maxwell J. *Philosophy and Linguistic Analysis*. Pittsburgh: Duquesne University Press, 1959. The entire book is well worth reading as it traces the development of analytic philosophy and devotes a chapter to each of the leading philosophers in this tradition. The last chapter points out the value and weakness of analytic philosophy in the light of traditional philosophy.

Copleston, Frederick. *Contemporary Philosophy*. Westminster, Md.: The Newman Press, 1956. The first half of this paperback, pp. 1–101, deals with British philosophy and includes a discussion of the meaning of the terms predicated of God. The second half of the book deals with existentialism.

Pitcher, George. *The Philosophy of Wittgenstein*. Englewood Cliffs, N.J.: Prentice-Hall, 1964. The most recent and complete book on Wittgenstein, it should be read in its entirety but especially the following chapters: "On Life and Character" (1); "Picture Theory" (4); "Facing the Consequences" (on Solipsism-6); "Puzzlement and Philosophy" (8); "Mind and Its Place in Language" (11); and the last chapter, "Philosophy" (13).

Pole, D. *The Later Philosophy of Wittgenstein*. New York: Oxford University Press, 1958. This is a critical study of Wittgenstein's *Philosophical Investigations*. All of the chapters would help in understanding this difficult work, and especially the following: "Linguistic Approach to Philosophy" (1); "Inner Experience" (3); "Difficulties in Wittgenstein's Philosophy" (4). The last chapter discusses the work of John Wisdom.

Urmson, J. O. *Philosophical Analysis: Its Development Between the Two World Wars*. Oxford: Oxford University Press, 1956. This is a very short but thorough history of the transition from logical atomism to logical positivism, its downfall and the rise of contemporary philosophical analysis. The whole book (200 pages) should be read.

PART FIVE

Introduction

Historical Background

Major Themes in Phenomenology and Existentialism

Summary: Man and Being

Readings

EXISTENTIALIST AND PHENOMENOLOGICAL THOUGHT:

Husserl

Merleau-Ponty

Sartre

Brunner

Marcel

Heidegger

EDITED BY

Robert Sokolowski

THE CATHOLIC UNIVERSITY OF AMERICA

EXISTENTIALIST AND PHENOMENOLOGICAL THOUGHT:

Husserl *— founder of phenomenology*

Merleau-Ponty

Sartre

Brunner *— person: the highest type of being*

Marcel *—— christian existentialist*

Heidegger *— temporality*

Introduction

themes in phenomenology + existentialism

1. *The body + its space*
2. *expression + speech*
3. *Time*
4. *Emotion*
5. *negation + freedom*
6. *understanding persons + explanation*
7. *Decision structures personality*

Historical Background

The strong emphasis contemporary thought places on the philosophy of man is largely due to the success enjoyed by phenomenology and existentialism. Both these philosophical movements, which have come to dominate continental European thought in the twentieth century, are focused on man. The human subject is taken by them as the foundation of all philosophy, and is also the chief object of their concern and study.

It is true that with René Descartes (1596–1650) philosophy began to turn to man as its focal point. Medieval philosophy before Descartes had been orientated towards being: towards the world as created, finite being, and towards God as pure, uncreated existence. Man was given his place within this framework. He was accorded the respect and attention he deserved as the image and likeness of God, but still was given a subordinate place in the medieval synthesis. Descartes changed this by beginning his philosophy with man, with the *cogito*. Everything else, both the world and God, finds entrance into his philosophy only through man's consciousness, which is the foundation and guarantee of everything that is to be accepted as true and valid. Descartes' turn to the human subject led to a basic reorientation of philosophy, and all the main currents of thought after him have been centered on man.

552

And yet, both phenomenologists and existentialists claim that previous philosophies of man were not radical enough. They did not probe deeply enough into the nature of man, and in one way or another they tried to reduce man to something else. Phenomenology and existentialism thus claim to go farther than Descartes and his successors in giving man the unique status that belongs to him.

How do they do this? We can appreciate the different approaches taken by phenomenology and existentialism by using the classical distinction between man's knowledge and his will. We can consider phenomenology to be chiefly concerned with man as knower. It tries to show that human consciousness differs from everything else in the world, and that it cannot be treated in terms of the structures and laws that hold for nonconscious reality. Existentialism, on the other hand, is primarily concerned with man as a source of freedom and spontaneous activity. It shows man that he has an originality and responsibility that cannot be reduced to impersonal forces, institutions, or economic and social laws. Classifying phenomenology and existentialism in this way is only provisional, for knowing and deciding are two activities of a single human agent and overlap in many ways. The two philosophical movements also have much in common and often cannot be distinguished, but our classification does express the general tendency of each, and if prudently used it will not be misleading.

Phenomenology

Edmund Husserl (1859–1938) is the founder of modern phenomenology, and the publication of his *Logical Investigations* in 1900 and 1901 marks the beginning of this movement. Husserl started groups of phenomenologists at Göttingen, where he taught from 1901 to 1916, and at Freiburg, where he remained from 1916 until his death in 1938. Another important phenomenological circle arose, quite independently of Husserl, at Munich. During the first decades of this century German philosophy was marked by neo-Kantian groups, some notable philosopher-psychologists, and personalist thinkers like Max Scheler (1874–1928). Before long Husserl's phenomenology ranked with the chief philosophical movements in that country, and it contributed very much to the man who has become the dominant figure in contemporary German thought, Martin Heidegger (b. 1889). Phenomenology remained a predominantly German school of thought until the late 1930s when the work of Maurice Merleau-Ponty (1908–61), Jean-Paul Sartre (b. 1905), and more recently Paul Ricoeur (b. 1913) brought about an especially strong development in France. Since 1960 extensive translations and studies have made this philosophical movement more accessible to American readers.

The first volume of Husserl's *Logical Investigations* contains a critique of what he called "psychologism," a doctrine that he continued to attack in various ways throughout his career. Basically, psychologism amounts to an attempt to reduce human consciousness to the status of an ordinary thing in the world. Its extreme form is found in behaviorist psychologists who try to explain human knowing by means of causal laws, as though consciousness could be inserted as another item in the chains of material causality that exist among objects in the world. Specifically, Husserl rejected the attempt made by some psychologists to explain logical and mathematical laws purely in terms of psychological processes. They tried, for example, to reduce the logical principle of contradiction or the Pythagorean theorem to simple empirical generalizations of how men happen to think at certain times and under certain conditions. Against this, Husserl argued that logic and mathematics have an ideal structure of their own that is not reducible to psychological or anthropological laws. The domain of consciousness has a structure and rules proper to itself and cannot be treated by the methods of empirical science, for these are appropriate only to the objects of consciousness. They cannot be applied to consciousness itself.

Although psychologism is found in its most blatant form in behaviorist psychology, Husserl felt that it was also found in different degrees in practically every philosopher of the past, including Descartes. Even Descartes, he claimed, could not get away from the temptation of treating the ego as a "piece of the world." Although Descartes tried to separate mind from matter, he still thought of mind as a thinking *thing,* and thus inserted it among the things of the world. He was, in Husserl's opinion, not radical enough in his treatment of the ego. Consciousness should be conceived as wholly different from the world, and a science of consciousness should devise entirely new terms, laws, and structures that are proper to the ego. It should not try to apply the tools of objective, world-directed sciences to the study of consciousness.

One of the aims of phenomenology is to study human consciousness and to elaborate the new terminology and laws that are proper to it. Husserl's descriptions of intentionality, sensations, internal time, his analysis of various acts of consciousness, are all carried out in order to describe subjectivity. But is this all that phenomenology is supposed to do? Does it deal only with subjectivity, leaving the world entirely outside its scope? Not at all, for when phenomenology describes the ego, the basic structure it finds there is the *intentionality* of consciousness. Consciousness is never closed upon itself. In its very nature it is always consciousness *of* something. The ego cannot be conceived except as faced with objects that are other than itself. In this way, through the essential intentionality of consciousness, the world is brought into the field of phenomenology.

Phenomenology, therefore, considers the world in a special way, precisely as an object of intentionality. It examines things in the way they appear to consciousness; it studies them specifically as phenomena; it is the science of their appearing. Other sciences do not do this. They take things as independent realities, as existing apart from consciousness and as related among themselves by certain causal laws. Such sciences entirely neglect a whole dimension of things; they neglect to examine how things appear. Phenomenology proposes to take this task upon itself, and in doing so, claimed Husserl, it will furnish a foundation for other sciences because it will be describing the appearances that are the basis for laws formulated in physics, biology, sociology, and other sciences.

Thus phenomenology has another focal point. It not only studies subjectivity, but also analyzes the world as it appears to subjectivity. It studies consciousness and reality in their correlation to one another. In doing this it does not put consciousness back as another object in the world. It does not revert to psychologism, because it maintains a fundamental, irreducible duality between consciousness and the world. The two are connected only by the intentionality of consciousness, not by any laws of objective causality.

Husserl's concept of the relation between consciousness and the world can be compared to the relationship between the eye and the field of vision. The seeing eye can never itself be an object in the field of vision. It is fundamentally different from what it sees. The field of vision, however, is correlated to the eye. There can be no field of vision without the eye, for an object seen is constituted *as an appearance* only when there is an eye to see it. There is a correlation between the two in which they remain fundamentally distinct and yet imply one another. Consciousness and reality, according to Husserl, are also basically distinct and yet mutually related by intentionality. In fact, reality is dependent upon consciousness in order to become a phenomenon, for unless there is consciousness present, reality does not carry on its process of appearing. To express this, Husserl said that consciousness "constitutes" reality.

Phenomenology thus has two focal points: (a) consciousness and (b) reality as it appears to consciousness. The task of phenomenology is to describe various regions of reality in the way they appear to consciousness, and to show what activity consciousness must carry out in order to let such regions of reality appear. It must study the constitution of physical reality, social reality, artistic reality, and the like, and thus formulate a "phenomenology" of these and other regions of human experience. This is the world-directed focal point. As regards its focus on subjectivity, phenomenology must describe its structures and activities and show how these function to constitute reality. Thus it is a philosophy of man, but since it considers man in the context of his world, it is a philosophy of man's world as well.

Consciousness and the world comprise one of the basic dualities of phenomenology. Another duality, which is important for the readings we have selected, is that between scientific reality and what Husserl called the *Lebenswelt*. This term is literally translated by "life world," but perhaps its overtones would be better conveyed in English by "lived world." It refers to that area of our experience that lies before conceptualization—before predicates are formulated and judgments are made in a scientific, rigorous way. It refers to ordinary, as opposed to scientific, experience.

Husserl said that the empirical sciences use technical concepts, many of which are artificially formulated. With these exact concepts, and especially with the use of mathematical formulae, empirical sciences are able to build an intricate network of laws and structures that tell us much about reality. He claimed, however, that we must not accept such technical concepts naively. Their origins must be questioned, for they are not made in a void but arise from the more primitive, nontechnical notions present in ordinary human experience, in the lived world. The rigorous concepts of space used in relativity theory, for instance, ultimately arise from the lived experience of space that we all have because of our corporeal nature. Phenomenology must study such primitive experience and show how the exact sciences arise from it.

Husserl felt that phenomenology can even investigate pre-predicative experience, that is, the preconceptual lived awareness we have of various regions of reality. Some of his followers, especially Merleau-Ponty, have carried out excellent analyses of this elusive area of consciousness.

As a final note in this general introduction to phenomenology, we should mention that besides carrying on a constant battle with psychologism, Husserl also continually fought against the Kantian distinction between phenomenon and the "thing in itself." For Husserl, the appearances that consciousness perceives are not a veil or barrier behind which another sort of reality hides. Appearances are the manifestation of reality. They are not a third entity between the ego and its object; they simply *are* the object as it appears. Another point of difference is that Husserl did not say, as Kant did, that structures and categories are imposed on reality by consciousness. Husserl did admit that there are structures, laws, and essences in what we experience, but he insists that they arise from experience itself. They are not imposed a priori by the mind. In both these respects, phenomenology opens up new possibilities for realistic philosophy on the contemporary scene.

Existentialism

Just as phenomenology tries to preserve man's consciousness and knowing from being reduced to the laws and structures of worldly reality, so existentialism tries to save man's will, his responsibility and originality, from being transformed into impersonal forces. Whereas phenomenology began with the twentieth century, existentialism appeared as early as the middle of the nineteenth century in the person of Søren Kierkegaard (1813–55). In him it took the form of a struggle to keep man from being swallowed up by the Hegelian absolute reason, which was understood or misunderstood by Kierkegaard to be an anonymous, cosmic process in which the individual man and his salvation are sacrificed to the development of the whole. We also find in Kierkegaard a strong critique of institutions, in particular of the Danish Established Church, which he felt was an obstacle to the fulfillment and salvation of the Christian. Finally, there is a strong religious aspect to his thought, for he felt that the final justification of man could be made only in the anguished, blind choice of faith in Christ; man cannot save himself. This religious note will be present in all existentialists in either a positive or a negative way; theistic existentialism grounds the dignity and freedom of man in God, while atheistic existentialism claims with equal insistence that belief in God necessarily stifles man and is the chief barrier to his own independent fulfillment.

Friedrich Nietzsche (1844–1900) also belongs in the existentialist tradition. The individual he exalted is the extraordinary, creative personality, who despises popular values and laws and writes his own morality, guided only by the initiative of his own power and strength. Franz Kafka (1883–1924), with his pathetic, despairing complaints about the small individual bewildered and crushed by massive government and business, also fits in this tradition. His works often proved to be accurate prophecies of dictatorial states in the twentieth century. Gabriel Marcel (b. 1889), who experienced first-hand the anonymous impersonalism of war during World War I, is the prime representative of Christian existentialism. Jean-Paul Sartre and Albert Camus (1913–60), who wrote just before World War II and during the occupation of France, developed a sense of rebellion and nihilism that marks much of the postwar existentialist writing. Both espoused atheism because of a conviction that human freedom is impossible if an omnipotent God exists. Martin Buber (1878–1965), steeped in the Judaic tradition of a personal God, described the "I-Thou" relationship and the philosophy of "encounter" that have become common coin in contemporary religious and philosophical literature. In Germany Karl Jaspers (b. 1883) began his career in psychoanalysis, a field in which man is too often reduced to a bundle of subconscious drives, and moved into a distinctive, original form of existentialism in which the highest concern is for man's individual freedom and creativity. Emmanuel Mounier (1905–50) in France and August Brunner (b. 1894) in Germany are sometimes classed as "personalists" because their thought is focused on the nature and structure of personal being. The problems they discuss and the doctrine they teach have much in common with existentialism.

Some of the existentialists, such as Kafka and Camus, are more literary figures than professional philosophers, and some straddle both fields. Marcel and Sartre are as celebrated for their plays as for their systematic philosophical writings.

As this historical survey indicates, existentialism covers a vast array of thinkers. Artists and academicians, theists and atheists, optimists and pessimists—all still have certain general traits in common. They stress the dignity of the individual; they remind man of his inalienable freedom and responsibility to be what he is. They take a position in philosophy. Their thought is more rhetorical, more exhortative than the calm scientific detachment of phenomenology. They deal with values and wish to communicate the values in which they believe.

Yet despite this difference in orientation between phenomenology and existentialism, the two currents of thought have come together and reinforced one another, most notably in France. The phenomenological method is used by existentialists as a way of describing the structure of consciousness, freedom, values, and action. Marcel's description of the virtues and Sartre's of the emotions and imagination are important contributions to theoretical analysis, and they shed light on man's activity and freedom as well.

The selection of readings in this volume is directed chiefly towards presenting the structure of human consciousness and freedom; the readings themselves do not probe deeply into how the existentialists say man should actually exercise his freedom. Rather, they give the theoretical foundations, the human structures that make freedom possible, and thus place greater stress on the phenomenological than on the existential aspects of the philosophy of man. The latter sphere of action is more thoroughly treated in *Approaches to Morality,* the ethics volume of this series.

Major Themes in Phenomenology and Existentialism

The themes treated in phenomenology and existentialism are noticeably different from those discussed in the other philosophies of man in this volume. The problem of knowledge, the attempt to justify the reality of what we know, is conspicuously absent in phenomenology, which begins with the assumption that the intentionality of consciousness puts us into contact with reality. It then goes on to describe the ways in which reality appears to consciousness, but feels no need to *prove* that it does appear. The problem of the unity of man's body and soul is also not directly faced in phenomenology. Rather than try to prove that man is a unified being, phenomenology simply describes the various aspects of his conscious experience. It analyzes both the corporeal and spiritual dimensions in human awareness and insists that they are both experienced in a single, unified consciousness.

The problem of freedom is extensively treated in existentialism. Usually the main concern is to describe the experience of freedom, but often an attempt is made to show what it is in human consciousness that makes freedom possible. Both Merleau-Ponty's section on the mobility of the body and Sartre's on negativity have reference to the explanation of freedom. Finally, the problem of human immortality is generally not treated in strictly phenomenological analysis. Phenomenology is more concerned with describing what is directly experienced than with inquiry into the metaphysical nature of the human soul and its existence after death, which is of course not accessible to phenomenological analysis. Phenomenological data could be used in discussing the problem of immortality, but then it would be in the context of metaphysical argument and no longer in the realm of pure description.

Since the phenomenological philosophy of man is concerned primarily with describing how man experiences his existence in the world, the basic phenomenological themes attempt to articulate various aspects of man's experience. Of basic importance is the awareness we have of our body and its mobility, which make it possible for human consciousness to exist among the physical things of this world. This is discussed in our first selection by Merleau-Ponty. But the simple experience of our body is not yet a fully human awareness because it lacks the structure and meaningfulness that are needed if consciousness is to be more than a mute, animal-like awareness. Hence it is necessary to investigate the role that language and expression play in man's experience of himself in the world; without these there can be no truly human existence.

Practically every phenomenologist holds that the most fundamental structure in human consciousness is its temporality. The constantly changing flow of inner time and the ability of consciousness to remain the "same" throughout this flow make all other factors in human consciousness possible. Even mobility in bodily space, speech and expression, and history and tradition are rooted in temporality.

But man's being in the world is not only that of a knower. He also is the subject of desire and action, and here his experience of the emotions is of prime importance. They open his consciousness to values in the world; they prompt him to desire and achievement. According to the phenomenologists, the emotions are not only subjective states of man; they also modify his relationship to the world, as Sartre shows in the first selection we have from his writings.

Man's action is not only determined by his emotions. He also possesses freedom—the ability of assenting to values or denying them, the capacity to choose among various goods. This subject is treated in the second selection by Sartre on freedom and negativity. It is a phenomenological analysis that also brings us into the realm of existentialism by dealing with the foundations of human activity. Sartre feels that human freedom is bound up with what he calls "negativity" or "nothingness"—the dissatisfaction and unrest that are at the heart of existence and desire.

Free human existence is further elaborated, from another viewpoint, in the selection by Brunner. In what can again be called a phenomenological and an existential study, the dimension of personal human existence is analyzed. This selection goes a step beyond the levels of existence treated so far. Man is described not merely in his awareness of the body and space, as an entity capable of speech, or as a consciousness structured by time and attracted to the world by emotion; he is described as a person capable of assuming responsibility, deciding his own destiny, and entering into relationships with others in a community.

Personal human existence has many facets that can be described phenomenologically. The development of virtue is one facet. Virtue—the habit of doing good—is the repercussion that a proper use of freedom has upon our own existence. Different virtues call for different types of analysis. The first selection by Marcel gives us a description of fidelity, which is closely linked with human freedom. As always, the chief aim is to describe how the virtue of fidelity is experienced in human awareness. Another dimension of personal existence is the community. A solitary man is not a man. How we are related to others and how we are to foster our relations so that they become more and more personal, more and more human, are discussed in Marcel's second selection. The analysis of man's conscious being is thus carried from his primitive, lived experience of bodily space into the complex personal relationships that he has with other men.

The philosophy of man cannot stop with descriptions of the various levels in man's existence; it must go one step further and describe man's relation to being. All the dimensions of human existence previously described must be related to being, and the philosophy of man must be followed by metaphysics. Indeed, the philosophy of man can only be appreciated when the study of being—metaphysics—has been understood.

The Body and Its Space

The phenomenological studies of Maurice Merleau-Ponty are an attempt to probe deeper and deeper into Husserl's problem of the *Lebenswelt,* the area of ordinary, lived experience that arises prior to scientific conceptualization. His first selection is an analysis of space. The rigorous spatial concepts of geometry are all ultimately rooted in the primitive, lived experience we have of spatiality. Physical scientists tend to overlook this personal space because they consider it too subjective, and yet all objective space is ultimately constituted as a superstructure to our lived space and can never be understood unless the primary experiential space has been clarified.

Merleau-Ponty's analysis of space comes down to an analysis of corporeal space. The space that we experience in a living way is basically the spatiality of our own body and the primitive type of space the body first arranges in the world. All spatial structures ultimately refer back to the "here," which is our body. The body is the condition for objective space. In phenomenological terms it forms the "horizon" that is a necessary condition for the objective spatiality of objects.

It is very difficult to grasp the idea of the lived space of the body. We tend to think spontaneously of lived space in terms of the objective space of things, but this is not how we are immediately aware of it. Merleau-Ponty's analyses show the peculiarities of corporeal space and describe how it becomes the ground for all objective space. For example, I know "where" a pain in my leg is, even though my eyes may be closed and I may not be able to locate this feeling in relation to any external objects. There is an immediate, lived, phenomenal space that I have in my own corporeal extension, and the coordinates in this "internal" space are not the same as those we use for external objects. In fact, my internal space really sets up a very primitive but basic set of coordinates by which all external objects are spatialized. It introduces the lived experience of up and down, right and left, forward and backward, here and there, and scientific space is simply a careful, intelligent elaboration of these. If we are going to carry out a phenomenology, a description of things in their way of appearing to us, then lived spatiality is certainly one of the fundamental aspects of this science.

Furthermore, the body is something of a spatial paradox. When I touch one of my hands with the other, a very paradoxical thing occurs. My body then acts as the organizer of space, for the *touching* hand sets up a pattern of coordinates originating from the ultimate "here," which is the center of my consciousness. At the same time my *touched* hand is being treated as an object in that space. My body can thus be both the designer of space and a passive object in that space. The body is both subject and object. Because of this paradoxical character, it can serve as a bridge between consciousness and the world. It puts consciousness into the world.

Merleau-Ponty showed that lived space is not constituted if the body stays still. A necessary condition for spatiality is motion. Again, this is so basic and primitive that we easily overlook it, but the things we see would simply be flat color patches if we did not have the kinesthetic power of introducing our body among them. Our corporeal mobility constitutes things in perspective, and this is simply rudimentary space.

Husserl and Merleau-Ponty both insisted that spatiality is not a subjective obstacle or barrier to our knowledge of things. Immanuel Kant (1724–1804) called space an a priori form of sensibility and gave the impression that if we could somehow get away from space, if we could look around it, we might have a chance of getting at the things in themselves. Such an idea is vigorously rejected by the phenomenologists. Space is real; it belongs to the world of things. In one respect, our bodies are things in the world, and when we experience our own corporeal space and then constitute objective, worldly space, we are experiencing the true character of material, extended being. There is no "better" or more accurate way to see things, because they truly exist in spatiality. To try to conceive them or even to talk about them in any other way is meaningless.

Husserl tended to keep consciousness basically apart from the body. He maintained a rather strong distinction between what he called the "transcendental ego," or pure consciousness, and the "psychological ego," which we could compare to the lived experience of the body. Merleau-Ponty differed from him by reducing consciousness to the lived corporeal experience. This for him is an absolute, the ultimate source of all conceptualization and the starting point for philosophical study. For Merleau-Ponty, man *is* lived awareness of corporeality. This is the experiential, phenomenological definition of man and the source of all his other characteristics. French phenomenologists often call man an *esprit incarné* (incarnate or embodied spirit), and Merleau-Ponty's conception of man as conscious corporeality has kept this term in use.

Expression and Speech

Merleau-Ponty's concept of man is well illustrated in the way he thought of speech and expression. He rejected the idea that speech is an external tag that we put on internal activities called "thoughts." He felt that such a dualistic position would cut man into two parts: the internal spiritual part and the external bodily one. Expression is simply the activity of the human body, but it is carried out with meaning and sense. Speech is a special form of expression. It too is a physical activity, a process of the body, performed with meaning and according to logical rules. The meaning is what distinguishes it from a mere animal-like response to a situation, but the meaning cannot exist apart from corporeal expression. There is no such thing as pure thinking in man.

Here again Merleau-Ponty tried to get behind ossified forms of speech to the living experience that is their source. Speech is a crystallization, a coalescence of living experience. It is falsified if we make it a dead letter by breaking it away from such experience. Merleau-Ponty thus gave us a concrete approach to the treatment of language, and in some other works he has made fine observations on the nature of painting. Phenomenology can offer profitable analyses of all forms of expression, including music, mimicry, dance, fiction, and poetry, by showing what sort of pre-predicative, lived experience is involved in each and by indicating what type of crystallization of meaning occurs in forming the special type of expression that each has.

To say that language sometimes becomes a dead letter does not mean that it is an obstacle to man. Phenomenologists agree that language makes humanity possible. Lived experience must coalesce into the fixed forms of expression and language; if this does not occur human experience would have no stability. Every experience and every thing that we meet would be new and different if we did not have the word between ourselves and what we experience. The word organizes and structures our experience into meaningful patterns and provides the element of fixity that is needed to keep us from a chaos of change.

Speech also makes the growth of knowledge possible; if we could not husband the results of our earlier experience into the stable forms of words, there would be no way for us to fit new events into growing patterns. The historical nature of man is closely tied up with his ability to speak. His social nature is also conditioned by speech, because through words he assumes the inherited wisdom of his society and makes his contribution to it. His insights are deposited for society when they become expressed. To take man's symbols and language away from him is like removing all the branches from a tree—what is left cannot stay alive and is not even called a tree any more. In considering man as a symbol-making and speech-using being, Merleau-Ponty repeated a theme that runs through all of phenomenology.

Man as Structured by Time

Merleau-Ponty's treatment of time owes much to Husserl and Heidegger. The importance temporality has in phenomenology is shown by the title of Heidegger's major work, *Being and Time* (1927). The meaning of the title is that being and time are to be joined together. Being is essentially temporal. Man, as the knower of being, is also temporal. His temporality is not something extra added to him; he does not first exist as a substance and then acquire temporality as a characteristic. Rather, temporality is what makes it possible for him to be man. But how is this temporality to be described?

Let us first consider the present instant. Merleau-Ponty used Heidegger's term *ek-stase,* which is from a Greek compound term whose literal sense is to "stand out" or to "open out." The present instant of human consciousness is such an *ek-stase.* The present is not a closed unit, an atom with clearly defined borders before and after. The present is rather an opening; it expands into the future (by protention) and maintains the past (by retention). When I listen to a piece of music my consciousness is not divided into minute static units that rapidly follow one another, each being an individual, isolated atom. Rather my consciousness is continually anticipating the imminent turn of melody and continually preserving the phases that have just elapsed. If this were not so I would not be able to experience the tune as a whole. I would be concerned only with each atom of music as it came into my mind and then would expel it as I moved on to the next unit. The conscious present is not like this; it is elastic, expanded into the future and the past.

This *ek-static* way in which man exists is the basis for his freedom. If man were captivated each instant by what is immediately present to him, he would not have the possibility of focusing his consciousness elsewhere. He would not be aware of the mobility of his consciousness or of his power to guide the direction it takes.

This much is true of our experience of the immediate present. If we take a broader view we see that man is also temporal in the sense that even his remote past has a way of being present to him. Things that happened years ago that may have sunk into oblivion are still operative in his present action and thought. Man's consciousness and the meanings he constitutes bear what Husserl called a "sedimented" history. Every man has lived through his own childhood and youth and has gone through experiences that structure him as a man. All these things enter into his consciousness and personality. A material thing like a stone can go through various events over and over and remain exactly the same stone because it does not have the temporality of man. A man is changed by what happens to him. He bears his past within himself because his present consciousness retains what is past. And yet he is never condemned by his past, he never entirely loses the possibility of changing or redeeming his past, because his present is also open upon the future.

The temporal factors that we have described for the individual man also operate on a public scale. We build not only upon our own individual past but also upon the centuries that make up the history of man. Likewise we plan not only our own future but also work for the future of humanity. This dimension is called the historicity of man.

Human temporality is not a passive thing. Man is not just an inert object caught up in a flow of time. He actively creates temporality by bringing the process of timing into the world. It is his consciousness that protends into the future and retains the past; his consciousness is this temporality. If man is totally without consciousness he loses his temporality, and though physiological changes may occur in him he is no longer a historical being. His historicity is achieved only through his living presence—through his *ek-static* way of being in the world.

Man and Emotion

A rationalistic form of philosophy would be inclined to downgrade the place of the emotions in man, seeing them as a barrier to clear thinking and as the intrusion of "lower" bodily elements into the pure realm of reason. Phenomenology, with its sensitivity to the corporeal nature of man and with its concern for the concrete situation as a starting point for philosophical analysis, has a much higher estimation of the role of emotions in the conscious life of man.

The phenomenological concept of intentionality makes it possible to avoid treating emotions as something purely subjective. They are not only subjective states of our psyche but have an objective reference. Man has many forms of intentionality, many ways of being in the world—in work, in social relations, in play, through knowledge, and as a biological entity that strives to keep alive. Each of these intentionalities is surrounded by a host of needs or tendencies, and each of these in turn is cushioned by a pattern of emotion or affectivity, which can be either positive (when the need is satisfied) or negative (when the need is frustrated). Good food brings positive affectivity when it satisfies our tendency of hunger; physical dangers bring the negative affectivity of fear when they threaten to frustrate our tendency to keep ourselves alive. Even the "pure intellect" has its affectivity in the joy of discovering truth and in the irritation of not being able to solve a problem.

As Sartre says, the emotions work a magical transformation of the world. A man whose tendency towards social acceptance and status has been frustrated through a personal catastrophe becomes filled with gloom. His gloom is not only inside himself—by virtue of the intentionality of consciousness it pervades his whole world. Everything is colored by sadness, and the people and things he meets are under this pall. So, too, the world sings for a happy man.

This emotional coloring of the world should not be considered necessarily misleading, false, or as an obstacle to truth. First, it serves to uncover values in the world. Many human values would pass unnoticed and undesired if it were not for the affectivity that draws us to them. Secondly, the emotions act as a spur to make us realize values and ambitions. A young boy who wants "emotionally" to become an aviator and whose world is now colored with the emotive anticipation of such a career will work to make that coloring of the world come about. Thus the emotions produce a certain falseness in the world that is necessary for human achievement; the falseness presents the world as man wants it to be and as man can make it but as different from what it really is. Reason and planning have to work here as well, but the emotional incentive is important both at the beginning of a project, when its need and value have to be discovered, and throughout its fulfillment, when the emotions can serve as a prop to keep the work going during difficult times. Thirdly, the emotions promote the social life of man by keeping him open to the world. They seek the fulfillment of the tendencies they accompany, and such satisfaction cannot be found in the man himself. He must enter into relations with the world and with others. His emotions can keep him from the proud isolation of someone who is a world unto himself.

The emotions become misleading and harmful if they make us blind to reality. Emotions have the tendency to take complete possession both of our world and of our consciousness, and if they go too far they can totally sever us from reality. When this occurs we no longer have the delicate balance of emotion and reason that works so well to promote our being in the world; instead we have the domination of emotion with reason and reality left behind. Then we do live in a narcissistic dream world in which we are incapable of rational evaluation and action. But such deviation is not inherent in the essence of emotion and should not make us overlook the importance that emotion has for our life with others in the world.

Negativity and Freedom

The selection from Sartre's *Being and Nothingness* (1943) is included for two reasons. First, it affords an excellent example of pre-predicative phenomenological analysis. Sartre is concerned to show the origins of negation. Negation as found in judgments ("This is not white," "Peter is not sick," etc.) is not the primary case of negation. Prior to this, on a more primitive, lived scale, there is a pre-predicative experience of negation. Sartre's phenomenological description of looking for his friend Pierre in a café and *not* finding him there is a little masterpiece of style and sensitivity.

Sartre concludes that our consciousness is what brings negativity into the world. Apart from man there would be no negation. Beings without consciousness are simply there. They do not have the expectation that goes beyond what is immediately given and then enables them to say, "This is *not* what I mean." Only human consciousness can break out of being, break out of what is there before it and say "no" to what is there. Without consciousness there would be only the fullness of being. In pre-Socratic philosophy, the atomists claimed that being was a plenum, a dense fullness that was broken up and differentiated only by the void; Sartre's human consciousness works like the atomists' void—it introduces negativity and emptiness into the world.

This takes us to the second reason for selecting this passage. Sartre's concept of man as the source of nothingness is the basis for his existentialist concept of what man is, and at this point we move from the realm of phenomenological description into full existentialism. Man is the source of nothingness, and hence somehow *is* nothingness. He is not simply being, for being is silent and satisfied with what is. Man wants what is not, he wants to create and achieve, and he is the merchant of negation and dissatisfaction. Hence the title *Being and Nothingness* refers to the two domains of reality: objective being and the nothingness that is human consciousness.

Sartre's concept of human freedom is closely linked with the idea of nothingness. Man is free precisely because he is not yet determined as a being. He must create and structure himself by his own choices. If he were already there as a finished substance, there would be nothing left for him to do and there would be no room for freedom. As it is, claims Sartre, he creates himself if he exercises his freedom and is not led along by custom and the crowd, in which case he would degenerate into a mechanical function and no longer be a free man. Sartre's dictum, "Existence precedes essence," summarizes this concept of freedom. Man simply exists at first; he must create his own essence and make himself into what he is.

Sartre's basic reason for atheism is in this concept of freedom. He maintains that if God exists there is a pattern in the divine mind for man to follow—man is determined by God to be in a certain way. Therefore there is no room for freedom; if everything is already fixed for us by a divine intellect and will, we only go through the motions of being free.

By way of criticism, we might say that what Sartre rejects is a rationalistic concept of God as is found in Leibniz or Spinoza, where events are prearranged by a comprehensive divine plan. According to this concept, creation is left to follow the scenario fixed by divine reason. Christian tradition and theology have a less rationalistic concept of the creator and conceive of a God who allows man to share in his own creative process by realizing human values and bringing about fuller dimensions of the human personality. Man also brings newness into the world through scientific progress and economic development, all in conjunction with the creative and providential power of God.

In the passage we have selected Sartre also treats a theme that has been found in existentialists since Kierkegaard: the distinction between fear and anguish. Fear is an emotion experienced in reference to a definite, concrete object: I am afraid of the fierce dog coming towards me. Anguish or dread is more amorphous. It does not have any specific object, but is a state of uneasiness and terror that is not provoked by a threat coming from without but from within. I am in dread of my own nothingness because I know that I may not achieve what I want to do. My nothingness is not only a source of action and success, but it may also be the source of failure and defeat, and I am always aware of this permanent risk that accompanies all that I do. The distinction between fear and anguish is sensitively developed by Sartre, who has a fine though perhaps one-sided awareness of the tragic element in man.

The Nature and Understanding of Persons

Sartre's concept of man is opposed by the personalistic philosophy expressed in our selection from the work of August Brunner. Brunner builds his philosophy around the concept of person as the highest type of being we experience. Far from being a nothingness, the person ontologically exists more intensely than objective impersonal being. He becomes nothingness only if we try to grasp him with methods and analyses derived from the material or biological spheres of existence. When we do this he eludes our grasp and is then "nothing," but the fault is ours for not looking for him in the right way. Brunner gives a thorough treatment of how persons are manifest to us.

The pivot of his analysis is the distinction between *verstehen* (to understand) and *erklären* (to explain), which has been classical in German philosophy since G. W. F. Hegel (1770–1831) and Wilhelm Dilthey (1833–1911). Understanding operates in our knowledge of persons. When we know the network of goals, motives, character traits, and choices that go into a person's activity, then his action is understandable to us. Explanation works in our knowledge of the material world by means of causal laws and by showing the parts out of which a physical whole is made.

To illustrate this distinction: A husband understands the actions of his wife because he has come to know the pattern of motives and goals in which her personality acts. Suppose that at a certain time her actions suddenly become unintelligible to him; she may become very harsh and erratic and no longer be the same person. If some physical illness is the cause of her actions, they can no longer be understood, but must be explained. Her personal motives and goals no longer make her actions intelligible, and her personality does not reveal itself in her actions. Physical and biological causes must now explain them.

Personal understanding can thus be described as the act of putting ourselves in the place of another, of seeing his world and pattern of goals, values, and motives as he has constituted them, and of being able to see *why* he acts in a certain way. This requires a certain liberality and freedom on our part, an ability to step out of our own world and to appreciate that of another. It also requires that the person we are trying to understand be willing to reveal his world to us; in a person's freedom, it is possible for him to refuse disclosure of his personality to certain other people. If this occurs, the others have no way of understanding him as a person, for such personal knowledge must be freely granted. There is no way of forcing it.

Understanding is a very concrete, individual way of knowing a person. We cannot generalize it. We come to know only a few people with deep understanding, and we realize that every person must be understood as an individual, with his own world and pattern of values. Explanation, on the other hand, works in generalities. It universalizes, forming rules that can be applied to all cases without concern for the individuality of the items involved. There are many other ways of articulating the difference between understanding and explanation, and Brunner does so with deep insight into the structure of personal existence and personal knowledge. He shows that knowledge of persons is chronologically the first type of knowing we have; it is only with great difficulty that other forms of knowledge disengage themselves from the categories of thought proper to personal thinking.

This special form of understanding is necessary to know persons because persons exist in a special way. Persons are not simply further links in the causal chains that tie material reality together. They involve a spontaneity and originality that make each one unique and irreducible to the others.

Person and Decision

One of the characteristics of personal existence is found in the first selection we have from the works of Gabriel Marcel. To exist as a person is never a finished process. Personal existence is always a power that is given to us, but we must actualize and fulfill it by our own decision. No one can do this for us because personal existence means precisely assuming values and choices through our own freedom of decision. Thus the structure of our personality becomes formed through the decisions we make. Someone who formulates all his decisions on the basis of financial values gradually becomes an avaricious person, and all his actions become colored by money. Another person who makes choices out of service to others becomes fundamentally structured by generosity.

We are responsible for the structure of our personality because human decisions transcend the moment in which they are made. Man is not just a bundle of ever changing psychological states. When he commits himself to a certain course of action, this decision remains with him in the future. This is why promises make sense. The human person transcends time not only in his knowledge, which can abstract from the here and now, but also in his will, which can determine himself to act even after the present situation has passed. This is part of the historicity of man.

Marcel meditatively analyzes this aspect of human decision in his description of the virtue of fidelity. Even when I no longer feel like visiting my sick friend, I realize that I have promised to see him again and that he needs my company. The bond of fidelity to my own decision, to my own personality as I have structured it by my promise, demands that I carry out what I said I would do.

Freedom is closely tied up with fidelity. Freedom is not best exemplified in the liberty of choice; it is most profound in what we might call the "freedom of perseverance," that is, the willingness to stay with our decision if it was made in truth. This does not entail a proud stubbornness or an unwillingness to change when conditions really demand a new approach. It means the will to persevere in a choice if that choice was made on the basis of true values, even though subsequent conditions and feelings may make the decision very difficult to maintain. The more intense our personal existence, the greater our fidelity to truth will be.

Interpersonal Relationships

Human decisions and the formation of personality are not solitary processes; they require the presence of other persons. An isolated individual cannot exercise personal existence. He needs the tradition that others offer him, the values and intellectual insights that they teach, and the generosity and strength of personality that they exemplify for him. Marcel articulates this social dimension of human existence in terms of family relationships, especially the relationship between father and son. Here we have something that in one way can be considered a very material, worldly reality—the biological process of reproduction that is the basis for the relationship of father and son. But this biological relationship is only the foundation for a whole network of other factors that true human fatherhood implies: education, guidance, nourishment, companionship, and all the acts of mutual generosity that accompany these.

The same occurs in all our manifold relations to others. Living in the world necessarily sets us into many relations with other people; we depend on one another for food, work, entertainment, friendship, education, travel, and even to stay alive and healthy. Like the biological aspect of fatherhood, these relations are objective and material, but they can serve as the basis for higher human contact with others, in which we mutually enrich and deepen our personalities as well as satisfy our needs. It lies within our freedom to make these relations truly human and personal.

Thus, our freedom and our decisions do not operate in a void. They function upon relations and materials that are given to us in the human situation into which we are born. We can assume our relationships and act according to their true nature, or we can rebel against them and create our own standards. Rebellion may be necessary if a given relationship has become falsified by the customs of men and the revolt is geared towards restoring or discovering the true nature of the relation. But to rebel is folly if

570 / EXISTENTIALIST AND PHENOMENOLOGICAL THOUGHT

one tries to do away with relationships that man needs. This is not freedom according to truth, but an arbitrary and false decision. The complex of human relations in which our personal beings develop is an essential factor in the constitution of our personalities, but it entails a pattern of responsibilities we must assume if we are to live in truth.

Summary: Man and Being

The phenomenological philosophy of man that we have presented thus far is chiefly a description of the structure of consciousness and of the human person as an origin of action. Philosophically, we cannot stop with this. Because of the intentionality of consciousness and because human action is ultimately geared toward revealing the truth of things, man is essentially related to being. Martin Heidegger stresses that man is the place where being becomes revealed. Man is the only entity that can question being and inquire into its structure.

Man's experience of his *corporeal space* allows him to exercise mobility and to structure mathematical space, but since it introduces him into the world of physical reality, it also sets the stage where man will discover being. The use of *speech* and *expression* enables man to structure his own experience meaningfully, but it also makes it possible for him to approach being with the wisdom and insight that historical tradition deposits for him in the language he uses. Through speech he can express in a permanent form the discoveries he himself makes about being. *Temporality* is not only the basic structure of human existence and history; it also makes possible the process of inquiry in which man enables being to manifest itself to him.

The *emotions* are modifications of human consciousness, but they also prompt man to discover those aspects of the truth of being that we call values. They help him to discover the goodness of being and persuade him to act in the world in such a way as to bring greater good and truth into reality. Even the *negativity* in man, his restlessness and dissatisfaction, serves the truth of being by making man unhappy with what has already been acquired and anxious to achieve more.

In regard to *personal existence,* it is by respecting the truth of things and of other persons that we come to live more intensely ourselves. The personal *decision* that Marcel speaks of not only serves to structure our own personality in a certain way; it also endows us with the perseverance and strength of will that are necessary if we are to seek out the truth of being. And, finally, *interpersonal relationships* exist not merely for the sake of enjoyable companionship and pleasant friends, but ultimately for the sake of finding and living in truth. The truth of being is not manifest to anyone in pure isolation; it appears to man only in the context of a community, where he finds the language and the tradition that enable him to understand being.

Man carries out his role as "shepherd of being," as Heidegger puts it, by virtue of the structures we have described. Temporality, corporeal space, intersubjectivity, decision, the emotions, and especially speech, which Heidegger calls "the house of being," are all factors that open man to being and allow him to live according to truth. Thus the philosophy of man that we have elaborated is a preface to the examination of being, and philosophical anthropology is the first step in metaphysics.

Glossary

ANGUISH:

Insecurity and terror coming not from fear of any precise object outside one's self but from the realization of one's own nothingness, of one's own inherent possibility of failure and defeat.

CONSTITUTION:

Process by which an object becomes a phenomenon for intentional consciousness. The term also refers to the network of intentional acts that consciousness must carry out in order to allow a given object to appear as phenomenon.

DASEIN:

Heidegger's name for human existence taken as that in which being is called into question.

EK-STASE:

Term applied to the conscious temporal present to indicate that it is not a closed, isolated atomic unit, but that it "opens out" into the future (by "protention") and the past (by "retention"). Man's existence is *ek-static,* i.e., essentially temporal, essentially opened to the future and past in the present instant.

EN SOI:

Term used by Sartre to refer to objective material reality that exists in itself as a brute, impenetrable datum with no awareness of itself. It is opposed to the *pour soi,* consciousness, which exists for itself, that is, with awareness of its own existence.

EPOCHÉ:

For Husserl, this is the first step toward beginning phenomenology. It means specifically suspending judgment about the natural, objective world. This suspension (which is not a sceptical doubt) forces us to turn our attention to the conscious ego. It also helps us to see the whole world as the intentional correlate to consciousness.

EXISTENCE:

Sometimes used technically by existentialist writers to refer to the way man exists, as opposed to the way of being of things. Usually connotes the temporal, *ek-static* being of man, because it can be derived from the same Greek terms.

HORIZON:
Whenever we perceive or know anything, the object we focus attention on must stand out against a surrounding background, which itself is not a focal point of attention. This background is often called "horizon."

INTENTIONALITY:
Structure by which consciousness is never self-enclosed or isolated, but always consciousness *of* something; by virtue of intentionality, consciousness is essentially directed to an object other than itself.

INTERSUBJECTIVITY:
Existence of the ego with others in a community of consciousness.

LIVED WORLD (*Lebenswelt*):
The world that is experienced in an ordinary, prescientific way.

NATURAL ATTITUDE:
For Husserl, the naive, ordinary attitude one has before adopting the phenomenological attitude. The natural attitude asserts the existence and structure of objective reality without considering it as correlative to, and hence to some extent dependent upon, consciousness.

NOTHINGNESS:
Used by Sartre to refer to human consciousness as the source of negativity in the world. Only man, by his unfulfilled intentions and expectations, brings negativity into the world.

PHENOMENA:
Objects considered in their manner of appearing to consciousness.

PHENOMENOLOGY:
Science that describes how objects appear to consciousness, and what consciousness must do to make them appear.

REDUCTION:
Husserl's "transcendental reduction" is the shift in attention that is necessary at the beginning of phenomenology. By it we turn away from the objective world and focus on the sphere of consciousness. We "restrict" or "reduce" our area of attention to the conscious ego and to the world as the correlate of the ego.

TEMPORALITY:
Structure by which consciousness opens upon the future and retains its past. Temporality is the most fundamental structure of consciousness, according to most phenomenologists.

TEMPORALIZATION:
Process by which consciousness constitutes the dimensions of past, present, and future.

UNDERSTANDING (*verstehen*):
Type of knowledge we have of other persons, as opposed to the causal explanations (*erklären*) we give of impersonal things. Involves the comprehension of motives, values, and actions.

WORLD:

Used by phenomenologists to refer to the totality of existents, not really as something that we can ever focus on or know directly but simply as the general background against which all individual entities appear. Being in the world (*In der Welt Sein; être au monde*) is a characteristic of consciousness whereby it necessarily finds itself immersed in a world, directed toward objects, and surrounded by the general horizon of a world. Consciousness cannot know itself except in such a presence in the world.

Edmund Husserl

EDMUND HUSSERL was born in 1859 in Moravia, then part of Austria. He first studied science and mathematics and moved into philosophy via problems he found in treating the origins of arithmetic. He was also influenced to enter philosophy by his teacher Franz Brentano, an important German thinker at the turn of the century. Husserl began to lecture at Halle in 1887, obtained a position at Göttingen in 1901, and moved to Freiburg in 1916, where he remained until his retirement in 1928. He continued to live in that city until his death in 1938. His life and interests were mainly centered on academic and philosophical matters. His personal writings, class lectures, philosophical notebooks and meditations, and the manuscripts he prepared for various occasions, are preserved at the Husserl Archives at Louvain, Belgium, where the edition of his unpublished material and the reedition of some of his published works are carried on. *The Crisis of the European Sciences* was written during the last years of his life and published posthumously in 1954.

Man and His World

48. Anything that is—whatever its meaning and of whatever region—is an index of a subjective system of correlation.[1]

[*The remarks in italics are inserted by the editor to outline the ideas contained in Husserl's text. Husserl begins this section by observing that although men have long realized that things appear different to different persons, no one has ever seen that we can make a scientific study of the correlation between the knowing person and the appearances of things to him.*]

In this exclusive preoccupation with the multiplicities of subjective ways of appearing through which the world is presented to us, we now

---

[1] Any object of consciousness, no matter to what type (region) of reality it may belong, is correlated to (a) a definite pattern of appearances and (b) a definite pattern of subjective, conscious acts that must be performed in order to make the object appear. Husserl says the object is an "index" for such patterns. [R.S.]

From a forthcoming translation of Edmund Husserl, *Die Krisis der europaischen Wissenschäften,* to be published by Northwestern University Press. Reprinted by permission of the publisher.

gradually arrive—even though we have really considered only the world we directly perceive, indeed only physical bodies in that world—at the insight that we are not dealing merely with contingent matters of fact. Rather, no conceivable human being, no matter how different we imagine him to be, could ever experience a world in ways of being given different from the constantly changing relativity we have sketched out: as a world presented to him in the life of his consciousness and in community with other human beings. The fact which is naively accepted as obvious, that each person sees things and the world in general as they appear to him, concealed, as we now realize, a great horizon of remarkable truths whose uniqueness and systematic inter-connection never entered the philosophical purview. The correlation between world (the world of which we always speak) and subjective manners of givenness never evoked philosophical wonder (that is, prior to the first breakthrough of "transcendental phenomenology" in the *Logical Investigations* [2]), in spite of the fact that it had come forward noticeably even in pre-socratic philosophy and among the Sophists—though here only as a theme for sceptical argumentation. This correlation never incited philosophical interest of its own, which could have made it the object of a scientific treatment proper to it. Philosophers were confined by the obviousness of the fact that a thing appears differently to each person.

[*Husserl now states that appearances of things can be scientifically studied by phenomenology. Appearances are not a chaotic mass; they have a structure. Each type of object has its special structure, its own typology, of appearances. Each has its own way of being given to consciousness. We can discover laws governing these structures of appearance.*]

But as soon as we begin to examine carefully the "how" of the appearance of a thing in its actual and possible variation,[3] and to pay consistent attention to the correlation it comprises between *appearance* and *that which appears as such:* and if we consider the variation as a variation of validity [4] for the intentionality of the ego-subjects and their social interrelation, we are forced to recognize a fixed typology with ever-widening ramifications. It applies not only to perceiving, to bodies and to the penetrable depths of immediate sensation, but to any and every being within the spatio-temporal world and to its subjective manners of givenness. In this

---

[2] Husserl often uses the Kantian term "transcendental" phenomenology to name his philosophy, thus distinguishing it from mere psychological analysis of consciousness. On the *Logical Investigations,* see the Introduction to this section. [R.S.]

[3] When we consider the actual patterns of appearances a thing does show, or when we consider the possible patterns it could show. [R.S.]

[4] The term "validity" refers to those objects that are accepted by consciousness as "valid," that is, true, acceptable, verified. Such validity requires more than simple appearance; it requires the stronger appearance of direct evidence. Each type of reality has its own way of "verifying" itself. [R.S.]

correlation with its own manners of givenness, which are by no means merely sensate in character, each being is within a possible experience, and each has its modes of validity and its particular manners of synthesis. Experience, self-evidence, is not an empty generality, but is differentiated according to the species, genera and regional categories of beings and also according to all spatio-temporal characteristics. A being with any concrete or abstract, real or ideal meaning has its manners of self-givenness and, on the side of the ego, its manners of intention in modes of validity; to this belong the manners of the subjective variation of these modes in syntheses of individual-subjective and intersubjective agreement and discrepancy. We also foresee (as even the first trials made clear in a preliminary way) that this confusingly manifold typology of correlations, comprising further differentiations at every turn, is not merely a generally established fact, but rather that the factual announces an essential necessity which, with the proper method, can be translated into essential generalities, into an immense system of novel and highly astounding *a priori* truths.

[*Every object has a whole network of ways in which it can be given to consciousness; consider for example how water appears to us. We can look at it from a distance or from close by; we can touch it, freeze it, swim in it, drink it, vaporize it, measure how fast it flows or falls. All these are various appearances water shows to us; water itself is the unitary object and sense, the "synthesis" that endures throughout all these changing experiences. A full phenomenological analysis of our experience of water would delineate all the conceivable ways it can appear to us; this would be the "ideal generality of actual and possible experiential manners of givenness" Husserl talks about. Every actual experience of water is an actualization of only one of these ways of appearing. But when one way is actualized, the others remain in the background as a horizon, a potential set of other ways in which water can appear.*]

No matter where we turn, every being that is valid for me and every conceivable subject as existing in actuality is thus correlatively—and with essential necessity—an index of its own systematic multiplicities. Each one indicates an ideal generality of actual and possible experiential manners of givenness, each of which is an appearance of this same being; so that every actual, concrete experience brings about, from this total multiplicity, a harmonious development of manners of givenness which, as a continuum, fulfills the experiencing intention. The total multiplicity of manners of givenness, however, is itself a horizon of possibly realizable developments, as opposed to the development in progress; and as such it belongs to each experience, or to the intention which is operative within it. For each subject this intention is the *cogito;* the manners of givenness (understood in the widest sense) constitute its *cogitatum* according to the "what" and the "how"; and the manners of givenness, furthermore, bring to "presentation" the one and the same being which is their unity.[5]

49. Preliminary concept of transcendental consitution as "original formation of meaning." The restricted character of the exemplary analyses carried out so far; an indication of further horizons of interpretation.

[*Husserl now shows that phenomenological analysis must develop many complications. On the part of the knower, it cannot remain with the solitary individual. It must take him as a member of intersubjective society. On the part of the object, it cannot remain with an individual thing. It must look into the other objects that exist in relation to any individual thing, and must ultimately probe into the nature of the whole world as a universal background against which all individual objects appear.*]

We see how far we must take all this when we realize that, while we are dealing with the total intentional accomplishment, having many levels, of the subjectivity in question, it is not that of the isolated subject. We are dealing, rather, with the whole of the intersubjectivity which is brought together in the accomplishment—and here the concepts of "what is," of "manners of givenness," of "syntheses," etc. are repeatedly relativized. Again and again we realize that, beginning with the superficially visible, the manners of appearing belonging to the unifying multiplicities are themselves unities of multiplicities which lie deeper, and which are also constituted through appearances, so that we are led back to an obscure horizon—which, however, can still be opened up through methodical inquiry. All the levels and strata through which the syntheses are interwoven, intentionally overlapping from subject to subject, form a universal unity of synthesis; through it the objective universe comes to be—the world [6] as it is concretely and vividly given (and presented for all possible *praxis* [7]). In this regard we speak of the "intersubjective constitution" of the world, meaning by this the total system of manners of givenness, however hidden, and also of modes of validity for egos; through this constitution, if we systematically uncover it, the world as it is for us becomes understandable as a structure of meaning formed out of elementary intentionalities. The being of these intentionalities themselves is nothing but one meaning-formation operating together with another, "constituting" new meaning through synthesis. And meaning is never anything but meaning in modes of validity, that is, as related to intending ego-subjects which effect validity.

---

[5] In this sentence Husserl speaks of three things: (1) the *cogito* (I think), the consciousness intentionally directed to an object; (2) the *cogitatum* (that which is thought), the appearance presented to consciousness; (3) the "one and same being" that manifests itself in the appearances. [R.S.]

[6] See *World* in the Glossary in this section. [R.S.]

[7] *Praxis*: human action. [R.S.]

[*Thus the ultimate aim, Husserl continues, is to explain our experience of objects (and their appearance to us) by showing the elementary intentions and appearances that constitute them. This is the deepest form of explanation man can achieve, even though it is itself not free of some areas of vagueness and obscurity.*]

Intentionality is a title which stands for the only actual and genuine way of explaining, making comprehensible. To go back to the intentional origins and unities of the formation of meaning is to proceed toward a comprehension which, once achieved (which is of course an ideal case), would leave no meaningful question unanswered. But every serious and genuine move from a "ready-made being" [8] back to its intentional origins gives us, in respect to those strata already uncovered and the clarification of what is accomplished in them, an understanding which, though merely relative, is yet an actual understanding as far as it goes.

QUESTIONS FOR STUDY AND DISCUSSION

1. Explain: Every type of reality has its own form of evidence, its own way of being given to consciousness.
2. In what way is an object a synthesis of appearances?
3. Let us suppose that a certain object appears to us in a certain way. What does it mean to say that other possible ways of appearing remain in the background, as a horizon, during the appearance that actually takes place?
4. How does phenomenology try to "explain" an object?

---

[8] We must start with beings that are accepted naively and unquestioningly as something there before us ("ready-made being") and investigate the acts of conscious intentionality that have allowed it to become an object for us. [R.S.]

Maurice Merleau-Ponty

MAURICE MERLEAU-PONTY was born in 1908. After teaching at French lycées and the University of Lyons, he came to the Sorbonne in 1949. In 1952 he took the chair that was once occupied by Henri Bergson at the Collège de France and thus became the youngest person ever to be appointed professor at that institution. *Phenomenology of Perception,* written in 1945, is his major work. Although philosophy and psychology were his chief fields of study, his writings show the breadth of his interests, which spread to linguistics, art, sociology, and politics. In the latter, he was at first closely allied with Sartre, but during the last few years of his life moved towards a more moderate socialist position. His death in 1961 at the age of fifty-three brought to an end one of the most brilliant and still promising careers in contemporary philosophy.

The Body and Its Space

Let us first of all describe the spatiality of my own body. If my arm is resting on the table I should never think of saying that it is *beside* the ash-tray in the way in which the ash-tray is beside the telephone. The outline of my body is a frontier which ordinary spatial relations do not cross. This is because its parts are inter-related in a peculiar way: they are not spread out side by side, but enveloped in each other. For example, my hand is not a collection of points. In cases of allocheiria,[1] in which the subject feels in his right hand stimuli applied to his left hand, it is impossible to suppose that each of the stimulations changes its spatial value on its own account. The various points on the left hand are transferred to the right as relevant to a total organ, a hand without parts which has been suddenly displaced. Hence they form a system and the space of my hand is not a mosaic of spatial values. Similarly my whole body for me is not an assemblage of organs juxtaposed in space. I am in undivided possession of it and I know

---

[1] A disorder of sensation in which sensations are referred to the wrong part of the body. [C.S.]

Merleau-Ponty often makes use of psychological data to illustrate his ideas. [R.S.]

From pp. 98–106 of Maurice Merleau-Ponty, *Phenomenology of Perception,* translated by Colin Smith. © 1962 by Humanities Press, Inc. Reprinted by permission of Humanities Press, Inc., and Routledge and Kegan Paul Ltd., London.

where each of my limbs is through a *body image* in which all are included. But the notion of body image is ambiguous, as are all notions which make their appearance at turning points in scientific advance. They can be fully developed only through a reform of methods. At first, therefore, they are used only in a sense which falls short of their full sense, and it is their immanent development which bursts the bounds of methods hitherto used. "Body image" was at first understood to mean a *compendium* of our bodily experience, capable of giving a commentary and meaning to the internal impressions and the impression of possessing a body at any moment. It was supposed to register for me the positional changes of the parts of my body for each movement of one of them, the position of each local stimulus in the body as a whole, an account of the movements performed at every instant during a complex gesture, in short a continual translation into visual language of the kinaesthetic and articular impressions of the moment. When the term body image was first used, it was thought that nothing more was being introduced than a convenient name for a great many associations of images, and it was intended merely to convey the fact that these associations were firmly established and constantly ready to come into play. The body image was supposed gradually to show itself through childhood in proportion as the tactile, kinaesthetic and articular contents were associated among themselves or with visual contents, and more easily evoked them. Its physiological representation could then be no more than a focus of images in the classical sense. Yet in the use made of it by psychologists, it is clear that the body image does not fit into this associationist definition. For example, in order that the body image may elucidate allocheiria, it is not enough that each sensation of the left hand should take its place among generic images of all parts of the body acting in association to form around it, as it were, a superimposed *outline* of the body; these associations must be constantly subject to a single law, the spatiality of the body must work downwards from the whole to the parts, the left hand and its position must be implied in a comprehensive bodily *purpose* and it must originate in that purpose, so that it may at one stroke not only be superimposed or brought down on to the right hand, but actually become the right hand. When we try to elucidate the phenomenon of the phantom limb by relating it to the body image of the subject, we add to the accepted explanations, in terms of cerebral tracks and recurrent sensations, only if the body image, instead of being the residue of habitual cenesthesis,[2] becomes the law of its constitution. If a need was felt to introduce this new word, it was in order to make it clear that the spatial and temporal unity, the inter-sensory or the sensori-motor unity of the body is, so to speak, *de jure,* that it is not confined to contents actually and fortuitously associated in the course of our experience, that it is in some way anterior to them and makes their association possi-

---

[2] The experience we have of primitive sensations like bits of color, sounds, and feelings. [R.S.]

ble. We are therefore feeling our way towards a second definition of the body image: it is no longer seen as the straightforward result of associations established during experience, but a total awareness of my posture in the intersensory world, a "form" in the sense used by Gestalt phychology.[3] But already this second definition too is superseded by the analyses of the psychologists. It is inadequate to say that my body is a form, that is to say a phenomenon in which the totality takes precedence over the parts. How is such a phenomenon possible? Because a form, comparable to the mosaic of a physico-chemical body or to that of "cenesthesis," is a new type of existence. The fact that the paralysed limb of the anosognosic [4] no longer counts in the subject's body image, is accounted for by the body image's being neither the mere copy nor even the global awareness of the existing parts of the body, and by its active integration of these latter only in proportion to their value to the organism's projects. Psychologists often say that the body image is *dynamic*. Brought down to a precise sense, this term means that my body appears to me as an attitude directed towards a certain existing or possible task. And indeed its spatiality is not, like that of external objects or like that of "spatial sensations," a *spatiality of position*, but a *spatiality of situation*. If I stand in front of my desk and lean on it with both hands, only my hands are stressed and the whole of my body trails behind them like the tail of a comet. It is not that I am unaware of the whereabouts of my shoulders or back, but these are simply swallowed up in the position of my hands, and my whole posture can be read so to speak in the pressure they exert on the table. If I stand holding my pipe in my closed hand, the position of my hand is not determined discursively by the angle which it makes with my forearm, and my forearm with my upper arm, and my upper arm with my trunk, and my trunk with the ground. I know indubitably where my pipe is, and thereby I know where my hand and my body are, as primitive man in the desert is always able to take his bearings immediately without having to cast his mind back, and add up distances covered and deviations made since setting off. The word "here" applied to my body does not refer to a determinate position in relation to other positions or to external co-ordinates, but the laying down of the first co-ordinates, the anchoring of the active body in an object, the situation of the body in face of its tasks. Bodily space can be distinguished from external space and envelop its parts instead of spreading them out, because it is the darkness needed in the theatre to show up the performance, the background of somnolence or reserve of vague power against which the gesture

---

[3] One of the basic tenets of Gestalt psychology is that human experience is not made up of individual, discrete sensations (such as bits of sound, color, and texture), but that such basic sensations coalesce in human consciousness to form larger patterns or figures (*Gestalt* in German). These larger patterns or forms cannot be reduced to the basic sensations. Merleau-Ponty tries to see whether the experience of the body is such a form. [R.S.]

[4] Anosognosia is a refusal to admit one's own sensory defects, impairment of mobility, or disease. [R.S.]

and its aim stand out, the zone of not being *in front of which* precise beings, figures and points can come to light. In the last analysis, if my body can be a "form" and if there can be, in front of it, important figures against indifferent backgrounds, this occurs in virtue of its being polarized by its tasks, of its *existence towards* them, of its collecting together of itself in its pursuit of its aims; the body image is finally a way of stating that my body is in the world. As far as spatiality is concerned, and this alone interests us at the moment, one's own body is the third term, always tacitly understood, in the figure-background structure.[5] and every figure stands out against the double horizon of external and bodily space. One must therefore reject as an abstraction any analysis of bodily space which takes account only of figures and points, since these can neither be conceived nor be without horizons.

It will perhaps be replied that the figure-background structure or the point-horizon structure themselves presuppose the notion of objective space; that in order to experience a display of dexterity as a figure *against* the massive background of the body, the hand and the rest of the body must be linked by this relationship of objective spatiality, so that the figure-background structure becomes once again one of the contingent contents of the universal form of space. But what meaning could the word "against" have for a subject not placed by his body face to face with the world? It implies the distinction of a top and a bottom, or an "orientated space." When I say that an object is *on* a table, I always mentally put myself either in the table or in the object, and I apply to them a category which theoretically fits the relationship of my body to external objects. Stripped of this anthropological association, the word *on* is indistinguishable from the word "under" or the word "beside." Even if the universal form of space is that without which there would be for us no bodily space, it is not that by which there is one. Even if the form is not the *setting in which,* but the *means whereby* the content is posited, it is not the sufficient means of this act of positing as far as bodily space is concerned, and to this extent the bodily content remains, in relation to it, something opaque, fortuitous and unintelligible. The only solution along this road would be to recognize that the body's spatiality has no meaning of its own to distinguish it from objective spatiality which would do away with the content as a phenomenon and hence with the problem of its relation to form. But can we pretend to discover no distinctive meaning in the words "on," "under," "beside," or in the dimensions of orientated space? Even if analysis discovers in all these relationships the universal relation of externality, the self-evidence of top

---

[5] The "figure-background structure" refers to the fact that we can never focus our consciousness on any figure or shape without having it silhouetted against a background, which itself is not the object of our direct focus. The author claims here that the body is needed as a third factor in order to allow the figure-background structure to appear. In the next lines, Merleau-Ponty talks about the "point-horizon structure" and the same thing is meant; we cannot focus on a given point unless it stands out against a horizon. See *Horizon* in the Glossary in this section. [R.S.]

and bottom, right and left, for the person who has his being in space, prevents us from treating all these distinctions as nonsense and suggests to us that we should look beneath the explicit meaning of definitions for the latent meaning of experiences. The relationships between the two spaces would therefore be as follows: as soon as I try to posit bodily space or bring out its meaning I find nothing in it but intelligible space. But at the same time this intelligible space is not extracted from orientated space, it is merely its explicit expression, and, when separated from that root has no meaning whatsoever. The truth is that homogeneous space can convey the meaning of orientated space only because it is from the latter that it has received that meaning. In so far as the content can be really subsumed under the form and can appear as the content *of* that form, it is because the form is accessible only through the content. Bodily space can really become a fragment of objective space only if within its individuality as bodily space it contains the dialectical ferment to transform it into universal space. This is what we have tried to express by saying that the point-horizon structure is the foundation of space. The horizon or background would not extend beyond the figures or round about it, unless they partook of the same kind of being as it, and unless they could be converted into points by a transference of the gaze. But the point-horizon structure can teach me what a point is only in virtue of the maintenance of a hither zone of corporeality from which to be seen, and round about it indeterminate horizons which are the counterpart of this spectacle. The multiplicity of points or "here's" can in the nature of things be constituted only by a chain of experiences in which on each occasion one and no more of them is presented as an object, and which is itself built up in the heart of this space. And finally, far from my body's being for me no more than a fragment of space, there would be no space at all for me if I had no body.

If bodily space and external space form a practical system, the first being the background against which the object as the goal of our action may stand out or the void in front of which it may *come to light,* it is clearly in action that the spatiality of our body is brought into being, and an analysis of one's own movement should enable us to arrive at a better understanding of it. By considering the body in movement, we can see better how it inhabits space (and, moreover, time) because movement is not limited to submitting passively to space and time, it actively assumes them, it takes them up in their basic significance which is obscured in the commonplaceness of established situations. We should like to analyse closely an example of morbid motility which clearly shows the fundamental relations between the body and space.

A patient whom traditional psychiatry would class among cases of psychic blindness is unable to perform "abstract" movements with his eyes shut; movements, that is, which are not relevant to any actual situation, such as moving arms and legs to order, or bending and straightening a finger. Nor can he describe the position of his body or even his head, or the passive movements of his limbs. Finally, when his head, arm or leg is touched, he cannot identify the point on his body; he cannot distinguish two points of contact on his skin even as much as three inches apart; and he cannot recognize the size or shape of objects placed against his body. He manages the abstract movements only if he is allowed to watch the limb required to perform them, or to go through preparatory movements involving the whole body. The localization of stimuli, and recognition of objects by touch also become possible with the aid of the preparatory movements. Even when his eyes are closed, the patient performs with extraordinary speed and precision the movements needed in living his life, provided that he is in the habit of performing them: he takes his handkerchief from his pocket and blows his nose, takes a match out of a box and lights a lamp. He is employed in the manufacture of wallets and his production rate is equal to three quarters of that of a normal workman. He can even without any preparatory movement, perform these "concrete" movements to order. In the same patient, and also in cerebellar cases, one notices a dissociation of the act of pointing from reactions of taking or grasping: the same subject who is unable to point to order to a part of his body, quickly moves his hand to the point where a mosquito is stinging him. Concrete movements and acts of grasping therefore enjoy a privileged position for which we need to find some explanation.

Let us examine the question more closely. A patient, asked to point to some part of his body, his nose for example, can only manage to do so if he is allowed to take hold of it. If the patient is set the task of interrupting the movement before its completion, or if he is allowed to touch his nose only with a wooden ruler, the action becomes impossible. It must therefore be concluded that "grasping" or "touching," even for the body, is different from "pointing." From the outset the grasping movement is magically at its completion; it can begin only by anticipating its end, since to disallow taking hold is sufficient to inhibit the action. And it has to be admitted that a point on my body can be present to me as one to be taken hold of without being given in this anticipated grasp as a point to be indicated. But how is this possible? If I know where my nose is when it is a question of holding it, how can I not know where it is when it is a matter of pointing to it? It is probably because knowledge of where something is can be understood in a number of ways. Traditional psychology has no concept to cover these varieties of consciousness of place because consciousness of place is always, for such psychology, a positional consciousness, a representation, *Vor-stellung*, because as such it gives us the place as a determination of the objective world and because such a representation either is or is not, but, if it is, yields the object to us quite unambiguously and as an end identifiable through all its appearances. Now here, on the other hand, we have to create the concepts necessary to convey the fact that bodily space may be given to me in an intention to take hold without being given in an intention to know. The patient is conscious of his bodily space as the matrix of his habitual action, but not as an objective setting; his body is at his disposal as a means of ingress into a familiar surrounding, but not as the means of expression of gratuitous and free spatial thought. When ordered to perform a concrete movement, he first of all repeats the order in a questioning tone of voice, then his body assumes the general position required for the task; finally he goes through the movement. It is noticeable that the whole body is involved in it, and that the patient never cuts it down, as a normal subject would, to the strict minimum. To the military salute are added the other external marks of respect. To the right hand pantomime of combing the hair is added, with the left, that of holding a mirror; when the right hand pretends to knock in a nail, the left pretends to hold the nail. The explanation is that the order is taken quite seriously and that the patient manages to perform these concrete movements to order only provided that he places himself mentally in the actual situation to which they correspond. The normal subject, on giving, to order, a military salute, sees in it no more than an experimental situation, and therefore restricts the movement to its most important elements and does not throw himself into it. He is using his body as a means to play acting; he finds it entertaining to pretend to be a soldier; he escapes from reality in the rôle of the soldier just as the actor slips his real body into the "great phantom" of the character to be played. The normal man and the actor do not mistake imaginary situations for reality, but extricate their real bodies from the living situation to make them breathe, speak and, if need be, weep in the realm of imagination. This is what our patient is no longer able to do. In the course of living, he says "I experience the movements as being a result of the situation, of the sequence of events themselves; myself and my movements are, so to speak, merely a link in the whole process and I am scarcely aware of any voluntary initiative . . . It all happens independently of me." In the same way, in order to make a movement to order he places himself "in the affective situation as a whole, and it is from this that the movement flows, as in real life." If his performance is interrupted and he has the experimental situation recalled to him, all his dexterity disappears. Once more kinetic initiative becomes impossible, the patient must first of all "find" his arm, "find," by the preparatory movements, the gesture called for, and the gesture itself loses the melodic character which it presents in ordinary life, and becomes manifestly a collection of partial movements strung laboriously together. I can therefore take my place, through the medium of my body as the potential source of a certain number of familiar actions, in my environment conceived as a set of *manipulanda* [6] and without, moreover, envisaging my body or my surrounding as objects in the Kantian sense, that is, as systems of qualities linked by some intelligible law, as transparent entities, free from any attachment to a specific place or time, and ready to be named or at least pointed out. There is my arm seen as sustaining familiar acts, my

---

[6] *Manipulanda*: things to be handled and used. [R.S.]

body as giving rise to determinate action having a field or scope known to me in advance, there are my surroundings as a collection of possible points upon which this bodily action may operate,—and there is, furthermore, my arm as a mechanism of muscles and bones, as a contrivance for bending and stretching, as an articulated object, the world as a pure spectacle into which I am not absorbed, but which I contemplate and point out. As far as bodily space is concerned, it is clear that there is a knowledge of place which is reducible to a sort of co-existence with that place, and which is not simply nothing, even though it cannot be conveyed in the form of a description or even pointed out without a word being spoken. A patient of the kind discussed above, when stung by a mosquito, does not need to look for the place where he has been stung. He finds it straight away, because for him there is no question of locating it in relation to axes of co-ordinates in objective space, but of reaching with his phenomenal hand a certain painful spot on his phenomenal body,[7] and because between the hand as a scratching potentiality and the place stung as a spot to be scratched a directly experienced relationship is presented in the natural system of one's own body. The whole operation takes place in the domain of the phenomenal; it does not run through the objective world, and only the spectator, who lends his objective representation of the living body to the acting subject, can believe that the sting is perceived, that the hand moves in objective space, and consequently find it odd that the same subject should fail in experiments requiring him to point things out. Similarly the subject, when put in front of his scissors, needle and familiar tasks, does not need to look for his hands or his fingers, because they are not objects to be discovered in objective space: bones, muscles and nerves, but potentialities already mobilized by the perception of scissors or needle, the central end of those "intentional threads" which link him to the objects given. It is never our objective body that we move, but our phenomenal body, and there is no mystery in that, since our body, as the potentiality of this or that part of the world, surges towards objects to be grasped and perceives them.[8] In the same way the patient has no need to look for a theatre of action and a space in which to deploy these concrete movements: the space is given to him in the form of the world at this moment; it is the piece of leather "to be cut up"; it is the lining "to be sewn." The bench, scissors, pieces of leather offer themselves to the subject as poles of action; through

---

[7] The hand or body as it appears in immediate, lived consciousness. [R.S.]

[8] It is not a question of how the soul acts on the objective body, since it is not on the latter that it acts, but on the phenomenal body. So the question has to be reframed, and we must ask why there are two views of me and of my body: my body for me and my body for others, and how these two systems can exist together. It is indeed not enough to say that the objective body belongs to the realm of "for others," and my phenomenal body to that of "for me," and we cannot refuse to pose the problem of their relations, since the "for me" and the "for others" co-exist in one and the same world, as is proved by my perception of an other who immediately brings me back to the condition of an object for him. [M.M.-P.]

their combined values they delimit a certain situation, an open situation moreover, which calls for a certain mode of resolution, a certain kind of work. The body is no more than an element in the system of the subject and his world, and the task to be performed elicits the necessary movements from him by a sort of remote attraction, as the phenomenal forces at work in my visual field elicit from me, without any calculation on my part, the motor reactions which establish the most effective balance between them, or as the conventions of our social group, or our set of listeners, immediately elicit from us the words, attitudes and tone which are fitting. Not that we are trying to conceal our thoughts or to please others, but because we are literally what others think of us and what our world is. In the concrete movement the patient has a positing awareness neither of the stimulus nor of his reaction: quite simply he is his body and his body is the potentiality of a certain world.

. . .

The analysis of bodily space has led us to results which may be generalized. We notice for the first time, with regard to our own body, what is true of all perceived things: that the perception of space and the perception of the thing, the spatiality of the thing and its being as a thing are not two distinct problems. The Cartesian and Kantian tradition already teaches us this; it makes the object's spatial limits its essence; it shows in existence *partes extra partes,* and in spatial distribution, the only possible significance of existence in itself.[9] But it elucidates the perception of the object through the perception of space, whereas the experience of our own body teaches us to realize space as rooted in existence. Intellectualism clearly sees that the "motive of the thing" and "the motive of space"[10] are interwoven, but reduces the former to the latter. Experience discloses beneath objective space, in which the body eventually finds its place, a primitive spatiality of which experience is merely the outer covering and which merges with the body's very being. To be a body, is to be tied to a certain world, as we have seen; our body is not primarily *in* space: it is of it. Anosognosics who describe their arm as "like a snake," long and cold, do not, strictly speaking, fail to recognize its objective outline and, even when the patient looks unsuccessfully for his arm or fastens it in order not to lose it, he *knows* well enough where his arm is, since that is where he looks for it and fastens it. If, however, patients experience their arm's space as something alien, if generally speaking I can feel my body's space as vast or minute despite the evidence of my senses, this is because there exists an

[9] *Partes extra partes:* parts outside of parts, the classical scholastic term used to denote the spatiality of physical objects. Both Kant and Descartes saw the necessary connection between the spatiality and the essence of physical objects. In different ways, both philosophers identify spatial structure with the essence of physical things. They equate the spatial "parts" of a thing with the thing's essence. [R.S.]

[10] Motive is used here in the sense of pattern or structure, much as the term "motif" is used in music. The structure of physical things and the structure of space are intrinsically interwoven. [R.S.]

affective presence and enlargement for which objective spatiality is not a sufficient condition, as anosognosia shows, and indeed not even a necessary condition, as is shown by the phantom arm. Bodily spatiality is the deployment of one's bodily being, the way in which the body comes into being as a body. In trying to analyse it, we were therefore simply anticipating what we have to say about bodily synthesis in general.

We find in the unity of the body the same implicatory structure as we have already described in discussing space. The various parts of my body, its visual, tactile and motor aspects are not simply co-ordinated. If I am sitting at my table and I want to reach the telephone, the movement of my hand towards it, the straightening of the upper part of the body, the tautening of the leg muscles are superimposed on each other. I desire a certain result and the relevant tasks are spontaneously distributed amongst the appropriate segments, the possible combinations being presented in advance as equivalent: I can continue leaning back in my chair provided that I stretch my arm further, or lean forward, or even partly stand up. All these movements are available to us in virtue of their common meaning. That is why, in their first attempts at grasping, children look, not at their hand, but at the object: the various parts of the body are known to us through their functional value only, and their co-ordination is not learnt. Similarly, when I am sitting at my table, I can instantly visualize the parts of my body which are hidden from me. As I contract my foot in my shoe, I can see it. This power belongs to me even with respect to parts of the body which I have never seen. Thus certain patients have the hallucination of their own face *seen from inside*. It has been possible to show that we do not recognize our own hand in a photograph, and that many subjects are even uncertain about identifying their own handwriting among others, and yet that everyone recognizes his own silhouette or his own walk when it is filmed. Thus we do not recognize the appearance of what we have often seen, and on the other hand we immediately recognize the visual representation of what is invisible to us in our own body. In heautoscopy [11] the double which the subject sees in front of him is not always recognized by certain visible details, yet he feels convinced that it is himself, and consequently declares that he sees his double. Each of us sees himself as it were through an inner eye which from a few yards away is looking at us from the head to the knees. Thus the connecting link between the parts of our body and that between our visual and tactile experience are not forged gradually and cumulatively. I do not translate the "data of touch into the language of seeing" or *vice versa*—I do not bring together one by one the parts of my body; this translation and this unification are performed once and for all within me: they are my body itself. Are we then to say that we perceive our body in virtue of its law of construction, as we know in ad-

---

[11] An illness in which the patient perceives his own body as outside himself. He "sees his own double." [R.S.]

vance all the possible facets of a cube in virtue of its geometrical structure? But—to say nothing at this stage about external objects—our own body acquaints us with a species of unity which is not a matter of subsumption under a law. In so far as it stands before me and presents its systematic variations to the observer, the external object lends itself to a cursory mental examination of its elements and it may, at least by way of preliminary approximation, be defined in terms of the law of their variation. But I am not in front of my body, I am in it, or rather I am it. Neither its variations nor their constant can, therefore, be expressly posited. We do not merely behold as spectators the relations between the parts of our body, and the correlations between the visual and tactile body: we are ourselves the unifier of these arms and legs, the person who both sees and touches them. The body is, to use Leibnitz's term, the "effective law" of its changes. If we can still speak of interpretation in relation to the perception of one's own body, we shall have to say that it interprets itself. Here the "visual data" make their appearance only through the sense of touch, tactile data through sight, each localized movement against a background of some inclusive position, each bodily event, whatever the "analyser" which reveals it, against a background of significance in which its remotest repercussions are at least foreshadowed and the possibility of an intersensory parity immediately furnished. What unites "tactile sensations" in the hand and links them to visual perceptions of the same hand, and to perceptions of other bodily areas, is a certain style informing my manual gestures and implying in turn a certain style of finger movements, and contributing, in the last resort, to a certain bodily bearing.[12] The body is to be compared, not to a physical object, but rather to a work of art. In a picture or a piece of music the idea is incommunicable by means other than the display of colors and sounds. Any analysis of Cézanne's work, if I have not seen his pictures, leaves me with a choice between several possible Cézannes, and it is the sight of the pictures which provides me with the only existing Cézanne, and therein the analyses find their full meaning. The same is true of a poem or a novel, although they are made up of words. It is well known that a poem, though it has a superficial meaning translatable into prose, leads, in the reader's mind, a further existence which makes it a poem. Just as the spoken word is significant not only through the medium of individual words, but also through that of accent, intonation, gesture and facial expression, and as these additional meanings no longer reveal the speaker's thoughts but the source of his thoughts and his fundamental manner of being, so poetry, which is perhaps accidentally narrative and in that way informative, is essentially a variety of existence. It is distinguishable from the cry, because the cry makes use of the body as nature gave it to us: poor in expressive means; whereas the poem uses language, and even a particu-

---

[12] The mechanics of the skeleton cannot, even at the scientific level, account for the distinctive positions and movements of my body. [M.M.-P.]

lar language, in such a way that the existential modulation, instead of being dissipated at the very instant of its expression, finds in poetic art a means of making itself eternal. But although it is independent of the gesture which is inseparable from living expression, the poem is not independent of every material aid, and it would be irrecoverably lost if its text were not preserved down to the last detail. Its meaning is not arbitrary and does not dwell in the firmament of ideas: it is locked in the words printed on some perishable page. In that sense, like every work of art, the poem exists as a thing and does not eternally survive as does a truth. As for the novel, although its plot can be summarized and the "thought" of the writer lends itself to abstract expression, this conceptual significance is extracted from a wider one, as the description of a person is extracted from the actual appearance of his face. The novelist's task is not to expound ideas or even analyse characters, but to depict an inter-human event, ripening and bursting it upon us with no ideological commentary, to such an extent that any change in the order of the narrative or in choice of viewpoint would alter the *literary* meaning of the event. A novel, poem, picture or musical work are individuals, that is, beings in which the expression is indistinguishable from the thing expressed, their meaning, accessible only through direct contact, being radiated with no change of their temporal and spatial situation. It is in this sense that our body is comparable to a work of art. It is a focal point of living meanings, not the function of a certain number of mutually variable terms. A certain experience of touch felt in the upper arm signifies a certain feeling in the forearm and shoulder along with a certain appearance of the same arm, not because the various tactile perceptions among themselves, or the tactile and visual ones, are all involved in one intelligible arm, as the different facets of a cube are related to the idea of a cube, but because the arm seen and the arm touched, like the different segments of the arm, together *perform* one and the same action.

Just as we saw earlier that motor habit threw light on the particular nature of bodily space, so here habit in general enables us to understand the general synthesis of one's own body. And, just as the analysis of bodily spatiality foreshadowed that of the unity of one's own body, so we may extend to all habits what we have said about motor ones. In fact every habit is both motor and perceptual, because it lies, as we have said, between explicit perception and actual movement, in the basic function which sets boundaries to our field of vision and our field of action. Learning to find one's way among things with a stick, which we gave a little earlier as an example of motor habit, is equally an example of perceptual habit. Once the stick has become a familiar instrument, the world of feelable things recedes and now begins, not at the outer skin of the hand, but at the end of the stick. One is tempted to say that through the sensations produced by the pressure of the stick on the hand, the blind man builds up the stick along with its various positions, and that the latter then mediate a second order object, the external thing. It would appear in this case that perception is always a reading off from the same sense-data, but constantly accelerated, and operating with ever more attenuated signals. But habit does not *consist* in interpreting the pressures of the stick on the hand as indications of certain positions of the stick, and these as signs of an external object, since it *relieves us of the necessity* of doing so. The pressures on the hand and the stick are no longer given; the stick is no longer an object perceived by the blind man, but an instrument *with* which he perceives. It is a bodily auxiliary, an extension of the bodily synthesis. Correspondingly, the external object is not the flat projection or invariant of a set of perspectives, but something towards which the stick leads us, and the perspectives of which, according to perceptual evidence, are not signs, but aspects. Intellectualism cannot conceive any passage from the perspective to the thing itself, or from sign to significance otherwise than as an interpretation, an apperception, a cognitive intention. According to this view sense-data and perspectives are at each level contents grasped as (*aufgefasst als*) manifestations of one and the same intelligible core. But this analysis distorts both the sign and the meaning; it separates out, by a process of objectification of both, the sense-content, which is already "pregnant" with a meaning, and the invariant core, which is not a law but a thing: it conceals the organic relationship between subject and world, the active transcendence of consciousness, the momentum which carries it into a thing and into a world by means of its organs and instruments. The analysis of motor habit as an extension of existence leads on, then, to an analysis of perceptual habit as the coming into possession of a world. Conversely, every perceptual habit is still a motor habit and here equally the process of grasping a meaning is performed by the body. When a child grows accustomed to distinguishing blue from red, it is observed that the habit cultivated in relation to these two colours helps with the rest. Is it, then, the case that through the pair blue-red the child has perceived the meaning: "colour"? Is the crucial moment of habit-formation in that coming to awareness, that arrival at a "point of view of colour," that intellectual analysis which subsumes the data under one category? But for the child to be able to perceive blue and red under the category of colour, the category must be rooted in the data, otherwise no subsumption could recognize it in them. It is necessary that, on the "blue" and "red" panels presented to him, the particular kind of vibration and impression on the eye known as blue and red should be represented. In the gaze we have at our disposal a natural instrument analogous to the blind man's stick. The gaze gets more or less from things according to the way in which it questions them, ranges over or dwells on them. To learn to see colours is to acquire a certain style of seeing, a new use of one's own body; it is to enrich and recast the body image. Whether a system of motor or perceptual powers, our body is not an object for an "I think," it is a grouping of lived-through meanings which moves towards its equilibrium. Sometimes a new cluster of meanings is formed: our former movements are integrated into a fresh motor entity, the first visual data into a fresh sensory entity, our natural powers suddenly come together in a richer meaning, which hitherto has been merely foreshadowed in our perceptual or practical field, and which has made itself felt in our experience by no more than a certain lack, and which by its coming suddenly reshuffles the elements of our equilibrium and fulfills our blind expectation.

QUESTIONS FOR STUDY AND DISCUSSION

1. When a man learns to walk with a cane, the cane is said to become an "extension" of his body. How does the cane modify his corporeal space?
2. How does the lived space of an experienced airplane pilot differ from that of a watchmaker? How are they the same? Has the activity of these men had any repercussions on their primitive experience of space?
3. Would it be true to say that a musician has an "artistic" dimension in his experience of space that a person who is not a musician lacks?
4. Analyze the experience one would have of an anesthetized arm as an illustration of the difference between lived space and the space of the world. Does the factor of mobility play a role here?
5. How can a project or a task to be done give perspective, meaning, and structure to one's lived experience of space?

Expression and Speech

If speech presupposed thought, if talking were primarily a matter of meeting the object through a cognitive intention or through a representation, we could not understand why thought tends towards expression as towards its completion, why the most familiar thing appears indeterminate as long as we have not recalled its name, why the thinking subject himself is in a kind of ignorance of his thoughts so long as he has not formulated them for himself, or even spoken and written them, as is shown by the example of so many writers who begin a book without knowing exactly what they are going to put into it. A thought limited to existing for itself, independently of the constraints of speech and communication, would no sooner appear than it would sink into the unconscious, which means that it would not exist even for itself. To Kant's celebrated question, we can reply that it is indeed part of the experience of thinking, in the sense that we present our thought to ourselves through internal or external speech. It does indeed move forward with the instant and, as it were, in flashes, but we are then

From pp. 177–90 of Maurice Merleau-Ponty, *Phenomenology of Perception,* translated by Colin Smith. © 1962 by Humanities Press, Inc. Reprinted by permission of Humanities Press, Inc., and Routledge and Kegan Paul Ltd., London.

left to lay hands on it, and it is through expression that we make it our own. The denomination of objects does not follow upon recognition; it is itself recognition. When I fix my eyes on an object in the half-light, and say: "It is a brush," there is not in my mind the concept of a brush, under which I subsume the object, and which moreover is linked by frequent association with the word "brush," but the word bears the meaning, and, by imposing it on the object, I am conscious of reaching that object. As has often been said, for the child the thing is not known until it is named, the name is the essence of the thing and resides in it on the same footing as its colour and its form. For pre-scientific thinking, naming an object is causing it to exist or changing it: God creates beings by naming them and magic operates upon them by speaking of them. These "mistakes" would be unexplainable if speech rested on the concept, for the latter ought always to know itself as distinct from the former, and to know the former as an external accompaniment. If it is pointed out in reply that the child learns to know objects through the designations of language, that thus, given in the first place as linguistic entities, objects receive only secondarily their natural existence, and that finally the actual existence of a linguistic community accounts for childish beliefs, this explanation leaves the problem untouched, since, if the child can know himself as a member of a linguistic community before knowing himself as thinking about some Nature, it is conditional upon the subject's being able to overlook himself as universal thought and apprehend himself as speech, and on the fact that the word, far from being the mere sign of objects and meanings, inhabits things and is the vehicle of meanings. Thus speech, in the speaker, does not translate ready-made thought, but accomplishes it.[1] *A fortiori* must it be recognized that the listener receives thought from speech itself. At first sight, it might appear that speech heard can bring him nothing: it is he who gives to words and sentences their meaning, and the very combination of words and sentences is not an alien import, since it would not be understood if it did not encounter in the listener the ability spontaneously to effect it. Here, as everywhere, it seems at first sight true that consciousness can find in its experience only what it has itself put there. Thus the experience of communication would appear to be an illusion. A consciousness constructs— for *x*—that linguistic mechanism which will provide another consciousness with the chance of having the same thoughts, but nothing really passes between them. Yet, the problem being how, to all appearances, consciousness learns something, the solution cannot consist in saying that it knows everything in advance. The fact is that we have the power to understand over and above what we may have spontaneously thought. People can speak to us only a language which we already understand, each word of a difficult

---

[1] There is, of course, every reason to distinguish between an authentic speech, which formulates for the first time, and second-order expression, speech about speech, which makes up the general run of empirical language. Only the first is identical with thought. [M.M.-P.]

text awakens in us thoughts which were ours beforehand, but these meanings sometimes combine to form new thought which recasts them all, and we are transported to the heart of the matter, we find the source. Here there is nothing comparable to the solution of a problem, where we discover an unknown quantity through its relationship with known ones. For the problem can be solved only if it is determinate, that is, if the cross-checking of the data provides the unknown quantity with one or more definite values. In understanding others, the problem is always indeterminate [2] because only the solution will bring the data retrospectively to light as convergent, only the central theme of a philosophy, once understood, endows the philosopher's writings with the value of adequate signs. There is, then, a taking up of others' thought through speech, a reflection in others, an ability to think *according to others* which enriches our own thoughts. Here the meaning of words must be finally induced by the words themselves, or more exactly, their conceptual meaning must be formed by a kind of deduction from a *gestural meaning,* which is immanent in speech. And as, in a foreign country, I begin to understand the meaning of words through their place in a context of action, and by taking part in a communal life—in the same way an as yet imperfectly understood piece of philosophical writing discloses to me at least a certain "style"—either a Spinozist, criticist or phenomenological one—which is the first draft of its meaning. I begin to understand a philosophy by feeling my way into its existential manner, by reproducing the tone and accent of the philosopher. In fact, every language conveys its own teaching and carries its meaning into the listener's mind. A school of music or painting which is at first not understood, eventually, by its own action, creates its own public, if it really *says* something; that is, it does so by secreting its own meaning. In the case of prose or poetry, the power of the spoken word is less obvious, because we have the illusion of already possessing within ourselves, in the shape of the common property meaning of words, what is required for the understanding of any text whatsover. The obvious fact is, however, that the colours of the palette or the crude sounds of instruments, as presented to us in natural perception, are insufficient to provide the musical sense of music, or the pictorial sense of a painting. But, in fact, it is less the case that the sense of a literary work is provided by the common property meaning of words, than that it contributes to changing that accepted meaning. There is thus, either in the man who listens or reads, or in the one who speaks or writes, a *thought in speech* the existence of which is unsuspected by intellectualism.

To realize this, we must turn back to the phenomenon of speech and reconsider ordinary descriptions which immobilize thought and speech, and

---

[2] Again, what we say here applies only to first-hand speech—that of the child uttering its first word, of the lover revealing his feelings, of the "first man who spoke," or of the writer and philosopher who reawaken primordial experience anterior to all traditions. [M.M.-P.]

make anything other than external relations between them inconceivable. We must recognize first of all that thought, in the speaking subject, is not a representation, that is, that it does not expressly posit objects or relations. The orator does not think before speaking, nor even while speaking; his speech is his thought. In the same way the listener does not form concepts on the basis of signs. The orator's "thought" is empty while he is speaking and, when a text is read to us, provided that it is read with expression, we have no thought marginal to the text itself, for the words fully occupy our mind and exactly fulfil our expectations, and we feel the necessity of the speech. Although we are unable to predict its course, we are possessed by it. The end of the speech or text will be the lifting of a spell. It is at this stage that thoughts on the speech or text will be able to arise. Previously the speech was improvised and the text understood without the intervention of a single thought; the sense was everywhere present, and nowhere posited for its own sake. The speaking subject does not think of the sense of what he is saying, nor does he visualize the words which he is using. To know a word or a language is, as we have said, not to be able to bring into play any pre-established nervous network. But neither is it to retain some "pure recollection" of the word, some faded perception. The Bergsonian dualism of habit-memory and pure recollection [3] does not account for the near-presence of the words I know: they are behind me, like things behind my back, or like the city's horizon round my house, I reckon with them or rely on them, but without having any "verbal image". In so far as they persist within me, it is rather as does the Freudian Imago which is much less the representation of a former perception than a highly specific emotional essence, which is yet generalized, and detached from its empirical origins. What remains to me of the word once learnt is its style as constituted by its formation and sound. What we have said earlier about the "representation of movement" must be repeated concerning the verbal image: I do not need to visualize external space and my own body in order to move one within the other. It is enough that they exist for me, and that they form a certain field of action spread around me. In the same way I do not need to visualize the word in order to know and pronounce it. It is enough that I possess its articulatory and acoustic style as one of the modulations, one of the possible uses of my body. I reach back for the word as my hand reaches towards the part of my body which is being pricked; the word has a certain location in my linguistic world, and is part of my equipment. I have only one means of representing it, which is uttering it, just as the artist has only one means of representing the work on which he is engaged: by doing it. When I imagine Peter absent, I am not aware of contemplating an image

---

[3] Henri Bergson (1859–1941) distinguishes sharply between "habit-memory" (habits that a person acquires and that are a memory of the past when acquired, even though the person is not clearly aware of them as deriving from his past) and "pure recollection" (a clear, conscious attempt to bring the past back to consciousness). Merleau-Ponty claims that our knowledge of words is made up of a combination of both of these. [R.S.]

of Peter numerically distinct from Peter himself. However far away he is, I visualize him in the world, and my power of imagining is nothing but the persistence of my world around me. To say that I imagine Peter is to say that I bring about the pseudo-presence of Peter by putting into operation the "Peter-behavior-pattern." Just as Peter in imagination is only one of the modalities of my being in the world, so the verbal image is only one of the modalities of my phonetic gesticulation, presented with many others in the all-embracing consciousness of my body. This is obviously what Bergson means when he talks about a "motor framework" of recollection, but if pure representations of the past take their place in this framework, it is not clear why they should need it to become actual once more. The part played by the body in memory is comprehensible only if memory is, not only the constituting consciousness of the past, but an effort to reopen time on the basis of the implications contained in the present, and if the body, as our permanent means of "taking up attitudes" and thus constructing pseudo-presents, is the medium of our communication with time as well as with space.[4] The body's function in remembering is that same function of projection which we have aready met in starting to move: the body converts a certain motor essence into vocal form, spreads out the articulatory style of a word into audible phenomena, and arrays the former attitude, which is resumed, into the panorama of the past, projecting an intention to move into actual movement, because the body is a power of natural expression.

These considerations enable us to restore to the act of speaking its true physiognomy. In the first place speech is not the "sign" of thought, if by this we understand a phenomenon which heralds another as smoke betrays fire. Speech and thought would admit of this external relation only if they were both thematically given, whereas in fact they are intervolved, the sense being held within the word, and the word being the external existence of the sense. Nor can we concede, as is commonly done, that speech is a mere means of fixation, nor yet that it is the envelope and clothing of thought. Why should it be easier to recall words or phrases than thoughts, if the al-

---

[4] ". . . when I awoke like this, and my mind struggled in an unsuccessful attempt to discover where I was, everything would be moving around me through the darkness, things, places, years. My body, still too heavy with sleep to move, would make an effort to construe the form which its tiredness took as an orientation of its various members, so as to induce from that where the wall lay and the furniture stood, to piece together and to give a name to the house in which it must be living. Its memory, the composite memory of its ribs, knees, and shoulder-blades offered it a whole series of rooms in which it had at one time or another slept; while the unseen walls kept changing, adapting themselves to the shape of each successive room that it remembered, whirling madly through the darkness. . . . My body, the side upon which I was lying, loyally preserving from the past an impression which my mind should never have forgotten, brought back before my eyes the glimmering flame of the night-light in its bowl of Bohemian glass, shaped like an urn and hung by chains from the ceiling, and the chimney-piece of Sienna marble in my bedroom at Combray, in my great-aunt's house, in those far-distant days which, at the moment of waking, seemed present without being clearly defined." (Proust, *Swann's Way*, I, trans. C. K. Scott Moncrieff, Chatto and Windus, pp. 5–6.) [M.M.-P.]

leged verbal images need to be reconstructed on every occasion? And why should thought seek to duplicate itself or clothe itself in a succession of utterances, if the latter do not carry and contain within themselves their own meaning? Words cannot be "strongholds of thought," nor can thought seek expression, unless words are in themselves a comprehensible text, and unless speech possesses a power of significance entirely its own. The word and speech must somehow cease to be a way of designating things or thoughts, and become the presence of that thought in the phenomenal world, and, moreover, not its clothing but its token, or its body. There must be, as psychologists say, a "linguistic concept" (*Sprachbegriff*) or a word concept (*Wortbegriff*), a "central inner experience, specifically verbal, thanks to which the sound, heard, uttered, read or written, becomes a linguistic fact." Certain patients can read a text, "putting expression into it," without, however, understanding it. This is because the spoken or written words carry a top coating of meaning which sticks to them and which presents the thought as a style, an affective value, a piece of existential mimicry, rather than as a conceptual statement. We find here, beneath the conceptual meaning of the words, an existential meaning which is not only rendered by them, but which inhabits them, and is inseparable from them. The greatest service done by expression is not to commit to writing ideas which might be lost. A writer hardly ever re-reads his own works, and great works leave in us at a first reading all that we shall ever subsequently get out of them. The process of expression, when it is successful, does not merely leave for the reader and the writer himself a kind of reminder, it brings the meaning into existence as a thing at the very heart of the text, it brings it to life in an organism of words, establishing it in the writer or the reader as a new sense organ, opening a new field or a new dimension to our experience. This power of expression is well known in the arts, for example in music. The musical meaning of a sonata is inseparable from the sounds which are its vehicle: before we have heard it no analysis enables us to anticipate it; once the performance is over, we shall, in our intellectual analyses of the music, be unable to do anything but carry ourselves back to the moment of experiencing it. During the performance, the notes are not only the "signs" of the sonata, but it is there through them, it enters into them.[5] In the same way the actress becomes invisible, and it is Phaedra who appears. The meaning swallows up the signs, and Phaedra has so completely taken possession of Berma that her passion as Phaedra appears the apotheosis of ease and naturalness.[6] Aesthetic expression confers on what it expresses an existence in itself, installs it in nature as a thing perceived and accessible to all, or conversely plucks the signs themselves—the person of the actor, or the colours and canvas of the painter—from their empirical existence and bears them off into another world. No one will deny that here the process

---

[5] Proust, *Swann's Way*, II, trans. C. K. Scott Moncrieff, p. 185. [M.M.-P.]
[6] Proust, *The Guermantes Way*, I, pp. 55 and ff. [M.M.-P.]

of expression brings the meaning into being or makes it effective, and does not merely translate it. It is no different, despite what may appear to be the case, with the expression of thoughts in speech. Thought is no "internal" thing, and does not exist independently of the world and of words. What misleads us in this connection, and causes us to believe in a thought which exists for itself prior to expression, is thought already constituted and expressed, which we can silently recall to ourselves, and through which we acquire the illusion of an inner life. But in reality this supposed silence is alive with words, this inner life is an inner language. "Pure" thought reduces itself to a certain void of consciousness to a momentary desire. The new sense-giving intention knows itself only by donning already available meanings, the outcome of previous acts of expression. The available meanings suddenly link up in accordance with an unknown law, and once and for all a fresh cultural entity has taken on an existence. Thought and expression, then, are simultaneously constituted, when our cultural store is put at the service of this unknown law, as our body suddenly lends itself to some new gesture in the formation of habit. The spoken word is a genuine gesture, and it contains its meaning in the same way as the gesture contains its. This is what makes communication possible. In order that I may understand the words of another person, it is clear that his vocabulary and syntax must be "already known" to me. But that does not mean that words do their work by arousing in me "representations" associated with them, and which in aggregate eventually reproduce in me the original "representation" of the speaker. What I communicate with primarily is not "representations" or thought, but a speaking subject, with a certain style of being and with the "world" at which he directs his aim. Just as the sense-giving intention which has set in motion the other person's speech is not an explicit thought, but a certain lack which is asking to be made good, so my taking up of this intention is not a process of thinking on my part, but a synchronizing change of my own existence, a transformation of my being. We live in a world where speech is an *institution*. For all these many commonplace utterances, we possess within ourselves ready-made meanings. They arouse in us only second order thoughts; these in turn are translated into other words which demand from us no real effort of expression and will demand from our hearers no effort of comprehension. Thus language and the understanding of language apparently raise no problems. The linguistic and intersubjective world no longer surprises us, we no longer distinguish it from the world itself, and it is within a world already spoken and speaking that we think. We become unaware of the contingent element in expression and communication, whether it be in the child learning to speak, or in the writer saying and thinking something for the first time, in short, in all who transform a certain kind of silence into speech. It is, however, quite clear that constituted speech, as it operates in daily life, assumes that the decisive step of expression has been taken. Our view of man will remain superficial so long as we fail to go back to that origin, so long as we fail to find, beneath the chatter of words, the primordial silence, and as long as we do not describe the action which breaks this silence. The spoken word is a gesture, and its meaning, a world.

Modern psychology has demonstrated that the spectator does not look within himself into his personal experience for the meaning of the gestures which he is witnessing. Faced with an angry or threatening gesture, I have no need, in order to understand it, to recall the feelings which I myself experienced when I used these gestures on my own account. I am not well able to visualize, in my mind's eye, the outward signs of anger, so that a decisive factor is missing for any association by resemblance or reasoning by analogy, and what is more, I do not see anger or a threatening attitude as a psychic fact hidden behind the gesture, I read anger into it. The gesture *does not make me think* of anger, it is anger itself. However, the meaning of the gesture is not perceived as the colour of the carpet, for example, is perceived. If it were given to me as a thing, it is not clear why my understanding of gestures should for the most part be confined to human ones. I do not "understand" the sexual pantomime of the dog, still less of the cockchafer or the praying mantis. I do not even understand the expression of the emotions in primitive people or in circles too unlike the ones in which I move. If a child happens to witness sexual intercourse, it may understand it although it has no experience of desire and of the bodily attitudes which translate it. The sexual scene will be merely an unfamiliar and disturbing spectacle, without meaning unless the child has reached the stage of sexual maturity at which this behaviour becomes possible for it. It is true that often knowledge of other people lights up the way to self-knowledge: the spectacle outside him reveals to the child the meaning of its own impulses, by providing them with an aim. The example would pass unnoticed if it did not coincide with the inner possibilities of the child. The sense of the gestures is not given, but understood, that is, seized upon by an act on the spectator's part. The whole difficulty is to conceive this act clearly without confusing it with a cognitive operation. The communication or comprehension of gestures comes about through the reciprocity of my intentions and the gestures of others, of my gestures and intentions discernible in the conduct of other people. It is as if the other person's intention inhabited my body and mine his. The gesture which I witness outlines an intentional object. This object is genuinely present and fully comprehended when the powers of my body adjust themselves to it and overlap it. The gesture presents itself to me as a question, bringing certain perceptible bits of the world to my notice, and inviting my concurrence in them. Communication is achieved when my conduct identifies this path with its own. There is mutual confirmation between myself and others. Here we must rehabilitate the experience of others which has been distorted by intellectualist analyses, as we shall have to rehabilitate the perceptual experience of the thing. When I perceive a thing, a fireplace for example, it is not the concordance of its various aspects which leads me to believe in the existence of the fireplace as the flat projection and collective significance of all these perspectives. On the contrary I perceive the thing in its own self-evident completeness and this is what gives me the assurance that, in the course of perceptual experience, I shall be presented with an indefinite set of concordant views. The identity of the thing through perceptual experience is only another aspect of the identity of one's own body throughout exploratory movements; thus they are the same in kind as each other. Like the body image, the fireplace is a system of equivalents not founded on the recognition of some law, but on the experience of a bodily presence. I become involved in things with my body, they co-exist with me as an incarnate subject, and this life among things has nothing in common with the elaboration of scientifically conceived objects. In the same way, I do not understand the gestures of others by some act of intellectual interpretation; communication between consciousnesses is not based on the common meaning of their respective experiences, for it is equally the basis of that meaning. The act by which I lend myself to the spectacle must be recognized as irreducible to anything else. I join it in a kind of blind recognition which precedes the intellectual working out and clarification of the meaning. Successive generations "understand" and perform sexual gestures, such as the caress, before the philosopher makes its intellectual significance clear, which is that we lock within itself a passive body, enwrap it in a pleasurable lethargy, thus imposing temporary respite upon the continual drive which projects it into things and towards others. It is through my body that I understand other people, just as it is through my body that I perceive "things." The meaning of a gesture thus "understood" is not behind it, it is intermingled with the structure of the world outlined by the gesture, and which I take up on my own account. It is arrayed all over the gesture itself—as, in perceptual experience, the significance of the fireplace does not lie beyond the perceptible spectacle, namely the fireplace itself as my eyes and movements discover it in the world.

The linguistic gesture, like all the rest, delineates its own meaning. This idea seems surprising at first, yet one is forced to accept it if one wishes to understand the origin of language, always an insistent problem, although psychologists and linguistics both question its validity in the name of positive knowledge. It seems in the first place impossible to concede to either words or gestures an immanent meaning, because the gesture is limited to showing a certain relationship between man and the perceptible world, because this world is presented to the spectator by natural perception, and because in this way the intentional object is offered to the spectator at the same time as the gesture itself. Verbal "gesticulation," on the other hand, aims at a mental setting which is not given to everybody, and which it is its task to communicate. But here what nature does not provide, cultural background does. Available meanings, in other words former acts of expression, establish between speaking subjects a common world, to which the words being actually uttered in their novelty refer as does the gesture to the perceptible world. And the meaning of speech is nothing other than the way in which it handles this linguistic world or in which it plays modulations on the keyboard of acquired meanings. I seize it in an undivided act which is as short as a cry. It is true that the problem has been merely shifted one stage further back: how did the available meanings themselves come to be constituted? Once language is formed, it is conceivable that speech may have meaning, like the gesture, against the mental background held in common. But do syntactical forms and vocabulary, which are here presupposed, carry their meaning within themselves? One can see what there is in common between the gesture and its meaning, for example in the case of emotional expression and the emotions themselves: the smile, the relaxed face, gaiety of gesture really have in them the rhythm of action, the mode of being in the world which are joy itself. On the other hand, is not the link between the word sign and its meaning quite accidental, a fact demonstrated by the existence of a number of languages? And was not the communication of the elements of language between the "first man to speak" and the second necessarily of an entirely different kind from communication through gesture? This is what is commonly expressed by saying that gesture or emotional pantomime are "natural signs," and the word a "natural convention." But conventions are a late form of relationship between men; they presuppose an earlier means of communication, and language must be put back into this current of intercourse. If we consider only the conceptual and delimiting meaning of words, it is true that the verbal form—with the exception of endings—appears arbitrary. But it would no longer appear so if we took into account the emotional content of the word, which we have called above its "gestural" sense, which is all-important in poetry, for example. It would then be found that the words, vowels and phonemes are so many ways of "singing" the world, and that their function is to represent things not, as the naïve onomatopoeic theory had it, by reason of an objective resemblance, but because they extract, and literally express, their emotional essence. If it were possible, in any vocabulary, to disregard what is attributable to the mechanical laws of phonetics, to the influences of other languages, the rationalization of grammarians, and assimilatory processes, we should probably discover in the original form of each language a somewhat restricted system of expression, but such as would make it not entirely arbitrary, if we designate night by the word "nuit," to use "lumière" for light. The predominance of vowels in one language, or of consonants in another, and constructional and syntactical systems, do not represent so many arbitrary conventions for the expression of one and the same idea, but several ways for the human body to sing the world's praises and in the last resort to live it. Hence the *full* meaning of a language is never translatable into another. We may speak several languages, but one of them always remains the one in which we live. In order completely to assimilate a language, it would be necessary to make the world which it expresses one's own, and one never does belong to two worlds at once.[7] If there is such a thing as universal thought, it is achieved by taking up the effort towards expression and communication in *one* single language, and accepting all its ambiguities, all the suggestions and overtones of meaning of which a linguistic tradition is made up, and which are the exact measure of its power of expression. A conventional algorism—which moreover is meaningful only in relation to language—will never express anything but nature without man. Strictly speaking, therefore, there are no conventional signs, standing as the simple notation of a thought pure and clear in itself, there are only words into which the history of a whole language is compressed, and which effect communication with no absolute guarantee, dogged as they are by incredible linguistic hazards. We think that language is more transparent than music because most of the time we remain within the bounds of constituted language, we provide ourselves with available meanings, and in our definitions we are content, like the dictionary, to explain meanings in terms of each other. The meaning of a sentence appears intelligible throughout, detachable from the sentence and finitely self-subsistent in an intelligible world, because we presuppose as given all those exchanges, owed to the history of the language, which contribute to determining its sense. In music, on the other hand, no vocabulary is presupposed, the meaning appears as linked to the empirical presence of the sounds, and that is why music strikes us as dumb. But in fact, as we have said, the clearness of language stands out from an obscure background, and if we carry our research far enough we shall eventually find that language is equally uncommunicative of anything other than itself, that its meaning is inseparable from it. We need, then, to seek the first attempts at language in the emotional gesticulation whereby man superimposes on the given world the world according to man. There is here nothing resembling the famous naturalistic conceptions which equate the artificial sign with the natural one, and try to reduce language to emotional expression. The artificial sign is not reducible to the natural one, because in man there is no natural sign,

---

[7] "In my case, the effort for these years to live in the dress of Arabs, and to imitate their mental foundation, quitted me of my English self, and let me look at the West and its conventions with new eyes: they destroyed it all for me. At the same time I could not sincerely take on the Arab skin: it was an affectation only. Easily was a man made an infidel, but hardly might he be converted to another faith. I had dropped one form and not taken on the other, and was become like Mohammed's coffin in our legend. . . . Such detachment came at times to a man exhausted by prolonged physical effort and isolation. His body plodded on mechanically, while his reasonable mind left him, and from without looked down critically on him, wondering what that futile lumber did and why. Sometimes these selves would converse in the void; and then madness was very near, as I believe it would be near the man who could see things through the veils at once of two customs, two educations, two environments." (T. E. Lawrence, *The Seven Pillars of Wisdom*, Jonathan Cape, pp. 31–2.) [M.M.-P.]

and in assimilating language to emotional expressions, we leave untouched its specific quality, if it is true that emotion, viewed as a variation of our being in the world, is contingent in relation to the mechanical resources contained in our body, and shows the same power of giving shape to stimuli and situations which is at its most striking at the level of language. It would be legitimate to speak of "natural signs" only if the anatomical organization of our body produced a correspondence between specific gestures and given "states of mind." The fact is that the behaviour associated with anger or love is not the same in a Japanese and an Occidental. Or, to be more precise, the difference of behaviour corresponds to a difference in the emotions themselves. It is not only the gesture which is contingent in relation to the body's organization, it is the manner itself in which we meet the situation and live it. The angry Japanese smiles, the westerner goes red and stamps his foot or else goes pale and hisses his words. It is not enough for two conscious subjects to have the same organs and nervous system for the same emotions to produce in both the same signs. What is important is how they use their bodies, the simultaneous patterning of body and world in emotion. The psycho-physiological equipment leaves a great variety of possibilities open, and there is no more here than in the realm of instinct a human nature finally and immutably given. The use a man is to make of his body is transcendent in relation to that body as a mere biological entity. It is no more natural, and no less conventional, to shout in anger or to kiss in love than to call a table "a table." Feelings and passional conduct are invented like words. Even those which, like paternity, seem to be part and parcel of the human make-up are in reality institutions. It is impossible to superimpose on man a lower layer of behaviour which one chooses to call "natural," followed by a manufactured cultural or spiritual world. Everything is both manufactured and natural in man, as it were, in the sense that there is not a word, not a form of behaviour which does not owe something to purely biological being—and which at the same time does not elude the simplicity of animal life, and cause forms of vital behaviour to deviate from their pre-ordained direction, through a sort of *leakage* and through a genius for ambiguity which might serve to define man. Already the mere presence of a living being transforms the physical world, bringing to view here "food," there a "hiding place," and giving to "stimuli" a sense which they have not hitherto possessed. *A fortiori* does this apply to the presence of a man in the animal world. Behaviour creates meanings which are transcendent in relation to the anatomical apparatus, and yet immanent to the behaviour as such, since it communicates itself and is understood. It is impossible to draw up an inventory of this irrational power which creates meanings and conveys them. Speech is merely one particular case of it.

What is true, however—and justifies the view that we ordinarily take of language, as being in a peculiar category—is that, alone of all expressive processes, speech is able to settle into a sediment and constitute an acquisi-

604 / MAURICE MERLEAU-PONTY

tion for use in human relationships. This fact cannot be explained by pointing out that speech can be recorded on paper, whereas gestures or forms of behaviour are transmitted only by direct imitation. For music too can be written down, and, although there is in music something in the nature of an initiation into the tradition, although, that is, it would probably be impossible to graduate to atonal music without passing through classical music, yet every composer starts his task at the beginning, having a new world to deliver, whereas in the realm of speech, each writer is conscious of taking as his objective the same world as has already been dealt with by other writers. The worlds of Balzac and Stendhal are not like planets without communication with each other, for speech implants the idea of truth in us as the presumptive limit of its effort. It loses sight of itself as a contingent fact, and takes to resting upon itself; this is, as we have seen, what provides us with the ideal of thought without words, whereas the idea of music without sounds is ridiculous. Even if this is pushing the principle beyond its limits and reducing things to the absurd, even if a linguistic meaning can never be delivered of its inherence in some word or other, the fact remains that the expressive process in the case of speech can be indefinitely reiterated, that it is possible to speak about speech whereas it is impossible to paint about painting, and finally that every philosopher has dreamed of a form of discourse which would supersede all others, whereas the painter or the musician does not hope to exhaust all possible painting or music. Thus there is a privileged position accorded to Reason. But if we want to understand it clearly, we must begin by putting thought back among the phenomena of expression.

QUESTIONS FOR STUDY AND DISCUSSION

1. Is it possible to think without the use of our corporeality? What is the "bodily" aspect in the thought of a mathematician who, motionless and with eyes closed, tries to solve a problem?
2. Is there any thinking involved in playing a violin?
3. Can men think more effectively when additional physical means of expression are found, such as oils for painting, refined musical instruments, or computers? Do these items help man think more profoundly?
4. To what degree is it true to say that people who speak different languages experience different worlds?
5. Why should Merleau-Ponty say that a writer hardly ever rereads his own works?

Man as Structured by Time

In so far as, in the preceding pages, we have already met time on our way to subjectivity, this is primarily because all our experiences, inasmuch as they are ours, arrange themselves in terms of before and after, because temporality, in Kantian language, is the form taken by our inner sense, and because it is the most general characteristic of "psychic facts." [1] But in reality, and without prejudging what the analysis of time will disclose, we have already discovered, between time and subjectivity, a much more intimate relationship. We have just seen that the subject, who cannot be a series of psychic events, nevertheless cannot be eternal either. It remains for him to be temporal not by reason of some vagary of the human make-up, but by virtue of an inner necessity. We are called upon to conceive the subject and time as communicating from within. We can now say of temporality what we said earlier about sexuality and spatiality, for example: existence can have no external or contingent attribute. It cannot be anything—spatial, sexual, temporal—without being so in its entirety, without taking up and carrying forward its "attributes" and making them into so many dimensions of its being, with the result that an analysis of any one of them that is at all searching really touches upon subjectivity itself. There are no principal and subordinate problems: all problems are concentric. To analyse time is not to follow out the consequences of a pre-established conception of subjectivity, it is to gain access, through time, to its concrete structure. If we succeed in understanding the subject, it will not be in its pure form, but by seeking it at the intersection of its dimensions. We need, therefore, to consider time in itself, and it is by following through its internal dialectic that we shall be led to revise our idea of the subject.

We say that time passes or flows by. We speak of the course of time. The water that I see rolling by was made ready a few days ago in the mountains, with the melting of the glacier; it is now in front of me and makes its way towards the sea into which it will finally discharge itself. If time is similar to a river, it flows from the past towards the present and the future. The present is the consequence of the past, and the future of the present. But this often repeated metaphor is in reality extremely confused. For, *looking at the things themselves,* the melting of the snows and what

---

[1] Merleau-Ponty is very much influenced by Husserl's *Phenomenology of Internal Time-Consciousness.* [R.S.]

From pp. 410–28 of Maurice Merleau-Ponty, *Phenomenology of Perception,* translated by Colin Smith. © 1962 by Humanities Press, Inc. Reprinted by permission of Humanities Press, Inc., and Routledge and Kegan Paul Ltd., London.

results from this are not successive events, or rather the very notion of event has no place in the objective world. When I say that the day before yesterday the glacier produced the water which is passing at this moment, I am tacitly assuming the existence of a witness tied to a certain spot in the world, and I am comparing his successive views: he was there when the snows melted and followed the water down, or else, from the edge of the river and having waited two days, he sees the pieces of wood that he threw into the water at its source. The "events" are shapes cut out by a finite observer from the spatio-temporal totality of the objective world. But on the other hand, if I consider the world itself, there is simply one indivisible and changeless being in it. Change presupposes a certain position which I take up and from which I see things in procession before me: there are no events without someone to whom they happen and whose finite perspective is the basis of their individuality. Time presupposes a view of time. It is, therefore, not like a river, not a flowing substance. The fact that the metaphor based on this comparison has persisted from the time of Heraclitus to our own day is explained by our surreptitiously putting into the river a witness of its course. We do this already when we say that the stream discharges *itself,* for this amounts to conceiving, where there is merely a thing entirely external to itself, an individuality or interior of the stream which manifests itself outside. Now, no sooner have I introduced an observer, whether he follows the river or whether he stands on the bank and observes its flow, than temporal relationships are reversed. In the latter case, the volume of water already carried by is not moving towards the future, but sinking into the past; what is to come is on the side of the source, for time does not come from the past. It is not the past that pushes the present, nor the present that pushes the future, into being; the future is not prepared behind the observer, it is a brooding presence moving to meet him, like a storm on the horizon. If the observer sits in a boat and is carried by the current, we may say that he is moving downstream towards his future, but the future lies in the new landscapes which await him at the estuary, and the course of time is no longer the stream itself: it is the landscape as it rolls by for the moving observer. Time is, therefore, not a real process, not an actual succession that I am content to record. It arises from *my* relation to things. Within things themselves, the future and the past are in a kind of eternal state of pre-existence and survival; the water which will flow by tomorrow *is* at this moment at its source, the water which has just passed *is* now a little further downstream in the valley. What is past or future for me is present in the world. It is often said that, within things themselves, the future is not yet, the past is no longer, while the present, strictly speaking, is infinitesimal, so that time collapses. That is why Leibniz was able to define the objective world as *mens momentanea,*[2] and why Saint Augustine, in

---

[2] *Mens momentanea:* an instantaneous state of the mind. Leibniz is guilty, according to Merleau-Ponty, of an "atomistic" concept of time. Each instant, and the state of

order to constitute time, required, besides the presence of the present, a presence of the past and of the future. But let us be clear about what they mean. If the objective world is incapable of sustaining time, it is not because it is in some way too narrow, and that we need to add to it a bit of past and a bit of future. Past and future exist only too unmistakably in the world, they exist in the present, and what being itself lacks in order to be of the temporal order, is the not-being of elsewhere, formerly and tomorrow. The objective world is too much of plenum for there to be time. Past and future withdraw of their own accord from being and move over into subjectivity in search, not of some real support, but, on the contrary, of a possibility of not-being which accords with their nature. If we separate the objective world from the finite perspectives which open upon it, and posit it in itself, we find everywhere in it only so many instances of "now." These instances of "now," moreover, not being present to anybody, have no temporal character and could not occur in sequence. The definition of time which is implicit in the comparisons undertaken by common sense, and which might be formulated as "a succession of instances of *now*" has not even the disadvantage of treating past and future as presents: it is inconsistent, since it destroys the very notion of "now," and that of succession.

We should, then, gain nothing by transferring into ourselves the time that belongs to things, if we repeated "in consciousness" the mistake of defining it as a succession of instances of now. Yet this is what psychologists do when they try to "explain" consciousness of the past in terms of memories, and consciousness of the future in terms of the projection of these memories ahead of us. The refutation of "physiological theories" of memory, in Bergson for example, is undertaken in the domain of causal explanation; it consists in showing that paths in the brain and other bodily expedients are not adequate causes of the phenomena of memory; that, for example, nothing can be found in the body to account for the order of disappearance of memories in cases of progressive aphasia.[3] The discussion conducted on these lines certainly discredits the idea of a bodily storage of the past: the body is no longer a receptacle of engrams,[4] but an organ of mimicry with the function of ensuring the intuitive realization of the "intentions" of consciousness. But these intentions cling on to memories preserved "in the unconscious," and the presence of the past in consciousness remains a simple factual presence; it has passed unnoticed that our best reason for rejecting the physiological preservation of the past is equally a reason for rejecting its "psychological preservation," and that reason is that no preservation, no physiological or psychic "trace" of the past can make consciousness of the past understandable. This table bears traces of

the world at each instant, is conceived as a clearly determined, atomic unit. Each instant would lack the "flow" that Merleau-Ponty says should characterize time. [R.S.]

[3] A psychic disorder involving loss or impairment of the ability to use written or spoken language. [R.S.]

[4] The trace left psychologically upon the memory by a stimulus or experience. [R.S.]

my past life, for I have carved my initials on it and spilt ink on it. But these traces in themselves do not refer to the past: they are present; and, in so far as I find in them signs of some "previous" event, it is because I derive my sense of the past from elsewhere, because I carry this particular signifi- cance with myself. If my brain stores up traces of the bodily process which accompanied one of my perceptions, and if the appropriate nervous influx passes once more through these already fretted channels, my percep- tion will reappear, but it will be a fresh perception, weakened and unreal perhaps, but in no case will this perception, which is present, be capable of pointing to a past event, unless I have some other view of my past which enables me to recognize it as memory, which runs counter to the hypothe- sis. If we now go on to substitute "psychic traces" for physiological ones, and if our perceptions are preserved in an unconscious, the difficulty will be the same as before: a preserved perception is a perception, it continues to exist, it persists in the present, and it does not open behind us that dimen- sion of escape and absence that we call the past. A preserved fragment of the lived-through past can be at the most no more than an occasion for thinking of the past, but it is not the past which is compelling recognition; recognition, when we try to derive it from any content whatever, always precedes itself. Reproduction presupposes re-cognition, and cannot be un- derstood as such unless I have in the first place a sort of direct contact with the past in its own domain. Nor can one, *a fortiori,* construct the future out of contents of consciousness: no actual content can be taken, even equivo- cally, as evidence concerning the future, since the future has not even been in existence and cannot, like the past, set its mark upon us. The only con- ceivable way, therefore, of explaining the relation of future to present is by putting it on the same footing as that between present and past. When I consider the long procession of my past states, I see that my present is al- ways passing, and I can anticipate this passage, treat my immediate past as a remote one, and my actual present as past: ahead of it is then a vacuum, and this is the future. Looking ahead would seem in reality to be retro- spection, and the future a projection of the past. But even if, *per impossible,* I could construct consciousness of the past with transferred presents, they certainly could not open a future for me. Even if, in fact, we form an idea of the future with the help of what we have seen, the fact remains that, in order to pro-ject it ahead of us, we need in the first place a sense of the future. If prospection is retrospection, it is in any case an anticipatory retro- spection, and how could one anticipate if one had no sense of the future? It is said that we guess "by analogy" that this inimitable present will, like all the others, pass away. But for there to be an analogy between presents that have elapsed and the actual present, the latter must be given not only as present, it must already announce itself as what will soon be past, we must feel the pressure upon it of a future intent on dispossessing it; in short the course of time must be primarily not only the passing of present to past, but also that of the future to the present. If it can be said that all prospection is anticipatory retrospection, it can equally well be said that all retrospection is prospection in reverse: I know that I was in Corsica before the war, because I know that the war was on the horizon of my trip there. The past and the future cannot be mere concepts abstracted by us from our perceptions and recollections, mere denominations for the actual series of "psychic facts." Time is thought of by us before its parts, and temporal relations make possible the events in time. Correspondingly it is necessary for the subject not to be himself situated in it, in order to be able to be present in intention to the past as to the future. Let us no longer say that time is a "datum of consciousness"; let us be more precise and say that consciousness unfolds or constitutes time. Through the ideal nature of time, it ceases to be imprisoned in the present.

But does it enjoy an opening on to a past and a future? It is no longer beset by the present and by "contents," it travels freely from a past and a future which are not far removed from it, since it constitutes them as past and future, and since they are its immanent objects, to a present which is not near to it, since it is present only in virtue of the relations which consciousness establishes between past, present and future. But then has not a consciousness thus freed lost all notion of what future, past and even present can possibly be? Is not the time that it constitutes similar in every detail to the real time the impossibility of which we have demonstrated; is it not a series of instances of "now," which are presented to nobody, since nobody is involved in them? Are we not always just as far away from understanding what the future, the past and the present, and the passage between them, can possibly be? Time as the immanent object of a consciousness is time brought down to one uniform level, in other words it is no longer time at all. There can be time only if it is not completely deployed, only provided that past, present and future do not all three have their being in the same sense. It is of the essence of time to be in process of self-production, and not to be; never, that is, to be completely constituted. Constituted time, the series of possible relations in terms of before and after, is not time itself, but the ultimate recording of time, the result of its *passage,* which objective thinking always presupposes yet never manages to fasten on to. It is spatial, since its moments co-exist spread out before thought [5]; it is a present, because consciousness is contemporary with all times. It is a setting distinct from me and unchanging, in which nothing either elapses or

---

[5] In order to arrive at authentic time, it is neither necessary nor sufficient to condemn the spatialization of time as does Bergson. It is not necessary, since time is exclusive of space only if we consider space as objectified in advance, and ignore that primordial spatiality which we have tried to describe, and which is the abstract form of our presence in the world. It is not sufficient since, even when the systematic translation of time into spatial terms has been duly stigmatized, we may still fall very short of an authentic intuition of time. This is what happened to Bergson. When he says that duration "snowballs upon itself," and when he postulates memories in themselves accumulating in the unconscious, he makes time out of a preserved present, and evolution out what is evolved. [M.M.-P.]

happens. There must be another true time, in which I learn the nature of flux and transience itself. It is indeed true that I should be incapable of perceiving any point in time without a before and an after, and that, in order to be aware of the relationship between the three terms, I must not be absorbed into any one of them: that time, in short, needs a synthesis. But it is equally true that this synthesis must always be undertaken afresh, and that any supposition that it can be anywhere brought to completion involves the negation of time. It is indeed the dream of philosophers to be able to conceive an "eternity of life," lying beyond permanence and change, in which time's productivity is pre-eminently contained, and yet a thetic consciousness *of* time which stands above it and embraces it merely destroys the phenomenon of time. If we are in fact destined to make contact with a sort of eternity, it will be at the core of our experience of time, and not in some non-temporal subject whose function it is to conceive and posit it. The problem is how to make time explicit as it comes into being and makes itself evident, having the *notion* of time at all times underlying it, and being, not an object of our knowledge, but a dimension of our being.

It is in my "field of presence" in the widest sense—this moment that I am spending working along with, behind it, the horizon of the day that has elapsed, and, in front of it, the evening and night—that I make contact with time, and learn to know its course. The remote past has also its temporal order, and its position in time in relation to my present, but it has these in so far as it has been present itself, that it has been "in its time" traversed by my life, and carried forward to this moment. When I call up a remote past, I reopen time, and carry myself back to a moment in which it still had before it a future horizon now closed, and a horizon of the immediate past which is today remote. Everything, therefore, causes me to revert to the field of presence as the primary experience in which time and its dimensions make their appearance unalloyed, with no intervening distance and with absolute self-evidence. It is here that we see a future sliding into the present and on into the past. Nor are these three dimensions given to us through discrete acts: I do not form a mental picture of my day, it weighs upon me with all its weight, it is still there, and though I may not recall any detail of it, I have the impending power to do so, I still "have it in hand." In the same way, I do not think of the evening to come and its consequences, and yet it "is there," like the back of a house of which I can see only the façade, or like the background beneath a figure. Our future is not made up exclusively of guesswork and daydreams. Ahead of what I can see and perceive, there is, it is true, nothing more actually visible, but my world is carried forward by lines of intentionality which trace out in advance at least the style of what is to come (although we always wait, perhaps to the day of our death, for the appearance of *something else*). The present itself, in the narrow sense, is not posited. The paper, my fountain-pen, are indeed there for me, but I do not explicitly perceive them. I do not so much perceive objects as reckon with an environment; I seek support in my tools, and am at my task rather than confronting it. Husserl uses the terms protentions and retentions for the intentionalities which anchor me to an environment. [6] They do not run from a central *I*, but from my perceptual field itself, so to speak, which draws along in its wake its own horizon of retentions, and bites into the future with its protentions. I do not pass through a series of instances of now, the images of which I preserve and which, placed end to end, make a line. With the arrival of every moment, its predecessor undergoes a change: I still have it in hand and it is still there, but already it is sinking away below the level of presents; in order to retain it, I need to reach through a thin layer of time. It is still the preceding moment, and I have the power to recapture it as it was just now; I am not cut off from it, but it would not belong to the past unless something had altered. It is beginning to be outlined against, or projected upon, my present, whereas it *was* my present a moment ago. When a third moment arrives, the second undergoes a new modification; from being a retention it becomes the retention of a retention, and the layer of time between it and me thickens. One can, as Husserl does, represent this phenomenon diagrammatically. In order to make it complete, the symmetrical perspective of protentions would have to be added. Time is not a line, but a network of intentionalities. [7]

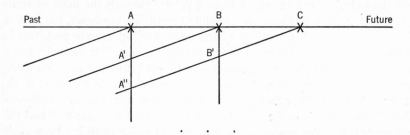

[6] In Husserl's terminology, protention is the opening of consciousness upon the future; it is the immediate, lived anticipation consciousness has of the future. Retention is the opening upon the past; the lived, immediate awareness we have of what has just occurred and elapsed from the present awareness. See *Ek-stase* in the Glossary in this section. [R.S.]

[7] Merleau-Ponty adapts this diagram from Husserl's *Phenomenology of Internal Time-Consciousness,* trans. by J. S. Churchill and with Introd. by C. O. Schrag (Bloomington, Ind.: Indiana University Press, 1964), p. 49. As it stands here, the meaning would be as follows: the present moment is not closed and atomic but opens out to future and past. The diagram is supposed to illustrate this. Consider the point C as the present moment moving toward the future (toward the right side of the diagram). At this moment, consciousness also includes retention of the past moments A and B. But it includes them as modified, as "just past" or "just elapsed," with A being experienced as prior to B. This is shown by the diagonal line C—B'—A". The present moment C opens out along the direction of this diagonal line; it holds past moments in retention.

Thus the horizontal line represents successive "present moments." The vertical lines represent successive modifications undergone by a given moment as it sinks into

It will doubtless be maintained that this description and this diagram do not bring us one step nearer to a solution. When we pass from A to B, and then on to C, A is projected or outlined as A′ and then as A″. For A′ to be recognized as a retention or *Abschattung* of A, and A″ of A′, and even for the transformation of A into A′ to be experienced as such, is there not needed an identifying synthesis linking A, A′, A″ and all other possible *Abschattungen,* and does this not amount to making A into an ideal unity as Kant requires? And yet we know that with this intellectual synthesis there will cease to be any time at all. A and all previous moments of time will indeed be identifiable by me, and I shall be in a way rescued from time which runs them into one another and blurs their identity. But at the same time I shall have lost all sense of before and after which is provided by this flux, and nothing will any longer serve to distinguish the temporal sequence from spatial multiplicity. Husserl introduced the notion of retention, and held that I still have the immediate past in hand, precisely for the purpose of conveying that I do not posit the past, or construct it from an *Abschattung* really distinct from it and by means of an express act; but that I reach it in its recent, yet already elapsed, thisness. What is given to me is not in the first place A′, A″, or A‴, nor do I go back from these "outlines" to their original A, as one goes back from the sign to its significance. What is given to me is A transparently visible through A′, then the two through A″, and so on, as I see a pebble through the mass of water which moves over it. There are certainly identifying syntheses, but only in the express memory and voluntary recollection of the remote past, that is, in those modes derived from consciousness of the past. For example, I may be uncertain about the date of a memory: I have before me a certain scene, let us suppose, and I do not know to what point of time to assign it, the memory has lost its anchorage, and I may then arrive at an intellectual identification based on the causal order of events, for example, I had this suit made before the armistice, since no more English cloth has been available since then. But in this case it is not the past itself that I reach. On the contrary, for when I rediscover the concrete origin of the memory, it is because it falls naturally into a certain current of fear and hope running from Munich to the outbreak of war; it is, therefore, because I recapture time that is lost; because, from the moment in question to my present, the chain of retentions and the overlapping horizons coming one after the other ensure an unbroken continuity. The objective landmarks in relation to which

_____

the past. The diagonal lines represent the way such modified past moments are retained in subsequent present moments.

The German term *"Abschattungen,"* which occurs in the next few lines, literally means shades or silhouettes. Here it is used in a special way to denote the various modifications a given instant undergoes. It refers to the various aspects or appearances a given instant can present to consciousness. More generally, *Abschattungen* refers to the pattern of appearances in which a given object is manifest to consciousness. [R.S.]

I assign a place to my recollection in the mediatory identification, and the intellectual synthesis generally, have themselves a temporal significance only because gradually, step by step, the synthesis of apprehension links me to my whole actual past. There can, therefore, be no question of assimilating the latter to the former. The fact that the *Abschattungen* A' and A'' appear to me as *Abschattungen* of A, is not to be explained by the fact that they all participate in an ideal unity A, which is their common ground. It is because through them I obtain the point A itself, in its unchallengeable individuality, which is for ever established by its passage into the present, and because I see springing from it the *Abschattungen* A', A'' . . . In Husserl's language, beneath the "intentionality of the act," which is the thetic consciousness of an object,[8] and which, in intellectual memory for example, converts "this" into an idea, we must recognize an "operative" intentionality (*fungierende Intentionalität*) which makes the former possible, and which is what Heidegger terms transcendence. My present outruns itself in the direction of an immediate future and an immediate past and impinges upon them where they actually are, namely in the past and in the future themselves. If the past were available to us only in the form of express recollections, we should be continually tempted to recall it in order to verify its existence, and thus resemble the patient mentioned by Scheler, who was constantly turning round in order to reassure himself that things were really there—whereas in fact we feel it behind us as an incontestable acquisition. In order to have a past or a future we do not have to bring together, by means of an intellectual act, a series of *Abschattungen,* for they possess a natural and primordial unity, and what is announced through them is the past of the future itself. Such is the paradox of what might be termed, with Husserl, the "passive synthesis" of time—and of a term which is clearly not a solution, but merely a pointer to the problem.

Light begins to be shed on the problem if we remember that our diagram represents an instantaneous cross-section of time. What there really is, is not a past, present and future, not discrete instants A, B and C, nor really distinct *Abschattungen* A', A'', B', nor finally a host of retentions on the one hand and protentions on the other. The upsurge of a fresh present does not *cause* a heaping up of the past and a tremor of the future; the fresh present *is* the passage of future to present, and of former present to past, and when time begins to move, it moves throughout its whole length. The "instants" A, B and C are not successively *in being,* but *differentiate* themselves from each other, and correspondingly A passes into A' and thence into A''. In short, the system of retentions collects into itself at each instant what was, an instant earlier, the system of protentions. There is, then, not a multiplicity of linked phenomena, but one single phenomenon of lapse. Time is the one single movement appropriate to itself in all its

[8] An awareness that is clearly and explicitly focused on the object in question. We must also have an operative consciousness, which is an implicit temporal awareness at the base of our clear, explicit consciousness. [R.S.]

parts, as a gesture includes all the muscular contractions necessary for its execution. When we pass from B to C, there is, as it were, a bursting, or a disintegration of B into B′, of A′ into A″, and C itself which, while it was on the way, announced its coming by a continuous emission of *Abschattungen,* has no sooner come into existence than it already begins to lose its substance. "Time is the means offered to all that is destined to be, to come into existence in order that it may no longer be." It is nothing but a general flight out of itself, the one law governing its centrifugal movements, or again, as Heidegger says, an *ek-stase.* While B becomes C, it becomes also B′; and simultaneously A which, while becoming B, had also become A′, lapses into A″. A, A′ and A″ on the one hand, and B and B′ on the other, are bound together, not by any identifying synthesis, which would fix them at a point in time, but by a transitional synthesis (*Übergangssynthesis*), in so far as they issue one from the other, and each of these projections is merely one aspect of the total bursting forth or dehiscence. Hence time, in our primordial experience of it, is not for us a system of objective positions, through which we pass, but a mobile setting which moves away from us, like the landscape seen through a railway carriage window. Yet we do not really believe that the landscape is moving; the gate-keeper at the level crossing is whisked by, but the hill over there scarcely moves at all, and in the same way, though the opening of my day is already receding, the beginning of my week is a fixed point; an objective time is taking shape on the horizon, and should therefore show up in my immediate past. How is this possible? How is it that the temporal *ek-stase* is not an absolute disintegration in which the individuality of the moments disappears? It is because the disintegration undoes what the passage from future to present had achieved: C is the culmination of a long concentration which has brought it to maturity; as it was being built up, it made its approach known by progressively fewer *Abschattungen,* for it was approaching *bodily.* When it came into the present it brought with it its genesis, of which it was merely the ultimate expression, and the impending presence of what was to come after it. So that, when the latter comes into being and pushes C into the past, C is not suddenly bereft of its being; its disintegration is for ever the inverse or the consequence of its coming to maturity. In short, since in time being and passing are synonymous, by becoming the past, the event does not cease to be. The origin of objective time, with its fixed positions lying beneath our gaze, is not to be sought in any eternal synthesis, but in the mutual harmonizing and overlapping of past and future through the present, and in the very passing of time. Time maintains what it has caused to be, at the very time it expels it from being, because the new being was announced by its predecessor as destined to be, and because, for the latter, to become present was the same thing as being destined to pass away. "Temporalization is not a succession (*Nacheinander*) of ecstases. The future is not posterior to the past, or the past anterior to the present. Temporality temporalizes itself as future-which-lapses-into-the past-by-coming-into-the-present." [9] Bergson was wrong in *explaining* the unity of time in terms of its continuity, since that amounts to confusing past, present and future on the excuse that we pass from one to the other by imperceptible transitions; in short, it amounts to denying time altogether. But he was right to stick to the continuity of time as an essential phenomenon. It is simply a matter of elucidating this. Instant C and instant D, however near they are together, are not indistinguishable, for if they were there would be no time; what happens is that they run into each other and C becomes D because C has never heen anything but the anticipation of D as present, and of its own lapse into the past. This amounts to saying that each present reasserts the presence of the whole past which it supplants, and anticipates that of all that is to come, and that by definition the present is not shut up within itself, but transcends itself towards a future and a past. What there is, is not a present, then another present which takes its place in being, and not even a present with its vistas of past and future followed by another present in which those vistas are disrupted, so that one and the same spectator is needed to effect the synthesis of successive perspectives: there is one single time which is self-confirmatory, which can bring nothing into existence unless it has already laid that thing's foundations as present and eventual past, and which establishes itself at a stroke.

The past, therefore, *is* not past, nor the future future. It exists only when a subjectivity is there to disrupt the plenitude of being in itself, to adumbrate a perspective, and introduce non-being into it. A past and a future spring forth when I reach out towards them. I am not, for myself, at this very moment, I am also at this morning or at the night which will soon be here, and though my present is, if we wish so to consider it, this instant, it is equally this day, this year or my whole life. There is no need for a synthesis externally binding together the *tempora* [10] into one single time, because each one of the *tempora* was already inclusive, beyond itself, of the whole open series of other *tempora,* being in internal communication with them, and because the "cohesion of a life" is given with its *ek-stase.* The passage of one present to the next is not a thing which I conceive, nor do I see it as an onlooker, I perform it; I am already at the impending present as my gesture is already at its goal, I am myself time, a time which "abides" and does not "flow" or "change," which is what Kant says in various places. This idea of a time which anticipates itself is perceived by common sense in its way. Everyone talks about Time, not as the zoologist talks about the dog or the horse, using these as collective nouns, but using it as a proper noun. Sometimes it is even personified. Everyone thinks that there is here a single, concrete being, wholly present in each of its manifestations, as is a man in each of his spoken words. We say that there is time as we

---

[9] Martin Heidegger, *Being and Time,* trans. by John Macquarrie and Edward Robinson (New York: Harper & Row, 1962), p. 401. [R.S.]

[10] *Tempora:* plural of the Latin *tempus,* time. Refers to the various "streams of conscious temporality" that make up individual persons. [R.S.]

say that there is a fountain: the water changes while the fountain remains because its form is preserved; the form is preserved because each successive wave takes over the functions of its predecessor: from being the thrusting wave in relation to the one in front of it, it becomes, in its turn and in relation to another, the wave that is pushed; and this is attributable to the fact that, from the source to the fountain jet, the waves are not separate; there is only one thrust, and a single air-lock in the flow would be enough to break up the jet. Hence the justification for the metaphor of the river, not in so far as the river flows, but in so far as it is one with itself. This intuition of time's permanence, however, is jeopardized by the action of common sense, which thematizes or objectifies it, which is the surest way of losing sight of it. There is more truth in mythical personifications of time than in the notion of time considered, in the scientific manner, as a variable of nature in itself, or, in the Kantian manner, as a form ideally separable from its matter. There is a temporal style of the world, and time remains the same because the past is a former future and a recent present, the present an impending past and a recent future, the future a present and even a past to come; because, that is, each dimension of time is treated or aimed at *as* something other than itself and because, finally, there is at the core of time a gaze, or, as Heidegger puts it, an *Augen-blick, someone* through whom the word *as* can have a meaning.[11] We are not saying that time is for someone, which would once more be a case of arraying it out, and immobilizing it. We are saying that time *is* someone, or that temporal dimensions, in so far as they perpetually overlap, bear each other out and ever confine themselves to making explicit what was implied in each, being collectively expressive of that one single explosion or thrust which is subjectivity itself. We must understand time as the subject and the subject as time. What is perfectly clear, is that this primordial temporality is not a juxtaposition of external events, since it is the power which holds them together while keeping them apart. Ultimate subjectivity is not temporal in the empirical sense of the term: if consciousness of time were made up of successive states of consciousness, there would be needed a new consciousness to be conscious of that succession and so on to infinity. We are forced to recognize the existence of "a consciousness having behind it no consciousness to be conscious of it" [12] which, consequently, is not arrayed out in time, and in which its "being coincides with its being for itself." We may say that ultimate consciousness is "timeless" (*zeitlose*) in the sense that it is not intratemporal.[13] "In" my present, if I grasp it while it is still living and with all that implies, there is an *ek-stase* towards the future and towards

---

[11] A play on the German word *Augenblick*, which means instant or moment. If the word is broken down, it becomes *Auge* (eye) and *Blick* (gaze, glance); a moment is a "glance of the eye." Thus the moment requires conscious awareness. Again the author stresses the intrinsic union between temporality and consciousness. [R.S.]

[12] Husserl, p. 117. [R.S.]

[13] *Ibid.*, p. 159. [R.S.]

the past which reveals the dimensions of time not as conflicting, but as inseparable: to be at present is to be always and for ever. Subjectivity is not in time because it takes up or lives through time, and merges with the cohesion of a life.

Are we coming back in this way to a kind of eternity? I belong to my past and, through the constant interlocking of retentions, I preserve my oldest experiences, which means not some duplicate or image of them, but the experiences themselves, exactly as they were. But the unbroken chain of the fields of presence, by which I am guaranteed access to the past itself, has the essential characteristic of being formed only gradually and one step at a time; each present, in virtue of its very essence as a present, rules out the juxtaposition of other presents and, even in the context of a time long past, I can take in a certain period of my past life only by unfolding it anew according to its own *tempo*. The temporal perspective with its confusion of what is far removed in time, and that sort of "shrinkage" of the past with oblivion as its ultimate limit, are not accidents of memory, and do not express the debasement into empirical existence of a consciousness of time theoretically all-embracing, but its initial ambiguity: to retain is to hold, but at a distance. Once again, time's "synthesis" is a transitional synthesis, the action of a life which unfolds, and there is no way of bringing it about other than by living that life, there is no seat of time; time bears itself on and launches itself afresh. Time as an indivisible thrust and transition can alone make possible time as successive multiplicity, and what we place at the origin of intratemporality is a constituting time. When we were engaged above in describing the overlapping of time by itself, we were able to treat the future as a past only by qualifying it as a past to come, and the past as a future only by calling it a future which has occurred; this means that when we came to put all time on the same footing, we had to reassert the originality of each perspective, and derive this quasi-eternity from the event. What does not elapse in time is the lapse of time itself. Time restarts itself: the rhythmic cycle and constant form of yesterday, today and tomorrow may well create the illusion that we possess it immediately, in its entirety, as the fountain creates in us a feeling of eternity. But the generality of time is no more than one of its secondary attributes and provides only an inauthentic view of it, since we cannot get as far as conceiving a cycle without drawing a distinction, in terms of time, between the point of arrival and the point of departure. The feeling for eternity is a hypocritical one, for eternity feeds on time. The fountain retains its identity only because of the continuous pressure of water. Eternity is the time that belong to dreaming, and the dream refers back to waking life, from which it borrows all its structures. Of what nature, then, is that waking time in which eternity takes root? It is the field of presence in the wise sense, with its double horizon or primary past and future, and the infinite openness of those fields of presence that have slid by, or are still possible. Time exists for me only because I am situated in it, that is, because I become aware of myself as already committed to it, because the whole of being is not given to me incarnate, and finally because one sector of being is so close to me that it does not even make up a picture before me—I cannot *see* it, just as I cannot see my face. Time exists for me because I have a present. It is by coming into the present that a moment of time acquires that indestructible individuality, that "once and for all" quality, which subsequently enables it to make its way through time and produce in us the illusion of eternity. No one of time's dimensions can be deduced from the rest. But the present (in the wide sense, along with its horizons of primary past and future), nevertheless enjoys a privilege because it is the zone in which being and consciousness coincide. When I recall an earlier perception, or when I imagine a visit to my friend Paul who is in Brazil, my aim, it is true, is the past itself in its true place, or Paul himself in the world, and not some interposed mental object. Nevertheless my act of representation, unlike the experiences represented, is actually present to me; the former is perceived, the latter are merely represented. Either a former or a potential experience, in order that they may appear to me, need to be borne into being by a primary consciousness, which in this case is my inner perception of recollection or imagination. We said above that we need to arrive at a consciousness with no other behind it, which grasps its own being, and in which, in short, being and being conscious are one and the same thing. This ultimate consciousness is not an eternal subject perceiving itself in absolute transparency, for any such subject would be utterly incapable of making its descent into time, and would, therefore have nothing in common with our experience: it is the consciousness of the present. In the present and in perception, my being and my consciousness are at one, not that my being is reducible to the knolwedge I have of it or that it is clearly set out before me—on the contrary perception is opaque, for it brings into play, beneath what I know, my sensory fields which are my primitive alliance with the world—but because "to be conscious" is here nothing but "to belong to," and because my consciousness of existing merges into the actual gesture of "ex-sistence." It is by communicating with the world that we communicate beyond all doubt with ourselves. We hold time in its entirety, and we are present to ourselves because we are present to the world.

That being the case, and since consciousness takes root in being and time by taking up a situation, how are we then to describe it? It must be a comprehensive project, or a view of time and the world which, in order to be apparent to itself, and in order to become explicitly what it is implicitly, that is, consciousness, needs to unfold itself into multiplicity. We must avoid conceiving as real and distinct entities either the indivisible power, or its distinct manifestations; consciousness is neither, it is both; it is the very action of time-creation—of "flux," as Husserl has it—a self-anticipatory movement, a flow which never leaves itself. Let us try to give a better description with the help of an example. The novelist or psychologist who fails to go back to ultimate origins and accepts time-creation as something ready made, sees consciousness as a multiplicity of psychic facts among which he tries to establish causal relations. For example, Proust shows how Swann's love for Odette *causes* the jealousy which, in turn, *modifies* his love, since Swann, always anxious to win her from any possible rival, has no time really to look at Odette. In reality, Swann's consciousness is not a lifeless setting in which psychic facts are produced from outside. What we have is not jealousy aroused by love and exerting its own counter-influence, but a certain way of loving in which the whole destiny of that love can be discerned at a glance. Swann has a liking for Odette's person, for that "spectacle" that she is, for her way of looking, of modulating her voice, and for the way a smile comes to her lips. But what *is* having a liking for someone? Proust tells us when speaking of another love: it is the feeling of being shut out of the life of the beloved, and of wanting to force one's way in and take complete possession of it. Swann's loves does not cause him to *feel* jealousy. It *is* jealousy already, and has been from the start. Jealousy does not produce a change in the quality of love: Swann's feeling of pleasure in looking at Odette bore its degeneration within itself, since it was the pleasure of being the only one to do so. The set of psychic facts and causal relationships is merely an outward manifestation of a certain view that Swann takes of Odette, a certain way of belonging to another. Swann's jealous love ought, moreover, to be related to the rest of his behaviour, in which case it might well appear as itself a manifestation of an even more general existential structure, which would be Swann's whole pesonality. Conversely all consciousness as a comprehensive project is outlined or made manifest to itself in those acts, experiences and "psychic facts" in which it is recognized. Here is where temporality throws light on subjectivity. We shall never manage to understand how a thinking or constituting subject is able to posit or become aware of itself in time. If the *I* is indeed the transcendental Ego of Kant, we shall never understand how it can in any instance merge with its wake in the inner sense, or how the empirical self still remains a self. If, however, the subject is identified with temporality, then self-positing ceases to be a contradiction, because it exactly expresses the essence of living time. Time is "the affecting of self by self": what exerts the effect is time as a thrust and a passing towards a future; what is affected is time as an unfolded series of presents; the affecting agent and affected recipient are one, because the thrust of time is nothing but the transition from one present to another. This *ek-stase,* this projection of an indivisible power into an outcome which is already present to it, is subjectivity. The primary flow, says Husserl, does not confine itself to being: it must necessarily provide itself with a "manifestation of itself" (*Selbster-scheinung*), without our needing to place behind it a second flow which is conscious of it. It "constitutes itself as a phenomenon in itself." [14] It is of the essence of time to be not only actual time, or time which flows, but also

---

[14] *Ibid.,* p. 109. [R.S.]

time which is aware of itself, for the explosion or dehiscence of the present towards a future is the archetype of the *relationship of self to self,* and it shows up an interiority or ipseity. Here a light bursts forth, for here we are no longer concerned with a being which reposes within itself, but with a being the whole essence of which, like that of light, is to *make visible.* It is through temporality that there can be, without contradiction, ipseity, significance and reason. That is seen even in the commonly held notion of time. We mark out the phases or stages of our life; for example, we consider everything that bears a significant relationship to our concerns at the moment as part of our present, thus recognizing implicitly that time and significance are but one thing. Subjectivity is not motionless identity with itself: as with time, it is of its essence, in order to be genuine subjectivity, to open itself to an Other and to go forth from itself. We must not envisage the subject as constituting, and the multiplicity of its experiences or *Erlebnisse* as constituted; we must not treat the transcendental Ego as the true subject and the empirical self as its shadow or its wake. If that were their relationship to each other, we could withdraw into the constituting agency, and such reflection would destroy time, which would be left without date or place. The fact that even our purest reflection appears to us as retrospective in time, and that our reflection on the flux is actually inserted into that flux, shows that the most precise consciousness of which we are capable is always, as it were, affected by itself or given to itself, and that the word consciousness has no meaning independently of this duality.

Nothing said of the subject is false: it is true that the subject as an absolute presence to itself is something we cannot circumvent, and that nothing could happen to it of which it did not bear within itself the lineaments. It is also true that it provides itself with symbols of itself in both succession and multiplicity, and that these symbols *are* it, since without them it would, like an inarticulate cry, fail to achieve selfconsciousness. It is here that what we provisionally termed the passive synthesis becomes clarified. A passive synthesis is a contradiction in terms if the synthesis is a process of composition, and if the passivity consists in being the recipient of multiplicity instead of its composer. What we meant by passive synthesis was that we make our way into multiplicity, but that we do not synthesize it. Now time-creation, or temporalization, satisfies by its very nature these two conditions: it is indeed clear that I am not the creator of time any more than of my heart-beats. I am not the initiator of the process of temporalization; I did not choose to come into the world, yet once I am born, time flows through me, whatever I do. Nevertheless this ceaseless welling up of time is not a simple fact to which I am passively subjected, for I can find a remedy against it in itself, as happens in a decision which binds me or in the act of establishing a concept. It withholds me from what I was about to become, and at the same time provides me with the means of grasping myself at a distance and establishing my own reality as myself. What is called passivity is not the acceptance by us of an alien reality, or a causal action exerted upon us from outside: it is being encompassed, being in a situation —prior to which we do not exist—which we are perpetually resuming and which is constitutive of us. A spontaneity "acquired" once and for all, and one which "perpetuates itself in being in virtue of its being acquired" [15] is nothing other than time and subjectivity. It is time, since a time without its roots in a present and thence a past would no longer be time, but eternity. Heidegger's historical time, which flows from the future and which, thanks to its resolute decision, *has* its future in advance and rescues itself once and for all from disintegration, is impossible within the context of Heidegger's thought itself: for, if time is an *ek-stase,* if present and past are two results of this *ek-stase,* how could we ever cease to see time from the point of view of the present, and how could we finally escape from the inauthentic? It is always in the present that we are centred, and our decisions start from there; they can therefore always be brought into relationship with our past, and are never motiveless, and, though they may open up a cycle in our life which is entirely new, they still have to be subsequently carried forward, and afford only a temporary reprieve from dispersion. There can therefore be no question of deriving time from spontaneity. We are not temporal beings *because* we are spontaneous and because, as consciousnesses, we tear ourselves away from ourselves. On the contrary, time is the foundation and measure of our spontaneity, and the power of out-running and of *"néantiser"* [16] which dwells within us and is ourselves, is itself given to us with temporality and life. Our birth, or, as Husserl has it in his unpublished writings, our "generativity," is the basis both of our activity or individuality, and our passivity or generality—that inner weakness which prevents us from ever achieving the density of an absolute individual. We are not in some incomprehensible way an activity joined to a passivity, an automatism surmounted by a will, a perception surmounted by a judgement, but wholly active and wholly passive, because we are the upsurge of time.

QUESTIONS FOR STUDY AND DISCUSSION

1. In what sense can we say that remembering involves reliving and reopening the past?
2. Comment on the following way of distinguishing between space and time: in space, a point never can contain any other points within itself, whereas in conscious time each present point contains all the rest.
3. Why does Merleau-Ponty say that there is no temporality in purely material being, apart from consciousness?
4. Why does Merleau-Ponty say man is both wholly active and wholly passive as regards temporality?

---

[15] Jean-Paul Sartre, *Being and Nothingness,* trans. by Hazel E. Barnes (New York: Philosophical Library, 1956), p. 149. [R.S.]
[16] *néantiser:* producing a negative entity. [C.S.]
  See Sartre's development of negativity. [R.S.]

Jean-Paul Sartre

JEAN-PAUL SARTRE was born in Paris in 1905. He taught at lycées in Laon
and Le Havre for a short time and traveled throughout Europe and the
Near East from 1929 until 1934, when he returned to a teaching post.
He ended his academic career in 1944 when he resigned from the lycée
where he taught in Paris, and since then he has devoted himself to writing
and to the journal he founded, *Les Temps Modernes*. Besides his philosophical works, he has also written plays, novels, and the dialogues for
several films. Gifted with a brilliant style, he was awarded the Nobel prize
for literature in 1964 but, feeling that his work would be judged not for
itself but as the product of a Nobel prize winner, he refused to accept it.
He was involved in the French resistance during World War II and has
been active in leftist political causes. The first part of his autobiography,
The Words, appeared in 1964. He now lives in Paris and continues to
publish both philosophical and dramatic works.

Man and Emotion

Perhaps what will help us in our investigation is a preliminary observation
which may serve as a general criticism of all the theories of emotion which
we have encountered. . . . For most psychologists everything takes place
as if the consciousness *of* the emotion were first a reflective consciousness,
that is, as if the first form of the emotion as a fact of consciousness were to
appear to us as a modification of our psychic being or, to use everyday language, to be first perceived as a *state of consciousness.* And certainly it is
always possible to take consciousness of emotion as the affective structure
of consciousness, to say "I'm angry, I'm afraid, etc." But fear is not originally consciousness *of* being afraid, any more than the perception of this
book is consciousness *of* perceiving the book. Emotional consciousness is,
at first, unreflective, and on this plane it can be conscious of itself only on
the non-positional mode. Emotional consciousness is, at first, consciousness *of* the world. It is not even necessary to bring up the whole theory in
order clearly to understand this principle. A few simple observations may
suffice, and it is remarkable that the psychologists of emotion have never

From pp. 50–77 of Jean-Paul Sartre, *The Emotions: Outline of a Theory,* translated by
Bernard Frechtman. Copyright 1948 by Philosophical Library, Inc. Reprinted by
permission of the publisher.

thought of making them. It is evident, in effect, that the man who is afraid is afraid *of* something. Even if it is a matter of one of those indefinite anxieties which one experiences in the dark, in a sinister and deserted passageway, etc., one is afraid *of* certain aspects of the night, of the world. And doubtless, all psychologists have noted that emotion is set in motion by a perception, a representation-signal, etc. But it seems that for them the emotion then withdraws from the object in order to be absorbed into itself. Not much reflection is needed to understand that, on the contrary, the emotion returns to the object at every moment and is fed there. For example, flight in a state of fear is described as if the object were not, before anything else, a flight *from* a certain object, as if the object fled did not remain constantly present in the flight itself, as its theme, its reason for being, *that from which one flees*. And how can one talk about anger, in which one strikes, injures, and threatens, without mentioning the person who represents the objective unity of these insults, threats, and blows? In short, the affected subject and the affective object are bound in an indissoluble synthesis. Emotion is a certain way of apprehending the world. . . . The subject who seeks the solution of a practical problem is outside in the world; he perceives the world every moment through his acts. If he fails in his attempts, if he gets irritated, his very irritation is still a way in which the world appears to him. And, between the action which miscarries and the anger, it is not necessary for the subject to reflect back upon his behavior, to intercalate a reflective consciousness. There can be a continuous passage from the unreflective consciousness "world-acted" (action) to the unreflective consciousness "world-hateful" (anger). The second is a transformation of the other.

To understand better the meaning of what is to follow, it is necessary that the reader bear in mind the essence of *unreflective behavior*. There is too great a tendency to believe that action is a constant passing from the unreflective to the reflective, from the world to ourself. We perceive the problem (unreflectiveness-consciousness *of* the world); then we perceive ourself as having the problem to solve (reflection); on the basis of this reflection we conceive an action insofar as it ought to be carried on *by us* (reflection), and then we go into the world to carry out the action (unreflective), no longer considering anything but the object acted upon. Then, all new difficulties, all partial checks which might require a restriction of adaptation, again send us to the reflective plane. Hence, a constant going and coming, which is constitutive of action.

Now it is certain that we can reflect on our action. But an operation *on* the universe is carried out most often without the subject's leaving the unreflective plane. For example, at this moment I am writing, but I have no consciousness of writing. Will it be said that habit has made me unconscious of the movements my hand is making as it forms the letters? That would be absurd. Perhaps I have the habit of writing *particular* words in a *particular* order. In a general way, one should distrust explaining things by

ascribing them to habit. In reality, the art of writing is not at all unconscious. It is a present structure of my consciousness. Only, it is not conscious *of* itself. To write is to take an active consciousness *of the words*
insofar as they are born under my pen. Not of words insofar as they are
written by *me:* I intuitively grasp the words insofar as they have this structural quality of issuing *ex nihilo,* and yet of not being creators of themselves, of being passively created. At the very moment that I form one
of them, I do not pay attention to each solitary stroke that my hand
forms; I am in a special state of waiting, creative waiting; I wait for
the word—which I know in advance—to borrow the hand which writes
and the strokes which it forms in order that it may realize itself. To be
sure, I am not conscious of the words in the same way as when I look over
someone's shoulders and read what he is writing. But that does not mean
that I am conscious of myself as writing. The essential differences are as
follows: first, my intuitive apprehension of what my neighbor is writing is
of the type called "probable evidence." I perceive the words which his
hand forms well in advance of its having completely formed them. But at
the very moment when, on reading "indep . . . ," I intuitively perceive
"independent," the word "independent" is given as a probable reality (in
the manner of the table or the chair). Contrariwise, my intuitive perception
of the words I am writing delivers them to me as certain. It is a matter of a
somewhat special certainty; it is not certain that the word "certainty"
which I am in the act of writing is going to appear (I may be disturbed,
may change my mind, etc.), but it is certain that if it appears, it will appear
as such. Thus the action constitutes a class of certain objects in a probable
world. Let us say, if you will, that insofar as they are real, future objects,
they are probable, but insofar as they are potentialities of the world, they
are certain. In the second place, the words which my neighbor is writing
make no demands; I contemplate them in their order of successive appearance as I would look at a table or a clothes-hanger. On the other hand,
the words which I write are *exigences.*[1] The very way I perceive them
through my creative activity constitutes them as such; they appear as potentialities *having to be realized.* Not having to be realized *by me.* The *I*
does not appear here at all. I simply sense the traction which they exert. I
feel their exigence objectively. I see them realizing themselves and at the
same time demanding to be realized further. I may very well *think* that the
words which my neighbor is forming are demanding their realization from
him. I do not *feel* this exigence. On the other hand, the exigence of the
words which I form is directly present; it has weight and it is felt. They tug
at my hand and guide it. But not in the manner of live and active little
demons who might actually push and tug at it; they have a passive exigence. As to *my hand,* I am conscious of it in the sense that I see it directly
as the instrument by which the words realize themselves. It is an object in

---

[1] They contain an almost impersonal demand to be formed in a certain way. [R.S.]

the world, but at the same time, it is present and lived. Here I am at the moment hesitating: shall I write "therefore" or "consequently"? That does not at all imply that I stop and think about it. Quite simply, the potentialities "therefore" and "consequently" appear—as potentialities—and come into conflict. We shall try elsewhere to describe in detail the world acted upon. The thing that matters here is to show that action as spontaneous unreflective consciousness constitutes a certain existential level in the world, and that in order to act it is not necessary to be conscious of the self as acting—quite the contrary. In short, unreflective behavior is not unconscious behavior; it is conscious of itself non-thetically,[2] and its way of being thetically conscious of itself is to transcend itself and to seize upon the world as a quality of things. Thus, one can understand all those exigences and tensions of the world which surrounds us. Thus, one can draw up a "hodological" map of our *Umwelt*,[3] a map which varies as a function of our acts and needs. Only, in normal and adapted action, the objects "to be realized" appear as having to be realized in certain ways. The means themselves appear as potentialities which demand existence. This apprehension of the means as the only possible way to reach the end (or, if there are *n* means, as the only *n* possible means, etc.) can be called a pragmatistic intuition of the determinism of the world. From this point of view, the world around us—what the Germans call *Umwelt*—the world of our desires, our needs, and our acts, appears as if it were furrowed with strict and narrow paths which lead to one or the other determined end, that is, to the appearance of a created object.

Naturally, there are decoys and traps scattered around here and there. This world might be compared to the moving plates of the coin-making machines on which the ball-bearings are made to roll; there are paths formed by rows of pins, and often, at the crossings of the paths, holes are pierced through. The ball-bearings must travel across a determined route, taking determined paths and without falling into the holes. This world is *difficult*. This notion of difficulty is not a reflective notion which would imply a relationship to me. It is there, on the world; it is a quality of the world which is given in the perception (exactly like the paths toward the potentialities and the potentialities themselves and the exigences of objects: books having to be read, shoes having to be assembled, etc.); it is the noematical [4] correlative of our activity whether undertaken or only conceived.

---

[2] Implicitly, without being directly focused upon. [R.S.]

[3] *Umwelt:* the "world surrounding us" and facing our consciousness. A "hodological map" of this world would be a description of various values and needs experienced in this world and the means necessary to satisfy them. The term "hodological" is taken from Kurt Lewin, who wrote extensively in psychology. The term is rarely used in phenomenology. [R.S.]

[4] The term "noema" is often used by phenomenologists to denote that which is an object of consciousness, with the meaning it has for consciouness. Thus the "noematical correlative of our activity" is the meaning various objects in the world take for our consciousness when we attempt to carry out projects or actions upon them. They

At present, we can conceive of what an emotion is. It is a transformation of the world. When the paths traced out become too difficult, or when we see no path, we can no longer live in so urgent and difficult a world. All the ways are barred. However, we must act. So we try to change the world, that is, to live as if the connection between things and their potentialities were not ruled by deterministic processes, but by magic. Let it be clearly understood that this is not a game; we are driven against a wall, and we throw ourselves into this new attitude with all the strength we can muster. Let it also be understood that this attempt is not conscious of being such, for it would then be the object of a reflection. Before anything else, it is the seizure of new connections and new exigences. The seizure of an object being impossible or giving rise to a tension which cannot be sustained, consciousness simply seizes it or tries to seize it otherwise. In itself there is nothing strange about this change in the direction of consciousness. We find a thousand examples of similar transformations in activity and perception. For example, to look for a face concealed in a picture puzzle ("where is the gun?") is to lead ourselves perceptibly into the picture in a new way, to behave before the branches, the telegraph poles and the image *as* in front of a gun, to realize the eye movements which we would make in front of a gun. But we do not grasp these movements as such. An intention which transcends them and whose hyle [5] they constitute directs itself through them upon the trees and the poles which are seized as "possible guns" until suddenly the perception crystallizes and the gun appears. Thus, through a change of intention, as in a change of behavior, we apprehend a new object, or an old object in a new way. There is no need to start by placing ourselves on the reflective plane. The vignette's inscription serves directly as motivation. We seek the gun without leaving the unreflective plane. That is, a potential gun appears—vaguely localized in the image. The change of intention and behavior which characterizes the emotion must be conceived in the same manner. The impossibility of finding a solution to the problem objectively apprehended as a quality of the world serves as motivation for the new unreflective consciousness which now perceives the world otherwise and with a new aspect, and which requires a new behavior—through which this aspect is perceived—and which serves as hyle for the new intention. But the emotive behavior is not on the same plane as the other behaviors; it is not *effective*. Its end is not really to act upon the object as such through the agency of particular means. It seeks by itself to confer upon the object, and without modifying it in its actual structure, another quality, a lesser existence, or a lesser presence (or a greater existence, etc.). In short, in emotion it is the body which, directed by consciousness, changes its relations with the world in order that the world may change its

---

become "difficult," "easy," "to be done quickly," or "to be avoided." Such noemas only arise when we try to accomplish something or when we engage in activity. [R.S.]
[5] Husserl's term for sensory data. [R.S.]

qualities. If emotion is a joke, it is a joke we believe in. A simple example will make this emotive structure clear: I extend my hand to take a bunch of grapes. I can't get it; it's beyond my reach. I shrug my shoulders, I let my hand drop, I mumble, "They're too green," and I move on. All these ges-tures, these words, this behavior are not seized upon for their own sake. We are dealing with a little comedy which I am playing *under* the bunch of grapes, through which I confer upon the grapes the characteristic of being "too green" which can serve as a substitute for the behavior which I am unable to keep up. At first, they presented themselves as "having to be picked." But this urgent quality very soon becomes unbearable because the potentiality cannot be realized. This unbearable tension becomes, in turn, a motive for foisting upon the grapes the new quality "too green," which will resolve the conflict and eliminate the tension. Only I cannot confer this quality on the grapes chemically. I cannot act upon the bunch in the ordi-nary ways. So I seize upon this sourness of the too green grapes by acting disgusted. I magically confer upon the grapes the quality I desire. Here the comedy is only half sincere. But let the situation be more urgent, let the incantatory behavior be carried out with seriousness; there we have emo-tion.

For example, take passive fear. I see a wild animal coming toward me. My legs give way, my heart beats more feebly, I turn pale, I fall and faint. Nothing seems less adapted than this behavior which hands me over de-fenseless to the danger. And yet it is a behavior of *escape*. Here the fainting is a refuge. Let it not be thought that this is a refuge *for me,* that I am trying to save *myself* in order not to *see* the wild animal *any more.* I did not leave the unreflective level, but, lacking power to avoid the danger by the normal methods and the deterministic links, I denied it. I wanted to annihilate it. The urgency of the danger served as motive for an annihilat-ing intention which demanded magical behavior. And, by virtue of this fact, I did annihilate it as far as was in my power. These are the limits of my magical action upon the world; I can eliminate it as an object of con-sciousness, but I can do so only by eliminating consciousness [6] itself. Let it not be thought that the physiological behavior of passive fear is pure dis-order. It represents the abrupt realization of the bodily conditions which ordinarily accompany the transition from being awake to sleeping.

The flight into active fear is mistakenly considered as rational behavior. Calculation is seen in such behavior—quick calculation, to be sure—the calculation of someone who wants to put the greatest possible distance be-tween himself and danger. But this is to misunderstand such behavior, which would then be only prudence. We do not flee in order to take shelter; we flee for lack of power to annihilate ourselves in the state of fainting. Flight is a fainting which is enacted; it is a magical behavior which consists

---

[6] Or at least by modifying it; fainting is the transition to a dream consciousness, that is, "unrealizing." [J.-P.S.]

of denying the dangerous object with our whole body by subverting the vectorial structure of the space we live in by abruptly creating a potential direction on the *other side*. It is a way of forgetting it, of denying it. It is the same way that novices in boxing shut their eyes and throw themselves at their opponent. They want to eliminate the existence of his fists; they refuse to perceive them and by so doing symbolically eliminate their efficacity. Thus, the true meaning of fear is apparent; it is a consciousness which, through magical behavior, aims at denying an object of the external world, and which will go so far as to annihilate itself in order to annihilate the object with it.

Passive sadness is characterized, as is well known, by a behavior of oppression; there is muscular resolution, pallor, coldness at the extremities; one turns toward a corner and remains seated, motionless, offering the least possible surface to the world. One prefers the shade to broad daylight, silence to noise, the solitude of a room to crowds in public places or the streets. "To be alone with one's sorrow," as they say. That is not the truth at all. It is a mark of good character to seem to meditate profoundly on one's grief. But the cases in which one really cherishes his sorrow are rather rare. The reason is quite otherwise: one of the ordinary conditions of our action having disappeared, the world requires that we act in it and on it *without that condition*. Most of the potentialities which throng it (tasks *to* do, people *to* see, acts of daily life *to* carry out) have remained the same. Only the means of realizing them, the ways which cut through our "hodological space" have changed. For example, if I have learned that I am ruined, I no longer have the same means at my disposal (private auto, etc.) to carry them out. I have to substitute new media for them (to take the bus, etc.); that is precisely what I do not want. Sadness aims at eliminating the obligation to seek new ways, to transform the structure of the world by a totally undifferentiated structure. In short, it is a question of making of the world an affectively neutral reality, a system in total affective equilibrium, of discharging the strong affective charge from objects, of reducing them all to affective zero, and, by the same token, of apprehending them as perfectly equivalent and interchangeable. In other words, lacking the power and will to accomplish the acts which we had been planning, we behave in such a way that the universe no longer requires anything of us. To bring that about we can only act upon our self, only "dim the light," and the noematical correlative of this attitude is what we call *Gloom;* the universe is gloomy, that is, undifferentiated in structure. At the same time, however, we naturally take the cowering position, we "withdraw into ourselves." The noematical correlative of this attitude is *Refuge.* All the universe is gloomy, but precisely because we want to protect ourselves from its frightening and limitless monotony, we constitute any place whatever as a "corner." It is the only differentiation in the total monotony of the world: a stretch of wall, a bit of darkness which hides its gloomy immensity from us.

Active sadness can take many forms. But the one cited by Janet (the psychasthenic who became hysterical because she did not want to confess) can be characterized as a *refusal.* The question is, above all, one of a negative behavior which aims at denying the urgency of certain problems and substituting others. The sick person wanted Janet's feelings to be moved. That means she wanted to replace the attitude of impassive waiting which he adopted by one of affectionate concern. That was what she wanted, and she used her body to bring it about. At the same time, by putting herself into a state which made confession impossible, she cast the act to be performed out of her range. Thus, as long as she was shaken with tears and hiccups, any possibility of talking was removed. Therefore, the potentiality was not eliminated in this case; the confession remained "to be made." But she had withdrawn from the sick person; she could no longer *want* to do it, but only *wish* to do it some day. Thus, the sick person had delivered herself from the painful feeling that the act was *in her power,* that she was free to do it or not. Here the emotional crisis is the abandoning of responsibility. There is magical exaggeration of the difficulties of the world. Thus, the world preserves its differentiated structure, but it appears as unjust and hostile, because it demands *too much* of us, that is, more than it is humanly possible to give it. The emotion of active sadness in this case is therefore a magical comedy of impotence; the sick person resembles servants who, having brought thieves into their master's home, have themselves tied up so that it can be clearly seen that they could not have prevented the theft. Only, here, the sick person is tied up by himself and by a thousand tenuous bonds. Perhaps it will be said that this painful feeling of freedom which he wants to get rid of is necessarily of a reflective nature. But we do not believe it, and all one need do is observe himself to be aware of this: it is the object which is given as having to be created *freely,* the confession which is given as both *having* to and *being able* to be made.

Of course, there are other functions and other forms of active sadness. We shall not insist upon anger, which we have already spoken of at some length and which, of all the emotions, is perhaps the one whose functional role is most evident. But what is to be said about joy? Does it enter into our description? At first sight it does not seem to, since the joyous subject does not have to defend himself against a change which belittles him, against a peril. But at the very beginning, we must first distinguish between joy-feeling, which represents a balance, an adapted state, and joy-emotion. But the latter, if we consider it closely, is characterized by a certain impatience. Let it be understood that we mean by that that the joyous subject behaves rather exactly like a man in a state of impatience. He does not stay in one place, makes a thousand plans which he immediately abandons, etc. In effect, it is because his joy has been aroused by the appearance of the object of his desires. He is informed that he has acquired a considerable sum of money or that he is going to see again someone he loves and whom he has not seen for a long time. But although the object is "imminent," it is not yet there, and it is not yet *his*. A certain amount of time separates him from the object. And even if it is there, even if the longed-for friend appears on the platform of the station, still it is an object which only yields itself little by little, though the pleasure we have in seeing it is going to lose its edge; we shall never get to the point of holding it there before us as our absolute property, of seizing it at one swoop as a totality (nor will we ever, at one swoop, realize our new wealth as an instantaneous totality. It will yield itself through a thousand details and, so to speak, by *"Abschattungen"* [7]). Joy is a magical behavior which tends by incantation to realize the possession of the desired object as instantaneous totality. This behavior is accompanied by the certainty that the possession will be realized sooner or later, but it seeks to anticipate this possession. The divers activities of joy, as well as muscular hypertension and slight vaso-dilatation, are animated and transcended by an intention which aims through them at the world. This seems easy; the object of our desires appears near and easy to possess. Each gesture is a further approbation. To dance and sing for joy represent symbolically approximate behavior, incantations. By means of these the object, which one could really possess only by prudent and, in spite of everything, difficult behavior, is possessed at one swoop—symbolically. Thus it is, for example, that a man who has just been told by a woman that she loves him, can start dancing and singing. By doing this he abandons the prudent and difficult behavior which he would have to practice to deserve this love and make it grow, to realize slowly and through a thousand little details (smiles, little acts of attentiveness, etc.) that he possesses it. He even abandons the woman who, as a living reality, represents precisely the pole of all his delicate behavior. He grants himself a respite; he will practice them later. For the moment, he possesses the object by magic; the dance mimics the possession.

Yet we cannot be satisfied with these few remarks. They have allowed us to appreciate the functional role of emotion, but we still do not know very much about its nature.

We must first note that the few examples we have just cited are far from exhausting the variety of emotions. There can be many other kinds of fear, many other kinds of sadness. We merely state that they all are tantamount to setting up a magical world by using the body as a means of incantation. In each case the problem and the behavior are different. To grasp its significance and its finality it would be necessary to know and analyze each particular situation. Generally speaking, there are not four major types of emotion. There are many more, and it would be useful and fruitful to classify them. For example, if the fear of the timid person is suddenly moved to anger (a change of behavior motivated by a change of situation), this is not an ordinary type of anger; it is *fear* which has been *surpassed*. This does not at all mean that it is in some way reducible to fear. It simply

---

[7] *Abschattungen*: term used by Husserl to name the various aspects or profiles in which an object appears to us. See pp. 611–12, note 7. [R.S.]

retains the antecedent fear and makes it enter its own structure. It is only when one has been convinced of the functional structure of emotion that he will come to understand the infinite variety of emotional consciousness. On the other hand, it is proper to insist upon a fact of major importance: behavior pure and simple *is not emotion,* and pure and simple consciousness of this behavior is not emotion either. Indeed, if it were so, the finalist character of emotion would appear much more clearly, and on the other hand, consciousness would easily be able to free itself from it. Moreover, there are false emotions which are not behavior. If someone gives me a gift which only half interests me, it is possible that I may make an external show of intense joy, that I may clap my hands, that I may jump, that I may dance. However, all this is a comedy. I shall let myself be drawn into it a little, and it would be inexact to say that I *am not* joyful. However, my joy is not real. I shall drop it, I shall cast it off as soon as my visitor has parted. This is exactly what we shall call a *false* joy, bearing in mind that falseness is not a logical characteristic of certain propositions, but an existential quality. In the same way I can have false fear or false sadness. Nevertheless, these false states are distinguished from those of the actor. The actor mimics joy and sadness, but he *is neither* joyful *nor* sad because this kind of behavior is addressed to a fictitious universe. He mimics behavior, but he is not behaving. In the different cases of false emotion which I have just cited, the behavior is not sustained by anything; it exists by itself and is voluntary. But the situation is real, and we conceive it as demanding this behavior. Also, by means of this behavior we intend magically to invest real objects with certain qualities. But these qualities are false.

That need not mean that they are imaginary or that they must necessarily annihilate themselves later. Their falseness arises out of an essential weakness which *presents itself* as violence. The agreeableness of the object which was just given to me exists as an exigence much more than as a reality; it has a sort of parasitic and tributary reality which I strongly feel. I know that I make it appear upon the object by a kind of fascination; let me cease my incantations and it will immediately disappear.

True emotion is quite otherwise; it is accompanied by belief. The qualities conferred upon objects are taken as true qualities. Exactly what is meant by that? Roughly this: the emotion is undergone. One cannot abandon it at will; it exhausts itself, but we cannot stop it. Besides, the behavior which boils down to itself alone does nothing else than sketch upon the object the emotional quality which we confer upon it. A flight which would simply be a journey would not be enough to establish the object as being horrible. Or rather it would confer upon it the formal quality of *horrible,* but not the matter of this quality. In order for us truly to grasp the horrible, it is not only necessary to mimic it; we must be spell-bound, flooded by our own emotion; the formal frame of the behavior must be filled with something opaque and heavy which serves as matter. We understand in this situation the role of purely physiological phenomena: they represent the *seriousness* of the emotion; they are phenomena of belief. They should certainly not be separated from behavior. At first, they present a certain analogy with it. The hyper-tension of fear or sadness, the vaso-constrictions, the respiratory difficulties, symbolize quite well a behavior which aims at denying the world or discharging it of its affective potential by denying it. It is then impossible to draw exactly a borderline between the pure difficulties and the behavior. They finally enter with the behavior into a total synthetic form and cannot be studied by themselves; to have considered them in isolation is precisely the error of the peripheric theory. And yet they are not reducible to behavior; one can stop himself from fleeing, but not from trembling. I can, by a violent effort, raise myself from my chair, turn my thought from the disaster which is crushing me, and get down to work; my hands will remain icy. Therefore, the emotion must be considered not simply as being enacted; it is not a matter of pure demeanor. It is the demeanor of a body which is in a certain state; the state alone would not provoke the demeanor; the demeanor without the state is comedy; but the emotion appears in a highly disturbed body which retains a certain behavior. The disturbance can survive the behavior, but the behavior constitutes the form and signification of the disturbance. On the other hand, without this disturbance, the behavior would be pure signification, an affective scheme. We are really dealing with a synthetic form; *in order to believe* in magical behavior it is necessary to be highly disturbed.

In order to understand clearly the emotional process with consciousness as the point of departure, it is necessary to bear in mind the twofold character of the body, which is, on the one hand, an object in the world and, on the other, something directly *lived* by consciousness. We can then grasp the essential point: emotion is a phenomenon of belief. Consciousness does not limit itself to projecting affective signification upon the world around it. It *lives* the new world which it has just established. It lives it directly; it is interested in it; it endures the qualities which behavior has set up. This signifies that when, with all paths blocked, consciousness precipitates itself into the magical world of emotion, it does so by degrading itself; it is a new consciousness facing the new world, and it establishes this new world with the deepest and most inward part of itself, with this point of view on the world present to itself without distance. The consciousness which is roused rather resembles the consciousness which is asleep. The latter, like the former, is thrown into a new world, and transforms its body as synthetic totality in such a way that it can live and grasp this new world through it.

In other words, consciousness changes the body, or, if you like, the body—as a point of view on the universe immediately inherent in consciousness—puts itself on the level of behavior. There we have the reason why physiological manifestations are, at bottom, very trivial disturbances; they resemble those of fever, of angina pectoris, of artificial over-excitement, etc. They simply represent the total and commonplace disturbance of the body as such (the behavior alone will decide whether the disturbance will be in "diminution of life" or in "enlargement"). In itself it is nothing; quite simply, it represents an obscuring of the point of view of consciousness on things *insofar* as consciousness realizes this obscuring and *lives it spontaneously*. Of course, we mean by this obscuring a synthetic totality and not something piecemeal. But on the other hand, as the body is a thing among things, a scientific analysis will be able to distinguish in the "biological-body" or the "thing-body" troubles localized in such or such an organ.

Thus the origin of emotion is a spontaneous and lived degradation of consciousness in the face of the world. What it cannot endure in one way it tries to grasp in another by going to sleep, by approaching the consciousness of sleep, dream, and hysteria. And the disturbance of the body is nothing other than the lived belief of consciousness, insofar as it is seen from the outside.

QUESTIONS FOR STUDY AND DISCUSSION

1. How do nonintentional moods such as irritability coming from a lack of sleep differ from intentional emotions like fear? Would a sore arm be an intentional or a nonintentional feeling?
2. Can we go through the experience of a strong emotion such as anger and all the while reflect upon our experience in order to be able to describe it?
3. Can we contrive to make ourselves feel an emotion, or are we chiefly passive in being overcome by it?
4. How can emotion prevent us from acting rationally in some instances?

Negativity and Freedom

NEGATIONS [1]

Someone will object that being-in-itself can not furnish negative replies. Did not we ourselves say that it was beyond affirmation as beyond negation? Furthermore ordinary experience reduced to itself does not seem to disclose any non-being to us. I think that there are fifteen hundred francs in

---

[1] Sartre sets up the problem of the origin of negation in the following terms: he admits the obvious fact that men do make negative judgments. But is negation *only* a characteristic of judgments, and hence only a characteristic of speech? Is it only a "logical" reality? Or, on the other hand, does it have a foundation in some sort of real, metaphysical negativity? Sartre will choose the latter, and will ground negation in man. [R.S.]

From pp. 6–12 and 21–35 of Jean-Paul Sartre, *Being and Nothingness,* translated by Hazel E. Barnes. © 1956 by Philosophical Library, Inc. Reprinted by permission of the publisher.

my wallet, and I find only thirteen hundred; that does not mean, someone will tell us, that experience had discovered for me the non-being of fifteen hundred francs but simply that I have counted thirteen hundred-franc notes. Negation proper (we are told) is unthinkable; it could appear only on the level of an act of judgment by which I should establish a comparison between the result anticipated and the result obtained. Thus negation would be simply a quality of judgment and the expectation of the questioner would be an expectation of the judgment-response. As for Nothingness, this would derive its origin from negative judgments; it would be a concept establishing the transcendent unity of all these judgments, a propositional function of the type, "X is not."

We see where this theory is leading; its proponents would make us conclude that being-in-itself is full positivity and does not contain in itself any negation. This negative judgment, on the other hand, by virtue of being a subjective act, is strictly identified with the affirmative judgment. They can not see that Kant, for example, has distinguished in its internal texture the negative act of judgment from the affirmative act. In each case a synthesis of concepts is operative; that synthesis, which is a concrete and full event of psychic life, is operative here merely in the manner of the copula "is" and there in the manner of the copula "is not." In the same way the manual operation of sorting out (separation) and the manual operation of assembling (union) are two objective conducts which possess the same reality of fact. Thus negation would be "at the end" of the act of judgment without, however, being "in" being. It is like an unreal encompassed by two full realities neither of which claims it; being-in-itself, if questioned about negation, refers to judgment, since being is only what it is—and judgment, a *wholly* psychic positivity, refers to being since judgment formulates a negation which concerns being and which consequently is transcendent. Negation, the result of concrete psychic operations, is supported in existence by these very operations and is incapable of existing by itself; it has the existence of a noema-correlate;[2] its *esse* resides exactly in its *percipi*. Nothingness, the conceptual unity of negative judgments, can not have the slightest trace of reality, save that which the Stoics confer on their "lecton."[3] Can we accept this concept?

The question can be put in these terms: Is negation as the structure of the judicative proposition at the origin of nothingness? Or on the contrary is nothingness as the structure of the real, the origin and foundation of negation? Thus the problem of being had referred us first to that of the question as a human attitude, and the problem of the question now refers us to that of the being of negation.

---

[2] As Sartre uses the term here, to say that negation is a "noema-correlate" would mean that it exists only as an object of consciousness. It would have no existence in itself, apart from consciousness; its "being" (*esse*) is "to be perceived" (*percipi*), in Berkeley's famous phrase. On the concept of noema, see pp. 624–25, note 4. [R.S.]

[3] An abstraction or something with purely nominal existence . . . . [H.E.B.]

It is evident that non-being always appears within the limits of a human expectation. It is because I expect to find fifteen hundred francs that I find *only* thirteen hundred. It is because a physicist *expects* a certain verification of his hypothesis that nature can tell him no. It would be in vain to deny that negation appears on the original basis of a relation of man to the world. The world does not disclose its non-beings to one who has not first posited them as possibilities. But is this to say that these non-beings are to be reduced to pure subjectivity? Does this mean to say that we ought to give them the importance and the type of existence of the Stoic "lecton," of Husserl's noema? We think not.

First it is not true that negation is only a quality of judgment. The question is formulated by an interrogative judgment, but it is not itself a judgment; it is a pre-judicative attitude. I can question by a look, by a gesture. In posing a question I stand facing being in a certain way and this relation to being is a relation of being; the judgment is only one optional expression of it. At the same time it is not necessarily a person whom the questioner questions about being; this conception of the question by making of it an intersubjective phenomenon, detaches it from the being to which it adheres and leaves it in the air as pure modality of dialogue.[4] On the contrary, we must consider the question in dialogue to be only a particular species of the genus "question;" the being in question is not necessarily a thinking being. If my car breaks down, it is the *carburetor,* the *spark plugs, etc.,* that I question. If my watch stops, I can question the watchmaker about the cause of the stopping, but it is the various mechanisms of the watch that the watchmaker will in turn question. What I expect from the carburetor, what the watchmaker expects from the works of the watch, is not a judgment; it is a disclosure of being on the basis of which we can make a judgment. And if I *expect* a disclosure of being, I am prepared at the same time for the eventuality of a disclosure of a non-being. If I question the carburetor, it is because I consider it possible that "there is nothing there" in the carburetor. Thus my question by its nature envelops a certain pre-judicative comprehension of non-being; it is in itself a relation of being with non-being, on the basis of the original transcendence; that is, in a relation of being with being.

Moreover if the proper nature of the question is obscured by the fact that questions are frequently put by one man to other men, it should be pointed out here that there are numerous non-judicative conducts which present this immediate comprehension of non-being on the basis of being —in its original purity. If, for example, we consider *destruction,* we must recognize that it is an *activity* which doubtless could utilize judgment as an instrument but which can not be defined as uniquely or even primarily judicative. "Destruction" presents the same structure as "the question." In a sense, certainly, man is the only being by whom a destruction can be ac-

---

[4] "Modality of dialogue" is simply a characteristic of discourse, not a reality of any sort. [R.S.]

complished. A geological plication, a storm does not destroy—or at least they do not destroy *directly;* they merely modify the distribution of masses of beings. There is no *less* after the storm than before. There is *something else.* Even this expression is improper, for to posit otherness there must be a witness who can retain the past in some manner and compare it to the present in the form of *no longer.* In the absence of this witness, there is being before as after the storm—that is all. If a cyclone can bring about the death of certain living beings, this death will be destruction only if it is experienced as such. In order for destruction to exist, there must be first a relation of man to being—*i.e.,* a transcendence; and within the limits of this relation, it is necessary that man apprehend one being as destructible. This supposes a limiting cutting into being by a being, which, as we saw in connection with truth, is already a process of nihilation. The being under consideration is *that* and outside of that *nothing.* The gunner who has been assigned an objective carefully points his gun in a certain direction *excluding* all others. But even this would still be nothing unless the being of the gunner's objective is revealed as *fragile.* And what is fragility if not a certain probability of non-being for a given being under determined circumstances. A being is fragile if it carries in its being a definite possibility of non-being. But once again it is through man that fragility comes into being, for the individualizing limitation which we mentioned earlier is the condition of fragility; *one* being is fragile and not *all* being, for the latter is beyond all possible destruction. Thus the relation of individualizing limitation which man enters into with *one* being on the original basis of his relation to being causes fragility to enter into this being as the appearance of a permanent possibility of non-being. But this is not all. In order for destructibility to exist, man must determine himself in the face of this possibility of non-being, either positively or negatively; he must either take the necessary measures to realize it (destruction proper) or, by a negation of non-being, to maintain it always on the level of a simple possibility (by preventive measures). Thus it is man who renders cities destructible, precisely because he posits them as fragile and as precious and because he adopts a system of protective measures with regard to them. It is because of this ensemble of measures that an earthquake or a volcanic eruption can *destroy* these cities or these human constructions. The original meaning and aim of war are contained in the smallest building of man. It is necessary then to recognize that destruction is an essentially human thing and that *it is man* who destroys his cities through the agency of earthquakes or directly, who destroys his ships through the agency of cyclones or directly. But at the same time it is necessary to acknowledge that destruction supposes a prejudicative comprehension of nothingness as such and a conduct *in the face of nothingness.* In addition destruction although coming into being through man, is an *objective fact* and not a thought. Fragility has been impressed upon the very being of this vase, and its destruction would be an irreversible absolute event which I could only verify. There is a transphenomenality of non-being as of being.[5] The examination of "destruction" leads us then to the same results as the examination of "the question."

But if we wish to decide with certainty, we need only to consider an example of a negative judgment and to ask ourselves whether it causes non-being to appear at the heart of being or merely limits itself to determining a prior revelation. I have an appointment with Pierre at four o'clock. I arrive at the café a quarter of an hour late. Pierre is always punctual. Will he have waited for me? I look at the room, the patrons, and I say, "He is not here." Is there an intuition of Pierre's absence, or does negation indeed enter in only with judgment? At first sight it seems absurd to speak here of intuition since to be exact there could not be an intuition of *nothing* and since the absence of Pierre is this nothing. Popular consciousness, however, bears witness to this intuition. Do we not say, for example, "I suddenly saw that he was not there." Is this just a matter of misplacing the negation? Let us look a little closer.

It is certain that the café by itself with its patrons, its tables, its booths, its mirrors, its lights, its smoky atmosphere, and the sounds of voices, rattling saucers, and footsteps which fill it—the café is a fullness of being. And all the intuitions of detail which I can have are filled by these odors, these sounds, these colors, all phenomena which have a transphenomenal being. Similarly Pierre's actual presence in a place which I do not know is also a plenitude of being. We seem to have found fullness everywhere. But we must observe that in perception there is always the construction of a figure on a ground. No one object, no group of objects is especially designed to be organized as specifically either ground or figure; all depends on the direction of my attention. When I enter this café to search for Pierre, there is formed a synthetic organization of all the objects in the café, on the ground of which Pierre is given as about to appear. This organization of the café as the ground is an original nihilation. Each element of the setting, a person, a table, a chair, attempts to isolate itself, to lift itself upon the ground constituted by the totality of the other objects, only to fall back once more into the undifferentiation of this ground; it melts into the ground. For the ground is that which is seen only in addition, that which is the object of a purely marginal attention. Thus the original nihilation of all the figures which appear and are swallowed up in the total neutrality of a *ground* is the necessary condition for the appearance of the principal figure, which is here the person of Pierre. This nihilation is given to my intuition; I am witness to the successive disappearance of all the objects which I look at—in particular of the faces, which detain me for an instant (Could this be Pierre?) and which as quickly decompose precisely because they "are not" the face of Pierre. Nevertheless if I should finally discover Pierre, my intuition would be filled by a solid element, I should

---

[5] "Transphenomenality" of negation means that it is more than a mere appearance or phenomenon. It has a certain objective reality. [R.S.]

be suddenly arrested by his face and the whole café would organize itself around him as a discrete presence.

But now Pierre is not here. This does not mean that I discover his absence in some precise spot in the establishment. In fact Pierre is absent from the *whole* café; his absence fixes the café in its evanescence; the café remains *ground;* it persists in offering itself as an undifferentiated totality to my only marginal attention; it slips into the background; it pursues its nihilation. Only it makes itself ground for a determined figure; it carries the figure everywhere in front of it, presents the figure everywhere to me. This figure which slips constantly between my look and the solid, real objects of the café is precisely a perpetual disappearance; it is Pierre raising himself as nothingness on the ground of the nihilation of the café. So that what is offered to intuition is a flickering of nothingness; it is the nothingness of the ground, the nihilation of which summons and demands the appearance of the figure, and it is the figure—the nothingness which slips as a *nothing* to the surface of the ground. It serves as foundation for the judgment—"Pierre is not here." It is in fact the intuitive apprehension of a double nihilation. To be sure, Pierre's absence supposes an original relation between me and this café; there is an infinity of people who are without any relation with this café for want of a real expectation which establishes their absence. But, to be exact, I myself expected to see Pierre, and my expectation has caused the absence of Pierre *to happen* as a real event concerning this café. It is an objective fact at present that I have *discovered* this absence, and it presents itself as a synthetic relation between Pierre and the setting in which I am looking for him. Pierre absent haunts this café and is the condition of its self-nihilating organization as ground. By contrast, judgments which I can make subsequently to amuse myself, such as, "Wellington is not in this café, Paul Valéry is no longer here, *etc.*"—these have a purely abstract meaning; they are pure applications of the principle of negation without real or efficacious foundation, and they never succeed in establishing a *real* relation between the café and Wellington or Valéry. Here the relation "is not" is merely *thought*. This example is sufficient to show that non-being does not come to things by a negative judgment; it is the negative judgment, on the contrary, which is conditioned and supported by non-being.

How could it be otherwise? How could we even conceive of the negative form of judgement if all is plenitude of being and positivity? We believed for a moment that the negation could arise from the comparison instituted between the result anticipated and the result obtained. But let us look at that comparison. Here is an original judgment, a concrete, positive psychic act which establishes a fact: "There are 1300 francs in my wallet." Then there is another which is something else, no longer it but an establishing of fact and an affirmation: "I expected to find 1500 francs." There we have real and objective facts, psychic, and positive events, affirmative judgments. Where are we to place negation? Are we to believe that it is a pure and simple application of a category? And do we wish to hold that the mind in itself possesses the *not* as a form of sorting out and separation? But in this case we remove even the slightest suspicion of negativity from the negation. If we admit that the category of the "not" which exists *in fact* in the mind and is a positive and concrete process to brace and systematize our knowledge, if we admit first that it is suddenly released by the presence in us of certain affirmative judgments and then that it comes suddenly to mark with its seal certain thoughts which result from these judgments—by these considerations we will have carefully stripped negation of all negative function. For negation is a refusal of existence. By means of it a being (or a way of being) is posited, then thrown back to nothingness. If negation is a category, if it is only a sort of plug set indifferently on certain judgments, then how will we explain the fact that it can nihilate a being, cause it suddenly to arise, and then appoint it to be thrown back to non-being? If prior judgments establish fact, like those which we have taken for examples, negation must be like a free discovery, it must tear us away from this wall of positivity which encircles us. Negation is an abrupt break in continuity which can not in any case *result* from prior affirmations; it is an original and irreducible event. Here we are in the realm of consciousness. Consciousness moreover can not produce a negation except in the form of consciousness of negation. No category can "inhabit" consciousness and reside there in the manner of a thing. The *not,* as an abrupt intuitive discovery, appears as consciousness (of being), consciousness of the *not.* In a word, if being is everywhere, it is not only Nothingness which, as Bergson maintains, is inconceivable; for negation will never be derived from being. The necessary condition for our saying *not* is that non-being be a perpetual presence in us and outside of us, that nothingness haunt being.

But where does nothingness come from? If it is the original condition of the questioning attitude and more generally of all philosophical or scientific inquiry, what is the original relation of the human being to nothingness? What is the original nihilating conduct?

. . .

THE ORIGIN OF NOTHINGNESS

It would be well at this point to cast a glance backward and to measure the road already covered. We raised first the question of being. Then examining this very question conceived as a type of human conduct, we questioned this in turn. We next had to recognize that no question could be asked, in particular not that of being, if negation did not exist. But this negation itself when inspected more closely referred us back to Nothingness as its origin and foundation. In order for negation to exist in the world and in order that we may consequently raise questions concerning Being, it is necessary that in some way Nothingness be given. We perceived then that Nothingness can be conceived neither *outside of* being, nor as a complementary, abstract notion, nor as an infinite milieu where being is suspended. Nothingness must be given at the heart of Being, in order for us to be able to apprehend that particular type of realities which we have called *négatités*.[6] But this intra-mundane Nothingness cannot be produced by Being-in-itself; the notion of Being as full positivity does not contain Nothingness as one of its structures. We can not even say that Being excludes it. Being lacks all relation with it. Hence the question which is put to us now with a particular urgency: if Nothingness can be conceived neither outside of Being, nor in terms of Being, and if on the other hand, since it is non-being, it can not derive from itself the necessary force to "nihilate itself," *where does Nothingness come from?*

If we wish to pursue the problem further, we must first recognize that we can not grant to nothingness the property of "nihilating itself." For although the expression "to nihilate itself" is thought of as removing from nothingness the last semblance of being, we must recognize that only *Being* can nihilate itself; however it comes about, in order to nihilate itself, it must *be*. But Nothingness *is not*. If we can speak of it, it is only because it possesses an appearance of being, a borrowed being, as we have noted above. Nothingness is not, Nothingness "is made-to-be," Nothingness does not nihilate itself; Nothingness "is nihilated." It follows therefore that there must exist a Being (this can not be the In-itself) of which the property is to nihilate Nothingness, to support it in its being, to sustain it perpetually in its very existence, *a being by which nothingness comes to things*. But how can this Being be related to Nothingness so that through it Nothingness comes to things? We must observe first that the being postulated can not be passive in relation to Nothingness, can not receive it; Nothingness could not *come* to this being except through another Being—which would be an infinite regress. But on the other hand, the Being by which Nothingness comes to the world can not *produce* Nothingness while remaining indifferent to that production—like the Stoic cause which produces its effect without being itself changed. It would be inconceivable that a Being which is full positivity should maintain and create outside itself a Nothingness or transcendent being, for there would be nothing in Being by which Being could surpass itself toward Non-Being. The Being by which Nothingness arrives in the world must nihilate Nothingness in its Being, and even so it still runs the risk of establishing Nothingness as a transcendent in the very heart of immanence unless it nihilates Nothingness in its being *in connection with its own being*. The Being by which Nothingness arrives in the world is a being such that in its Being, the Nothingness of its Being is in question. *The being by which Nothingness comes to the world must be its*

---

[6] "There is an infinite number of realities which are not only objects of judgment, but which are experienced, opposed, feared, etc., by the human being and which in their inner structure are inhabited by negation, as by a necessary condition of their existence. We shall call them *négatités*." (Sartre, *Being and Nothingness*, p. 21.) *Négatité* could be considered the objective correlate to the negativity in human consciousness. [R.S.]

own Nothingness. By this we must understand not a nihilating act, which would require in turn a foundation in Being, but an ontological characteristic of the Being required. It remains to learn in what delicate, exquisite region of Being we shall encounter that Being which is its own Nothingness.

We shall be helped in our inquiry by a more complete examination of the conduct which served us as a point of departure. We must return to the question. We have seen, it may be recalled, that every question in essence posits the possibility of a negative reply. In a question we question a being about its being or its way of being. This way of being or this being is veiled; there always remains the possibility that it may unveil itself as a Nothingness. But from the very fact that we presume that an Existent can always be revealed as *nothing,* every question supposes that we realize a nihilating withdrawal in relation to the given, which becomes a simple *presentation,* fluctuating between being and Nothingness.

It is essential therefore that the questioner have the permanent possibility of dissociating himself from the causal series which constitutes being and which can produce only being. If we admitted that the question is determined in the questioner by universal determinism, the question would thereby become unintelligible and even inconceivable. A real cause, in fact, produces a real effect and the caused being is wholly engaged by the cause in positivity; to the extent that its being depends on the cause, it can not have within itself the tiniest germ of nothingness. Thus in so far as the questioner must be able to effect in relation to the questioned a kind of nihilating withdrawal, he is not subject to the causal order of the world; he detaches himself from Being. This means that by a double movement of nihilation, he nihilates the thing questioned in relation to himself by placing it in a *neutral* state, between being and non-being—and that he nihilates himself in relation to the thing questioned by wrenching himself from being in order to be able to bring out of himself the possibility of a non-being. Thus in posing a question, a certain negative element is introduced into the world. We see nothingness making the world irridescent, casting a shimmer over things. But at the same time the question emanates from a questioner who in order to motivate himself in his being as one who questions, disengages himself from being. This disengagement is then by definition a human process. Man presents himself at least in this instance as a being who causes Nothingness to arise in the world, inasmuch as he himself is affected with non-being to this end.

These remarks may serve as guiding thread as we examine the *négatités* of which we spoke earlier. There is no doubt at all that these are transcendent realities; distance, for example, is imposed on us as something which we have to take into account, which must be cleared with effort. However these realities are of a very peculiar nature; they all indicate immediately an essential relation of human reality to the world. They derive their origin from an act, an expectation, or a project of the human being; they all indicate an aspect of being as it appears to the human being who is engaged in the world. The relations of man in the world, which the *néga-tités* indicate, have nothing in common with the relations *à posteriori* which are brought out by empirical activity. We are no longer dealing with those relations *of instrumentality* by which, according to Heidegger, objects in the world disclose themselves to "human reality." Every *négatité* appears rather as one of the essential conditions of this relation of instrumentality. In order for the totality of being to order itself around us as instruments, in order for it to parcel itself into differentiated complexes which refer one to another and which can *be used,* it is necessary that negation rise up not as a thing among other things but as the rubric of a category which presides over the arrangement and the redistribution of great masses of being in things. Thus the rise of man in the midst of the being which "invests" him causes a world to be discovered. But the essential and primordial moment of this rise is the negation. Thus we have reached the first goal of this study. Man is the being through whom nothingness comes to the world. But this question immediately provokes another: What must man be in his being in order that through him nothingness may come to being?

Being can generate only being and if man is inclosed in this process of generation, only being will come out of him. If we are to assume that man is able to question this process—*i.e.,* to make it the object of interrogation —he must be able to hold it up to view as a totality. He must be able to put himself *outside of* being and by the same stroke weaken the structure of the being of being. Yet it is not given to "human reality" to annihilate even provisionally the mass of being which it posits before itself. Man's *relation* with being is that he can modify it. For man to put a particular existent out of circuit is to put himself out of circuit in relation to that existent. In this case he is not subject to it; he is out of reach; it can not act on him, for he has retired *beyond a nothingness.* Descartes following the Stoics has given a name to this possibility which human reality has to secrete a nothingness which isolates it—it is *freedom.* But freedom here is only a name. If we wish to penetrate further into the question, we must not be content with this reply and we ought to ask now, What is human freedom if through it nothingness comes into the world?

It is not yet possible to deal with the problem of freedom in all its fullness. In fact the steps which we have completed up to now show clearly that freedom is not a faculty of the human soul to be envisaged and described in isolation. What we have been trying to define is the being of man in so far as he conditions the appearance of nothingness, and this being has appeared to us as freedom. Thus freedom as the requisite condition for the nihilation of nothingness is not a *property* which belongs among others to the essence of the human being. We have already noticed furthermore that with man the relation of existence to essence is not comparable to what it is for the things of the world. Human freedom precedes essence in man and makes it possible; the essence of the human being is suspended in his freedom. What we call freedom is impossible to distinguish from the *being* of "human reality." Man does not exist *first* in order to be free *subsequently;* there is no difference between the being of man and his *being-free.* This is not the time to make a frontal attack on a question which can be treated exhaustively only in the light of a rigorous elucidation of the human being. Here we are dealing with freedom in connection with the problem of nothingness and only to the extent that it conditions the appearance of nothingness.

What first appears evident is that human reality can detach itself from the world—in questioning, in systematic doubt, in sceptical doubt, in the *epoché,*[7] *etc.*—only if by nature it has the possibility of self-detachment. This was seen by Descartes, who is establishing doubt on freedom when he claims for us the possibility of suspending our judgments. . . . It is also in this sense that Hegel asserts the freedom of the mind to the degree that mind is mediation—*i.e.,* the Negative. Furthermore it is one of the trends of contemporary philosophy to see in human consciousness a sort of escape from the self; such is the meaning of the transcendence of Heidegger. The intentionality of Husserl and of Brentano has also to a large extent the characteristic of a detachment from self. But we are not yet in a position to consider freedom as an inner structure of consciousness. We lack for the moment both instruments and technique to permit us to succeed in that enterprise. What interests us at present is a temporal operation since questioning is, like doubt, a kind of behavior; it assumes that the human being reposes first in the depths of being and then detaches himself from it by a nihilating withdrawal. Thus we are envisaging the condition of the nihilation as a relation to the self in the heart of a temporal process. We wish simply to show that by identifying consciousness with a causal sequence indefinitely continued, one transmutes it into a plenitude of being and thereby causes it to return into the unlimited totality of being—as is well illustrated by the futility of the efforts to dissociate psychological determinism from universal determinism and to constitute it as a separate series.

The room of someone absent, the books of which he turned the pages, the objects which he touched are in themselves only *books, objects; i.e.,* full actualities. The very traces which he has left can be deciphered as traces of him only within a situation where he has been already posited as absent. The dog-eared book with the well-read pages is not by itself a book of which Pierre has turned the pages, of which he no longer turns the pages. If we consider it as the present, transcendent motivation of my perception or even as the synthetic flux, regulated by my sensible impressions, then it is merely a volume with turned down, worn pages; it can refer only to itself or to present objects, to the lamp which illuminates it, to the table which holds it. It would be useless to invoke an association by contiguity as Plato does in the *Phaedo,* where he makes the image of the absent one

---

[7] See *Epoché* in the Glossary in this section. [R.S.]

appear on the margin of the perception of the lyre or of the cithara which he has touched. This image, if we consider it in itself and in the spirit of classical theories, is a definite plenitude; it is a concrete and positive psychic fact. Consequently we must of necessity pass on it a doubly negative judgment: subjectively, to signify that the image *is not* a perception; objectively, to deny that the Pierre of whom I form the image *is here* at this moment.

This is the famous problem of the characteristics of the true image, which has concerned so many psychologists. . . . Association, we see, does not solve the problem; it pushes it back to the level of reflection. But in every way it demands a negation; that is, at the very least, a nihilating withdrawal of consciousness in relation to the image apprehended as subjective phenomenon, in order to posit it precisely as being only a subjective phenomenon.

Now I have attempted to show elsewhere [8] that if we posit the image *first* as a renascent perception, it is radically impossible to distinguish it *subsequently* from actual perceptions. The image must enclose in its very structure a nihilating thesis. It constitutes itself qua image while positing its object as existing *elsewhere* or *not existing*. It carries within it a double negation; first it is the nihilation of the world (since the world is not offering the imagined object as an actual object of perception), secondly the nihilation of the object of the image (it is posited as not actual), and finally by the same stroke it is the nihilation of itself (since it is not a concrete, full psychic process.) In explaining how I apprehend the absence of Pierre in the room, it would be useless to invoke those famous "empty intentions" of Husserl, which are in great part constitutive of perception. Among the various perceptive intentions, indeed, there are relations of *motivation* (but motivation is not causation), and among these intentions, some are full (*i.e.,* filled with what they aim at) and others empty. But precisely because the matter which should fill the empty intentions *does not exist,* it can not be this which motivates them in their structure. And since the other intentions are full, neither can they motivate the empty intentions inasmuch as the latter are empty. Moreover these intentions are of psychic nature and it would be an error to envisage them in the mode of things; that is, as recipients which would first be given, which according to circumstances could be emptied or filled, and which would be by nature indifferent to their state of being empty or filled. It seems that Husserl has not always escaped the materialist illusion. To be empty an intention must be conscious of itself as empty and precisely as empty *of* the exact matter at which it aims. An empty intention constitutes itself as empty to the exact extent that it posits its matter as non-existing or absent. In short an empty intention is a con-

---

[8] Sartre is referring to his early work, *Imagination; A Psychological Critique,* trans. and with Introd. by Forrest Williams (Ann Arbor, Mich.: University of Michigan Press, 1962). The original was written in 1936. [R.S.]

sciousness of negation which transcends itself toward an object which it posits as absent or non-existent.

Thus whatever may be the explanation which we give of it, Pierre's absence, in order to be established or realized, requires a negative moment by which consciousness in the absence of all prior determination, constitutes itself as negation. If in terms of my perceptions of the room, I conceive of the former inhabitant who is no longer in the room, I am of necessity forced to produce an act of thought which no prior state can determine nor motivate, in short to effect in myself a break with being. And in so far as I continually use *négatités* to isolate and determine existents—*i.e.,* to think them—the succession of my "states of consciousness" is a perpetual separation of effect from cause, since every nihilating process must derive its source only from itself. Inasmuch as my present state would be a prolongation of my prior state, every opening by which negation could slip through would be completely blocked. Every psychic process of nihilation implies then a cleavage between the immediate psychic past and the present. This cleavage is precisely nothingness. At least, someone will say, there remains the possibility of successive implication between the nihilating processes. My establishment of Pierre's absence could still be determinant for my regret at not seeing him; you have not excluded the possibility of a determinism of nihilations. But aside from the fact that the original nihilation of the series must necessarily be disconnected from the prior positive processes, what can be the meaning of a motivation of nothingness by nothingness? A being indeed can *nihilate itself* perpetually, but to the extent that it nihilates itself, it foregoes being the origin of another phenomenon, even of a second nihilation.

It remains to explain what this separation is, this disengaging of consciousness which conditions every negation. If we consider the prior consciousness envisaged as motivation, we see suddenly and evidently that *nothing* has just slipped in between that state and the present state. There has been no break in continuity within the flux of the temporal development, for that would force us to return to the inadmissible concept of the infinite divisibility of time and of the temporal point or instant as the limit of the division. Neither has there been an abrupt interpolation of an opaque element to separate prior from subsequent in the way that a knife blade cuts a piece of fruit in two. Nor is there a *weakening* of the motivating force of the prior consciousness; it remains what it is, it does not lose anything of its urgency. What separates prior from subsequent is exactly *nothing*. This nothing is absolutely impassable, just because it is nothing; for in every obstacle to be cleared there is something positive which gives itself as about to be cleared. The prior consciousness is always *there* (though with the modification of "pastness"). It constantly maintains a relation of interpretation with the present consciousness, but on the basis of this existential relation it is put out of the game, out of the circuit, between parentheses—exactly as in the eyes of one practicing the phenomenological *epoché,* the world both is within him and outside him.

Thus the condition on which human reality can deny all or part of the world is that human reality carry nothingness within itself as the *nothing* which separates its present from all its past. But this is still not all, for the *nothing* envisaged would not yet have the sense of nothingness; a suspension of being which would remain unnamed, which would not be consciousness of suspending being would come from outside consciousness and by reintroducing opacity into the heart of this absolute lucidity, would have the effect of cutting it in two. Furthermore this nothing would by no means be negative. Nothingness, as we have seen above, is the ground of the negation because it conceals the negation within itself, because it is the negation as being. It is necessary then that conscious being constitute itself in relation to its past as separated from this past by a nothingness. It must necessarily be conscious of this cleavage in being, but not as a phenomenon which it experiences, rather as a structure of consciousness which it is. Freedom is the human being putting his past out of play by secreting his own nothingness. Let us understand indeed that this original necessity of being its own nothingness does not belong to consciousness intermittently and on the occasion of particular negations. This does not happen just at a particular moment in psychic life when negative or interrogative attitudes appear; consciousness continually experiences itself as the nihilation of its past being.

But someone doubtless will believe that he can use against us here an objection which we have frequently raised ourselves: if the nihilating consciousness exists only as consciousness of nihilation, we ought to be able to define and describe a constant mode of consciousness, present *qua* consciousness, which would be consciousness of nihilation. Does this consciousness exist? Behold a new question has been raised here: if freedom is the being of consciousness, consciousness ought to exist a consciousness of freedom. What form does this consciousness of freedom assume? In freedom the human being *is* his own past (as also his own future) in the form of nihilation. If our analysis has not led us astray, there ought to exist for the human being, in so far as he is conscious of being, a certain mode of standing opposite his past and his future, as being both this past and this future and as not being them. We shall be able to furnish an immediate reply to this question; it is in anguish that man gets the consciousness of his freedom, or if you prefer, anguish is the mode of being of freedom as consciousness of being; it is in anguish that freedom is, in its being, in question for itself.

Kierkegaard describing anguish in the face of what one lacks characterizes it as anguish in the face of freedom. But Heidegger, whom we know to have been greatly influenced by Kierkegaard, considers anguish instead as the apprehension of nothingness. These two descriptions of anguish do not appear to us contradictory; on the contrary the one implies the other.

First we must acknowledge that Kierkegaard is right; anguish is distinguished from fear in that fear is fear of beings in the world whereas anguish is anguish before myself. Vertigo is anguish to the extent that I am afraid not of falling over the precipice, but of throwing myself over. A situation provokes fear if there is a possibility of my life being changed from without; my being provokes anguish to the extent that I distrust myself and my own reactions in that situation. The artillery preparation which precedes the attack can provoke fear in the soldier who undergoes the bombardment, but anguish is born in him when he tries to foresee the conduct with which he will face the bombardment, when he asks himself if he is going to be able to "hold up." Similarly the recruit who reports for active duty at the beginning of the war can in some instances be afraid of death, but more often he is "afraid of being afraid;" that is, he is filled with anguish before himself. Most of the time dangerous or threatening situations present themselves in facets; they will be apprehended through a feeling of fear or of anguish according to whether we envisage the situation as acting on the man or the man as acting on the situation. The man who has just received a hard blow—for example, losing a great part of his wealth in a crash—can have the fear of threatening poverty. He will experience anguish a moment later when nervously wringing his hands (a symbolic reaction to the action which is imposed but which remains still wholly undetermined), he exclaims to himself: "What am I going to do? But what am I going to do?" In this sense fear and anguish are exclusive of one another since fear is unreflective apprehension of the transcendent and anguish is reflective apprehension of the self; the one is born in the destruction of the other. The normal process in the case which I have just cited is a constant transition from one to the other. But there exist also situations where anguish appears pure; that is, without ever being preceded or followed by fear. If, for example, I have been raised to a new dignity and charged with a delicate and flattering mission, I can feel anguish at the thought that I will not be capable perhaps of fulfilling it, and yet I will not have the least fear in the world of the consequences of my possible failure.

What is the meaning of anguish in the various examples which I have just given? Let us take up again the example of vertigo. Vertigo announces itself through fear; I am on a narrow path—without a guard-rail—which goes along a precipice. The precipice presents itself to me as *to be avoided;* it represents a danger of death. At the same time I conceive of a certain number of causes, originating in universal determinism, which can transform that threat of death into reality; I can slip on a stone and fall into the abyss; the crumbling earth of the path can give way under my steps. Through these various anticipations, I am given to myself as a thing; I am passive in relation to these possibilities; they come to me from without; in so far as I am also an object in the world, subject to gravitation, they are *my* possibilities. At this moment *fear* appears, which in terms of the situation is the apprehension of myself as a destructible transcendent in the midst of transcendents, as an object which does not contain in itself the origin of its future disappearance. My reaction will be of the reflective order; I will pay attention to the stones in the road; I will keep myself as far as possible from the edge of the path. I realize myself as pushing away the threatening situation with all my strength, and I project before myself a certain number of future conducts destined to keep the threats of the world at a distance from me. These conducts are *my* possibilities. I escape fear by the very fact that I am placing myself on a plane where *my own* possibilities are substituted for the transcendent probabilities where human action had no place.

But these conducts, precisely because they are *my* possibilities, do not appear to me as determined by foreign causes. Not only is it not strictly certain that they will be effective; in particular it is not strictly certain that they will be adopted, for they do not have existence sufficient in itself. We could say, varying the expression of Berkeley, that their "being is a sustained-being" and that their "possibility of being is only an ought-to-be-sustained." [9] Due to this fact their possibility has as a necessary condition the possibility of negative conduct (*not* to pay attention to the stones in the road, to run, to think of something else) and the possibility of the opposite conduct (to throw myself over the precipice). The possibility which I make *my* concrete possibility can appear as my possibility only by raising itself on the basis of the totality of the logical possibilities which the situation allows. But these rejected possibles in turn have no other being than their "sustained-being"; it is I who sustain them in being, and inversely, their present non-being is an "ought-not-to-be-sustained." No external cause will remove them. I alone am the permanent source of their nonbeing, I engage myself in them; in order to cause *my* possibility to appear, I posit the other possibilities so as to nihilate them. This would not produce anguish if I could apprehend myself in my relations with these possibles as a cause producing its effects. In this case the effect defined as my possibility *would be strictly* determined. But then it would cease to be *possible;* it would become simply "about-to-happen." If then I wished to avoid anguish and vertigo, it would be enough if I were to consider the motives (instinct of self-preservation, prior fear, *etc.*), which make me reject the situation envisaged, as *determining* my prior activity in the same way that the presence at a determined point of one given mass determines the courses followed by other masses; it would be necessary, in other words, that I apprehend in myself a strict psychological determinism. But I am in anguish precisely because any conduct on my part is only *possible;* and this means that while constituting a totality of motives *for* pushing away that situation, I at the same moment apprehend these motives as not sufficiently effective. At the very moment when I apprehend my being as *horror* of the precipice, I am conscious of that horror as *not determinant* in relation to my possible con-

---

[9] On the reference to Berkeley, see p. 634, note 2. [R.S.]

duct. In one sense that horror calls for prudent conduct, and it is in itself a pre-outline of that conduct; in another sense, it posits the final developments of that conduct only as possible, precisely because I do not apprehend it as the *cause* of these final developments but as need, appeal, *etc.*

Now as we have seen, consciousness of being is the being of consciousness. There is no question here of a contemplation which I could make after the event, of an horror already constituted; it is the very being of horror to appear to itself as "not being the cause" of the conduct it calls for. In short, to avoid fear, which reveals to me a transcendent future strictly determined, I take refuge in reflection, but the latter has only an undetermined future to offer. This means that in establishing a certain conduct as a possibility and precisely because it is *my* possibility, I am aware that *nothing* can compel me to adopt that conduct. Yet I am indeed already there in the future; it is for the sake of that being which I will be there at the turning of the path that I now exert all my strength, and in this sense there is already a relation between my future being and my present being. But a nothingness has slipped into the heart of this relation; I *am* not the self which I will be. First I am not that self because time separates me from it. Secondly, I am not that self because what I am is not the foundation of what I will be. Finally I am not that self because no actual existent can determine strictly what I am going to be. Yet as I am already what I will be (otherwise I would not be interested in any one being more than another), *I am the self which I will be, in the mode of not being it.* It is through my horror that I am carried toward the future, and the horror nihilates itself in that it constitutes the future as possible. Anguish is precisely my consciousness of being my own future, in the mode of not-being. To be exact, the nihilation of horror as a *motive,* which has the effect of reinforcing horror as a *state,* has as its positive counterpart the appearance of other forms of conduct (in particular that which consists in throwing myself over the precipice) as *my* possible *possibilities.* If *nothing* compels me to save my life, *nothing* prevents me from precipitating myself into the abyss. The decisive conduct will emanate from a self which I am not yet. Thus the self which I am depends on the self which I am not yet to the exact extent that the self which I am not yet does not depend on the self which I am. Vertigo appears as the apprehension of this dependence. I approach the precipice, and my scrutiny is searching for myself in my very depths. In terms of this moment, I play with my possibilities. My eyes, running over the abyss from top to bottom, imitate the possible fall and realize it symbolically; at the same time suicide, from the fact that it becomes a *possibility* possible for *me,* now causes to appear possible motives for adopting it (suicide would cause anguish to cease). Fortunately these motives in their turn, from the sole fact that they are motives of a possibility, present themselves as ineffective, as non-determinant; they can no more *produce* the suicide than my horror of the fall can *determine me* to avoid it. It is this counter-anguish which generally puts an end to anguish by transmuting it into indecision. Indecision in its turn, calls for decision. I abruptly put myself at a distance from the edge of the precipice and resume my way.

The example which we have just analyzed has shown us what we could call "anguish in the face of the future." There exists another: anguish in the face of the past. It is that of the gambler who has freely and sincerely decided not to gamble any more and who when he approaches the gaming table, suddenly sees all his resolutions melt away. This phenomenon has often been described as if the sight of the gaming table reawakened in us a tendency which entered into conflict with our former resolution and ended by drawing us in spite of this. Aside from the fact that such a description is done in materialistic terms and peoples the mind with opposing forces (there is, for example, the moralists' famous "struggle of reason with the passions"), it does not account for the facts. In reality—the letters of Dostoevsky bear witness to this—there is nothing in us which resembles an inner *debate* as if we had to weigh motives and incentives before deciding. The earlier resolution of "not playing anymore" is always *there,* and in the majority of cases the gambler when in the presence of the gaming table, turns toward it as if to ask it for help; for he does not wish to play, or rather having taken his resolution the day before, he thinks of himself still as not wishing to play anymore; he believes in the effectiveness of this resolution. But when he apprehends then in anguish is precisely the total inefficacy of the past resolution. It is there doubtless but fixed, ineffectual, surpassed by the very fact that I am conscious *of* it. The resolution is still *me* to the extent that I realize constantly my identity with myself across the temporal flux, but it is no longer *me*—due to the fact that it has become an object *for* my consciousness. I am not subject to it, it fails in the mission which I have given it. The resolution is there still, I *am* it in the mode of not-being. What the gambler apprehends at this instant is again the permanent rupture in determinism; it is nothingness which separates him from himself; I should have liked so much not to gamble anymore; yesterday I even had a synthetic apprehension of the situation (threatening ruin, disappointment of my relatives) as *forbidding me* to play. It seemed to me that I had established a *real barrier* between gambling and myself, and now I suddenly perceive that my former understanding of the situation is no more than a memory of an idea, a memory of a feeling. In order for it to come to my aid once more, I must remake it *ex nihilo* and freely. The not-gambling is only one of my possibilities, as the fact of gambling is another of them, neither more nor less. *I must rediscover* the fear of financial ruin or of disappointing my family, *etc.,* I must re-create it as experienced fear. It stands behind me like a boneless phantom. It depends on me alone to lend it flesh. I am alone and naked before temptation as I was the day before. After having patiently built up barriers and walls, after enclosing myself in the magic circle of a resolution, I perceive with anguish that *nothing* prevents me from gambling. The anguish *is me* since by the very fact of taking my position in existence as consciousness of being, I make myself *not to be* the past of good resolutions *which I am.*

It would be in vain to object that the sole condition of this anguish is ignorance of the underlying psychological determinism. According to such a view my anxiety would come from lack of knowing the real and effective incentives which in the darkness of the unconscious determine my action. In reply we shall point out first that anguish has not appeared to us as a *proof* of human freedom; the latter was given to us as the necessary condition for the question. We wished only to show that there exists a specific consciousness of freedom, and we wished to show that this consciousness is anguish. This means that we wished to established anguish in its essential structure as consciousness of freedom. Now from this point of view the existence of a psychological determinism could not invalidate the results of our description. Either indeed anguish is actually an unrealized ignorance of this determinism—and then anguish apprehends itself in fact as freedom —or else one may claim that anguish is consciousness of being ignorant of the real causes of our acts. In the latter case anguish would come from that of which we have a presentiment, a screen deep within ourselves for monstrous motives which would suddenly release guilty acts. But in this case we should suddenly appear to ourselves as *things in the world;* we should be to ourselves our own transcendent situation. Then anguish would disappear to give away to *fear,* for fear is a synthetic apprehension of the transcendent as dreadful.

This freedom which reveals itself to us in anguish can be characterized by the existence of that *nothing* which insinuates itself between motives and act. It is not *because* I am free that my act is not subject to the determination of motives; on the contrary, the structure of motives as ineffective is the condition of my freedom. If someone asks what this *nothing* is which provides a foundation for freedom, we shall reply that we can not describe it since it *is not,* but we can at least hint at its meaning by saying that this nothing is made-to-be by the human being in his relation with himself. The nothing here corresponds to the necessity for the motive to appear as motive only as a correlate of a consciousness *of* motive. In short, as soon as we abandon the hypothesis of the contents of consciousness, we must recognize that there is never a motive *in* consciousness; motives are only *for* consciousness. And due to the very fact that the motive can arise only as appearance, it constitutes itself as ineffective. Of course it does not have the externality of a temporal-spatial thing; it always belongs to subjectivity and it is apprehended as *mine.* But it is by nature transcendence in immanence, and consciousness is not subject to it because of the very fact that consciousness posits it; for consciousness has now the task of conferring on the motive its meaning and its importance. Thus the *nothing* which separates the motive from consciousness characterizes itself as transcendence in immanence. It is by arising as immanence that consciousness nihilates the nothing which makes consciousness exist for itself as transcendence. But we see that the nothingness which is the condition of all transcendent negation can be elucidated only in terms of two other original nihilations: (1) Consciousness *is not* its own motive inasmuch as it is *empty* of all content. This refers us to a nihilating structure of the pre-reflective *cogito*. (2) Consciousness confronts its past and its future as facing a self which it is in the mode of not-being. This refers us to a nihilating structure of temporality.

There can be for us as yet no question of elucidating these two types of nihilation; we do not at the moment have the necessary techniques at our disposal. It is sufficient to observe here that the definitive explanation of negation can not be given without a description of self-consciousness and of temporality.

What we should note at present is that freedom, which manifests itself through anguish, is characterized by a constantly renewed obligation to remake the *Self* which designates the free being. As a matter of fact when we showed earlier that my possibilities were filled with anguish because it depended on *me* alone to sustain them in their existence, that did not mean that they derived from a *Me* which to itself at least, would first be given and would then pass in the temporal flux from one consciousness to another consciousness. The gambler who must realize anew the synthetic apperception of a *situation* which would forbid him to play, must rediscover at the same time the *self* which can appreciate that situation, which "is in situation." This *self* with its *a priori* and historical content is the *essence* of man. Anguish as the manifestation of freedom in the face of self means that man is always separated by a nothingness from his essence. We should refer here to Hegel's statement: *"Wesen ist was gewesen ist."* Essence is what has been. Essence is everything in the human being which we can indicate by the words—that *is*. Due to this fact it is the totality of characteristics which *explain* the act. But the act is always beyond the essence; it is a human act only in so far as it surpasses every explanation which we can give of it, precisely because the very application of the formula "that is" to man causes all that is designated, *to have-been*. Man continually carries with him a pre-judicative comprehension of his essence, but due to this very fact he is separated from it by a nothingness. Essence is all that human reality apprehends in itself as *having been*. It is here that anguish appears as an apprehension of self inasmuch as its exists in the perpetual mode of detachment from what is; better yet, in so far as it makes itself exist as such. For we can never apprehend an *Erlebnis* [10] as a living consequence of that *nature* which is ours. The overflow of our consciousness progressively constitutes that nature, but it remains always behind us and it dwells in us as the permanent object of our retrospective comprehension. It

---

[10] *Erlebnis:* experience. [R.S.]

is in so far as this nature is a demand without being a recourse that it is apprehended in anguish.

In anguish freedom is anguished before itself inasmuch as it is instigated and bound by nothing.

QUESTIONS FOR STUDY AND DISCUSSION

1. What is the relation between negativity and questioning?
2. Why does Sartre say that only man really destroys or annihilates, and that natural forces such as storms or floods do not?
3. In what way does Sartre distinguish between the statements, "Pierre is not in this café," and "Wellington is not in this café"? They are both negative statements; how do they differ?
4. Does freedom depend on negativity, or does negativity depend on freedom? Explain.
5. Can animals have fear? Can they have anguish? What is it in man that makes him different from animals in this respect?

August Brunner

AUGUST BRUNNER was born in 1894 in Alsace. He is a member of the Society of Jesus and has taught in several Jesuit institutions in England, on the Continent, and the Near East. He now is one of the editors of *Stimmen der Zeit,* an important German review, in which he publishes frequently. His major work is *Stufenbau der Welt,* which was published in Germany in 1950.

The Nature and Understanding of Persons

PRIOR CONDITIONS TO UNDERSTANDING [1]

A dialogue is possible only between persons, between beings possessing a self—a self that exists through its own being and not simply in the thought of another. For the acts of speaking and understanding which constitute a conversation imply a certain self-possession, and this in turn rests upon self-existence. Thus personal existence implies self-existence and independence. In addition, it means being an originative source and not merely a confluence of physical and psychic operations; for words are meaningful only when an answer is not simply an effect stimulated by a quantum of physical energy received by the listener. Rather, the person guides, restrains or plays out this energy with a view to meaning, to a totality that does not have the simple nature of such energy. The answer always includes a certain newness which has its source and beginning in the initiative of the one who answers; otherwise the reply would be a reciprocal physiological reaction and not meaningful speech. Hence the person is, in a certain way, an ultimate, a central point, a beginning that radiates out in various relationships, freely turns to this or that, and pursues ends set for itself by itself.

The person can be grasped only when he so turns to other persons and to things. If he were directly accessible in himself then he would be delivered over to anyone who comes along. He would possess no self, but would

---

[1] In this selection the English terms "understanding" or "to understand" are always used to translate the German *verstehen,* which has the technical meaning explained in the Introduction to this section. [R.S.]

From pp. 89–107 of August Brunner, *Erkenntnistheorie.* Copyright 1948 by J. P. Bachem, Cologne. This selection translated by Robert Sokolowski. Reprinted by permission of the publisher.

654

be everybody's thing. But he is not a being in the world, something we run into in the world; rather he is a being that *has* a world and freely reveals himself in and through his world. Each person is a central point that possesses its world and exists in itself; he projects himself into the world of things by his power of ordering and disposing them. Thus he is never a means, never a mere sample of a species that could be replaced by any other sample; for this would be to overlook the newness and originality of the person, that is, his very being as a person.

Thus to know a person as such means to be aware of these characteristics essential to his being. If these do not come at least implicitly to the fore, then we have simply come to know a thing to which we may perhaps attribute consciousness; we do not know a person.

Grasping these characteristics need not be, and in most cases is not, a reflexive act. It shows itself simply in the fact that we see, in the speech and action of the other, a meaningful process guided by him according to patterns of meaning and goals, and that we enter into these patterns. We do not see in his speech and action merely a senseless process guided by associations, as would be the case where mental illness or drunkenness make self-possession totally or partially impossible and thus give physiological or physical factors full play. To know a person means to put ourselves at the source-point of his meaningful behavior, and to go along with him from there to that which he intends. Thus understanding implies the recognition of the selfhood and independence of the other person. In this we have a direct contact with reality. It means I must allow the other to remain in his independence and his difference from me, that I must not degrade him by arranging him as a pure means in my own goals and categories. I must not try to bring him into line with my own conceptions but must leave him free in his own proper otherness. For this reason every idealism runs aground on the problem of understanding, if not in theory then at least in fact.

But man is not pure self. The self is only the deepest nucleus of his being. Around it lie various regions that are more or less directly subject to his self-possession. They become the more impersonal, thing-like, the more they escape the direct domination of the self. These regions or levels of the person become proportionally more external and they are no longer the person himself. But in his freedom the person can subject himself to these regions. He can see in them his own self and make their interests and needs his own. He can thus either keep his personal existence as pure as possible and truly be himself in his decision and his own impetus; or he can place his personal existence in the service of things and thus devalue it, allowing himself to be driven instead of deciding for himself. But even the most intimate self of man always remains bound to the impersonal regions of his being and thus projects into the world of things.

This fact explains how the person, who can be grasped only in his radiation into the world and never as an object, can show forth so many different aspects and yet be completely overlooked behind what emanates from him. Only thus can we explain how man can explicitly deny the existence of person or else reduce it to a chance bundle of relations, even though constantly affirming it by implication. No one sees in his own self a simple conjunction of relations, but finds there an independent source of radiation. And we grasp the person of another only by going along with his intentions, by taking him as an ultimate source and central point from which various ramifications issue forth. The latter, because they are more thing-like, can then be treated as immediate objects. We have this in the case of speech. The person of another is given as a self along with his speech.

But often we are more interested in the impersonal aspects of a man by which he enters into a harmful or beneficial relation with us. Then the self of the other man comes through to us more weakly, it recedes more and more, and we take him more and more as a thing. The limit lies in a behavior that uses others as things with no rights and treats a man as something that has meaning only in the measure that he serves as means to our own ends, something that can no longer have a self. Such behavior does not measure up to reality, it falsifies the person, and hence is immoral.

But since man is not a pure person he can, as we have said, never withdraw to a pure personal existence, turned away from all extra-personal levels of existence. For he cannot rip himself away from the drives arising from the subpersonal in him; rather he controls them and puts them to the service of what is higher, and thus makes himself constantly more free and independent.

Thus the measure of personal existence is given in proportion to the freedom of each individual. Furthermore only to the degree that he is in possession of his own self is he able to act as a self towards others, recognize them as selves, and thus admit their own personal existence. For to go beyond one's own aims, cares and wishes, to recognize the self-conscious-ness and the rights of others—all this stands in opposition to the interests and fears that arise from one's own subpersonal levels, which selfishly desire to use everything as means in their own service. For this there must be a control exercised by the self, which only then becomes a true self in this apparent and so-called selflessness.

So it is clear that grasping other persons as such can occur in many different degrees: from the selfless allowance of another to be himself in his own right, without concern for what I might want from him, to the almost total muffling of this other self by means of pretensions, self-interest and concern for one's own aims, counting others more and more only as means or as obstacles, and thus putting my own wishes in the place of reality.

Another factor, conditioned again by the subpersonal element, is the inertia of imagination and thought which contents itself with general schemas and will not or cannot assume the effort of self-originated think-ing. Our corporeally conditioned sensory knowledge is not elastic enough to match the unique newness of what is given to it, especially in the case of persons. It has to content itself with schemas that more or less accurately represent important characteristics and then suppress the rest. Thus no schema is adequate to the unique and individual reality. It is a generalization at the cost of certain aspects of the uniqueness of the thing known. Spiritual knowledge can nevertheless go beyond this and grasp the concrete better in its individuality, but to do so requires a dedication that most are incapable of and often do not even want. Blunting the newness of real beings in this way is practically inconsequential in our knowledge of material things for reasons we will discuss later; though in a lesser degree, it is still inconsequential when we deal with plants and animals, but it does hinder us from taking the personal existence of others fully into account. In place of the unique, individual self we get simply a member of a class, one that can be replaced by any other.

To know a person as such means to grant him recognition. It means leaving him free in his own unique, inimitable way of existing, taking him not as I would like to have him, but as he is in his self-existence, which is not created by me or dependent upon me. It means doing so without concern for my own advantage or disadvantage. It means to forget one's self in order to be there entirely for the other, to affirm him in the uniqueness of his self and in the best of his potentialities. We ourselves feel insulted when others see in us only means to an end and examples of a species.

What we have described is love in its proper sense, having freed itself from self-interest.[2] Naturally such a love does not prevent us from carrying out social functions towards others, making demands on them and watching over their fulfillment, even reprimanding and punishing. But all this is permeated and even commanded by the consideration of another person as such. It does not remain stuck in mere routine nor caught up in self-interests.

For such behavior the reality of what is given as real can never seriously become a question. We maintain that the problem of knowledge could have become acute and really taken seriously only when people's interests turned away from the personal to the impersonal, to the material, and began to think about all other reality in categories proper to the impersonal and material. This came about in the era when the natural sciences enjoyed universal dominion.

It is clear that such selfless behavior is difficult and therefore rare. It hands us over so to speak with no defenses to others, it helplessly exposes our own dear and important interest to great dangers, but it does so in order to gain the highest values. Since it is grounded as much as possible on the self, such behavior is never—or at best only slightly—a matter of habit; rather it demands new initiatives day after day, over and again new heroism, which cannot even take pleasure in itself as the public heroism of the warrior can. Thus it is purer and more personal than the latter. But the

---

[2] St. Augustine, *De diversis quaestionibus*, c. 71 (Migne: *Patrologia Latina*, Vol. 40, Column 82): *Nemo nisi per amicitiam cognoscitur*: No one can be known except through friendship. [A.B.]

depths of personal existence and hence the depths of reality itself reveal themselves only to such initiative.

Such behavior does not fabricate the object of its knowledge; it is diametrically opposed to such construction. Reality appears in it rather as something given; the person of the other is inexplicable in its existence, it is ever a new wonder that we find before us. Only to the degree that the subpersonal schemas squeeze in between the knower and reality can reality appear to be a construction, the objectivation of our own categories of thought. And indeed when such schemas are used, thought does become largely a construction. Thus our knowledge of other persons stays between two extremes, of which neither ever—or hardly ever—becomes realized: between conceiving the concrete self in his pure uniqueness, and misconceiving him as a mere means, a thing.

The case is no different for the knowledge of our own persons. Our own self has to be experienced as a self, as an origin, source of control, self-existence and initiative. But this is possible only in the measure that we really are these things, only in the measure that we consciously and freely make our own decisions in accordance with meanings and motives of the highest type, instead of allowing our decisions to be taken away from us or prescribed for us by inertia, habit and passion. Everything that drags us along only half willing lessens our self-existence because it does not have its beginning and ground in our self, but is the operation of something more or less impersonal. Thus it is clear that knowledge of our own depths is bound up with that of others, and each conditions the other because on both sides the same condition is required: full spiritual freedom. The results of the first part of our book thus find their confirmation and basis.

We must repeat, however, that this is a question of living and unreflective knowledge, not at all of scientific or philosophical knowledge, which belong to another level. (The areas of religion and morality, however, are directly linked to this sphere of self-existence.) Grasping this knowledge in a living way is a still prior condition to all the other conditions we have described. If someone will not carry out the initiative that is demanded because it seems too hard for him, or if through lassitude he has become incapable of such initiative, then these areas remain closed to him; they do not exist for him, not because our behavior creates reality but because it is the condition for our conscious, knowing entrance into it.

Whatever depends so much on the behavior of one's own self cannot be transferred and communicated like a mere thing. The knowledge we speak of is personal also in the new sense that it becomes a part of the knower once he carries it out himself in an original way. It can of course be mediately passed on to others, but in a way that matches its original character: it must be originally achieved by everyone who wants to learn it. Each one must carry out this knowledge himself, but he can do so prompted by the example and the living words of someone who has himself accomplished it and can point out its possibility. The second knowledge is then a "reproduction" of the first in the sense that each man must carry out or "produce" on his own account what the first man has already done. But this reproduction is easier than the very first approach; it now has a certain guidance and incentive. It is still costly, but its price is less than the first. It still remains one's own living knowledge and personal possession, "existential truth," immediately affecting our own existence and working through our behavior. Personal life is nourished by these truths. It is nourished on general and abstract truths only in the measure that they become concrete and living knowledge, existential truth for each man, through his own effort.

These truths have a living influence on the areas of religion and morality, which are so close to the person. We can thus see why the meaning of religion and morality will be very highly valued by those who are deeply concerned with the personal life of man.

It would be an unjust exaggeration to reject every general truth as useless or false. For the content of existential truth is indeed individual and tailored to the unique case of this man, but according to the law of analogy, which holds for all being, there is no reality that is totally different from the others, that shows no similarity of greater or lesser degree with other beings. Such a common aspect can be freed from an individual case, made independent and thus turned into a general truth that could be passed on in communication. In this process it has lost its immediate existentiality, but through personal appropriation it can regain it.

At any rate, as long as we stay on the level of general truth, it is not existential. This explains the fact that someone can approach a religion such as Christianity or Buddhism in the impersonal way of a scholar without sharing in the religious conviction that is there. Still, such knowledge lacks the final deep element, the religious moment. For a religion is not just a matter for reason, not just a philosophical system, even if it may contain elements for one. It is above all a life, which as a human life involves cognitions and convictions. But only life, only one's own experience, can make us know this life in what is most proper to itself. It would be folly to want to share in this experience through a sort of psychological experiment, by behaving as if one shared in this conviction. Religious behavior is marked by the absoluteness of its pledge, by the pledge of one's whole person, and this is irreconcilably opposed to any "as if." This presents a problem for the history of religions. It is partly solved through the scholar's own similar experiences which make it possible for him to understand a behavior that is more or less like his own. The richer and deeper one's own religious experience is, the better one is situated to understand the proper essence of another religion, other things being equal.

The knowledge of personal being is thus tied to a certain prior condition that we might call acquiescence to reality. It is absolutely required on this level of being. For other levels it is only a question of not setting your own fantasies in the place of reality. Apart from this, things are readily accessible to man's spontaneous knowledge, all the more so in proportion as they are more material, more purely things. As regards matter there is need for no particular personal activity besides the proper use of intellect. Everything here is simply a matter of talent and hard work. This is clearest in mathematical knowledge, which is totally independent of any moral and personal behavior of the knower. Platonism, with its interest in the moral and religious personality of man, stressed the importance of such behavior right from the beginning, but overgeneralized the need for it in all fields of knowledge.

The question whether every error is a sin arises in connection with this. Obviously such a relationship could only come into question in a field such as we have discussed, that of the knowledge of personal existence. In the field of things there is no essential relation between error and sin, only perhaps an accidental one. The most common sources of error in knowing things are simply the weakness and limitation of our power of knowing. Also, deficiencies in our knowledge are often unconsciously increased because the schemata of our perception and imagination are so imprecise, as we have often mentioned. But an intrinsic connection between sin and error exists only where knowledge depends upon a behavior that must be freely assumed, and where the knower through his own guilt cannot or will not carry out such behavior; that is, only in the field of personal being. But even here we should not state any general law too strictly. In this sphere also there can be errors without any guilt, even if we should consider such personally guiltless errors as ultimately coming from original sin.

Until now we have spoken only of the conditions that the knower must have for knowledge of personal beings as such. But these do not suffice. The person is self-possession and excludes any arbitrary control by others. Hence there also exist, in the case of this level of being, conditions in the subject to be known. The subject must open himself, he must will to reveal himself, or else neither the activity nor the knowing power of the knower will be of any help. Every person is a sanctuary to which he alone allows entrance. But the behavior we have described, respectful love, invites the subject to disclose himself and does not force him. The more personal a certain reality is, the less it is open to all, the more it must be freely given in an attitude of reciprocal familiarity. A bond of familiarity, an inner sharing of personal interests, are the results of such personal revelation. This familiarity is bound up with certain spatial and temporal conditions that are summarized in the concept of "presence"; but whereas such presence is sufficient for the knowledge of things, in the sphere of personal being it is only one aspect in the presence of personal self-revelation and personal openness to such revelation. Here too all degrees of familiarity are possible, and the richness and depth of knowledge is measured out accordingly.

This condition, which is valid only on the level of personal existence, has often been generalized and applied to the knowledge of things, and led thinkers to objectify a sort of spiritual being in things, which would then reveal itself as essentially similar to the knower. This essential similarity between knower and known is obviously only a projection, into these lower levels, of that familiarity which is a precondition for the disclosure and understanding of personal being. Only in personal being is it true, to a certain degree, that like is known only by like; and even this likeness is not to be taken in a mathematical sense, but as the personal familiarity that must be maintained by both parties.

Obviously these preconditions of knowledge, required both in the knower and the one known, are realized to an appreciable degree only now and then and only towards a few persons. They are never really brought to perfection. Still, such knowledge is of the greatest importance. It is under its influence that the personal and spiritual life of man arises within the family. All other forms of knowing thus bear the traces of their origin in this type. Only very slowly do they disengage what is proper to themselves from their entanglement with personal knowledge. We saw above how the knowledge of things is still filled with categories taken from this area of knowledge. And through it we enter into immediate, sure contact with reality in itself; we saw in the first part of the book how even the knowledge we have of things is tied up with personal knowledge as regards its existential value. Thus its depths are the standard for measuring the depths of our grasp of reality, even though it does not match the extension and the scientific comprehension found in our knowledge of things.

We go beyond the narrow circle of familiarity when we run into social roles, functions that are more or less intimately tied up with the individual personal being who carries them out, roles that allow his personality to manifest itself in greater or lesser degree. Thus we have acquaintances, colleagues, or simply fellow members of a social group. They enter into contact with us as politicians, officials, artists; others play economic roles such as manufacturers, salesmen, workers and managers. Each of these functions assumes the personal aspect of its bearer, but not all in the same immediacy. There are functions that touch almost directly the personal element in their bearer, and others that by nature are only loosely tied up with it. This is not the place to go into these relationships and the personal and social problems that they pose. Only one thing is important: the personal being of the man bearing a function must always be present somehow in the background if we wish to grasp a man as such and not degrade him to a mere thing. The more impersonal a function is the easier it is to replace the functionary, the easier it is to stick him into a general class, even going so far as a general category like "man." But even here the presence of a unique personality in every member still remains. This personality can come to the fore when we come to appreciate the man personally; through his strength and goodness he can assert himself in his true nature sometimes even in functions that are hardly personal at all. Thus even a general concept can become a personal name, as do the names "Father" and "Mother." No one who uses them just intends to classify his own parents as mere instances of the general concepts of father and mother. These various points are important for the theory of concepts.

THE STRUCTURE OF UNDERSTANDING

It is to be expected that the understanding of persons matches the level of being in its structure; this is indeed the case. The person is self-existence, something that does not belong to a subject as its act or property. In this self-existence he is the ground and source of acts, behavior and inclinations through which he relates to other persons and to things in a way appropriate to each. The person is thus also "outside" himself and directed towards other things; he has his existence in this direction he takes upon himself, in this striving after goals. There is a hierarchy among these goals. A goal at this or that moment is determined by a more comprehensive goal; this in turn can be a means to the realization of another still more permanent and more encompassing goal. Transient acts and behavior are thus the application of permanent attitudes, which themselves are determined by the character of the person; his character in turn is one of the possibilities that a person has. Through this ordering of goals above and below one another there comes about a unity in the existence of a person. This unity reflects the person's self-possession throughout the changes in life, and is made possible by this self-possession. By their own influence alone, changing conditions and accidents would bring about only a chaotic, undirected process. But by relying on his own self the person can force through, in greater or lesser degree, his own intention and his own being. He forces the multitude of events that come upon him into his own direction and thus realizes, in greater or lesser degree, a unified course in his life. The more strength he has to dominate and have his way instead of passively being dragged here and there, the more meaningful is his personality. Thus the person as self-existence is a power, ability, and potentiality that freely determines itself. He has possibilities and realizes them in any situation. These possibilities are the expression of the capacity to force one's self through subpersonal factors; they are a person's strength of being.

Goals and possibilities thus form a unity determined by the person. But this unity acquires a special structure because of the bond between the center of a person with the other levels of existence about him. The pure personal unity becomes a totality that spreads about the man and provides a place in which he can appear. This is the personal world of each and every man. The person does not belong to this world, but bears it. Through his acts and behavior he projects into this world. The person approaches everything he meets with his own conceptions, evaluations and attitudes, and this is what makes such a contact a real "meeting." Everything is colored by him to a certain degree, everything "belongs" to him.

This gives us the basic elements of understanding. It is clear and has often been mentioned that the person is not open for others to grasp arbitrarily. If this were so, he would no longer be a self. He is thus not an object in the way a thing is. He cannot be approached purely in his own self because he does not exist in a pure state as a person, but only as bound up with subpersonal levels that form the bridge to his personal world. In and through this world the person is grasped as the ground that gives life, takes positions, sets and follows goals, and maintains itself throughout all change; he is grasped as an ultimate.

We have already pointed out the special way in which persons are manifest in the case of speech. In listening and speaking the meaning, that which the speaker means, is grasped as something rational; not merely a causal factor, but an intention directed at a goal. Understanding thus means to grasp the action of a man as something determined by a goal he has set for himself; it means ordering the momentary goal in a wider pattern, just as words are ordered into a sentence and a sentence again into the unity of the speech determined by a given situation. By organizing such goals, all truly human activity points back to the self, which considers the situation it is in, grasps various possibilities, and freely chooses among them. When an activity or behavior can no longer be ordered into a personal unity, then mere causes appear in the place of motivating goals. Such causes were not absent before this, of course, but they disappeared from sight because the meaning dominated them. This is the case with the purely sensory sound of a word, which is entirely overcome by the meaning. Likewise when asked, "Why are you going there?" no one would answer by enumerating the nerve reactions and muscular motions of his legs. Such an explanation would presume that meaningful understanding is impossible, and would treat the man as mentally hindered by sickness or delirium. This predominance of final causality in understanding is the reason we are so doggedly prone to use final causes as explanations everywhere, even where they have no place.

Understanding, we may repeat, means to put one's self in the place of the person to be understood, and thence to see his world as a coherent unity that is borne and determined by him. As pure understanding, this does not yet imply any agreement or disagreement. Putting one's self in the place of another in this way is made possible naturally by the selfhood, the self-possession of the person. It will succeed to the degree that a man can free himself from himself and see reality with the eyes of another. This happens in various degrees, as we have pointed out in the preceding section.

Obviously, taking the place of another in this way is the only mode of knowing proper to persons. The person does not become an object as a thing does, but is grasped in his being as a ground and origin when we "go along with" him. The person is thus perceptible only in and through relations, behavior and acts. He can never be cut off from them. The person hovers like the atmosphere in such understanding, penetrating and encompassing everything but hardly perceptible itself. For this reason he escapes any search that tries to grasp him after the manner of an object, and tries to dissolve him into a bundle of relations and "causal interactions." The person can be grasped only as the final ground and source penetrating through such things; he can be grasped only in the emanation of such relationships and interactions from himself.

To understand thus means to take something immediately present to us and to see it in its relationship to a meaning. This first, immediate meaning is then to be ordered into a more comprehensive one, and so on higher and higher until we come to the unity of the person, as he declares himself in his world. At this point understanding reaches its upper limit. The existence and unicity of this person cannot be understood any further; it can only be taken as a fact that grounds all understanding. Likewise, the purely physical presence of something that bears meaning, for example, the sound as such in speech, forms a lower limit for understanding that cannot be crossed. Understanding can move only between these two limits. Thus a double moment of pure facticity is implied and presupposed by all understanding, but it does not become a conspicuous factor except in cases where understanding fails to work properly.

An important result of this is the fact that knowledge does not coincide with understanding, as some theories that want to understand everything implicitly maintain. Knowledge goes far beyond understanding. Understanding is chronologically the first form of knowing and is humanly speaking the most important, but its area of application is very limited. Primitive people and naive thought, however, believe that they can understand everything. Primitive explanations of nature work only with the categories of finality and therefore see the expression of personal beings in all natural phenomena. When something unusual happens in nature they take it to be the result of caprice or chance, and they feel that relatively rare and startling events that show a pattern of some sort are brought about by menacing powers. And even now, pure efficient causes can scarcely be conceived; we always cover them up and falsify them by putting goal-directed action into them. Thus philosophically a critique of finality in our thinking is absolutely necessary.

The sphere of meaning we can grasp immediately is also very restricted. It is not at all immediately apparent that everything, including the beings and events that go beyond the sphere of persons, has a meaning. This would entail that all beings are tied together in a pattern of meanings and goals that surpasses them all, a pattern that belongs to a primary personal being, that is, to a personal God, whose existence would be immediately shown. Even if such a proof were possible, all beings would still not be understandable to us, each with its proper sense, for we could never place ourselves in the position of an infinite personal being and look out from his point of view upon everything as fused into a unity of meaning. Any attempt to do this with our finite methods would yield only self-deception. Only God himself can say anything about the particular intention he is pursuing with a given being or event. The proof of the existence of a personal God only gives us the certainty that there is a meaning present in everything, a meaning that surpasses us and is generally hidden from us, one that we can only believe in as regards its individual elements.

Understanding a real person usually occurs in the following way. We approach him knowing that he exists as a person. This means that we consider him a self, a source and ground, from which the unity of a world emanates. This preconception however is empty, or only filled with previous experiences. Slowly, in dealing with the person, this emptiness becomes filled, and the prejudices we had from earlier experiences are replaced by reality. More and more our own constructions get driven away by the independent being of the other person; the concept of truth that we have elaborated above is confirmed in this. It is easy to see that this concrete knowledge is a progressive synthesis, through which all the new additions of knowledge are written into the personality we come to know more completely and profoundly. The ideal goal of this synthesis would be the exhaustive knowledge of a concrete person.

Since understanding allows us to grasp the intentions and originality of the person along with certain sensibly perceptible aspects, it always contains a double moment. A purely physical event or being is taken as a bearer of meaning, as something taken up by a self that transcends and dominates the physical aspect and sets its own goals. If we are going to deal with understanding, then a reference to the person must be grasped along with the purely material or physiological reality. Then the way the facts are cannot be explained any longer simply by giving the efficient causes, because these causes no longer work in total independence. In fact their existence is practically submerged in the total structure of meaning.

Still the connection of efficient causes remains unbroken; the free action of the man simply enters as a new cause along with the others, but as an efficient cause that, in its strength and direction, is measured out to reach a goal through the confluence of all the other causes. Because man controls himself and his action, and to the extent that he does so, he can prescribe a measure to the intensity of his own causal action, while physical causes always work at full capacity. Materialism and determinism look only to the chain of efficient causes and deny the governing influence of a person's free determination. But they cannot help implicitly recognizing it, for they attribute to their own words and systems a meaning that is supposed to be understandable to others and could never be simply linked on to the chain of pure efficient causes.

At times men have tried to explain understanding by means of other "simpler" forms of knowledge. But this fails because understanding is chronologically the first type of knowledge we have, and other forms of knowing separate themselves from it only with great difficulty. The latter should rather be considered as derived and deficient forms of understanding, as forms in which certain aspects become more emphasized and then break away when the higher and unifying aspects are weakened or disappear. But explaining a higher whole by giving the simpler elements out of which it is put together has a place only on the level of the material. We will study the reasons for this later.

There is another attempt to explain understanding that we must reject, one found in Dilthey for example. Understanding is taken as a type of projection of one's own states into the other. This presupposes, as do so many epistemologies since the time of Descartes, that self-knowledge is essentially easier than knowledge of others. According to this, we would understand the smile of another as an expression of joy because we ourselves smile when we feel happy. Unfortunately, each man's own facial expression, the sound of his own voice, the particular style of his own bearing, are all unknown to the man himself. How could a child, when learning to understand its mother, make a comparison that even most adults are incapable of! Understanding is rather the beginning, the awakening of the personal and spiritual in man, an awakening that can be prepared by innate instinct patterns but always represents something totally new in the face of them.

Let us remark finally that understanding does not mean reliving another's experience. To relive someone's experience may include genuine or supposed understanding, but it does not involve taking the place of another person as a matter of knowledge; it is rather a matter of feeling and emotion, trying to make yourself feel as though *you* were being affected instead of seeing someone else affected. This type of thing is far removed from the certitude and objectivity of understanding. Understanding always remains aware of the otherness prevailing between knower and known, while reliving tries to do away with this distinction and tries to make yourself just like the other. Community between persons is not promoted by blurring their otherness like this; rather it would be dissolved if the fusion could be pushed all the way, for there would be no more plurality to be united in a community. True community consists rather in having a common world, being directed towards similar goals with the same attitude towards reality, all this coming from the similarity of our personal depths. It must be unreflexive and without conscious, reflexive choice. Such personal depths become similar under the workings of similar influences; they do not simply arise from the nature common to all men. They can only be historical forces.

KNOWLEDGE AND COMMUNITY

The person is not a unity that stands alone. Though it sounds strange in the abstract, we must affirm that the person is simultaneously the most closed and the most open of all beings, and both these aspects condition the person. He is closed in the sense that he possesses himself as a self and can forbid all others entrance into his innermost sphere; also, that in this self-possession the person sharply marks himself off from all that is not himself. He can never confuse one of his own present acts with that of someone else. Only a personal being can, in the strict sense, set himself in opposition, distinguish himself from everything that he is not and truly call it "the other." For the person alone is a self. On the lower levels of being the borderlines of an individual being become more and more unclear until they practically vanish even in the lower animals and plants; for here a new entity can be formed out of a mere part of an individual being. And on the level of material reality the concept of an individual being becomes completely questionable.

But the person, as a self, is open and stands in relation to others. Precisely because he remains firmly in himself in this way, he can turn towards others without suffering loss to himself. He can turn wherever he wishes. And he lives in such turning toward others, which takes place through communication and coexistence. It is the person alone who can be the subject of a relation in the full sense, who relates himself to others and does so consciously. On the lower levels of being even the category of relation becomes weaker and weaker and is hardly perceptible at all.

Through the relations of knowledge and will a variegated net of influences is spun out between persons, though we are usually not at all clearly aware of its operation. From the very beginning everyone is tied up in such a net that educates and forms him. The more internal and permanent the exchange between the same persons, the more comprehensive and deep will this influence become; an ever greater togetherness of knowing, judging, evaluation and rejection will be created through the formation of the most intimate ground of the self, as we have seen above. Thus arises the community spirit of a group. The group is then in turn included in a larger one that also has its own spirit, but because it now encompasses several other subordinate groups, it no longer has the exclusivity that they have. Despite its aspects of similarity, it allows room for many differences. Since interaction between persons is carried out through the intermediary of the body, its possibility depends on certain corporeal conditions such as spatial and temporal presence. These factors tend to restrict the community to a narrower scope.

This common spirit which founds the community is called "objective spirit" by Hegel, the first philosopher to discover it, because he considers it something objective, transcending the individual. Hegel saw in it a spiritual, individual substance that moved itself spontaneously according to the laws of knowledge, while individuals were only moments in it, moments in which it realized itself. As against Hegel we insist that this objective spirit has no proper self, and that no self can be a moment in a higher self. The freedom of individual persons is really only a word in Hegel, and if he were consistent he would have to exclude all responsibility in this totality which progresses according to necessary logical laws. But we adequately account for this objective spirit by the relations among persons who make up a community. In this way it transcends any individual member and is relatively, though never absolutely, independent of this or that individual. It can thus appear to him as a foreign, objective power, but this happens only when the individual rebels against the spirit of a community. He then begins to experience the power of the other persons.

Another overemphasis in Hegel is the fact that he saw in the powers that move this spirit only purely spiritual powers, and especially forces of thought. In reality, forces of all different types are operative in it, everything that has influence on human life: personal elements, spiritual, vital, biological and economic. Its unity is founded on the unity of the persons who bear it.

As a result of this unity, every influence that a given person carries out in a certain field changes not only this field, but the entire person too, who then works as so changed within the objective spirit. Thus there arises a constant exchange in the objective spirit between these influences, and the unity that is constantly being destroyed is always being restored. This movement has something of the logical motion of thesis, antithesis and synthesis, but it is only a similarity. Still, Hegel handled his logical law with such breadth and plasticity that in many cases he did come close to the true movement.

Thus every change of the objective spirit is mirrored in each of its regions, and if we follow a given individual field in its development we get a sort of projection of the total motion on the field in question. This explains the fact that attempts are made over and over again to explain historical motion by means of one particular type of causality. We must mention too that individual fields do not follow the total motion all in the same way, and the motion in each field is not equally original. But we must not develop this point here.

The community is founded upon individual persons. Hence it has a structure that is similar to that of persons. Like these, it has a certain unity amid change, a certain self-identity, but without a self. In order to understand it we must, just as in the case of persons, put ourselves in the direction of its aspirations, evaluations, and the attitudes it takes, we must look from its point of view upon its possibilities and what it has made of them. But in doing so we do not come to a self; rather, as Hegel and Dilthey have correctly seen, we come to a loose net of relationships, to a purely mobile pattern of causes that are borne by persons. The community has no being in itself but rests on the being of persons, who all too often are swallowed up in it. Thus the person as such is not founded upon the community but the community upon the person, of whom it realizes only one aspect, his social side. We admit that the individual person always comes after the community, for he is born into the community and fostered by it; but this is so only because the person always finds other persons there before himself. Still, community is not something externally added to the person, but a part, a moment of himself. Individual and community are two sides of a person that are manifest in every activity of his, though in different degrees.

Every individual thus takes his part in the promotion or the perversion of the community. But the contribution of most just gets lost in the crowd, and only a few men, the great men, carry out an influence that can later be historically perceived.

From what we have said we can conclude that the influence of the community on our knowledge is very deep, even though this influence is usually not perceived, or only perceived by persons who belong to another community. The community receives a new born child through the family and forms his knowledge and thinking through education. It furnishes him with that irreplacable tool needed for all spiritual life, language, and in doing so gives him a treasury of experience, but also outfits him with a special way of approaching reality. Thus an immense store of experience and knowledge, much too large for any individual to find the time, strength and opportunity to achieve, is dropped in his lap. Without this tradition there would be no culture and man would be an animal, not man. But through this the predispositions and abilities of the community become fixed and formed for good, and work themselves into all knowledge. Even someone who turns against the spirit by which he was formed begins his rebellion as a person who has been formed by it.

Every community is historical. The purely natural elements are indeed a foundation for it, and it can form itself only within that which nature allows, but the specific formation that is achieved is the work of historical forces. Thus in all knowledge there is a historical moment, which need not be purely subjective. The distinctions of natural versus historical and objective versus subjective do not coincide, but cut across one another.

Although the role of the community is of greatest importance, the individual as such does not therefore sink into insignificance, to a simple operation, to a moment of the community. Rather he assumes what the community offers him in a personal way, enriches it through his own experience, makes it of greater or lesser value, and thus constantly works along with the development of the community that he bears within himself. It is a heritage that is ever living and ever to be revived. It lives only through the force and the will of the individual, just as he can only live in a community. Thus individual and community as such are abstractions that never exist in the pure state. Only persons are real, and they are simultaneously individual and social because of their existence as selves. But just as we previously found a balance among the various levels that belong to a person, so now we find, for the same reasons, a balance between the individual and communitarian moments of the person. Therefore over the long run one does not gain at the loss of the other; instead each suffers when the other is weakened. The greater value individuals have, the more they can offer the community; the higher the community stands, the easier individuals can assume a higher level of spiritual existence. We must always balance off both sides of the person to bring about the best in each.

QUESTIONS FOR STUDY AND DISCUSSION

1. Why does Brunner feel that the problem of knowledge (i.e., the suspicion that we do not really know reality) cannot be seriously entertained in the case of our understanding of other persons?
2. Is it true to say that one man can be more a person than another?
3. In what way can personal existence and understanding be communicated? Would language alone suffice for such communication? Do you think that language alone suffices for any sort of communication?
4. Can we know ourselves apart from our presence in the world and our relations to others?
5. What is the difference between a thing in the world and a person who has a world?
6. In what way does personal causality differ from and yet work along with material efficient causes?
7. In what way is the person subordinated to the community? How is the community subordinated to the person?

Gabriel Marcel

GABRIEL MARCEL was born in Paris in 1889. His father was active in the
French diplomatic and artistic world. Marcel's teaching career has been
relatively brief; he taught intermittently at French lycées from 1911 until 1922, and again from 1939 to 1941. The recipient of many literary
awards, he has been writing for the stage since 1911, and his plays and
philosophical works earned him an appointment to the French Academy
in 1952. His innate sensitivity to human values and his distrust of tech-
nological, impersonal society must have been sharpened by his experience
in World War I, when he worked with the Red Cross in attempting to
locate missing persons. He became a Roman Catholic in 1929, and is
today considered the chief representative of Christian existentialism.

Person and Decision

I promised C—— the other day that I would come back to the nursing
home where he has been dying for weeks, and see him again. This promise
seemed to me, when I made it, to spring from the inmost depths of my
being. A promise moved by a wave of pity: he is doomed, he knows it, he
knows I know it. Several days have gone by since my visit. The circumstances which dictated my promise are unchanged; I have no room for self-
deception about that. I should be able to say—yes, I even dare assert—that
he still inspires the same compassion in me. How could I justify a change
in the state of my feelings, since nothing has happened since which could
have the power to alter them? And yet I must in honesty admit that the pity
I *felt* the other day, is today no more than a theoretical pity. I still judge
that he is unhappy and that it is right to be sorry for him, but this is a
judgment I should not have dreamed of formulating the other day. There
was no need. My whole being was concentrated into an irresistible impulse
towards him, a wild longing to help him, to show him that I was on his
side, that his sufferings were mine. I have to recognise that this impulse no
longer exists, and it is no longer in my power to do more than imitate it by
a pretence which some part of me refuses to swallow. All that I can do is to
observe that C—— is unhappy and alone and that I cannot let him down;

From pp. 47–56 of Gabriel Marcel, *Being and Having,* translated by Katherine Farrer.
Reprinted by permission of the Beacon Press. Copyright © 1951 Beacon Press.

also, I have promised to come back; my signature is at the foot of the bond and the bond is in his possession.

The silence I feel within me is strangely different from that other cry of pity from the heart; yet it does not seem to me altogether mysterious. I can find a good enough explanation for it in myself and the rhythm of my moods. But what is the good? Proust was right: we are not at our own disposal. There is a part of our being to which strange, perhaps not altogether conceivable, conditions give us sudden access; the key is in our hands for a second; and a few minutes later the door is shut again and the key disappears. I must accept this fact with shame and sorrow.

But this commitment that I took upon myself the other day—surely it rested upon my ignoring, and wrongly ignoring, these fluctuations and interruptions in my states? Surely it was rather presumptuous of me to assert that, on such-and-such a day in the future, I should still feel the same compassion which pierced me to the heart when I stood by the sick bed? Or did I really make no such claim at the time, did I really mean that a certain material fact—my visit—would take place after a certain interval? What shall I answer? I must not accept this alternative. I did not *ask* myself whether the feeling that impelled me towards him was going to die down like a fountain or the shape of a melody. *A fortiori* I could not commit myself to feeling tomorrow as I did yesterday.

But suppose I leave aside whatever I was conscious of at that fleeting moment, and suppose I try to discover what my promise means in so far as it was an act. Then I am bound to recognise that it contains a decree so daring that it surprises me now. Allowing for the possibility of exterior conditions which may put it out of my power to keep my promise, I have admitted, however implicitly, that the state of my feelings was capable of alteration, but I decided at the same time that this eventual alteration was something of which I should not take account. Between the being who dares to say "I" and who has attributed to himself the power to bind *himself* (I bind *myself*)—between him and the endless world of causes and effects which simultaneously escape from my own jurisdiction and from all rational prevision, there is an intermediate realm, where events take place which are not in accordance with my desires or even with my expectation; yet I reserve to myself the right and the power to abstract from these events in my actions. This power of real abstraction is at the very core of my promise: this is what gives it its peculiar weight and worth. I will make an effort to fix my attention on this central datum, and not yield to the vertigo which threatens to overwhelm me when I see the gulf opening at my feet: in fact, what is this body of which I am at once master and slave? Can I, without folly or insincerity, relegate it to the huge foreign empire which eludes my grasp? But I cannot completely include it, either, in that subject realm where my own decree gives me the power to discount any of its contents. It seems to me equally true to say that I am and am not responsible for these bodily fluctuations; both assertions seem accurate to me, and both ridiculous. I will question myself no further on this point; enough to have recognised that in binding myself by a promise I have acknowledged the presence of an inner hierarchy, consisting of a ruling principle, and a life whose details remain unpredictable, but which the principle subjects to itself, or, still more accurately, which it pledges itself to keep under its yoke.

I cannot help seeing that here I am repeating one of the commonplaces most often explored by the wisdom of antiquity; but perspective plays us strange tricks: what seemed self-evident long ago takes on, in my eyes today, a paradoxical aspect. And what is more, I cannot help wondering if this decree will not be called a shocking act of violence by the supporters of that ethic of transparent honesty which I hear most commonly professed around me. Is not the very language of "abstracting" or "discounting" (which I have had to use several times) enough to breed considerable disquiet? How can I justify this dictatorship which I claim to exercise over my future actions, in the name of some present state? Where does this authority come from, and what lays claim to it? Am I not oversimplifying, when I distinguish from my present a subject which claims to go beyond it in a mental dimension which is not to be confused with duration, and which I can hardly figure out, even in idea? To look more closely, is not my present itself making an arbitrary claim to a sort of eternity of right? But in that case falsehood is established at the very heart of my life. For this pretended "eternity of right" no corresponding continuity of fact can be found; and it seems that I am brought up against the following disconcerting alternatives. At the moment of my commitment, I either (1) arbitrarily assume a constancy in my feelings which it is not really in my power to establish, or (2) I accept in advance that I shall have to carry out, at a given moment, an action which will in no way reflect my state of mind when I do carry it out. In the first case I am lying to myself, in the second I consent in advance to lie to someone else.

Shall I seek reassurance by telling myself that these are just a cloud of subtleties concealing a really very simple problem, which life will make it its own business to solve?

I cannot be content with such a lazy answer; the less so, since I can imagine at this moment a dozen cases where the problem is still the same, but where its terms are of a kind which proclaim its seriousness even to the most careless thinker. To swear fidelity to a creature, to a group, to an idea, even to God—in every case, is not this to expose ourselves to the same disastrous dilemma? Is not any promise whatever rooted in a state of mind which is entirely of the moment, and whose permanence nothing can guarantee?

When I look at it like this, the very nature of fidelity seems to me suddenly covered by a thick veil; I can no longer understand what meaning the term "commitment" has ever had for me. And now I call to mind once more the memory of all the disappointments, all the hatreds of myself and others which were the ordinary results of too hasty promises. Were they mere accidents? or must we see them, on the contrary, as the natural effects of a most inexcusable presumption? At what price are they to be avoided? If we are to remain tied by our inward bond, must we not learn to shut our eyes to the contorted but fateful life-process which only a feeble sight will fail to discern beneath the accumulations of habit? To swear fidelity—whatever the object to which the vow is taken—what is it really but committing myself to ignore the deepest part of my being, to learn the art of duping myself constantly with tricks that I play upon myself, for my own deception? Indeed, can a commitment exist that is not a betrayal?

But there is no betrayal which is not a repudiation of fidelity. Is there, then, such a thing as a basic fidelity, a primal bond, which I break every time I make a vow which in the least degree concerns what I vaguely call my soul? (Obviously there is no question here of vows about mere matters of the most outward and socialised activity, where I am as it were using a tool ready to my hand.) This primal bond can only be what some people have taught me to call fidelity to myself. Myself, they will say, is what I betray when I so bind myself. Myself: not my being but my becoming; not what I am today but what I shall perhaps be tomorrow. Here the mystery thickens. How can I be faithful, or again how can I be unfaithful, to the Me whom today cannot know, and only the future will reveal? Surely they mean me to understand just this; that I must keep myself at the disposal of the unknown Me, so that one day he can come into my place without meeting any resistance from the Me that I still am, but shall in that second have ceased to be? They are just asking me to lend myself to the game, and not in the least to stiffen my muscles and resist. The word fidelity has certainly undergone a change here! It now sketches no more than a lazy acquiescence, a graceful passivity. Well, but who prescribes it for me? this unknown whose prestige is entirely due to the fact that he does not yet exist? Amazing privilege for the unborn! But at least the privilege must be recognised, and once more I am in the dark. For the act by which this privilege of my future being is so consecrated is in fact part of my present: so we admit a value in the future in so far as it is a future which is attached to my present state, but which is nevertheless distinct from it, since it somehow has control of its successor.

Shall I yield to the temptations of dialectic? Shall I admit that it is really my present state which is denied and claims to be transcended? Surely we cannot help regarding this as a manipulation to be mistrusted, since it implies, suppose I allow it, some sort of truth which transcends the life-process and is capable of serving as its foundation. But if this is so, there is no further question of my lending myself unresistingly to the current of my moods of the moment. Something which forms no part of them rules their caprices, perhaps a law. And it is my business to remain faithful to this law or unity. Terminology, however, threatens once more to lead me into error. This unity is just me; it is a single unvarying principle—whether form or reality—which insists upon its own continuity. The fidelity is no longer to a life-process, a "becoming," for this is meaningless, but to a *being* which I can see no possibility of distinguishing from myself. And so I escape from the mirage of a tomorrow which loses its colour as it sharpens its outlines.

Have I at last found the way out? Have I escaped from the horns of the dilemma which seemed to forbid me to be sincere and faithful at once? The solution which occurs to me is not just a logical invention; a very simple word describes the hidden spring of the action by which I bind myself. To make it a point of honour to fulfil a commitment—what else is this but putting an accent on the supra-temporal identity of the subject who contracts it and carries it out? And so I am brought to think that this identity has a validity in itself, whatever the content of my promise may be. This identity is the one important thing to maintain, however absurd the particular commitment may appear, to the eyes of a spectator, through my rashness or weakness in undertaking it. However overwhelmingly men of sense object, however often my friends remonstrate, I shall take no notice; I have promised and will keep my word. Perhaps my persistence will even be proportionally strengthened as the carrying out of the promise looks to myself and others more and more like the fulfilment of a wager.

But if this is so, the particular object, were it God himself, to which fidelity binds its votaries, must remain a pure accident, a sort of pretext. It cannot enter the closed circle in which the will returns upon herself in her effort after the demonstration of her own power.

But I cannot really confuse this attachment of the soul to its own glory —the most arid, strained, and irritable of all the forms of self-love—with that which I have all my life called Fidelity. It cannot be pure chance that fidelity shows itself in its most unmistakable garb among those who have, on the contrary, the least concern to cut a figure in their own eyes. The face of a servant or a farm-labourer is its place of revelation for me. What can be the ground of so ruinous a confusion of two spiritual states, when the most superficial judgment will assure me that they are forever incompatible? How can we help seeing that a fidelity to another of which I was myself the ground, the spring, and the centre—that such a fidelity as this would expose yet again, by the furtive act of substitution it reveals, the lie at the heart of that existence which it shapes?

How to get out of this deadlock? I must again tackle the precise problem, the dilemma, which I stated at the beginning; especially the problem of fidelity vowed to a person. I must refuse the choice of alternatives (continuity of the inner disposition or insincerity of action). I cannot base my argument on the effort of my own will. I must admit, then, that something unalterable is implied in the relation itself. Must see further into the nature of this unalterable: where do I start if I am go get hold of it? Need to start from Being itself—from commitment to God.

It is an act of transcendence having its ontological counterpart in the hold God has over me. This hold is the term in relation to which even my freedom is ordered and defined.

The mysterious relation between grace and faith exists wherever there is fidelity; and wherever a relation of this sort fails to appear, there is room for no more than a shadow of fidelity, a mere constraint imposed upon the soul, although it may be both culpable and full of lies.

A philosophy which refuses me the possibility of grasping anything but what it calls my "states of consciousness" is seen to be manifestly false when we confront it with the spontaneous and irresistible assertion which forms, as it were, the ground-bass of human knowledge. In the same way, the contention that fidelity, despite appearances, is never more than a mode of pride and self-regard, unquestionably robs of their distinctive character the loftiest experiences that men think they have known. The correlation which unites these two "ventures" cannot be over-stressed. I believe I see a centre of light here; I feel I must try to get nearer to it. And I believe that if a refutation can be attempted in the one case, it should also be possible in the other, and along the same line of thought.

When I say that I am unable to grasp any knowledge which transcends my states of consciousness, am I not lazily opposing this knowledge (a knowledge disappointing and even deceptive, since it contains a claim it cannot make good) to a knowledge which is not actually given, but which is at the very least ideally conceived, and, unlike the first, touches a reality independent of the mind which construes it? Without this axis of reference, however imaginary I may consider it, it is clear that the expression "my states of consciousness" is emptied of its meaning, since that meaning is only definite if it remains restrictive. The important question to ask is: how can I conceive of a knowledge thus irreducible to that which according to this hypothesis I really enjoy? or even, a deeper question, do I actually conceive of it? If I admit that perhaps I do not conceive of it, that is enough to make the insecure doctrine which I claimed to preach fall to the ground at once. But it is scarcely in my power to understand how the idea of a real knowledge, i.e. a reference to Being, could come to birth inside a world of pure states of consciousness. And so I begin to find a secret way of escape in the outer bailey of that tall keep in which I pretended to im- mure myself. Shall I not be forced to recognise from now onwards that this very idea is, as it were, the indelible mark which another order has left upon me?

The same is true of fidelity. Across the attachments which the I vows to itself lies the shadow of another fidelity, and only the fact that I have first conceived it enables me to deny its existence myself. But if it has been given me to conceive it at all, surely this is because I have dimly experi- enced it, whether in myself or in others? Surely it is no accident that I use those things which I affect no longer to believe in, as the models for my tentative picture of personal reality, even while I allege that the distinctive character of this reality is the continually renewed effort of coherence and balance between its two aspects?

Am I not, moreover, justified in mistrusting the actual nature of the set by which I claim to gather up into myself the roots or links of all fidelity? How can I help seeing that such a dogged and determined contempt of evidence cannot have its origin in experience, however central and however hidden you suppose it to be: it can only originate in prejudice, in the act of fundamental negation by which I banish the Real to infinity, and then dare to usurp its place and dress myself up in its stolen attributes—degrading them, it is true, in the process.

Can we only rescue fidelity at this price? I think it would be a thousand times better if I resolved to see in it nothing but a survival, a lingering shadow which melts right away under the light of thought. Better that than to set up such idolatry at the centre of my life.

Although I would not venture to assert that the connection can be observed in every case, yet I cannot fail to notice that where Fidelity is at her most unmistakable, where her face shines with clearest light, she goes hand in hand with a character as opposed to Pride as anything we can imagine. Patience and Humility gaze from the depths of her eyes. Patience and Humility; virtues whose very names today are forgotten, and whose true nature is further darkened to our sight with every step forward in man's technical and impersonal equipment, his logical and dialectical equipment with the rest.

The alliance of these three virtues into a unity—the unity of a being whose ever-changing structure psychology has no power to fathom—could not exist, could not even be thought of, in a purely personal system: where the self, and only the self, was the centre for those roots and links with reality, which uphold the commitments which Life may inspire us to undertake.

QUESTIONS FOR STUDY AND DISCUSSION

1. The reason why every commitment entails a risk is that our future states are not totally under our own control. How does Marcel express the changeableness and elusiveness that our future has toward ourselves?
2. Marcel asks himself whether undertaking a commitment means that I either "lie to myself" or "lie to someone else." What does he mean by these "lies"?
3. In what way can fidelity to one's self become proud and stubborn, looking for one's own glory?
4. Is it necessary to refer our fidelity to another person if we are to avoid making it merely a matter of proud, stoic self-mastery?
5. Can the unchangeableness of God be the basis for the permanence of our act of fidelity?

Interpersonal Relationships

In the latter part of the last chapter we saw that in some sense or other, certainly so far in a rather obscure sense, it does seem possible to transcend the opposition between the flux of successive images and the timelessness of the abstract concept; and if that opposition can be transcended at a supratemporal level, that is, at the level of time's other dimension of depth or inwardness, it follows that I must think of myself not merely as somebody thrust into the world at a moment of time that can be historically located, but also as bound to those who have gone before me in some fashion that cannot be brought down to a mere linkage of cause and effect. It is from this point of view that we ought to consider what I have elsewhere called the mystery of the family bond; which is itself, for that matter, only a particular expression of that general mystery of being to which we shall be devoting our attention in my second volume. No doubt, of course, it does seem rather odd to deal with a particular expression of the mystery of being before treating the whole subject generally. But we must not forget that our task is that of a quest or an investigation, following up successive clues, and not that of the didactic exposition of the consequences and corollaries that would follow from the acceptance of certain initial axioms or the proof of certain initial theorems.

It ought to be noticed, before we go on any further, that the point of view from which we are considering the reality of the family bond is what might be called a metasociological one. I mean, simply, that we are going deeper than sociology does. Sociology, so long as it remains at its own proper level, cannot begin to state our kind of problem: which is, in fact, our old problem, "What am I? And how is it that I am able to ask myself what I am?", with a new face.

We are living today, to be sure, or at least so it seems, in a world in which the notion of sonship, and the notion of fatherhood too, are tending to be emptied of that richness of meaning which they possessed for other societies. The philosophy that is tending to triumph today is the old philosophy of the eighteenth century, of the *Aufklärung*,[1] in a new dress. For that philosophy, the metaphysical reality of sonship is one superstition among many others and ripe for the rubbish-heap. It is important therefore for us to get a firm grasp of the almost completely negative conception of

---

[1] *Aufklärung:* Enlightenment. [R.S.]

From pp. 197–206 of Gabriel Marcel, *The Mystery of Being,* translated by G. S. Fraser. Copyright 1950 by Henry Regnery Company. Reprinted by permission of Henry Regnery Company and The Harvill Press Ltd., London.

sonship which is tending to define itself and to assert its authority before our eyes. It seems to define itself, in fact, basically in terms of a refusal—a refusal to acknowledge the existence in life, in the fact of being alive, of a value that allows us to think of life as a gift. The old French expression "devoir le jour à"—to owe the light of day to—would never be used by anybody today. It is not enough to say that it has become rather trite to talk of owing the light of day to one's parents. The notion, or rather the feeling, that these words express is no longer experienced except in a residual fashion. There are certain basic reasons for this state of affairs; the most obvious of them, on the face of it, is that to be alive in such a tragic and such a threatened world as ours seems to many people not a gift but a penalty—but, a penalty, after all, pronounced by whom? And a penalty for what crime? Can one be justly punished for an offence that one is not aware of having committed? But this is not the whole story. Let us look at it from the side of fatherhood, as well as from that of sonship. In very many cases, is not the act of begetting a child something unpremeditated, the act of somebody who is not behaving in a responsible fashion, and who is very far from taking upon himself everything that his act will entail for somebody who never asked to be born? It is precisely this affirmation, reinforced by a question and by an exclamation, "I never asked to be born, by what right—by what right!—has life been inflicted on me?" that lies at the roots of that contemporary nihilism, to which I shall have to come back much later. You will not have failed to notice, however, that we here touch again upon a state of affairs which took up our attention in chapter two. What we should notice particularly, however, is that from this negative perspective, this perspective of refusal, the bond between father and son gradually tends to lose every spiritual quality; it is conceived of now merely, in a rather vague fashion, as a somewhat obscure objective relationship, which can be of interest, from a strictly technical point of view, to the biologist alone. We might say that we are witnessing a more and more general disavowal of fatherhood, but a disavowal, paradoxically, mainly pronounced by sons. But naturally the process becomes to some extent reciprocal; when sons deny the rights of fathers, fathers are likely to refuse to acknowledge that they have any responsibility towards sons.

I know that I probably seem to be painting a rather gloomy picture here. In the majority of cases this basic situation of estrangement between father and son is masked by customary tolerance and ordinary human decency; but it breaks through to the surface in a very striking way in contemporary literature. In a body of work like that of Sartre's, a body of work whose importance cannot be brushed aside, this situation of estrangement emerges in a most definite shape; one might even say that Sartre's world is one where fatherhood, whether as a fact or as a value, has actually ceased to exist; it would be no exaggeration, in fact, to call this a world in which a man claims, in Sartre's slightly technical phraseology, to *choose himself* as the son of X, and therefore equally to *reject himself* as the son of X. But in relation to the general body of human traditions of feeling and behaviour, this is an innovation of a completely revolutionary sort. It is, in the most exact sense of the word, an impious innovation; and it is not by mere chance that Orestes, in Sartre's very first play, has the *beau rôle* just in that (not in spite of the fact that) he is the murderer of his mother.

It is rather important to ask ourselves how, or rather where, we are going to take our stand when we are faced with such a refusal to recognize life as a gift and therefore to acknowledge the metaphysical reality of sonship. It is pretty clear, at least, that we cannot simply condemn such refusals as infringing certain rules of morality, which we assert to be self-evident and beyond discussion; if we are to protest against this kind of nihilism, it can only be in the name of a sort of depth of reality which the nihilism refuses to recognize and, as it were, blots from view; it was just this very depth, in fact, that I was trying to make manifest in my essay, *Homo Viator*. This deep reality, that nihilism ignores, has to do with this same act of recognition and acknowledgement whose central importance for our thesis I have so often underlined. It is essential to the very notion of being a father that one should recognize one's son, and acknowledge him to be one's son; and to that of being a son, that one should recognize and acknowledge one's father's fatherhood. But I am not talking at this point, naturally, of recognition in the merely legal sense. I am not envisaging the case of the man who may be forced to recognize, and to contribute to the support of, a casually begotten bastard; what we are concerned with is a much deeper and more intimate kind of recognition—and a kind of recognition that is bound up with an activity of a very actual and very vital kind. If a man, in fact, fails to show any real interest in his child, he is behaving as if he did not recognize the child as his own; we are within our rights in saying that in such a case the father does *not* recognize the child, and even that real fatherhood is lacking, at least in the human sense of the term; from a purely biological point of view, in so far as heredity is a scientific fact, it continues of course, to manifest itself, whether or not the biological father behaves like a human father. But really, of course, the notion of fatherhood has its true and full meaning only at the human level; dogs, for instance, those casual and promiscuous creatures, are not really fathers in the human sense, though there are certain animal species—one thinks particularly of birds—in whose behaviour there is something like an anticipatory sketch of human fatherhood. We ought to be aware, however, that in such cases we are always interpreting bird behaviour on the analogy of human behaviour; human behaviour, as we intimately experience it, is our point of departure.

What has just been said of fatherhood might also be said of sonship—though, while the father has often in the past refused to acknowledge the son, it is only in our own days that the son, except in very exceptional circumstances, has refused to acknowledge the father. What is also misleading is the notion of a moral imperative, a notion really springing in the last analysis from the Ten Commandments: "Honour thy father and thy mother that thy days may be long upon the land which the Lord thy God giveth thee." Reflection shows us, however, that this commandment can have meaning only against the background of certain given structural social conditions; in a world that had become entirely proletarianized, the given conditions would tend to abolish this commandment or at least to rob it of any concrete significance. This is not to say that in such conditions one would be within one's rights in not honouring one's father, but more profoundly that an entirely proletarianized world would produce an increasing number of beings who in their very depths would feel themselves as being fatherless—as being *nobody's sons, Fils de Personne* to quote the title of a contemporary French play [2]—and who would feel this even though the individual who had physically begotten them were still alive.

It seems clear, therefore, that the notion of human fatherhood is one that is applicable within fairly strict limits; at one end of the scale it disappears to leave in its place a mere biological phenomenon; at the other end the biological phenomenon disappears without destroying the essentials of human fatherhood; I am thinking of the case of adoption—and here, too, we must look beyond legal definitions, for there can be legal adoption without the accomplishment of that spiritual act of which I am always thinking, and on the other hand the act can be accomplished in cases where legal adoption, for one reason or another, is impossible. The words "spiritual act" here should be taken in their strongest possible sense; one does not become the adoptive father of somebody merely through having a sudden impulse of affection, but only through a self-commitment to which one will have to remain faithful in spite of almost certainly inevitable lapses of interest, disappointments, and setbacks. Ought we to conclude, however, from the possibility of becoming a father by adoption, that it is necessary to make a radical distinction between spiritual and biological fatherhood? That, I think, would be a very rash thing to do. On the contrary, we ought to maintain that in normal circumstances the separation of the two kinds of fatherhood is something that ought not to be brought about, and even ought not to be able to be brought about; where there is such a separation it is because of some flaw in the individual's physical framework or social situation. But let us be wary about what we intend to convey here by the word "normal"; I am not thinking of a norm in an abstract sense, some formal rule of ethics whose basis would be hard to discover and which would subsist somehow or other beyond the world of everyday experience, but rather to a certain fullness of life which, when spiritual fatherhood is separated from biological fatherhood, becomes something for which the reflective consciousness feels a certain homesickness. Thus parents who have adopted a child, and who love the child with all their heart, cannot fail to feel a certain regret, except in very exceptional cases, that it is not

---

[2] By Henry de Montherlant. [G.M.]

the child of their own bodies. The exceptional cases I have in mind are those where, if the child was physically their own, they would risk transmitting to it certain hereditary weaknesses; but a satisfaction of that kind is, after all, an extremely relative satisfaction—taking its rise in something that is in itself a smart, a wound, a humiliation.

It is, in fact, very possible that in our actual world a dissociation between the spiritual and the biological is becoming quite generally operative; but this is only one more proof that our world is a broken world; it is only a broken world that could give rise to such practices, for instance, as artificial insemination.

Such topics, to some of my readers, may seem strangely alien to the kind of investigation to which this volume is devoted. Such readers, however, I believe, are the victims of a mere illusion, an illusion which consists in the last analysis of adhering to that conception of the spirit as something at the opposite extreme from the flesh, or as something completely transcending the flesh, against which I have never ceased to protest. In a very general fashion indeed, one might say that the difficulty we have had, in the course of these lectures, continually to confront lies in the very fact that the spiritual seems to wish to claim for itself the dignity of a separate existence, whereas in a deeper sense it only constitutes itself effectively *as* spirit on condition of becoming flesh. The example, that we have taken already, of adoption is very significant in this new regard; adoptive parents only really become parents on condition that they lavish on their adopted child the most actual, the most material, and the most humble cares and services, the same which they would have bestowed upon him if they had really engendered him. In this sense adoption is a kind of grafting of the flesh on to the spirit, and it cannot be anything else; it is wonderful that it should be possible at all, and in fact its possibility shows up better than anything else the limits of every philosophy of life that claims to base itself on purely biological considerations.

Yet, on the other hand, nothing can give us a more intense feeling of insecurity and strangeness than this human situation of ours; the situation of a being placed at the point of juncture, or of co-articulation, of the vital and the spiritual. It is not a matter of the sense of strangeness that would be felt by an observer of the situation from the outside—but of the strangeness that is felt from within by somebody who recognizes the situation as his own. Let us recall, for that matter—what goes without saying to anybody who has grasped the significance of these investigations of ours—that the very notion of observing the situation from the outside is, in this context, a meaningless one. It is of the very nature of our situation that it can be grasped only from within its own depths. But at the same time—and here we touch again on a point made at the very beginning of this volume —in a world like our own, which is becoming more and more completely subjected to the dominion of objective knowledge and scientific technique, everything, by an almost fatal necessity, tends to fall out as if this observation of our situation from the outside were a real possibility. From that falsely objective point of view, the very phrase "spiritual reality" is in danger of becoming emptied of all meaning; or rather what is still *called* "spiritual reality" is offered for our consideration as a mere superstructure, an epiphenomenal garment that masks, and rather thinly masks, a basic hurrying of matter: it might be demonstrated that an assumption of this sort, shared by both parties, is the mainspring of that strange convergence so often noted by scientists, at least in France, of strictly biological generalizations, on the one hand, with Marxist speculations on the other. Both biologists and Marxists are seeking to arrive at an interpretation of life at the purely objective level; only, unfortunately, the kind of objectiveness they are aiming at entails a preliminary, and complete, elimination of the subject as such.

We know of course that we are not, from our own point of view in these lectures, to understand the notion of the subject as it has traditionally been understood by idealist philosophers. Neither the transcendental ego of Kant nor the monad of Leibniz has any place in our argument. It is precisely in order to underline that fact that I have been emphasizing the notion of the family bond and its mysterious character. At the point we have now reached, it is on this new and difficult notion of *mystery* that we must concentrate: it is the notion in which this whole first volume logically culminates, and it is around this notion, as a starting point, that the lectures in my second volume will be built up.

When I talk about the mystery of the family bond some of my readers, I fancy, are disconcerted. The family is an institution; it is a fact; it is something which can be studied, at least in some of its aspects, by the methods of positive science. In talking about its *mystery,* am I not bringing in a touch of vague literary floweriness at a level of discourse where such battered ornaments of speech have no proper place? However, as we have seen already, the situation with which we are concerned, in our special context, is one whose true nature can be grasped or acknowledged only from the inside; there are no objective statements that can be made about it from the outside, for by definition it is *our* situation, the situation we cannot get outside of. That is why the kind of writer who makes the mystery of the family palpable to us is always, for example, the novelist rather than the historian of social institutions. However, though these remarks help to clear the ground a little, we have not yet succeeded in giving the term "mystery" that very precise and almost technical sense which alone can justify its introduction into the vocabulary of a philosopher.

Perhaps the shortest way towards our needed definition of the notion of mystery would be to begin by working out the distinction, at the spiritual level, between what we call an *object* and what we call a *presence*. Here, as always, we are taking as our starting point certain very simple and immediate experiences, but experiences which philosophy, until our own day, has always tended to overlook. We can, for instance, have a very strong feeling that somebody who is sitting in the same room as ourselves, sitting quite near us, someone whom we can look at and listen to and whom we could touch if we wanted to make a final test of his reality, is nevertheless far further away from us than some loved one who is perhaps thousands of miles away or perhaps, even, no longer among the living. We could say that the man sitting beside us was in the same room as ourselves, but that he was not really *present* there, that his *presence* did not make itself felt. But what do I mean by presence, here? It is not that we could not communicate with this man; we are supposing him neither deaf, blind, nor idiotic. Between ourselves and him a kind of physical, but merely physical, communication is possible; the image of the passing of messages between a reception point and an emission point, which we have rejected on several other occasions, is in fact quite applicable here. Yet something essential is lacking. One might say that what we have with this person, who is in the room, but somehow not really present to us, is communication without communion: unreal communication, in a word. He understands what I say to him, but he does not understand *me:* I may even have the extremely disagreeable feeling that my own words, as he repeats them to me, as he reflects them back at me, have become unrecognizable. By a very singular phenomenon indeed, this stranger interposes himself between me and my own reality, he makes me in some sense also a stranger to myself; I am not really myself while I am with him.

The opposite phenomenon, however, can also take place. When somebody's presence does really make itself felt, it can refresh my inner being; it reveals me to myself, it makes me more fully myself than I should be if I were not exposed to its impact. All this, of course, though nobody would attempt to deny that we do have such experiences, is very difficult to express in words; and we should ask ourselves why. The fact is that the notion of the *object,* as such, is linked in our minds with a whole set of possible practical operations (*"This* object is a typewriter, and this, and this, and this, etc. are what you do with it. . . .") that can be taught and that can thus be regarded as generally communicable. But these considerations do not apply, in any sense at all, to the notion of the *presence,* as such. It would be quite chimerical to hope to instruct somebody in the art of *making his presence felt*: the most one could do would be to suggest that he drew attention to himself by making funny faces! The whole business would be rather like teaching a woman how to have charm. It is as clear as can be that the notion of a *lesson in charm* is a self-contradictory one (one could have lessons in deportment, etiquette, and so on, but one can know about these things without having charm, and one can have charm without knowing about these things). In fact the whole notion of teaching charm, as of teaching people to make their presence felt, is the very height of absurdity.

QUESTIONS FOR STUDY AND DISCUSSION

1. Marcel uses the father-son relationship as an example in his treatment of human relationships. Take another basic relation, such as the economic one of buyer to seller or the political one of governor to governed, and show how it must be made into a truly human relationship.
2. How does Marcel avoid the pitfalls of (1) angelism, where man is taken as a pure spirit operating with no physical or corporeal basis; (2) materialism, where the corporeal relation is everything and there is no need to elevate or ennoble it with a spiritual dimension?
3. What is the difference between being present to another person and merely being in the same place with him?
4. How does Marcel feel about the contemporary world's position toward human relations like that of father and son? Do you agree with him? What about other forms of human relations? What aspects of the modern world have improved the possibilities of human relationships?

Martin Heidegger

MARTIN HEIDEGGER was born in 1889 and received some of his early education from the Jesuits. He studied at the University of Freiburg and began to lecture there in 1915. In 1923 he became professor at Marburg and in 1928 returned to Freiburg to replace Husserl, who retired that year. He taught there until 1944, served as rector of the University for a brief time, and in 1952 became professor emeritus. He now lives near Freiburg and gives public lectures on very rare occasions. In the last fifteen years he has published a great number of short treatises, many of which stem from lectures and seminars he held earlier in his career. His major work, *Being and Time,* appeared in 1927. It is one of the most important philosophical works in this century.

Man and Being

THE TWOFOLD TASK IN WORKING OUT THE QUESTION OF BEING
METHOD AND DESIGN OF OUR INVESTIGATION

The Ontological Analytic of Dasein [1] as Laying Bare the Horizon for an Interpretation of the Meaning of Being in General

In designating the tasks of "formulating" the question of Being, we have shown not only that we must establish which entity is to serve as our primary object of interrogation, but also that the right way of access to this entity is one which we must explicitly make our own and hold secure. We have already discussed which entity takes over the principal role within the question of Being. But how are we, as it were, to set our sights towards this entity, Dasein, both as something accessible to us and as something to be understood and interpreted?

In demonstrating that Dasein is ontico-ontologically prior,[2] we may

---

[1] The "ontological analytic" is the examination of consciousness not from a psychological or purely cultural point of view, but from the ontological standpoint: treating consciousness in its fundamental relationship to being. [R.S.]

[2] Heidegger makes use of the terms "ontic" (referring to the study of matters of fact, not profound enough to reach the dimension of being), "ontological" (concerning the analysis of being itself), "ontico-ontological" (combination of both), and "pre-

From pp. 36–40 of *Being and Time* by Martin Heidegger. Translated by John Macquarrie and Edward Robinson. Harper & Row, Publishers, 1962. Reprinted by permission of Harper & Row, Publishers, and SCM Press Ltd., London.

have misled the reader into supposing that this entity must also be what is given as ontico-ontologically primary not only in the sense that it can itself be grasped "immediately," but also in that the kind of Being which it possesses is presented just as "immediately." Ontically, of course, Dasein is not only close to us—even that which is closest: we *are* it, each of us, we ourselves. In spite of this, or rather for just this reason, it is ontologically that which is farthest. To be sure, its ownmost Being is such that it has an understanding of that Being, and already maintains itself in each case as if its Being has been interpreted in some manner. But we are certainly not saying that when Dasein's own Being is thus interpreted pre-ontologically in the way which lies closest, this interpretation can be taken over as an appropriate clue, as if this way of understanding Being is what must emerge when one's ownmost state of Being is considered as an ontological theme. The kind of Being which belongs to Dasein is rather such that, in understanding its own Being, it has a tendency to do so in terms of that entity towards which it comports itself proximally and in a way which is essentially constant—in terms of the "world." In Dasein itself, and therefore in its own understanding of Being, the way the world is understood is, as we shall show, reflected back ontologically upon the way in which Dasein itself gets interpreted.

Thus because Dasein is ontico-ontologically prior, its own specific state of Being (if we understand this in the sense of Dasein's "categorial structure") remains concealed from it. Dasein is ontically "closest" to itself and ontologically farthest; but pre-ontologically it is surely not a stranger.

Here we have merely indicated provisionally that an Interpretation of this entity is confronted with peculiar difficulties grounded in the kind of Being which belongs to the object taken as our theme and to the very behaviour of so taking it. These difficulties are not grounded in any shortcomings of the cognitive powers with which we are endowed, or in the lack of a suitable way of conceiving—a lack which seemingly would not be hard to remedy.

Not only, however, does an understanding of Being belong to Dasein, but this understanding develops or decays along with whatever kind of

---

ontological" (the unrefined, lived experience we have of being and our relation to being; not reflective and verbalized enough to be true ontology). The point he makes is as follows: in the analysis of being, we must first treat Dasein, human consciousness, because Dasein is prior to being both ontically and ontologically. We are to analyze Dasein in its relationship to being. But how can we focus our attention on Dasein? Is it difficult to do so?

Ontically, Dasein is close to ourselves and easy to grasp, because it is identical with ourselves. We are the same "thing" as Dasein. But this is an ontic, superficial statement; it does not yet show *ontologically* how we are identified with Dasein. To examine Dasein ontologically, in its relationship to being, is a long, difficult road; Dasein is ontologically very "far" from us.

And yet, we do have a lived, unreflective awareness of Dasein's relation to Being. We experience it pre-ontologically. We have this much to start with and must elaborate our ontology on this basis. [R.S.]

Being Dasein may possess at the time; accordingly there are many ways in which it has been interpreted, and these are all at Dasein's disposal. Dasein's ways of behaviour, its capacities, powers, possibilities, and vicissitudes, have been studied with varying extent in philosophical psychology, in anthropology, ethics, and "political science," in poetry, biography, and the writing of history, each in a different fashion. But the question remains whether these interpretations of Dasein have been carried through with a primordial existentiality comparable to whatever existentiell primordiality they may have possessed. Neither of these excludes the other but they do not necessarily go together. Existentiell interpretation can demand an existential analytic,[3] if indeed we conceive of philosophical cognition as something possible and necessary. Only when the basic structures of Dasein have been adequately worked out with explicit orientation towards the problem of Being itself, will what we have hitherto gained in interpreting Dasein get its existential justification.

Thus an analytic of Dasein must remain our first requirement in the question of Being. But in that case the problem of obtaining and securing the kind of access which will lead to Dasein, becomes even more a burning one. To put it negatively, we have no right to resort to dogmatic constructions and to apply just any idea of Being and actuality to this entity, no matter how "self-evident" that idea may be; nor may any of the "categories" which such an idea prescribes be forced upon Dasein without proper ontological consideration. We must rather choose such a way of access and such a kind of interpretation that this entity can show itself in itself and from itself. And this means that it is to be shown as it is *proximally and for the most part*—in its average *everydayness*. In this everydayness there are certain structures which we shall exhibit—not just any accidental structures, but essential ones which, in every kind of Being that factical Dasein may possess, persist as determinative for the character of its Being. Thus by having regard for the basic state of Dasein's everydayness, we shall bring out the Being of this entity in a preparatory fashion.

When taken in this way, the analytic of Dasein remains wholly oriented towards the guiding task of working out the question of Being. Its limits are thus determined. It cannot attempt to provide a complete ontology of Dasein, which assuredly must be constructed if anything like a "philosophical" anthropology is to have a philosophically adequate basis.[4]

If our purpose is to make such an anthropology possible, or to lay its

---

[3] "Existentiell" analysis: the examination of the actual states that Dasein has acquired. History, anthropology, biography, etc., carry out such an analysis, which is factual and less profound than "existential" analysis, which examines the basic characteristics of Dasein's existence, the characteristics it always and essentially has. [R.S.]

[4] The ambiguity of the pronominal references in this sentence and the one before it, reflects a similar ambiguity in the German. (The English-speaking reader should be reminded that the kind of philosophical "anthropology" which Heidegger has in mind is a study of man in the widest sense, and is not to be confused with the empirical sciences of "physical" and "cultural" anthropology.) [J.M., E.R.]

ontological foundations, our Interpretation will provide only some of the "pieces," even though they are by no means inessential ones. Our analysis of Dasein, however, is not only incomplete; it is also, in the first instance, *provisional*. It merely brings out the Being of this entity, without Interpreting its meaning. It is rather a preparatory procedure by which the horizon for the most primordial way of interpreting Being may be laid bare. Once we have arrived at that horizon, this preparatory analytic of Dasein will have to be repeated on a higher and authentically ontological basis.

We shall point to *temporality* as the meaning of the Being of that entity which we call "Dasein." If this is to be demonstrated, those structures of Dasein which we shall provisionally exhibit must be Interpreted over again as modes of temporality. In thus interpreting Dasein as temporality, however, we shall not give the answer to our leading question as to the meaning of Being in general. But the ground will have been prepared for obtaining such an answer.

We have already intimated that Dasein has a pre-ontological Being as its ontically constitutive state. Dasein *is* in such a way as to be something which understands something like Being. Keeping this interconnection firmly in mind, we shall show that whenever Dasein tacitly understands and interprets something like Being, it does so with *time* as its standpoint. Time must be brought to light—and genuinely conceived—as the horizon for all understanding of Being and for any way of interpreting it. In order for us to discern this, *time needs to be explicated primordially as the horizon for the understanding of Being, and in terms of temporality as the Being of Dasein, which understands Being.* This task as a whole requires that the conception of time thus obtained shall be distinguished from the way in which it is ordinarily understood. This ordinary way of understanding it has become explicit in an interpretation precipitated in the traditional concept of time, which has persisted from Aristotle to Bergson and even later. Here we must make clear that this conception of time and, in general, the ordinary way of understanding it, have sprung from temporality, and we must show how this has come about. We shall thereby restore to the ordinary conception the autonomy which is its rightful due, as against Bergson's thesis that the time one has in mind in this conception is space.

"Time" has long functioned as an ontological—or rather an ontical—criterion for naïvely discriminating various realms of entities. A distinction has been made between "temporal" entities (natural processes and historical happenings) and "non-temporal" entities (spatial and numerical relationships). We are accustomed to contrasting the "timeless" meaning of propositions with the "temporal" course of propositional assertions. It is also held that there is a "cleavage" between "temporal" entities and the "supra-temporal" eternal, and efforts are made to bridge this over. Here "temporal" always means simply being "in time"—a designation which, admittedly, is still pretty obscure. The fact remains that time, in the sense of "being in time," functions as a criterion for distinguishing realms of

Being. Hitherto no one has asked or troubled to investigate how time has come to have this distinctive ontological function, or with what right anything like time functions as such a criterion; nor has anyone asked whether the authentic ontological relevance which is possible for it, gets expressed when "time" is used in so naïvely ontological a manner. "Time" has acquired this "self-evident" ontological function "of its own accord," so to speak; indeed it has done so within the horizon of the way it is ordinarily understood. And it has maintained itself in this function to this day.

In contrast to all this, our treatment of the question of the meaning of Being must enable us to show that *the central problematic of all ontology is rooted in the phenomenon of time, if rightly seen and rightly explained,* and we must show *how* this is the case.

If Being is to be conceived in terms of time, and if, indeed, its various modes and derivatives are to become intelligible in their respective modifications and derivations by taking time into consideration, then Being itself (and not merely entities, let us say, as entities "in time") is thus made visible in its "temporal" character. But in that case, "temporal" can no longer mean simply "being in time." Even the "non-temporal" and the "supra-temporal" are "temporal" with regard to their Being, and not just privatively by contrast with something "temporal" as an entity "in time," but in a *positive* sense, though it is one which we must first explain. In both pre-philosophical and philosophical usage the expression "temporal" has been pre-empted by the signification we have cited; in the following investigations, however, we shall employ it for another signification. Thus the way in which Being and its modes and characteristics have their meaning determined primordially in terms of time, is what we shall call its *"Temporal"* determinateness. Thus the fundamental ontological task of Interpreting Being as such includes working out the *Temporality of Being.* In the exposition of the problematic of Temporality the question of the meaning of Being will first be concretely answered.

Because Being cannot be grasped except by taking time into consideration, the answer to the question of Being cannot lie in any proposition that is blind and isolated. The answer is not properly conceived if what it asserts propositionally is just passed along, especially if it gets circulated as a free-floating result, so that we merely get informed about a "standpoint" which may perhaps differ from the way this has hitherto been treated. Whether the answer is a "new" one remains quite superficial and is of no importance. Its positive character must lie in its being *ancient* enough for us to learn to conceive the possibilities which the "Ancients" have made ready for us. In its ownmost meaning this answer tells us that concrete ontological research must begin with an investigative inquiry which keeps within the horizon we have laid bare; and this is all that it tells us.

If, then, the answer to the question of Being is to provide the clues for our research, it cannot be adequate until it brings us the insight that the specific kind of Being of ontology hitherto, and the vicissitudes of its inquiries, its findings, and its failures, have been necessitated in the very character of Dasein.

Letter on Humanism

. . .

Sartre formulates, on the other hand, the basic principle of existentialism as this: existence precedes essence, whereby he understands *existentia* and *essentia* in the sense of metaphysics, which since Plato has said *essentia* precedes *existentia*.[5] Sartre reverses this phrasing. But the reversal of a metaphysical phrase remains a metaphysical phrase. As such it remains with metaphysics in the oblivion of the truth of Being. For though philosophy may determine the relationship between *essentia* and *existentia* in the sense of the controversy of the Middle Ages or in the sense of Leibniz or others, one must first of all ask, through what destiny of Being this difference in Being as *esse essentiae* and *esse existentiae* precedes thought. It remains to be considered why this question about the destiny of Being has never been asked and why it could never be thought. Or isn't this a sign of the oblivion of Being that there is this difference between *essentia* and *existentia?* We may suppose that this destiny does not lie in a mere neglect by human thought, let alone in an inferior capacity of earlier western thought. The difference—hidden in its essential source—between *essentia* (essentiality) and *existentia* (actuality) dominates the destiny of Western history and of all the history determined by Europe.

Sartre's key phrase on the superiority of *existentia* over *essentia* undoubtedly justifies the name "existentialism" as a suitable title for this philosophy. But the key phrase of "existentialism" has not the least thing in common with the same phrase in *Sein und Zeit* [*Being and Time*]; apart from the fact that in *Sein und Zeit* a phrase about the relationship between *essentia* and *existentia* cannot yet be expressed, for there we are concerned with settling something preliminary. This, as can be seen from what has been said, is done there rather clumsily. What is yet to be said today might, perhaps, become an impulse to guide the essence of man to attend in thought to the dimension of the truth of Being, which pervades it. Yet even this can only happen for the dignity of Being and for the benefit of *Dasein* which man endures in existing; not for the sake of man, but that through his works civilization and culture may be vindicated.

In order that we today, however, may arrive at the dimension of the truth of Being, we have first of all to make clear how Being concerns man and how it claims him. Such an essential experience happens to us when it

---

[5] On the use of essence and existence, see the Introduction to this section, p. 566. [R.S.]

From pp. 280–83 of Martin Heidegger, *Letter on Humanism*, translated by Edgar Lohner, in *Philosophy in the Twentieth Century*, edited by William Barrett and Henry Aiken. © Copyright 1962 by Random House, Inc. Reprinted by permission.

dawns upon us that man is, as long as he exists. Let us say this first in the language of tradition, which says: the ex-sistence [6] of man is his substance. For this reason in *Sein und Zeit* the following phrase often recurs: "the 'substance' of man is existence" (p. 153, 255, 362). But "substance" is already understood according to the history of Being, the blanket translation of οὐσία,[7] a word which designates the presence of one present and at the same time very often signifies with a mysterious ambiguity what is present. If we think of the metaphysical term "substance" in this sense, which in *Sein und Zeit* is already suggested because of the "phenomenological destruction" realized there (cf. p. 25), then the phrase "the 'substance' of man is ex-sistence" does not say anything other than that the way in which man is essentially in his own essence moving toward Being, is that he stands outside himself within the truth of Being. Through this essential determination of man the humanistic interpretations of man as *animal rationale,* as "person," or as an intellectual, spiritual, corporeal, being, are not declared wrong, nor rejected. The only thought is rather that the highest humanistic determinations of the essence of man do not yet come to know the authentic dignity of man. In this the thinking in *Sein und Zeit* runs counter to humanism. But this opposition does not mean that such thinking would make common cause with the opposite of the human and espouse the inhuman, defend inhumanity and degrade the dignity of man. Humanism is opposed because it does not set the *humanitas* of man high enough. However, the essential dignity of man does not lie in the fact that he is as the "subject" of beings, their substance, so that as the despot of Being he may let the character of beings dissolve into an "objectivity" that is much too loudly praised.

Man is rather "cast" by Being itself into the truth of Being, in order that he, ex-sisting thus, may guard the truth of Being; in order that in the light of Being, beings as beings may appear as what it is. Whether and how it appears, whether and how God and the gods, history and nature, enter, presenting and absenting themselves in the clearing of Being, is not determined by man. The advent of beings rests in the destiny of Being. For man, however, the question remains whether he finds what is appropriate to his essence to correspond to his destiny; according to this, as an ex-sisting person, he has to guard the truth of Being. Man is the guardian of Being. The thinking in *Sein und Zeit* proceeds towards this, when ecstatic existence only is experienced as "care" (cf. § 44a).

Yet Being—what is Being? It is Itself. Future thought must learn to experience and to express this. "Being" is neither God nor the basis of the world. Being is further from all that is being and yet closer to man than every being, be it a rock, an animal, a work of art, a machine, be it an angel or God. Being is the closest. Yet its closeness remains farthest from

---

[6] See *Existence* in the Glossary in this section. [R.S.]

[7] Greek term for substance. [R.S.]

man. Man first clings always and only to beings. But when thought represents beings as beings it no doubt refers to Being. Yet, in fact, it always thinks only of beings as such and never of Being as such. The "question of Being" always remains the question of beings. The question of Being still does not get at what this captious term means: the question seeking for Being. Philosophy, even when critical, as in Descartes and Kant, always follows the procedure of metaphysical representation. It thinks from beings to beings with a glance in passing at Being. For the light of Being already implies each departure from beings and each return to them.

Metaphysics, however, knows the clearing of Being as the looking toward what is present in its appearance (ἰδέα), or critically as what is seen of the external aspect of the categorical representation from the side of subjectivity. This means: the truth of Being as the clearing itself remains concealed from metaphysics. This concealment, however, is not a defect of metaphysics, but the treasure of its own richness, which is withheld and yet held up to it. The clearing itself, however, is Being. Within the destiny of Being the clearing grants a view to metaphysics, a view from which all that is present is attained by man as he presents himself to it, so that man himself can only attain Being . . . through intellection. . . .

Or to proceed in more straightforward fashion perhaps: What relation has Being to ex-sistence? Being itself is the relationship, insofar as It retains and reunites ex-sistence in its existential (i.e. ecstatic) essence—as the place of the truth of Being amidst the beings. Since man as an existing one comes to stand in this relationship which Being itself professes to be, insofar as he, man, ecstatically stands it, i.e. insofar as he, caring, takes over, he fails to recognize at first the closest and clings to the next closest. He even believes that this is the closest. Yet closer than the closest and at the same time, for ordinary thought, farther than his farthest is closeness itself: the truth of Being.

The oblivion of the truth of Being under the impact of beings, which is not considered in its essence, is the sense of "decadence" in *Sein und Zeit*. This word does not signify the fall of man, understood as in a "moral philosophy" that has been secularized; this word states an essential relationship between man and Being within the relation of Being to man's essence. In view of this, the terms "authenticity" and "un-authenticity" do not signify a moral-existential or an "anthropological" distinction, but the "ecstatic" relation of man's essence to the truth of Being, which is still to be realized and up to now has remained concealed from philosophy. But this relation, such as it is, does not derive from ex-sistence, but the essence of ex-sistence derives existential-ecstatically from the essence of the truth of Being.

The unique thought that *Sein und Zeit* attempts to express, wants to achieve, is something simple. As such, Being remains mysterious, the plain closeness of an unobtrusive rule. This closeness is essentially language itself. Yet the language is not merely language, insofar as we imagine it at the most as the unity of sound-form (script), melody and rhythm and meaning. We think of sound-form and script as the body of the word; of melody and rhythm as the soul and of meaning as the mind of language. We generally think of language as corresponding to the essence of man, insofar as this essence is represented as *animal rationale,* i.e. as the unity of body-soul-mind. But as in the *humanitas* of the *homo animalis* ex-sistence remains concealed and through this the relation of the truth of Being to man, so does the metaphysical-animal interpretation of language conceal its essence from the point of view of the history of Being. According to this, language is the house of Being, owned and pervaded by Being. Therefore, the point is to think of the essence of language in its correspondence to Being and, what is more, at this very correspondence, i.e., the dwelling of man's essence.

Man, however, is not only a living being, who besides other faculties possesses language. Language is rather the house of Being, wherein living, man ex-sists, while he, guarding it, belongs to the truth of Being.

Thus, what matters in the determination of the humanity of man as ex-sistence is not that man is the essential, but that Being is the essential as the dimension of the ecstatic of ex-sistence. This, however, is not the spatial dimension. All that is spatial and all time-space is essentially dimensional, which is what Being itself is.

The essence of man, however, consists of being more than mere man, insofar as this mere man is represented as a rational animal. "More" must not be understood here in an additive sense, as if the traditional definition of man were to remain as the basic definition, in order to undergo an expansion through an addition of the existential. The "more" means: more original and, therefore, in essence more essential. But here the mysterious is manifest: man is in his thrownness.[8] This means that man is as the ex-sisting counter-throw of Being even more than the *animal rationale,* insofar as he is less related to the man who is conceived from subjectivity. Man is not the master of beings. Man is the shepherd of Being. In this "less" man does not suffer any loss, but gains, because he comes into the truth of Being. He gains the essential poverty of the shepherd whose dignity rests in the fact that he was called by Being itself into the trueness of his truth. This call comes as the throw, from which stems the thrownness of the *Dasein.* Man is in his essence (from the point of view of the history of Being) that being whose Being as ex-sistence consists of dwelling in the nearness of Being. Man is the neighbor of Being.

But no doubt, you have wanted to reply for some time now, does not

---

[8] By the "thrownness" that characterizes man, Heidegger means that Dasein finds himself as already projected into existence, already thrown into reality. He does not bring himself into existence; he is "put there." But once in existence, Dasein sets up other projects and brings other things about; he carries out a "counter-throw." Thus Dasein has a certain initiative and dominance over being, but not a total one, because he does not master his own beginning. [R.S.]

such thinking think precisely of the *humanitas* of the *homo humanus?* Does it not think of this *humanitas* in such a decisive meaning as no metaphysics has thought or even can think of it? Is not this "humanism" in an extreme sense? Certainly. It is the humanism that thinks of the humanity of man from the nearness to Being. But it is at the same time the humanism for which not man, but the historical essence of man in his derivation from the truth of Being, is playing. But does not the ex-sistence of man then stand and fall in this game at the same time? Indeed, it does.

In *Sein und Zeit* (p. 62) it is said that all questioning of philosophy "strikes back into existence." But existence is here not the actuality of the *ego cogito.*[9] Nor is it the actuality of subjects that act with and for each other and in this way come into their own. "Ex-sistence" is basically different from all *existentia* and "existence," the ec-static dwelling in the nearness of Being. It is the guardianship, i.e. the concern of Being. Since in this thinking something simple is to be thought, it is very difficult to represent it by traditional philosophy. Yet the difficulty does not consist of indulging in a particular profundity and of forming complex conceptions, but it conceals itself in stepping back and letting thought take up a skillful inquiry and abandon the trained opinions of philosophy.

It is everywhere believed that the effort in *Sein und Zeit* has ended up a blind alley. We won't discuss this opinion here. The thought, which in the above mentioned essay attempted a few steps, has not yet passed beyond *Sein und Zeit.* But perhaps it has in the meantime come a little bit more into its own. As long as philosophy, however, occupies itself only with constantly obstructing possibilities, with engaging in matters of thought—i.e. the truth of Being—, so long is it perfectly secure from the danger of ever breaking down at the hardness of its matter. So the "philosophizing" about the failure is separated by an abyss from a failing thought. If a man should be fortunate in this, no misfortunes would occur. For him it would be the only gift that thought could receive from Being.

Yet this too is important: the matter of thinking is not reached by talking about "the truth of Being" and of "the history of Being." Everything depends upon bringing into language the truth of Being and letting thought penetrate this language. Perhaps then language requires far less precipitate utterance than correct silence. Yet who amongst us today would like to imagine that his attempts at thought were at home on the path of silence? If it goes far enough, our thought might perhaps point to the truth of Being and to it as what is to be thought. In this way it would be more than anything else removed from mere suspicion and opinion and be allotted to the already rare handiwork of script. The matters, in which something is, even if they are not determined for eternity, come in due time.

Whether the realm of the truth of Being is a blind alley or whether it is

---

[9] *Ego cogito:* the "I think"; consciousness. [R.S.]

the free dimension in which freedom saves its essence, each one may judge for himself after having tried to go his appointed way or blaze a better; that is, one in more accord with the question. On the next to the last page of *Sein und Zeit* are the words "the *dispute* in regard to the interpretation of Being (i.e. not of the existent, nor of the Being of man) cannot be straightened out, *because it has not even been begun*. And in the end one cannot 'pick a quarrel,' for the beginning of a dispute requires some equipment. Only towards that is the investigation aimed." These words retain their validity even after two decades. Let us also in the coming days be voyagers to the neighborhood of Being. The question which you put helps to clarify the way.

You ask: *Comment redonner un sens au mot "Humanisme"?* "How can one restore meaning to the word humanism?" Your question not only presupposes that you want to retain the word "humanism," but it also contains the admission that the word has lost its meaning.

It has lost it through the realization that the essence of humanism is metaphysical and this now means that metaphysics not only does not ask the question of the truth of Being, but even abstracts asking it, insofar as metaphysics persists in its oblivion of Being. The thought, however, that leads to this realization of the questionable essence of humanism has at the same time brought us to think of the essence of man more originally. In view of this more essential *humanitas* of the *homo humanus,* the possibility follows of restoring to the word humanism an historical meaning that is older than what "history" considers the oldest. This restoration is not to be understood as though the word humanism were without meaning at all and a mere *flatus vocis*.[10] The *"humanum"* in the word points to the *humanitas,* the essence of man. The "ism" indicates that the essence of man would like to be understood essentially. The word "humanism" has this meaning as a word. This requires first that we experience the essence of man more originally; and then show in what degree this essence becomes in its own way a destiny. The essence of man rests in ex-sistence. This essence desires from Being itself, insofar as Being raises man as the ex-sisting one for the guardianship of the truth of Being. "Humanism" means now, should we decide to retain the word: the essence of man is essential for the truth of Being, and apart from this truth of Being man himself does not matter. So we think of a "humanism" of a strange sort. The word offers a term which is a *lucus a non lucendo*.[11]

Should one still call "humanism" this view which speaks out against all

---

[10] *Flatus vocis:* a word with no real meaning or objective reference. [R.S.]

[11] *Lucus a non lucendo:* Latin phrase often used to denote misleading or erroneous derivation of words. Literally it means that a grove of trees (*lucus*) gets its name from not being light (*a non lucendo*). This is false etymology, although it appears correct superficially. Heidegger here implies that the word "humanism" is similarly misleading; it gets its ultimate meaning not simply from humanity or man, as we would superficially expect, but from man's relation to being. Humanism is ultimately grounded in being. [R.S.]

earlier humanism, but which does not at all advocate the in-human? And this only in order to swim perhaps in the dominant currents, which are stifled in a metaphysical subjectivism and find themselves drowned in the oblivion of Being? Or should thought, resisting the word "humanism," make an effort to become more attentive to the *humanitas* of the *homo humanus* and what grounds this *humanitas?* So, if the world-historical moment has not already gone that far itself, a reflection might be awakened that would not only think of man, but of the "nature" of man, and even more than this of his nature, the original dimension in which the essence of man, determined as coming from Being itself, is at home.

.   .   .

QUESTIONS FOR STUDY AND DISCUSSION

1. Can psychology, anthropology, ethics, politics, etc., give a satisfactory explanation of *Dasein* (human existence) is no ontological analysis of man has been carried out? Why?
2. How important is temporality for understanding man as related to being? Use Merleau-Ponty's analysis of time to elucidate the role of temporality.
3. In his *Letter on Humanism,* why does Heidegger say that being is closest and yet farthest from man?
4. According to Heidegger, what is the deepest basis upon which a true humanism must be built?
5. Could man carry out his role as the shepherd of being, as the place where being becomes known, without language? Can anything else take the place of language?

TOPICS FOR DISCUSSION AND TERM PAPERS

A.

1. Recent phenomenologists have shown a particular interest in the problem of hermeneutics, the science of interpreting monuments and written texts from past ages as a basis for history. Use the various themes developed in this section to shed light on what we do when we interpret an ancient text. Show first how the text is a reflection of someone's world, and then show how we must go about understanding it. Make use of the concepts of speech and expression, man and his world, temporality, understanding of persons, and man and being.

2. Heidegger says that man's basic role is to allow being to appear to him. How do the emotions function in bringing this about?

3. Show how community and language function reciprocally in allowing man to discover the truth of being.

4. Can man exist in a human way outside of a community? Could he make any decisions or choices entirely apart from a community?

5. Relate the emotions to symbolism and expression. If emotion is a magical transformation of the world, as Sartre says, how could various art forms be used to carry out this transformation is a sophisticated, intelligent way?

6. Use the concept of temporality and as many other phenomenological concepts as possible to argue whether or not present-day Western civilization is Greek in thought and Roman in law.

7. Does humanity evolve automatically under the laws of social development or does it need great men with extraordinary powers of intellect and will to make it progress? Does human development necessarily bring with it a deeper comprehension of being?

8. Does a person who makes one quick decision after another and changes his mind very frequently become a better person because he exercises his freedom so much?

9. Is there such a thing as a "sacred" place, a "sad" place, a "joyful" place? How would we experience such places in our lived experience of space?

10. Show how bodily mobility is necessary not only for the constitution of space, but also for expression and speech, for temporality, and for emotion. Is bodily mobility a necessary substratum for the possibility of human freedom?

B.

1. How does phenomenology compare the human body to material things? How does Cartesian philosophy, with its doctrine of man as a spirit in a machine, compare the human body to material things? Compare the phenomenological concepts of body and consciousness to the Aristotelian concept of soul as form of the body.

2. Compare the existentialist doctrine of human decision as that which constitutes and forms personal existence with the Marxist concept of work and

labor as constitutive of humanity. Both of these traditions claim that man must "create himself" in some way; is there any place for such self-formation in the scholastic tradition? Is there any place for it in empiricist conceptions of man? How does it compare with what pragmatism says about man making himself?

3. Compare the phenomenological concept of the lived world (*Lebenswelt*) with the notion of ordinary language in Wittgenstein. Contrast the explanations of man as a speech-using being given in phenomenology and linguistic analysis. At what point of Aristotelian and Thomistic philosophy of man would the problem of language make itself felt? How does Hegel describe the process by which the spirit externalizes and expresses itself?

4. Compare Sartre's analysis of the emotions with the scholastic concept of sensible appetites. How does each account for human freedom vis-à-vis the emotions? Do the empiricist and naturalist philosophies of man make room for such freedom? Do the scholastic and empiricist philosophies of man take into account the intentionality of emotions?

5. How does each of the traditions represented in this volume answer this question: What is man supposed to do with his existence?

6. How does each of the traditions represented in this volume evaluate man's history? How seriously does each take history and temporality? In examining each tradition, note whether it considers history to be an essential factor in the being and formation of man, or whether it takes it as something added superficially to man's existence.

RECOMMENDED READINGS

Primary Sources

Arendt, Hanna. *The Human Condition.* Garden City, N.Y.: Doubleday & Co., 1959. Very highly recommended. An excellent and original use of phenomenological and classical Greek concepts, after the fashion of Heidegger, to describe human existence and activity.

Heidegger, Martin. *Being and Time.* Trans. by John Macquarrie and Edward Robinson. New York: Harper & Row, 1962. It is difficult to indicate selections since the entire work must be studied if any single part is to be properly understood. However, on the basis of the selections given in this volume, the following passages may be approached first: pp. 78–168, on the concept of being in the world and being with others; pp. 279–311, on temporality as related to death, a theme of special importance in Heidegger's early thought.

————. *Kant and the Problem of Metaphysics.* Trans. by James S. Churchill. Bloomington, Ind.: Indiana University Press, 1962. Section IV, pp. 209–55, is a concise statement of how Heidegger feels the philosophy of man is the first step of metaphysical analysis of being. Supposes some understanding of Kant.

————. *Letter on Humanism,* trans. by Edgar Lohner, in *Philosophy in the Twentieth Century.* Ed. by William Barrett and Henry Aiken. New York: Random House, 1962. II, 270–302. A statement of how Heidegger's philosophy provides a basis for "humanism" and maintains the dignity of man.

Husserl, Edmund. *Cartesian Meditations.* Trans. by Dorion Cairns. The

Hague: Martinus Nijhoff, 1960. Of Husserl's larger writings, this work should be studied first. It is somewhat easier than the others and provides a concise summary of his phenomenology from a time when his thought was fully matured.

————. *Phenomenology and the Crisis of Philosophy.* Trans. and with Introd. by Quentin Lauer. New York: Harper & Row, 1965. This volume contains two parts. One is an essay written by Husserl in 1911, "Philosophy as a Rigorous Science." The definitive form of phenomenology was just taking shape in his mind at that time, and this essay sets up the program that Husserl was to pursue in his later studies. Part II is a lecture entitled "Philosophy and the Crisis of European Man," given by Husserl in 1935. Husserl is extremely difficult to read at first, and these two works are probably the most accessible for a first orientation to his thought.

Jaspers, Karl. *Man in the Modern Age.* Trans. by Eden and Cedar Paul. Garden City, N.Y.: Doubleday & Co., 1957. Analysis of man's contemporary relationship to such factors as mass society, the state, culture, education, and technology. Establishes some contacts between the philosophy of man and human affairs in the world.

Marcel, Gabriel. *Creative Fidelity.* Trans. and with Introd. by Robert Rosthal. New York: Farrar, Straus & Giroux, 1964. A collection of meditations on the aspects of concrete human existence that Marcel writes about: faith, personality, fidelity, and human action.

————. *The Existential Background of Human Dignity.* Cambridge, Mass.: Harvard University Press, 1963. This volume contains the William James Lectures delivered at Harvard in 1961–62. Besides treating various aspects of human existence, Marcel makes many references to his earlier work and thought; this book thus provides a retrospective commentary on his own thinking.

Merleau-Ponty, Maurice. *Signs.* Trans. and with Introd. by Richard C. McCleary. Evanston, Ill.: Northwestern University Press, 1964. A collection of essays. Of special interest are: "Indirect Language and the Voices of Silence," on artistic creativity; "On the Phenomenology of Language"; and two essays on the relation between phenomenology and sociology, "The Philosopher and Sociology" and "From Mauss to Claude Lévi-Strauss."

Mouroux, Jean. *The Meaning of Man.* Trans. by A. H. G. Dowens. New York: Doubleday & Co., 1961. An attractive statement of Christian personalism with emphasis on the religious dimension of man.

Polanyi, Michael. *Personal Knowledge.* New York: Harper & Row, 1964. Although not usually classed as an existentialist, Polanyi's expression of topics usually treated by phenomenologists and existentialists compares favorably with the best writings in those traditions. In this book, Ch. 4, "Skills," Ch. 5, "Articulation," Ch. 7, "Conviviality," and Ch. 8, "The Logic of Affirmation," are especially recommended.

Ricoeur, Paul. *Fallible Man.* Trans. by Charles Kelbley. Chicago: Henry Regnery Co., 1965. The first major English translation of the work of this leading contemporary French phenomenologist. It is a phenomenological analysis of the human experience of finitude and guilt.

Sartre, Jean-Paul. *Existentialism and Human Emotions.* Trans. by Bernard Frechtman. New York: Philosophical Library, 1957. The first part of this volume, "Existentialism," is a translation of Sartre's popular essay, *L'existen-*

tialisme est un humanisme, in which he tries to show how his philosophy maintains human values.

————. *The Psychology of Imagination.* Trans. anonymously. New York: Citadel Press, 1961. A sensitive analysis of the "transforming" power of imagination. Some good descriptions of symbolism, mimicry, dreams, and art.

Scheler, Max. *Man's Place in Nature.* Trans. and with Introd. by Hans Meyerhoff. New York: Farrar, Straus & Giroux, 1962. Analysis of the grades of life found in plants, psyche, and spirit, and of the types of action consequent upon them. First published in 1927, it represents Scheler's final thought and tends to disjoin spirit from the human psyche and body.

Commentaries

Barral, Mary Rose. *Merleau-Ponty: The Role of the Body-Subject in Interpersonal Relations.* Pittsburgh: Duquesne University Press, 1965. A description and restatement of the major themes found in *Phenomenology of Perception,* especially the experience of the body, sexuality, communication and speech, and intersubjectivity. Easy to understand, could be used as an introductory guide to this work of Merleau-Ponty.

Collins, James. *The Existentialists: A Critical Study.* Chicago: Henry Regnery Co., 1952. Separate chapters are devoted to the thought of Sartre, Jaspers, Marcel, and Heidegger. The book begins with a chapter about the origins of existentialism and ends with a chapter summarizing five existentialist themes.

Desan, Wilfrid. *The Marxism of Jean-Paul Sartre.* Garden City, N.Y.: Doubleday & Co., 1965. A study of Sartre's later philosophy with emphasis on his relation to Marxism. The problem of social reality and existence in the community is studied.

————. *The Tragic Finale: An Essay on the Philosophy of Jean-Paul Sartre.* New York: Harper & Row, 1960. Analysis of themes found in Sartre's earlier thought, especially in *Being and Nothingness.*

Kaufmann, Walter. *Nietzsche.* New York: Meridian Books, 1956. The standard English work on Nietzsche. Part III, "Nietzsche's Philosophy of Power," pp. 181–286, contains material relevant to existential philosophy of man.

Langan, Thomas. *The Meaning of Heidegger.* New York: Columbia University Press, 1959. A less technical treatment than Richardson's work. Problems of the philosophy of man are emphasized on pp. 3–85.

Lauer, Quentin. *Phenomenology: Its Genesis and Prospect.* New York: Harper & Row, 1965. A clear treatment of the major themes in Husserl's work, with a final chapter giving a very brief description of Scheler, Heidegger, Sartre, and Merleau-Ponty.

Luijpen, William A. *Existential Phenomenology.* Trans. anonymously. Pittsburgh: Duquesne University Press, 1960. This work is not a study of any specific thinker, but attempts an original statement of the major phenomenological and existentialist themes of knowledge, intersubjectivity, and freedom.

Richardson, William J. *Heidegger: Through Phenomenology to Thought.* The Hague: Martinus Nijhoff, 1963. The most extensive study of Heidegger published to date in any language. For the philosophy of man, pp. 1–160, covering *Being and Time* and *Kant and the Problem of Metaphysics,* are most relevant.

Spiegelberg, Herbert. *The Phenomenological Movement: A Historical Introduction*, 2nd ed. rev. 2 vols. The Hague: Martinus Nijhoff, 1965. A very comprehensive and authoritative history of phenomenology with clear, systematic treatment of all major and minor thinkers in this tradition, a summary of contemporary trends, and extensive bibliographical notices and factual information. This is the main reference work for phenomenology and phenomenological existentialism.

Strasser, Stephan. *Phenomenology and the Human Sciences*. Trans. by John R. Kanda. Pittsburgh: Duquesne University Press, 1963. An attempt to show the differences between phenomenology and psychology in particular, and the ways in which they can complement one another.

Thévenaz, Pierre. *What Is Phenomenology?* Ed. and trans. by James M. Edie. Chicago: Quadrangle Books, 1962. A collection of articles and essays on certain themes in phenomenology. The first article, pp. 37–92, which bears the same title as the book, discusses the way in which Husserl, Sartre, and Merleau-Ponty conceive of the science of phenomenology.

Tymieniecka, Anna-Teresa. *Phenomenology and Science in Contemporary European Thought*. New York: Farrar, Straus & Giroux, 1962. The author shows that phenomenology is not antiscientific, but that it insists there are other ways of explaining reality besides the methods followed by natural sciences.